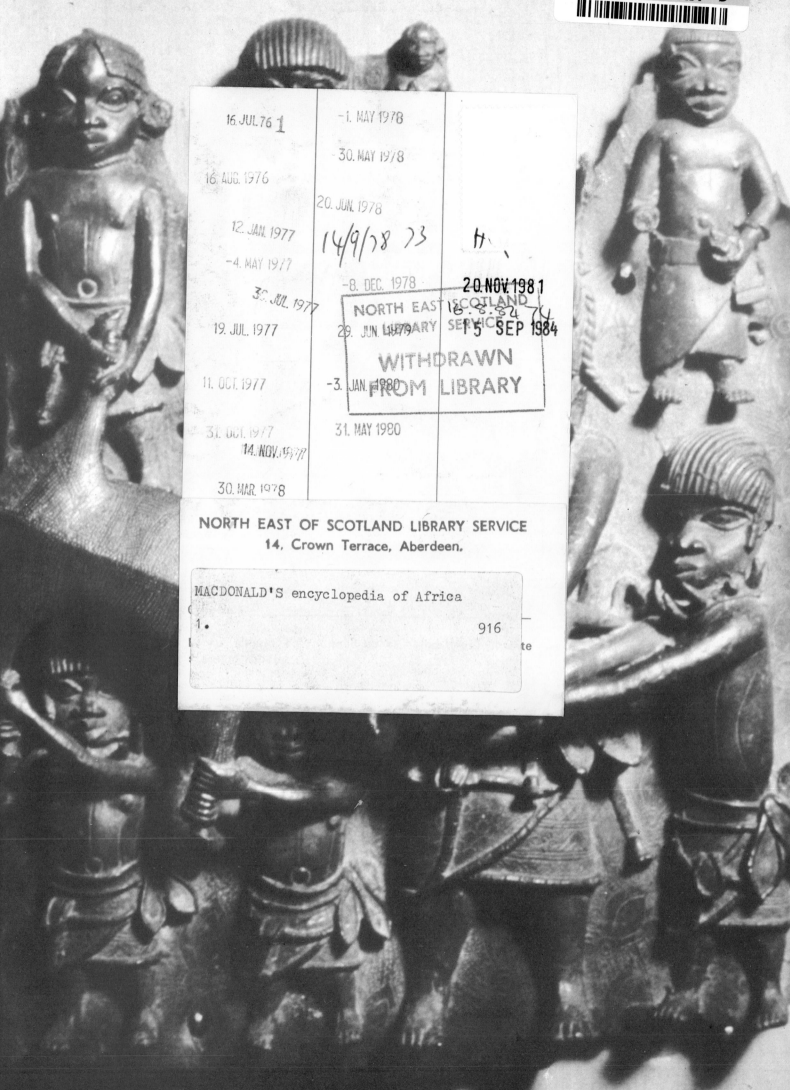

MACDONALD'S ENCYCLOPEDIA OF

AFRiCA

MACDONALD'S ENCYCLOPEDIA OF
AFRiCA

Macdonald Educational

Contents

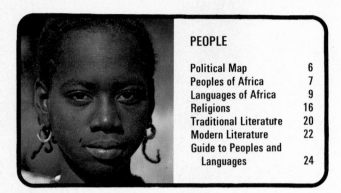

PEOPLE

Political Map	6
Peoples of Africa	7
Languages of Africa	9
Religions	16
Traditional Literature	20
Modern Literature	22
Guide to Peoples and Languages	24

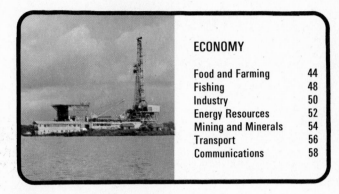

ECONOMY

Food and Farming	44
Fishing	48
Industry	50
Energy Resources	52
Mining and Minerals	54
Transport	56
Communications	58

GAZETTEER

Gazetteer of Places, an alphabetical guide to the countries, chief towns and other features of Africa   86

916
1.

ECOLOGY

Map of Vegetation Regions	129
Vegetation	130
Wildlife	136
National Parks	149

HISTORY

Africa Past and Present   164

GOVERNMENT

Government and Diplomacy   192

First published in 1976 by
Macdonald Educational Limited,
Holywell House, Worship Street,
London EC2

Printed in England by Waterlow (Dunstable) Ltd.

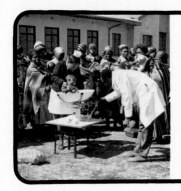

SOCIAL SERVICES

Education 60
Health and Medicine 70

THE LAND

The Land: Landscapes,
   Lakes and Rivers 78
Weather and Climate 82
Geology and Soils 84

THE ARTS

Early Art 150
Art Today 158
Music and Dance 160

SPORT

Sport 162

FAMOUS PEOPLE

Who's Who, an
   alphabetical guide
   to famous African
   personalities 200

Bibliography 216
Acknowledgements 217
Index 218

Political Map

Editor's Note
The names of countries and towns used throughout this book are those which are generally accepted in the Black African States of the continent. Zimbabwe is therefore used to denote the British colony of Rhodesia, and the name Namibia denotes South-West Africa.

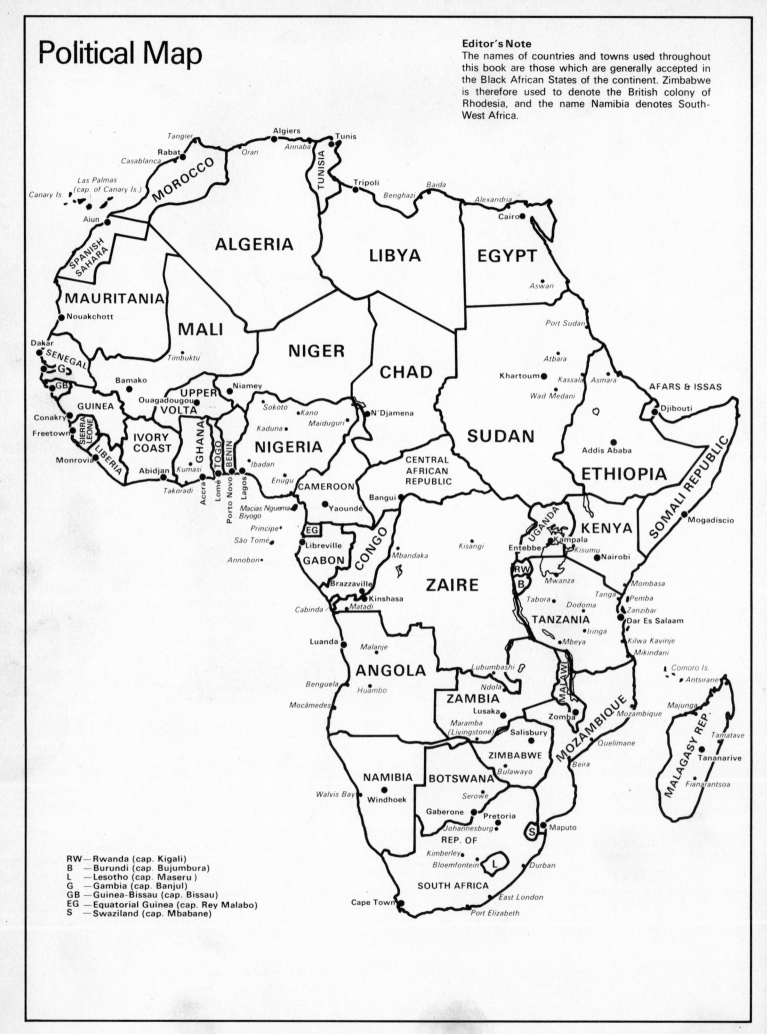

RW — Rwanda (cap. Kigali)
B — Burundi (cap. Bujumbura)
L — Lesotho (cap. Maseru)
G — Gambia (cap. Banjul)
GB — Guinea-Bissau (cap. Bissau)
EG — Equatorial Guinea (cap. Rey Malabo)
S — Swaziland (cap. Mbabane)

PEOPLES OF AFRICA

Africa is the second largest continent in the world (only Asia is bigger). Although Africa has an area three times that of Europe, its population of more than 400 millions is only two-thirds of Europe's. These people are divided into more than 1,000 different ethnic groups. All these groups, some of which have less than 100 members, have different languages, social customs, religions and ways of life. The vast size of the continent and the geographical barriers, such as mountains, deserts, forests and lakes, have tended to isolate groups of people from each other. Because of the isolation of one group from all the others, the people had no need for a common language and each group's language developed separately. Each group regarded the languages spoken by other groups as 'wrong'. Even today, some Bushmen in the Kalahari refuse to believe that anyone whom they do not personally know could speak their language.

The total isolation of groups from one another began to end when the Arabs first crossed the Sahara with their caravans. The arrival of the Europeans, with their roads, railways, telegraph wires and steamboats further reduced the importance of natural barriers and distances. Despite the improvement in communications, the number of ethnic groups and dialects is not decreasing. Ethnicity, one of the major problems faced by modern national governments, has not disappeared with independence. The reasons for this can be traced back to the way of life of people before the coming of the Europeans. The Tuaregs of the Sahara, the Masai of the Kenyan and Tanzanian steppes and the pygmies of Zaire were all adapted to surviving in the harsh surroundings in which they lived. They accepted the hyaenas, jackals, leopards and lions as natural hazards which they had to live with, in much the same way that people in western society accept the dangers of the motor car. In the same way, they were afraid of other peoples, or else they despised them. For example, the Bedouins of the desert still despise men who do not follow the austere life that they lead—herding camels, hunting gazelles, and eating locusts and dates. The Somali

▲ On special occasions, women in Nigeria dress their hair in an elaborate way, wear colourful dresses and often coral beads. Nigeria has a long tradition of art and personal adornment.

▲ A class of cheerful primary school girls in the South Nyanza region of Kenya. Education is changing the social roles of women.

◄ A mother and child in Zambia. Increased health facilities, including clinics for mothers and children, have contributed much to the welfare of families throughout Africa.

are feared as raiders by their neighbours in Kenya and Ethiopia. The Bantu speaking peoples in South Africa once feared the Bushmen, who poisoned their wells and killed their cattle. Until the 1870s, the Kikuyu of Kenya sought safety from raiding Masai in the sanctuary of the forests. Even if they did not fear each other, each group regarded others with suspicion. Even today, villagers have been known to flee with their goods into the forests at the approach of government tax collectors.

Africa is still underpopulated and any group of people who are oppressed, afraid or merely over-crowded may leave one area and start a new life in another less densely inhabited region. This process has produced more than 1,000 languages in Africa over the years. As the process continues, the languages split up into different dialects. When one group splits into two, it may only take two generations before the two new groups are speaking different dialects. As with languages, each group believes that its dialect is the correct way of speaking. Occasionally, a large ethnic group may absorb a smaller weaker group mostly by conquest. When this happens, the smaller group will become *bilingual* (speaking two languages equally well).

Most modern African states south of the Sahara enclose a large number of different languages within their borders. Many people would object to seeing any language other than their own becoming the sole national language of their country. For this and other reasons, many independent African nations are continuing to use the language of the former colonial power as their official language. More important, no African language, except Swahili, Hausa and Malagasy, has an adequate vocabulary for technical and administrative purposes.

Africa presents a considerable problem to students of the social, cultural and environmental behaviour of man, his physical characteristics and his distribution. To study the people of Africa, scholars want first to classify them. The main factor which distinguishes the different ethnic groups from each other is the difference in language. Distinctions of religion, economic life and social behaviour are not precise enough for the purpose of accurate classification. Often peoples speaking one language show

POPULATION DISTRIBUTION

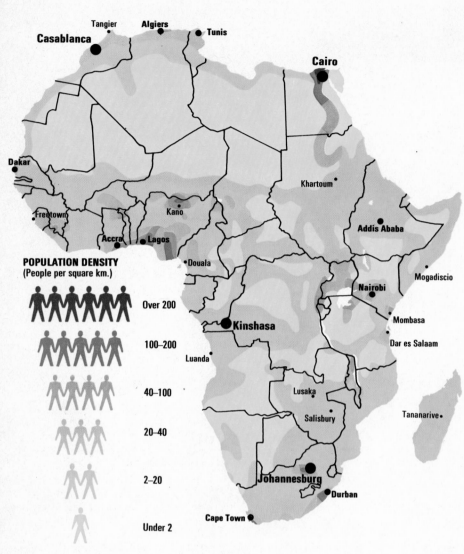

Tangier Algiers Tunis
Casablanca
Cairo
Dakar
Khartoum
Freetown Kano
Addis Ababa
Accra Lagos
Douala
Mogadiscio
Nairobi
Kinshasa
Mombasa
Luanda
Dar es Salaam
Lusaka
Salisbury
Tananarive
Johannesburg
Durban
Cape Town

POPULATION DENSITY
(People per square km.)

Over 200

100–200

40–100

20–40

2–20

Under 2

▲ The map shows the distribution of people in Africa. It can be seen that orange and yellow are the dominant colours on the map, indicating that vast areas of Africa have a population density of less than 20 people to a square kilometre. The black dots show major concentrations of peoples in large cities. The largest dots indicate places with more than 1,000,000 inhabitants; the medium-sized dots are places with populations of more than 500,000; and the smallest dots are cities with over 100,000 inhabitants.

different racial features, while elsewhere people belonging to one racial group speak different languages.

While the people of Africa south of the Sahara are basically Negroid in racial character, many of them are of mixed ancestry. Some types, such as the pygmies of Zaire, have retained their racial but not their linguistic characteristics. The invasions of the Arabs in North Africa and, to a lesser extent, the Europeans in the south, have brought about a mixed racial heritage. For example, people in Ethiopia and Somalia show evidence of Arab ancestors, as do the Swahili in East Africa and the Fulani of West Africa. Few 'pure' Bushmen or Hottentots now remain. Most of them have mixed with the Bantu-speaking peoples. Madagascar, in spite of its isolation, is inhabited by people who have roots in Africa, Arabia, India and, predominantly, Indonesia. The Coloureds of South Africa are the result of intermarriage between European colonists, Malays (brought from Asia as slaves to work on farms) and Africans.

Africans practise many different religions. A few are *monotheists*, worshipping one High God as in Christianity or Islam. Others are *polytheists*, worshipping many gods. Some ethnic groups are spirit worshippers, while others revere their ancestors and make sacrifices to them. The sun, the moon and the natural elements of thunder, wind and rain, are regarded as supernatural forces in some places and are appeased with prayers and sacrifices. Some peoples have mystic relationships with their totem animals—that is, they believe they descend from an animal ancestor. *Animists* believe that inanimate objects, such as stones and trees, are alive and they worship the spirits which they believe live in them. Many people either do not conform to any rigid religion or they practise a mixture of several. For example, some who call themselves Muslims will also worship spirits.

Africa is made up of many different environments—savanna, woodland, forest and so on. The people who live in the various conditions lead a way of life adapted to their surroundings. The Somali are nomadic herdsmen, wandering over the sparse vegetation of Somalia, southern Ethiopia and northern Kenya with their cattle in search of grass. Where the land is more fertile, people live in villages and cultivate staple food crops, such as maize or cassava. The Nkundo of central Zaire live by hunting the animals of the forest, catching them with cunningly devised traps. Peoples who live in coastal regions often live by fishing, as do those who live near the great lakes and rivers. The *fellahin* (peasants) of Egypt carry on the same traditional farming methods along the banks of the River Nile which are shown on the beautiful wall paintings in the ancient Egyptian pyramids.

As with race and religion, the economic ways of life of Africa cannot be divided into neat and tidy compartments. While some peoples do follow one occupation, such as cattle herding, to the exclusion of all others, most people combine different means of livelihood. Nearly all Africans keep goats in addition to whatever other animals or crops they may raise. Many peoples who grow crops also hunt. The economic way of life of a people is not only determined by the tradition of the people themselves, but also dictated by the environment in which they live. Because the natural surroundings influence the economic way of life, they also influence the cultural habits of the people. A cattle-owning people value cattle highly as status symbols and as a measure of wealth but their economy may also depend on hunting and growing crops.

Scholars have also tried to classify African ethnic groups into *patriarchies* (father-dominated societies) and *matriarchies* (mother-dominated). However, many groups do not fit into either of these categories. Therefore, it can be seen why it is difficult to identify the many different groups who live in Africa by their race, religion, economic way of life or social behaviour. The classification by language is the most accurate and easily understood method of identifying ethnic groups.

LANGUAGES OF AFRICA

The main groups of languages are those spoken in Africa south of the equator, West Africa, North-East Africa and North Africa. Africa south of the equator is mainly Bantu speaking, with the exception of parts of western South Africa and south-western Africa where Khoi-San languages are spoken. The Malagasy language is of Asian origin.

West Africa south of the Sahara contains what is now called the 'fragmentation belt' between the Atlantic and the Sahara. Several language families are represented in this area and in addition there are a number of isolated language groups.

In North-East Africa, including Sudan and Ethiopia, various language families are found, including the Semitic languages of Ethiopia, the Nilotic languages and the Cushitic languages.

In the Sahara and North Africa, the Berber and Arabic languages are spoken. Arabic is the language of trade, communication, religion and culture.

Africa South of the Equator

South of a line from Cameroon in the west to Uganda and the northern Kenyan coast in the east, most languages and dialects belong to one large family called Bantu languages. Bantu is a word meaning 'people'. The prefix *ba-* indicates that this is a plural word. The word *muntu* has the same root (*ntu*) with *mu-* indicating a singular word—that is, 'a person'. Forms of this word occur throughout

Sultan Ahmed's tomb (c. 1880), at Witu, Kenya, has the oldest known Swahili inscription.

East, Central, and Southern Africa. For example, the South African Zulu word for 'the people' is *a-bantu* and the cognate East African Swahili word is *watu*, 'people'.

Bantu languages, however, are not so alike that someone who speaks one Bantu language can understand someone speaking another. Vocabulary and pronunciation differences are so great that this is not possible. But the chief characteristic of Bantu languages, which enable them to be grouped in one family, is that the words are built up by prefixes and suffixes around a set of related word roots. Various examples of this form of word construction are given below.

Bantu languages are spoken in three main areas: East, Central and Southern Africa. However, within this chiefly Bantu language region, a few people, including Bushmen and Hottentots, speak non-Bantu languages.

East Africa

Swahili is the most important Bantu language of East Africa and also the easiest to learn. But its vocabulary is larger than that of any other African language. Some dialects of Swahili are important because each is used as a *lingua franca* (common language of communication) by Bantu people throughout East Africa, eastern Zaire, Rwanda and Burundi, and as far south as northern Mozambique. Swahili is even used on the Comoro Islands off the East African coast. Another reason for the importance of Swahili is that some ancient and much modern literature has been written in it.

The name of the country Uganda in East Africa is the Swahili form of *Buganda*, a province within the country. *Bu-* is a prefix which, when attached to a word stem, indicates the land of a people (in this case, the land of the *Ganda*). The prefix *ba-* indicates the people themselves. Thus, *Baganda* means the people of *Buganda*. One person in Buganda is called a *Muganda*, the *mu-* prefix being the same as in the word *muntu*.

Swahili is the most important language in Kenya and Tanzania, although the Swahili spoken in these countries is not exactly the same. In fact, 14 dialects of Swahili occur, the most important being:

1. **Kenya Coast Literary Swahili** This ancient language dating back to the 17th century is the one in which a mainly Islamic literature still continues to be written. It is still spoken along the coast of Kenya and has its centres in Mombasa, Malindi and Lamu.

2. **Tanzania Standard Swahili** This dialect is the one in which most Christian and general administrative documents are written. It is also the language of modern, western-type literature.

3. **Kiungwana or Congo Swahili** This form of Swahili is used in the eastern provinces of Zaire,

People from the four main African language groups. 1. Zulus speak a Bantu language. 2. A Gambian from West Africa. 3. An Ethiopian from North-East Africa. 4. A Moroccan from North Africa.

where it is widely spoken. The chief centres of this form of Swahili are the cities of Kivu, Shaba (formerly Katanga) and Kisangani. It is also understood in Burundi.

All these three dialects are understood from one region to another. Radio broadcasts are therefore suitable for all listeners throughout this large area.

4. **Ki-Ngazija** This is the form of Swahili as spoken on the Comoro Islands. This dialect is rather different in phonetic forms, but its written literature is very close to Kenya Coast Literary Swahili.

Swahili is now an extensive language, not only because it has adopted many words from Arabic, English, Hindustani and Portuguese, but also because it has coined many modern words. Examples are *garimoshi*, 'a steam train' (literally waggon smoke); *motokaa*, 'motor car' (fire [and you] sit [near it]); and *jokofu*, 'refrigerator' (an oven [but it makes] dead [water, that is, ice]).

An example of how Swahili is constructed is illustrated by the following proverb:
Ku-m-pa a-li-ye-ku-pa si ku-pa, ni ku-lipa 'To give to him that gave to you is not giving, it is repaying'.

The word *ku-m-pa* literally means 'to give him'. *Pa* is the root of the verb: 'give'. *Ku-* is the infinitive prefix common to most Bantu languages. It also occurs in *ku-lipa*, 'to pay'. The *-m-* in ku-m-pa is the infix for the third person singular (him). The subject form is *a-* in *a-li-ye*, in which *li-* indicates the past tense and *-ye* the relative infix. *Si* means 'it is not'. *Ni* means 'is', 'it is'.

Central Africa

In Rwanda, the chief language is Rwanda or Ruanda. This melodious and rich Bantu language is spoken by about two million people. These people have an elaborate poetic tradition, especially in epic and praise (eulogistic) poetry which is recited at court. Most of these poems have been lost but some have been preserved in collections made by European scholars.

In Burundi, the chief language is Rundi. This language is mutually intelligible with the language of Rwanda. Ancient literary traditions still exist in Burundi, but less is known about them even than in Rwanda.

The national language of Zaire is now Lingala, the language of the army. It comes from the region around the Middle Zaire River. Although it has a comparatively small vocabulary, the language contains many colourful expressions. For example, *Mayele ma mwasi, maleki mondele* 'The cunning of a woman surpasses even that of a white man'. The prefix *ma-* in *mayele*, 'wisdom', is repeated after *mayele*, and can be translated as 'of'. The same prefix is again used in the word *maleki*, so linking the verb *leki* (surpasses, literally 'leaves behind') with the subject *mayele*. This form of construction, using prefixes, is characteristic of Bantu languages.

A larger cluster of dialects is spoken in the 'armpit' of the Zaire River, what was once commonly called the Congo Basin. Bantu-speaking peoples were

---

English words adopted by Swahili
The following words describe parts of a car:
boneti: bonnet
bureki: brake
buti: boot
enjini: engine
habu: hub
kilachi: clutch
liva: lever
madigadi: mudguards
waipa: windscreen wiper
bampa: bumper

A Fulani girl. The language of the Fulani is widely spoken throughout West Africa. ▼

A Zambian teacher instructs a class in reading. Zambia's languages belong to the Bantu group. ▼

---

forced into this densely forested region by pressure from peoples from the north-east. These groups have been named the Mongo-Nkundo peoples. Most of the known literature of these peoples is in the Nkundo dialect. Outstanding among these oral traditions is the great epic of Lianja, a mysterious ancestor-hero, who is the son of the God of death and is reborn after he is killed by his enemies by entering spiritually into the womb of his wife. This long epic reflects the strange Zairese philosophy of *metempsychosis*, the rebirth of the father from the womb of his wife. He and his brothers, together with his mysterious sister-wife, live through uncanny adventures on fishing and hunting expeditions, when they meet weird creatures in the forest. The Mongo-Nkundo dialects are melodious, full of vowels with rising and descending tones.

Cameroon, together with the extreme eastern region of Nigeria (formerly part of the British Cameroons), is ethnically one of the most complex parts of Africa. In the southern Cameroon live large numbers of groups of Bantu peoples. Some groups have as few as 50 members. The other peoples of Cameroon speak many completely different languages, some of which have never been described. Others have been briefly described by missionaries or used for translations of the Bible, or often only one of the gospels. Among these tongues, the chief Bantu languages are Yaoundé, also called Ewondo or Mbulu, and Duala.

Bamum is one of the languages spoken in central Cameroon. In the early 1900s, the king of Bamum devised an original script for the language, making Bamum one of the few African tongues to have developed a written form of its own without the influence of either the Arabs or the Europeans. Northern Cameroon is also extremely complicated linguistically. Fulani, Arabs, and other peoples are among the many ethnic groups who live there.

The Mbundu are the chief ethnic group of Angola. Their language, which belongs to the Bantu group, uses the prefix *ki-* to indicate 'the manner in which' something is done. Thus *Kimbundu* means 'the way in which the Mbundu speak'—that is, the Mbundu language. In Kimbundu the prefix *a-* signifies a plural. One of the groups who speak Kimbundu is called the Ngola. The plural of Ngola is Angola—the name of the country. The Mbundu have a large folklore of legends and songs, an example of which is shown below.

Other Angolan languages include Umbundu, which is completely different from Kimbundu. Umbundu is spoken in the Central Highlands. In

---

A Mbundu Song
A girl finally finds her lover after many adventures. But, alas, he is bewitched and lies in a magic sleep. Unable to wake him, she sings:
Eme ngalami ni menia (I have no water)
O menia mu ngala namu, masoshi (The water which I have is tears)
Se uandala, zuela (If you please, speak)

the north, Ki-Kongo is spoken in and around San Salvador, the capital of the medieval Kingdom of Kongo.

South Africa

Malawi was once called Nyasaland, which meant 'Land of the Lake'. Its language was called Nyanja or chi-Nyanja (the language of the lake) where it has the Bantu prefix ki- which sounds like chi- in Nyanja. Nyanja is now called chi-Chewa. Malawi, or Maravi, is the name of an ancient kingdom of the Shire region mentioned in Portuguese sources of the 16th century. An example of a proverb in chi-Chewa is: *Wagona ku moto ndiye aona kutentha* 'He sits near the fire, he feels the burning'. The 'fire' may refer to the chief—that is, the man who is closest to his master knows his moods and so benefits from his knowledge. The proverb may also refer to any personal experience. For example, before you set out on a journey you should ask the advice of a man who has already seen the place.

In Zimbabwe, the Bantu language Shona is spoken by more than three quarters of the population. Shona has several major dialects, Karanga, Zezuru and Korekore. There are also two closely related languages, Kalanga and Ndau, which were once dialects of Shona. Shona has a growing body of literature, with poems, short stories, proverbs, fables, and some novels.

Some typical features of Bantu languages can be illustrated from Shona. For example, *ku-wona* in Shona and many other Bantu languages means 'to see'. *Ku-* indicates the infinitive, in the same way that 'to' is used in English. The root of the verb is *-won* (see). The ending *-a* indicates the positive. From this root, Bantu languages form a long list of other words, for example, *ku-won-is-a* (causative)—to make see, to show. From this word is derived *Mu-won-is-i*, a noun indicated by the prefix *Mu-*, and a profession indicated by the suffix *-i*. The word therefore means 'a person who shows' or 'a guide'. *Ku-won-er-a* means 'to see by means of something'. *Chi-* indicates a thing, and so the derivative *chi-won-er-o* means 'a thing by means of which one sees' or 'a similarity'. *Chi-won-is-o* means 'something that shows or illustrates', so it is the word for 'an example'.

Other words from the same root include *Ku-won-ek-a* which means 'to be visible'. The derivative *chi-won-ek-o* means 'appearance'. *Ku-won-an-a* means 'to see each other'. *Ku-won-w-a* means 'to be seen'. The infix *-w-* indicates the passive, and so *ku-won-is-w-a* means 'to be shown'. *Ku-won-is-an-a* combines the *-is* and *-an-* infixes, so it means 'to show each other'.

The main cluster of Bantu languages in South Africa is called Nguni. It was previously named after the Zulu Caffir, the Caffirs being now named the Xhosa or, for those readers who cannot pronounce the characteristic 'click', the Khosa. An offshoot of Zulu is Ndebele, which is so close to Zulu as to be mutually comprehensible. It is now spoken in the northern and central Transvaal. The

Moroccan	اَلْحَمْدُ لِلَّهِ الَّذِي هَدَانَا لَهٰذَا وَالِسَلاَ مِ وَالصَّلَاة
Hausa	وَنَرْشِينَ آبَابُرَنِ هَوْرَس كُوقَارِيا سَنْشِرْ عَرَيْسْ ثُنْزَاقِنْ
Swahili	بَعَدَ خِلِ نَصَلاَةٍ تَوْخَبِسْ كَدَ كَتْلُنْ مُوْلِدِ نِطَقَّرِ
Tuareg	ⵜ ⴳⵔⵉ ⵣⵏⵣ ⵥⵉ ⵯ ⵣ⵿ⴷⵏⴻ ⵉ⵿⵿
Vai	ꗬꗡꗨꗳ ꔢꗶꔤ ꗷꕚꗋꕞꗰ ꕢꕞ
Mende	ꖌꗝꔧꗱ ꕱꖁꔻꕞꕤ ꕪꕜꖀꕞꕱꔟꖸ
Bamum	ꚰꚡꚢꚣ ꚤꚥꚦ ꚧꚨꚩꚪꚫ ꚬ⵿ ꚭꚮ
Coptic	Ⲡⲁⲓⲣⲏϯ ⲅⲁⲣ ⲁ̀ ⲫϯ ⲙⲉⲛⲣⲉ ⲡⲓⲕⲟⲥⲙⲟⲥ ϩⲱⲥⲧⲉ ⲡⲉϥϣⲏⲣⲓ
Ancient Egyptian	𓁀 𓏏 𓁐 𓆓 𓈖 𓅓 𓆓 𓉐
Fulfulde	غَطْ غَرْطُ أُحْوُوجِكْ بَبّ پِجِ هْڲ يَبّ تَنْوَ جَبّ ع غُرْمَ تَپْلِجْ جَبّ
Amharic	ስጌዓዋ። ቀጸዓዋ። ኃይለ። ሥላሴ። ንጉሥ። ነገሥት። ዘኢትዮጵያ። አዜይ። አጼ። ይስ።

▲ Examples of written scripts used in a selection of African languages.

▲ Zulus speak a Bantu language. This language has adopted some English words (see the table below).

English words adapted to Zulu
izingilazi: glasses
izipayisi: spices
isipinashi: spinach
imotokali: motor car
isipanji: sponge
isipuni: spoon
isitimela: steamer
ililoli: lorry

biggest concentration of Ndebele split from the Zulus in the mid 1800s under their king Mzilikazi and wandered northward. They defeated the Shona peoples in Central Rhodesia and settled there. The Ndebele were defeated by the British in 1893.

Zulu is especially expressive and elegant, making it suitable for poetry, song and other literary works. An example of Zulu is a short poem by Otty Mandhlayiso:

Imbali yimbali ngokuqhakaza
icimezile yimbali ngokushiwo

The poem means:
'A flower is a flower only when bursting open. When closed, she is a flower only in name.'

The poem was written when the poet's friend was departing and the unexpressed concept behind the poem is that friendship comes to life only when two friends meet; when they are apart, it is friendship in name only: the poet needs to feel his friend's presence.

The Zulu language, like Swahili, has adopted many English words. The words have been modified to suit the rules of Bantu languages, as shown in the box. Zulu has no 'r' and the prefix *ili-* before *-loli* is worth noting.

From such combinations of English words with simplified Bantu grammar, another language sprang up. It developed during the first period of mining and plantation activity in the days of British South Africa. This language is called 'Basic Bantu', or Fanagalo (from *fana ga lo*, meaning 'just like this'). In this language, the rather complex Zulu grammar is drastically simplified.

Afrikaans is the first official language of South Africa. It is derived from Dutch. By the 1800s, the spoken language of the settlers, whose ancestors came from Holland, Flanders, and northern Germany, showed marked differences from Standard Dutch. It was called *Afrikaans Nederlands*, or

'African Dutch'. Today Afrikaans is spoken by 60
per cent of the people of European origin and by
most of the Coloureds (people of mixed origin).

Botswana is the country of the *Be*-tswana people.
One member of the nation is called a *Mo*-tswana
and the language is *Se*-tswana.

Through eastern Botswana runs an important
railway, linking Cape Town and Kimberley with
Bulawayo in Zimbabwe and Ndola in the Copper
Belt of Zambia. The railway has inspired a poem
in a Transvaal dialect, which is part of the Northern
Sotho group. Experts distinguish between the
North Sotho (or Suthu) dialects and the closely
related dialects of Lesotho, which is usually called
Southern Sotho (or Suthu), or Se-sotho. The poem
is called *Setimela*, a word that comes from the
English word 'steamer'. The poem is written as
though the train were an African chief, singing a
song praising himself. The first few lines are:

Ke nna lehokolodi le leso
(I am the black centipede)
lepopoduma, ledumela teng
(the mighty roarer, thundering inside)
leputlelele, la-nko ye ntsho
(the rusher with a black nose)
Note how, with typical Bantu style, the *le*- prefix of

the word for 'centipede' is repeated at the start of
every word group, creating natural alliteration.

The Malagasy Republic

The people of the island of Madagascar speak a
non-Bantu language, with variations of dialect from
area to area. The official language is Hova, the
language of the Merina people, the central and
most numerous ethnic group. Hova is now called
Malagasy, a word derived from the French word
Malgache. (The French colonized Madagascar in
the late 1800s.) The people of Madagascar are
descendants of immigrants from South-East Asia,
the African mainland, and Arabia. Malagasy is, by

A table showing Afrikaans
words and their
meanings. If the
Afrikaans words are
compared to Standard
Dutch, from which the
language was derived,
the two languages now
seem very dissimilar. ▼

ANIMALS			
Standard Dutch	Afrikaans	Literal meaning	English
Kameleon	trap-soetjies	'tread carefully'	chamelon
impala	rooibok	'red-buck'	impala
nÿlpaard	seekoei	'sea-cow'	hippopotamus
giraf (ziraf)	kameelpêrd	'camel-horse'	giraffe
zebra	kwagga	(from Hottentot)	zebra
ongedierte	goggas	(from Hottentot)	vermin
bruine hyena	strandwolf	'beach wolf'	brown hyena
neushoorn	renoster	(from English)	rhinoceros
python	luisland	'lazy snake'	python
serval kat	tierboskat	'tiger-forest-cat'	serval cat
gnoe	wildebees	'wild bovine'	gnu
miereneter	erdvark	'earth-pig'	antbear
ichneumon	muishond	'mouse dog'	mongoose
stekelvarken	ystervark	'iron pig'	porcupine
sabel antiloop	swartwitpens	'black-white-stomach'	sable antelope
egel	krimpvarkie	'shrink piglet'	hedgehog
FRUITS			
djamboe	koejavel		guava
mandarÿn	nartjie		tangerine
sinaasappel	lemoen		orange

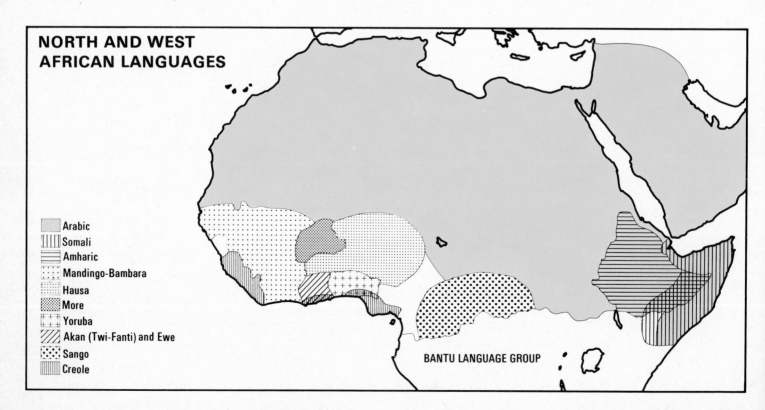

**NORTH AND WEST
AFRICAN LANGUAGES**

- Arabic
- Somali
- Amharic
- Mandingo-Bambara
- Hausa
- More
- Yoruba
- Akan (Twi-Fanti) and Ewe
- Sango
- Creole

BANTU LANGUAGE GROUP

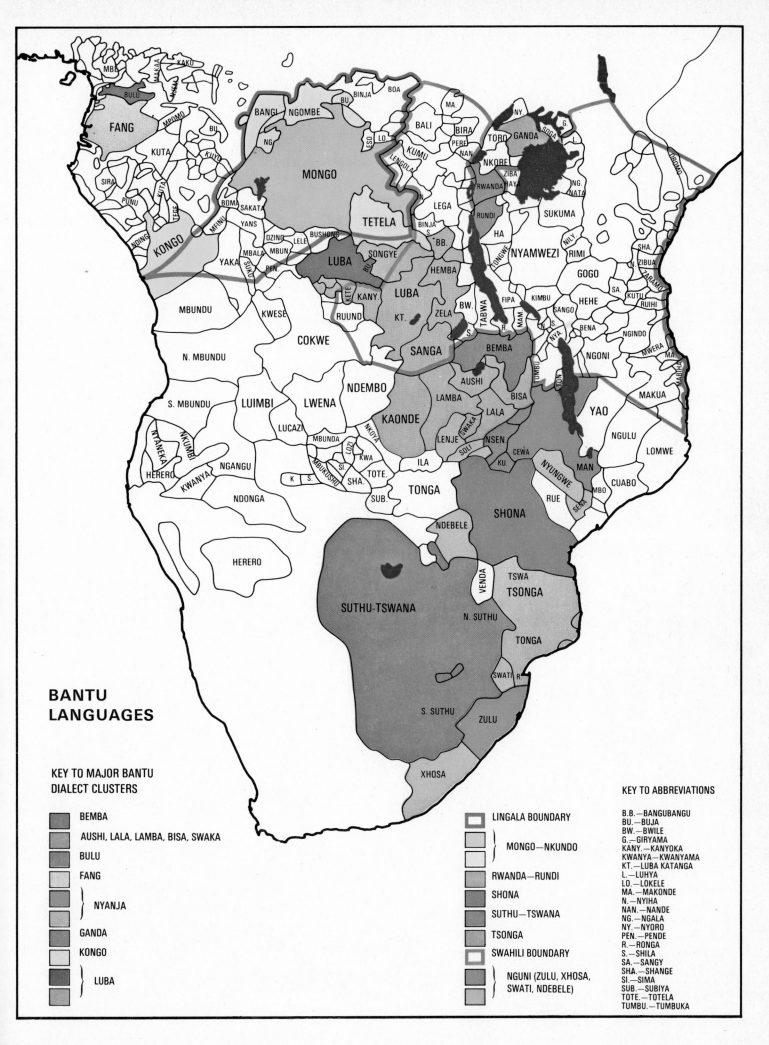

BANTU
LANGUAGES

KEY TO MAJOR BANTU DIALECT CLUSTERS

- BEMBA
- AUSHI, LALA, LAMBA, BISA, SWAKA
- BULU
- FANG
- } NYANJA
- GANDA
- KONGO
- } LUBA

- LINGALA BOUNDARY
- } MONGO—NKUNDO
- RWANDA—RUNDI
- SHONA
- SUTHU—TSWANA
- TSONGA
- SWAHILI BOUNDARY
- NGUNI (ZULU, XHOSA, SWATI, NDEBELE)

KEY TO ABBREVIATIONS

B.B.—BANGUBANGU
BU.—BUJA
BW.—BWILE
G.—GIRYAMA
KANY.—KANYOKA
KWANYA—KWANYAMA
KT.—LUBA KATANGA
L.—LUHYA
LO.—LOKELE
MA.—MAKONDE
N.—NYIHA
NAN.—NANDE
NG.—NGALA
NY.—NYORO
PEN.—PENDE
R.—RONGA
S.—SHILA
SA.—SANGY
SHA.—SHANGE
SI.—SIMA
SUB.—SUBIYA
TOTE.—TOTELA
TUMBU.—TUMBUKA

origin, an oriental language. It is related to Malay and other Indonesian languages.

Malagasy is the national language and the language of the capital Tananarive. It is used in primary schools. Malagasy has an extensive and advanced literature, including poetry, literary criticism, and works on history and geography.

It is quickly developing a vocabulary of scientific terms and is the only language in French-speaking Africa which is sufficiently developed to be used side by side with French as the official and cultural language. In some rural areas, people have resisted the introduction of Malagasy, preferring to speak their own dialects. However, the government is gradually converting people to speaking the national language. New words in Malagasy have been derived by putting together existing words.

West Africa

One group of West African languages is called the West Atlantic group. This group includes Fula

---

Malagasy Words
fo-n-kari: cruelty (literally heart-of-cat)
lala-m-bi: railway (road of iron)
lala-nd-ra: artery (road of blood)
lala-nd-rano: canal (road of water)
lala-m-po: desire (road of heart)
lala-nd-rivotra: windpipe (road of wind)
mena-sofina: a European (red ears)

(or Peul or Fulfulde), the language of about four million Fulani or Fulbe people, who are spread over a large part of West Africa. The Fulani, who are herdsmen, live in eastern Senegal, eastern Guinea, Mali, southern Niger, northern Nigeria, and even in northern Cameroon. They are darker than the Arabs, but lighter than the Africans of the forest belt to the south. A French name for the Fulani, *Toucouleur*, comes from the name *Tukulor*, which the western Fulani use to describe themselves. (It does not mean 'of all colours'.)

The Fulani call their language *Ful-ful-de* a word derived from Ful-be, which they use to describe themselves. In the word *Ful-be* the suffix *-be* denotes 'people'. The singular of *Ful-be* is *Pulo*. Most words have a different initial consonant in the singular and plural, so a plural word differs at both the beginning and the end.

Another West Atlantic language is spoken by the Wolof people of Senegal. The Wolof call their country Jolof, a word derived from Olof, the name of the language. Their word for 'love' is *sopa*; 'to be loved' is *sopu*; *sopul* is 'not to love'; and *sopalu* is 'to make love'.

Mande languages are spoken in Mali and surrounding states. One group called Mande-Fu (*fu* is the word for 'ten') includes Susu on the Guinea coast, Mende in Sierra Leone, and Kpelle and Loma in Liberia. The main group is the Mande Tan (*tan* is their word for 'ten') which includes Vai in Liberia. The one widely spread language of this group is Mande-kan, 'the Mande language' which

---

Mande Words
kan-tigi: a faithful person who keeps his word (language master)
kan-fila-tigi: a swindler or imposter (double language master)
faa: power (sabre)
faa-ma: king (a sabre-owning person)
faama-ya: royalty
faa-nta: poor (sabre-lacking)
faanta-ya: poverty
faama-muso: queen
nisi-muso: cow (bovine-female)
nisi-bombo: cow pox (bovine pimples)

Modern More Words
set-em-tore: sewing machine (literally sew-I-myself)
gulsed-em-tore: typewriter (write-I-myself)
yind-em-tore: gramophone (sing-I-myself)

Ewe Words
adzudzo-vu: steamer (smoke-boat)
yaame-vu: aeroplane (air-boat)
didi-we-nuglo-nu: telegraph (far-place-writing-thing)
did-we-nuwo-nu: telephone (far-place-speech-thing)

---

is spoken by the Mande and Mali-nke (Mali people), by the Dyula traders in the south (Ivory Coast), and by people as far as the boundaries of Nigeria. They are often called the Bambara by Europeans, Bamana by themselves, and Malel by the Arabs. This confusing collection of names is comparable in Europe to the Germans, called Deutsche by themselves, Allemands by the French, Tedeschi by the Italians, Tyskar by thé Swedes, and Nemci by the Czechs. The Mande language is extremely flexible. It is often called kan-gbe—the language of clarity.

The Gur languages include Senufo on the western borders of Upper Volta and to the north the Dogon. About two million Mosi people belong to this group. They inhabit the savanna regions in the northern part of Upper Volta. The Mosi people, called Mossi by the French and Mo-se by themselves, speak a language called More. This language uses compound words to express modern terms, as shown in the box.

A large and important group of West African languages is called the Kwa group. Kwa languages include the Akan language, with its dialects Twi and Fante. Akan is best known as the language of the kingdom of Ashante in Ghana. Although its speakers are proud of their language, it has not achieved more than local official status in Ghana, where English is still the chief language of education and administration. The people call their own language *Twii-kasa* (the Twi language). It is governed by *kasa-mmara* (language law), the Twi-Akan word for grammar. From the last half of the word *kasa-mmara*, one makes the word *mmara-hye* (literally law-fixing) which means legislation. The legislator is a *mmara-hye-fo* (law-fix-man). The trespasser is *mmara-ton-fo* (law-twist-man). He is fined with *mmara-ton-de* (*de* is money) for 'twisting' the law (*mmara*). By this method thousands of new words can be formed.

In Togo, the chief language is Ewe, which is related to the Akan-Twi group. The similarity between them is shown by the way in which new words are made from combining existing words. Examples are shown in the box.

With a population of more than 67 millions, Nigeria has a larger population than any other country in Africa. In southern Nigeria, and in the capital Lagos, Yoruba is the main language. Words for every need can also be constructed in Yoruba. For example, by adding a negative prefix *ài-* to words, new words are formed with an abstract meaning. *Ai-kú* literally means 'not-die' and this is the word for 'immortality'; and *ài-mò* (not-know) means 'ignorance'. Modern concepts or inventions are combinations of existing words. For example, *okò-ilè* means 'boat (on) land'—that is, railway. Yoruba and Nupe, a language spoken farther north can also be written in Arabic script. Yoruba also has an extensive literature in Roman script and is one of the most important literary languages in the whole of modern Africa.

Bini or Edo is the language spoken in Benin state.

To the east of the Niger River, more than 3,000,000 people speak Igbo (also called Ibo). Igbo is the chief contact language of the Eastern region of Nigeria. One characteristic of Igbo is that several words can derive from one root form. Examples are shown in the box.

The eastern part of Nigeria and most of Cameroon are inhabited by hundreds of small groups, each with its own quite distinct language. Many of these languages have never been described and many have never been written down. North of this area, Islam has had a great influence on the culture of the people. Such languages as Fula (described above) and Hausa have literatures in Arabic script. Hausa is the chief language of northern Nigeria. More people in West Africa speak it as their first language than any other tongue. It is also used as a contact or *market language*. It is spoken in such countries as Niger, Benin (Dahomey), Cameroon, and even Ghana. The code of laws of Northern Nigeria have been translated into Hausa from English. Hausa is likely to become an official language, side by side with English.

Hausa has adopted many hundreds of words from Arabic and English, and this fact makes it one of the richest of all African tongues. For example, the Hausa word for 'soldier' is *soja* from the English 'soldier'.

North-East Africa

The Nilotic family of languages are spoken in southern Sudan, Uganda and western Kenya. They probably originated in the central Sudan. The southern Nilotic sub-family group comprises Alur-Acholi-Lango in Zaire and northern Uganda and Luo in Kenya. The Alur are tall people, lighter coloured than their neighbours. They live on the western banks of Lake Mobutu Sese Seko and the Nile, where that river leaves the lake. Numbering some 200,000, they straddle the Uganda-Zaire border. The Alur reached their present home from the Nile valley to the north about 100 years ago. The Alur language is one of the purest of Nilotic tongues and it has an extremely interesting oral literature.

In the western Sudan, Nilotic languages include Thuri, Bodho, Cholo, Bor, and Lwo or Jur (Giur). In the eastern Sudan, they include Shilluk and Burun-Jumjum-Maban. In western Ethiopia, the Nilotic tongue Anuak is spoken. Nilotic languages are characterized by a preference for monosyllabic

> **Igbo words from the root -che**
> *ichè:* to think
> *echichè:* thought
> *uchè:* mind, common sense
> *ochè:* thinker
> *nchè-ta:* remembrance, reminiscence

> **Hausa Words**
> *jirgin-wuta:* steamboat (boat of fire)
> *jirgin-sama:* aeroplane (boat of sky)
> *gida-n-gizo:* prison (house of spiders)
> *gida-n-kudi:* bank (house of money)

> **Arabic Words Using the Three Radical Consonants** *ktb*
> *kitab:* a book
> *kataba:* he wrote
> *kutubiyya:* a library
> *katib:* a scribe
> *ma-ktab:* office
> *aktaba:* he dictated
> *uktiba:* he took down dictation
> *mukatib:* correspondent

◀ A Falasha woman photographed outside Gondar, Ethiopia. The Falasha practise Judaism.

word-roots, a verbal conjugation system with prefixes for persons and with tones for tenses, and plural formation by suffixes or vowel alterations.

Dinka and Nuer are two separate dialect groups and sub-families of the Nilotic family. Dinka has four main dialects, one of which, Rek, is the most widely used in commerce and education. The oral literature of the Dinka is rich, especially their songs.

Ethiopia has several interesting languages. One of them, Ge'ez, is now extinct but it is still recited in Ethiopian Christian services. Amharic, the language of the Amharas in central Ethiopia, is still written with the ancient Ge'ez script. With 251 characters, this script is difficult to master. Amharic, called Amarinya by the Amharas, is the language of the imperial court and thus Ethiopia's official language. About five million Ethiopians speak it as a first language and it is also spoken by most other Ethiopians as a second language.

The Oromo language is spoken by over 12 million Galla people in Ethiopia and northern Kenya. In the 16th and 17th centuries, the Galla were a powerful people who menaced the Amharas to the north. Some Galla have been converted to Islam, but the Christian Bible, too, has been translated into the Galla language.

The Somali language is spoken everywhere throughout Somalia except in the southern tip, where Swahili is spoken. Somali is also spoken in the south-eastern corner of Ethiopia. The Somali government recently agreed on an orthography for the language with Roman letters. Previously, only Arabic script had been used. The Somali language is being adapted for modern times. For example the word *wargeys* (literally information conveyor) is the new word for newspaper; and *dayachgacmeed* (hand-made moon) is the word for spacecraft.

Northern Africa

With more than 100 million speakers, Arabic is seventh among the world's most spoken languages. With more than 80 million speakers in Africa, Arabic is Africa's most spoken language. Besides the Arabs, many other Africans in Chad, Eritrea, Mali, Niger, Senegal, Somalia and Zanzibar use Arabic as their contact language with the outside world.

Like all Semitic languages, Arabic is based on the principle that every word must have three *radical* (root) consonants and that the vowels indicate the grammatical function of the word. The order of the consonants embodies the essential meaning of the word. In a dictionary words are grouped under the three radical consonants, such as *ktb* in *kitab* (book). All derivative words using *ktb* are assembled together.

English words adapted into Arabic have to be changed so that they have three consonants. For example, the English word 'jug' is adapted to become *jagg* (plural *jugug*). In the same way, jeep becomes *jiyb* (plural *juyub*). Because Arabic has no letter 'p', piston becomes *bistan* (plural *basatin*). *Taksi* (taxi) forms the plural *takasi*.

15

RELIGIONS

Africa has many religions. They include those introduced from the Middle East (Islam and Christianity) and the ethnic religions. It is possible that these ethnic religions may be more than a thousand in number.

Islam and Ethiopian and Coptic Christianity have more than a thousand years of tradition behind them in Africa. *Animistic* is a term used to describe many of the ethnic religions. Animism involves a belief in spirits that inhabit stones and rivers, trees and winds and other natural phenomena. However, each of Africa's many ethnic groups has its own unique religion, some of which are not animistic. This is why theologians talk of *ethnic religions*, when they wish to distinguish African religions from Christianity and Islam. In many cases, the ethnic religions are very different from Islam or Christianity.

Every group of people has its own culture. The culture of each group has its own spiritual values, which make life worthwhile. These values are the motivating source of the peoples' activities and among nearly all the peoples of Africa, these values include religious concepts. However, like many peoples in the modern world, some African peoples have become less interested in religion.

The study of religion starts from three basic principles. These principles are *belief, behaviour,* and most important, *purpose*. For example, the purpose of a Muslim is to attain Paradise, and the purpose of a mystic is to experience the Divine Presence. From these main goals in life come all other values. These values determine peoples' behaviour, affecting their ways of life and special activities, such as ritual.

Culture and Belief Most religions can be adopted by people of widely varying ways of life. For instance, Islam has been successful among the cattle-herding Fulani of the grasslands of West Africa. It has also thrived among the Dyula traders of West Africa, and the agricultural Hausa of northern Nigeria. Each of these peoples has its own history, and Islam took on a new shape in each case.

The same applies to Christianity. The Chagga Lutherans of Tanzania and the Kikuyu Presbyterians of Kenya are very different from the Monophysite Ethiopians, or the Roman Catholics in Zaire, to say nothing of independent Christian sects. The imported religions are given new shape in the context of African philosophy.

Christianity and Islam co-exist with traditional religions in many areas. *Below left* A Christian is baptised by total immersion at Brazzaville, Congo's capital. *Below right* A wooden carving representing a horseman. This Yoruba carving was used by worshippers during rituals.

Bottom left A Muslim mosque at Malindi, Kenya. *Bottom right* A group of Ethiopian Coptic Christian priests.

▲ A *nkisi*, or religious symbol, from the region north of the mouth of the River Zaire. The carvings have great ritual power. This thick-set figure inspires fear and the pieces of iron in the shoulders and chest add to its power.

A statuette of a fertility goddess from Congo. Such statuettes were important in traditional religions. ▼

Belief in a Supreme Being Not all the peoples of Africa believe in one Creator, the 'High God'. No trace of such a belief exists among some peoples. Among others, however, the idea of a Creator is most elaborate.

It seems that wherever a clearer idea of one God existed, it has spread over a vast area. The idea was given new impetus by the introduction of Christianity and Islam. Christianity spread over much of North Africa, northern Sudan and Ethiopia during the first few hundred years of the Christian era. It survived in the Ethiopian Empire. It was brought to the coasts of West, South and East Africa from the late 1400s onwards.

Islam spread through North Africa from AD 640 onwards. Flourishing cities in East and West Africa were centres of Islamic culture in the 1100s. The ancient West African empires of Mali and Ghana had Muslim rulers, though the traditional African religions were practised by a very large proportion of the West African peoples.

The concept of a distant Creator, who seldom interferes in the lives of men, seems to develop as societies grow more complex. In less advanced societies, this idea is only a vague notion. It becomes very developed where *rationality* (the use of reason) is greater. This theory is supported by the fact that names for the One God are remarkably similar in groups of unrelated or distantly related languages. For example, *Nyame* or *Nyambe*, the root form (radical) of a word for God, is used from Ghana to Zaire. The word *Kalunga* (God) comes from western Angola and probably means *ocean*. This word is used as far inland as south-eastern Zaire, where it now means *spirit*.

In Zambian languages, the word *Lesa* is used for God. This word originally meant *rain*. Similarly, *Ngai*, or God, means *rain* in Masai. The Kikuyu took over this word and reinterpreted it to mean *the Divider*.

God, Natural Phenomena and Spirits The origin of the idea of God in natural phenomena seems more distinctly African. Words for 'sun' and 'sky' seem to develop a secondary meaning of God in Cameroon and some parts of Tanzania, Kenya and Zambia. The words for 'water' or 'river' seem to be the original meanings of some East African words for God. For example, *Adroa* or *Androa* (river) is used for God by the Lugbara in Uganda. In Zulu, *Umhlanga* is the *reed* from which men came. The Zulu word *Unkulunkulu*, which is now used for God, seems to have meant *ancestor*. In some languages of the forest belt, such as the Ubangi–Shari group and some which are spoken in Cameroon, the word for God seems to be the same as *forest*. This may explain a saying in Zaire: 'We get everything from the forest.' It seems that the oldest idea of God is often connected with water and vegetation.

In many other languages, the word for God is not clearly separated from the word for spirit. The Swahili word *Mulungu* or *the Good One*, (*Mungu* in modern Swahili) was adopted as the word for God by many East African peoples. This word has a plural form which means *idols*. The word *Modimo* in Tswana and Sotho means God and spirit. The same applies to the word *Jok* in Alur, Acholi, Luo and Lango, all Nilotic languages of East Africa. *Jok* means God, spirit, spirits and spirit-energy. (See also the chapters on *Peoples of Africa*, page 7, and *Languages of Africa*, page 9.)

The Forest God in some regions along the Zaire River may have originally been the Hunter God. The Hunter God is not always clearly distinguished from the tribal ancestor, who, in many cases is identical with the *culture hero*. Through myths, the culture hero is the forefather of the people. He is sometimes thought of as a clan leader who invented the bow and arrow, and traps and snares. He may also have given his people cattle and cassava, or taught them how to fish with nets, fish traps, lines or poison. In later myths, the God-figure may gradually be separated from the hero-figure. In such myths, God first taught the art of hunting or hoeing to the hero-figure. However, the original forms of these mythical beings are very shadowy and remote.

Acts of Worship After belief and purpose in religion comes action. This takes the form of worship, the performance of rituals, the reciting of prayers or formulae, sacrifices, or good deeds. Such acts lose their meaning without belief and purpose. They become repetitions of the remembered past. This happens in many religions. However, many purely African religions are still very much alive. Most Ashanti villagers worship a High God, whom they call *Onyame*. In every town where a chief lives, a priest works full time in the service of God.

Among many African peoples, the chief himself is often the leading priest. Indeed, this holy office is often what makes a qualified man become a chief. In some parts of Uganda, only the rainmaker (or priest), who has the magic power to placate the Rain-God, is worthy of royal office. Among the Ngbandi of northern Zaire, on the other hand, the priesthood is hereditary. It passes to the eldest male heir, irrespective of whether the chieftainship is held by the same person.

In many regions, the priesthood is granted after a long period of apprenticeship. Apprentices are initiated into the secret lore and magic rites. In some cases, priests can be recruited only from certain families and never from the common people. In other cases, priests select novices who show signs of a mysterious quality. This quality is called in some African languages: 'receptive to becoming the seat of God', or the 'wife of God'. The expression *wife of God*, does not mean that the medium who from time to time is dominated or 'possessed' by the God, must be a woman. It means only that the novice is like a woman in relation to the Godhead. In Islam, as in Christianity, religious ceremonies are only conducted by men. But in many West African religions, a woman can and, in some cases, must perform the ritual to propitiate or appease God.

Rites Ceremonies are solemn occasions which are usually composed of a number of rites. These acts are mostly accompanied by certain words and phrases, which are sometimes spoken in a special language. Rites must be performed at special times and places. Otherwise, the rites will not be valid and the Divinity will not be propitiated.

The chief purpose of rites is to please the powerful spirit. The people may wish for prosperity, children, cattle, health and long life. Rites may also be performed to prevent dangers, such as sickness, floods, drought, famine and death. These disasters may be, or may already have been, caused by God or by an evil spirit. In many cases, people believe that God punishes people for their sins by causing disasters. These sins may simply be the neglect of sacrifices for the spirits, or of obligatory prayers to God, or immorality, as defined in every religion.

Gods and Spirits Gods have stronger personalities than spirits. They have a more marked place in the mythology of the people. For example, the gods of the ancient Greeks, Egyptians and Hindus are remembered because each has a distinct character and myths are told about them.

Spirits are more vague. They are shadowy forces or are undefinable feelings that make us shiver. They are phosphorescent vapours in the forest, the bamboo bush that crackles in the night wind from the sea, or the Zaire River that splashes mysteriously.

▲ A dance mask used in boys' initiation ceremonies among the western Bapende people of south-western Zaire. Initiation ceremonies were part of the religious training of young people in many areas.

An elaborate shrine at Bondoukou in the Ivory Coast, showing the influence of Christianity on local religions. ▼

Many African gods still show signs of links with the kingdom of nature. For example, there is the mother hippopotamus of the Ronga people in Mozambique and some groups along the Wele-Ubangi. These gods are similar to ancient Egyptian gods, such as Thoueris, the Nile goddess of protection, who had the shape of a hippo. The revered animal may sometimes be a God or an ancestor. For example, the Makere in Zaire believe that they are descended from the chimpanzee. Other groups believe that their ancestor was the leopard or the crocodile and never eat their flesh.

Spirit Possession Many people believe that it is dangerous to antagonize an ancestral spirit—that is, the spirit of parents or grandparents who live near the homes of their descendants. Failure to make correct sacrifices may anger a spirit. Disease may be the result. There is an elaborate 'spirit possession cult' in many parts of Africa. In this cult, spirits sometimes talk through a man or woman, called a *medium*. The priest or diviner has the magic power to make the God or spirit descend into the body of the medium. The spirit then speaks through the medium's mouth. It may speak a language that the medium does not know. But the words of that language are correctly pronounced by the medium who acts as a temporary body for the God or spirit. Such things have actually happened. But whether the spirit was really there is a matter of belief.

Belief and Morality Because man's purpose is the basis of his beliefs, his life has a fixed direction and is filled with religious activities. These include prayers and ritual slaughter of goats or cows, dance rites, songs and recitals, processions and other festive or solemn gatherings. Every community of people, knowing that it belongs together, feels that such activities are essential. Belonging together is the result of belief. It is the cause of a good purpose, a good moral life, good deeds and so on.

Such faith forms the strongest basis of morality—that is, the wish to be good and to avoid evil. With the exception of criminals, who exist in all societies, all men want to be good, or to be seen as good, or both. This holds people together in a community and makes life progress.

Taboos and Totemism Hunting tribes wanted the God of the wilderness to favour them. Their prayers asked him to 'send the game in the hunters' direction'. Connected with hunting there were certain forbidden acts or taboos. If these taboos were broken, then the God might become angry and keep the game hidden from the hunters and they would go home empty handed.

Early man did not consider himself to be superior to the rest of nature. Indeed, he identified himself with one of his fellow creatures. For instance, the Transvaal Suthu stress this identity in an animal dance, when each clan performs a special dance in

honour of the animal. If it is their custom 'to dance the lion', the clan will confirm 'we are lions'. Similarly, the Venda in North Transvaal do the python dance. In Uganda, the crane dance and the monkey dance are performed. The characteristic movements of the animals are often imitated, but this is not necessary in all cases. The Kamba in Kenya are divided into Leopards, Jackals, Hyaenas, Hawks and other clans. Among the Lovedu in North Transvaal, there are Elephants, Crocodiles, Bush Dogs, Impalas and Porcupines. Among the Nandi of Kenya, clansmen do not claim descent from any human founder. But they do claim to be brothers of their clan animal or *totem*.

Through the totem, there exists a mystical brotherhood between all members of the clan. Among the Nuer of central Sudan, some clans 'respect' lions, because someone of that clan, having killed a lion who attacked his sheep, started to behave like a lion. This meant that the lion spirit had put a spell on the man. A sheep had to be sacrificed to the lion spirit to remove the spell.

Some scholars have suggested that the totem system is not directly related to the animals, but to the spirits of the animals. However, there remains the problem: what is a spirit? Although spirits are said to exist everywhere in all African countries, there is, inevitably, a great lack of information about these spirits.

Christianity has had a considerable effect on the culture of many communities in Africa. *Bottom left* The Anglican cathedral at Lusaka, Zambia. *Below left* A Sunday school at Masasi, Tanzania. *Bottom right* A child reading Christian literature that has been translated into Swahili.

TRADITIONAL LITERATURE

More than a thousand languages are spoken in Africa by as many peoples. Each group of peoples has its own rich traditions. Parents and grandparents have passed on the traditions by word of mouth to their children, and in some cases special tutors instructed children in sacred, often secret lore. Accounts of past history, moral rules, stories and poems were often not written down. They survived, however, because they were learned word for word by each generation. In Africa, many men know long epic poems by heart.

Today, however, fewer and fewer young people have as much time as their ancestors for 'tribal lore' and unfortunately the older men who still retain these traditions are also becoming fewer and fewer. As a result, irreplaceable treasures of *oral*—that is spoken—literature are being lost at an alarming rate.

Since the 1800s various scholars, most of them missionaries, began to write down the traditional lore of peoples among whom they lived. Because of the work of the missionaries, the beauty of much oral literature has been preserved. Many books have been filled with texts, translations and commentaries. More recently, some African scholars and writers, in the first place in Hausa, Igbo, Kongo, Sotho, Swahili, Shona, Yoruba and Zulu, have written down their oral literature, sometimes in their own language, or sometimes in the English or French languages.

Early Written Literatures Some African peoples have an interesting cultural heritage with a very ancient written literature. The best known example of an old written literature is Ethiopic. This literature was written in Ge'ez, a language which is now extinct, although it is still recited for religious purposes in Ethiopia. Three living Semitic languages, Amharic, Tigre and Tigrinya, are written in Ethiopic characters which may derive from ancient South Arabian inscriptions. Tigrinya is a descendant of the old Abyssinian language, but it is Amharic which has the oldest literature of any living language in Africa. Coptic, an even older language with an extensive Christian literature, can no longer be regarded as a living language.

Literature in Arabic Script Other African peoples with a written literature are those that have come under the influence of Islamic learning. Arabic is not only important as a spoken language, but it has also been widely used for written literature. For example, the Somalis had no written literature in their own language. Although there is a rich variety of oral literature, Somali scholars had always composed their *written* works in the Arabic language. In October, 1972, scholars finally agreed on a form of *orthography* (accepted spellings) for Somali in Roman script. This will mark a milestone in Somali history: it will open the way to the creation of a modern written literature out of oral tradition and poetry.

PROVERBS FROM AFRICA

The dog you did not feed will not hear your call (Zaire)
Leave the handling of the gun to the hunter (Angola)
Let the jealous man envy you: his grief at your joy is enough punishment for him (Arabic)
A man of power may be right or wrong, but he is always right (Bambara)
The man you offered no coffee will be the one you meet when you are in need (Buganda)
When cat and mouse make an alliance, shopkeeper watch your wares (Egypt)
A guest is like a river: he should not be stagnant (Kikuyu)
A kind person is the one who is kind to a stranger (Kongo)
No man will starve in his mother's house (Liberia)
People are like plants in the wind: they bow down and rise up again (Malagasy Republic)
The tree remembers, the axe does not remember (*Meaning:* the victim of an insult remembers, the offender forgets) (Shona)
He who takes his time does not fall (Somali)
Praise the palm-wine tapster and he will dilute the wine (Swahili)
When you see a fly, it comes from the dirt (Tsonga, Transvaal)
If you never offer palm-wine to your uncle, you will not learn many proverbs (Yoruba)

Mali also has very little written literature in the local Mande (Mandingue) language. The scholars write in Arabic, although the poets keep up the tradition of memorized compositions of long epics and other songs in the Mande language. In the many dialects of the Mande group (Mandingo, Bambara, Dyula, Malinke), there are hundreds of stories and many long epics, some of them commemorating the exploits of the national hero Sundjata. The Mande peoples still have a separate guild or caste (*dyeli-ya* in Mande) for professional troubadours, or poet-musicians. The Berbers have the *amdyaz*, a professional poet, wandering reciter and singer of tales.

The most important written literature in West Africa is in Hausa, the language of northern Nigeria and neighbouring areas of Niger. Hausa literature in Arabic script is called *Ajami*. It is mainly in verse. The main categories are hymns to the Prophet Muhammad, sermons in verse about hell and paradise, versified doctrine, morality and law.

Oral poetry is a very old tradition of the Hausa people. It is performed with music by professional singing poets (*mawaka*). The poems either contain praise (*yabo*), or they can mock and make fun of their subjects, in *zambo*. The subjects of poetry may be great men and rulers who pay the poets and performers. Poems may also concern farming, hunting, politics, and wrestling, and are sometimes specially made up for religious and spiritual occasions.

The most important musical instrument used with oral poetry is the talking drum (*kalangu*), which can imitate the different tones of the human voice. Stringed instruments such as the *molo* and *garaya* also provide music with the poetry.

In Fula (Fulani or Peul), there are chronicles, some other histories and poetry in Arabic script, although most Fula poetry is oral. One manuscript in Arabic script has been found written in the Dagomba or Dagbane language of northern Ghana. Writings in Kanuri, the language of the ancient Bornu empire around Lake Chad, have been discovered. They date back to the 1600s. Nupe in western Nigeria also uses Arabic script, but little is known of its literature. This also applies to Yoruba, which is spoken in the same region. Some fat, handwritten volumes in Arabic script have recently been discovered, but research into these volumes is only beginning. Malagasy, the language of the Malagasy Republic, has also been written in Arabic characters. Malagasy written literature includes stories and magic charms, as well as Islamic texts.

Swahili Literature The language with the most extensive literature in Arabic script is Swahili. More than 20,000 pages have been collected. Most texts are in verse, even on such topics as dogma and duties. Swahili also has the most elaborate epic literature of Africa. More than 70 long poems contain heroic, religious and allegorical legends. Many people recite these poems from memory, so the oral and written traditions are united. In Kenya and Tanzania, many people write in Swahili and a modern Swahili literature in Roman script is quickly developing. One of the leading modern Swahili writers was Shaaban Robert (1911–62). He wrote children's stories, a biography and verses called *Utenzi wa Vita vya Uhur (Epic on the war for Freedom)*. Other writers of the Swahili language were M. S. Abdulla, Mathias Mnyampala and Sheikh Kaluta Amri Abedi.

Other Languages African authors also write fiction today in Zulu and Xhosa (South Africa). Sotho (Lesotho), Yoruba and Hausa in Roman script (Nigeria), Nyanja or Chewa (Malawī) and Ganda (Luganda in Buganda). Many other modern African writers such as those who write in the Hausa and Yoruba languages make use of traditional subjects.

Literature in four of the main languages of Zaire (Kongo, Mongo-Nkundo, Ngbandi-Sango and Luba) has been published by missionaries who collected oral literature. The most outstanding is the long cycle of miraculous exploits of the hero-ancestor Lianja in Nkundo. According to legend, Lianja was born, fully armed, through his mother's shin.

Some people will help you put your basket on your head so that they can see what's in it (Zulu)

Traditional themes and forms Heroes are plentiful in African epics. There is King Liongo, the hero-poet of Swahili songs, who possibly lived in the Middle Ages and who, according to legend, could only be killed by a copper needle introduced into his navel; there is Antar, the black poet and fighter of the Sahara Arabs; there is Abu Zaidi and his Banu Hilali who conquered North Africa; there is Anansi, the spider, in Ghana, who travelled with the slaves to the New World; and the Tula among the Azande of the Southern Sudan, who is a mythical hero with divine powers. Kabundi (the martin, of the Luba in Zaire) and Ucakijana (the mongoose, of Zulu legends) are rogue-heroes and tricksters, like the fox in Frankish fables. Nwanpfundla, among the Tsonga of southern Mozambique, is a hare, similar to Brer Rabbit in the United States.

Animal fables generally tell of how an animal trickster, such as a hare, spider or tortoise, overcomes more powerful opponents.

Traditional African literature also includes countless proverbs, riddles and funny expressions. There are also songs for every occasion, from dirges to lullabies, including fishing songs, herdings songs, hoeing songs, hunting songs, picking songs, pounding songs and rowing songs. Both dirges and dance songs often play a part in religious life.

AN AFRICAN FABLE

In Nyanja, there is a proverb *Chifundo chidaapa nkwale*, which means 'Kindness killed the partridge.' It is illustrated by the following fable:

A strong wind blew a bush fire toward a river. In the bush lived lizards, waterbucks, birds and snakes. A puff adder realized the danger. He asked a partridge to give him a lift to the other side of the river. The partridge and the puff adder had not always been on good terms, but finally the partridge agreed to help. The kind bird took up a stick. He told the puff adder to bite on the middle of it. The partridge then took up the stick at both ends and flew across the river. The snake was safe.

Some time later, the puff adder was hungry. He thought it would be a good idea to eat the partridge, because it would be easy to catch him. The snake told the trusting partridge that he wanted to go home. The partridge replied that he was not in a hurry. The snake pretended to be impatient. The partridge was still undecided when the snake bit him. The poison swiftly spread through the body of the partridge and he died. The snake ate him, not caring to remember that he owed his life to the bird. He preferred to eat him rather than ask for another favour.

The proverb 'Kindness killed the partridge' is sometimes used by a person to someone asking a favour. The person asking the favour is then obliged to return the money or the object he has borrowed. Otherwise, he will be compared to the puff adder.

This story was told to Dr. Jan Knappert of the School of Oriental and African Studies, University of London by a Zambian, S. G. Mpandoki. When the story was finished, another man who had been listening, suggested a different meaning. He said that a girl might quote the proverb when she was approached by a young man. In this way, she would appeal to the young man's gentleness and sense of responsibility. This may well be the origin of the fable. Snakes are often used as male symbols, and the partridge has female characteristics, such as kindness and truthfulness.

MODERN LITERATURE

One of the more astonishing developments of the last 20 years in Africa has been the sudden and dramatic flowering of literature in the languages of the former colonial powers (English, French and Portuguese). This literature complements the more limited circulation of books written in ethnic languages such as Swahili, Yoruba, Igbo, Chinyanja, Bemba, Kikuyu and Dholuo.

The Colonial Age Apart from the formal English verse composed by Olaudah Equiano, an 18th-century slave, such literature usually had political origins. But in East Africa there was Jomo Kenyatta's classical piece of cultural nationalism, *Facing Mount Kenya*, first published in 1938; Julius Nyerere's fine speeches and writings on terminal colonialism and socialism *(Ujamaa)*; Tom Mboya's *Freedom and After* and Oginga Odinga's *Not Yet Uhuru*. In West Africa there were Kwame Nkrumah's books on neo-colonialism and African unity (including his autobiography *I Speak of Freedom*), Chief Obafemi Awolowo's *Path to Nigerian Freedom* and Nnamdi Azikiwe's *Zik*.

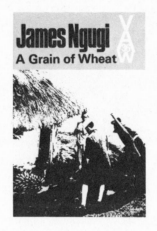

After independence The main themes of this new literature included the countryman coming to the town, the return of the young man who has been to Europe for his education and the dilution of African culture by European influences. In West Africa the major contemporary literary figures are, in Nigeria: Chinua Achebe, novelist and poet; the late Christopher Okigbo (a poet killed during the Nigerian civil war); Gabriel Okara, novelist and poet; J. P. Clark, poet, dramatist and essayist; Cyprian Ekwensi, novelist; Wole Soyinka, dramatist and novelist; Nkem Nwankwo, novelist; Amos Tutuola, traditional storyteller; Onuora Nzekwu, novelist; Ola Rotimi, dramatist; Michael Echeruo, poet and literary critic, and Elechi Amadi, novelist. In Ghana there are Ayi Kwei Armah, novelist; J. C. de Graft,

The brilliant young Nigerian writer, Chinua Achebe, winner of many literary awards. ▶

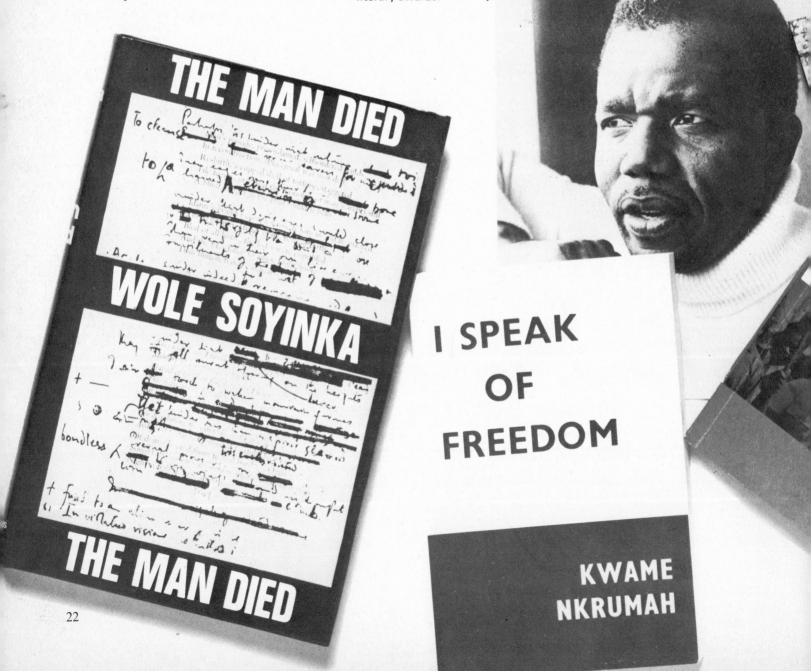

22

dramatist; Ama Ata Aidoo, dramatist; Efua Sutherland, dramatist, and Cameron Duodo, novelist. There is also the Gambian novelist Lenrie Peters and the Sierra Leonean poet and short story writer, Abioseh Nicol, and his compatriots, the novelist William Conton, the dramatist R. Sarif Easmon and the critic Eldred Jones. In East Africa the major figures are Okot p'Bitek, the Ugandan poet and novelist; Ngugi wa Thiongo, the Kenyan novelist and playwright; Austin Bukenya, the Ugandan novelist; the Kenyan novelists and short story writers, Grace Ogot, Leonard Kibera and his brother Sam Kahiga; Taban Lo Liyong, the Ugandan poet and literary critic, the playwrights Kenneth Watene from Kenya and John Ruganda and Robert Serumaga from Uganda; the Kenyan novelist Meja Mwangi and the Ugandan poet Okello Oculi.

South Africa There is a growing literature in both English and Afrikaans which consists firstly of

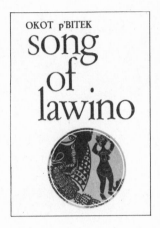

attacks upon the social system by writers often now in exile and secondly of nostalgic but hopeless writings about the political situation. These include the works of Peter Abrahams, Athol Fugard, Alan Paton and Laurens van der Post, the poetry of Dennis Brutus and the work of Lewis Nkosi, Bloke Madisane and Bessie Head.

French African Literature Authors are deeply concerned with cultural integrity. President Senghor of Senegal is one of the finest contemporary poets and his followers include Birago Diap, David Diap and Conte Saidon. From Cameroon come the novelists Mongo Beti and Ferdinand Oyono.

Portuguese African Literature The long guerilla struggle for freedom produced a dozen first-class war poets who also became political leaders. From Angola came Agostinho Neto, Antonia Jacinto, Viriato da Cruz, Arnaldo Santos and Fernando Costa Andrade; from Mozambique, Marcellino dos Santos, Armando Guebuza, Jorge Rebelo and Jose Craveirinha; and from Guinea-Bissau, Onesimo Silveira and Mario Cissoko.

South African writer, Nadine Gordimer.

GUIDE TO PEOPLES AND LANGUAGES

Scholars estimate that more than 2,000 names are used for peoples and languages in Africa. Each name may have several forms, spelled according to the language in which it is used.

This guide was largely derived from the published reference works of the International African Institute and from the documentation available in its London office, which is, as yet, unpublished. In *Africa Bibliography: Series A* are listed, initially by region and country, all works known to the Institute on the ethnology, sociology and linguistics of the various peoples. The Institute has also produced some sixty volumes in its *Ethnographic Survey of Africa*. Each volume gives a summary of the available information on African peoples or groups of related peoples and also provides a bibliography. Information on all known languages and dialects of Africa is provided by four volumes in the series *Handbook of African Languages: La langue berbère* (André Basset); *Languages of West Africa* (D. Westermann and M. A. Bryan); *The Non-Bantu Languages of North-eastern Africa* (A. N. Tucker and M. A. Bryan); and *The Bantu Languages of Africa* (M. A. Bryan).

The present guide does not claim to be a comprehensive work, but it does contain every name used as a heading in the Institute's card catalogue, supplemented by numerous cross-references and also additional names obtained from the *Ethnographic Survey of Africa* and the *Handbook of African Languages*. The minimum information given is the country or area in which the people live, any figure available as to their number (often based on antiquated sources), and the type of languages which they speak.

Entries on terms relating to African peoples and their languages are also included as entries in the guide. A comprehensive system of cross-references (e.g. CLASS LANGUAGES) is provided to help readers to find their way through this complex pattern of languages.

Abe, a people living in Ivory Coast. They number 25,000 and speak a language belonging to the KWA language family.

Abulu, a people living in north-eastern Zaire numbering 1,450. The Abulu speak a MORU-MANGBETU language.

Abure, a people who live in Ivory Coast. They number 8,200 and speak a KWA language.

Achipawa (Achifawa), a Nigerian people living near the Niger River numbering 16,800. They speak a CLASS LANGUAGE of Nigeria.

Acholi (Acoli), a people who live in northern Uganda and Sudan numbering 216,000. They speak a NILOTIC LANGUAGE of the South Lwo group.

Adangme, a Ghanaian people, number more than 100,000. They speak a KWA language.

Adele, a people living in Togo to the north of the town of Kposo.

Adhola, people living in Uganda and Kenya. They number 73,000 and they speak a NILOTIC LANGUAGE of the South Lwo group.

Adja, a people living in Togo, where they number 3,000, and in Benin (Dahomey). They speak a dialect of the EWE language.

Adyukru, a people living in Ivory Coast. They number 21,000 and speak a WEST ATLANTIC LANGUAGE.

Afar (Adal) or (Danakil) are groups of nomadic herdsmen in Ethiopia and in the Territory of Afars and Issas. They number 109,000 and they speak Afar, a CUSHITIC LANGUAGE.

Afitti, a people living in the Nuba Hills of Sudan. They number 3,000. Their language belongs to the NYIMANG group.

Afrikaans is the first official language of South Africa. It is spoken by 60 per cent of the people of European origin and by most of the Coloureds. Although derived from Standard Dutch, the language has many marked differences. It was called 'African Dutch' or *Afrikaans Nederlands*.

Afusare (Hill Jerawa), a Nigerian people living in the Benue-Plateau State.

Agau is a language group of CUSHITIC LANGUAGES made up of BILIN, KHAMIR, QWARA and AWIYA languages.

Agbor, a people living in southern Nigeria.

Aghem, a people living in the part of Nigeria which was formerly British Cameroon.

Agni see ANYI.

Ahanta is a dialect of ANYI.

Ahizi (Aizi), a people living around the Ebrie Lagoon in Ivory Coast. They speak either a KWA or KRU language.

Ahlon, a small group of people, numbering less than 1,000, living in the central hills of Togo.

Akaju, a people living in southern Nigeria.

Akan is the collective name for the group of dialects that comprises Twi (Tsi) and Fante. It also includes the dialects spoken in the old kingdom of Ashanti (Central Ghana).

Akebu, a people living in Togo.

Akem (Akyem) is a dialect of Twi.

Akpafu, a people living in the region of Buëm in Togo. They number 1,500 and they speak a TOGO REMNANT LANGUAGE.

Akwa, a Congolese people who speak a BANTU LANGUAGE.

Akwapem is a dialect of Twi.

Akye (Atye), a people living in Ivory Coast. They number 60,000 and speak a KWA language.

Alaba, a people living in south-western Ethiopia. They number 40,000 and speak a CUSHITIC LANGUAGE of the Sidamo language group.

Aladian, a people living in Ivory Coast. They number 8,000 and speak a KWA language.

Alawa are a Tanzanian people who number 11,300. Together with the IRAQW, they form an ISOLATED LANGUAGE GROUP.

Alur, a people living on the western banks of lake Mobutu Sese Seko and the Nile and on the Uganda–Zaire border. They number about 200,000 and speak Alur, a NILOTIC LANGUAGE.

Amadi see MA.

Amarani, a people living in Somalia. They speak MBALAZI, a dialect of SWAHILI.

Amarinya see AMHARIC.

Amar Kokke, a people in south-western Ethiopia, speak a language of the BAKO language group.

Amba (Bwisi), a Uganda people living in the region of Bwamba. They number 34,500 and speak a BANTU LANGUAGE.

Ambo, a people living in Namibia. They speak a BANTU LANGUAGE.

Ambo, a Zambian people living on the banks of the Lukushashi River. They number 10,000 and speak a BANTU LANGUAGE.

Amengi, a people living in Zaire. They speak MORU-MANGBETU.

Amharic is the official language of Ethiopia. It is spoken as a first language by 5,000,000 people and as a second language by about 20,000,000 people. Amharic is the Standard language of the Shoa province, where it is called Amarinya. Amharic belongs to the SEMITIC LANGUAGE family and is written in a modified form of the GE'EZ script used by medieval authors.

Amu, the people living on Lamu Island off Kenya. Their language is a dialect of SWAHILI.

Anaguta, a people living in southern Nigeria.

Angas, a people living in the Benue-Plateau State of Nigeria. They number 55,200 and they speak a NON-CLASS LANGUAGE.

Angba, a people living in Orientale Province in Zaire. Their language is a dialect of BWA.

Ángolares, a people living on the island of São Tomé.

Animere, a people living in Togo. They speak a dialect related to TEM.

Antaifasy, 'the people of the sandy beach', a Malagasy people living on the east coast of the island of Madagascar. They number over 30,000.

Antaimoro, a Malagasy people living on Madagascar numbering about 211,000.

Antaisaka, a Malagasy people of the east coast of southern Madagascar numbering about 300,000.

Antambahoaka, a Malagasy people living on Madagascar numbering 22,000 people. They claim an Arab origin from Mecca.

Antankara, 'People on the Rock', a Malagasy people living on the extreme northern point of Madagascar, between Amber Cape and the River Sambirano. The Antankara are partly descended from Arab traders. They number 30,000.

Antanosy, a Muslim people living on the south-eastern coast of the island of Madagascar. They number 15,000.

Anuak (Yambo), a people living in southern Sudan and Ethiopia. They number 216,000 and speak a NILOTIC LANGUAGE of the North Lwo language group.

Anufo, a people living in Togo, where they number 16,000, and in Ghana, where there are 11,000 of them. They speak a KWA language that is also spoken by the Cakosi people.

Anyi (Agni) is a language spoken in various dialects by about 79,000 people in Ivory Coast and Ghana. It is a KWA language.

Anyi-Baule, the collective name for a group of peoples who inhabit the eastern part of the Ivory Coast.

Apagibeti are a number of BANTU LANGUAGE dialects spoken by peoples living in the Equateur province of Zaire.

ARABS: The Arab influence in Africa is shown by the many mosques found throughout the continent. This mosque is at Fez, in Morocco.

Arabic, a northern SEMITIC LANGUAGE originally spoken in Arabia. The ARAB conquests brought Arabic to North Africa. Arabic is spoken by over 80,000,000 people in Africa alone and is Africa's most important language. Arabic is also spoken widely in Mauritania, Niger, Chad, and the Sudan. There are 28 letters in the Arabic alphabet. The language structure is based on the principle that most word-roots have three consonants, e.g. k-t-b. The meanings of word-roots are varied by vowel changes and the addition of other letters. For example, *Kataba* meaning 'he wrote' becomes, in the passive, *Kutiba*, 'it is written'. *Kitâb* means 'a book', (plural *Kutub*). *Kataba kitâb* means 'he wrote a book'. By adding *-iyya* to *Kutub*, 'books', the word becomes *Kutubiyya*, 'library'. The elegant Arabic script, which dates from about the 5th century, is written from right to left. Arabic is the official language of Islam and all readings from the Koran are in Arabic. The Arabic language has greatly influenced the original North African languages. Many Arabic words have become part of languages such as SWAHILI.

Arabs, the people of Arabia, many of whom now live in Africa. In 640 A.D. Egypt fell to Arab invaders who introduced the ARABIC language and the religion of Islam. Raids towards the west preceded the Arab conquests of Libya, Tunisia and Morocco. The Arabic language was also spread by nomadic Arab peoples such as the BEDOUINS who moved about with their camel herds in the desert areas. Arab traders settled further south along the east coast and influenced the SWAHILI people and language. The Arabs have influenced much of western Africa. Arabic is the official language in all parts of North Africa; part of north-eastern Nigeria was settled by the Shuwa Arabs; the Abbala and Baggara Arab groups became camel and cattle herders in the north of the Central African Republic.

Arago, a Nigerian people who live north of the Benue River. They number 8,800 and their language is IDOMA.

Arbore, a people and language of south-western Ethiopia, north of Lake Stephanie. The Arbore number 3,000 and their language belongs to the CUSHITIC LANGUAGE group.

Argobba, an Ethiopian people of between 2,000 and 2,500 members. They speak a language belonging to the SEMITIC LANGUAGE family.

Ari, a people living in Ivory Coast. They number 11,000 and they speak a KWA language.

Asante see ASHANTI.

ASHANTI: Elders of the Ashanti people of Ghana playing music on horns.

Ashanti, an important people living in central Ghana. They number more than 2,000,000 and speak AKAN (Twi-Fante). The traditional Ashanti economy is based on agriculture. This has been developed into the production of cash crops, such as cocoa, fruit, rubber and kolanuts.

Asu (Athu), a people living in Tanzania, where they number 99,000. A few Asu also live in Kenya.

Asua, a group of pygmies living in north-eastern Zaire among the Maele, Abulu and Popoi peoples.

Aten (Ganawuri), a Nigerian people living in the area of Jos. They number 4,000 and they speak a CLASS LANGUAGE.

Atwot (Atuot), a group of people living in southern Sudan in the Lakes district near Yirrol. The group has 31,600 members. Their dialect belongs to the NUER dialect cluster of the NILOTIC LANGUAGES.

Auni (Auo), a people living in South Africa and Botswana. They speak a Bushman language (see KHOI-SAN).

Aushi (Ushi), a Zambian people who live on the banks of the Luapula River. They number 29,000 and they speak a BANTU LANGUAGE.

Avatime, a people who live in seven villages in the central Togo Hills. They speak a TOGO REMNANT LANGUAGE.

Avikam, a people living in Ivory Coast. They number 9,000 and speak a KWA language.

Avukaya see MORU.

Awiya, an Ethiopian people who speak a CUSHITIC LANGUAGE.

Azande see ZANDE

Azer, a people living in Mali. They speak a dialect related to SONINKE.

Azza, a people living in Niger.

Baageto, a people living in Cameroon. They number about 1,700 and speak a BANTU LANGUAGE.

Babi, a people living in Congo.

Babong, a people living in Cameroon. They number about 1,200 and speak a BANTU LANGUAGE.

Babukur, a people living in Sudan. They speak BOGURU, a BANTU LANGUAGE.

Babute see VUTE.

Baca, a Bantu-speaking people living in Natal, South Africa (see BANTU LANGUAGES).

Bachada, a people living in south-west Ethiopia. They speak a language of the BAKO group.

Bachama, people and language on the Benue River in Nigeria.

Bade, a people living in Bornu State, Nigeria. They number 32,000 and speak a language of the CHADO-HAMITIC LANGUAGE group.

Bafaw (Bafo), a people living on the borders between Nigeria and Cameroon. They number 2,400 and speak a BANTU LANGUAGE.

Bafia, a group of people with 18,000 members in central Cameroon. They speak a BANTU LANGUAGE.

Baga, a people living in the coastal region of Guinea. They number 50,000 and speak a WEST ATLANTIC LANGUAGE.

Bagam, a people living in Cameroon. They speak a CLASS LANGUAGE of the BAMILEKE group.

Baganda see GANDA.

Bagirmi, a people living in Chad. They number 25,000 and speak a language of the BONGO BAGIRMI language group.

Bago, a people living in Togo. They speak TEM.

Bahima see TUTSI.

Bai (Bari) a group of people living in southern Sudan which has 2,500 members. They speak a Sere-Mundu language, one of the Ndogo-Sere language group.

Baiso, a people living in Ethiopia.

Bajuni (Gunya, Tikuu), a people living in the coastal regions of southern Somalia, and on the islands situated between Mogadiscio and Pate. They speak a dialect of SWAHILI.

Baka, a people living in southern Sudan in the region of Maridi and in Zaire. They number 3,000 and speak a language belonging to the BONGO-BAGIRMI language unit.

Bakja, a people living in Cameroon. They number 14,000 and speak a BANTU LANGUAGE.

Bako, a people living in Ethiopia to the east of the Omo River. Their language is one of an ISOLATED LANGUAGE GROUP.

Bakogo, a people living in Cameroon. They number 20,000 and speak a BANTU LANGUAGE.

Bakoko, a people living in Cameroon. They speak a BANTU LANGUAGE.

Bakolle, a small number of people living in south-east Nigeria. They number 307 and speak a BANTU LANGUAGE.

Bakundu, a people living in the part of Nigeria which was formerly British Cameroon. They speak a BANTU LANGUAGE.

Bakwe (Bakwo), are a group of people, with 2,500 members, who live in Liberia. Their language forms a dialect cluster of the KRU language.

Bakwele (Bekwil), a people of Congo who number 5,000. They speak a BANTU LANGUAGE.

Bakweri (Bakwele, Kpe), a people living in south-east Nigeria. They have 15,600 members and speak a BANTU LANGUAGE.

Balante (Balanta), a people living in Guinea-Bissau and in Senegal. They number 154,000 and speak a WEST ATLANTIC LANGUAGE.

Bale, a people living in the Eastern Province of Zaire.

Balengi, a people living in Equatorial Guinea.

Balese, a people living in north-east Zaire. Numbering 20,100, they speak a language of the Mangbutu-Efe group.

Bali, a people living in the part of Nigeria which was formerly British Cameroon. They speak a CLASS LANGUAGE.

Bali (Baali), a people living in the Eastern Province of Zaire. They number 37,700 and speak a BANTU LANGUAGE.

Balom, a people of central Cameroon. They number 4,000 and speak a BANTU LANGUAGE.

Balong, a group of people with 4,400 members who live on the border between Nigeria and Cameroon.

Baluba see LUBA.

Bambala see BURJI.

Bambara (Bammana), a widespread people who live in Mali, Guinea, Senegal, Ivory Coast, Upper Volta and Mauritania. They number more than 1,000,000, with most of them—835,000—living in Mali. Their language is part of the Malinke-Bambara-Dyula cluster of the Mande family.

Bamboko, a people living in south-east Nigeria and Cameroon. They number 1900 and speak a BANTU LANGUAGE.

Bambuti see MBUTI.

Bamileke, a large group of people living in Cameroon. The group has 455,000 members and they speak a CLASS LANGUAGE.

Bamum, a people living in central Cameroon. They number about 80,000 and speak a CLASS LANGUAGE.

Bana, a people living in Cameroon. They number 8,000 and speak a CLASS LANGUAGE.

Banda, the name given to a large number of peoples who live in Central African Republic and speak one of the Banda-Gbaya-Ngbandi languages.

Bandala, a people who live in southern Sudan.

Bandem, a people who live in Cameroon and Nigeria. They speak a BANTU LANGUAGE.

Bandi (Gbande), a people living in Liberia. They number 35,000 and speak a MANDE language.

Bandia, a people living in Zaire. They speak Pa-Zande.

Baneka, a people living in Cameroon. They number 3,000 and speak a BANTU LANGUAGE.

Banen, a people of central Cameroon. They number 28,000 and speak a BANTU LANGUAGE.

Bangala, 1. a people living in scattered villages along the Middle Zaire and lower Ubangi rivers. 2. a language spoken in parts of north-eastern Zaire as a trade language.

Bangba, a group of people who live in the eastern province of Zaire. The group has 29,000 members and they speak various dialects of SERE-MUNDU.

Bangbinda, a small group of people living in Sudan and Zaire. They speak NGBINDA.

Bango are a people living in the eastern province of Zaire.

Bangubangu, a people living in Kivu province, Zaire. They speak a BANTU LANGUAGE.

Banjun, a people living in Nigeria and Cameroon.

Bankon (Abo), are a people living in Cameroon. They number 10,200 and speak a BANTU LANGUAGE.

Banna, a people living in south-west Ethiopia. They speak the language belonging to the Bako language group.

Banoho are a people of Cameroon. They speak a BANTU LANGUAGE.

Bantu Languages, a family of languages which are spoken between Duala in the Cameroon and the Kei River in South Africa, between Barawa in Somalia and Omaruru in Namibia. There are 84 groups of Bantu languages. Each group may have between one and ten languages. There are, in total, about 400 different Bantu languages divided into some 1600 dialects. All these languages and their dialects have the same characteristics (see CLASS LANGUAGES). Also in Bantu languages there are words which are common to almost all the groups and individual languages.

Banyun, a people living in Guinea-Bissau and Senegal. They number 18,000 and speak a WEST ATLANTIC LANGUAGE.

Bara, a Malagasy people living in south-west Madagascar numbering 200,000.

Barabaig are a group belonging to the TATOGA cluster of peoples who live in Tanzania. They number 36,000.

Barambo (Barambu), a people living in the eastern province of Zaire and in Sudan. Numbering 46,000, they speak a language related to ZANDE.

Barea, a people living in Eritrea. They number 15,000 and their language makes up an ISOLATED LANGUAGE GROUP.

Bargu (Bariba), a widespread people who live in north-east Togo, northern Benin (Dahomey), and Kwara state in Nigeria. They number 240,000 and speak a GUR language.

Bari, a people and language of southern Sudan. The Bari number 35,000 and the language is a member of the NILO-HAMITIC group and has six dialects.

Bariba see BARGU.

Barue, a people living in Nigeria and Cameroon. They number 4,700 and speak a BANTU LANGUAGE.

Barundi, a name for the two groups of people living in Burundi, the HUTU and the TUTSI. They speak RUNDI, a BANTU LANGUAGE.

Barwe are a people of Mozambique.

Basa (including Basa Komo and Basa Kaduna), a people living in central Nigeria. They number 67,500 and they speak a CLASS LANGUAGE of Nigeria.

Basari see BASSARA.

Baseda (Basila, Winjiwinji), a people living in Dahomey.

Basekwe, a people living in Equatorial Guinea.

Basic Bantu see FANAGALO.

Basketo, a people who live in south-west Ethiopia. They speak a CUSHITIC LANGUAGE belonging to a dialect cluster of the OMETO group.

Bassa, a people of Liberia. They have 150,000 members and speak a dialect of KRU.

Bas(s)a-Komo, a people living in Nigeria. They speak a CLASS LANGUAGE dialect belonging to the KAMUKU dialect cluster.

Bassa (Nigeria) see BASA.

Bassari 1. a section of the Tenda people who live on the borders of Guinea and Senegal, and also in Gambia. They number 7,600 and speak a WEST ATLANTIC LANGUAGE. 2. a people living in northern Togo. They number 22,000 and they speak the TYAM language.

Bata, a people of West Africa. 15,000 of them live in Cameroon and 23,000 live in Nigeria. Their language forms a dialect cluster (see LANGUAGE FAMILY).

Batanga see NOHO-PUKO.

Bati, a small group of people who live in Cameroon. They speak a BANTU LANGUAGE.

Baule, a people living in Ivory Coast and Ghana. They number 373,000 and their language, Baule, forms part of the KWA language group.

Bayele, a people living in Equatorial Guinea.

Bazantche (Gbazantche), a people who live in Benin (Dahomey). They speak a KWA language.

Bebele (Bamuele) live in Cameroon. They number 18,000 and speak a BANTU LANGUAGE.

Bedawiye (Bedanje, Beja) is a CUSHITIC LANGUAGE spoken in Eritrea in Ethiopia. It is spoken by the Beni Amer and a number of related groups.

Bedik, a people living in Senegal.

Bedouin, 'People of the desert', nomadic ARABS living in the deserts of North Africa, Egypt, Syria and Arabia. They speak the ARABIC language and follow the Islamic faith. Bedouins live by raising flocks of sheep, goats and herds of cattle and camels.

Beja see BEDAWIYE.

Beke, a people who live in Zaire. They speak a BANTU LANGUAGE.

Bekwil (Bakwele), a people living in Congo and Gabon. Numbering 5,000, they speak a BANTU LANGUAGE.

Beli, a people living in southern Sudan. They number 7,300 and speak a dialect of BONGO-BAGIRMI.

BEDOUIN: A Bedouin girl from Tunisia.

Belle, a people who live in Liberia.

Bemba, a large group of people living in Zambia, numbering 140,000. Another 30,000 Bemba live in Zaire. They speak a BANTU LANGUAGE which acts as a LINGUA FRANCA in the Zambian copperbelt.

Bembe, a people living in the Kivu province of Zaire. They speak a BANTU LANGUAGE belonging to the LEGA group.

Bena, a people living in Tanzania. They number 158,000 and speak a BANTU LANGUAGE.

Bena Tubeya, a people living in Zaire and Angola. Numbering 20,000, they speak Rund, a BANTU LANGUAGE.

Bende, a people living in Tanzania. They number 6,800 and speak a BANTU LANGUAGE.

Bene (Bane), a people living in Cameroon. This group has 60,000 members. They speak a BANTU LANGUAGE.

Benga is the name given to small groups of people scattered throughout Gabon and the mainland of Equatorial Guinea. They speak a BANTU LANGUAGE.

Benge, a people who live in Zaire's Eastern province. They speak a BANTU LANGUAGE.

Benin was an ancient kingdom in Nigeria. See EDO.

Berba, a people living in Togo. The 44,000 members of this group speak a dialect of the GURMA cluster.

Berbers, a large group of peoples and languages of North Africa. There are over 4,000,000 Berbers in Morocco alone and, excluding the TUAREGS, there are about 3,000,000 Berbers in Algeria. The name 'Berber' came long ago from the Greeks who called these peoples 'Barbarous' because they did not speak Greek. Their language is very different from any other known language group. The Berber language is often called Hamitic. It was spoken throughout North Africa before the ARAB invasions scattered the Berber peoples. Their agricultural settlements on the plains were destroyed and many of the Berber groups are now nomadic herders. In Egypt, Siwa is the only place where a Berber language, Siwi, is still spoken.

In Libya, where the Berbers had developed their own alphabet, only a few Berbers remain living in the south and west. In Tunisia, Algeria and Morocco groups of Berbers live in the mountains. There they still follow their traditional ways of life and are famous for their fine leather-work and woven woollen rugs and garments.

Berta, a people living in Sudan and Ethiopia. They number 20,000. Their language forms an ISOLATED LANGUAGE GROUP.

Besme, a people living in Chad. They speak a language belonging to the SOMRAI group.

Bete (Betegbo), a language spoken in Ivory Coast by 153,000 people. The language forms a dialect cluster of KRU.

Bethen, a people living in Cameroon. They speak a BANTU LANGUAGE.

Beti, a people living in Cameroon. They number 401,000.

Betsileo, 'the invincible people', are a Malagasy people living south of the MERINA. They number 800,000.

BERBER: A Berber shepherdess from Morocco.

Betsimisaraka, 'Inseparable People', a people living along the east coast of the island of Madagascar. They mainly live by fishing and number 900,000.

Betzinga (Bacenga), a people living in Cameroon. Numbering 10,000, they speak a BANTU LANGUAGE.

Bezanozano, 'people with many tresses', a cattle-herding people in Madagascar numbering 44,000.

Biafada, a people living in Guinea-Bissau. They number 11,850 and speak a WEST ATLANTIC LANGUAGE belonging to the MANDYAK group.

Bideyat, a people living in Chad and Sudan. They speak an EAST SAHARAN LANGUAGE.

Bidyo, a people living in Chad. They number about 13,000 and speak a CHADO-HAMITIC LANGUAGE belonging to the Sokoro-Mubi Group.

Bidyogo (Bijago), a people living in Guinea-Bissau. The Bidyogo group has 10,000 members. They speak a WEST ATLANTIC LANGUAGE of the MANDYAK group.

Bila, a people living in Zaire. They number 5,650 and speak a BANTU LANGUAGE.

Bilala (Bulala), a people living in Chad. They number 35,000 and speak a language belonging to the KUKA dialect cluster of the BONGO-BAGIRMI language.

Bili, a people who live in Zaire. They number 5,000 and speak a BANTU LANGUAGE.

Bilin (Bogos), a people living in Eritrea in Ethiopia. Numbering 24,500, they speak a CUSHITIC LANGUAGE.

Bima, a people living in the region of south-east Nigeria which was formerly British Cameroon. They speak a BANTU LANGUAGE.

Bini see EDO.

Binji, a people who live in Zaire. They number about 64,000 and speak a BANTU LANGUAGE.

Binza, a people living in Zaire. They speak a BANTU LANGUAGE.

Bira, a group of people who live in Zaire and Uganda. The group, who number 39,000, are divided into plains Bira and mountain Bira, who live in the Ruwenzori mountains. They both speak a BANTU LANGUAGE.

Birifor, a people living in northern Ghana and Upper Volta. They number 90,000 and speak a GUR language.

Birked, a Nubian people who live in Sudan and Chad. They speak ARABIC.

Birom, a people living in the Benue-Plateau state of Nigeria in the region of Jos. They number between 40,000 and 100,000. They speak a CLASS LANGUAGE.

Birwa, a people who live in the Transvaal province of South Africa. They speak a BANTU LANGUAGE of the SHONA group.

Bisa (Biisa), a people living in Zambia in the region of the River Luangwa. They number 41,000 and speak a BANTU LANGUAGE.

Bitare is a CLASS LANGUAGE spoken in south-eastern Nigeria.

Bizhi, a people living in Zambia. They number 1,800 and speak a BANTU LANGUAGE belonging to the Ila-Tonga group.

Bo (Boka), a people of Upper Volta.

Bobangi, a people living in the Equateur province of Zaire. They speak a BANTU LANGUAGE.

Bobo, a widespread group of people, of whom about 120,000 live in Mali and 169,000 live in Upper Volta. They speak a number of dialects of GUR.

Bodiman, a people who live in Cameroon. They number 2,000 and speak a Coastal Bantu language.

Bodo is the name given to a small group of people who are scattered throughout Central African Republic, Sudan and Zaire.

Bogongo, a people living in Central African Republic. They speak a BANTU LANGUAGE.

Boguru, a small group of people living in Sudan and Zaire. They speak a BANTU LANGUAGE which is also spoken by the Babukur and the Bagbele peoples.

Boki, a people living in the region of south-eastern Nigeria which was formerly British Cameroon. They number 86,000 and speak a CLASS LANGUAGE.

Boko, a people who live in Zaire and speak a BANTU LANGUAGE.

Bolewa, a people living in Nigeria in the region of Bauchi and Bornu. They number 32,000 and speak a CHADO-HAMITIC LANGUAGE.

Bolia, a people who live in Zaire. They speak a BANTU LANGUAGE.

Boloki, a people living in the Equateur province of Zaire. They speak a BANTU LANGUAGE.

Bolondo, a people who live in Zaire. They speak a BANTU LANGUAGE.

Boma, a people living in the Bandundu province of Zaire. They number 8,000 and speak a BANTU LANGUAGE.

Bomboko, a people living in south-eastern Nigeria. They number 2,000 and speak a BANTU LANGUAGE.

Bomboli live in Zaire. They speak a dialect of Lobala, a BANTU LANGUAGE.

Bomitaba, a people who live in Congo.

Bomvana, a people who live in South Africa. They speak a dialect of XHOSA.

Bomwali, a people who live in Congo. They speak a BANTU LANGUAGE.

Bondei, a people living in Tanzania. They number 28,300 and speak a BANTU LANGUAGE.

Bonjo see MONJOMBO.

Bondongo, a people who live in Congo.

Bongili, a people living in Congo who speak a BANTU LANGUAGE.

Bongo, a people who live in southern Sudan. They speak a BONGO-BAGIRMI language. They number 5,000.

Bongo-Bagirmi, a group of languages spoken in the south-western part of the Sudan and across the border of the Central African Republic. The main sub-groups include Bagirmi, Bongo, Kresh and Sara. Single units of Bongo-Bagirmi are Sinyar and Kara.

Boni (Waboni), a people living in Somalia.

Bonkeng, a people who live in Cameroon. They number 1,700 and speak a BANTU LANGUAGE.

Boong, a people who live in Congo. They number 6,000 and speak a BANTU LANGUAGE.

Bor Belanda, a people who live in southern Sudan in the region of Raffili and Tembura. They number 3,000 and speak a NILOTIC LANGUAGE of the northern LUO group.

Bori see MORU.

Bowili, a small group of people who live in Togo in the region of Buëm. They number 600 and speak a TOGO REMNANT LANGUAGE.

Bozo, a people living in Mali. They number 30,000 and speak a dialect of Soninke.

Brong, a people who live in Ivory Coast. They number 21,500 and they speak a dialect of GUANG.

Bua, a people who live in Chad. They number 10,700. Their language forms an isolated group.

Bube (Bubi), the main group of people living on the island of Macias Nguema Biyoga, formerly called Fernando Poo (total population 61,500). They also live in Gabon, where there are 4,000 of them. They speak a BANTU LANGUAGE.

Budja, a people who live in the Equateur province of Zaire. They speak a BANTU LANGUAGE.

Budu, a people who live in the Province Orientale of Zaire. They number 83,000 and speak a BANTU LANGUAGE.

Buduma (Yedina), a people living in Chad on islands on Lake Chad. They number 30,500 and speak a CHADO-HAMITIC LANGUAGE.

Budya (Buja), 1. a people living in Zimbabwe. They speak a dialect of Korekore, a BANTU LANGUAGE, belonging to the SHONA language group.

Bugombe, a people living in Zaire. They number 12,300 and speak a BANTU LANGUAGE.

Builsa, a people living in northern Ghana. They number 53,500.

Buja, a people who live in Zaire. They number 100,000 and speak a BANTU LANGUAGE.

Bujeba, a people who live in Equatorial Guinea.

Bulom (Sherbro), a people who live in Sierra Leone. They number 167,000. Their dialects form a dialect cluster of the WEST ATLANTIC LANGUAGES.

Bulu, a people who live in Cameroon. They number 184,000 and speak a BANTU LANGUAGE.

Bunda, a people who live in Angola.

Bungu, a people living in Tanzania in the region of Lake Rukwa. They number 15,000 and speak a BANTU LANGUAGE.

Bura, a people living in Nigeria, where they number 72,000 and in Cameroon, where they number 16,500.

Buraka, a people who live in Congo and in Central African Republic. They speak a dialect of SERE-MUNDU.

Burji (Bambala), a people living in south-western Ethiopia and in Kenya. They number 200,000 and speak a CUSHITIC LANGUAGE.

Burun, a people who live in the Gezira region of Sudan. They number 26,000 and speak a NILOTIC LANGUAGE of the north LUO group.

Burungi, a people who live in Tanzania in the region of Mbulu and Kondoa. They number 9,000. Their language forms an ISOLATED LANGUAGE GROUP with the IRAQW language.

Busa are a large group of people. About 100,000 live in Upper Volta, 27,000 in Ghana, 16,000 in Benin (Dahomey) and 11,000 in Nigeria. They speak a Mande-Fu language.

Bushmen see KHOI-SAN.

Bushongo, a Bantu people of central ZAIRE. They speak KUBA.

Buso, a small group of people who live in Chad. They number less than 50 and speak the BUA language.

Butawa, a people who live in the region of Bauchi and Kano in Nigeria. They number 9,000 and they speak a CLASS LANGUAGE of Nigeria.

Buyi, a people who live in the Kivu province of Zaire. They speak a BANTU LANGUAGE.

Buzu, a people living in Niger.

Bviri (Biri, Belarda, Gumba), a people who live in southern Sudan. They number 16,000 and speak a dialect of the SERE-MUNDU group.

Bwa, a people who live in Zaire and speak a BANTU LANGUAGE.

Bwela, a people who live in Zaire and speak a BANTU LANGUAGE.

Bwile, a people who live in Tanzania in the region of Lake Mweru. They number 5,000 and speak Tabwa, a BANTU LANGUAGE.

Bwisi, a people who live in Uganda and Zaire in the Ruwenzori Mountains. They number 6,000 and speak a BANTU LANGUAGE.

Chado-Hamitic Languages, a family of languages spoken in Nigeria and Chad. The main member of the family is HAUSA.

Chaga (Shaka), a group of people living in Tanzania. They number 360,000 and they speak a BANTU LANGUAGE.

Chagga see Chaga.

Chamba, a people and language of Nigeria in the region of Benue and Adamawa. The language, which is a NON-CLASS LANGUAGE, forms a dialect cluster (see LANGUAGE FAMILY).

Chara, a people who live in south-western Ethiopia. Their language forms a dialect cluster (see LANGUAGE FAMILY) of the OMETO language group.

Chawai, a people who live in the region of Zaria in Nigeria. They number 22,000 and speak a CLASS LANGUAGE.

Cheke, a people living in Nigeria and Cameroon. They speak a language belonging to the Bata group.

Chewa, a people living in southern Malawi and areas of western Mozambique. The Chewa language, also called Chinyanja, is important in Malawi and is spoken by about 1,000,000 people.

Chikunda see KUNDA.

Chishinga, a people living in Zambia near the Luapula river. They speak a BANTU LANGUAGE.

Chleuh is the name given to a group of BERBER dialects.

Chofa, a people living in Zaire, where they number 2,400.

Chok, a people living in Zaire. They number 9,500.

Chokwe (Cokwe) are a widespread group of people living in central Africa. 350,000 Chokwe live in Zaire, 338,000 in Angola and 25,000 in Zambia. They speak a BANTU LANGUAGE which belongs to the Chokwe-Lunda group.

Chopi, a people who live in Mozambique. They speak a BANTU LANGUAGE.

Chuka, a people living in Kenya, are a sub-group of the Meru and are related to the Kikuyu. They number 18,500 and speak a BANTU LANGUAGE.

Cile, a people who live in south-western Tanzania. They number 8,000.

Cimba, a people living in Namibia and Angola. They speak a dialect of HERERO.

Cinga, a people who live in Cameroon, where they number 15,500. They speak a BANTU LANGUAGE.

Class Languages. Some languages have nouns that are divided into groups or classes of nouns, e.g. animals, plants, parts of the body etc. These languages are called 'class languages'. The classes are expressed by different prefixes or suffixes. Usually there are pairs of classes. In Swahili: *m*tu means person, *wa*tu means people. The prefix m- is singular and called 'class 1', wa- is plural and is called 'class 2'. In many languages, class 2 has the form *ba*. Therefore the names for some peoples are: *Ba*kongo, *Ba*rundi, *Ba*suto. In some languages the classes are indicated by suffixes. For example, in DAGOMBA bi*a* meaning child becomes bi*he*, children. Adjectives, pronouns, verb forms and interrogatives may agree with the subject noun of a sentence. For example in Swahili:

sing. *Ki*tu *ki*-le *ki*zuri *ki*dogo *ki*li *ki*pi?
    Thing that beautiful little it-was what?
plural *Vi*tu *vi*-le *vi*zuri *vi*dogo *vi*li *vi*pi?

Click Languages use a characteristic 'click' sound made by the tongue against the roof of the mouth. These languages include XHOSA, ZULU, and languages of the Khoi (Hottentots) and San (Bushmen). See KHOI-SAN.

Coniagui see KONYAGI.

Creole languages are spoken in Africa, the West Indies or in the Indian Ocean (e.g. Mauritius), by a people of mixed descent, some of whose ancestors were Africans, some Europeans. The majority of words in a Creole language are taken from the European 'base' language, i.e. one of the old 'Colonial' languages: Portuguese, Spanish, Dutch, French and English. Since those peoples, in the days of slavery, had no other language in common, they had to use the European language, which they were never properly taught. As a result, the Creole language gradually developed. The name Creole is from the Portuguese word *creolho* for a servant.

Cuabo (Chwabo), a group of people who live in the Quelimane-Mlanje mountains of Mozambique. They speak a BANTU LANGUAGE.

Cushitic (Kushitic) Languages are spoken by about 20,000,000 people in and around the north-eastern 'horn' of Africa. This family of languages is often divided into seven groups. The Eastern group consists of SOMALI, GALLA, BONI and RENDILLE. The Central group, which is spoken in Eastern Ethiopia and Eritrea, consists of AFAR, SAHO and AGAU (Agaw). In the north, around the north-eastern part of the Sudan and south-eastern regions of Egypt, a distinct sub-group of the Cushitic family is spoken. This sub-group is known as BEDAWIYE or Beja. The western group consists of JANJERO, KAFA and MAJI which are collectively called OMOTIC. The south-western group of Cushitic languages are GELABA (Merille), ARBORE, KONSO and GIDOLE. A lesser-known group of Cushitic languages is spoken in Ethiopia. This group includes SHINASHA, MAO and BURJI (Bambala). Sidamo is another Ethiopian sub-group of the Cushitic language family. Darasa is the main dialect of SIDAMO.

Daba, a people living in Cameroon. They number 30,000. They speak a Chadic language which forms part of a dialect cluster (see LANGUAGE FAMILY).

Dagaba, a people who live in northern Ghana. They number 119,000.

Dagari (Dagati), a people living in Ghana and Upper Volta. They number 120,000 and speak a dialect of GUR.

Dago see DAJU.

Dagomba (Dagbamba), a people and language of northern Ghana around Tamale and Yendi. They number about 200,000. Dagomba is a dialect of GUR. See also MOSSI.

Dai, a people living in Chad. They number 600 and speak an EAST SAHARAN LANGUAGE belonging to the BUA group.

Daju, a people living in Chad in the region of Wadai, and in Sudan around Darfur. They number 67,000. Their language forms an ISOLATED LANGUAGE GROUP.

Dakakari, a people living in northern Nigeria in the Middle Niger region. They number 161,000 and speak a CLASS LANGUAGE of Nigeria.

Dakpa, a people living in Central African Republic. They speak a Banda language.

Dama (Damara, Damaqua, Bergdama), a people living in Namibia. They speak NAMA, a Hottentot language.

Dan (Gio, Yakuba), a people living in north-eastern Liberia and in Ivory Coast. They number 100,000 and are connected with the Guru.

Danakil see AFAR.

Dangaleat, a people who live in Chad. They number 16,000 and speak a CHADO-HAMITIC LANGUAGE.

Darasa, a people living in south-western Ethiopia. They number about 80,000 and speak a CUSHITIC LANGUAGE belonging to the SIDAMO group.

Darfur see FUR.

Dari, a people living in Chad who speak a CHADO-HAMITIC LANGUAGE.

Daza, a people living in Chad and Niger. They number 78,000 and speak an EAST SAHARAN LANGUAGE.

De (Dewoi, Do), a people living in Liberia. The De speak a dialect of KRU.

Delo, a people living in Togo. They speak TEM.

Dendi is the dialect of SONGHAI. It is spoken by about 27,500 people in Niger and Dahomey and by a few people in Nigeria.

Dengese see NDENGESE.

Dhaiso, a people living in Tanzania. They speak a BANTU LANGUAGE.

Dia (Djia), a people living in Bandundu province in Zaire. They speak a BANTU LANGUAGE.

Dialect Cluster see LANGUAGE FAMILY.

Diawambe, a people who live in Mali.

Dida, a people living in Ivory Coast. They number 56,000 and speak Bete.

Didinga, a people and language of the Sudan-Ethiopian border. The Didinga number 2,850 and the language belongs to the Didinga-Murle group.

Digo, a people who live in Kenya and Tanzania, where they number 32,150. They speak a BANTU LANGUAGE.

Dime, a people who live in south-western Ethiopia. They number 3,000 and speak a language belonging to the Bakó group.

Dimuk, a people living in northern Nigeria.

Dinka, a large group of people living in Southern Sudan. Dinka is also the name of a cluster of dialects related to the NILOTIC LANGUAGE family. These dialects are spoken by over 200,000 people in the central Sudan, mostly west of the Nile, along the Bahr el Ghazal river and its tributaries. Dinka has four main dialects: Padang and Bor in the north and south along the Nile; Rek and Agar in the west and centre of the region. Rek is the dialect most widely used in schools and for commerce.

Diriku (Mbogedu), a people living in Angola, Namibia and Botswana. They speak a dialect of KWANGALI, a BANTU LANGUAGE.

Djerma-Songhai see ZARMA.

Doba, a people living in south-western Ethiopia.

Doe (Dohe), a people living in Tanzania. They are related to the Zaramo people.

Doghosie, a people living in Ivory Coast. They number 7,500 and speak either the SENUFO or LOBI language.

Dogon, a people living in Mali and Upper Volta. They number 226,000 and speak Dogon, a GUR language. The Dogon people have their own religion, architectural style and culture.

Doko, a people living in the Equateur province of Zaire. They speak a BANTU LANGUAGE.

Dompago, a people living in the region of the Togo-Benin (Dahomey) border. They number 14,000 and they speak TEM.

Dondo 1. a people living in Congo. 2. a people living in Rhodesia.

Dongo 1. a people living in Zaire. They number 5,000. Their language is Mba. 2. see NDONGO.

Dongola, a people living in Sudan in the Nile Valley. They speak Dongoli, a NUBIAN LANGUAGE.

Dorobo, a small group of people who live in the forests of Kenya and Tanzania. They speak a dialect of KALENJIN, a NILO HAMITIC LANGUAGE.

Duala, a people who live in Cameroon. They number 23,000 and they speak a BANTU LANGUAGE.

Duka (Dukawa, Dukauchi), a people living near Kontagora and Zuru in the Middle Niger region of northern Nigeria. They number 20,000 and they speak a CLASS LANGUAGE of Nigeria.

Dukunz, a people who live in Ethiopia.

Duma 1. a people who live in Gabon. They number 10,000 and they speak a BANTU LANGUAGE. 2. a people who live in Zimbabwe. They speak a dialect of KARANGA, a BANTU LANGUAGE belonging to the SHONA group.

Dungulin, a people who live in Chad. They number 16,300.

Duru, a people who live in Cameroon in the region of Adamawa. They number 16,000 and they speak a NON-CLASS LANGUAGE belonging to the CHAMBA group.

Dyakanke, a people who live in Senegal. They speak SONINKE.

Dyalonke see YALUNKA.

Dyan, a people living in Upper Volta. They speak a dialect of LOBI.

Dyawara (Diawara), is the name given to a section of the SONINKE people.

Dye, a people living in north-western Togo.

Dyerma see ZARMA.

Dyola (Diola), a people living in Senegal, where they number 115,000, and in Gambia where they number 20,000. They speak a WEST ATLANTIC LANGUAGE.

Dyula (Jula, Dioula), a people living in Ivory Coast and Upper Volta. They number 140,000 and they speak a MANDE dialect, belonging to the Malinke-Bambara-Dyula dialect cluster (see LANGUAGE FAMILY).

Dyumba, a small group of people who live in Gabon. They speak a BANTU LANGUAGE.

Dzing (Ding), a people living in Bandundu province in Zaire. They speak a dialect of YANSI, a BANTU LANGUAGE.

East-Saharan languages are spoken in Chad, the Central African Republic and the north-eastern part of Nigeria. The main members of this group are Kanuri-Kanembu, Tubu-Tuda (Toubou-Teda) and Zaghawa.

Edo is a language belonging to the KWA family. It is also known as Benin. It is spoken by about 1,000,000 people in Nigeria in the region of Benin, Ishan and Kukuruku.

Efe, a group of PYGMIES who live among the BALESE people in Zaire. They number 10,000.

Efik, a people and language of southern Nigeria near Calabar and of the region which was formerly part of British Cameroon. The Efik people are related to the IBIBIO and they are traditionally fishermen and traders. The Efik language belongs to a language group which includes Ibibio. Efik has become the literary language of the area.

Egede, a people living in Nigeria in the area where the Benue river joins the Niger river. They number 70,000 and they speak a language related to IDOMA.

Eki, a people living in Cameroon. They number 2,900 and they speak a BANTU LANGUAGE.

Ekoi, a people who live in Nigeria near Calabar and Ogoja. They number 94,000 and they speak a large number of dialects of a CLASS LANGUAGE.

Ekot Ngba, a people who live in Cameroon.

Ekumbe, a people who live in south-eastern Nigeria in the region which was formerly part of British Cameroon. They number 850 and speak a BANTU LANGUAGE.

Eliri, a small group of people who live in Sudan. They number 400. Their language is KOALIB-TAGOI.

Embu, a people who live in Kenya to the south-east of Mount Kenya. They are closely related to the KIKUYU and speak a BANTU LANGUAGE.

Enya, a people who live in the Province Orientale of Zaire. They speak a BANTU LANGUAGE.

Eton, a people who live in Cameroon. They number 111,700 and they speak a BANTU LANGUAGE.

Etsako, nine related groups of people who live in the Mid-West State of Nigeria. They number 45,000 and they speak EDO.

Etulo, a small group of people who live among the TIV people in Nigeria. Their language is IDOMA.

Etung, a people who live in southern Nigeria.

Ewe, an important language in the Republic of Togo and in eastern Ghana. About 2,000,000 people speak Ewe. There is literature in Ewe.

Ewondo (Yaoundé), a people who live in Cameroon. They number 93,000 and they speak a BANTU LANGUAGE.

Fa' (Fak, Balom), a people who live in Cameroon. They number 3,900 and they speak a BANTU LANGUAGE.

Fa d'Ambu, a people who live on Macias Nguema Biyoga, formerly called Fernando Poo.

Falasha, a Jewish people who live in the Qemant region of Ethiopia. They speak KAYLA and QWARA, which are dialects of the CUSHITIC LANGUAGE group.

Fali, a people who live in the mountainous regions of Cameroon. They number 37,000 and they speak a NON-CLASS LANGUAGE.

Fanagalo (Fanekalo, Fanakalo), a PIDGIN language spoken throughout a wide area of South Africa. Fanagalo is also called Basic Bantu. Many of the words came from ZULU and XHOSA, with additions from English and AFRIKAANS.

Fang, a people who live in Cameroon, Equatorial Guinea, Gabon and Congo. They number 216,000 and speak a BANTU LANGUAGE.

Fante see AKAN.

Fanya, a people who live in Chad. They number 1,500. They speak BUA.

Feroge, a group of peoples who live in western Sudan in the area of Raga. They number 2,500 and they speak a dialect of SERE-MUNDU.

Fingo, a people who live in Cape Province, South Africa.

Fipa, a people who live in Tanzania on the shores of Lake Tanganyika. The Fipa number 86,500 and speak a BANTU LANGUAGE.

FANTE: These Fante boys speak a dialect that belongs to the Akan group of dialects.

FULA: *Above* A Fula (or Fulani) mother and child. The Fula live in western Africa from Senegal in the west to northern Cameroon in the east. The Fula of northern Cameroon are called Fulbe. *Below* A group of Fulbe musicians are seen playing in the centre of a village.

Fiyadikkya, a people and language of Egypt, near the border with Sudan. Fiyadikkya is a NUBIAN LANGUAGE.

Fokeng, a people who live in Lesotho.

Fon, a people who live in Benin (Dahomey). Together with the AJA, they number 836,000. They speak a dialect of EWE.

Frafra is a name given to the TALENSI, NAMNAM and GURENSI peoples.

Fula or **Fulani,** a people living in West Africa between Senegal and northern Cameroon. The Fulani number about 4,000,000. Many Fulani live a nomadic life. The Fulani speak Fulfulde, a CLASS LANGUAGE. The Fulani of the northern Cameroon are often called Fulbe. Another name for Fulani is Peul.

Fulbe see FULA.

Fuliru (Fuliro), a people who live in the Kivu province of Zaire. They number 56,000 and they speak a BANTU LANGUAGE.

Fumu, a small group of people who live in Congo. They number 200 and they speak a BANTU LANGUAGE.

Fung, a people who live in the Sudan.

Fungor, a people who live in the Nuba Hills in Sudan. Numbering 2,400, they speak the KOALIB-TAGOI language.

Fungwe, a people who live in Zimbabwe.

Fur (Konjara), a people and language of the Dar-Fur region of Sudan and also of Chad. The Fur number about 300,000. Their language forms an ISOLATED LANGUAGE GROUP. From the year 1500 until 1874, the Fur were ruled by sultans of the Keira dynasty.

Furu, a people who live in the Equateur province of Zaire. Numbering 5,000, they speak a BONGO-BAGIRMI language of the Kresh language group.

Gã, or **Gan,** a people who live in Ghana in the area of Accra. Groups of Gã also live in Togo and along the coast of Benin (Dahomey). The Gã language is used as a literary language.

Gablai, a fishing people who live in Chad. They are few in number. They speak a language belonging to the SOMRAI group.

Gabri, a people who live in Chad. Their language belongs to the SOMRAI group.

Gade, a people who live in northern Nigeria.

Gafat is an almost extinct SEMITIC LANGUAGE which is spoken in Ethiopia.

Gagu, a section of the KWENI people.

Galla, or **Oromo,** a people living in Ethiopia numbering over 12,000,000. In the 16th and 17th centuries there were important Galla kingdoms. After a series of wars with the Ethiopians and the SWAHILI, the Galla eventually became part of the Kingdom of Ethiopia. The Galla people are mainly farmers, growing crops and raising cattle, but some groups are nomadic herders. Some groups of Galla people follow their traditional religion. Some are Muslims while others are Christians. The Galla people speak different dialects of a language belonging to the CUSHITIC LANGUAGE group.

Gallinas see VAI.

Galwa, a people who live in Gabon. They number 2,000 and speak a BANTU LANGUAGE.

Gam, a people who live in Chad. They speak a language belonging to the SOMRAI group.

Gan see GÃ.

Ganawuri see ATEN.

Ganda (Baganda) are the people of a formerly important kingdom called Buganda which gave its name to Uganda. They number about 2,000,000 and speak a BANTU LANGUAGE called Luganda. Luganda has an extensive literature. Eight newspapers are published in Luganda. The Ganda have an interesting history, their kingdom being based on a strong dynasty of kings (Kabaka).

Ganza, a people who live in Sudan and in the Dar Fung region of Ethiopia. They number 1,000. Their language forms an ISOLATED LANGUAGE GROUP.

Gardulla, a people living in south-western Ethiopia. They speak a CUSHITIC LANGUAGE.

Garwe, a people who live in Zimbabwe. They speak a dialect of NDAU, a BANTU LANGUAGE.

Gbanyang, a people who live in northern Ghana. They speak a dialect belonging to the DAGOMBA dialect cluster (see LANGUAGE FAMILY) of GUR.

Gbanziri, a people who live in Central African Republic and in Zaire, where there are 150 of them. They speak a dialect which belongs to the Buraka-Gbanziri dialect cluster (see LANGUAGE FAMILY) of the SERE-MUNDU language.

Gbari (Gwari), a people who live in north-western Nigeria near the Niger river. Numbering 200,000, they speak a language of the KWA group.

Gbati, a people living in Zaire. They number 820 and speak a BANTU LANGUAGE.

Gbaya (Gbeya), a large number of dialects and peoples of the Central African Republic. There are about 600,000 Gbaya-speaking people.

Gbigbil, a people living in Cameroon. Numbering 6,200, they speak a BANTU LANGUAGE.

Ge'ez is the classical SEMITIC LANGUAGE of Ethiopia. It is the language of the Coptic Christian Church. It has a religious literature dating back to the middle ages but it is no longer spoken.

Gelaba (Merille), a people who live in Ethiopia around the northern shores of Lake Turkana. Numbering 2,100, the Gelaba speak a CUSHITIC LANGUAGE.

Gere, a people who live in Ivory Coast.

Gerze (Guerzé) see KPELLE.

Gidar, a people who live in Cameroon, where they number 40,000, and in Chad, where they number 7,500.

Gidole, a people and language in south-western Ethiopia. Gidole is a CUSHITIC LANGUAGE.

Gimira, a people living in south-western Ethiopia. Numbering 20,000, they speak a CUSHITIC LANGUAGE.

Gio see DAN.

Gisiga, a people living in Cameroon. They number 44,000. Their language belongs to the Daba dialect cluster of the Matakam-Mardera language group (see LANGUAGE FAMILY).

Gisu (Gishu, Masaba), a people living in Kenya and in Uganda on the western slopes of Mount Elgon, where they number 250,000. They speak a BANTU LANGUAGE.

Go (Rurede), a people living in Zaire. They number 24 and speak Stedi, a GUR language.

Godye (Godia), a people who live in Ivory Coast. They number 2,000. They speak a dialect belonging to the BETE dialect cluster (see LANGUAGE FAMILY).

Gofa, a people who live in south-western Ethiopia. They speak a dialect of WALAMO.

Gogo, a people living in Tanzania. Numbering 340,000, they speak a BANTU LANGUAGE.

Gola, a people who live in western Liberia, where there are 150,000 of them, and in Sierra Leone, where they number 8,500. They speak a WEST ATLANTIC LANGUAGE.

Golo, a people living in Sudan in the Wau Mboro region, where they number 4,000. They also live in Central African Republic, where they are called the Vita. They speak a Banda-Gbaya-Ngbandi language.

Gonde, a people who live in Cameroon and Nigeria. They number 22,000.

Gonja see GUANG.

Gorowa, a people living in Tanzania. They number 17,500. Their language forms an ISOLATED LANGUAGE GROUP with IRAQW.

Gove (Gova), a people who live in Zimbabwe. They speak a dialect of ZEZURU.

Grebo live in eastern Liberia. They speak a dialect of KRU.

Grusi is the name applied to the KASENA, ISALA and other peoples living in northern Ghana and also in Upper Volta. They number 144,000. Their dialects form a dialect cluster of GUR.

Guang (Gonja), a people who live in northern Ghana. Their language forms a dialect cluster of KWA.

Gula, a people living in Chad.

Gule, a people who live in Sudan to the west of Roseires. Their language forms an ISOLATED LANGUAGE GROUP.

Gumba, a legendary people who lived in Kenya.

Gumuz (Gumus, Gunza), a people living in Ethiopia. Their language forms an ISOLATED LANGUAGE GROUP.

Gun (Gŭ), a people who live in Benin (Dahomey). They speak a dialect of EWE.

Gungawa, a people who live on the banks of the River Niger near Yauri and Borgu. They number 15,000 and speak a CLASS LANGUAGE of Nigeria. They are fishermen.

Gur, a language group of Upper Volta.

Gurage, a group of peoples speaking SEMITIC LANGUAGES in Ethiopia. The Gurage number 350,000.

Gure, a people who live in Nigeria in the region of Zaria. Numbering 3,800, they speak a CLASS LANGUAGE.

Gurensi (Nakanse), a people living in northern Ghana and Upper Volta. They number 105,000 and speak GUR.

Gurma (Gurmantche), a people who live in Upper Volta, Togo and Benin. They number 127,000 and their language forms a dialect cluster of GUR.

Guro see KWENI.

Gusii, a people who live in south-western Kenya, where they number 255,000, and Tanzania, where they number 3,400. They speak a BANTU LANGUAGE.

Gwa, a people who live in Ivory Coast. They number 6,000 and they speak KWA.

Gwama, a people who live in south-western Ethiopia.

Gwamba, a people who live in the Transvaal, South Africa and in Mozambique. They speak a dialect of TSONGA, a BANTU LANGUAGE.

Gwari see GBARI.

Gweno, a people who live in Tanzania. They speak a BANTU LANGUAGE.

Gwere, a people living to the east of Lake Kyoga in Uganda. Numbering 83,200, they speak a BANTU LANGUAGE.

Ha, a people living in north-western Tanzania. They number 330,000 and they speak a BANTU LANGUAGE.

Habab is the name given to a section of the Beit Asgeda people. They speak TIGRE.

Haddad, a people who live in Chad.

Hadimu, a people who live on the island of Zanzibar. They speak a dialect of SWAHILI.

Hadiya (Gudella), an Ethiopian people, who live in the south-west of the country. They speak a CUSHITIC LANGUAGE belonging to the SIDAMO group.

Hadjerai, a people who live in Chad.

Hadzapi (Hadza), a small group of hunters and gatherers who live in Tanzania in the area of Kondoa and Mbulu. They speak a CLICK LANGUAGE.

Haha see HA.

Hamba, a people living in the Kasai province, Zaire.

Hamej, the name given by the ARABS to various groups of Dar Fung peoples.

Hangaza, a Tanzanian people. They number 54,500 and they speak a BANTU LANGUAGE.

Hanya, a people who live in Angola.

Harari, a people of SEMITIC LANGUAGE of Ethiopia in the area of Harar. The Harari number 35,000. Harari literature is mainly concerned with religious subjects such as hymns, and the history and laws of Islam.

Hausa, a people and language of West Africa. Hausa is the most important West African language and it is estimated that it is spoken by about 20,000,000 people, most of whom are Muslims. It is the official language of northern Nigeria. It is spoken in the large cities of Jos, Kano and Sokoto, north as far as the edge of the Sahara, west, as a trade language, in Benin (Dahomey) and Ghana and east into the Cameroon. Hausa has adopted many hundreds of words from ARABIC and English and has a rich literature written in Arabic script.

Havu, a people living in the Kivu province of Zaire. The Havu number 50,000 and speak a BANTU LANGUAGE.

Haya, a people who live in western Tanzania. Numbering 370,000 they speak a BANTU LANGUAGE.

Hehe, a Tanzanian people. They number 286,000 and speak a BANTU LANGUAGE.

Heiban, a people who live in the Nuba Hills in Sudan. They number 2,500 and they speak a dialect of KOALIB-TAGOI.

Heikum (Hainum), a people who live in Namibia. They speak a dialect of NAMA.

Hemba, a people who live in Shaba province, Zaire. They speak a BANTU LANGUAGE.

Hera (Here), a people of Zimbabwe. They speak a dialect of MANYIKA, which belongs to the SHONA group of BANTU LANGUAGES.

Herero, a group of peoples living in Namibia. The Herero number about 100,000 and speak a BANTU LANGUAGE. They are mainly cattle-breeders.

Higi, a people who live in south-eastern Nigeria, where they number 4,000. They also live in Cameroon, where they are known as the KAPSIKI. They speak a Chadic language.

Hima, a people who live in Rwanda and Zaire. They number 4,000 and they speak a BANTU LANGUAGE.

Hlengwe, a people of Zimbabwe who speak a BANTU LANGUAGE.

Hlubi, a people who live in Lesotho and Cape Province, South Africa. They speak a BANTU LANGUAGE.

Hoho see HA.

Holo (Holu), a people who live in Angola. They number 12,000 and they speak a BANTU LANGUAGE.

Holoholo, a people who live in south-eastern Zaire and in Tanzania, where they number 2,100. They speak a BANTU LANGUAGE.

Homa, a people who live in Sudan. They are few in number. They speak a BANTU LANGUAGE.

Hororo (Mpororo), a people living in Uganda. They speak a form of NKORE, a BANTU LANGUAGE.

Hottentot see KHOI-SAN.

Humbe, a people living in Angola. They speak a dialect of NYANEKA, a BANTU LANGUAGE.

Humbu, a people who live in the Bas Zaire and Bandundu provinces of Zaire.

Hunde, a people who live in the Kivu province of Zaire. They number 33,600. They speak a dialect of TEMBO, a BANTU LANGUAGE.

Hungu, a people who live in Angola. They number 61,500 and speak a dialect of KONGO, a BANTU LANGUAGE.

Hurutse, a people who live in the Transvaal and Cape Province of South Africa. They speak TSWANA.

Hutu (Bahutu), a people living in Rwanda and Burundi.

Ibibio, a large group of people who live in the Calabar and Rivers States of southern Nigeria. They number more than 1,000,000 and they speak a NON-CLASS LANGUAGE.

Ibibio-Efik, a cluster of closely-related dialects spoken by some 200,000 people in southern central Nigeria. Efik is the main dialect. Although Efik is only spoken by some 10,000 people, it is accepted by speakers of other Ibibio dialects as the literary language.

Ibo see IGBO.

Idoma, a people and (NON-CLASS) LANGUAGE of the Benue-Plateau State of Nigeria. The Idoma number 250,000.

Igala, a people who live in the Benue-Plateau State of Nigeria. They number 200,000 and they speak a dialect of YORUBA.

Igbira (Kwotto), a people who live in Nigeria in the region where the Benue River joins the Niger River. Numbering 148,000, they speak dialects of the KWA group of languages.

Igbo (Ibo), a people and language of Nigeria. The Igbo are one of the major peoples of Nigeria. The Igbo language is spoken by about 4,000,000 people in the East Central State. It is often grouped with the KWA language family.

Ijaw (Ijo), a group of peoples and a language of south and south-west Nigeria. The Ijaw people number about 156,000 and live in groups which include the Okrikan, Nembe, Kolokuma, Atisa and Warri. Ijaw is a CLASS LANGUAGE with dialects which vary from group to group.

Ikuhane, a people who live in Zambia. They number 3,000 and speak a BANTU LANGUAGE.

Ila, a Zambian people. Numbering 13,000, they speak a BANTU LANGUAGE.

Indri, a people living in southern Sudan in the region of Rega. The Indri number about 700. They speak a SERE-MUNDU language, belonging to the FEROGE language group.

Ineme, a people living in the Kukuruku division of Nigeria's Mid-Western State. They number 5,800 and they speak EDO.

Ingassana (Tabi), a people who live in the Tabi Hills of Sudan. They number 20,000. Their language forms an ISOLATED LANGUAGE GROUP.

Iraqw, a people who live in Tanzania in the region of Mbulu. They number 100,000. Their language forms an ISOLATED LANGUAGE GROUP.

Irenge, a people who live in the Lafit Hills of southern Sudan.

Irigwe, a Nigerian people who live in the region of Jos. Numbering 12,000, they speak a CLASS LANGUAGE.

Isala (Sisala), a people who live in northern Ghana, where they number 40,000 and in Upper Volta, where they number 3,000. They speak a dialect which belongs to the GRUSI dialect cluster of GUR.

Ishan, a people who live in Nigeria to the north-east of Benin City. Numbering 183,000, they speak a dialect of Bini.

Isoko, a Nigerian people who live in the region of the delta of the Niger River. They number 33,000, and they speak a dialect of the KWA language group.

Isolated Language Group, a term used to describe languages, dialect clusters or language groups, where no other related languages or language groups have been found.

Issa (Isa), a people living south of Djibouti. They speak a dialect of SOMALI.

Isuwu (Subu), a people who live in the part of south-eastern Nigeria which was formerly part of British Cameroon. They number 140 and they speak a Coastal Bantu language.

Itsekiri (Jekri), a people who live in Nigeria to the north-west of the delta of the River Niger. They number between 20,000 and 25,000. They speak a dialect of YORUBA.

Ivbiosakon is the name given to a group of 17 groups of people who live in south-west Kukuruku division of Nigeria's Mid-Western State. They number 185,000 and they speak EDO.

Iwa, a people who live in Zambia near the border with Tanzania. Numbering 13,750, they speak a BANTU LANGUAGE.

Iyembe, a people who live in Zaire in the provinces of Bas-Zaire and Bandundu.

Jaba, a people who live near Zaria in northern Nigeria. Numbering 25,400, they speak a CLASS LANGUAGE.

Janjero, an Ethiopian people who speak a CUSHITIC LANGUAGE, known also as Janjero, of the Omotic sub-group.

Jarawa, a Nigerian people who live in the Benue-Plateau State. They are divided into 'Plains' and 'Hills' Jarawa. They speak a dialect in the Jar dialect cluster.

Jawunde see EWONDO.

Jegel, a people living in Chad, where they number 9,200.

Jekri see ITSEKIRI.

Jen (Dza), a people who live in Nigeria in the region of Adamawa. They speak a NON-CLASS LANGUAGE.

Jerawa live in Nigeria in the region of Jos and Bauchi. They speak a CLASS LANGUAGE.

Jimi, a people living in Cameroon. They number 2,000 and they speak NJEM.

Jita, a people living in Tanzania. Numbering 71,400, they speak a BANTU LANGUAGE.

Jompre see KUTEV.

Jongor, a people who live in Chad. They number 26,000 and they speak a CHADO-HAMITIC LANGUAGE belonging to the Sokoro-Mubi language group.

Jukun (Kororofawa), a Nigerian people who live in the region of Benue and Adamawa. They number 32,000 and they speak a NON-CLASS LANGUAGE.

Juman, a people who live in Chad, where they number 720. They speak a language belonging to the Kim dialect cluster of the SOMRAI language group.

Kaa, a people who live in Cameroon. They number 5,300 and they speak a BANTU LANGUAGE.

Kaalong (Mbong), a small group of people living in Cameroon. They number only 50. They speak a BANTU LANGUAGE.

Kabakaba Dunjo live in Chad. They number 17,000 and they speak a dialect of BONGO-BAGIRMI.

K'abena, a people numbering several thousand who live in south-western Ethiopia. They speak a CUSHITIC LANGUAGE belonging to the SIDAMO group.

Kabre, a people living in Togo. Together with the Lama or LAMBA and NAWDEMBA peoples, they number 269,000. They speak TEM.

Kabwari, a Zairian people who live on the north-west shore of Lake Tanganyika. They speak a BANTU LANGUAGE.

Kachama (Haruro), a people who live in south-western Ethiopia. They number 150 and they speak a CUSHITIC LANGUAGE belonging to the dialect cluster of the OMETO group.

Kadara (Ajure), a Nigerian people who live in the region of Zaria. They number 17,800.

Kadugli (Kudugli, Dhalla), a people who live in the Sudan. They number between 18,000 and 19,000. They speak one of the KADUGLI-KRONGO languages.

Kadugli-Krongo, a group of languages spoken in central Sudan in the southern Nuba Hills area. It consists of Kadugli, Miri, Tulishi, Keiga, Tumma, Katcha, Tumtum and Krongo. Each language has only a few hundred speakers.

Kafa (Kaffa), a people and CUSHITIC LANGUAGE of the one-time kingdom of Kaffa, now in Ethiopia. The Kafa language is also spoken by the Bosha, Mucha and Shekka peoples.

Kagoro (Bambara), a people who live in northern Nigeria in the region of Zaria. Numbering 9,300, they speak a dialect related to KATAB.

Kaguru (Kagulu), a people who live in the Eastern Region of Tanzania. Numbering 87,000, they speak a BANTU LANGUAGE.

Kahe, a Tanzanian people, who number 1,800. They speak a BANTU LANGUAGE.

Kahugu, a people who live in northern Nigeria. They number 1,200 and they speak a CLASS LANGUAGE.

Kaiku, a people who live in Zaire in the region of Beri. They speak a BANTU LANGUAGE.

Kajure (Ajure), a people who live in Nigeria in the region of Zaria. They number 17,800.

Kaka (Kako, Yaka), a people who live in Cameroon, where they number 37,000, and also in Congo. They speak a BANTU LANGUAGE.

Kakwa, a widespread people who live in southern Sudan, Uganda and Zaire. They number 54,000. They speak a dialect of BARI.

Kalanga, a people and BANTU LANGUAGE of Zimbabwe. The Kalanga language belongs to the SHONA group.

Kalenjin, a language group and people of Kenya. Kalenjin has two main languages, NANDI and Kipsikis, and several dialects.

Kaleri, a people who live in northern Nigeria.

Kamasya (Tuken), a people who live in Kenya in the area of Baringo. Numbering 40,400, they speak a dialect of NANDI, a NILO-HAMITIC LANGUAGE.

Kamba. 1. a people who live in Congo. 2. a people living in Kenya in the region of Machakos and Kitui. They number 1,400,000 and they speak a BANTU LANGUAGE.

Kambari, a people who live in northern Nigeria in the Middle Niger region. They number 67,000 and speak a CLASS LANGUAGE of Nigeria.

Kambatta, a people who live in south-western Ethiopia. They speak a CUSHITIC LANGUAGE, belonging to the SIDAMO group.

Kamdang, a people living in Sudan. Numbering 2,900, they speak a dialect of KADUGLI-KRONGO.

Kami, a people who live in the Eastern Region of Tanzania. They speak a BANTU LANGUAGE.

Kamuku is the name given to a group of peoples living in the Middle Niger region of Nigeria. The group includes the Kamuku, Baushi, Ngwe, Po Pongo and Ura Tochipo peoples. In all, they number 25,000. They speak a CLASS LANGUAGE of Nigeria.

Kanakuru, a people who live in northern Nigeria in the region of Bornu and Adamawa. Numbering 11,300, they speak a CHADO-HAMITIC LANGUAGE.

Kande, a very small group of people who live in Gabon. They speak a BANTU LANGUAGE.

Kanembu, a people who live in Chad, where they number 60,000, and in Niger and Nigeria. Their language is KANURI.

Kanga, a people living in the Miri Hills of Sudan. They number 6,000 and they speak KADUGLI-KRONGO.

Kango (Likango) live in Zaire's Province Orientale. They speak a BANTU LANGUAGE. The Kango are mostly fishermen.

Kanu, a people living in Zaire. They number 3,500 and they speak a BANTU LANGUAGE.

Kanuri, an EAST SAHARAN LANGUAGE and a large group of people who live in northern Nigeria in the region of Bornu, Kano, Sokoto and Zaria. The Kanuri also live in Niger. They number about 1,000,000. At one time, they were ruled by kings.

Kanyoka, a people who live in Zaire in Kasai province. They speak a BANTU LANGUAGE.

Kaondé, a people living in Zambia and Zaire. Numbering 38,000, they speak a BANTU LANGUAGE.

Kapsiki, a people living in the Mandara Mountains of Cameroon, where they number 22,500. They also live in Nigeria, where they are known as HIGI. They speak a Chadic language.

Kara. 1. a people who live in the Equateur province of Sudan. Their language is BONGO-BAGIRMI. 2. a people living in Tanzania. The group has 30,700 members. They speak a dialect belonging to the KEREWE dialect cluster (see LANGUAGE FAMILY).

Karagwe, a people who live in Tanzania. They speak a BANTU LANGUAGE.

Karamojong, a group of seven peoples who live in the Karamojong district of Uganda. These peoples are the Karamojong, Sie, Dodos, Turkana, Toposa, Donyiro and Jiye. Together, they number 214,000. They speak a NILO-HAMITIC LANGUAGE belonging to the TESO language group.

Karanga, a people and language of Zimbabwe. Karanga is a BANTU LANGUAGE belonging to the SHONA group.

Kare (Kari), a people who live in eastern Zaire and Central African Republic. They number between 4,000 and 5,000. They speak a BANTU LANGUAGE.

KareKare, a people who live in northern Nigeria in the region of Bauchi, Bornu and Kano. Numbering 39,000, they speak a CHADO-HAMITIC LANGUAGE.

Kari, a people who live in Cameroon and Chad. They number 40,000 and they speak a NON-CLASS LANGUAGE.

Kasele, a people living in Togo. They number 20,000 and they speak a GUR language of the GURMA dialect cluster.

Kasena, a people who live in Upper Volta, where they number 41,000, and in Ghana, where they number 33,000. They speak a GUR language belonging to the GRUSI dialect cluster.

Katab, a group of ten peoples who live near Zaria in northern Nigeria. Numbering 7,000, they speak a CLASS LANGUAGE of Nigeria.

Katcha (Dholubi), a people living in Sudan. They number 5,700 and they speak KADUGLI-KRONGO.

KARAMOJONG: This group of seven peoples in Uganda and Kenya includes the Turkana, seen here fishing.

Katla, a people who live in the Nuba Hills of Sudan. They number 8,500. Their language forms part of an ISOLATED LANGUAGE GROUP.

Kayla (Kailinya), a people and CUSHITIC LANGUAGE of Ethiopia.

Kayunga, a small group of people living in Zaire. They number about 600.

Kazibati, a people who live in Zaire. They number 365 and they speak a dialect of NGBANDI.

Kebbawa, a people who live in northern Nigeria.

Kebu (Akebu), a people who live in Togo and speak a CLASS LANGUAGE.

Kebu, a people who live in the Province Orientale of Zaire.

Keiga, a Sudanese people who live to the north of Miri. They number 6,000 and they speak KADUGLI-KRONGO.

Keiga Jirru, a people living in the Nuba Hills of Sudan. They number 1,500. Their language belongs to the TEMEIN language group.

Kela, a people who live in the Kasai province of Zaire. They number between 80,000 and 100,000. They speak a BANTU LANGUAGE.

Kele. 1. a very small group of people who live in Gabon. They speak a BANTU LANGUAGE. 2. a Zairian people, who number 2,400. 3. a people who live in the province Orientale of Zaire. The Kele (Lokeke) number 26,000, and speak a BANTU LANGUAGE.

Keliko see MORU.

Kemant (Qemant), a people living in Ethiopia on the shores of Lake Tana. They speak a CUSHITIC LANGUAGE.

KANURI: A Kanuri girl who lives in a province of northern Nigeria.

Kenga, a people who live in Chad. They number between 20,000 and 25,000. Their language is BONGO-BAGIRMI.

Kentu, a people living in Nigeria in Benue-Plateau State and in the region which was formerly part of British Cameroon. They number 6,300 and they speak a NON-CLASS LANGUAGE.

Kenuz, a Nubian people who live in Egypt in the Nile Valley. They speak Kenuzi, a NUBIAN LANGUAGE.

Kenyi, a people of Uganda, who speak a BANTU LANGUAGE.

Kera, a people who live in Cameroon. They number 15,000 and they speak a NON-CLASS LANGUAGE.

Kerewe, a Tanzanian people who number 31,300. They speak a BANTU LANGUAGE.

Kerre, a people living in south-western Ethiopia. Their language belongs to the BAKO language group.

Kete, a people living in Zaire. They number 12,900 and they speak a BANTU LANGUAGE.

Keyo (Elgeyo), a Kenyan people who number 40,400. They speak a dialect of KALENJIN, a NILO-HAMITIC LANGUAGE.

Kgalagadi (Kxalaxari), a people who live in Botswana. Their language is TSWANA, a BANTU LANGUAGE.

Kgatla (Khatla, Kxatla), a people living in the Transvaal, South Africa and in Botswana. They speak TSWANA, a BANTU LANGUAGE.

Khamir, a people living in Ethiopia who speak a CUSHITIC LANGUAGE.

Khamta, a people living in Ethiopia. They speak a CUSHITIC LANGUAGE.

Khasonke (Kassonke, Kasso), a people who live in Mali. They number 53,000. They speak a MANDE language belonging to the Malinke-Bambara-Dyula dialect cluster.

Khoi-San is the collective name for the Khoi (Hottentots) and San (Bushmen) in Southern Africa and for their languages. The languages, culture and history of the two peoples are very different. The largest group of Khoi, numbering about 30,000, are the NAMA who live in Namibia. Most of the people speak Nama, a Khoi 'CLICK' LANGUAGE but some speak AFRIKAANS. Most of the Nama still follow their traditional way of life, hunting and keeping cattle and fat-tailed sheep.

The San people, called Bushmen, live mainly in and around the Kalahari Desert, in Botswana and Namibia. Together, they number no more than 20,000 and speak several distinct languages. The San live and hunt in small groups and have no permanent villages. They are expert hunters, using bows and throwing sticks.

Khomani, a people who live in the Cape Province of South Africa. They speak a Bushman language (see KHOI-SAN).

Khwakkhwa (Qwa-Qwa), a people who live in Lesotho.

Kibet, a people who live in Chad. They number between 16,000 and 17,000. Their language, Kibet, belongs to the TAMA language group.

Ki-Chaga (Tschagga), see CHAGA.

Kichi, a people who live in Tanzania, to the west of Matumbi. They speak a BANTU LANGUAGE.

Kiga, a people who live in Uganda. The group has 460,000 members and they speak a BANTU LANGUAGE.

Kikuyu, a Bantu people living in Kenya (calling themselves Agekoyo) and their language. The Kikuyu number more than 2,000,000. They originally lived in the area between Mt. Kenya and Nairobi but they now live in all parts of Kenya. The Kikuyu economy used to be based on goats and crop-growing, mainly maize, sweet potatoes, sugar cane, millet and beans. Even before independence the Kikuyu farmers had begun to grow commercial crops, such as coffee and pyrethrum. The traditional Kikuyu religion is based on belief in a high God called Ngai, 'The Divider', who lives above Mt. Kenya. Some Kikuyus, however, have adopted Catholicism, or Islam, and many are Protestants.

Kilba, a people who live in Cameroon. Numbering 20,000, they speak a Chadic language resembling MARGI.

Kim, a group of people who live in Chad. They number 4,500 and they speak a language belonging to the SOMRAI language group.

Kimbu, a Tanzanian people who number 31,150. They speak a BANTU LANGUAGE.

Kimbundu, a people who live in Angola. They number 110,500 and they speak a BANTU LANGUAGE.

Kinga. 1. a Chadic people numbering 20,700. 2. a people living in Tanzania in the region of Lake Nyasa. Numbering 57,000, they speak a BANTU LANGUAGE.

Kipsikis, a people living in Kenya. They number 157,200 and they speak a dialect of KALENJIN, a NILO-HAMITIC LANGUAGE.

Kisi, a Tanzanian people who number 3,600. They speak a BANTU LANGUAGE.

Kissi (Kisi), a people who live in Guinea (164,000), Sierra Leone (35,000), and Liberia (25,000). They speak a WEST ATLANTIC LANGUAGE.

Kitosh (Vukusu), a people who live in Kenya. They speak a BANTU LANGUAGE. See GISU.

Kiungwana see SWAHILI.

Koalib, the name of the peoples who live in the hills to the west of Abri in Sudan. They number 25,000. They speak KOALIB-TAGOI.

Koalib-Moro is a group of CLASS LANGUAGES spoken in the Nuba and Moro hills in Sudan. The Group is made up of the languages of the Koalib, Heiban, Laro, Otoro, Shwai, Tira, Moro and Fungor peoples.

Koalib-Tagoi, a large language group of the Nuba Hills in Sudan. The unit is made up of LAFOFA and the KOALIB-MORO, TALODI-MASAKIN, and TEGALI-TAGOI language groups.

Kobi, a people who live in the Ruwenzori Mountains of Uganda. They speak a BANTU LANGUAGE.

Kofyar, a people living in northern Nigeria.

Koki, a very small group of people living in Uganda. They speak a BANTU LANGUAGE.

Kom (Nkom, Bikom, Bamekom), a people who live in south-eastern Nigeria. Numbering 15,000, they speak a CLASS LANGUAGE.

Koma, a people living in the Sudanese–Ethiopian border. The group has 3,000 members. Their language forms an ISOLATED LANGUAGE GROUP.

Kombe (Ngumbi), a people who are scattered along the coasts of Cameroon and Rio Muni. They speak a BANTU LANGUAGE.

Konabem, a people living in Cameroon who number 3,000. They speak a BANTU LANGUAGE.

Konda, a people living in Zaire in the Bas-Zaire and Bandundu provinces.

Konga (Ka), a people who live in Angola.

Kongo, a people (Bakongo) and BANTU LANGUAGE (Kikongo) of Zaire. The Kongo people number about 4,000,000 and are the largest group in Zaire. Most of the Kongo are farmers, growing cassava, maize, sweet potatoes and bananas. Cash crops such as coffee and cocoa are now grown and many people work in large towns. There are more than 50 dialects of the Kongo language. There is an official trade language known as 'Government Kikongo', Kileta or Ikeleve. In Brazzaville and nearby areas, the language is called Kituba or Mono-Kutuba.

Konjo (Konzo), a people who live in Uganda on the slopes of the Ruwenzori Mountains. Numbering 107,000, they speak a BANTU LANGUAGE.

Konkomba (Kokomba), a people who live in Ghana and in Togo. They number 49,000 and they speak a dialect in the GURMA cluster of the GUR language group.

KHOI-SAN: This group includes Hottentots and Bushmen. The Bushmen are expert hunters (*below left*). Their paintings (*below right*) are well known.

32

Kono, a people who live in Sierra Leone, where they number 80,000. Small groups of Kono also live in Liberia. They speak a MANDE language which is closely related to VAI.

Konongo, a Tanzanian people, numbering 20,500. They speak a dialect of Nyamirezi, a BANTU LANGUAGE.

Konso, a people and CUSHITIC LANGUAGE of Ethiopia to the south of Lake Cimao, and also of Kenya.

Kony, a people living in Kenya on the slopes of Mount Elgon. Together with the SAPEI and the POKOT peoples, they number 24,000. They speak a dialect of KALENJIN, a NILO-HAMITIC LANGUAGE.

Konyagi (Coniagui), a people who live on the Guinea-Senegal border. The group has 10,600 members, and is a section of the TENDA people. They speak a WEST ATLANTIC LANGUAGE.

Konzo see KONJO.

Korana (Kora), a people living in Griqualand West, South Africa. They speak a Hottentot language (see KHOI-SAN).

Koranko (Kuranko), a people who live in Sierra Leone, where they number 73,500, and in Guinea, where they number 36,500. They speak a dialect belonging to the Malinke-Bambara-Dyula dialect cluster of the MANDE language.

Korekore, a people and BANTU LANGUAGE of Zimbabwe and Angola. Korekore belongs to the SHONA language group.

Korio, a people living in south-western Ethiopia.

Koro, a group of people living in northern Nigeria to the north-east of the Middle Niger River. The Koro group has 31,500 members.

Kosi (Bakosi, Nkosi), a group of people living in Cameroon, where they number 1,850. They also live in the part of Nigeria which was formerly British Cameroon. The Kosi speak a BANTU LANGUAGE.

Kota. 1. a people who live in Central African Republic. Together with the NGANDO people, they number 2,900. They speak a BANTU LANGUAGE. 2. a people who live in Gabon and Congo. Numbering 28,000, they speak a BANTU LANGUAGE.

Kotoko, a people who live in Cameroon, Chad and Nigeria. They number 31,000 and speak a CHADO-HAMITIC LANGUAGE.

Kotokoli, the name of the TEM-speaking peoples of northern Togo.

Koyo, a Congolese people who speak a BANTU LANGUAGE.

Koyra, a people who live in south-western Ethiopia. They speak a CUSHITIC LANGUAGE which forms a dialect cluster within the OMETO language group.

Kpala, a people living in north-western Zaire. They speak SERE-MUNDU.

Kpe see BAKWERI.

Kpelle, a large group of people living in Liberia and Guinea. They number 500,000 and they speak a MANDE language.

Kposa (Akposso), a Togolese people who speak a CLASS LANGUAGE.

Kra, a people living in eastern Liberia. They speak KRU.

Kran, a people who live in Liberia and Ivory Coast. They number 100,000 and they speak a dialect of KRU.

Kresh, a people who live in Equateur province in southern Sudan. They number 8,000. Their language is BONGO-BAGIRMI.

Krim, a section of the BULOM people who number 44,600.

Krio see CREOLE.

Krobo, a dialect of KWA which is spoken by the ADANGME people.

Krongo, a people living in the Moro Hills in Sudan. They number 10,000. They speak KADUGLI-KRONGO.

Kru, a family of languages spoken in Liberia and along the Ivory Coast. These languages are strongly tonal with mainly monosyllabic roots. The main members are: Kru, Bassa, Kran and Grebo.

Kuba. 1. a people who live in Congo and speak a BANTU LANGUAGE. 2. a Zairian people who number 73,200. They speak a BANTU LANGUAGE.

Kudawa, a people who live in Nigeria between Bauchi and Kano. The group has 2,200 members. They speak a CLASS LANGUAGE of Nigeria.

Kuka, a Chadic people who number 33,700. Their dialects form a dialect cluster (see LANGUAGE FAMILY) of the BONGO-BAGIRMI language.

Kuku, a people who live in southern Sudan on the Kajo Kaji plateau, and also in Uganda. They number 26,000. They speak a dialect of BARI, a NILO-HAMITIC LANGUAGE.

Kukuruku, a people who live in Nigeria's Mid-Western State. They number 185,000. They speak EDO, a KWA language.

Kukwa, a people living in Congo. They number 11,000 and speak a BANTU LANGUAGE.

Kukwe (Kuke), a Tanzanian people who live north of Lake Nyasa. They are a section of the NYAKYUSA people and they speak a BANTU LANGUAGE.

Kulango, a people who live in Ivory Coast and Ghana. They number 40,000. Their language is GUR.

Kulu, a people living in northern Nigeria.

Kumam, a Ugandan people who live in the Teso and Lango districts. They number 56,000. They speak a NILOTIC LANGUAGE of the South Lwo language group.

Kumu, a people who live in Zaire. They number 59,000 and they speak a BANTU LANGUAGE.

Kunama, a people who live in Eritrea in Ethiopia. They number 30,000. Their language forms an ISOLATED LANGUAGE GROUP.

Kunante, a people living in Guinea-Bissau. They number 6,000 and speak a WEST ATLANTIC LANGUAGE.

Kunda (Cikunda), a people living in Mozambique and Malawi, where they number 72,800, and also in Zambia, where they number 27,000. They speak a BANTU LANGUAGE.

Kunda, a people who live in Shaba province in Zaire. They speak a BANTU LANGUAGE.

Kung, a San people who live in south-eastern Angola, Namibia and Botswana. They speak a CLICK LANGUAGE.

Kunta, a nomadic people who live in Mali.

Kurama, a people living in the region of Zaria in northern Nigeria. They number 11,000.

Kuria (Kulia), a people who live in Tanzania, where they number 65,000, and in Kenya, where they number 30,000. They speak a BANTU LANGUAGE.

Kurtey, a people related to the SONGHAI.

Kurumba, a people who live in Upper Volta. They number 80,000 and they speak a dialect belonging to the GRUSI dialect cluster (see LANGUAGE FAMILY).

Kurunga, a people living in Chad. Their language belongs to the MABA group.

Kusasi, a people who live in northern Ghana, where they number 93,000, and in Upper Volta, where they number 8,000. Their dialect belongs to the DAGOMBA dialect cluster of GUR.

Kushankuru, a people who live on the Sudan-Ethiopia border in the region of Dar Fung.

Kusu, a Zairian people who live in Kivu province. They number 26,000 and speak a BANTU LANGUAGE.

Kutev (Jompre), a people who live in the Benue-Plateau State of Nigeria. They number 15,600 and speak a CLASS LANGUAGE.

Kutu, a people who live in the Eastern Region of Tanzania. They number 18,000 and they speak a BANTU LANGUAGE.

Kuturmi (Ada), a people who live near Zaria in Nigeria. They number 2,000.

Kuulwe, a people in south-western Tanzania. They number 3,000.

Kuyu, a people living in Congo.

Kwa, a large family of West African languages spoken in eastern Ivory Coast, Ghana, Togo, Benin (Dahomey) and Nigeria. The members of the family include: AKAN (Twi-Fante), BAULE, ANYI, and NZIMA.

Kwaa, a people of Liberia who speak KRU.

Kwahu, a people living in Ghana.

Kwakum, a people who live in Cameroon. They number several thousand and speak a BANTU LANGUAGE.

Kwala, a people who live in Congo. They speak a BANTU LANGUAGE.

Kwandi, a Zambian people who number 2,500. They speak a BANTU LANGUAGE belonging to the Luyana language group.

Kwangali, a people and BANTU LANGUAGE of Namibia and Angola.

Kwangwa, a people who live in Zambia. They number 25,500 and they speak a BANTU LANGUAGE spoken by the LOZI.

Kwanyama (Kuanyama), a people who live in Angola and Namibia. They speak a BANTU LANGUAGE.

Kwaya (Zegbe), a dialect of the BETE dialect cluster.

Kwe. 1. a people living in Botswana. Kwe is also the Khoi (Hottentot) suffix meaning 'people' and is put on the ends of words naming several peoples. 2. a people who live in Congo. They speak a BANTU LANGUAGE.

Kwena, a people living in Botswana and in the Transvaal, South Africa. They speak TSWANA.

Kweni (Guro), a people who live in Ivory Coast. They number 83,000 and they speak a MANDE language.

Kwere, a Tanzanian people who live in the Eastern region of the country. They number 40,000 and speak a BANTU LANGUAGE.

Kyama, a people who live in Ivory Coast. They number 11,600 and speak KWA.

Labwor, a people living in the Labwor Hills of northern Uganda. They number 5,300. They speak a NILOTIC LANGUAGE belonging to the South Lwo group.

Lafofa, a people living in the Eliri Hills in Sudan. They number 2,500 and they speak KOALIB-TAGOI.

Laka (Lak, Lag), a people living in Chad, where they number 40,000, and in Cameroon.

Lala. 1. a cluster (see LANGUAGE FAMILY) of dialects spoken in the area of Adamawa in Nigeria. It is a CLASS LANGUAGE spoken by the Yungur (17,200), Lala (9,700), Roba (1,300) and Binna (2,300) peoples. 2. a South African people who live in Zululand. They speak a dialect of the ZULU language. 3. a people living in Zambia, where they number 50,000, and in Zaire, where they number 10,000. They speak Lala, a BANTU LANGUAGE.

Lali, a Congolese people who speak a BANTU LANGUAGE.

Lamba. 1. a people who live in Togo, where, together with the Kabre and Nawdemba, they number 269,000. They also live in Benin (Dahomey). They speak TEM. 2. a people who live in Zambia, where they number 22,000, and in Zaire, where they number 10,000. They speak Lamba, a BANTU LANGUAGE.

Lambya, a people who live in Tanzania where they number 7,500, and also in Malawi. They speak a BANTU LANGUAGE.

Landogo see LOKO.

Landoma (Landuma), a people living in Guinea who number 12,500. They speak a WEST ATLANTIC LANGUAGE.

Lange, a people who live in Zaire and speak a BANTU LANGUAGE.

Langi (Rangi, Irangi), a people who live in Tanzania. They number 95,400 and they speak a BANTU LANGUAGE.

Lango. 1. a people who live in northern Uganda. They number 276,000 and speak a NILOTIC LANGUAGE belonging to the South Lwo group. 2. a people who live in southern Sudan in an area south-east of Torit. They number 15,000 and they speak a dialect of Lotuko, a NILO-HAMITIC LANGUAGE.

Langu, a people living in Zaire. They number 950.

Language Family and Dialect Cluster. There are more than a thousand languages in Africa. A few hundred of these can be grouped together in 'families' of related languages. The term 'family' means that, at some time in the past, there was only one language spoken by a single group of possibly related people. When a 'family' becomes a clan, then a tribe, then a nation, small groups of peoples and their languages are absorbed. These languages become dialects of the main language family. All the larger groups of peoples, such as the ARABS, HAUSA, SOMALI and SWAHILI, have in the past absorbed smaller groups. Where there is no dominant group in a region, clans and families break away to form their own villages. The Bantu people spread out across Africa like this, forming hundreds of communities. Each community developed its own language, which in turn ramified into a dialect cluster. In some cases single nations were created from groups who spoke different dialects, such as the kingdoms of Lesotho, Botswana and KwaZulu.

The established African language families are: BANTU, BERBER, CUSHITIC (East), GUR, KWA, MANDE, NILOTIC (South-West), SEMITIC, TOGO REMNANT and WEST ATLANTIC. Language scholars still disagree over the structure of other language families. There are smaller units such as *dialect clusters*. In Europe, there are official or 'standardized' languages for each country. In Africa the following languages are standardized: AFRIKAANS, AMHARIC, ARABIC, HAUSA, IBO, LUGANDA, NDEBELE, RUNDI, RWANDA, SHONA, SOMALI, SUTHU, SWAHILI, TIGRINYA, TSONGA, TSWANA, VENDA, XHOSA, YORUBA and ZULU. Agreement on Somali spelling only dates from 1973 and full agreement has not yet been reached on Swati or Luganda. General agreement has not been reached on any of the other languages. Even the major dialect clusters, such as Kongo Luba, Nyanja and Mongo-Nkundo, have no generally accepted spelling. Dialect clusters may grow into separate *language groups*, e.g. DUTCH-AFRIKAANS and RWANDA-RUNDI. *Language groups* are, therefore, more closely related than *language families* which are older and more ramified.

Lari, a Congolese people who speak a dialect of KONGO, a BANTU LANGUAGE.

Laro, a people who live in the Nuba Hills of Sudan. They number 3,600 and they speak KOALIB-TAGOI.

Lebi, a people who live in Shaba province, Zaire.

Lebu, a people living in the coastal regions of Senegal. The group has 36,000 members. They speak a dialect of WOLOF.

Lefana (Lelemi), a people living in Togo in the regions of Buëm and Borada. They number less than 3,000. Their language is a TOGO REMNANT LANGUAGE.

Lega, a people who live in the Kivu province of Zaire. They number at least 45,000. They speak a BANTU LANGUAGE.

Lele. 1. a people who live in Chad and speak NANCERE. 2. a people who live in Zaire. They number 26,000 and they speak a BANTU LANGUAGE belonging to the KUBA language group.

Lemba, (Remba), a people living in Zimbabwe.

Lendu, a people who live in Zaire and Uganda. They number 160,000. Their language is related to MORU-MANGBETU.

Lengola, a people living in the Province Orientale of Zaire. They speak a BANTU LANGUAGE.

Lenje, a Zambian people who number 40,500. They speak a BANTU LANGUAGE belonging to the Ila language group.

Letswalo, a people who live in Transvaal, South Africa. They speak a BANTU LANGUAGE related to the SHONA language group.

Leya, a people living in Zambia. They number 3,800 and speak a BANTU LANGUAGE.

Libinza, a people who live in Zaire and speak a BANTU LANGUAGE.

Liguri, a people who live in the Nuba Hills in Sudan. They number 2,000. Their language belongs to the Daju language group.

Likila, a group of people who live in Zaire. They speak a BANTU LANGUAGE.

Liko, a people living in Zaire who number 26,000. They speak a BANTU LANGUAGE.

Likpe (Mu), a people who live in Togo in the region to the east of Buëm. They number 3,000 and they speak a TOGO REMNANT LANGUAGE.

Lima, a Zambian people who number 9,000. They speak a BANTU LANGUAGE.

Limba. 1. a group of people who live in Guinea and in Sierra Leone, where they number 174,000. They speak a WEST ATLANTIC LANGUAGE. 2. a people living in Cameroon (Malimbe). They number 3,700 and they speak a BANTU LANGUAGE.

Lingala, a BANTU LANGUAGE spoken in central Zaire. It is based on Bobangi but has adopted many French words. It was used by traders, officials and administrators. It is now the most important language in Central Zaire.

Lingua Franca, a common language which is used by people of different language groups, e.g. HAUSA, SWAHILI.

Lobala, a people living in Zaire. They speak a BANTU LANGUAGE.

Lober see BIRIFOR.

Lobi, a people and language of Upper Volta and Ivory Coast. The Lobi number 211,000. The language forms a dialect cluster of GUR.

Lobo, a people who live in the Equateur province of Zaire. They speak a BANTU LANGUAGE.

Logba, a people living in Togo. They number less than 2,000. Their language is a TOGO REMNANT LANGUAGE.

Logo see MORU.

Logoli (Ragoli, Maragoli), a Kenyan people who speak a BANTU LANGUAGE.

Loi, a people who live in Zaire and speak a BANTU LANGUAGE.

Loko (Landogo, Luko, Lokko). 1. a people living in Sierra Leone who are closely related to the MENDE. They number 70,000. Their language belongs to the Mande-Fu language group of MANDE. 2. a people who live in south-eastern Nigeria in the region of Ogoja. They number 20,000. They speak a CLASS LANGUAGE which is also spoken by the YAKO people.

Lokoya, a people who live in southern Sudan in the area to the north of Torit. They number 12,000. Their language is a dialect of LOTUKO, a NILO-HAMITIC LANGUAGE.

Lolobi, a people living in Togo, who speak a TOGO REMNANT LANGUAGE.

Loma (Toma), a people who live in Liberia and Guinea. They number 260,000. They speak a MANDE language belonging to the Mande-Fu language group.

Lombi. 1. a group of people who live in Nigeria in the region which was formerly part of British Cameroon. They number 1,050 and they speak a BANTU LANGUAGE. See LUMBI.

Lomotwa, a people who live in Shaba province in Zaire. Their language is a dialect of BEMBA, a BANTU LANGUAGE.

Lomwe, a people living in Mozambique to the south of the River Lurio. They number 38,000 and they speak a BANTU LANGUAGE.

Long (Elong), a people who live in Nigeria and Cameroon. They number 4,000 and they speak a BANTU LANGUAGE.

Longarim, a people living in the Boya Hills of southern Sudan. They number about 900. Their language belongs to the Didinga-Murle language group.

Longuda, a Nigerian people who live in the regions of Adamawa and Bauchi. The group has 12,000 members. They speak a CLASS LANGUAGE.

Losengo, a people living in Zaire. They speak a BANTU LANGUAGE.

Lotuho (Latuka, Lotuko), a people and language of southern Sudan in the area of Torit. The Lotuho number 35,000. They speak a NILO-HAMITIC LANGUAGE.

Lovale see LWENA.

Lovedu (Lobedu, Lubedu), a people living in the Transvaal, South Africa. They speak a language closely related to PEDI.

Lozi (Rotse, Luyana, Kololo), the name of 25 groups of people living in Zambia and Botswana. They speak a BANTU LANGUAGE.

Luba, the collective name for two different Zaire dialects. These are Tshiluba in Kasai, spoken by the Baluba-Kas and Kiluba in Katanga, spoken by the Baluba-Kat. Speakers of the Luba dialects number about 3,000,000.

Luchazi (Lucazi), a group of people living in Angola and Zambia. They number 60,000. Their language is a BANTU LANGUAGE belonging to the Chokwe-Lunda language group.

Luganda see GANDA.

Lugbara, a people who live in Uganda and Zaire. They number 240,000 and speak MORU-MANGBETU.

Luguru (Ruguru), a people and language of the eastern part of Tanzania. Together with the KAMI, they number 202, 300. They speak a BANTU LANGUAGE.

Luhya (Lujia), a people who live in Kenya, where they number over 1,500,000. The Luhya also live in Uganda. They speak a BANTU LANGUAGE.

Luimbi, an Angolan people who number only a few hundreds. They speak a BANTU LANGUAGE belonging to the Chokwe-Lunda language group.

Luko see LOKO.

Lukolwe, a Zambian people who number 9,350. They speak a BANTU LANGUAGE belonging to the Nkoya language group.

Lulua, a people who live in the Kasai province of Zaire. They speak Luba.

Luluba (Olu'bo), a group of people who live in the Luluba hills of southern Sudan. The group has 4,000 members. Their language is MORU-MANGBETU.

Lumbi, (Barumbi) a people who live in Zaire where they number 8,350. They speak MORU-MANGBETU.

Lumbu. 1. a people who live on the borders between Gabon and Congo. They number 12,000 and they speak a BANTU LANGUAGE. 2. a people who live in the Shaba province of Zaire. 3. a Zambian people who number 1,950. They speak a BANTU LANGUAGE belonging to the Ila-Tonga language group.

Luna, a people who live in Zaire. They speak a BANTU LANGUAGE.

LOZI: A group of Lozi musicians. The Lozi live in Zambia and Botswana. Their language has many traditional fables or *matangu*.

Lunda, a people living in Shaba province in Zaire, Angola and Zambia. The Southern Lunda, who live in Zambia, number 63,000. The Lunda speak a BANTU LANGUAGE belonging to the Chokwe-Lunda language group.

Lundu, a people living in the part of Nigeria which was formerly British Cameroon. They number 6,200 and they speak a BANTU LANGUAGE.

Lundwe, a people living in Zambia. They number 3,500 and speak a BANTU LANGUAGE belonging to the Ila-Tonga language group.

Lungu, a people living in Zambia. They speak a BANTU LANGUAGE.

Lungwa (Rungwa), a Tanzanian people who live to the north-west of Lake Rukwa. The Lungwa number about 7,200. They speak a BANTU LANGUAGE.

Luntu, a people who live in the Kasai province of Zaire. They number 100,000. Their language is SONGE, a BANTU LANGUAGE.

Luo, a people in West Kenya numbering over 1,700,000. They are one of the main groups of people living in Kenya and they speak a NILOTIC LANGUAGE, Dho-Luo. This is a very melodic language and the Luo are famous for their songs. Traditionally the Luo are farmers, growing maize, millet and cassava. Now they also raise cattle and grow cash crops, such as cotton.

Lushange, a people living in Zambia. They speak a BANTU LANGUAGE of the Nkoya language group.

Luwata see BERBERS.

Luyi (Luyana), a Zambian people who number 3,300. They speak a BANTU LANGUAGE.

Lwena (Luena), a people who live in Angola and Zambia. They number 90,000. They speak a BANTU LANGUAGE belonging to the Chokwe-Lunda language group.

Lwo, collective name for two groups of Nilotic languages. Acholi, Alur Lango, Luo and others belong to South-Lwo.

Lyele (L'ele), a people who live in Upper Volta. They number 61,000. Their language belongs to the GRUSI dialect cluster of GUR.

Ma (Amadi) a people who live in Zaire. They number 4,700 and they speak the MBA language.

Maba, a mountain people living in Chad. They number 56,700. Their language belongs to an ISOLATED LANGUAGE GROUP.

Mabale, a people living in the Equateur Province of Zaire. They speak a BANTU LANGUAGE.

Maban, a people living in southern Sudan. They number 20,000 and speak a NILOTIC LANGUAGE belonging to the north Lwo group.

Mabendi, a people who live in the forests of Zaire. Their language is Lese. See BALESE.

Mabisanga, a people living in north-eastern Zaire. They number 4,000 and they speak MORU-MANGBETU.

Mada. 1. a people living in Cameroon. They number 9,500. 2. a people who live in the Benue-Plateau State of Nigeria. They number 23,400 and speak a CLASS LANGUAGE belonging to the JERAWA language cluster.

Ma'di, a people who live in Uganda and in Sudan. Together with the LUGBARA people, they number 240,000. Their language is MORU-MANGBETU.

Maele, a people living in north-eastern Zaire. They number 13,100 and speak MORU-MANGBETU.

Mahafaly, a Malagasy people living on the island of Madagascar numbering 90,000.

Mahamid, a people who live in Chad.

Mahas, a people who live in Sudan near the border with Egypt. They speak Mahasi, a NUBIAN LANGUAGE.

Mahi, a people who live in Benin (Dahomey). They number 12,000 and speak a dialect of EWE.

Maji, a people living in south-western Ethiopia. They number between 6,000 and 7,000. They speak a CUSHITIC LANGUAGE.

Maju (Maidjuwu), a people who live in north-eastern Zaire. They number 8,200 and speak MORU-MANGBETU.

Makaa, a people of Cameroon. They number 51,600 and speak a BANTU LANGUAGE.

Makere, a people living in north-eastern Zaire. They number 17,500 and speak MORU-MANGBETU.

Makoa, a Malagasy people living on the west side of the island of Madagascar. They number 67,000.

Makoma, a Zambian people who number 7,600. Their language is LOZI, a BANTU LANGUAGE.

Makonde, a Tanzanian people who live in the coastal regions and on the borders with Mozambique. They number 380,000 and speak a BANTU LANGUAGE.

Makua, a people who live in Mozambique to the south of the Rovuma River, and in Tanzania, where they number 40,000. They speak a BANTU LANGUAGE.

Malagasy, a people and language of the Malagasy Republic (Madagascar). The Malagasy people number over 5,000,000. They are descendants of the Indonesians who travelled to Madagascar during the early Middle Ages. The Malagasy language is related to Indonesian languages and the official dialect is that of the MERINA people. This dialect was originally called Hova. There are 16 ethnic groups living in the Malagasy Republic. See entries on: ANTAIFASY; ANTAISAKA; ANTANKARA; ANTANOSY; BARA; BETSILEO; BETSIMISARAKA; BEZANOZANO; ONJATSY; SAHAFATRA; SAKALAVA; SIHANAKA; TANALA, TSIMIHETY.

Malila, a people living in Tanzania. They number 17,400 and speak a BANTU LANGUAGE.

Malinke see MANDE-MANDINGO.

Mambila, a people who live in the Adamawa region of Nigeria and in Cameroon. They number 15,800. They speak a NON-CLASS LANGUAGE of Nigeria.

Mambwe, a people living in Tanzania where they number 21,400, and in Zambia where they number 25,100. They speak a BANTU LANGUAGE.

Mamprusi, a people who live in northern Ghana and in Togo. They number 85,000. Their language belongs to the DAGOMBA dialect cluster of GUR.

Mamvu, a people who live in north-eastern Zaire. They number 24,000 and speak a language belonging to the Manbutu-Efe language group.

Mamvu-Mangutu, a group of languages spoken in north-eastern Zaire.

Manda, a people living to the north-east of Lake Nyasa in Tanzania. They speak a BANTU LANGUAGE.

Mandara, a people who live in Cameroon and in Nigeria in the region of Bornu. They number 16,800 and speak a Chadic language.

Mande, a language group of Mali which includes Mandinka, Bambara and Dyula.

Manding see MANDE.

Mandingo, a people and language of Gambia. The language is a western dialect of MANDE.

Mandyak, a people who live in Guinea, where they number 71,700 and in Senegal, where they number 12,000. They speak a WEST ATLANTIC LANGUAGE.

Mangala, a language which has developed from BOLOKI in Zaire. It acts as a common language for many small groups of people who speak different languages and dialects in north-eastern Zaire.

Manganja, a people who live on the border between Mozambique and Malawi. They speak a BANTU LANGUAGE.

Mangaya, a Sudanese people who live in the south of the country in the region of Raga. They number only about 300 and speak a SERE-MUNDU language.

Mangbai, a people who live in Cameroon, where they number about 3,000 and a village in Chad where they number about 1,000. They speak a NON-CLASS LANGUAGE.

Mangbele, a people living in north-eastern Zaire. 8,000 Mangbele speak a MORU-MANGBETU language and 5,000 speak a dialect of Majogo-Bangba.

Mangbetu, a people living in north-eastern Zaire. They number 9,000 and they speak MORU-MANGBETU.

Mangbutu, a Zairian people who number 8,700. They speak a MORU-MANGBETU language.

Mangisa, a people living in Cameroon, where they number 14,000. They speak a BANTU LANGUAGE.

Manja, the name given to dialects in the GBAYA dialect cluster (see LANGUAGE FAMILY) and the peoples who speak them in Central African Republic.

Mano (Manon), a people living in Liberia and Guinea. They number 150,000 and they speak a MANDE language.

Manya, the name used by the LOMA and BANDI in Liberia to describe the MANDE speakers who live among them.

MASAI: The Masai live in Kenya and Tanzania.

Manyika, a people and language of Zimbabwe and Mozambique. Manyika is a BANTU LANGUAGE belonging to the SHONA dialect cluster.

Mao, a people who live in south-western Ethiopia. They number 10,000. One section of the Mao speak a language which forms an ISOLATED LANGUAGE GROUP. The others speak a CUSHITIC LANGUAGE.

Mararit, a people and language of Chad. The Mararit number 41,500 in Chad and 400 in Sudan. The language belongs to the TAMA language group.

Maravi, a name given to the NYANJA, CEWA and NSENGA peoples.

Marfa (Marba), a Chadic people, who live in the region of Wadai. They number 18,000 and they speak a dialect of MASALIT.

Margi, a people who live in Cameroon and in Nigeria in the Adamawa region. They number 60,000 and they speak a Chadic language.

Mari (Mhari), a people of Zimbabwe, who speak a dialect of KARANGA.

Market Language see PIDGIN.

Masa, a people living in Cameroon and Chad. They number 43,000 and they speak a CHADO-HAMITIC LANGUAGE.

Masai (Maasai), a people and language of the Great Rift Valley of southern Kenya and northern Tanzania. The Masai number less than 200,000 and their language belongs to the NILO-HAMITIC LANGUAGE group. Originally the warring Masai were cattle-herders and the milk and blood from their cattle forms their traditional diet. Now the Kenyan and Tanzanian governments are encouraging the Masai to make permanent agricultural settlements.

Masakin, a people living in Sudan. They number 9,600 and they speak a KOALIB-TAGOI language.

Masalit, a people and language of the Wadai region of Chad. They number 66,500 in Chad and 27,000 in the Dar Fur region of Sudan. Their language belongs to the Maba language group.

Mashasha, a people living in Zambia. They number 13,100 and they speak a BANTU LANGUAGE belonging to the Nkoya language group.

Mashi, 1. a people who live in Zambia. They number 4,500. They speak LOZI, a BANTU LANGUAGE. 2. a Bantu-speaking people in eastern Zaire.

Masongo, a people who live in south-western Ethiopia. They number 6,000 and they speak a language belonging to the Didinga-Murle language group. (See DIDINGA.)

Matabele see NDEBELE.

Matakam, a people who live in the Mandara Mountains in Cameroon. They number 10,000. Their language forms a dialect cluster (see LANGUAGE FAMILY) of the Chadic language.

Matambwe, a Tanzanian people who number 16,000. They speak a BANTU LANGUAGE.

Matengo, a people who live in Tanzania. They number 57,600 and they speak a BANTU LANGUAGE.

Matumbi, a people living in Tanzania. They number 40,600 and they speak a BANTU LANGUAGE.

Mau (Mauka), a people living in Ivory Coast. They speak a dialect closely related to MALINKE.

Mauri, a people who live in Niger.

Maviha, a people living in Mozambique. They speak a BANTU LANGUAGE.

Mawer, a people living in Chad.

Mayogo, a people who live in the Province Orientale of Zaire. They number 41,000 and speak a SERE-MUNDU language.

Mba, a people and language of the Province Orientale of Zaire. They number 16,000. The Mba language forms an ISOLATED LANGUAGE GROUP.

Mbagani, a people who live in Zaire's Kasai province. They speak a BANTU LANGUAGE.

Mbala. 1. a Zambian people who number 7,000. They speak a BANTU LANGUAGE belonging to the Ila Tonga language group. 2. a people (also called Bushongo) who live in Zaire. The group has 16,700 members. They speak a BANTU LANGUAGE belonging to the Kuba language group.

Mbama (Mbamba, Bakota), a Congolese people who number 12,000. They speak a BANTU LANGUAGE.

Mbangwe, a people who live in Congo. They number 2,000 and they speak a BANTU LANGUAGE.

Mbanza (Mbanja), a people who live in Zaire. They number 81,000 and they speak BANDA.

Mbare, a people who live in Zimbabwe and Zambia.

Mbata, a group of people who live in the Bas-Zaire and Bandundu provinces of Zaire. They speak a BANTU LANGUAGE belonging to the KONGO language group.

Mbati (Isongo), a people living in Central African Republic. They number 15,200 and they speak a BANTU LANGUAGE.

Mbede (Mbete), a people living in Gabon, where they number 20,000 and in Congo, where they number 35,000. They speak a BANTU LANGUAGE.

Mbembe. 1. a people living in Nigeria. They number 2,900 and they speak a NON-CLASS LANGUAGE. 2. a people who live in the region of Ogoja in Nigeria. They number 43,000 and they speak a CLASS LANGUAGE.

Mbene, a people living in Cameroon who number 150,000. They speak a BANTU LANGUAGE.

Mbesa, a people who live in the Province Orientale in Zaire. They speak a BANTU LANGUAGE.

Mbete, a people who live in Congo, where they number 35,000, and in Gabon, where there are 20,000 of them. They speak a BANTU LANGUAGE.

Mbimu, a people living on the border between Nigeria and Cameroon. They number 7,500 and they speak a BANTU LANGUAGE.

Mbire, a people living in Zimbabwe. They speak a dialect of ZEZURU, which belongs to the SHONA group of the BANTU LANGUAGES.

Mbo. 1. a people who live in Nigeria and Cameroon. They number 16,500 and speak a BANTU LANGUAGE. 2. a Zairian people who number 2,100. They speak a BANTU LANGUAGE.

Mbogedu see DIRIKU.

Mboko, a Congolese people who speak a BANTU LANGUAGE.

Mbole (Bambuli), a people living in the Kasai province of Zaire. They number between 90,000 and 100,000. They speak a BANTU LANGUAGE.

Mbomotaba, a people who live in Congo and speak a BANTU LANGUAGE.

Mbonge, a people who live in Nigeria. They number 6,000 and they speak a BANTU LANGUAGE.

Mboshi, a people who live in Congo and speak a BANTU LANGUAGE.

Mbowe, a Zambian people who number 5,300. Their language is LOZI, which belongs to the Luyana group of the BANTU LANGUAGES.

Mbudza, a people who live in Zaire and speak a BANTU LANGUAGE.

Mbugu, a people living in Tanzania. Their language forms an ISOLATED LANGUAGE GROUP.

Mbugwe, a people who live in Tanzania. They number 7,400 and they speak a BANTU LANGUAGE.

Mbui (Yi), a people living in Angola. They speak KIMBUNDU, a BANTU LANGUAGE.

Mbukushu, a people who live in Angola, the Caprivi Strip of Namibia and in Botswana. They speak a BANTU LANGUAGE.

Mbum, a people living in the Bandundu province of Zaire. They speak a dialect of YANSI, a BANTU LANGUAGE.

Mbunda, a people who live in Angola and Zambia, where they number 23,700. They speak a BANTU LANGUAGE.

Mbundu see KIMBUNDU, UMBUNDU.

Mbunga, a Tanzanian people who live between the Ruaha and Rufiji rivers. They number 10,000 and they speak a BANTU LANGUAGE.

Mbuti (Bambuti), a people living in the Ituri forest of Zaire. They are PYGMIES. They speak a BANTU LANGUAGE.

Mbwela, an Angolan people who speak a BANTU LANGUAGE belonging to the CHOKWE-LUNDA group.

Mbwela (Mbwera), a Zambian people who number 4,050. They speak a BANTU LANGUAGE belonging to the Nkoya language group.

Megye (Medje, Meje), a people who live in the Province Orientale of Zaire. They number 30,000 and they speak MORU-MANGBETU.

Mejime (Medzime), a Cameroonian people who number 2,700. They speak a BANTU LANGUAGE.

Mekaf, a people who live in the part of Nigeria which was formerly British Cameroon. They speak a CLASS LANGUAGE.

Mekan (Sufo), a people who live in Ethiopia to the south of the Akobo River. Their language belongs to the Dindinga-Murle language group.

Mende, a language of the Mande-Fu sub-group of the MANDE language family. It is spoken by over 600,000 people in the south-eastern part of Sierra Leone.

Merille see GELABA.

Merina, a people living in Imérina, the central province of the Malagasy Republic (Madagascar). They number about 1,000,000 and speak MALAGASY, which is related to Indonesian languages. The Merinas are descended from Indonesian people who began settling on Madagascar before 700 A.D. They probably travelled from Indonesia in out-rigger canoes. The language of the Merinas has now become the official language of Malagasy. It has an extensive literature.

Meroitic, the name of an ancient people and language of Sudan, known only from undeciphered inscriptions at Meroe.

Meru, a people who live in Kenya, to the north-west of Mount Kenya. They number 350,000 and they speak a BANTU LANGUAGE. They are closely related to the KIKUYU.

Metyibo, a people living in Ivory Coast. They number 3,000 and they speak a KWA language.

Mfinu, a people who live in the Bandundu province of Zaire. They speak a BANTU LANGUAGE.

Midob, a Sudanese people who live in the region of Dar Fur. They number 1,800. Their language belongs to the NUBIAN LANGUAGE group.

Mihavani, a people living in Mozambique.

Milembwe, a people who live in the Kasai province of Zaire.

Miltu, a Chadic people who speak the BUA language.

Mimi, a people who live in Chad in the region of Wadai. They number 16,200. Their language forms an ISOLATED LANGUAGE GROUP.

Mindumo, a Congolese people who number 4,000. They speak a BANTU LANGUAGE.

Minya (Minyanka), a people living in Ivory Coast. They speak a dialect closely related to MALINKE.

Minyanka, the name given to a section of the SENUFO people of Mali. They number 36,000.

Miri, a people who live in the Miri Hills of Sudan. They number 14,000 and their language is KADUGLI-KRONGO.

Mishulundu, a Zambian people who live in Barotseland.

Mituku, a people who live in the Province Orientale of Zaire. They speak a BANTU LANGUAGE.

Mitumba, a people living in the Shaba province of Zaire.

Mmani (Mandenyi), a people who live in the coastal regions of Guinea. They speak a WEST ATLANTIC LANGUAGE.

Moba (B'moba), a people who live in Togo and Ghana. They number 90,000. Their dialect belongs to the GURMA dialect cluster of GUR.

Mofu, a people living in the Mandara Mountains of Cameroon. They number 16,000 and speak a Chadic language.

Mogogodo, a people who live in Kenya.

Mogum, a people who live in Chad and number 6,300. They speak a CHADO-HAMITIC LANGUAGE.

Mokpe (Baakpe, Bakwiri, Kweli, Kuili, Kwiri), a people who live in the part of Nigeria which was formerly British Cameroon. They number 15,600 and they speak a BANTU LANGUAGE.

Mondari (Mandari), a people living in southern Sudan in the region of Tombe-Terakeka. They number 36,000. They speak a dialect of BARI, a NILO-HAMITIC LANGUAGE.

Mongo. 1. a people who live in Nigeria and in Cameroon. They number 900. 2. a people who live in the Equateur province of Zaire. They number 80,000 and they speak a BANTU LANGUAGE.

Mongo-Nkundo, a collective name for a group of closely-related BANTU dialects in Zaire. They are spoken by more than 2,000,000 people.

Monjombo, a people living in Congo, Central African Republic and Zaire. They number 13,000 and they speak SERE-MUNDU.

Mono, a Cameroonian people who speak a NON-CLASS LANGUAGE.

Monokutuba, a national language of Congo.

Mora, the name used to describe 11 closely-related dialects spoken on the Mora Massif in Cameroon.

More see MOSSI.

Moro, a people who live in the Nuba Hills of Sudan. They number 18,000. Their language is KOALIB-TAGOI.

Morokodo, a people who live in the Amali district of southern Sudan. Their language is BONGO-BAGIRMI. Their dialect forms a dialect cluster together with the Biti, Wira and Nyamuta dialects.

Moru, a people living in Sudan. Together with the AVUKAYA, LOGO, KELIKO, BORI and NDO peoples, they number 83,000. Their language belongs to the Moru Ma'di language group of the MORU MANGBETU language.

Moru-Mangbetu, a group of languages spoken in southern Sudan and north-eastern Zaire. This group includes Moru-Madi, Lugbara (Uganda), Mangbutu-Efe, Mangbetu and Lendu.

Mossi, a people and large language group of Upper Volta. The More, TALENSI and DAGOMBA belong to the Mossi language group which is a sub-group of GUR. The Mossi number about 2,000,000 and are the largest group in Upper Volta.

Mpama, a people who live in the Equateur province of Zaire. They number 6,000 and they speak a BANTU LANGUAGE.

Mpondo, a South African people living in Pondoland. They speak a dialect of XHOSA, a BANTU LANGUAGE.

Mpongwe, a Gabonese people who number 1,000. They speak a BANTU LANGUAGE.

Mpoto, a people who live in Tanzania between Lake Nyasa and the Mozambique border. They speak a BANTU LANGUAGE.

Mubi, a people who live in Chad. They number 21,600 and they speak a CHADO-HAMITIC LANGUAGE belonging to the Sokoro-Mubi language group.

Mudogo, a Chadic people who number 8,300. Their language belongs to the Kuka dialect cluster of the BONGO-BAGIRMI language.

Muklete, a people who live in Cameroon. They number 8,500.

Mulimba (Limba, Melimba), a people who live in Cameroon. They number 3,700 and they speak a BANTU LANGUAGE.

MPONDO: The Mpondo girls are preparing for a dance. The Mpondo are a South African people.

Mumuye, a people who live in Nigeria in the region of Adamawa. They number 79,000 and they speak a NON-CLASS LANGUAGE.

Mundang, a people who live in Cameroon, where they number 25,500 and in Chad, where they number 60,000. They speak a NON-CLASS LANGUAGE belonging to the Mbum language group.

Mundu, a people living in Zaire, where they number 2,800 and in Sudan, where they number 1,850. Their language is SERE-MUNDU.

Mungo, a people who live in the part of Nigeria which was formerly British Cameroon. They number 1,000 and speak a BANTU LANGUAGE.

Murle (Beir), a people living in southern Sudan. They number 40,000 and speak a language belonging to the Didinga-Murle language group.

Murzu, a people who live in south-western Ethiopia.

Musei, a people living in Chad where they number 41,000, and in Cameroon where they number 7,000. Their language belongs to the Masa group of the CHADO-HAMITIC LANGUAGES.

Musgu (Musgum), a people who live in Cameroon in the region of the Lozone River, where they number 40,000. They also live in Chad. They speak a CHADO-HAMITIC LANGUAGE.

Mvele (Yezum), a people living in Cameroon who number 140,000. They speak a BANTU LANGUAGE.

Mvuba, a people who live in Zaire and in north-eastern Uganda. Their language belongs to the Mangbutu-Efe language group.

Mvumbo (Ngumba), a people who live in Cameroon and in Rio Muni. They speak a BANTU LANGUAGE.

Mwahet, a people living in Cameroon who number 2,400. They speak a BANTU LANGUAGE.

Mwenyi, a people who live in Zambia. They number 4,000 and speak LOZI, a BANTU LANGUAGE.

Mwera, a people who live in south-eastern Tanzania. They number 126,400 and speak a BANTU LANGUAGE.

Mweri see SUMBWA.

Myene, a Gabonese people who speak a BANTU LANGUAGE.

Nafana (Mfantra), a people who live in Upper Volta. They speak SENUFO, a cluster of dialects of the Gur language group.

Nago, the name given to the YORUBA people who live in Benin (Dahomey).

Nahoza, a people living in Tanzania.

Nalu, a people who live on both sides of the border between Guinea and Guinea-Bissau. They number 10,000 and they speak a WEST ATLANTIC LANGUAGE.

Nama, a people who live in Namibia. They number about 30,000 and they speak a Khoi (Hottentot) language (see KHOI-SAN).

Namchi (Do Ayo), a Cameroonian people who number 14,700. They speak a NON-CLASS LANGUAGE belonging to the Chamba language group.

Namnam, a people who live in the northern part of Ghana. They number 8,000 and they speak a dialect of GUR.

Nancere, a people living in Chad. They number 20,000 and their language belongs to the SOMRAI language group.

Nande, the name given to a number of related dialects of BANTU LANGUAGES including Mate and Kumbule, which are spoken in Zaire. About 22,500 people speak Nande dialects.

Nandi, a people who live in Kenya and number 112,900. They speak Nandi, a NILO-HAMITIC LANGUAGE which belongs to the Kalenjin group of languages, which also includes Kipsikis, Keyo, Tuken, Kony, Sabei (Sapiny) and Pokot (Suk).

Nanumba, a people living in northern Ghana and in Togo. They speak a dialect belonging to the DAGOMBA dialect cluster.

Nanzwa, a people who live in Zimbabwe.

Napagibetini, a number of BANTU LANGUAGE dialects which are spoken in Zaire.

Naron (Nhauru), a Botswanan people who number 3,000. They speak a Khoi (Hottentot) language (see KHOI-SAN).

Nata, a people who live in northern Tanzania. They number 9,500 and they speak a BANTU LANGUAGE.

Natemba, a people living near the border between Togo and Benin (Dahomey). They number 17,000 and their language is GUR.

Natioro, a people who live in Ivory Coast. They number 1,000 and speak a dialect of SENUFO.

Nawdemba (Naudeba), a people living in Togo in the region of Lama-Kara. Together with the LAMBA and KABRE peoples, they number 269,000. They speak TEM.

Ndaka, a people who live in the Province Orientale of Zaire. They number 4,750 and speak a BANTU LANGUAGE.

Ndali, a Tanzanian people who live at the northern end of Lake Nyasa. They number 50,000 and they speak a BANTU LANGUAGE.

Ndam, a people who live in Chad. They number 670 and they speak a language belonging to the SOMRAI language group.

Ndamba, a people who live in Tanzania. The group has 19,000 members. They speak a BANTU LANGUAGE.

Ndanda, a people who live in Zaire and speak a BANTU LANGUAGE.

Ndasa, a people living in Gabon.

Ndau, a people and language of Mozambique and Zimbabwe. Ndau is a BANTU LANGUAGE belonging to the SHONA language group.

Ndebele, a people and BANTU LANGUAGE of Zimbabwe and some parts of South Africa. The Ndebele number about 750,000. They split off from the ZULUS under Mzilikazi in the mid 1800s and moved north into 'Rhodesia'.

Ndembu (Ndembo), a people who live in Zambia and in Shaba province in Zaire. Their language is a dialect of LUNDA.

Ndengereko, a people who live in the region of Dar-es-Salaam in Tanzania. They number 53,300 and they speak a BANTU LANGUAGE.

Ndengese (Dengese), a people living in Zaire. They number 3,800 and speak a BANTU LANGUAGE belonging to the Kuba language group.

Ndo, a people who live on the border between Zaire and Uganda. They number 13,000 and their language is MORU-MANGBETU.

Ndobo, a people who live in Zaire and speak a BANTU LANGUAGE.

Ndogo, a people who live in western Sudan. They number 3,500. They speak Ndogo-Sere which forms a single language unit of the SERE-MUNDU languages.

Ndolo, a people who live in Zaire and speak a BANTU LANGUAGE.

Ndombe, a people who live in Angola and speak a BANTU LANGUAGE.

Ndonde, a people who live in Tanzania near the border with Mozambique. They number 12,100 and they speak a BANTU LANGUAGE.

NDEBELE: The Ndebele of Zimbabwe and South Africa decorate their homes with beautiful designs.

Ndonga, a people living in Namibia. They speak a BANTU LANGUAGE.

Ndongo (Dongo), a people who live in Angola. They were formerly a large group of people. But they now live in only three villages.

Ndoro, a people who live in Cameroon and in Nigeria in Benue-Plateau State. They number 1,200 and they speak a NON-CLASS LANGUAGE.

Nduka, a people who live in Chad and speak a BONGO-BAGIRMI language.

Ndundulu, a people who live on the border between Zambia and Angola. They number 22,000. Their language is LOZI, a BANTU LANGUAGE.

Ndunga, a people who live in the Equateur province of Zaire. They number 2,500 and they speak a language belonging to the Mba language group.

Nenu (Ninong), a Nigerian people who number 2,600. They speak a BANTU LANGUAGE.

Neyo, a people who live in Ivory Coast, where they number 4,500. They speak a dialect belonging to the BETE dialect cluster of KRU.

Ngala, see BANGALA, LINGALA.

Ngando. 1. a people who live in Central African Republic. Together with the KOTA, they number 2,900. They speak a BANTU LANGUAGE. 2. a people who live in the Equateur province of Zaire. They number 120,600 and they speak a BANTU LANGUAGE.

Ngare, a Congolese people who speak a BANTU LANGUAGE.

Ngasa, a people and language group of the north-eastern slopes of Mount Kilimanjaro, Tanzania. The Ngasa number 1,000 and they speak a NILO-HAMITIC LANGUAGE.

Ngayaba, a people who live in Cameroon. They number less than 1,000 and speak a BANTU LANGUAGE.

Ngazidja, a people living in the Comoro Islands. They speak a dialect of SWAHILI.

Ngbaka, a large number of peoples who live in Central African Republic and Zaire. The name also refers to the dialects which they speak. Their language group is Banda-Gbaya-Ngbandi.

Ngbandi, a people and language of the River Ubangi in northern Zaire. The group has about 200,000 members. Ngbandi is a Banda-Gbaya-Ngbandi language (see NGBAKA).

Ngbee, a people living in Zaire. They are few in number. They speak a BANTU LANGUAGE.

Ngbinda, a people and language of Sudan and Zaire. Ngbinda is a BANTU LANGUAGE. The people are also called the BANGBINDA people.

Ngbundu, a people who live in the Equateur province of Zaire. They number 9,000.

Ngee, a people living in Zaire. They speak a BANTU LANGUAGE.

Ngende, a Zairian people who number 7,600. They speak a BANTU LANGUAGE.

Ngengele (Gengele), a people who live in the Kivu province of Zaire. They speak LEGA, a BANTU LANGUAGE.

Nghwele, a Tanzanian people who speak a BANTU LANGUAGE.

Ngindo, a people who live in Tanzania. They number 85,200 and they speak a BANTU LANGUAGE.

Ngiri, a Zairian people who speak a BANTU LANGUAGE.

Ngizim, a people who live in Nigeria in the region of Bornu and Kano. The group has 39,000 members. They speak a CHADO-HAMITIC LANGUAGE.

Ngom, a people who live in Gabon. They number 11,000 and speak a BANTU LANGUAGE.

Ngoma, a people who live in the Shaba province of Zaire. Their language is BEMBA, a BANTU LANGUAGE.

Ngombe, a people who live in north-western Zaire. They number 155,000 and speak a BANTU LANGUAGE.

Ngonde see NYAKYUSA.

Ngondi, a people living in Central African Republic. They speak a BANTU LANGUAGE.

Ngongo, a Zairian people who speak a BANTU LANGUAGE.

Ngoni, the name of two peoples, one in Malawi and one in Tanzania. Their languages belong to the NGUNI sub-family of the BANTU LANGUAGE family.

Ngoro, a people who live in Cameroon. They number about 6,000 and speak a BANTU LANGUAGE.

Ngova, a people who live in Zimbabwe. They speak a dialect of KARANGA, a BANTU LANGUAGE belonging to the SHONA language group.

Ngul, a people living in the Kasai province of Zaire. They speak a BANTU LANGUAGE.

Ngulu (Nguru, Mihavane), a large group of people who live in Mozambique and Malawi, where they number 380,000. They speak a BANTU LANGUAGE belonging to the MAKUA language group.

Ngulu (Nguu, Nguru), a people living in eastern Tanzania. The group has 52,900 members. They speak a BANTU LANGUAGE belonging to the ZARAMO language group.

Ngungwel, a Congolese people who speak a BANTU LANGUAGE.

Ngurimi, a people who live in Tanzania. They number 11,800 and they speak a BANTU LANGUAGE.

Ngwaketse, a people who live in Botswana. They speak TSWANA, a BANTU LANGUAGE.

Ngwana, the Zairian name for SWAHILI.

Ngwane, a people who live in Natal province, South Africa.

Ngwato (Ngwatu), a people who live in Botswana. They speak TSWANA, a BANTU LANGUAGE.

Nielim (Iuwa), a people living in Chad. They number 2,000 and they speak the Bua language.

Nilo-Hamitic languages (Paranilotic), the collective name for a group of scattered languages spoken in East Africa between Kondoa, Tanzania and the River Tapari in southern Sudan. There are six groups: BARI, LOTUHO, TESO, NGASA, MASAI, and KALENJIN.

Nilotes are peoples who speak NILOTIC LANGUAGES. They live along the Nile and its tributaries and on the shores of lakes Mobutu Sese Seko (Lake Albert), Victoria and Kyoga. The Nilotes are mainly cattle farmers, hunters and fishermen. The main groups are the NUER, the DINKA, the ACHOLI-ALUR-LANGO, and the LUO.

Nilotic languages, a family of languages spoken in the Sudan, Uganda and Kenya. There are three main groups. 1. the Southern Nilotic sub-family group which consists of Acholi-Alur-Lango in Zaire and northern Uganda, Shilluk in the Sudan and Dhopadhola and Luo in eastern Uganda and western Kenya. 2. the western Sudan group consisting of Thuri, Bodho, Cholo, Bor and Lwo. 3. the Eastern Sudan group consisting of Burun-Jumjum-Maban. The Nilotic language structure is based on monosyllabic word-roots and a sytem of verbs with prefixes for persons and different tones for tenses. Plurals are formed by suffixes or alterations to vowels. DINKA and NUER are two separate dialect groups and sub-families of the Nilotic family. These languages are all spoken in central Sudan.

Nilyamba, a people living in Tanzania. They number 170,700 and they speak a BANTU LANGUAGE.

Ningawa, a people who live in Nigeria between Bauchi and Kano. They number 3,700 and they speak a CLASS LANGUAGE of Nigeria.

Njabi see NZEBI.

Njalgulgule, a people living in the Equateur province of Sudan. They number 1,000 and they speak a language belonging to the Daju language group.

Njem, a people living in Cameroon. They number 2,000 and they speak a BANTU LANGUAGE.

Njems, a branch of the Masai people.

Njiningi, a people living in Congo. They number 9,000 and they speak a BANTU LANGUAGE.

Njinju, a people living in Congo. This group of people has 9,000 members. They speak a BANTU LANGUAGE.

Nkangala, a people who live in Angola and speak a BANTU LANGUAGE.

Nkole see NKORE.

Nkomi, a people living in Gabon. They number 5,000 and speak a BANTU LANGUAGE.

Nkore (Nkole, Nyankore), a people who live in the Great Lakes region of Uganda. The group has 520,000 members and they speak a BANTU LANGUAGE.

Nkoya, a people living in Zambia. They number 18,500 and they speak a BANTU LANGUAGE belonging to the Nkoya language group.

Nkunda see NYANJI.

Nkundo, a people who live in the Equateur province of Zaire. They number 130,600 and speak a BANTU LANGUAGE.

Nkutshu, a group of people living in Zaire. The group is made up of KUKU and MBENGI peoples. They speak a BANTU LANGUAGE.

Nkuvu, a people who live in Shaba province, Zaire.

Noe (Nohwe), a people living in Zimbabwe. They speak a dialect of ZEZURU.

Noho-Puko, a people living in Cameroon, who number 2,000. They speak a BANTU LANGUAGE.

Non-class languages are isolated language groups spoken in eastern Nigeria and regions to the east of Nigeria. Scholars have found these languages difficult to classify. They cannot decide which family these languages belong to. See also CLASS LANGUAGES.

Nrebele, a people who live in the Transvaal, South Africa. Their language is a dialect of ZULU.

Nsaw (Bansaw, Nso), a people who live in the part of Nigeria which was formerly British Cameroon. They number 40,000 and speak a CLASS LANGUAGE.

Nsenga, a Zambian people who live on the Zambezi River and the Tanzanian/Zambian border. They number 45,000.

Nsibidi, a secret language and script of southern Nigeria.

Nsongo, a people who live in the Equateur province of Zaire. They are a section of the MBUNDU people.

Ntomba, a Zairian people who live in the province of Bas-Zaire. They number between 40,000 and 50,000. They speak a BANTU LANGUAGE.

Ntribu, a small Togolese group who number about 700 people.

Nuba see NUBIAN LANGUAGE.

Nubian language, a term used to describe three language groups. 1. a literary language written in Coptic script. This ancient Nubian language was used during the 8th to 11th centuries for Christian religious texts. 2. there are four modern Nubian dialects which are closely related to ancient Nubian. These are: KENUZI, FIYADIKKYA, MAHASI and DONGOLI. 3. Hill Nubian or Nuba is a series of scattered languages spoken in the Nuba mountains, south-central Sudan.

Nuer, a people and language of central Sudan. The Nuer number about 300,000. The Nuer language belongs to a separate branch of the NILOTIC LANGUAGE family. It has many dialects.

Nungu (Nunku) see MADA.

Nunu, a people who live in Zaire and speak a BANTU LANGUAGE.

Nupe, a Nigerian people and language of the area where the River Niger is joined by the River Benue. The Nupe people number 360,000 and the language belongs to the KWA group.

Nwenshi, a people who live in Zaire in Shaba province.

Nyakwai (Ngiakwai), a people living in Kenya and in Uganda. Their language is a dialect of KARAMOJONG, a NILO-HAMITIC LANGUAGE.

Nyakyusa (Konde, Ngonde), a people who live in Tanzania, where they number 192,000, and in Malawi where they number 62,000. In Malawi they are called Ngonde. They speak a BANTU LANGUAGE.

Nyala, a Kenyan people who live around the shores of Lake Victoria. They speak a BANTU LANGUAGE.

Nyali, a people living in the Province Orientale of Zaire. They number 12,500 and they speak a BANTU LANGUAGE.

Nyambo, a people who live in Tanzania, where they number 4,000, together with the KARAGWE. They also live in Rwanda.

Nyam-Nyam see ZANDE.

Nyamwanga (Mwanga), a people living in Tanzania and Zambia. They number 47,000 and they speak a BANTU LANGUAGE.

Nyamwezi, a Tanzanian people who number 413.000. They speak a BANTU LANGUAGE.

Nyaneka, a people and BANTU LANGUAGE of Angola.

Nyang, a people who live in Cameroon and speak a BANTU LANGUAGE.

Nyanga, a people who live in Kivu province in Zaire. They number 24,750, and speak a BANTU LANGUAGE.

Nyangbara, a people who live in southern Sudan. There are 18,000 of them. They speak a dialect of BARI, a NILO-HAMITIC LANGUAGE.

Nyangbo, a people who live in the hills of Togo. They number less than 2,000 and speak a TOGO REMNANT LANGUAGE.

Nyanja, a people living in Malawi. They number 312,500 and speak a BANTU LANGUAGE.

Nyankole see NKORE.

Nyankore see NKORE.

Nyaturu, a Tanzanian people who number 181,700. They speak a BANTU LANGUAGE.

Nyende, a people who live in Benin (Dahomey).

Nyengo, a people living in Angola and in Zambia, where they number 4,450. They speak a BANTU LANGUAGE.

Nyepu, a people who live in southern Sudan to the north-west of Kajo Kaji. They number 3,500 and they speak a dialect of BARI, which is a NILO-HAMITIC LANGUAGE.

Nyi, a people living in the Equateur province of Zaire.

Nyiha, a Tanzanian people living to the south of Lake Rukwa. They number 55,700 and they speak a BANTU LANGUAGE.

Nyika, a Kenyan people made up of nine different groups who live in the coastal areas of the country. They number 40,000 and they speak BANTU LANGUAGES.

Nyikoroma, a people who live in southern Sudan. They number 25,000.

Nyimang, a people living in the Nuba Hills of Sudan. They number 26,000. Their language forms an ISOLATED LANGUAGE GROUP. A small amount of literature is written in the Nyimang language.

Nyindu, a Zairian people who number 25,000. They speak a BANTU LANGUAGE.

Nyoo (Nyokon), a people who live in Cameroon. They number 3,900 and speak a BANTU LANGUAGE.

Nyoro, a Ugandan people who live in the region of the Great Lakes. They number 103,100 and speak a BANTU LANGUAGE.

Nyuli, a people who live in Uganda to the south of Mbale. They number 57,000 and speak a BANTU LANGUAGE.

Nyungwe, a people living in Tete province in Mozambique. They speak a BANTU LANGUAGE.

Nzakara, a people who live in Central African Republic and Zaire, where they number 3,000. They speak a dialect of ZANDE.

Nzebi, a people who live in Gabon and Congo. They number 20,000 and speak a BANTU LANGUAGE.

Nzima, a people living in southern Ghana and Ivory Coast. They speak a dialect from the Anyi-Baule dialect cluster, which is part of the KWA language group.

Nzwani, a people who live in the Comoro Islands. They speak a dialect of SWAHILI.

Oberi Okaime, a religious language and script used by a group of people who live in southern Nigeria.

Ogoni, a Nigerian people who live in the region of Calabar and Owerri. They number 76,300 and speak a dialect which is related to IBIBIO-EFIK.

Oli (Ewodi, Wouri, Wuri), a people living in Cameroon. They number 3,700 and they speak a Bantu language.

Oli, a people who live in the Bandundu province of Zaire. They speak NKUNDO, which is a BANTU LANGUAGE.

Olombo, a people living in the Province Orientale of Zaire. They number 10,400 and they speak a BANTU LANGUAGE.

Ombo, a people who live in the Kivu province of Zaire. They speak a BANTU LANGUAGE.

Ometo, a name meaning 'Men of the Omo (River)'. The word also refers to a group of CUSHITIC LANGUAGES spoken in south-western Ethiopia.

Omotic, the collective name for a group of CUSHITIC LANGUAGES consisting of JANJERO, KAFA and MAJI.

Onjatsy, a group of Muslim traders living on the north-eastern coast of Madagascar.

Oromo see GALLA.

Orri, a Nigerian people who live in the region of Ogoja. They number 25,000 and they are related to the IDOMA people.

Otoro, a people who live in the Nuba Hills of Sudan. They number 10,500 and their language is KOALIB-TAGOI.

Ovambo, see AMBO (Zambia).

Ovimbundu see UMBUNDU.

Paduko, a people who live in Cameroon to the south of the Mora Massif. They speak a Chadic language.

Pahouin, a name given to the group made up of the FANG, BETI, and BULU peoples.

Pajade see BADYARA.

Pambia, a people who live in Sudan, where they number 12,000, and also in Central African Republic. Their language is ZANDE.

Pande, a people who live in Central African Republic and Congo. They speak a BANTU LANGUAGE.

Pangwa, a Tanzanian people who live on the north-east shores of Lake Nyasa. They number 37,700 and speak a BANTU LANGUAGE.

Paranilotic see NILO-HAMITIC LANGUAGES.

Pari, a Sudanese people who live in the Equateur province. They number 7,000. Their language is ANUAK.

Peda (Hweda), a people who live in Benin.

Pedi (Northern SOTHO), a people who live in the Transvaal, South Africa. They number 500,000 and speak a BANTU LANGUAGE.

Pende, a people who live in the Bandundu province of Zaire. They speak KONGO.

Pere, a Zairian people who number 4,000.

Peul see FULA.

Phuti, a people who live in East Griqualand, South Africa and in Lesotho. They speak a BANTU LANGUAGE.

Pianga, a people living in Zaire. They number 2,900 and speak a BANTU LANGUAGE.

Pidgin, a term for simple market languages which have developed through trading. Pidgin English or Afro-English is spoken on the West coast of Africa. There is also a pidgin Swahili and pidgin Arabic. Fanagalo is a pidgin language which developed from ZULU and XHOSA. See also CREOLE.

Pilapila (including Taneka), a people living in Dahomey. They number 40,000 and speak a dialect belonging to the GURMA dialect cluster of GUR.

Pimbwe, a people who live on the north-west shores of Lake Rukwa in Tanzania. They number 11,500 and speak a BANTU LANGUAGE.

Podogo, a people living in Cameroon. The Podogo number 12,000 members.

Podzo, a people who live in Mozambique in the region of Beira. They number 4,600 and speak a BANTU LANGUAGE.

Pogoro (Pogolo), a people living in Tanzania. They number 63,200 and they speak a BANTU LANGUAGE.

Pojulu, a people living in southern Sudan and Zaire. They number 24,500. Their language is a dialect of BARI, a NILO-HAMITIC LANGUAGE.

Pok, a Kenyan people who live in the region of Mount Elgon. Together with the SAPEI and KONY peoples, they number 24,000. They speak one of the Kalenjin (NILO-HAMITIC) LANGUAGES.

Poke (Topoke), a people who live in Zaire. They number 46,000 and speak a BANTU LANGUAGE.

Poko (Bapuku), a people living in Cameroon, who speak a Coastal Bantu language.

Pokomo, a people who live in Kenya in the Tana Valley. They number 16,300 and speak a BANTU LANGUAGE.

Pokot, a people living in the Rift Valley in Kenya and in the region of Karamoja in Uganda. They number 60,800, and speak a NILO-HAMITIC LANGUAGE.

Pol, a people living in Cameroon. They number 2,200 and speak a BANTU LANGUAGE.

Pombo, a people who live in Angola. Their language is KONGO, a BANTU LANGUAGE.

Pomo, a Congolese people who speak a BANTU LANGUAGE.

Pondo, a Bantu people in South Africa.

Pongo, a people living in Cameroon. They number 6,600 and speak a Coastal Bantu language.

Popo see EWE.

Popoi, a people who live in north-eastern Zaire. They number 7,500 and their language is MORU-MANGBETU.

Poto, a people who live in the Equateur province of Zaire. They speak a BANTU LANGUAGE.

Punu, a people who live in Gabon and Congo. They number 46,000 and they speak a BANTU LANGUAGE.

Pygmies, several groups of people living in the equatorial forests of Zaire and Cameroon. They number several thousands and are characterized by their short stature (about five feet). They live by hunting and gathering wild fruits, insects and roots. Most pygmies speak BANTU LANGUAGES.

Qwara, a people living in the region near Lake Tana in Ethiopia. They speak a CUSHITIC LANGUAGE.

Rendile, a Kenyan people who speak a language closely related to SOMALI of the CUSHITIC LANGUAGE family.

Renge, a people who live in Rwanda and Burundi.

Reshe, a people who live in northern Nigeria on the Niger River. They number 5,000 and they speak a CLASS LANGUAGE of Nigeria.

Rimi see NYATURU.

Rolong, a people who live in South Africa, near the Botswana border. They speak a dialect of TSWANA.

Ron (Baron, Chala), a Nigerian people who number 11,600. They speak a NON-CLASS LANGUAGE.

Ronga, a people who live in Mozambique and South Africa. They speak a BANTU LANGUAGE.

Rongo, a people who live in Gabon. They number 2,000 and they speak a BANTU LANGUAGE. See TSONGA.

Rozwi, a people who live in Zimbabwe. They speak KALANGA, which belongs to the SHONA group of the BANTU LANGUAGES.

Rue, a people living in Mozambique and Zimbabwe. They speak a BANTU LANGUAGE.

Ruguru see LUGURU.

Ruihi, a Tanzanian people who live on the banks of the Rufiji River. They number 70,800 and speak a BANTU LANGUAGE.

Rukuba, a Nigerian people who live between Jos and Zaria. They speak a CLASS LANGUAGE.

Rund, a people who live in Zaire and Angola. The Rund number 20,000 and their BANTU LANGUAGE is also spoken by the BENA TUBEYA people.

Rundi (Ikirundi), the BANTU LANGUAGE of Burundi, spoken by more than 2,000,000 people.

Rungu, a people who live in Tanzania, where they number 9,600, and in Zambia, where they number 24,000. They speak a BANTU LANGUAGE.

Rurede see GO.

Rusha, a Tanzanian people who speak a BANTU LANGUAGE.

Rwanda, the BANTU LANGUAGE of Rwanda spoken by 2,000,000 people called the Banya-Rwanda. The language is very similar to RUNDI.

Sabanga, a people living in Central African Republic. They number less than 1,000 members. They speak the BANDA language.

Safwa, a Tanzanian people who number 63,000. They speak a BANTU LANGUAGE.

Sagara, a people who live in the Eastern region of Tanzania. They number 31,600 and speak a BANTU LANGUAGE.

Sahafatra, 'People of the Clearing', a people who live in south-east Madagascar. They number 25,000.

Saho, a CUSHITIC LANGUAGE and people. Saho is spoken by about 50,000 people in central Eritrea and in eastern Ethiopia.

PYGMIES: This group of pygmies live by hunting and gathering in the forests of Zaire.

Saint-Mariens, a people who live in Madagascar. They number 14,000 people.

Sakalava, 'Valley People', a people living on the western side of Madagascar numbering 400,000.

Sakata, a people who live in the Bas-Zaire province of Zaire. They speak a BANTU LANGUAGE.

Sala, a people living in Zambia. The group has 7,000 members. They speak a BANTU LANGUAGE belonging to the Ila-Tonga language group.

Salamat, a people who live in Chad.

Salampasu, a people living in the Kasai province of Zaire. They number 60,000 and speak SONGE, a BANTU LANGUAGE.

Sama, a people living in Angola. The group has 8,800 members. They speak KIMBUNDU, a BANTU LANGUAGE.

Samba, a people who live in Kivu province, Zaire.

Samburu, a Kenyan people who number 20,000. They speak a dialect of MASAI.

Sambyu, a people who live in Angola and Namibia. They speak a BANTU LANGUAGE.

Samia, a people who live in south-eastern Uganda, where they number 16,000, and in western Kenya, where they number 43,400. They speak a BANTU LANGUAGE.

Samo (Samogo, Sano), a people living in Upper Volta. The group has 120,000 members. They speak a MANDE language.

San see KHOI-SAN.

Sandawe, a Tanzanian people who live in the region of Kondoa. They number 23,400 and they speak a CLICK LANGUAGE.

Sanga, a people who live in the Shaba province of Zaire. They speak a BANTU LANGUAGE.

Sango. 1. a common language spoken throughout Central African Republic. The language is based on GBAYA, but many French words have been added to it. 2. a people living in Tanzania. They number 22,800 and speak a BANTU LANGUAGE.

Sangu, a people living in Gabon. The group has 18,000 members. They speak a BANTU LANGUAGE.

Sanhaja see BERBERS.

Sankani, a people who live in the Equateur province of Zaire.

Santrokofi, a people who live in Togo to the south of the town of Buëm. They number less than 1,000. They speak a TOGO REMNANT LANGUAGE.

Sanye, a people living in Kenya. Their language forms an ISOLATED LANGUAGE GROUP.

Sanza, a people who live in Zaire and in Uganda. They number 15,000 and speak a BANTU LANGUAGE.

Sapei (Sabei, Savei, Sebei, Sapiny), a people living in Kenya near Mount Elgon. Together with the KONY and POK peoples, they number 24,000. They speak a dialect of KALENJIN, a NILO-HAMITIC LANGUAGE.

Sara, a people who live in Chad and Central African Republic They number 47,000. Their language belongs to the BONGO-BAGIRMI dialect cluster.

Sara Gambai, a people living in Chad. They number 195,000 and speak a BONGO-BAGIRMI language.

Sara Kaba, a Chadic people who number 11,500. They speak BONGO-BAGIRMI.

Sarakolle see SONINKE.

Sara Mbai, a people who live in Chad. They number 59,000 and speak BONGO-BAGIRMI.

Sarwa. 1. a people living in Botswana. 2. a people living in Chad. They number 400 and they speak a BUA language.

Sayanci, a people who live in northern Nigeria.

Sebei see SAPEI.

Segeju, a Tanzanian people who speak a BANTU LANGUAGE.

Seidyanke, a people living in Guinea.

Sekiyani, a very small group of people living in Gabon. They speak a BANTU LANGUAGE.

Sekororo, a people who live in the Transvaal in South Africa. They speak a BANTU LANGUAGE related to the SHONA language group.

Sele, a people who live in Angola.

Selya (Seria), a people living to the north of Lake Nyasa in Tanzania. They speak a BANTU LANGUAGE. They are related to the NYAKYUSA people.

Semitic Languages, a family of languages spoken in North Africa, Egypt, Arabia, Palestine, Syria and Iraq. The only ancient Semitic language to remain today is Hebrew. Modern Semitic languages include: AMHARIC, ARABIC, GURAGE, HARARI and TIGRE.

Sena, a people who live in Mozambique and speak a BANTU LANGUAGE.

Senga, a people living on the banks of the River Luangwa in Zambia. They number 23,000 and speak a BANTU LANGUAGE.

Sengele, a Zairian people who speak a BANTU LANGUAGE.

Senufo (Senoufo), a large group of people and a language of Mali, Ivory Coast and Upper Volta. The Senufo number 760,000 and they speak dialects belonging to a cluster within the GUR languages.

Sere (Basiri, Shere, Shaire), a people who live in southern Sudan, Zaire and Central African Republic. They number 5,000 and their language belongs to the Ndogo-Sere single unit of the SERE-MUNDU languages.

Sere-Mundu, a group of languages spoken in the south-west Sudan and in north-eastern and north-western Zaire. The main sub-groups are: Ndogo-Sere, Feroge and Mundu-Ngbaka-Mabo.

Serer, a people who live in Senegal, where they number 306,500, and in Gambia, where they number between 2,000 and 4,000. They speak a WEST ATLANTIC LANGUAGE.

Sese (Sesse), a Ugandan people who live on the Sese Islands in Lake Victoria. They speak a BANTU LANGUAGE.

Sewa, a people in the Shaba province in Zaire and in Zambia. The group has 3,000 members. They are related to the LAMBA people.

Shaka see CHAGA.

Shambala (Shambaa, Sambaa), a people living in north-eastern Tanzania. They number 129,500 and speak a BANTU LANGUAGE.

Shanga, a people living near the mouth of the Sabi River, Mozambique. They speak a BANTU LANGUAGE.

Shanjo, a people who live in Zambia. They number 7,900 and speak LOZI, a BANTU LANGUAGE.

Shankwe (Shangwe), a people of Zimbabwe who speak a dialect of KOREKORE.

Shatt, a people who live in Kordofan province in Sudan. They number 8,000. Their language belongs to the Daju language group.

Shawasha, a people who live in Zimbabwe. They speak a dialect of ZEZURU which belongs to the SHONA group of the BANTU LANGUAGES.

SAMBURU: This Samburu woman lives in Kenya.

Sheni, a people living in the Zaria region of Nigeria.

Sherbro see BULOM.

Shi, a people who live in the Kivu province of Zaire. They number 109,800 and speak a BANTU LANGUAGE.

Shila, a people who live near Lake Mweru in Zambia, where they number 5,500, and also in Shaba province, Zaire. Their language is Tabwa, a BANTU LANGUAGE.

Shilluk, a people in eastern Sudan in Upper Nile province numbering 100,000. They speak a NILOTIC LANGUAGE belonging to the North Lwo language group. This language is similar to ALUR and ACHOLI.

Shinasha (Bworo), an Ethiopian people who speak a CUSHITIC LANGUAGE.

Shobwa, a people who live in Zaire, where they number 3,150.

Shona, a language group spoken by about 4,000,000 people. The main dialects are ZEZURU, KARANGA, MANYIKA and KOREKORE, NDAU and KALANGA. The two major dialects, Zezuru and Karanga, are to be combined but until agreement is reached, literature is being published in both.

Shu, a Zairian people. The group has 64,700 members and speak a BANTU LANGUAGE.

Shubi, a people who live in Tanzania, near the borders with Rwanda and Burundi. They number 74,000 and they speak a BANTU LANGUAGE.

Shuwa, an ARAB people living in north-east Nigeria.

Shwai, a people living in the Nuba Hills of Sudan. The group has 2,800 members. Their language is KOALIB-TAGOI.

Sidamo, a people who live in the region of the headwaters of the Juba River of south-western Ethiopia. They speak a CUSHITIC LANGUAGE.

Sidya (Sidyanka), a people who live in Guinea and Guinea-Bissau. They speak a dialect related to MALINKE.

Sigila, a people who live in Cameroon, east of Mora. They speak a CHADO-HAMITIC LANGUAGE.

Sihanaka, 'marsh people', a people living in northern Madagascar between Imérina and Tsimihety. They number 135,000.

Simaa, a people who live in Zambia. They number 9,100 and speak LOZI, a BANTU LANGUAGE.

Singa, a Kenyan people who live on the coast and on Rusinga Island. They speak a BANTU LANGUAGE.

Sinyar, a people living in Sudan near the border with Chad. Their language is BONGO-BAGIRMI.

Sira, a people living in Gabon. They number 17,000 and speak a BANTU LANGUAGE.

Sirikwa, a legendary people of Kenya.

So. 1. a people living in Cameroon who number 6,000. They speak a BANTU LANGUAGE. 2. a people who live in the Province Orièntale of Zaire. The group has 6,000 members. They speak a BANTU LANGUAGE.

Sobo, a Nigerian people who live in the Warri region. They number 108,000. Their language is KWA.

Soga, a large group of people living in Uganda. The group has 426,000 members and they speak a BANTU LANGUAGE.

Sokoro, a people who live in Chad. They number 4,100 and speak a CHADO-HAMITIC LANGUAGE.

Soli, a people living in Zambia. The group has 13,800 members. They speak a BANTU LANGUAGE belonging to the Ila language group.

Solongo, a people who live in Angola, where they number 1,700 and also in Zaire. Their language is a KONGO dialect.

Somali, a group of people and a CUSHITIC LANGUAGE of the Somali Republic (Somalia) and Eastern Ethiopia. The Somalis number about 4,000,000 of which about 99 per cent are Muslims. Traditionally, the Somalis are nomadic herdsmen, raising camels, goats, sheep and cattle. In some areas groups of Somalis have become settled farmers, growing maize, rice, millet and some fruit crops. The official orthography of the Somali language using the Roman alphabet was adopted in 1973.

Somba, a people who live in Benin (Dahomey). They number 72,000. Their dialect belongs to the GURMA dialect cluster of GUR.

Somrai, a people who live in Chad. Their language forms an ISOLATED LANGUAGE GROUP.

Songe, a people who live in the Kasai province of Zaire. They speak a BANTU LANGUAGE.

SUTHU: A Suthu (or Sotho) family living in Lesotho. The woman is taking grain from a storage basket.

Songhai, a people and language of the region from Western Niger to Mopti in Mali. The Songhai once had a great empire which flourished until about the 16th century. There are today less than 800,000 Songhai-speaking people. It is, however, still used as a trade language although it is not related to any other West African language. Zarma (Dyerma) is a close dialect of Songhai.

Songo, a people living in the Bas-Zaire and Bandundu provinces of Zaire. They speak a BANTU LANGUAGE.

Songola, a people who live in Zaire's Kivu province. Their language is LEGA.

Songomeno, a people who live in Zaire. They number between 30,000 and 40,000. They speak a BANTU LANGUAGE of the Kuba language group.

Songora, a people who live in Zaire. They number 1,270 and speak a BANTU LANGUAGE.

Soninke, a language spoken by a group of peoples living in eastern Senegal, northern Mali and as far as the borders of Upper Volta and Mauritania. These groups are: the Saracolle, Marka, Serahuli, Gajaga, Tubakai and Aswanik. Soninke belongs to the Mande-Tan sub-family of the MANDE language family.

Sonjo, a Tanzanian people who speak a BANTU LANGUAGE.

Sorat, a people who live in Uganda.

Sorkawa, a people who live in Niger.

Soruba-Kuyobe, a people living in Benin, where they number 5,000, and in Togo. They speak a dialect belonging to the GURMA dialect cluster of GUR.

Soso see SUSU.

Su (Isuwu, Bimbia, Isubu, Subu), a people who live in the part of Nigeria which was formerly British Cameroon. They number less than 500 and speak a BANTU LANGUAGE.

Subiya (Ikuhare), a Zambian people who number 2,950. They speak a BANTU LANGUAGE belonging to the Totela language group.

Subu see SU.

Sudie, a people living in Niger.

Suku, a people who live in the Bas-Zaire province of Zaire, where they number 74,250, and in Angola. They speak a language belonging to the KONGO language group.

Sukuma, a people living in Tanzania. They are a large group of people numbering about 1,250,000. They speak a BANTU LANGUAGE.

Sumbwa (Mweri), a people who live in Tanzania, where they number 76,400. They speak a dialect of Nyamwezi, a BANTU LANGUAGE.

Sundi, a people who live in Congo.

Sungor, a people and language of Chad. The Sungor number 21,000 in Chad and 9,000 in Sudan. Sungor belongs to the TAMA language group.

Suri, a people who live on the Borna Plateau of the Sudan and in Ethiopia. The group has 4,000 members. Their language belongs to the Didinga-Murle language group.

Surma (including Tid, Tirma, and Zelmamu), a people who live in Ethiopia.

Susu (Soso), a people who live in southern Guinea, where they number 238,000, and in Sierra Leone, where they number 49,000. They also live in Mali. Their different dialects form a dialect cluster in the Mande Fu language group of the MANDE family of languages.

Suthu, a BANTU LANGUAGE spoken by about 2,000,000 people in Lesotho and South Africa. Suthu literature contains works of poetry, novels, short stories and plays.

Swaga, a people who live in Zaire. They number 121,250 and speak a BANTU LANGUAGE.

Swahili, a people and language of East Africa, between Mogadiscio in Somalia, and Mozambique. There are about 1,000,000 people speaking Swahili as a first language. As many as 30,000,000 people in East Africa speak Swahili as a second language. It is one of the most important African languages. Swahili, sometimes called 'Coastal Bantu', has a basic BANTU LANGUAGE structure with more than 20,000 Arabic words. It also includes words from Persian, Portuguese, English, Urdu and Gujarati. The language has a unique literature which dates back to the early 17th century. This literature, mainly poetry, was written in Arabic script. The Swahili people are mainly fishermen and traders. The farmers grow rice, bananas, maize, millet, cassava and cash crops, such as fruits, coconuts and cloves. The Swahili are famous for their arts, crafts and music.

Swaka, a people who live in Zaire and Zambia. The group has 16,200 members. They speak a BANTU LANGUAGE.

Swase (Asosi), a people who live in the part of Nigeria, which was formerly British Cameroon. They number 3,000 and speak a BANTU LANGUAGE.

Swazi, a people living in Swaziland and adjacent parts of South Africa. They number about 1,000,000 and speak Swati, a BANTU LANGUAGE, close to ZULU. Most of the Swazi are farmers growing maize, millet, rice and cash crops. Many people now travel to South Africa to work.

Syan, a Ugandan people who number 10,000. They speak a BANTU LANGUAGE.

Tabwa (Taabwa), a people who live near Lake Mweru, in Zambia, where they number 8,000. They also live in the Shaba province of Zaire. They speak a BANTU LANGUAGE.

Tafi, a people living in Togo. They number less than 1,000 and speak a TOGO REMNANT LANGUAGE.

Tagbu, a people living in southern Sudan. They number 100. They speak a SERE-MUNDU language.

Tagoi, a people who live in the Nuba Hills of Sudan. They number 2,000 and they speak KOALIB-TAGOI.

Taita, a people living in Kenya and Tanzania. The group has 57,000 members. They speak a BANTU LANGUAGE.

Takemba, a people living in Togo. They speak a dialect belonging to the GURMA dialect cluster of GUR.

Talensi (Tallensi), a people who live in northern Ghana. They number 35,000 and they speak a GUR language. See also MOSSI.

Talinga, a people who live in the Ruwenzori Mountains in Uganda and Zaire. They speak a BANTU LANGUAGE.

Talodi, a people living in Sudan. The group has 1,200 members and they speak a KOALIB-TAGOI language.

Talodi-Masakin, a language group of the KOALIB-TAGOI languages. It is made up by the Talodi, Eliri, Masakin dialects, and by the 'Moro Hills' dialect cluster of Sudan.

Tama, a people living in Chad and Sudan. In Chad the Tama number 30,800. Their language belongs to an ISOLATED LANGUAGE GROUP. Tama is also the name of the language group which includes Sungor, Kibet and Mararit and is spoken by about 50,000 people.

Tambaro, a people who live in south-western Ethiopia. Their language belongs to the SIDAMO group of CUSHITIC LANGUAGES.

Tamberma see SOMBA.

Tambo, a people who live near the northern border of Zambia. They number 5,300 and they speak a BANTU LANGUAGE.

Tanala, 'People of the Forest', a people who live in eastern Madagascar, east of the BETSILEO. They are woodcutters and also grow rice. The Tanala number 237,000.

Tanga (Batanga), a people who speak a Bantu language in Cameroon.

Tangale, a people who live in the region of Bauchi in Nigeria. The group has 36,000 members. They speak a CHADO-HAMITIC LANGUAGE.

Tatoga (Taturu), several peoples living in Tanzania. In all, they number 64,000. The principal group are the BARABAIG people. The languages of the Tatoga form a dialect cluster of the NILO-HAMITIC LANGUAGES.

Taveta (Tuveta), a Kenyan people who speak a BANTU LANGUAGE.

Tawara, a people who live in Zimbabwe. They speak a dialect of KOREKORE, a language belonging to the SHONA language group of the BANTU LANGUAGES.

Teda (Tuda), a people who live in Chad, Niger and Libya, where they number 2,000. Together with the DAZA people, they number 31,000. They speak an EAST SAHARAN LANGUAGE.

Tegali, a people living in the Nuba Hills of Sudan. They number 22,000 and speak a KOALIB-TAGOI language.

Teke (Njiningi), a people who live in Congo and number 24,000. They speak a BANTU LANGUAGE.

Tem, a language spoken by the TEMBA people in northern Togo. It belongs to the GUR family of languages.

Temba, a people who live in northern Togo, where they number 52,000, and in Ghana, where they number between 14,000 and 18,000. They speak TEM.

Tembo, a people who live in Shaba province in Zaire. They number 15,000 and they speak a BANTU LANGUAGE.

Temein, a people who live in the Nuba Hills of Sudan. They number 2,300. Their language belongs to an ISOLATED LANGUAGE GROUP.

Temne (Timne), a people and language of Sierra Leone. The Temne number more than 500,000. The language belongs to the WEST ATLANTIC LANGUAGE group.

Tenda, a general name given to peoples of the region of the Senegal-Guinea border. These peoples include the BUYARA, KONYAGI, BASARI, Tenda Boeni and Tenda Maya.

Tera, a people who live in the region of Bornu and Bauchi in Nigeria. They number 18,500 and speak a Chadic language.

Teso (Iteso, Ateso), a people and language group of Kenya and Uganda. The Teso number 505,000 and they speak a NILO-HAMITIC LANGUAGE.

Tete, a Bantu-speaking people living round the city of Tete, Mozambique.

Tetela, a people who live in the Kasai province of Zaire. They number 30,000 and they speak a BANTU LANGUAGE.

Teuso, a people and ISOLATED LANGUAGE GROUP of the Timir forest, northern Kenya. The group has 2,500 members.

Teve (including the Gorongozi), a people who live in Mozambique. Their language is a dialect of MANYIKA, a BANTU LANGUAGE.

Tewi, a KRAN people who live in Liberia.

Tharaka, a Kenyan people who live on the north bank of the River Tana. They number 16,500 and they speak a BANTU LANGUAGE. They are a KIKUYU sub-group.

Thembu, a people who live in the Cape Province of South Africa. Their language is one of the XHOSA dialects.

Thonga (Tonga, Tsonga, Shangaan), a people who live in Mozambique and in the Transvaal, South Africa. They speak a BANTU LANGUAGE.

Thuri, a people living in southern Sudan. The group has 15,000 members. Their languages form a dialect cluster in the North Lwo group of the NILOTIC LANGUAGES. Other dialects which make up the cluster are Bodho, Colo and Manangeer.

Tid, an Ethiopian people who live near the border with Sudan.

Tigre, a SEMITIC LANGUAGE spoken in western Eritrea (in Ethiopia) and in the eastern Sudan. About 300,000 people speak the language.

Tigrinya, a SEMITIC LANGUAGE of Eritrea, Ethiopia and Sudan. The Tigrinya language is spoken by more than 1,000,000 people. It is the closest living language to ancient Ethiopic. Tigrinya, together with ARABIC, is an official language in Eritrea.

Tikar, a people who live in Nigeria, where they number 170,000, and in Cameroon, where they number 10,500. They speak a CLASS LANGUAGE.

Tikuu see BAJUNI.

Tima, a people who live in the Nuba Hills of Sudan. They speak a language belonging to the Katle language group.

Timne see TEMNE.

Tini, a people who live in Zaire. They number 15,000 and speak a BANTU LANGUAGE.

Tira, a Sudanese people who live in the Nuba Hills. Their language is KOALIB-TAGOI.

Tirma, a people who live in Ethiopia near the Sudanese border.

Tiv, a Nigerian people who live in Benue-Plateau State. They number 800,000 and they speak a CLASS LANGUAGE. Their language has some literature, including translations of the Bible.

Tlhaping, a South African people who live in the Cape Province. Their language is TSWANA.

Tlokwa, a people who live in the Transvaal, South Africa. They speak TSWANA.

Togo Remnant Languages are spoken in western Togo. They are so called because they appear to be the remaining scattered fragments of what may have been once a coherent cluster of languages.

Togoyo, a people living in southern Sudan in the region of Raga. They number only 20. They speak a SERE-MUNDU language.

Toma see LOMA.

Tombo, a people who live in Mali. Their language is DOGON.

Tonga. 1. a people living in Malawi on the shores of Lake Nyasa. They number 50,300 and speak a BANTU LANGUAGE. 2. a people who live in Mozambique. They speak Gitonga, a BANTU LANGUAGE. 3. a people who live in Zambia and Zimbabwe numbering between 70,000 and 110,000. They speak a BANTU LANGUAGE belonging to the Ila language group.

Tongwe, a people living in Tanzania. They number 7,900 and speak a BANTU LANGUAGE.

Toposa (including Dongiro), a semi-nomadic people who live in southern Sudan and northern Kenya. The group has 34,000 members. They speak a NILO-HAMITIC LANGUAGE belonging to the TESO language group.

Toriko, a people living in Zaire. They number 26,000 and speak Liko, a BANTU LANGUAGE.

Toro, a people who live in the Great Lakes region of Uganda. They number 183,500 and they speak a BANTU LANGUAGE.

Totela, a people living in Zambia. They number 14,160 and speak a BANTU LANGUAGE.

Toucouleur see FULANI.

Trade Language see PIDGIN.

Tsamai (Kule), a people living in south-western Ethiopia. They number 1,000 and speak a CUSHITIC LANGUAGE.

Tsamba, a people who live in the Bas-Zaire province of Zaire. Their language is KONGO, a BANTU LANGUAGE.

Tsangi, a Gabonese people numbering 10,000. They speak a BANTU LANGUAGE.

Tsayi, a people who live in Congo. They number 30,000 and speak a BANTU LANGUAGE.

Tsimihety, 'People of long, uncut hair', a people living on the north side of the central plateau of Madagascar. They number 390,000.

Tsogo, a people who live in Gabon. They speak a BANTU LANGUAGE.

Tsonga, a people and language of the eastern Transvaal and parts of Mozambique. The Tsonga language consists of a number of dialects which include Ronga, Shangane and Tswa.

Tsotso, an Angolan people who speak a BANTU LANGUAGE.

Tswa. 1. a people who live in Mozambique and speak a Tsonga dialect. 2. a people (Batswa) who live in the Equateur province of Zaire.

Tswana, a language and large group of people living in Botswana and adjacent areas of South Africa. The Tswana number more than 1,000,000. The Tswana language belongs to the Suthu-Tswana sub-family of the BANTU LANGUAGE family. Its dialects vary widely.

Tuareg (Touarègue), a BERBER people and language of the western Sahara. The Tuaregs number about 500,000 but as they are nomadic herdsmen it is difficult to know their exact numbers. Tuaregs are known as 'the people of the black veil' because of the veil worn as protection against the desert dust. The Tuaregs were originally farmers in West Libya and northern Tunisia. During the Middle Ages, however, the Tuaregs were driven south by the ARABS. They adapted to life in the desert, herding camels, sheep and goats and living in tents made of animal skins. The Tuaregs have preserved their own ancient script which is called Tifinagh.

Tubu, a people living in Chad and Niger. Together with the DAZA people, they number 200,000. They speak an EAST SAHARAN LANGUAGE.

Tuda see TEDA.

Tuken see KAMASYA.

Tula, a Nigerian people who live in the region of Bauchi, numbering 192,000.

Tulishi, a people who live in Sudan, where they number 2,500. They speak a KADUGLI-KRONGO language.

Tumak, a small group who live in Chad. Their language belongs to the SOMRAI language group.

Tumale, a Sudanese people who live in the Nuba Hills. Numbering 1,100, they speak a KOALIB-TAGOI language.

Tumbatu, a dialect of SWAHILI, which is spoken on Tumbatu Island, which lies to the north of Zanzibar.

TUAREG: This Berber lives in the western Sahara. He wears a veil across his face as protection against the desert sand.

Tumbuka, a people who live in Malawi and Zambia. They number 156,000 and they speak a BANTU LANGUAGE.

Tumbwe, a people who live in Shaba province, Zaire. They number 8,000 and they speak Lega, a BANTU LANGUAGE.

Tumma, a people living in Sudan. They number 4,200 and they speak a KADUGLI-KRONGO language.

Tumtum, a people who live in the Nuba Hills of Sudan. They number 1,300 and they speak a dialect of KADUGLI-KRONGO.

Tunya, a people living in Chad. They number 800. Their language is Bua.

Tupuri, a group of people who live near the River Lozone in Cameroon. The group has 130,000 members, who speak a NON-CLASS LANGUAGE.

Turkana, a people who live in north-western Kenya, extending into southern Sudan. They number between 70,000 and 80,000. They speak a NILO-HAMITIC LANGUAGE belonging to the TESO language group.

Turuka (Turka), a people who live in Ivory Coast. The group has about 25,000 members. Their dialect belongs to the LOBI dialect cluster.

Tusia, a people who live in Ivory Coast. They number 15,500. They speak a dialect belonging to the SENUFO dialect cluster.

Tutsi (Batutsi or Bahima), a people living in Rwanda and Burundi. Originally nomads, the cattle-herding Tutsi became a powerful group in the region, dominating the HUTU farmers. This social division has had an important effect on the politics of Rwanda and Burundi. The Tutsi speak BANTU LANGUAGES, RWANDA and RUNDI.

Twa. 1. a Zambian people who number 1,500. They speak a BANTU LANGUAGE related to Bemba. 2. a group of pygmies living in Burundi and in Uganda. They speak a form of RWANDA. 3. a Zairian people who number 3,800.

Twi-Fante see AKAN.

Twi-Kasa see AKAN.

Tyam, a people and language of northern Togo and Ghana. In Togo the Tyam number 38,000 and in Ghana they number 12,000.

Tyapi, a people who live in Guinea. They number 8,200 and they speak a dialect of Landoma.

Tyokossi, a people who live in Togo.

Udhuk, a Sudanese people who live in the region of Dar Fung. They number 5,000. Their language is part of an ISOLATED LANGUAGE GROUP.

Uldeme, a Cameroonian people who number 5,000.

Umbundu (Ovimbundu), a large group of people who live in Angola. The group has 1,331,000 members. They speak a BANTU LANGUAGE.

Unga, a Zambian people who number 14,000. They speak a BANTU LANGUAGE.

Ungwe, a people who live in Zimbabwe. Their language belongs to the SHONA group of the BANTU LANGUAGES.

Urhobo, a people living in the Niger Delta in Nigeria. The group has 209,000 members. Their language is KWA.

Vai (Gallinas), a people and language of northern Liberia and Sierra Leone. The group has 40,000 members. Vai is a MANDE language with its own script of more than 100 characters.

Vale, a people who live in Chad. They number 1,400 and they speak a BONGO-BAGIRMI language.

Venda, a people and BANTU LANGUAGE of the Transvaal, South Africa. The Venda also live in Zimbabwe. They number more than 350,000.

Vere, a people who live on the borders between Nigeria and Cameroon. Numbering 10,900, they speak a NON-CLASS LANGUAGE.

Vidunda, a people who live in the Eastern region of Tanzania. The group has 12,800 members who speak a BANTU LANGUAGE.

Vili. 1. a Gabonese people who speak a BANTU LANGUAGE. 2. a people who live in Congo. Their language is KONGO.

Vinza, a Tanzanian people who number 3,100. They speak a BANTU LANGUAGE.

Vita see GOLO.

Vora, a people who live in Central African Republic. They speak a BANTU LANGUAGE.

Vuma, a people living in Kenya.

Vute (Wute, Babute), a Cameroonian people who number 13,000. They speak a NON-CLASS LANGUAGE.

Waja, a Nigerian people who live in the region of Bauchi. The group has 20,000 members. They speak a CLASS LANGUAGE.

Wala, a people who live in northern Ghana. They number 26,000 and speak a GUR language.

Walamo, a people and CUSHITIC LANGUAGE of south-western Ethiopia. The Walamo number 225,000.

Wanda, a people who live to the south of Lake Rukwa in Tanzania. The group has 9,500 members. They speak a BANTU LANGUAGE.

Wandji, a people living in Gabon. They number 6,000 and speak a BANTU LANGUAGE.

Wangata, a Zairian people who live to the west of Lake Tumba. They speak a BANTU LANGUAGE.

Wanji, a people living in the Lake Nyasa region of Tanzania. Numbering 18,000, they speak a BANTU LANGUAGE.

Wasa (Wassaw), a people who live in Ghana.

Wasulu, a people who live in Guinea. There are 3,600 members of this group.

Wemenu, a people who live in Benin (Dahomey).

West Atlantic Languages, a geographical language group which includes TEMNE, SERER and WOLOF.

Woga, a Nigerian people who live near the border with Cameroon. Their language is Chadic.

Wogo, a people living in Niger.

Wolof, a large group of people and a language of Senegal. Wolof is spoken by about 1,000,000 people in western Senegal and is understood throughout the country. There is little written Wolof as most of the literature of Senegal is written in French. Wolof belongs to the WEST ATLANTIC LANGUAGE group.

Wongo, a Zairian people numbering 1,800.

Wovea (Bobea, Bota), a people who live in Nigeria and Cameroon. They number about 600 and they speak a Coastal Bantu language.

Wumbvu, a people who live in Gabon, numbering 4,000. They speak a BANTU LANGUAGE.

Wumu, a small group of people living in Zaire. They speak a BANTU LANGUAGE.

Wuong, a people who live in Congo and speak a BANTU LANGUAGE.

Xesibe, a people who live in East Griqualand in South Africa. They speak a dialect of XHOSA.

Xhosa, a large group of people and group of dialects of the eastern Cape Province and Transkei of South Africa. The Xhosa number nearly 4 million. The Xhosa dialects together with ZULU and SWATI belong to the NGUNI sub-family of the BANTU LANGUAGE family. The Xhosa dialects are spoken by several peoples in South Africa, such as the THEMBU. The language has many 'click' sounds, similar to those used in the languages of the KHOI-SAN. Cattle-raising is the traditional way of life of the Xhosa. Wars with white settlers over the possession of land continued for many years. Many Xhosa still farm the land in the traditional way but there are many who have also entered industry, commerce and the professions.

Xitonga see TSONGA.

Ya, a people who live in the Congo Republic. They speak a language belonging to the BANTU LANGUAGE family.

Yache, a Nigerian people who speak a CLASS LANGUAGE.

Yaka, a people who live in the Bas-Zaire province of Zaire, and in Angola. Their language is BANTU.

Yako, a people who live in Nigeria in the region of Ogoja. They number 20,000. They speak LUKO, a CLASS LANGUAGE

Yakoma, a people living in the Equateur province of Zaire.

Yakoro, a dialect of BOKI.

Yakuba see DAN.

Yala, a people living in southern Nigeria.

Yalna, a people living in Chad.

Yalunka (Dyalonke), a people who live in Guinea where they number 73,500, and in Sierra Leone, where they number 30,500. Their language is a dialect of Susu, a MANDE language.

Yambasa, a Cameroonian people who number 27,000. They speak a BANTU LANGUAGE.

Yangafek, a people living in Cameroon. They speak a BANTU LANGUAGE.

Yangere, a people living in Central African Republic. The group has 13,500 members. They speak the Banda language.

Yansi, a people and BANTU LANGUAGE of the Bandundu province of Zaire.

Yao, a people and BANTU LANGUAGE of south-eastern Malawi and northern Mozambique. The Yao number 281,200. Many of them are Muslims.

Yarse (Yansi), a people living in Upper Volta. They number 72,000. Their language is MOSSI.

Yasa, a people who live along the coast of Cameroon and Rio Muni. They are few in number. The Yasa speak a BANTU LANGUAGE.

Yaunde see EWONDO.

Yei. 1. a people who live in Botswana and speak a BANTU LANGUAGE. 2. a people living in Zambia.

Yeke, a people who live in Shaba province, Zaire.

Yela, a people who live in the Equateur province of Zaire. They speak a BANTU LANGUAGE.

Yemba, a people living in Angola.

Yendang, a dialect cluster (see LANGUAGE FAMILY) closely related to MUMUYE.

Yergum, a people who live in the Benue-Plateau State of Nigeria. They number 30,000 and speak a CLASS LANGUAGE.

Yewu, a people living in Zaire. They speak a dialect of the BANTU LANGUAGES.

Yira, a people who live in Zaire, where they number 1,700. They speak a BANTU LANGUAGE.

Yoabu, a people living on the border between Togo and Benin. Numbering 8,000, they speak Moa, which is a dialect in the GURMA dialect cluster.

Yombe, a people who live in the Bas-Zaire province of Zaire and in Congo. Their language is a dialect of KONGO.

Yoruba, an important people and language of Nigeria. Some 7,000,000 people speak Yoruba. It is one of the KWA languages of West Africa. Farming is the traditional way of life for the Yoruba people. They grow maize, yams, cassava, and other crops. The traditional Yoruba religion with its many gods is still followed, but many Yoruba people are now Christians or Moslems. The Yoruba language has an extensive literature of poetry, short stories, myths and proverbs.

Yulu-Binga, a people who live in southern Sudan. They number 3,000 and they speak a BONGO BAGIRMI language.

Zaghawa, a people living in Chad, where they number 27,000, and Sudan, where they number 41,000. They mainly speak an EAST SAHARAN LANGUAGE, but many of them speak the ARABIC language.

Zala, a people who live in south-west Ethiopia. They number between 15,000 and 20,000. Their language is a dialect of WALAMO, which belongs to the CUSHITIC LANGUAGE family.

Zanaki, a Tanzanian people who number 22,700. They speak a BANTU LANGUAGE.

Zanata see BERBER.

Zande (pl. Azande), a people living in the southern Sudan, Zaire and Central African Republic. They number about 1,000,000. Their language, Pa-Zande, makes up a single language unit. Dialects of Pa-Zande include Dio, Nzakara and Patri. There is little literature in Pa-Zande except stories about Tula, the spider-god.

Zaramo, a people and BANTU LANGUAGE of eastern Tanzania. The Zaramo number 183,000.

Zarma, a people who live in Niger (256,000) and Nigeria (12,500). They speak a dialect of the SONGHAI language.

Zaysse, a people living in south-western Ethiopia. Their language belongs to the OMETO group of the CUSHITIC LANGUAGES.

Zela, a people who live in the Shaba province of Zaire.

Zezuru, a people living in Zimbabwe. They speak Zezuru, a BANTU LANGUAGE belonging to the SHONA language group.

Ziba see HAYA.

Zigula (Zigua), a people who live in eastern Tanzania. They number 134,000 and speak a BANTU LANGUAGE.

Zilmamu, an Ethiopian people who are related to the SURMA.

Zimba. 1. a people who live in Mozambique. 2. a people who live in the Kivu province of Zaire. They number 50,000 and speak a BANTU LANGUAGE.

Zinza (Dzindza), a Tanzanian people who live on the south-west shores of Lake Victoria and on islands in the lake. They number 55,200 and they speak a BANTU LANGUAGE.

Zulgo, a people living in Cameroon who number 5,000.

Zulu, a large group of peoples living in the Natal province of South Africa. They number more than 4,000,000 and speak a BANTU LANGUAGE. The Zulu language is similar to XHOSA; it contains some 'click' sounds. There is an extensive literature in Zulu which includes histories, songs, poetry, novels, proverbs, and the famous *izibongo*, or praise songs in honour of the great Zulu Kings.

Zyoba, a people who live near Lake Tanganyika. They speak a BANTU LANGUAGE.

ZULU: A Zulu family living in a village in the Valley of a Thousand Hills, South Africa. There are many stories, poems and songs written in the Zulu language.

FOOD AND FARMING

The Importance of Farming

Farming is the most important single industry in Africa. It produces almost 36 per cent of the G.N.P., or *gross national product*—that is, the total value of all goods and services produced. It provides about 60 per cent of the export earnings, and employs 70 per cent of the total labour force. Yet Africa still imports agricultural produce worth £600 million every year.

According to the various national plans, only 20 to 30 per cent of total investment is spent on agricultural development. This figure is gradually increasing as more governments encourage agricultural development. A healthy agricultural economy is the foundation for future industrial expansion.

Agricultural productivity per person is only one-third of the world average. Increasing food production is offset by the rate of population growth, which averages more than 2.7 per cent per year. According to the United Nations Food and Agricultural Organization (F.A.O.), food production per person in Africa is less today than it was in the late 1950s, although agricultural produce for export has increased.

Subsistence Farming

Subsistence farming is the production of staple starch crops to provide food for the farmer and his family. More than 70 per cent of the cultivated land

▲ Workers in a rice field in the River Sebou basin, Morocco. This area is often affected by severe floods and dams are being built to control flooding and provide more agricultural land.

An Ethiopian farmer ploughs his land before planting sweet potatoes. Most people in Ethiopia live by subsistence farming.　▼

is still used for subsistence farming and most people are still employed in this type of activity.

The traditional method of farming involved the cultivation of a different area of land each year. When a piece of ground had been used to grow a crop, it was left *fallow* (unused) for a few years so that the soil could recover the nutrients which it had lost through cultivation. The increase in the population, however, has led to more people trying to live off the available fertile land. The fallow period has therefore become shorter as farmers have tried to extract a greater yield of crops from their land. Thus the land has less time to recover the natural elements which make it fertile. If the pressure on the land becomes too great, it will eventually become barren and unable to grow crops.

The slow growth rate of the African economy, at only 2.2 per cent each year, is said to be caused by the influence of subsistence farming. The subsistence farmer seldom has any surplus food to sell and, as a result, he has little money with which to buy other goods. In a country where subsistence farmers make up the bulk of the population, the level of buying and selling is low. Because few people have any money with which to buy things, industrialization is difficult to achieve. This farming system, however, can be used for the production of cash crops for export. The aim of many African countries is to improve the efficiency of subsistence farming.

Regional Subsistence Crops The staple food crops grown in subsistence farming are those which are suitable to the environment and which give the best food value in any particular environment. Africa can be divided into seven major regions on the basis of the staple food crops that are produced (see table: Regional Subsistence Crops).

From the brief survey shown, it is possible to understand the enormous influence of water supply. In fact, 60 per cent of the African continent is either steppe or desert with low and unreliable rainfall. Another 30 per cent is covered by the dry savanna lands of East and South Africa.

Livestock Many agricultural experts have stressed the need to introduce livestock farming into farming systems. The two main reasons for this are to improve the diet of the people and to obtain a supply of natural manure for the crops.

In the semi-desert areas, the rearing of livestock is almost the only occupation possible. In these areas, cattle and goats not only provide food for their masters, but also act as units for barter. As a result, people who raise livestock are interested more in breeding as many animals as possible than in using selective breeding methods to improve the quality of their stock. The mortality rate among livestock, especially in the drier areas, is very high. Droughts, such as the one which affected Senegal, Mali and Upper Volta in the early 1970s, have a devastating effect on the livestock population.

Overgrazing is a barrier to the improvement and expansion of livestock rearing. When food is scarce, livestock, particularly goats, will eat every available scrap of vegetation. This leads to soil erosion and the spread of desert conditions.

Cash Crop Farming

When they became independent, many African countries had an economy split into two sections. One section of the people enjoyed the wealth gained from exporting cash crops. Most people, however, remained as subsistence farmers. One of the major difficulties facing African agriculture today is how to extend the benefits of the modern cash crop system to traditional subsistence farming.

The future change from subsistence farming to

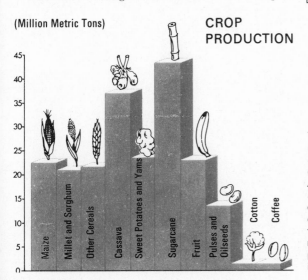

(Million Metric Tons)   CROP PRODUCTION

[Bar chart showing crop production: Maize (~22), Millet and Sorghum (~20), Other Cereals (~26), Cassava (~37), Sweet Potatoes and Yams (~43), Sugarcane (~20), Fruit (~29), Pulses and Oilseeds (~15), Cotton (~5), Coffee (~5)]

REGIONAL SUBSISTENCE CROPS

The Mediterranean coastal region of North Africa forms an area where wheat is the most important subsistence crop. This region is a transition zone between the Mediterranean climate and the Sahara desert.
The desert areas of Africa, particularly the Sahara, do not produce a dominant staple food crop. These huge areas are the home of nomads.
The dry north-west of Africa is an area where cereals, especially sorghum and millet are important. They can withstand long periods of drought and high temperatures.
The West African tropical rain forest area of Guinea, Sierra Leone and Liberia is an area where the basic food crop is rice.
Other forest areas of West and Central Africa grow various tropical root crops, such as cassava and sweet potatoes. Cassava is one of the most important tropical root crops.
The Great Lakes region supports plantains (green bananas), which form the basis of the food supply.
The savanna regions of East and South Africa produce maize as the staple crop. Maize gives a high yield under suitable climate and soil conditions.

Traditional and modern methods of irrigation are in use throughout the drier parts of Africa. *Above* Water wheels or *Sakia* in Sudan are made of wood and worked by oxen carrying water from the Nile. *Below* A modern bore hole provides water for cattle in North Senegal.

cash farming will create problems. Farmers tend to need more land to produce cash crops economically than they do to carry on subsistence agriculture. Also, some cash crops need several years of cultivation before they begin to give any yield. Practical problems, such as lack of equipment and transport difficulties will have to be overcome.

Cash crop farming is vital for economic development and industrialization. When a farmer changes from subsistence to cash crop farming, he earns money from his crops. He will then be able to buy manufactured goods. The increase in the demand for goods may cause the economy to expand.

Plantations and Smallholdings

Cash cropping in Africa is carried on both on plantations and on peasant smallholdings. Historically, the production of cash crops in most parts of the world has been on plantations, especially for bananas, cocoa, coffee and tea. The Tanzanian sisal industry is an example of cash cropping on plantations. In West Africa, however, the cocoa industry has been built up entirely by smallholders. Smallholdings are the most advanced form of farming carried on by peasants. In Africa, smallholdings have been responsible for the bulk of agricultural production.

Plantations often specialize in tree crops and usually only produce one crop. Examples include the rubber plantations of Liberia and Nigeria. The success of all cash crops, however, is vulnerable to fluctuations in prices on the international markets. Both systems, whether smallholdings or plantations, require diversification. The production of one or more secondary crops will support the farm if the main crop fails and also moderate the effects on the economy.

The Development of Agriculture

The importance of agricultural produce in the G.N.P. of Africa should not be under-estimated. Upper Volta, for example, relies on its livestock production, and live cattle provide 55 per cent of the total exports. Similarly, at least 75 per cent of the G.N.P. of Senegal and Gambia is provided by groundnut exports. The main problems for those countries which rely on agricultural products for their exports are the state of world demand and the difficulty of discovering new overseas markets.

Physical Problems of Farming in Africa Two severe physical problems limit agricultural development. First, the low or uncertain rainfall in many areas is a major obstacle. Secondly, African soils, which are rich in minerals but thin and infertile, lack several nutrients and are low in organic content. Tropical rain forest, which has fertile soil, covers eight per cent of Africa. In the past, the traditional method of farming different areas of land each year has reduced the importance of the poor soil. But as the pressure on the land increases, the poor quality of the soil takes on a greater importance.

The slopes of this tea plantation have been terraced to prevent soil from being washed away. Tea is an important cash crop in many African countries. ▼

◄ A worker gets his baskets ready for the grape harvest near Paarl, in South Africa.

These workers in Wollamo, Ethiopia are spreading coffee beans on drying trays. Coffee originated in north-east Africa and it is now exported to countries all over the world. ►

Farmers are being encouraged to grow cash crops such as tobacco. This will improve their own incomes and help their country's economy. ►

Solutions to Farming Problems The improvement of the water supply by irrigation and the introduction of a system of permanent fields used in rotation are two necessary steps which are already being taken. Agricultural development services have concentrated on four immediate issues: land tenure, crop improvement, crop protection and crop fertilization.

Land reform has, in some cases, brought about the splitting up of large estates to allow land ownership by the villagers. Small farmers are generally far more productive if they are cultivating land which they own than they are if they are cultivating land for which they pay rent. Crop improvement relies on research to produce more high-yielding varieties of plants. This research, however, has tended to concentrate upon cash crops rather than food crops. Land reform and crop improvement research schemes require the support of governments and often form part of the national plan.

The success of fertilizers and the protection of crops from pests and disease depend on the money

Some of the things that farmers must know about. Agricultural education is very important in modern Africa. Farmers must be taught new techniques to improve their crops. ▼

and equipment available and the extent of agricultural education. The establishment of co-operatives, such as the Vijiji Vya Ujamaa (self-help villages) in Tanzania, and irrigation schemes are very important in the development of African agriculture. Co-operatives aid the transition from traditional agriculture to commercial farming by giving credit, providing more efficient processing and marketing systems and by encouraging the use of modern methods. Irrigation schemes reduce the danger of drought, increase the amount of land which can be cultivated and encourage more productive farming techniques. Both factors allow a government to have stricter control over agriculture. This control can be used to put planning decisions into operation.

Because most people are poor, there is a low level of effective demand. The low income is caused by the low level of agricultural production. This, in turn, is controlled by one major factor—the lack of investment. Only increased investment can help break the vicious circle of poverty by providing the technology, machinery and scientific knowledge needed to develop a modern agricultural system.

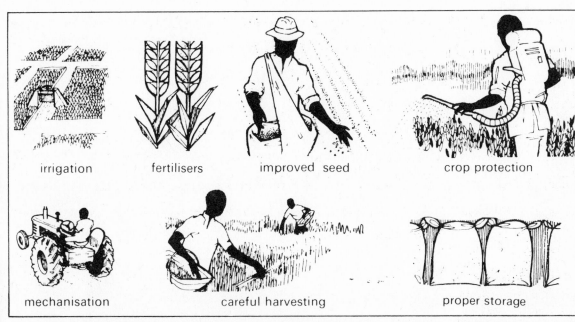

irrigation   fertilisers   improved seed   crop protection

mechanisation   careful harvesting   proper storage

Modern technology can be applied to the farmer's problems. *Below left* These tractors have special side wheels. They prevent the tractors from sinking into the thick mud of this rice field. *Below right* The use of fertilizers produces larger crop yields to feed more people.

FISHING

Fish is a major source of protein and is easy to obtain, but in most of Africa it remains an underdeveloped source of food. The continent's potential fish harvest is enormous. Deep sea fishing takes place off southern Africa and in the Indian Ocean. Coastal sea fishing is carried on in the Gulf of Guinea. Africa's vast lakes and huge rivers, and the artificial lakes, such as Volta and Kariba, are all rich fishing grounds. Fishing industries based upon artificial ponds are also being developed in many African countries. Yet, so far, only a few countries have begun to reach the potential harvests this rich source of food can provide. Such fish as tilapia breed easily and in large numbers, producing a tonne or more of fish per acre (about two-fifths of a hectare) of water per year. They have spread very quickly when introduced into the newly created man-made lakes.

Protein from Fish The nutritional importance of fish in diets cannot be overestimated. Fish provides animal protein and other ingredients often lacking. In some countries where the basic diet consists of a starch carbohydrate, such as cassava or maize, fish may well be the only source of protein. This is also true in traditional societies which own cattle but as yet have not come to use them as a regular source of food.

Fishing Industries of Africa

Most African countries give some attention in their development plans to improving techniques and increasing their fish harvest. International aid organizations, such as the United Nations Development Programme or the Food and Agricultural Organization, are involved in a number of fishing development schemes. On the whole, however, fishing still remains low on the list of development priorities.

Methods of fishing are a mixture of the traditional and the modern, with the traditional prevailing in most of the continent. A few countries have developed fishing as a major industry and export business. South Africa exports 90 per cent of its catch of anchovies, sardines and mackerel, as well as luxury items such as the Cape crawfish and octopus. In the Gulf of Guinea, Senegal has one of the most advanced fishing industries in Africa. It operates several fish canneries and earns about £5 million a year from fish exports. The industry employs about 100,000 people. On the other hand, Nigeria, with the largest population in Africa, harvests a mere 50,000 tonnes of fish a year.

Sea Fishing West African countries have greatly expanded their coastal fishing in recent years but they are handicapped in the development of deep sea fishing by the sheer expense of the operation. For this reason, Japanese or Norwegian deep sea trawlers fish off African waters, the large 'mother' vessel being maintained permanently in the fishing zone by small catcher vessels. Potential catches of fish are enormous and there is growing fear of overfishing, as well as the likelihood of a crisis about the extension of off-shore fishing rights. For example, Liberia in 1973 provided 80 per cent of its own fishing requirements and has one of the most modern fishing industries in Africa. However, its industry cannot afford even one deep sea trawler to enable it to compete with the major fishing countries, such as Russia, Japan or Poland, that operate off the Guinea coast. One such vessel could provide enough fish to supply the whole Liberian market.

Lake Fishing There are vast inland waters in Africa. Their total production of fish is at present less than that of the oceans, but it is economically often more important because the lakes, such as Lake Nyasa, are closer to densely populated areas. In this way the lakes act as a constant source of daily food.

Once a year, the Argungu fishing festival is held on a tributary of the River Niger near Sokoto, Nigeria. For most of the year, the river has few fish. But, on a given date, the 'keeper of the river' tells the fishermen that the river will be full of fish. The festival begins with as many as 5,000 fishermen taking part. The fishes which appear in great numbers in this strange way, are Nile perch which can weigh up to 70 kilos.

◀ One method of river fishing is to use wicker fish traps. These are positioned facing upstream so that fishes are washed into the traps by the current.

Togo fishermen haul their catch onto the beach. They are using a seine net. This type of net has sinkers on the bottom and floats on the top. The fish are caught within the net when the fishermen draw the ends ashore. ▼

INDUSTRY

Industry in African countries, with the exception of the Republic of South Africa, is in its infancy. According to 1968 United Nations statistics, Africa's manufacturing industries accounted for only 0.9 per cent of the world's total industrial output. African mining accounts for about half of the continent's total exports. In most African countries, industry is confined to the processing of minerals and other raw materials, such as timber, foodstuffs and textiles. The manufacturing industries produce basic necessities, such as clothes, shoes, soft drinks and beer, for the home markets.

South Africa is the most developed country in Africa, producing 40 per cent of the continent's total industrial output. In other countries, industrial growth is proceeding at a fast rate. But this high rate of growth is a reflection of the almost complete lack of any industrialization at the beginning of the 1960s.

In the early 1970s, about 26 per cent of Africa's gross national product (GNP)—the total value of all production, usually expressed in pounds sterling (£) or US dollars ($)—came from mining, manufacturing and construction. The percentage of the GNP coming from these sources in those countries which the United Nations classifies as *developed* is between 40 and 50 per cent. On average, agriculture accounts for 34 per cent of the GNP in African countries.

Manufacturing alone accounts for more than ten per cent of the GNP in only 15 African countries, of which South Africa and Egypt are the leaders. In the non-mining industries, the average factory is small, employing about 80 workers. Most factories process foodstuffs or chemicals, and Africa depends heavily on imports for the more sophisticated manufactured articles. For example, more than 35 per cent of all African imports consists of machinery or technical equipment.

The Main Industrial Nations

South Africa is the leading economic power of Africa. In 1972 the GNP was £5,900 million, which is about one quarter of the total for the whole continent. Manufacturing and construction made up about 25 per cent of this figure. South Africa has deposits of coal, copper, uranium and a wide range of other minerals. The discovery of diamonds in 1869 and gold in 1886 laid the foundations of South Africa's modern economy. Over the years, the country has benefited from vast inflows of capital from Britain and, more recently, the United States.

Since World War II, industrial development has increased greatly in South Africa. It has also become more varied. Among other industries, South Africa has a large automobile industry—a sure sign of an advanced industrial economy. Its annual income (per head) is between three and five times greater than that of the rest of Africa except Libya.

▲ Workers feed sisal fibres into a mechanical drier. Sisal is the main fibre cash crop in Kenya, Uganda and Tanzania.

◄ Workers control a machine which produces sweets at a factory in Nigeria. Most countries manufacture and process their own foodstuffs. They do not need to rely on importing expensive goods.

A Nigerian girl assembles a radio. The steady growth of industry has produced more and more skilled jobs. ▼

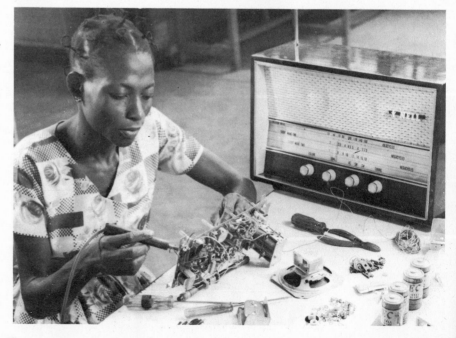

Other Economic Powers in Africa Egypt is the second most important economic power in Africa. Its industries include iron and steel, vehicle assembly and engineering. It has a GNP of £2,300 million and produces 25 per cent of Africa's manufactured goods.

Nigeria follows Egypt in importance, with a GNP of £2,200 million. Nigeria's rapidly expanding oil industry provides the base for future industrialization. Three North Africa countries, Algeria, Libya and Morocco, are among the most industrially advanced. Libya's oil wealth gives its small population the highest annual income per head in Africa.

Ghana has a high GNP of £940 million which gives an income per head of £100. Although this figure makes Ghana one of the wealthier countries, only one per cent of the national income comes from manufacturing. In common with many other African countries, Ghana's wealth comes from agriculture. On the other hand, about 25 per cent of the GNP of Zimbabwe comes from manufacturing. Zimbabwe produces about five per cent of Africa's total manufactures. Other leading industrial countries in Africa are Kenya, Zambia and Zaire.

Africa as a whole is still very poor by world standards. However, recent developments, especially the discovery of valuable mineral deposits in many countries, promise great economic expansion in the future. Power is essential for economic development, and the fact that Africa possesses about 40 per cent of the world's hydro-electric potential is another hopeful indication for the future. The huge Aswan, Kariba and Volta dams are already providing power for African industry. Other great hydro-electric projects are under construction in Zaire and southern Africa. The 2,000 megawatt Cabora Bassa Dam, which is built on the River Zambezi in Mozambique, is one of Africa's chief projects. (See the section on Hydroelectric power in the chapter on *Energy Resources*, pages 52–53.)

Problems of Industrialization Africa has plenty of land, vast mineral resources and great power potential. However, at present, much of Africa lacks sufficient capital and skilled personnel for industrial development. To compete economically in the modern world, industrial development has to be largely *capital intensive*. A capital intensive industry is one that makes full use of modern machinery, operated by relatively few workers. Large modern factories with modern machinery costs a great amount of money. The investment needed for capital intensive industry is not available in Africa at present and has to come from the developed countries of the world. But as the production of Africa's mineral resources grows, it will provide more African money for investment.

Another problem associated with capital intensive industry is that it does not provide as much employment as *labour intensive* industrialization, the alternative to capital intensive industrialization. Labour intensive industry depends on the use of a large, organized work force using sophisticated machinery. This method is usually slower and less efficient and most African planners favour capital intensive industrialization, because in modern terms it is more efficient.

Another problem of successful industrialization is the small size of the African home market in many countries. For example, a large steel mill is only viable if the steel produced can be sold. In small countries, the people do not have the money to buy steel goods, such as cars. A solution to this problem is the formation of economic unions between countries, such as the East African Common Market. With a larger market, a large-scale industrial enterprise, such as a steel mill, becomes an economic possibility.

The efficiency of Africa's agriculture has a major influence on industrial development. Every country has limited resources in terms of land, capital and work force. If all these resources are being used to provide food for the population in a subsistence farming economy, there will be no basis on which to build an industrial economy.

In the countries where the Africanization of foreign-owned businesses has taken place, it is essential that personnel should be trained in the technical and managerial skills needed to run large-scale businesses.

The Future

Apart from South Africa, the continent faces many problems over industrialization. Rapid and successful industrial development in Africa presents many economic problems. There is no intrinsic reason, however, why these should not be surmounted and the continent take its rightful place among the industrialized areas of the world. Africa's enormous natural resources are a powerful asset for industrial development throughout the continent. Africa has all the resources that it needs to develop great modern industrial centres. (See also chapters on *Mining and Minerals* and *Energy Resources*.)

▲ Fruit-growing and canning is becoming an important industry in many African countries.

As more foreign markets are found for exports, a large-scale industrial enterprise, such as this steel mill, becomes an economic possibility in Africa. ▼

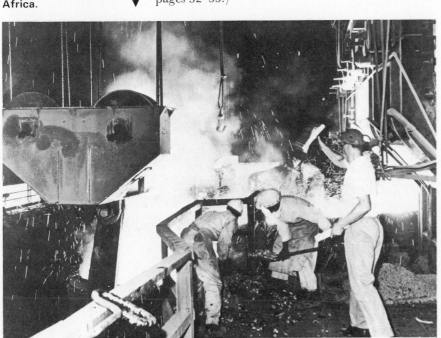

ENERGY RESOURCES

The economic development of Africa depends, to a great extent, on its domestic energy resources. An abundant supply of cheap power is essential for rapid industrial development. Many parts of Africa are rich in water power, oil and natural gas, although the potential of these resources has not yet been fully exploited.

Coal South Africa has by far the most productive coal-mining industry in Africa, and coal has played an extremely important part in the development of her economy. About 58 million tonnes (metric tons) of coal are mined in South Africa every year and coal generates 85 per cent of South Africa's electricity. In comparison, Zimbabwe's Wankie colliery, Africa's second largest producer, mines three million tonnes per year. Other countries with coalfields—Algeria, Morocco, Mozambique, Nigeria, Tanzania and Zaire—produce only a few hundred thousand tonnes annually, much of which is of poor quality.

Natural Gas Algeria has enormous reserves of natural gas at Hassi R'Mel in the central region of the country. The gas is transported by pipeline to the coast, where it provides the power for Algeria's expanding industries. Natural gas has also been found in Congo, Gabon, Morocco, Nigeria and Tunisia.

Oil In 1952, Libya was probably one of the poorest states in Africa. By 1968, oil exports had made it the richest in terms of income per person. Oil was first

Above and *right* Oil-drilling rigs in The Mid-West Region of Nigeria. Nigeria is the most important African oil producer after Libya.

discovered in the Libyan desert in 1959 and production began in 1962. Libya's oil exports are now about 1,000 million barrels annually.

Nigeria is the other great African oil producer. The revenue from oil, which is pumped up from offshore boreholes has given Nigeria a booming economy. The other major oil producing countries are Algeria, Angola, Gabon and Egypt.

The power derived from the vast oilfields of north and central Africa will make an enormous contribution to the development of the continent. Pipelines carrying oil to the countries without natural energy resources would bring great economic advantages to Africa as a whole.

Electricity from diesel fuel Many African countries still lack any great potential sources of energy, and for them the absence of cheap power is a major stumbling block to industrial development. In these countries, the main towns rely on electricity generated by small diesel power stations. This is an expensive and inefficient form of power production because the diesel fuel has to be imported and transported many kilometres inland using road or rail transport.

ENERGY RESOURCES

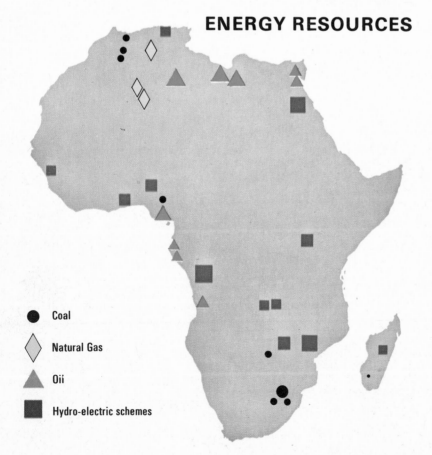

- ● Coal
- ◇ Natural Gas
- ▲ Oil
- ■ Hydro-electric schemes

PRODUCTION OF COAL 1971		PRODUCTION OF CRUDE PETROLEUM 1974 est.	
Country	Millions of metric tons	Country	Millions of metric tons
Southern Africa	58.816	Nigeria	112.000
Zimbabwe	3.089	Libya	77.000
Zambia	0.812	Algeria	49.000
Morocco	0.475	Gabon/Congo	13.000
Mozambique	0.323	Angola	8.500
Others	0.304	Egypt	7.500
		Tunisia	4.000
TOTAL	63.839	TOTAL	271.000

PRODUCTION OF NATURAL GAS 1971

Country	Thousands of millions of cubic metres
Algeria	2.965
Libya	0.465
Others	0.216
TOTAL	3.646

Hydro-electric power Without a doubt, Africa's greatest energy source is hydro-electric power and those countries with hydro-electric power stations are already able to sell surplus power to neighbouring countries. Because of the high cost of building dams and hydro-electric stations, hydro-electric power was generally not regarded as a practical possibility in Africa until the 1950s. Any industrial development that was to take place needed power, and this was in short supply. Experts have estimated that Africa possessed 40 per cent of the world's hydro-electric potential.

Major hydro-electric schemes The Kariba dam, constructed across the Zambezi river between 1955 and 1960, was Africa's first major hydro-electric dam. The Kariba dam's power output of 1,500 megawatts is fed into the grid system of the Central African Power Corporation. Zambia now supplies a further 600 megawatts to the Central African Power Corporation's grid from the new hydro-electric plant on the Kafue river.

At Inga, in Zaire, the first stage of what will be the world's largest hydro-electric complex was completed across the Zaire River in 1972. When this project is finished, it will have an output of 30,000 megawatts (20 times the output of the Kariba dam). Zaire already has more than 30 small hydro-electric stations producing electricity.

The Aswan High dam on the Nile in southeastern Egypt was opened in 1971. With an output of 2,100 megawatts, the Aswan High dam has the highest output of any single hydro-electric dam in Africa. The waters of the Nile backed up behind the dam form Lake Nasser. The water from this man-made lake has provided new areas for agricultural development.

Ghana's power comes from the Volta dam on the Volta river. This hydro-electric project began operation in 1965 with an output of 760 megawatts.

Nigeria's expanding industries need enormous amounts of electricity. Part of it comes from the Kainji dam on the Niger river. The total power output from the 12 generating units at Kainji is 960 megawatts.

Most of South Africa's electricity is generated by coal-fired power stations. However, two hydro-electric projects are under construction. The Orange River Scheme will take water through a series of tunnels to irrigate about 303,500 hectares (750,000 acres) of the waterless south-eastern Cape. A network of hydro-electric stations, with a total power output of 177 megawatts, is being incorporated into the scheme. The second hydro-electric project that will benefit southern Africa is the 2,000 megawatts Cabora Bassa dam being built across the Zambezi in Mozambique.

Some hydro-electric projects have provided the basis around which new communities have grown up, such as Jinja in Uganda. The Owen Falls dam at Jinja is situated on the Nile river at its exit from Lake Victoria. The hydro-electric plant, which has an output of 150 megawatts, provides power for many local industries.

▲ Hydro-electricity from large dams, such as Kariba, supplies much of Africa's power needs.

Coal is a cheap source of energy, because it needs little processing. The largest deposits in Africa are in Zimbabwe and South Africa. ▼

PRODUCTION OF HYDRO-ELECTRIC POWER 1971		
Country	Production in Thousand Million Kilowatt hours	Percentage of total African Production
Zimbabwe	5.622	21.1
Egypt	5.350	20.1
Zaire	3.437	12.9
Ghana	2.909	11.3
Nigeria	1.574	5.9
Morocco	1.498	5.6
Cameroon	1.139	4.2
Zambia	0.940	3.5
Uganda	0.813	3.0
Angola	0.605	2.3
Tanzania	0.325	1.2
Algeria	0.322	1.2
Kenya	0.319	1.2
Others	1.735	6.5
TOTAL	26.588	100.0

Source: United Nations: World Energy Supplies 1968–71

MINING AND MINERALS

The African continent is very rich in mineral resources, and the exploitation of these resources is, as yet, in its infancy. To those countries which are fortunate enough to have large deposits of minerals beneath their soil, the export of minerals provides an invaluable supply of foreign capital and investment, and a short cut to economic development. Taking the continent as a whole, mineral products account for about half of Africa's exports. The world's demand for minerals, especially metals, is increasing and known deposits are fast diminishing. Africa now produces about five per cent of the world's total mineral output, but this figure is sure to increase. Africa's vast untapped supply of minerals ensures the continent's future prosperity in the world.

At present, most of Africa's mineral wealth is exported. The income earned from mineral exports has played an important role in the economies of many developing African countries. The pattern of mineral production is likely to change over the next few decades. Increasing industrialization will create a demand for minerals for home markets and less will be exported.

The ancient Egyptians first mined copper and gold about 3000 BC. Today, we find that the most important part of Africa's metal production is still the mining of copper and gold. However, this state of affairs now appears to be changing. The mining of iron ore and bauxite (aluminium ore) is growing in importance, and is destined to play an important role in the economic future of Africa.

Gold is one of the heaviest metals, and, because of its rarity and durability, it has been used as money throughout the world for thousands of years. Today, more than half of the world's new gold comes from the mines of Ghana, Zimbabwe, South Africa and Zaire. The Witwatersrand area of Transvaal province, South Africa, is the most important gold field in the world. There, the gold is found as tiny specks in a belt of hard-cemented gravel beds, which stretch for more than 96 kilometres (60 miles) to the east and west of Johannesburg.

Copper The 'Copper Belt' of northern Zambia and the Zairian province of Shaba (formerly Katanga) contains the largest concentration of copper and cobalt minerals in the world. Indeed, Zambia's economy depends almost completely on mineral production. Between them, Zambia and Zaire produce more than 1,000,000 tonnes of copper metal per year. In addition, Zaire produces 70 per cent of the world's supply of cobalt.

Locating new deposits of copper is often a long and difficult process because there may be few indications on the surface of the presence of the metal underground. In recent years, several new deposits have been found in the Copper Belt by the systematic analysis of soil samples taken from wide areas. The discovery of high concentrations of copper and related minerals in some samples has led to the eventual discovery of ore deposits beneath the surface. Copper is mined both at the surface and underground. South Africa, Namibia and Uganda have copper mining industries.

The Witwatersrand in South Africa is the largest and most productive gold mining area in the world.
▼

PRODUCTION OF MINERALS IN AFRICA

Main Producing Countries	Production in 1971
GOLD	
South Africa	976,400 kilogrammes
Ghana	21,695 kilogrammes
Africa Total	1,012,000 kilogrammes
COPPER ORE	
Zambia	651,400 tonnes
Zaire	406,800 tonnes
South Africa	152,000 tonnes
Africa total	1,286,000 tonnes
DIAMONDS (uncut)	
Zaire	12,677,000 metric carats
South Africa	7,031,000 metric carats
Africa total	36,900,000 metric carats
CHROMIUM ORE	
South Africa	737,000 tonnes
Zimbabwe	Figures not available
Malagasy	62,200 tonnes
Africa total	990,000 tonnes
TIN	
Nigeria	6,731 tonnes
Zaire	6,447 tonnes
Africa total	18,600 tonnes
IRON ORE	
Liberia	16,728,000 tonnes
Mauritania	5,497,000 tonnes
South Africa	6,070,000 tonnes
Africa Total	38,500,000 tonnes

▲ Industrial diamonds from the famous Kimberley mine in the Cape Province, South Africa.

Diamonds Diamonds were discovered in Africa in 1866. A young boy found a pretty pebble on his father's farm in the Transvaal, South Africa, and gave it to his sister to play the game of 'five stones'. The 'pebble' was later found to be a 21.7 carat diamond. This discovery started the great rush of European prospectors to the area and eventually made South Africa the world's leading diamond producers. Africa now mines about three-quarters of the world's diamonds. The most famous diamond mine was established at Kimberley in Cape province. The mining activities at Kimberley have left a huge hole in the ground 1.2 kilometres wide (three-quarters of a mile) and almost half a kilometre (one-third of a mile) deep.

A diamond's value as a gemstone depends upon its brilliance, weight, colour and lack of impurities. Most smaller stones are of little use as gems, but they are useful as 'industrial diamonds'. Their extreme hardness enables them to be used as drill tips and

for cutting and grinding hard materials. Africa's largest production of industrial diamonds comes from Bakwanga in Zaire. There, the diamonds are dispersed through deposits of surface gravels. The gravel is scooped up by mechanical buckets and sent to treatment plants for the extraction of the diamonds. Diamonds are also mined in Angola, Botswana, Ghana, Namibia, Sierra Leone and Tanzania.

Chrome, Manganese and Vanadium Chromium ore (chromite) is found in the Great Dyke area of Zimbabwe and in the Bushveld of South Africa. These two sources supply 40 per cent of the world's chrome, which is used to strengthen and protect steels. Ghana is the leading producer of high quality manganese, another metal used by the steel industry. Large deposits of manganese ore are also found in the 'Kalahari' field in South Africa, near the border with Botswana. Vanadium, a rare metal used in the production of alloys, is found in the Bushveld and Namibia.

Tin Two important areas of tin ore (cassiterite) are the Jos plateau, in Nigeria, and eastern Zaire. The tin ore is processed in the mining areas. High pressure water jets sluice away the surrounding rock debris from the relatively heavy tin ore. Tin is used to provide a protective covering for other metals because it resists corrosion.

Iron Deposits of iron ore are abundant in Africa. However, the lack of industrial resources to process the ore and the difficulties of transporting it to sea ports for export have hindered the development of iron ore mining. Furthermore, the home market for metal goods in Africa is relatively undeveloped. Liberia, the largest exporter of iron, has an annual production of more than 23 million tonnes. Several countries have now set up their own smelters and steel works. These include Algeria, Ghana, Zimbabwe, South Africa and Egypt.

Aluminium Guinea is the leading African producer of bauxite, mining more than 2,500,000 tonnes annually. It is estimated that Guinea contains one-fifth of the world's high-grade bauxite deposits. Other bauxite producers include Sierra Leone, Ghana and Malawi. The refining of aluminium from bauxite needs huge amounts of electricity and up to the present most of the bauxite has been exported for processing. The development of Africa's great hydro-electric power resources will change this situation. Guinea has an aluminium refinery and Malawi is planning the construction of one.

Rarer Metals Africa produces a high proportion of the world's supply of rarer metals, such as beryllium, germanium, hafnium, lithium, niobium, platinum and uranium. South Africa and Zaire supply 35 per cent of the world's uranium, the raw mineral used for the generation of nuclear power. Radium, a metal far rarer than gold or diamonds, was, at one time, produced solely in Zaire as a by-product of the uranium industry. The total annual production of radium at that time was about one and a half ounces. Zaire and South Africa are the world's leading producers of germanium.

▲ Diamonds are taken from the gravel beds of rivers in Sierra Leone, a country rich in minerals.

Zambian copper ingots are lifted onto lorries prior to transportation. Zambia has the world's largest known reserves of copper. ▶

TRANSPORT

Before the 1800s, transport depended on sailing ships and the physical efforts of men and animals. The world consisted of a series of self-supporting societies linked together in order to exchange such luxuries as gold, ivory, porcelain or silks. The transport of bulky commodities was too costly when long-distance trade depended upon pack animals, head porterage, canoes or even the dhows that sailed between Africa, Arabia and India. The development of steam engines to drive ships and railway locomotives entirely changed international commerce. Today the world economy is based upon large-scale trading in all kinds of raw materials and manufactured goods.

During the 19th century, Africa's external trade developed slowly. Because the continent had few navigable rivers and lacked mechanical transport, the exchange of commodities and manufactured goods was limited to the areas around the ports or anchorages. From the end of the 19th century, the construction of railways and, later, the use of motor vehicles enabled people in the interior of the continent to take part in international trade. More recently, air transport has ended the isolation of even the remotest places.

Sea Transport Steamships caused a commercial revolution in the coastal states of Africa in the 1800s, because of the enormous output of certain valuable products. For example, Zanzibar monopolized the world clove market and West Africa developed overseas trade in palm oil. Sea transport no longer has such immediate importance for economic development, but it still carries the bulk of Africa's external trade. Such ports as Cape Town, Durban, Lagos and Mombasa have grown into large cities. Because European countries control most of the world's shipping, the establishment of national steamship companies, as in East Africa, Ghana and Nigeria, has proved a useful means of saving foreign exchange and of expanding trade and industry.

Inland Waterways Rapids and falls on most African rivers have always restricted their use as major transport routes. However, a few African rivers, such as the Niger, Nile and Senegal, provided the chief means of interior trade in the 1800s. Today, half a million tonnes of shipping operate on more than 11,200 kilometres (7,000 miles) of river in the Zaire basin. The Niger is navigable beyond Lokoja. Steamers serve almost 400 kilometres (250 miles) of the Gambia River, and lakes Nyasa, Tanganyika and Victoria have extensive shipping facilities.

Although water transport is inexpensive, Africa's waterways have declined in importance, because cargo has often to be carried around falls and shallows. Because this causes great difficulties, navigation on the Nile in the northern Sudan and on the Senegal River has been largely replaced by rail transport. The East African lake services have also suffered much from competition with road and rail transport. In 1963–4, a railway from Soroti to Pakwach replaced the ships used on lakes Mobutu Sese Seko and Kyoga.

Inland waterways are most important as a means of local transport in many areas, rather than as crucial arteries of commerce. However, the development of rapids for hydro-electric power projects may in the future be linked with the building of canals. This would improve navigation and either eliminate the trans-shipment of cargo or encourage the transport of goods in containers that might be transferred from shipping to road or rail services at the limit of navigation.

Rail Transport Railways made it far easier for areas in the African interior to engage in overseas trade. The building of main lines began north of the Sahara and south of the Zambezi during the 1870s. Around 1900, it began in the tropics. Today Africa has about 72,000 kilometres (45,000 miles) of railway. Almost one-third of this distance is in South Africa. Ten other countries, Nigeria, Zimbabwe, Zambia, Algeria, Egypt, Kenya, Uganda, Tanzania, Sudan and Zaire, have just under a

Above Repairing rain damage on an East African road to enable the bus to get through.
Below left Pack animals are still used in remote areas of East Africa. Camels carry equipment for locust control teams.
Bottom Aircraft enable passengers to travel great distances quickly and easily.

half of the total distance of track. The remaining 16,000 kilometres (10,000 miles) of line are spread between the other African states.

Because rail transport is suited to the movement of bulk commodities over long distances, it has had a great effect on economic progress in Africa. Railways made possible the growth of gold mining in South Africa, the development of copper reserves in Zaire and Zambia, and the export of such farm produce as Nigerian groundnuts (peanuts) and Ugandan cotton. Such ancient cities as Kano in Nigeria or Kumasi in Ghana expanded as they collected commodities from surrounding areas for shipment by rail to the coast. Elsewhere the transshipment of goods and produce created such centres as Kisumu in Kenya or Matadi in Zaire.

The most spectacular new line, completed in 1975, is the Uhuru railway between Dar es Salaam and Zambia. It was built jointly by Tanzania and Zambia with technical assistance from China. It will open up the southern parts of Tanzania for agricultural and industrial development and give Zambia another route to the sea.

Road Haulage The countryside, unable to finance the heavy costs of railway construction, continued to rely upon pack animals (mainly in grassland areas) and upon people carrying loads on their heads (mainly in forest areas). The building of

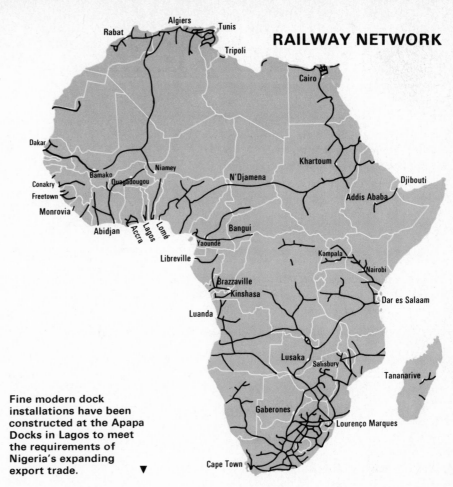

RAILWAY NETWORK

Fine modern dock installations have been constructed at the Apapa Docks in Lagos to meet the requirements of Nigeria's expanding export trade. ▼

motor roads made economic development in rural areas possible. From the 1920s, Africa developed an extensive road network. Local roads usually have an earth surface. They often become impassable during the rainy seasons. The main roads have either a gravel or a tar surface. Most countries are investing in the improvement of their trunk routes.

The motor vehicle proved ideally suited to African requirements. Businessmen found that road haulage required only a small investment but yielded high profits. Road transport widened the domestic economy, and an increasing share of local traffic travels by lorry. In recent years, heavy trailers have rivalled the railways in the haulage of bulk commodities between distant towns. The building of Pan-African highways such as the proposed Lagos–Mombasa highway will extend trade and the exchange of ideas.

Air Transport is especially suited to the carriage of passengers and high value goods. It has expanded rapidly in Africa. Cairo, Johannesburg, Lagos and Nairobi are among the world's most important airports. Such companies as Nigeria Airways and East African Airways have an international reputation. Internal air services have proved valuable in Africa, where surface transport is often slow or unreliable. However, aviation is not restricted to important routes between large cities. Light aircraft enable the provision of medical and other social services in the most isolated areas.

International routes, using fleets of jet aircraft on flights around the world, make a doubtful contribution to economic development because the aircraft have to be purchased at enormous cost.

COMMUNICATIONS

In earlier times, many African peoples had developed well-organized systems of communications by messengers, horns, tonal or 'talking' drums and other methods. But even as late as the nineteenth century, news travelled slowly, often distorted as it was passed on from group to group. Inadequate and unreliable information was the most severe problem that Africa experienced when it faced colonial rule.

Modern technology changed the value of information. Postal services and telecommunications enabled individuals to maintain close contact over great distances. Newspapers, although restricted to the literate minority, provided useful news coverage for the larger towns. However wireless broadcasting was the most significant change. It made news immediately available throughout Africa.

Postal Services Colonial governments originally established postal services to make their administration more efficient. But the public could use the system on the payment of a small postage charge. As more people learned to read and write, so correspondence became a popular means of communication. As the Swahili proverb says: 'A letter is half as good as a meeting'.

▲ People can communicate cheaply and easily by using the postal services.

Below left Newspapers and magazines are becoming more and more important in Africa as a means of communicating information. *Below right* Namibian children selling newspapers published in Afrikaans.

African towns are well provided with post offices. In outlying areas the situation is less satisfactory. There are few post offices. Because rural people now move about much more, there is an unsatisfied demand. By 1971 Kenya, Tanzania and Uganda had a combined total of 1,080 post offices, or one post office for approximately 32,000 people.

Telecommunications The Post Office has a monopoly of the telegraph and telephone services in Africa. From the earliest days of colonial rule, telegraphs linked important centres. Until the recent development of telex, however, the popularity of telephones caused a decline in the importance of the telegraph service.

Because the equipment is very expensive, telecommunications chiefly benefit the towns. Only wealthy individuals and such institutions as schools, businesses and government offices can afford telephones. But public demand is increasing. In many areas, the demand far exceeds the supply. For example, in Nigeria less than a quarter of those who need telephones actually have them. In towns telephones are an essential part of modern life. In 1968 there were just under 60,000 telephone sub-

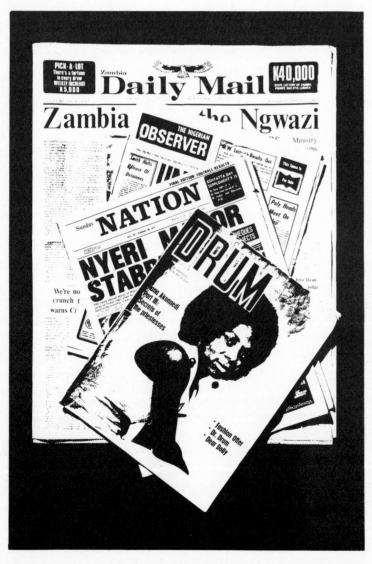

scribers in Kenya, Tanzania and Uganda who held more than 135 million local conversations and made more than 5 million long-distance calls. Recently there have been developments of new techniques in radio transmission, subscriber trunk dialling, and the relay of international messages by satellite. (It is likely that, as the relative cost of the service falls, the telephone system will attract more users.)

Newspapers The press in Africa reaches a small but growing and influential market. The continent has fewer than 200 daily newspapers, whose combined circulation is only about three million. (Some countries have no daily newspapers. Elsewhere, the size of the readership varies from the continental average of 1 person out of every 1,000. In Ghana it is 1 out of every 20 people, and in Morocco it is almost 1 out of every 10. Some 2,000 periodicals are also published in Africa, half of them in countries south of the Sahara.)

Difficulties of distribution limit the circulation and effectiveness of the press. Finance comes from governments, political parties or from overseas capital. The sale of the national newspapers, such as the *Daily Nation* in Kenya, *Daily News* in Tanzania, the *Voice of Uganda* in Uganda, the *Daily Times* and *The Observer* in Nigeria, or *The Daily Mail* in Zambia, is largely restricted to the bigger towns. Recently, improved distribution has made such papers increasingly available in rural areas.

Newspapers in vernacular languages, which are less adequately financed, emphasize matters of local interest. They are often published irregularly and serve both the city and the countryside.

One of the most popular columns in local newspapers is 'Reader's Letters', which gives readers the only outlet for their grievances and answers questions on all kinds of topics.

Newspapers are important in education. They can help people to judge the meaning of information. They enable people to improve their reading in their national language. They also encourage people to read other things, such as books and pamphlets. But competition from broadcasting has emphasized the need for a wide circulation to attract advertising revenue.

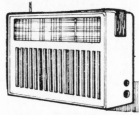

Audio-visual means of communication, such as films (*top*), radio (*centre*) and television (*bottom*), are used to teach students in modern schools and universities.

Broadcasting The world's first short wave wireless broadcasting station opened at Nairobi in 1928. Since then, radio has become the main source of news and the most effective advertising medium in Africa. From the late 1940s, production of cheap receiving sets made radio a popular means of mass communication. With the development of transistors in the late 1950s, the cost of receiving sets fell rapidly. Today there are few places where someone does not own a radio. All African states maintain a broadcasting service. For example, by 1969 Nigeria had 19 broadcasting stations and about 5,500,000 receiving sets. The estimated audience for radio broadcasts was about 30 million.

Radio broadcasts in vernacular languages, such as Dholu, Dinka, Fula, Lingala, Kikuyu and Boran, encourage the growth of national awareness even in the vast isolated areas. They allow governments to explain their viewpoints to their people. Most national broadcasting services in such commonly spoken languages as Arabic, English, Hausa and Swahili use short wave frequencies beamed from very powerful transmitters. This is partly because of the distances involved, but also because it minimises the interference of electrical disturbances in the atmosphere. Just as African programmes can be heard throughout the world, so people in Africa can receive short wave broadcasts from London, Moscow or Peking that give different interpretations of events and even contradictory facts.

Television Services have only a small coverage. In Uganda in 1968 there were only 6,111 licensed receiving sets. Transmissions entertain the wealthy few. But they also provide mass education when sets are placed in schools, social centres and similar institutions. Although most African states have television services, the development of suitable programmes has proved more difficult. Despite the growing number of programmes in such languages as Hausa and Swahili, services in most countries have to rely on imported material that can be irrelevant and very unsuitable for the needs of national development.

The Future Modern nations depend on communications. Post and telecommunications ensure that individuals may keep in touch and help government and business to run efficiently.

By using the press, wireless broadcasting and television, governments can mould the attitudes of society towards national endeavour and unity of purpose.

On the other hand, mass communications lead people to exaggerate fashions, to abandon traditional customs, and to oversimplify political problems so that they expect more than the government can provide and become dissatisfied. Although African governments control the media, mass entertainment and information can strain political, social and cultural institutions.

Above left The director of religious programmes makes a broadcast on Radio Tanzania. *Left* The modern broadcasting centre in Nairobi, Kenya.

EDUCATION

Education is essential for national development. In a slowly changing society, its purpose is to maintain the existing order. It also helps young people to fit into society as they find it. Africa today, however, is an area of rapid social change. Here education has a hard task. It must not only enable the individual to develop his gifts, but it must also ease the strains that arise when existing societies are upset by new social and economic forces. It must also assist the individual and the nation to stand on their own feet—education for self-reliance.

Pre-Colonial Education

In the original aliterate societies of Africa, young children were taught in the family circle. They learned the beliefs and behaviour that were expected of them. Girls learned from their mothers how to clean, cook and cultivate. They carried water and firewood, and helped to care for the babies. Boys went out with elder brothers to herd livestock and were instructed in hunting, fishing and fighting. As they grew older, children were taught what was expected of them as adult men and women. Their education ended with a stiff final examination. This was the initiation ceremony, which they had to pass before they were accepted as full members of the community.

This system was suited to the societies of that time. Children learned not merely how to be successful warriors, hunters or housewives. They also learned how to be good citizens. Their moral training was reinforced by their religion, so that they knew what might happen if their evildoing incurred the wrath of the gods or the ancestral spirits. However, the system was designed for a stable society, and discouraged change and experiment.

A similar type of education was once given in Europe. The characteristic institution of modern western education, the school or college, is of recent origin. This institution developed from the training given to young men who wanted to become priests. Only about 600 years ago, parents in England began to demand that their sons should attend school, although they had no intention of becoming priests. Education remained in the hands of the Church. Wealthy, pious men founded schools so that the benefit of the new education might be available for some poor children, as well as for the rich. Until the 1800s, illiteracy was widespread.

Early European Education in Africa

When the Europeans made their first settlements in Africa, they established small schools, like the charity schools in their own countries. Portuguese, Dutch, Danish and British chaplains taught a handful of children in the castles of the Gold Coast (now Ghana). Occasionally, a gifted boy would be sent to Europe for further education.

When serious missionary work began in Africa (1811 in Sierra Leone, 1827 in the Gold Coast, 1838 in Bechuanaland, 1842 in Nigeria, 1844 in Kenya and 1877 in Uganda), Christian missionaries used schools to develop their work. They wanted converts to be able to read the Bible. They needed to train African teachers. Both they and the colonial administrations also needed clerks who could write letters and keep accounts. For a long time, no one thought of providing more than this, and practically all education was conducted in local languages. Figures of school enrolment were low. This was partly because staff and funds were short, but mainly because few African parents in those days were interested in European education.

Developments in Europe After 1850, the attitude to education in Europe changed. Education was no longer regarded as a luxury for the rich or for the lucky few who won scholarships. People began to regard it as a universal right. They considered that the state had a duty to make education available to everyone. In 1870, for example, the British government first spent public money on providing primary schools. In 1902 it provided secondary schools. For many years, however, opportunities for secondary education remained limited, until after 1945.

This new attitude created many difficulties which are still far from being solved. The numbers of pupils have increased. The curriculum has become complicated. Some of the new subjects require elaborate equipment in laboratories and workshops. There is much specialization and new teaching methods. The system of public examinations has become large and complex.

To understand the problems in African education, we must bear in mind that all these changes in Europe took place during the colonial period. The year in which Britain first had state-financed secondary schools (1902) was also the year when the first European settlers arrived in Kenya.

People are the most valuable resource that any country has and children are especially important because they will create tomorrow's world. It is therefore essential that they receive a good education to give them the knowledge to help themselves and their countries.

In traditional societies, parents teach young people the skills and trades needed in their daily lives.

Problems for African Education

The chief difficulties for the development of African education are the isolation of many parts of the continent; lack of money; language problems; and the shortage of text-books.

Isolation The great size of Africa and the vast distances involved create many problems in education. For example, Sudan is ten times as large as Britain. Some areas are thinly populated and schools are far apart. In the rainy season, some schools become isolated.

Lack of Money The greatest difficulty of all is Africa's poverty. Even though they receive aid from overseas and may spend 30–40 per cent of their own revenue on education, African governments cannot provide all the schools and colleges that they need. There are insufficient buildings and equipment. Only a small proportion of pupils leaving primary schools will go on to a secondary school.

Below left This group of school-children in Botswana take a reading lesson out-of-doors. The school buildings provide only limited space so the children share the available rooms by operating a shift system.

Below right A great shortage of text-books still exists in local languages. Children often have to be taught an unfamiliar language as a medium of instruction.

There are not enough colleges of education or universities. As a result, much of the teaching in primary schools is done by inadequately trained teachers. Many pupils therefore begin their secondary schooling with a shaky foundation. There are not enough school inspectors. Some subjects that require specialist staff and equipment, such as art, music, science and crafts, cannot always be taught. Pupils have to be content to study subjects that can be learned from text-books, such as history and geography. However, lack of money also keeps many school libraries starved of books.

Language Problems Another difficulty is the considerable number of languages spoken within one country. Almost every African country is divided into 20 or more areas where quite different languages are spoken. Some of the most widely spoken languages have been used in schools. This clearly puts the children who speak one of the other languages at a disadvantage. Secondary school children in one country should surely be taught in the same language for at least two reasons. The first

reason is to develop a sense of common nationality. The second is to make it possible economically to provide text-books. But in which language, out of the twenty or more, should they be taught?

In many countries, no African language has yet been accepted as the national language. At present English or French, which were inherited from the former colonial powers, are used instead. As a result, children have to learn English or French in the primary school as a second language. They then use this language as the medium of instruction in the secondary school. However, even if they use English, French or an unfamiliar African language, they are still at a disadvantage.

Shortage of Text-Books Connected with the language problem is another difficulty—the shortage of suitable text-books. Much has been done in the last 30 years in producing text-books for African schools. But teachers in Africa still do not have a wide choice.

A high proportion of the teachers in African secondary schools and colleges of education are still teachers on short contracts. There is inevitably a lack of teachers with the experience required for writing text-books. For various reasons, books produced for schools in Europe are usually unsuitable for use in African schools. Some cannot be used because the writer's attitude arouses opposition among African readers. Non-African writers of history books in particular tend to make assumptions which are unacceptable to their African readers.

Other books may be unsuitable because of their language and style. An African pupil needs books whose subject matter is of the same grade as that provided for an English or French pupil of the same age. But because European languages are foreign to him, the African pupil may find a European text-book difficult to understand. Writers therefore need experience of producing material for pupils to whom English or French is a second language.

Colonial Education

Faced with these great difficulties, the colonial powers made slow progress in African education. Education was at first left entirely to missionary societies and other voluntary bodies. Colonial governments had no money to spare for social services. Many of them could not balance their budgets without grants from the metropolitan powers. It did not occur to tax-payers in Europe that they had any duty to provide funds for African education. Today education in many parts of Africa is still largely influenced by the systems established during the colonial period. The colonial powers used different systems.

French Colonial Education

In French West Africa education was systematically organized, but not extensively developed. At first much was left to the missionary societies. But in 1903 and 1912 a system of government schools was decreed. These schools were organized in three grades: the village school; the rural regional school or urban school; and the higher primary school. The schools were designed to teach the French language and arithmetic, with some training in agriculture and in crafts. Enrolment was usually limited. The colonial administration accepted only that number of pupils for whom it could foresee finding employment.

For example, at Dakar, in Senegal, there was one college, the William Ponty college. This college trained teachers and, after 1924, medical assistants also. In 1938 it had 220 students. In 1939 French West Africa had 310 village schools, 96 regional and 26 urban schools. In 1945 there were about 111,000 pupils attending schools in French West Africa. In French Equatorial Africa, education was even less developed.

Every country needs more than skilful masons, carpenters and mechanics. It needs professional men, businessmen, administrators and politicians. All of these must have skilled people to work under them. Every country also needs educated women. A great African, Dr. Aggrey, once said that educating a man was educating an individual, but that educating a woman was educating a family.

Belgian, German and Portuguese Colonial Education

Before 1914, the Belgians in the Congo (now Zaire) and the German colonial authorities seemed to have worked along the same lines. In German East Africa (1884–1916) Swahili was made the medium of instruction for the whole country. This provided Tanganyika (now Tanzania) with a national language. When the British took over Tanganyika from Germany in 1919, they were impressed to find that African staff were used to working from written instructions. In the Congo, the Belgians set up an extensive system of primary and craft schools, but there was not enough secondary education. The Belgians believed that if the Africans were trained to earn themselves a comfortable living, they would not be concerned with politics. In former Portuguese territories, Portuguese was the only medium of instruction, and all text-books were printed in Portuguese.

British Colonial Education

In British colonial Africa, missionary societies were left free to provide as much education as they could. They also received financial help from government funds. In the Gold Coast the first government grants were made to schools in 1882. A government department of education was established there in 1890. The first grant in Kenya, was made in 1922, but by then Kenya already had a few schools of its own.

Secondary schools run by the missions were opened in the Gold Coast in 1876, in Sierra Leone as early as 1845, in Uganda in 1904, and in Kenya in 1926. Although a government technical school and a teacher training college were opened in the Gold Coast in 1909, it was not until after World War I (1914–18) that any British colonial government opened its own secondary school. Makerere in Uganda was opened in 1922, and Achimota in the Gold Coast was opened in 1924. Both of them were intended to become full secondary schools.

Secondary schools in British tropical Africa were helped to maintain their academic standards by permitting their pupils to enter for British public examinations. During the 1930s the Cambridge Local Examinations Syndicate, in consultation with teachers in Africa, did much useful work in adapting syllabuses in biology, geography and some other subjects to suit the needs of African candidates. It was careful at the same time to maintain its academic standards. It therefore qualified successful candidates for entry to universities and professional bodies in Britain.

No restrictions were placed on Africans who wished to go to Britain or elsewhere for higher education. No government scholarships were granted before 1939. But Achimota College and some voluntary bodies awarded scholarships. The resulting group of professional men who had been at college in Britain provided a nucleus for the rising nationalist movement.

▲ Children manage without desks or chairs in a temporary building.

Girls in the playground of the Chikuni Mission at Monzi, Zambia. Missionary societies have provided both finance and teaching staff to many schools. ▼

Differences in Colonial Policy

An important difference between education in British colonies and in French or Belgian colonies was the place given to African languages.

In French-speaking Africa one of the main purposes of the schools was to produce African teachers with a good knowledge of the French language. To achieve this, African languages were banned from the classroom. Only French was permitted. This policy suited the convenience of the colonial power. But it had some justification on educational grounds. It greatly eased the problem of text-books. Once a pupil had mastered the language, he could read all French books. He then had no need for educational material in his mother tongue. The French thought that this great advantage outweighed the initial disadvantage of teaching young children in French from the very beginning of their school life.

The British argued differently. They were so impressed with the initial difficulty that their policy was to begin schooling in the children's mother tongue. English was introduced as a second language. The British believed that, by the end of the primary school course, a child would understand English well enough to use it as the medium of instruction.

The educational theory behind this idea was sound. But in practice the British could not carry out their scheme effectively. Out of some 400 languages spoken in British tropical Africa, only about 100 were ever used in school. There was little if any reading material in most of these languages. English was often inefficiently taught in primary

schools. Teachers in secondary schools had to spend too much of their time in remedying the deficiencies of the primary school's English teaching.

These defects were not apparent in the 1920s and 1930s, when enrolment in the primary schools was low and the proportion of trained teachers was high. But the defects became terribly plain when the primary school system expanded. The classes became large and most teachers were untrained.

One, good feature of secondary education in British Africa was that some African languages were accepted by the Cambridge Local Examinations Syndicate. In some secondary schools, efforts were made to cultivate the literary study of these languages. No similar work was undertaken in French schools. But a great impetus was given to African studies by the foundation in 1938 of the *Institut Français d'Afrique Noire* (now the *Institut Fondamental d'Afrique Noire*) at Dakar.

Primary reading books published in the Xhosa language of South Africa. Modern educational books have a strong visual content with simple text and colourful, interesting pictures. ▼

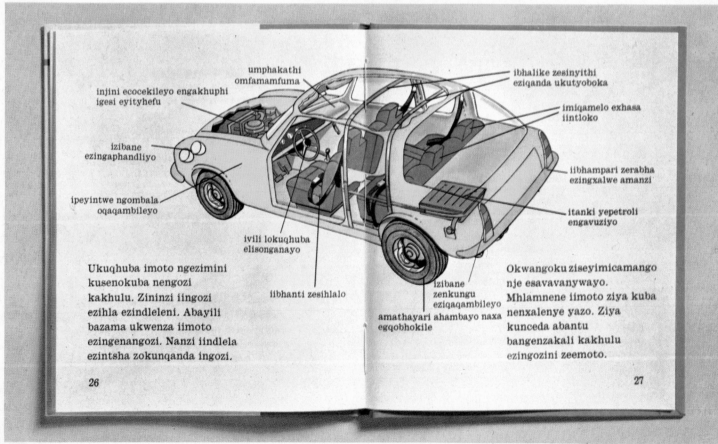

26

27

Education for Independence In spite of the distrust felt by senior British officials for 'bookish' education, the policy of the Colonial Office in London changed after World War I. The British government came to regard itself as a trustee for the African peoples. It believed that it was responsible for preparing its African colonies for independence, which it thought must inevitably come one day.

This policy was laid down for East Africa in a British government document called the *Devonshire White Paper* (1923). It was already being applied in West Africa, where there were no European settlers. In 1923, greatly to the benefit of education all over British tropical Africa, the Colonial Office set up an advisory committee on education. This committee began to issue professional advice to education departments in Africa and elsewhere.

Gradual Progress

African interest in European education increased slowly. In the Gold Coast, which was relatively wealthy, primary school enrolment rose from about 15,000 in 1902 to 50,000 in 1924, and 63,000 in 1935. In Kenya the figures were 2,000 in 1906, 43,000 in 1923, and about 100,000 in 1935. After 1935, the African demand for education increased. The Gold Coast enrolment rose to 185,000 in 1945 and to 301,000 in 1951. The enrolment in Kenya rose to 129,000 in 1938, 207,000 in 1946 and passed 500,000 in 1955.

One favourable result of the slow increase in enrolment before 1935 was that at first, at least in the more prosperous colonies, the British were able to make great improvements in quality. They provided better buildings and equipment, more training of teachers, and a higher proportion of trained teachers in primary schools. After 1935, however, quantity overtook quality.

When education came under the control of African statesmen, as for example in the Gold Coast in 1951, these ministers made universal primary education their first priority. They were prepared to accept a decline in inefficiency. They thought that any decline would be temporary and that schools would improve again, when funds were available and there were more trained teachers.

PROGRESS IN ENROLMENT IN EDUCATION
Figures are percentages of children in each age group.

	Primary		Secondary		Higher	
	1960	latest	1960	latest	1960	latest
Algeria	46	70	8	9	0.79	0.98
Angola	21	59	2	7	—	0.25
Benin (Dahomey)	26	36	2	4	—	0.08
Botswana	42	78	1	7	—	—
Central African Republic	35	75	1	4	—	—
Chad	15	27	0.4	2	—	—
Gabon	95	100	5	13	—	0.14
Ghana	38	56	2	5	0.18	0.65
Ivory Coast	46	72	2	10	0.10	1.02
Kenya	49	60	3	8	0.04	0.67
Liberia	38	64	2	11	0.56	1.23
Malawi	39	37	1	3	—	0.21
Mozambique	53	55	2	4	—	0.14
Niger	6	14	0.3	1	—	—
Nigeria	37	28	3	3	0.06	0.24
Senegal	27	44	3	?	0.50	0.90
Sierra Leone	22	32	3	8	0.18	?
South Africa	82	92	28	30	?	3.82
Sudan	17	25	5	9	0.38	0.87
Tanzania	25	37	2	3	—	0.13
Uganda	44	54	5	4	0.15	—
Zaire	72	100	3	11	?	0.68
Zambia	42	74	2	14	—	0.39
Zimbabwe	99	100	2	7	0.08	0.24

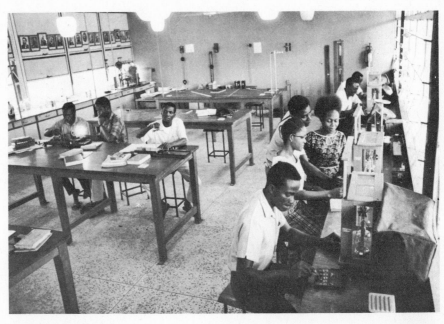

▲ The modern physics laboratory at the College of Education, University of Lagos. Many young people are encouraged to continue their education after school.

◀ A cookery demonstration in a school canteen. Adult education is considered to be of great importance today.

A trainee machinist in ▶ the machine shop of the Government Arts and Crafts Training Centre, Addis Ababa.

65

University Education

As early as 1920, a political movement, the Congress of British West Africa, called for a West African federal university. But there was little university or higher technical education in Africa before 1939. Fourah Bay College in Sierra Leone was affiliated to Durham University in England as early as 1876 and its students were able to obtain Durham degrees. In South Africa, there were opportunities for Africans to study at universities. Achimota in the Gold Coast was recognized by London University for civil and mechanical engineering, and produced its first graduate engineer in 1935.

In 1944, the British government appointed a commission to advise on the development of university education in its colonies. Through the work of this commission and of others, the British established universities at Ibadan, Khartoum, Makerere, Freetown, and Legon, near Accra. The multiracial university at Salisbury in Zimbabwe was founded somewhat later with help from Britain. Higher technical colleges were established at Nairobi, Kumasi, Enugu and elsewhere. Most of these were later recognized as universities. Funds for these new institutions were provided by Britain.

After independence the three East African governments abandoned the British idea of a federal East African university. They decided that each country should have its own university, and Makerere, Nairobi and Dar es Salaam were accordingly promoted.

Education and Society

In pre-colonial Africa education was carried on by the family and the clan. In the modern African states of today it is mainly carried on by the schools. How can the school and the family be kept in touch, so that the parents understand what the school is doing? How can the parents gain some benefit themselves from the schools?

Community development An educationist in Africa once said that if a village had a school, but was full of flies and mosquitoes then he knew that the school was not doing its job. In 1944, a British Colonial Office committee produced a report on what it called *mass education*, which is now usually called *community development*. This report recognized that ignorance and poverty produced apathy. People were used to hunger, sickness, flies and mosquitoes. It did not occur to them that anything could be done about these things. They thought that such matters should be dealt with by the government, if it cared.

The idea of community development is that people should be made to realize that they can help themselves. They can run adult literacy groups, build dams for watering cattle, drain marshes to get rid of mosquitoes, and build themselves village halls and clinics. In such ways the school and the village people could help each other. In 1952, an Anglo-African educational conference recommended that high priority should be given to such projects.

As the figures in the table on page 65 show,

▲ One of the impressive buildings of Nairobi University.

◄ President Nyerere of Tanzania addressing the University College at Nairobi when it was part of the University of East Africa.

Sir Seretse Khama, President of Botswana, on his way to give degrees to students at Roma University. ▼

African countries are making efforts to develop education. The figures show enrolment in primary, secondary, and higher education, expressed as a percentage of the number of children in each age group. In each group—primary, secondary or higher—the figures are given for 1960, and also for the latest available year, usually 1968 or 1969.

For comparison, the figures are also given for metropolitan Portugal. Portugal used to claim that her former African territories—Angola and Mozambique and others—were not colonies but provinces of the mother country. The figures show that educational development in these territories is more typical of Africa than of Europe.

In addition to formal education in schools and colleges, several African governments have large programmes of community development but a great deal still needs to be done. Much primary education is inefficient. Schooling is often regarded as a means of escaping from a village to a town, and a boy who cannot find a job in the town dares not go home and confess failure. Even the wealthy western countries are finding the continued expansion of school and college education a heavy burden. Africa will not have the funds or the personnel to be able to equip itself with a complete system of education along western lines. What then should be an African government's priorities?

Educational Priorities Education cannot be planned in isolation from other aspects of social policy. Most Africans live outside the towns. Until government revenues are greatly increased, most of them will have to be content with primary education. If farming could be made more productive, it would help greatly in increasing revenue. But people will not be persuaded to remain in the country, when all amenities of life, such as electricity, piped water, hospitals, cinemas and libraries, are concentrated in the towns. The villages must also be made comfortable, with projects of rural housing, water, electricity and other comforts. Community development projects could help greatly in this area. This is the basic thinking behind Julius Nyerere's famous policy of Ujamaa villages and Education for Self-reliance in Tanzania.

People in developed countries often say that education should enable an individual to develop his own gifts. But in Africa the family is more important than the individual. As a result, education is most needed as a service to society.

From this point of view planners must consider how many qualified people they can afford to train. They must also bear in mind that a balance should be kept between the higher grades and their subordinate staff, such as an engineer and his surveyors and draughtsmen. The laboratories and workshops in technical colleges should be full, not half empty. The primary and secondary schools must also produce enough students for training as teachers, and for filling the universities and higher technical colleges that exist. Some experts doubt the value of maintaining inefficient primary schools. Some argue that the number should be restricted to as many schools as can be properly staffed and equipped, and can effectively fulfil their function of teaching children. The numbers of primary schools can be increased as more money becomes available for equipment and more teachers are trained.

Those who leave primary school and go no further need not give up hope. School education should be supplemented by adult education perhaps along the lines of extension work elsewhere. Literature bureaux should provide cheap reading material and help people retain the literacy they acquired in school.

An educational system should be balanced. It should not be designed as a copy of something in Europe or the United States, but for Africa's own needs. African education was originally planned by Europeans. For many years, Africans were concerned with the idea of showing that they were the intellectual equals of their colonial rulers. They have now demonstrated that this is so and that stage is now past.

African countries can now afford to modify their school curricula and methods. They can set the standards they require. Education should not be designed to produce people who can fit into professional bodies in Europe but people who are useful in their own country. Education in Africa should be planned for national development.

◄ A Malawian farmer inspects his maize crop which is about to be harvested. He is taking part in the Lilongwe Land Development Programme. The aims of this project are to teach farmers how to increase their crop yields by using modern farming methods.

◄ Wives being taught how to grow tobacco plants by an agricultural adviser. More and more emphasis is being given to practical education for the community.

Student farmers listen to a lecture on crop cultivation at an agricultural college. ▼

EDUCATION IN NORTH AFRICA

Little is known about the system of education in Ancient Egypt, but it would have been closely linked to religious training. By 3000 BC the priests of Ancient Egypt knew how to read and write. They used *hieroglyphic* (sacred) script. *Demotic* script, used by ordinary people, developed from hieroglyphics. Archaeologists have found many thousands of *papyri* (documents written on paper made from papyrus reed) which show that many people knew how to read and write and that business deals as well as religious texts, were written down.

Egypt reached a high cultural standard under the Ptolemaic dynasty (323–30 BC) Scholars from other countries came to Egypt to study at the great Library of Alexandria. Greek and Coptic were the languages used. Coptic was the ancient language of Egypt written in Greek characters with some other

signs. As a whole, the Egyptian cities had a high degree of literacy. From the AD 100s to the AD 400s, some of the great early Christian theologians lived in Egypt. Known as the Alexandrines, they developed many of the Christian doctrines.

In the Roman North Africa, education was based on the Latin system. Private schools existed both in cities and small towns. The period of Roman domination in North Africa produced many distinguished scholars, of whom St. Augustine was one of the most outstanding.

In the AD 600s, the Muslim Arabs overran North Africa. More than a century passed before their traditions merged with the local traditions of learning. A new educational system, which had originally come from Iraq and Syria, grew up. Every town and village had schools. The most important function of the schools was to teach boys religious doctrine and

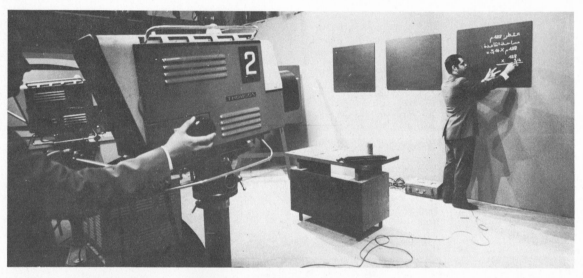

◀ The use of television and radio as teaching media is increasing in Africa. A lecturer in Tunis gives an arithmetic lesson by television.

Students sit a geography exam at the Training Institute for Secondary School Teachers, Omdurman, Sudan. ▼

to teach them to read the Koran. Grammar and arithmetic were also taught.

In the larger cities, *madrassahs*, or teaching mosques, were founded. They were, and still are, the universities of North Africa. The most celebrated madrassah is the al-Azhar in Cairo, which was founded in AD 972. It is still an important centre of learning and now accepts students from Africa south of the Sahara as well as from the Arab countries. Other important madrassahs are those at Fez, Marrakech and Qayrawan.

The universities of Egypt and North Africa were founded long before the first European universities, which were established in the 1200s. The main subjects were theology, philosophy, Islamic law and the natural sciences, including medicine. A degree course equivalent to a modern doctorate could take as long as 17 years to complete. The Islamic educa-

Below left A teacher taking an evening class in Rabat, Morocco, run by the 'Youth and Society' organization. This organization was formed by student and civil servant volunteers who teach basic subjects.

Below right An 8th-century book, the Koran of Sultan Shaban.

Bottom right A view of the courtyard of the al-Azhar, Cairo, one of the world's most famous teaching mosques.

tion system did not make any provisions for the education of women, although many learned to read and write at home.

During the colonial period, Algeria, Morocco and Tunisia fell under French dominance, and Egypt under British control. Schools and, eventually, universities of European type were set up alongside the traditional system. The first European-type schools, including medical and engineering colleges, were founded in Egypt during the reign of Khedive Muhammad Ali (1805–48).

Since independence, Algeria, Egypt, Libya, Morocco and Tunisia have all made considerable progress in developing education. The modern systems include primary and secondary schools, technical institutions and universities. In many of the educational institutions, women and girls receive equal opportunity with men and boys.

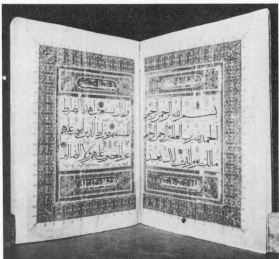

HEALTH AND MEDICINE

The challenge that faces those who care for the health of the people in Africa lies in understanding their real problems and finding solutions that work within the context of their own culture. Most of these solutions will be very simple, such as encouraging families to continue looking after their own sick, promoting good nutrition or advising a mother on weaning her child. Some will be more complicated, such as developing drugs for the treatment of leprosy or tuberculosis. Others will mean not adopting potentially harmful habits, such as bottle-feeding or over-independence on hospitals.

There are two broad attitudes to medicine and disease. The scientific-technological approach looks for specific explanations of disease, based on observations and tested by experiments. The traditional approach is connected with spiritual or psychological forces. In most societies, both approaches exist side by side. For example, in many parts of Africa technologically trained doctors are expected to treat broken bones or perform operations, but not mental illness which is the preserve of traditional healers. The Marabout of Senegal is a religious leader but he will also extract teeth and incise abscesses. The Mganga in East Africa is a herbalist and psychiatrist, as well as a spell-binder. Certainly many of the practices of traditional medicine, such as the use of experienced women for midwives can be both effective and mean that communities are responsible for their own health. The operation of boring a hole in the skull, or *trephining* to relieve brain pressure or let out evil spirits has been carried out for centuries by traditional healers in Ethiopia, Uganda and Nigeria without the use of the delicate equipment available to a trained brain surgeon. The Masai in Kenya stitched torn vessels with tendon. In Liberia, bone fractures have been treated by traction, with the limb fixed to the floor by pegs. Quinine from the bark of the cinchona tree was used to cure malaria long before the parasite which causes the disease was discovered.

Antibiotics used against infections, vaccines for smallpox and pesticides which stop the breeding of malaria-carrying mosquitos are powerful weapons against disease. But it is just as necessary to understand the conditions in which diseases flourish and the nature of beliefs about health and sickness. Technological resources, human and financial, for looking after health are scarce everywhere. Even Nigeria which assigns about 10 per cent of its budget to health care only has available £0.16 per person compared with about £120.00 in the U.S. But whatever the background, the task should be the same everywhere: to care for the sick, to attempt to cure and, above all, to prevent disease using the simplest measures. It is also very important that communications should be good enough for drugs and health programmes to be able to reach people in the remoter areas of Africa.

◀ A Xhosa woman holding up her X-ray plate. X-rays can be used to show bone fractures and diseased tissues in the human body.

Doctors examining Tunisian children for signs of trachoma. Trachoma is a virus infection affecting the eyes and often causing blindness. This infection is common in hot, dry areas where people have poor sanitation and unhealthy living conditions. ▶

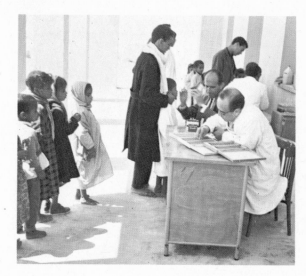

NOTE: SEE PAGE 77 FOR A GLOSSARY OF MEDICAL TERMS.

Health and Illness

The health of individuals and communities can be looked on as an *ecological system* made up of host, environment and disease agent. The disease agent can be a germ or a harmful alteration in the way of life. The disease agent has to be of sufficient intensity. The environment for the disease agent must be favourable and the resistance of the host must be overcome before there is illness. *Endemic* diseases are regularly present in many communities. Chronic malnutrition, malaria, tuberculosis, heart disease, anaemia are examples of endemic diseases. *Epidemic* diseases occur in sudden outbreaks. They include typhoid, smallpox, plague and measles. *Pandemic* diseases, such as influenza and cholera, sweep through large areas of the world.

Illness is easy enough to understand from one's own experience. Yet someone may feel healthy while the parasites of malaria are living in his blood cells or while the germ of tuberculosis is in his lungs. A child may look healthy to his parents because he is the same as all the other children in his family but all of them may be suffering from a poor diet.

TEN MAJOR DISEASES

Disease	Main Areas	Organism causing disease	Method of Spreading	Main Symptoms and Signs	Prevention or Treatment
Bilharzia	Egypt and North Africa, Sudan, North Ethiopia, Uganda, Congo, West Africa	Parasite	Life cycle in snails and water. Penetrates skin in water	Damage to involved tissue; bleeding from bladder and gut; in endemic areas much infection without signs	Kill snails; reduce contacts with infected water; chemotherapy
Cancer	All areas, especially 'ageing' population. Specific types found locally: i.e. jaw cancer in Ugandan children	Generally unknown: viruses sometimes responsible; radiation; chemicals	Non-communicable	Depends on part of body involved: cancer cells reproduce indiscriminately disorganizing tissues and spread to other parts of body, for example, lung to kidney or gut to liver	Surgery; cytoxic drugs; radiation
Dysentery (amoebic)	Tropics and Sub-tropics; North Africa	Parasitic amoeba	Contaminated food	Recurrent attacks; Mucus and blood-stained diarrhoea; usually painless	Improve sanitation; chemotherapy
Dysentery (bacillary)	Tropics and Sub-tropics; North Africa	Bacteria	Contaminated food and water; flies	Acute diarrhoea: colic and bloody mucus passed; dehydration; exhaustion. Mild cases are common	Improve hygiene; replace water loss; antibiotics
Filariasis	North Africa; West, Central and East Africa	Parasite worm	mosquito vector	Tissue inflammation and swelling generally involving legs	Elimination of vectors; chemotherapy
Leprosy	Nigeria, Congo, Central African Republic, Upper Volta, Benin (Dahomey)	Bacteria	Close contact for some time	Different types: 1) many bacteria; involving nasal mucosa, skin and nerves; lumps and areas of pigment loss or thickening in skin. 2) less bacteria; localized skin patches and nerves; loss of sensation, paralysis and gross deformities from damage to numbed areas	Immunization; chemotherapy
Malaria	Widely distributed; rare above 6,000 feet	Protozoan parasite (Several types: falciparum, vivax, malaria and ovale)	Mosquito vector; parasite migrates to salivary glands and infects at site of the bite	Symptoms depend on exposure of individual and community and type. Relapsing fevers; rigors; chronic or acute anaemia; enlargement of spleen with high mortality in non-immune infants; Blackwater fever	Eradication or control of the parasite by spraying breeding grounds or use of anti-malarial drugs
Trachoma	North Africa; Egypt; hot, dry areas with poor sanitation	Virus	Contact with infected cases and inadequate personal hygiene	Damage to the eye, initially the covering of the conjunctiva. Vessels spread over the cornea leading to loss of vision and eventually blindness, complicated by bacterial infection. In endemic areas mild or symptomless infections are common	Improve living conditions and water supply; reduce dust, dirt and flies; chemotherapy; surgical repair
Trypanosomiasis	A wide, patchy belt from Senegal and South Sudan to Okavango swamps in Botswana. Guinea, Ghana, Gambia, Nigeria, Sierra Leone, Congo and Cameroon	Protozoan parasite	Tsetse fly vector. Transmission depends on the number of man/fly contacts; animal reservoirs	Swelling at site of bite; Parasites in blood stream; later chronic, irregular fever, apathy, lethargy; involvement of central nervous system leading to confusion, falling asleep while eating and eventually coma. Time course varies	Clear areas of tsetse flies and reduce man/fly contacts; chemotherapy
Tuberculosis	Widespread	Bacteria	Direct infection; 'open' cases cough up bacteria in their sputum	Chronic disease; mild attacks protect in adult life; lungs affected, involvement leading to breathlessness, pneumonia, fluid in the chest and coughing up blood	BCG immunization treatment; Improved living conditions; Chemotherapy
Venereal Diseases Gonorrhoea	Worldwide	Bacteria	Sexual	*Male*—pain, discharge from urethra; swelling groin glands. *Female*—discharge from womb, infection of the tubes from the ovaries	Chemotherapy Treat carriers
Syphilis	Worldwide	Spirochaetes	Sexual	*Male*—sore at tip of penis. *Female*—sore at neck of womb. If untreated: rash; later involvement of brain and heart	High dose of penicillin; gonorrhoea and syphilis often treated at same time

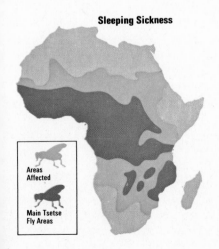

Sleeping Sickness

Areas Affected

Main Tsetse Fly Areas

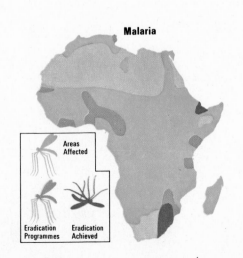

Malaria

Areas Affected

Eradication Programmes   Eradication Achieved

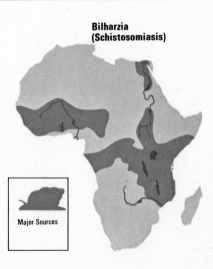

Bilharzia (Schistosomiasis)

Major Sources

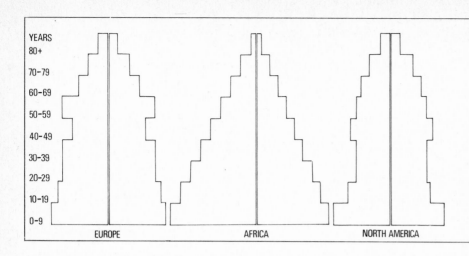

In Africa as a whole, between 40 and 50 per cent of the population are less than 15 years old. The African death rate is about double the English death rate but the birth rate is three times greater. The natural increase is, therefore, large. This means that although so many people are dying, the population is nevertheless increasing on average 2.5 per cent a year or doubling each 25–30 years.

YEARS
80+
70-79
60-69
50-59
40-49
30-39
20-29
10-19
0-9

EUROPE   AFRICA   NORTH AMERICA

◄ Chart showing the age-structure of populations in Europe, Africa and North America. The figures to the left show age groups. The pyramids show the proportion of the population in each age group.

Statistics about the Health of Populations

A healer or doctor compares our health as individuals with that of other people about whom he has experience. But he also needs to know something about the health and chances of getting particular diseases (risks) of whole communities. Such information about populations comes from a *census* which records births, deaths, marriages, occupations, and from records of diseases and population trends (*vital statistics*) kept by health workers.

The Geography of Diseases

The pattern of disease varies enormously across Africa. Dramatic killing diseases are present everywhere, together with minor complaints, such as colds, sore throats, skin diseases and earache.

In less privileged areas, illnesses are often associated with poverty, ignorance, inadequate feeding and frequent pregnancies and not so much due to the so-called 'tropical' diseases. In the richer regions, nutritional deficiency and infectious diseases due to inadequate waste disposal and contaminated water supplies are less common. But these regions show an increase in the 'degenerative' diseases, such as strokes and cancer, associated with ageing populations. Diseases of stress (heart attacks), diseases caused by industrial hazards (lung damage to miners, road traffic accidents) and diseases resulting from lack of exercise and overeating (obesity and sugar diabetes) are more evident in industrialized countries.

Diseases flourish because of a favourable natural or man-made environment or the presence of a suitable insect or animal carrier (*vector*). Trachoma is found mainly in the northern area towards the Mediterranean, while yellow fever occupies a broad band across the middle of Africa. The fly that transmits river blindness (onchocerciasis) breeds in fast-running streams mainly in Cameroon and Upper Volta. The tsetse fly transmits sleeping sickness (trypanosomiasis) and a mosquito malaria. Bilharzia (schistosomiasis) spreads around lakes or rivers where people come into contact with the snails which carry the disease.

Cancers also show marked regional variations. Cancer of the jaw occurs in Uganda. Cancer of the liver afflicts African people in southern Africa who cook in pots with a high iron content. Cancer of the gullet (oesophagus) attacks groups who drink beer fermented from maize. In such communities, this form of cancer is a common cause of death, yet neighbouring groups who ferment beer from millet have little oesophageal cancer.

Hereditary diseases, such as mental deficiency or dwarfism, are commoner in inbred societies. Some fevers found along the Mediterranean coast of Libya, Tunisia, Algeria and Morocco, which cause joint pains and kidney failure, are genetically transmitted. Sometimes hereditary disorders have beneficial effects. Sickle-cell anaemia, caused by an inherited defect in the haemoglobin (oxygen-carrying pigment) of the red blood cells, gives partial protection against malaria.

Kenyan children queue up to look through a microscope. They are looking at the parasite which causes *bilharzia*. ▼

Communicable and Infectious Diseases

The communicable and infectious diseases, together with malnutrition, are the most important health hazards to the people of Africa. Smallpox, diphtheria, whooping cough and influenza are spread by *direct transmission* from person to person. Tuberculosis is passed on through coughing and measles via droplets. Typhoid, cholera, the dysenteries and intestinal worms are spread through food and water contaminated by faeces or flies. *Indirect transmission* takes place when a stage of the *life-cycle* of the disease agent takes place outside the human host in a *vector* or carrier. This vector can be an insect, as with plague, yellow fever and malaria, or a snail as with bilharzia.

Typhoid, cholera, tetanus, tonsillitis, otitis media (infection of the middle ear), tuberculosis, leprosy and venereal disease are *bacterial diseases*. *Bacteria* destroy cells and may also produce poisons or *toxins* which travel in the blood stream away from the original site of entry into the body.

Smallpox, measles, mumps, polio, yellow fever, influenza and the common cold are *virus diseases*. *Viruses* are very small infective agents which multiply inside cells and destroy them. *Fungal infections* include ringworm and thrush (monilia).

Parasites live upon or in the body of another creature, the *host*, upon which they are dependent for their nourishment and ability to reproduce. The host can be man, animal, insect or plant. The parasite may be harmless or, by destroying vital parts or by its presence in large numbers, it may lead to illness or even the death of the host. Malaria parasites pass different parts of their life-cycle in the red-blood cells of man and in the stomach of the mosquito. The trypanosome parasite of sleeping sickness is carried by the tsetse fly. The bilharzia parasite lives in snails as well as in man. Loa-Loa, a worm infestation in West Africa which can attack the eye, is transmitted between man and monkeys in the rain forest by the mango fly.

Worm infestations include roundworm and pinworm which multiply in the gut when eaten with contaminated food. Tapeworm comes from inadequately cooked meat. Liver fluke occurs where sheep contaminate green vegetation. Hookworm penetrates generally through the exposed skin of bare feet and is a cause of anaemia, because the worm damages the lining of the intestines causing loss of blood.

Control of Disease

If the resources were available, many diseases could be prevented or at least their most damaging effects could be greatly reduced. Smallpox has been almost eradicated by immunization campaigns. An enormous improvement in the health and *quality of life* of the African people could be achieved simply by improving nutrition by growing more food. Much of the terrible toll taken by diseases, such as tuberculosis, malaria, typhoid and undernutrition, is not due to lack of knowledge but to a failure to apply this knowledge.

SOME COMMUNICABLE DISEASES

	Causative Organism	Mode of Spread	Main Symptoms and Signs	Prevention and Treatment
Cholera	Bacteria	Water	Acute watery diarrhoea, dehydration, collapse	Clean water; improve hygiene. Replace fluid loss
Diphtheria	Bacteria	Direct transmission	Sore throat with membrane blocking trachea; toxin causes heart damage	Immunization; antitoxin; chemotherapy
Infectious Hepatitis	Virus	Direct transmission: mosquitoes	Loss of appetite, fever, jaundice	Reduce reservoir of infection
Influenza	Virus	Droplet	Fever, headache, joint, back and muscle pains; secondary pneumonia	Immunization; chemotherapy
Leishmaniasis	Parasite	Sandfly	*Visceral*—chronic; fever, enlargement of the liver and spleen; anaemia; wasting *skin*—ulcerating sores	Control vector; chemotherapy
Loa Loa	Worm	Mango fly	'Calabar' swellings in skin or round joints; worms migrate under skin; microfilaria in circulation to eyes	Control vector; chemotherapy; remove adult worms
Onchocerciasis	Worm	Black fly	Skin nodules; thickened itching skin; eye involvement leads to blindness	Control vector; chemotherapy
Tetanus	Bacteria	Contaminated soil enters open wound	Toxin produces muscle tremors; later paralysis	Clean wounds; immunization; antitoxin; chemotherapy
Typhoid	Bacteria	Water	Fever; skin rashes; abdominal discomfort; gut perforation in severe cases	Improve water supplies; chemotherapy
Typhus	Rickettsia	Tick, louse	Fever; severe headache; rash; cerebral involvement with tremors and delirium	Control vector; chemotherapy
Yaws	Spirochaete	Direct contact	Involves skin, subcutaneous tissues and bone	Penicillin
Yellow fever	Virus	Mosquito	Acute fever; jaundice; protein loss in urine	Eradicate vector; vaccination

Insect carriers or *vectors* spread diseases. The anopheles mosquito carries malaria; the flea carries plague germs; the tsetse fly carries sleeping sickness. Modern pesticides help to destroy these dangerous insects.
▼

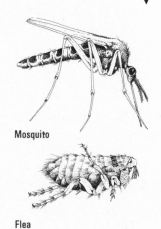

Mosquito

Flea

Tsetse Fly

Communicable diseases can be controlled by three main methods:

1. *Changing the environment* makes an area unsuitable for the disease carriers. For example, removing the wooded vegetation where the tsetse fly flourishes will control sleeping sickness. Draining the swampy breeding grounds of the mosquito will reduce malaria and yellow fever. Protecting wells from contamination by excreta from animals and men stops typhoid and cholera. If there are no infected rats in houses plague cannot spread.

2. *Changing habits or behaviour* may lead to less contact with harmful agents. Wearing shoes or sandals stops hookworm. Reducing bathing or washing clothes in infested water cuts down bilharzia. Stopping cigarette smoking reduces lung infection and cancer.

3. *Building up immunity* increases the resistance of the population. A person builds up his resistance by being well fed and also *actively* by coming into contact with a disease and surviving. Where malaria and tuberculosis are endemic, adults have a strong immunity and their attacks are often mild. The danger is that severe infections may be overwhelming the first time and so children, particularly if their resistance is already weakened by underfeeding, are most vulnerable. *Immunization* and *vaccination* are methods of *passively* or artificially giving protection against some infectious diseases.

Shortage of Food

Africa has millions of underfed people. Undernutrition occurs when the diet does not provide enough *calories*, the energy in food, or sufficient of the other constituents. *Malnutrition* means that some of the essential constituents, such as vitamins or protein, are lacking or not present in the right amounts even though there may be sufficient calories, say from carbohydrate, in the diet. *Famine* is severe food shortage affecting a whole region.

Foods contain varying amounts of protein, fat, carbohydrate and vitamin. A 'balanced' diet has them in the right proportions. Protein is used for building up cells, bones and muscles. Fat and carbohydrate provide stored reserves and food for energy. Vitamins control chemical reactions in cells that are responsible for body building and energy transfer.

One problem, which could be tackled, is that many foods, which form the major part of the diet of some societies, are cereals which contain much carbohydrate and little protein. The Baganda of Southern Uganda eat plantains as a staple diet, the Basotho maize and the Arabs rice. Customs also sometimes prevent young girls and pregnant women from eating eggs or drinking milk. This contributes to malnutrition, because young women, who are growing or 'feeding' a baby in their womb, most need the protein and calcium in these foods.

Malnutrition, in addition to its own harmful effects, contributes to a large number of deaths from infectious and communicable diseases in adults as well as in infancy and during childbirth. This happens because the resistance of a poorly nourished person to disease or suffering is much reduced. Improvement in nutrition needs the efforts of agriculturalists and preventive workers.

Children Under Five

The nutritional deficiency disorders of *kwashiorkor* (lack of protein) and *marasmus* (starvation from combined protein and calorie deficiency) most seriously affect young children. The survivors risk

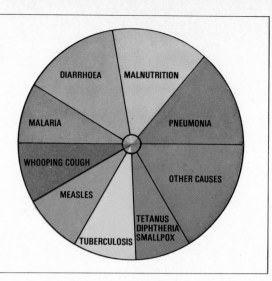

Between 15 and 20 per cent of the population of the less industrialized African countries are less than five years old. Yet deaths in this age group can be between 35 and 60 per cent of all deaths. For comparison, under-fives in Europe make up an average of 10 per cent of the population and only 7 per cent of all deaths. For the one to four year old age group, the death rate may be as high as 300 to 500 per 1,000. This appalling death rate is caused by a combination of malnutrition, diarrhoea, anemia, and such infections as pneumonia, malaria, measles, tuberculosis and tetanus.

permanently stunted growth and impaired mental development. It has to be remembered that these children will eventually make up the adult community.

Clinics, where mothers regularly bring their children of under five years old, have been set up in many countries including Botswana, Kenya, Lesotho, Malawi, Nigeria, Tanzania and Zambia. The mother attends once a month with her child, who is weighed and given vaccinations. She takes a chart home recording his progress. At Ilesha in Nigeria, after several years' experience with such an Under-Fives Clinic, mortality in childhood has dropped by 50 per cent.

Above Chart showing major causes of death in African children under five years. *Below left* These three babies are all nearly the same weight (2.75–3.25 kilos). The baby on the extreme right is new-born while the centre baby is two months old and the one on the left is aged four months. Doctors may not be aware that a child is undernourished unless they know the exact age.

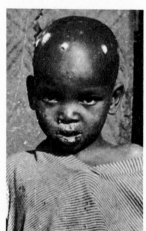

▲ This six-year-old Lesotho boy has the first signs of pellagra, a deficiency disease.

◄ Mothers and children wait for food and medical supplies in drought-stricken Ethiopia in 1974.

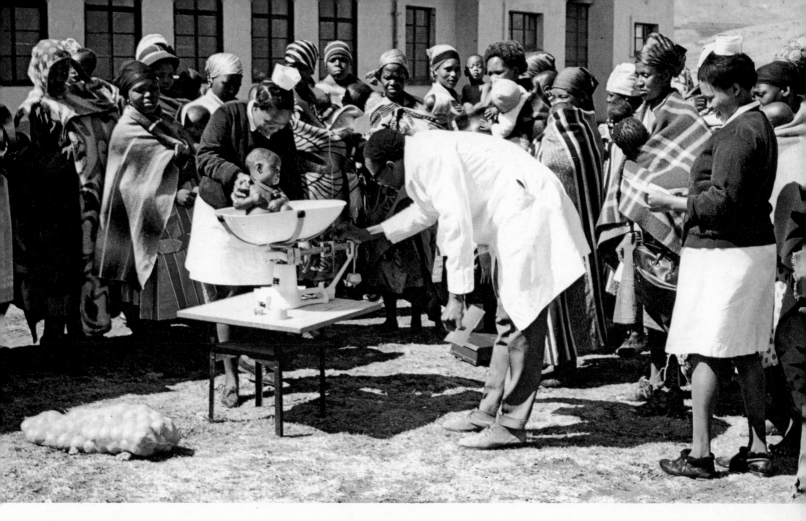

Spacing the Family

The large size of families in areas where food is scarce and living conditions are overcrowded is a major cause of high child mortality, anaemia and the premature death of women who have borne many children. In many parts of Africa, children are born into a family in quick succession. The dangers have long been recognized—*kwashiorkor* in the language of the Ga people in Ghana means 'the disease of the deposed baby'.

It is impossible to dictate the numbers of people in an 'ideal' family. Some parts of the continent could quite certainly support larger populations than they have now. But some form of *family spacing*— that is controlling the intervals between births—is probably necessary today to ensure the good health of most populations. Traditional societies some- times control the interval between pregnancies by such customs as the avoidance of intercourse while a woman is breast feeding. But modern techniques of birth control—the oral *contraceptive* pill, plastic coils in the womb (*intra-uterine devices I.U.D.'s*), rubber sheaths (*condoms*) for the man, used with a chemical that kills sperms which fertilize the egg (*spermicides*)—are far more efficient.

Man-made Hazards to Health

Man, unfortunately, continues to create an in- creasing number of hazards to his own health in addition to threats to plant and animal life. High technology, fast transport systems, radiation from new sources of energy, the vast problem of disposal of industrial wastes, accumulation of poisonous pesticides, and the unpredictable effects of changing

▲ **Mothers bring their babies to a clinic in Lesotho. The doctors and nurses examine and weigh the babies. They also advise the mothers on nutrition, immunization against disease and other health matters.**

Diagram showing the life cycle of the disease parasite which causes bilharzia. ▼

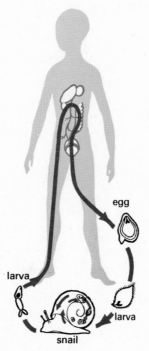

the natural environment, all have repercussions for the African people.

Every major man-made lake in Africa contains snails infected with the agents of bilharzia. Ten years after the completion of the Kariba dam, bilharzia affected 16 per cent of all age groups and 70 per cent of children living around the lake. Bilharzia from Lake Nasser is a danger hundreds of miles downstream in the Nile Valley. The wooded shorelines of the lakes may also attract the tsetse fly. Blackflies which transmit onchocerciasis breed in dam spillways. Irrigated areas have encouraged mosquitos in Sudan, the Kano plains and Kenya. Mosquitos also breed in water contained in old tins and car tyres in the urban areas.

In the mining industry, accidents from cutting machinery and rock falls are an obvious hazard. But dust particles also damage the lungs over many years causing *pneumoconiosis*, which leads to difficulty in breathing. Tuberculosis is common in crowded mining communities and cancer of the lung is a high risk among miners of asbestos and radioactive uranium.

Pollution of the environment is perhaps not yet recognized as a serious problem in Africa. But industries increasingly pour out smoke into the air and polluted water into the rivers and seas. Smoke and acidic sulphur dioxide fumes contribute to bronchitis; so does cigarette smoking. The motor car and the diesel engine are sources of harmful gases. Carbon monoxide, from exhaust fumes, dis- places oxygen from haemoglobin in the red blood cell. Road traffic accidents are also becoming an increasing cause of death and serious injury.

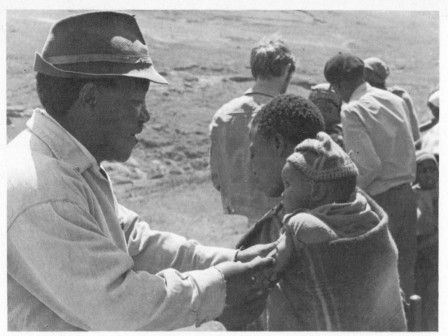

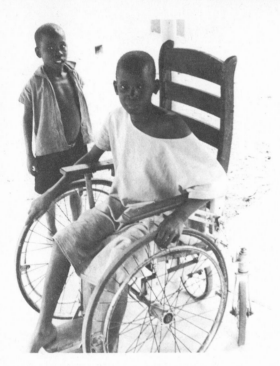

▲ A health visitor gives injections in a village which is suffering from a typhoid epidemic.

◄ A young boy uses a 'home-made' wheel chair made at Mkomaindo Hospital, Masasi, in Tanzania. Self-help schemes are essential in countries where doctors and equipment are in short supply.

CYCLES OF ILL-HEALTH

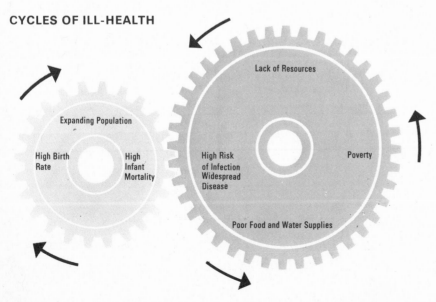

Expanding Population

High Birth Rate

High Infant Mortality

Lack of Resources

High Risk of Infection Widespread Disease

Poverty

Poor Food and Water Supplies

The World Health Organisation (W.H.O.)

The first article in the W.H.O. charter defines its aim as 'the attainment by all peoples of the highest possible level of health'. The W.H.O. operates as an independent agency of the United Nations. The regional office for Africa is in Brazzaville, capital of the Congo.

The W.H.O. has concentrated a great deal of effort in the field of *community health* in Africa. For example, vaccination and immunization schedules have been supported on a wide scale to combat smallpox, tetanus, diphtheria, tuberculosis and poliomyelitis. The organization has also developed curative programmes of drug treatments for tuberculosis, leprosy and yaws. Pesticides have been supplied for the eradication of the insect vectors of malaria and bilharzia.

Priorities in Care: Prevention or Cure?

The division of Africa into rich and poor nations is reflected as much in differing cultural views about health as by any other aspect of life. In any country, the city dweller can call on better professional, high-technology health services than the villager. But the villager can expect more support and care from his family when he is ill and, perhaps, more compassion and acceptance in his dying. The man with the means to buy his treatment has many, but not all, the advantages over the man with none.

Priorities are always difficult to establish because they mean concentrating effort on some areas and leaving others relatively untouched. But even rich nations cannot avoid these decisions. Evidence shows that the wealthier people become, the more demanding are their health 'wants'.

Curative services to treat people who are ill should be available for everyone. But this goal is difficult to achieve in practice because curative medicine is so costly. Furthermore, people still fall ill and the occurrence of new disease may only be reduced very slowly, if at all.

The preventive approach therefore aims to break the vicious circle of disease–treatment–more disease. Prevention is often cheap. The cost of treating one child with tuberculosis infection of the coverings of the brain equals the cost of protecting 7,000 children with anti-tuberculosis vaccine (BCG), and this vaccine also has an effect against leprosy. Prevention and simple forms of self-care involve everyone personally within the community itself rather than only those with illnesses who present themselves at clinics. Imagine a child who develops kwashiorkor after measles and then pneumonia. He needs a long stay in hospital, expensive drugs and plenty of food. Family spacing and a more balanced diet could have prevented the protein deficiency. Immunization could have prevented the measles and subsequent pneumonia.

Medical Resources: Distribution and Manpower

It is not easy to provide professional medical care of any but the most limited kind, when the money available to pay for it is often so restricted. With an annual income for each person of less than £30.00 it is probably impossible to provide basic health services on any but the most rudimentary scale. Ethiopia, Malawi, Tanzania and Lesotho fall into this group. Most African countries spend between £0.20 and £4.00 per head per year on health. For comparison, highly industrialized countries may spend between £40.00 and £100.

Distance is a most important factor determining whether patients can get treatment. It is a strange paradox that, while three-quarters of the people in Africa live in rural areas, most of the health services and doctors are in urban centres. In Ghana, for example, medical services cover only two-thirds of the people.

Hospitals can never by themselves provide a solution. Only a minority ever reach them and the cost of treatment is far too high for the money available. To give an idea of the range, treatment for an average illness costs about £21.00 at the national hospital in Nairobi compared with £0.26 at a rural health centre.

Health centres adapted to local conditions and situated in rural areas are one solution. The centres aim to bring at least some form of care within the range of most villagers. W.H.O. has proposed a minimum standard of one doctor and one health centre for every 10,000 people. The £5 million spent on the construction of the new hospital in Lusaka, Zambia, could have built 250 such centres. If each centre served 20,000 people, they would cover the entire population of Zambia.

Doctors Trained health workers at all levels are in desperately short supply. But the rural areas suffer from the shortage of doctors far more than the towns. In many areas, there is only one doctor for 25,000 people. In the northern states of Nigeria the ratio is as high as one doctor for 100,000 people. By comparison, the British National Health Service considers that a family doctor should have no more than 2,500 patients. The W.H.O. recommends a minimum of one doctor for 10,000 people. Britain and the United States have 12 to 16 times this minimum. Nigeria has half, Malawi one-fifth and Ethiopia one-tenth of W.H.O. minimum.

Medical Schools It takes six years to train a Western-style, scientifically-orientated doctor and the cost is very high. Although new schools are opening almost every year, the population is still increasing faster than new doctors are being trained, even in Nigeria which has recently been particularly active in opening medical schools. Each of the six universities in Nigeria has a medical school or college.

Nurses The situation of nurses is rather better. But nurses are only just beginning to be trained for a role outside hospitals. In some countries, such as Lesotho, nurse–doctor ratios are actually higher than in Europe because there are so few doctors.

Auxiliaries A practical approach, pioneered in Ethiopia and now used in Kenya, Tanzania, Zaire and Zambia, has been the training of para-medical staff or auxiliaries. Auxiliaries, health officers, and

DISEASES FOR WHICH IMMUNIZATION OR VACCINATION IS AVAILABLE

	Timing	Comments
Cholera	in epidemics	Partial protection only for 6 months.
Diphtheria	childhood	Combined with whooping cough and tetanus.
Measles	childhood	New: expensive.
Polio	childhood	Needs booster doses.
Smallpox	early	Needs booster doses.
Tetanus	childhood	Combined with diphtheria and whooping cough.
Tuberculosis	early	Also gives 80% protection against leprosy.
Typhoid	in epidemics	Partial protection for 6 months.
Whooping Cough	childhood	Combined with diphtheria and tetanus.
Yellow fever	early	Protection for 10 years.

The primary course usually involves several doses spaced at intervals to build up immunity. Repeat, or *booster* doses, given later keep up the level of protection.

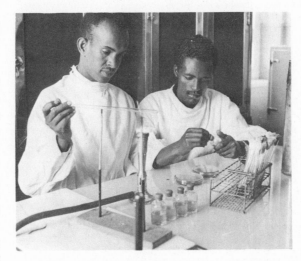

◄ Vaccine being tested in a laboratory in Addis Ababa. Vaccines, curative drugs and hospital services are very expensive. It is important, therefore, to tell communities about the causes of disease and how it can be prevented. Prevention is always better than cure.

A BRIEF GLOSSARY OF MEDICAL TERMS

Abdomen: part of the body containing all the organs between the chest and the pelvis
Anaemia: a deficiency or weakness of the blood. The commonest type is due to lack of iron
Antitoxin: a substance that neutralizes a toxin
Chemotherapy: a treatment with chemical drugs
Conjunctiva: white of eye
Delirium: a state of confusion, often seen with high fevers of long illness

Diarrhoea: frequent passing of liquid faeces
Endemic disease: a disease which occurs regularly in, and originates from, a particular area
Immunization: medical treatment which enables the body to produce protective antibodies
Parasite: an organism which lives on or in another organism (its host) and obtains food from it without benefiting, and often harming, the host

Penicillin: a type of drug known as an antibiotic used to attack germs or bacteria in the body
Pneumonia: an infection of the tissues of the lungs
Primary lesion: the first sign of a disease
Prophylaxis: prevention
Trachea: windpipe
Tremor: shaking, usually of the arms or legs
Toxins: poisons produced by some germs
Urethra: a tube that passes urine from the bladder

sanitarians are not substitutes for doctors, but they can be trained to perform a good deal of the simpler technical and diagnostic parts of his work. They can also give health education. It is much cheaper and quicker to train an auxiliary than a doctor. In China, this has been done on a national scale and each village has its own peasant 'barefoot doctor'.

New and simple ideas of this type reach out to people where they live and involve them directly. Such ideas are likely to determine the future pattern of health throughout Africa probably more than further technical advances, however tempting these may be.

THE LAND

Landscapes, Lakes and Rivers of Africa

Africa is the world's second largest continent and covers an area of 30.3 million square kilometres (11.7 million square miles). Because of its gigantic size, Africa often appears to be a region of wide horizons. Contrasts are rare and few physical barriers interrupt the almost limitless African landscape. The continent is made up of high plateau surfaces or tablelands in the east and south, whilst most of northern Africa is a low-lying region. The line dividing these areas, sometimes called *High* and *Low* Africa, runs roughly from the mouth of the Zaire River on the Atlantic coast, to the Gulf of Aden. South of this line, much of the land is over 910 metres (3,000 feet) above sea level. To the north of it most of the land is between 150 and 300 metres (500 and 1,000 feet) above sea level.

High Africa

The tablelands of High Africa were formed by forces within the earth's crust which, at various times, caused the occasional uplift and depression of giant blocks of land. Areas of ancient erosion surfaces, which were disturbed millions of years ago by a renewed uplift of the continent, are widespread in many parts of eastern and southern Africa.

Mountains of Ethiopia The most extensive area of highlands in Africa is in Ethiopia, where mountains rise to over 4,500 metres (15,000 feet). Here, Ras Dashen reaches 4,620 metres (15,158 feet). About 40 million years ago, an outburst of billions of tons of molten rock covered the area. Today, the deep gorges and flat-topped mountains of Ethiopia provide some of the most beautiful scenery in Africa. The BLUE NILE has cut its course through these volcanic rocks and those beneath them. North of the city of Addis Ababa, the river flows through a gorge which is more than 1,200 metres (4,000 feet) deep.

The Volcanoes of East Africa To the south of the Ethiopian highlands, a number of massive isolated volcanoes rise from the high East African plateau. The highest, Mount Kilimanjaro, is 5,895 metres (19,340 feet) above sea level. It stands on the Tanzanian border with Kenya. The snow-capped summit of the volcano, ringed with a collar of white cloud, can often be seen from more than 160 kilometres away. The other volcanoes of this group are Mount Kenya (5,200 metres—17,058 feet), Mount Meru (4,566 metres—14,979 feet) and Mount Elgon (4,321 metres—14,178 feet). These volcanoes were caused by the same earth movements which resulted from the magnificent African *rift valley* system (see the chapter on *Geology and Soils*, page 85, for a diagram of the East African Rift Valley System).

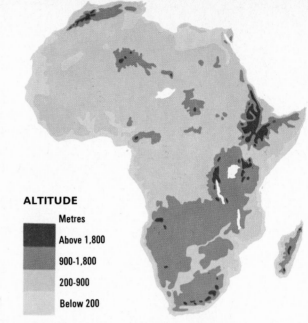

Right A map showing altitude and, *far right*, a map showing drainage patterns.

ALTITUDE

Metres

Above 1,800

900-1,800

200-900

Below 200

▲ The dramatic profile of Mount Kilimanjaro. At 5,895 metres, snow-capped Kilimanjaro is the highest mountain in Africa.

The Rift Valleys The rift valleys are a series of troughs in the African landscape. They were formed by the downward movement of one set of land blocks relative to another. The slumping and tilting of these land blocks has caused the formation of a series of wide valleys up to 64 kilometres (40 miles) wide and bounded by steep sides. The whole system stretches in a north-south direction for more than 4,800 kilometres (3,000 miles) from Mozambique in the south, through Tanzania, Kenya and Ethiopia, along the Red Sea and northwards into Syria. A western branch of the system passes through a zone occupied by a series of long lakes, of which Lake Tanganyika is the largest. To the east, another branch of the rift valley forms the steep north-facing slope in Somalia.

The Plateau of Southern Africa

The Plateau of Southern Africa The plateau extends more or less continuously south from East Africa to South Africa. Its southern limit is marked by the flat-topped Drakensberg range, which rise to heights of more than 3,350 metres (11,000 feet). Large tracts of the plateau of central-southern Africa are covered by thinly wooded, grassy plains called *savannas*. In southern Kenya and north-eastern Tanzania, an area known as the Masai Steppe stretches for over 560 kilometres (350 miles) from north to south. These savanna lands are broken by isolated piles of rounded, sun-blistered rock. Many game animals and groups of nomadic Masai herdsmen and their cattle inhabit the area.

Low Africa

Volcanoes and Mountain Ranges North of the plateau of High Africa the most striking mountain ranges are those of the Atlas mountains, which extend from Morocco to Algeria. Mount Toubkal, in Morocco, rises to 4,165 metres (13,665 feet). In the central Sahara area, two blocks of hard, erosion-resistant rocks form the mountain ranges of Ahaggar and Tibesti. Volcanic rocks are found in the Darfur province of western Sudan, where Jebel Mara reaches 3,070 metres (10,073 feet), and in Cameroon, where Mount Cameroon rises to 4,069 metres (13,350 feet). Mount Cameroon is the only point above 4,000 metres (13,080 feet) in western Africa south of the Sahara desert.

The main lowland areas of Africa are in northern Africa. A strip of low coastal plains runs around the continent. North of the West African coastal plains there is a humid belt of rain-forested hills. This passes into the drier plateau of the West African Sahel with its *inselberg* (isolated hills) landforms.

Deserts The greatest area of lowland is the wind-blown waste of the Sahára desert, which covers 9 million square kilometres (3.5 million square miles) of northern Africa. West of Cairo a large area of wind-scooped depressions go down to 128 metres (420 feet) below sea level. This remarkable area of

▲ Lava formations on the slope of Mount Meru, a volcano in the East Africa Rift Valley. The tree is covered with lichen, an organism formed by the association of two plants, an alga and a fungus.

salt marshes is known as the Qattara Depression. Some of the smaller basins in this area reach an abundant supply of water at 15 to 30 metres (50 or 100 feet) below sea level.

The largest desert area in southern Africa is the Kalahari basin, which covers large parts of Botswana and Namibia. The drainage of this generally dry area is internal and ends in the salty swamps of Lake Ngami and Lake Dow.

The drainage of the Chad basin of the southern Sahara is also internal. Lake Chad is fed from the south by the Shari River. It forms an area of swampy shallows and open water with no visible outlet. More than 725 kilometres (450 miles) to the north-east, a series of oases are fed by water provided by the underground drainage of Lake Chad.

The swirling sand dunes of the Great Erg in the Sahara. ▶

Lakes Lake Victoria is Africa's largest lake with an area of 69,452 square kilometres (26,828 square miles). It lies at the intersection of the Kenyan, Tanzanian and Ugandan borders. The lake, situated 1,134 metres (3,720 feet) above sea level, is one of the three largest in the world. In spite of its huge area, its greatest depth is only 82 metres (270 feet). The reason for the shallowness is that the lake occupies a slight depression on the plateau. This depression was caused by the sagging of the earth's crust between the two main branches of the Rift Valley System. Lake Victoria is the 'reservoir' of the Nile. It leaves the lake at Jinja where there is an important hydro-electric scheme.

Lake Tana, the source of the Blue Nile in Ethiopia, is the highest large lake in Africa. It lies over 1,830 metres (6,000 feet) above sea level and has an area of 3,626 square kilometres (1,400 square miles). Just south of the lake, the Blue Nile cascades over the Tississat waterfalls on its long journey through the rugged Ethiopian highlands to meet the White Nile at Khartoum.

A number of lakes form part of the main branch of the rift valley system. These include lakes Chamo, Eyasi, Manyara, Natron, Naivasha, and Turkana. Lakes lying in the western arm of the rift system are lakes Nyasa, Tanganyika, Kivu, Idi Amin Dada (formerly Edward) and Mobutu Sese Seko (formerly Albert). Lake Tanganyika is the second deepest lake in the world, with depths of more than 1,430 metres (4,700 feet). As well as the natural lakes, a number of man-made lakes have been created recently to provide sources of hydro-electric power. The largest of these are lakes Kariba (Zambia/Zimbabwe), Nasser (Egypt), and Volta (Ghana).

Rivers The main river systems of Africa are generally simple, due to the geologically young character of much of the land surface across which the rivers flow. There are eight great river systems with outlets to the surrounding oceans. They are the Nile, Zaire, Zambezi, Orange, Limpopo, Niger, Volta and Senegal rivers. African rivers are characterized by rapids and waterfalls, often where the plateau surface plunges down to the coast.

The Nile, with an overall length of 6,690 kilometres (4,157 miles), is Africa's longest river. It runs from south to north from Lake Victoria to its outlet at Alexandria on the Mediterranean coast. Considerable stretches of the Nile are navigable and steamer services operate on some of them. The river is the lifeline of the people of Egypt and Sudan, and a number of international agreements have been signed over the control of its waters.

The Nile leaves Lake Victoria just south of Jinja and follows a rocky course until it enters Lake Mobutu Sese Seko. From there, it flows over a very flat area, and spreads out into many small channels. This great expanse of papyrus swamps and lagoons, with thick floating islands of plant debris, is called the *Sudd.* The area is the site of a former lake similar in size to Lake Victoria. The water level of this lake rose until it overflowed its northern rim to allow the river to continue on its northward course.

At Khartoum, the White Nile is joined by the Blue Nile from the south-east. The seasonal variations of the Blue Nile's water level have caused extensive flooding along the banks of lower reaches of the main Nile River. Today the Nile is controlled by a number of man-made dams, the largest of which is the Aswan High Dam in Egypt. Broad strips

The steamer S.S. ▶ Liemba at Mpulunga on Lake Tanganyika. The lake is very suitable for shipping. At 1430 metres, it is the second deepest lake in the world.

An aerial view of the ▶ River Nile. The Nile is the longest river in Africa, flowing 6,690 kilometres from Lake Victoria to the sea.

◀ In March, the River Zambezi is swollen and fast-flowing. As its waters plunge over the Victoria Falls, fine spray rises several hundred metres.

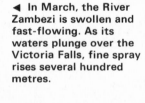

Graceful, fronded ▶ palms and glistening white sands make the East African shores among the most beautiful in the world.

of green cultivated land lie on either side of the lower reaches of the Nile. This land is irrigated by the Nile water.

The Zaire River has the largest drainage area of all the African rivers and is 4,371 kilometres (2,716 miles) long. Its drainage area lies almost entirely within the Republic of Zaire. The main river flows on a semi-circular course. Its most southerly tributary rises near the Zambian border and from there the river runs north to Kisangani. Then it sweeps westwards and south-westwards to its final entry into the Atlantic Ocean south-west of Matadi.

The Zaire has a wide network of tributaries and the river system is important as a transport medium. Large stretches of the rivers are navigable, including a 1,746 kilometre (1,085 mile) stretch of the Zaire itself from Kinshasa in the west to Kisangani in the north-east. Unfortunately, the river is not navigable immediately below Kinshasa.

Ocean-going ships are able to sail up the Zaire estuary 148 kilometres (92 miles) to the inland port of Matadi just below the falls. The estuary of the river is deep and a submarine channel goes out to sea for about 160 kilometres from the coast.

The Zambezi River rises in Angola and its 3,540 kilometre (2,200 mile) course drains water from a basin of more than 1,294,000 square kilometres (500,000 square miles). In its middle course are a number of falls and rapids, including the famous Victoria Falls. The 1,372 metre (4,500 feet) wide falls occur where the river plunges 107 metres (350 feet) over the edge of a block of hard, resistant volcanic rock. The continuous fine spray from the falls forms beautiful rainbows in the sunlight. Downstream from the falls, the 282-kilometre-long (175 miles) Lake Kariba temporarily interrupts the flow of the river. Near its outlet into the Indian Ocean the river is 8 kilometres wide.

The Orange River has one of the simplest river systems in Africa. It has only one main tributary, the Vaal River. The Orange River, which is more than 2,090 kilometres (1,300 miles) long, rises in the highlands of Lesotho and flows westwards to the Atlantic Ocean. Large stretches of the river are frequently dry, because much of its water is drawn off for irrigating farmlands.

The Coastal Lands The African coast has few inlets and few offshore islands. The island of Madagascar (now the Malagasy Republic) is the largest, with an area of 591,500 square kilometres (228,500 square miles). It is remarkable for its unique animal and plant life. It is separated from the mainland by the Mozambique Channel, which is more than 322 kilometres (200 miles) wide.

Many of the African shores are extremely beautiful and there are hundreds of miles of palm-lined beaches of white sand. Just off the coast of equatorial East Africa are remarkable natural breakwaters formed from the cemented shells of coral. These attractive coral reefs provide food and protection for a variety of colourful tropical fish which thrive in the warm waters. The reefs are a great attraction for tourists.

CLIMATE AND WEATHER

About three-quarters of Africa lies between the tropics of Cancer and Capricorn—two lines of latitude $23\frac{1}{2}°$ north and $23\frac{1}{2}°$ south of the equator. These lines of latitude enclose the only areas where the sun can appear directly overhead. Consequently much of the continent enjoys a warm *tropical* climate. Milder or temperate climates affect the Mediterranean coast of North Africa, southern Cape Province in South Africa, and some of the highland areas of the interior.

Temperatures

Climates are often described in terms of average temperature and rainfall. Over much of the continent, the temperature remains relatively constant, with most areas having a temperature of more than 20°C (68°F) throughout the year. However, variations in temperature are not unknown. They are surprisingly great in the deserts, where the temperature may drop by as much as 30°C (54°F) at night. Daytime temperatures in the Sahara are known to reach more than 44°C (111°F) in the shade.

Rainfall

The amount, distribution and reliability of the rainfall vitally affect the growth of vegetation and the extent of human activity in any particular area.

Pressure Zones and Rainfall The pattern of air movements over the continent governs the distribution of the main climatic regions. These air movements are largely responsible for the familiar, although often erratic, alternation between wet and dry seasons. Rain can be caused by the meeting of air streams at the surface. The result of this *convergence* of air streams is that some of the air is forced upwards, where it cools. As the air cools, the moisture in it condenses and forms droplets. When these droplets grow large enough, they fall as rain. The zones of convergence are areas of low atmospheric pressure or *low-pressure zones*, and are traditionally associated with rain. A *high-pressure zone* is an area affected by a descending air stream and an outward movement of air at the surface.

The Pattern of Seasonal Rains The air over the African continent has two sub-tropical high-pressure zones separated by an equatorial low-pressure zone, or *trough*. By January, the equatorial trough has moved far to the south of the equator to cover parts of southern Africa. By July, it has moved northward to lie over the southern part of the Sahara desert. A high-pressure cell bringing dry weather has now moved in over southern Africa from the east. Over northern Africa, the high-pressure zone known as the Azores High, which is responsible for the continuous dry weather over the Sahara, has moved northwards. This has allowed the rain-bearing south-westerly winds of the Atlantic Ocean to penetrate West Africa and move right across central Africa into Ethiopia.

▲ The continent of Africa is clearly visible in this photograph of the Earth, taken from space. The dry Sahara desert can be seen as the brown area in the north and the white areas are cloud formations. Such pictures give scientists much information about weather patterns.

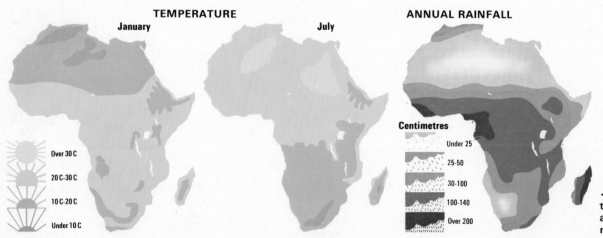

TEMPERATURE

January

July

Over 30 C
20 C-30 C
10 C-20 C
Under 10 C

ANNUAL RAINFALL

Centimetres

Under 25
25-50
30-100
100-140
Over 200

◄ Maps showing temperatures in January and July and the annual rainfall in Africa.

Variations in the Seasonal Rains The south to north movement of the relatively wet equatorial trough across Africa does not produce the even seasonal rainfall that might be expected. First, the effects of the equatorial trough are not felt in North Africa, where the Azores High provides almost continuous dry weather. Secondly, the coverging air streams, often at similar temperatures, do not generally meet along well-defined *fronts*, as is commonly the case when warm and cool air streams meet over Europe. This results in irregular zones of convergence and a very unreliable rainfall in many areas. These irregularities occur mostly in areas of scanty rainfall. In such areas, a few inches of rain can make all the difference between a successful harvest and a complete crop failure.

The Main Climatic Regions

The transition from one climatic region to another is generally gradual, but at least seven major climatic types occur. These climatic types are mainly related to rainfall and so they coincide roughly with the major vegetation boundaries. They are distributed in an almost symmetrical pattern north and south of the equator. The three most widespread types are the desert and semi-desert climates, the tropical savanna climate of the plateaux and the humid equatorial climate of the lush rain-forested areas. The tropical savanna climate affects a fifth of the continent and has greatly varying rainfall, ranging from 200 centimetres a year on the equatorial margins to 40 centimetres where it runs into the semi-desert climate.

The Effects of Altitude Altitude has a strong influence on climate. Even on the equator, isolated peaks, such as Mount Kilimanjaro, show a complete range of climatic conditions. There, one can climb up from the savanna plains through a rain forest belt and into a temperate zone before reaching the permanently snow-covered peak itself. In July, the temperature on the East African plateau at the equator is 11°C (27°F) lower than it is at the coast.

The Effect of Ocean Currents Climatic conditions on the African coast are often greatly influenced by oceanic currents. Off the East African coast, warm currents produce a humid coastal strip and the warm water encourages the growth of coral. On the other side of the continent, the cool Benguela current flows past the shores of south-western Africa and cold winds blowing from the sea remove moisture from the already parched Namib desert.

The cool Canaries current flows south-west along the north-western African coast, but is replaced to the south by the warmer Guinea current.

The Problem of Water Supplies

Rainfall is scanty over as much as three-quarters of sub-Saharan Africa and this presents an enormous problem to many of the people living there. It is vital that the maximum use is made of the available water supplies. Damming streams and digging wells are ways in which seasonal rainwater can be conserved and made more available for use.

Many areas have no permanent water table, and the search for underground water reservoirs requires a high degree of skill and knowledge of local conditions. Use is already being made of the great hydro-electric potential of the larger rivers and further schemes are under construction. All these various aspects of water conservation will help to increase productivity and general prosperity. (See the chapter on *Energy*, pages 52–53.)

Below left An ox found dying of thirst in a dried-up water hole. Failure of the rains during one season can cause hardship or even starvation for thousands of families. Lack of water is a serious problem in many areas.

Below right Flooding in areas such as the Sebou River Basin in Morocco, can damage thousands of hectares of crops. Modern dam-building methods are, however, now being used to reclaim this valuable land.

GEOLOGY AND SOILS

Africa is one of the earth's largest and most rigid land blocks. Its origins go back more than 3,000 million years. Scientists have recently suggested that it may have been formed by the joining up of a number of smaller continents. Africa's general geological structure was well established before 1,000 million years ago.

The Rocks of Africa The rocks of Africa include examples of all the three main rock groups—*igneous, sedimentary* and *metamorphic*. Igneous rocks are formed by the cooling of molten rock material or *magma*. Sedimentary rocks are produced by the deposition of fragments of existing rocks which have been weathered. Metamorphic rocks occur when igneous or sedimentary rocks are transformed under the influence of high temperatures, pressures and gases beneath the surface.

The oldest group of rocks on earth belong to the Precambrian period, which includes all rocks older than about 600 million years. This period covers about 85 per cent of the earth's geological history. In Africa, Precambrian rocks include formations of all the three major rock groups. Precambrian rocks outcrop over about one-third of the continent and underlie most of the remainder.

In many countries, geologists have detailed knowledge about the composition and distribution of the rocks. However, until recently, little was understood about their relationships with each other. Geologists have discovered that many of the structures seen in the very young rocks of the massively folded Alpine and Himalayan mountain ranges can also be seen in the Precambrian rocks of Africa. Presently-held views about these rocks were derived from existing knowledge about Alpine-type rock structures combined with accurate dating of many rock groups by radioactive methods. It is now thought that the whole of southern Africa was built up by a criss-cross series of mountain chains. These mountains are known as *fold belts*. Set within this pattern of fold belts are a number of ancient rigid blocks of very old rock.

Following the Precambrian period, structural changes took place in many parts of Africa. These changes were responsible for the important Mozambique fold belt of East Africa. Then followed a period of about 200 million years during which the land surface was steadily eroded. Layers of continental sediments were deposited in lagoons and shallow seas.

During this period of relative internal stability, a remarkable process was affecting the whole African continent. We know that, from the end of the Precambrian period onwards, the continents of Africa, Australia, India, Antarctica and South America were slowly converging. This movement of continents is called *continental drift*. It is probably caused by convection currents in the Earth's mantle, which underlies the crust. The currents may be caused by radioactive heat in the mantle. The continents finally joined up into one large continental mass which is known as *Gondwanaland*, the southern branch of a V-shaped super-continent known as *Pangaea*. Evidence for this theory is found in the rocks of the next great sedimentary sequence of rocks of Africa—the Karroo system. The coal-bearing Karroo rocks are an extensive series of mainly continental sediments, which reached their maximum development in South Africa. The remains of a plant species called *Glossopteris* were found in the coal beds of the Karroo. *Glossopteris* does not appear in the equivalent coal beds in Europe. However, it occurs in the coal beds of all

Below Mount Kenya, Africa's second highest mountain, is part of the great volcanic masses rising from the high plains of East Africa.

Bottom Erosion by wind and rain wears away soft rock. This often leaves unusual rock formations like this one at Epworth Mission, Zimbabwe.

the four other continental masses which are said to have belonged to Gondwanaland.

About 180 million years ago, volcanic activity indicated the start of the break up of the super-continent of Pangaea. The continents then began slowly to drift to their present positions. In southern Africa, long periods of erosion, with occasional uplift of the land, followed. North Africa began to subside and was eventually covered by the sea in many areas. Under these conditions, sandstones and limestones were built up on the sea floor. These deposits contain the valuable oil reserves of north and west Africa.

Continuous erosion of the rocks of southern Africa over a long period reduced the surface of the land to an almost level plain known as *peneplain*. Towards the end of the Tertiary period of geological history, more than twenty million years ago, Africa and Arabia were uplifted and widespread volcanic activity occurred in Ethiopia. This uplift was related to another phase of continental drift when the whole continent was driven against Europe. This caused the pushing up of the Alps in Europe and the formation of the Atlas mountains in Morocco.

The formation of the rift valley system of East Africa, with its associated volcanic activity, occurred as the land adjusted to the tension caused by the drifting apart of Africa and Arabia. These two land masses have moved apart by as much as 320 kilometres (200 miles) in the last twenty million years. (See the section on the Rift Valleys in the chapter on *The Land*, page 78.)

Soils Soils provide the basis for the development of farming. They consist of mineral particles which are graded according to size as stones, coarse sand, fine sand, silt and clay. Soils are not always easy to relate to the rocks from which they came in Africa. They are generally classified more according to climate.

Desert soils are the most closely related to rocks. Many of these raw mineral soils can hardly be considered as true soils, because they are almost useless for agriculture. At the edges of the deserts the semi-desert brown soils have a higher moisture content. They also contain some *humus*, the valuable vegetable mould which supports plant life.

The most widely developed soils in Africa are the iron-rich tropical soils which cover one-third of the continent. They are found extensively on the plateaux and are rarely very fertile. They are, however, commonly cultivated for shifting agriculture. (See the section on Subsistence Farming on page 44 of the chapter on *Food and Farming*.)

Soils along valley floors, such as the Nile alluvium, provide some of the most productive soils. Their development, however, is often dependent on an adequate supply of water to irrigate the crops.

One of Africa's main problems is soil erosion. This occurs when the soil is laid bare by such factors as fire, farming or overgrazing. The bare soil is exposed to the forces of the atmosphere, especially wind and rain. These forces strip away the soil, leaving rocky infertile land.

AFRICAN RIFT VALLEYS

RED SEA

ADDIS ABABA

L. Turkana

Mt Kenya

Mt Kilimanjaro

L. Victoria

L. Tanganyika

L. Nyasa

INDIAN OCEAN

▲ An aerial view of agricultural land in northern Tunisia which is being eroded by flood water. Soil erosion is one of Africa's most serious problems.

◄ The East African Rift Valley system was caused, millions of years ago, when blocks of land sank between roughly parallel *faults*, or cracks, in the earth's crust.

MAPS SHOWING THE MOVEMENTS OF CONTINENTS

200 million years ago

135 million years ago

65 million years ago

Today

85

GAZETTEER OF PLACES

Note: Place names in CAPITALS indicate that there is a separate entry on that place in this section. Names of people in CAPITALS are covered in the *Who's Who* section, starting on page 200.

ABA, a town in East Central State, Nigeria. It is a centre of a palm oil producing region in the rain forest. Pop. 131,000 (1963).

ABAYA, LAKE, covers an area of 1,840 square kilometres (720 square miles) in southern Ethiopia. It is the second largest of the lakes in the Rift Valley after Lake TURKANA.

ABBAI see BLUE NILE RIVER.

ABEOKUTA, capital of Abeokuta province, West Nigeria. Founded in 1830 by Egba Yoruba people seeking protection from Yoruba civil wars, it is now a trading and administrative centre.

ABIDJAN, capital of Ivory Coast since 1934. A trading and administrative centre, its port exports coffee, cocoa, lumber, pineapples and bananas. Pop. 360,000 (1965).

ABU SIMBEL: The rock temples were saved from the rising waters of Lake Nasser.

ABU SIMBEL, the site of two Egyptian temples cut 55 metres (185 feet) into solid rock. It dates from the reign of RAMESES II. The huge colossi at the front of the temples were moved by 1968 above the level of Lake NASSER, formed by the construction of the ASWAN HIGH DAM.

ACCRA, capital of Ghana and focus of communications. The city grew around three fortified European trading posts of the 1600s. It is the chief political, administrative and university centre of Ghana. The nearby harbour of Tema handles exports of cocoa and imports of manufactured goods. Pop. 758,000 (1968).

ADDIS ABABA, capital of Ethiopia. It lies on a plateau about 2,500 metres (8,000 feet) above sea level. The centre of government and commerce, the city has several imposing buildings, including the former official residence of the emperor (now deposed), the Haile Selassie I University, Africa Hall (headquarters of the U.N. Economic Commission for Africa) and the opera house. A railway connects the city with DJIBOUTI. Pop. 644,000.

ADOWA, town in northern Ethiopia where the Ethiopians defeated an Italian army in 1896. Adowa lies 1,800 metres above sea level.

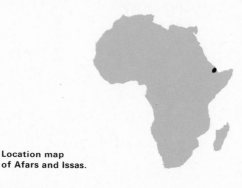

Location map of Afars and Issas.

AFARS AND ISSAS, overseas territory of France. Formerly called French Somaliland, it covers an area of 21,745 square kilometres (8,494 square miles) and has a population of about 126,000.

The two main groups of people are Somalis of the Issa clan and the Afar. About 9,000 Arabs and 7,000 Europeans also live in the country. The capital is DJIBOUTI. Most of the country is a desert plain, broken by inland mountain ranges. The economy depends on the nomadic livestock industry and the revenues from Djibouti free port, which also serves Ethiopia. French Somaliland was established in 1888 and the interior was opened up in the 1920s. It was heavily reinforced when Italy invaded Ethiopia in 1936. A referendum in 1967 decided that the territory should continue its alliance with France and remain part of the French Community. But, at the end of 1975, France announced that it intended to prepare the territory for independence.

AHAGGAR MOUNTAINS, southern Algeria. This large rocky plateau of the Sahara is around 1,000 metres (3,000 feet) high, rising to Mt. Taihat which is 2,750 metres (9,000 feet) high. The plateau is dissected by valleys cut by an ancient river system.

AIR MOUNTAINS, Niger. These mountains form a fertile and populous region in the Sahara. Cereals and dates are grown, and the mountains lie on an important caravan route. The population is mainly Tuareg.

AIUN, the newly built capital of Spanish Sahara. It lies 12 kilometres (8 miles) inland in the northern region of Saguia al-Hamra. Pop. 5,000.

ALBERT, LAKE see MOBUTU SESE SEKO, LAKE.

ALGERIA: The Roman ruins at Timgad in north-eastern Algeria.

ALEXANDRIA, the chief seaport of Egypt. It was founded in 332 BC by Alexander the Great, and was capital of Egypt for over 1,000 years. It was the world's greatest cultural centre 2,000 years ago and, before the rise of Constantinople, the greatest port and commercial centre. Little of antiquity remains in the modern city. The Mahmudiya canal connects the isthmus and peninsula, on which the city is built, with the NILE. Pop. 1,801,000.

AL FAYUM, a town and fertile oasis in Egypt, lies in a depression below sea level. It is irrigated with water from the NILE RIVER. Pop. 134,000 (1966).

Location map of Algeria.

ALGERIA, an independent republic in north Africa, bounded to the east by Tunisia and Libya, to the south by Niger, Mali and Mauritania, and to the west by Spanish Sahara and Morocco. The Mediterranean Sea lies to the north bordering Algeria's coastline which is 1,160 kilometres (725 miles) long. Covering an area of 2,348,895 square kilometres (917,537 square miles), Algeria has a population of 16,275,000.

People The population is almost entirely Muslim, consisting of Arabs and Berbers (including Kabyles and Tuaregs). About one million Europeans, mainly French, lived in Algeria before the country won its independence. However, most of them left in 1961–2. The capital of Algeria is ALGIERS. Other important towns include ORAN, Constantine, ANNABA and Sidi-Bel-Abbes.

Land and Economy Algeria is divided into three natural zones: the Mediterranean zone (or Tell Atlas); the steppes (or high plateau); and the Sahara (including the southern ranges of the Saharan Atlas). Algeria includes about 1,958,400 square kilometres (765,000 squares miles) of the arid Sahara. The habitable part of the country, where about four-fifths of the people live, is in the north near the coast. This region covers only about 204,800 square kilometres (80,000 square miles).

Most of Algeria is of limited value for farming. Much of the agricultural wealth comes from the fertile valleys and basins of the Mediterranean zone. There, rain falls during the winter months of the year. The chief crops of the coastlands are cereals. Vines are the chief commercial plant. Other Mediterranean crops include citrus fruits and olives. Elsewhere, forests and grazing land cover the mountains and steppes. Thick brush, myrtle and rosemary clothe the lower slopes. Esparto grass grows widely on the steppes. The east–west folds of the ATLAS MOUNTAINS act as barriers to climate and communications. They are cut by *wadis* (desert watercourses which are usually dry). On the steppes there are large muddy salt flats called *chotts*. Only drought resistant plants survive in the *ergs* (sand desert) and *hammada* (rock desert) of the south.

Immense deposits of oil and natural gas were found in the Sahara in 1952. A pipeline conveys oil from Hassi Messaoud in the Sahara to the Mediterranean port of Bougie. Natural gas is sent from Hassi R'Mel to Oran and Algiers, or to

Arzew in western Algeria to be liquefied. Oil production now exceeds 40 million metric tons a year. Phosphate is mined at Kouif, near Tebessa, and iron ore near the Tunisian border and in the Tell. Beni Saf, near Oran, is a specialist iron ore port. Iron and steel industries are being developed at Annaba, Oran and Algiers, which has automobile assembly plants. Manufacturing is, however, mainly limited to processing farm produce, fish canning and olive oil production.

Most of Algeria's trade is still with France. Exports include wine, barley, olives, fruits, dates, iron ore, phosphates, petroleum and natural gas. Imports are mainly food and manufactured articles. The three chief ports are Algiers, Oran, and Annaba, which also have international airports. There are 4,480 kilometres (2,800 miles) of railways. The road system includes more than 16,000 kilometres (10,000 miles).

Unit of Currency Dinar

History Phoenician trading posts were established as early as 800 BC along the Mediterranean coast. The most powerful settlement was CARTHAGE in present-day Tunisia, which was destroyed in 146 BC by the Romans. The Romans extended their control over the Mediterranean coast, and also penetrated inland. The Roman provinces in Algeria (called Africa) were overrun by the Vandals in the AD 400s and partly reconquered by the Byzantine Empire in 553. In 693 the Arabs brought the Berbers under control and into the Muslim world, and Arabic became the chief language. In 1533, the Ottoman Turks conquered the area and made it a province of the Ottoman Empire. In a sense, they created Algeria, because previously it had not had any united political existence. As the Ottoman empire declined, Algeria became more independent. The French annexed Algeria in 1831. It was the French who first gave the country its present name. However, many Algerians, such as the Arab chief ABD AL-KADIR, resisted French rule. The country was not finally subdued until the late 1800s.

Following World War I, a militant revolutionary movement, the Etoile Nord-Africaine (North African Star) came into being, together with other less extreme independence movements. The movements opposed France's racial and social policies. In 1937, the Etoile Nord-Africaine was transformed into a political party, the Algerian Peoples Party, but in 1939 it was banned because of alleged communist associations. After the liberation of France in 1944, several independence movements were operating in Algeria. Guerilla warfare began in 1954, and the Front de Libération (FLN) became dominant. In 1958 Europeans living in Algeria demanded the return of General de Gaulle to power in France. They hoped that de Gaulle would guarantee French rule in Algeria, but they were disappointed by his actions. Although the French were capable of containing the FLN, he did not accept the enormous cost of doing this. He regarded Algerian independence as a political necessity. An army revolt against de Gaulle's policies in April 1961 collapsed within a week. A terrorist movement led by the French General Salan to keep Algeria French petered out a year later. In 1962 Ahmed BEN BELLA, a leader of the FLN, was released from prison and became prime minister after Algeria gained independence from France on July 3, 1962. In the early 1960s, almost 1,000,000 French settlers left Algeria.

In July 1965, Ben Bella (then president) was overthrown by a Revolutionary Council led by Colonel Houari BOUMEDIENNE, following an army revolt. Since that time, Algeria's policies which are a mixture of socialism and Islam, have enjoyed great prestige in Africa and the Middle East.

Government Algeria is a one party state. The FLN nominates the president who is then elected by the people. The FLN also nominates candidates for the Assembly who are elected for five-year terms. There is universal suffrage for adults over 19 years of age.

ALGIERS, capital of Algeria. Founded in the 900s, it later became a pirate stronghold for 300 years until it was conquered by France in 1830. The original site was a series of islands called Al-Jazair, which were joined together to form an excellent harbour. An important coaling station in the days of steamships, it now exports oil, wine, grain and esparto grass. The old town which is dominated by a 16th century Kasbah contrasts with the European style of the new town. Pop. 943,000 (1966).

ANGOLA: a street in the Angolan town of Sa da Bandeira (Lubango).

Location map of Angola.

ANGOLA, formerly Portugal's largest overseas territory, is bounded by the Atlantic Ocean to the west, by Zaire to the north, by Zambia to the east and by Namibia (South-West Africa) to the south. Angola, including the enclave of Cabinda, covers an area of 770,161 square kilometres (481,351 square miles) and has a population of 5,798,000.

People The most numerous group of people are the Bantu, especially the Ovimbundu. Bushmen and Hottentots live in the south. The density of population is about 17 per square kilometre (11 per square mile). It is most dense in the ports and the highlands, but vast areas in the south and the east are virtually uninhabited. About 250,000 Portuguese settlers live in Angola. The capital is LUANDA. Other towns include BENGUELA, LOBITO, MELANGE, NOVA LISBOA (Huambo) and SA DA BANDEIRA (Lubango).

Land and Economy Behind the narrow coastal plain lie the Bie Plateau and the Luanda Highlands. From these areas, the land falls away eastwards to the Zaire and Zambesi basins. The southern region merges into the Kalahari.

The agricultural economy is based on coffee and maize. About 13 per cent of Africa's coffee comes from Angola, and the crop forms two-thirds of the territory's exports. Other cash crops include sugar cane, sisal and cotton. Maize is the chief food crop and an important export. It is grown chiefly by the peasants. Beans, cassava and peanuts are grown. In the south, the vegetation is mainly thorn and

scrub, but there are dense forests rich in oil palms and lumber in the north. The north is also the chief source of diamonds, found mainly near Dundo. Diamonds were once the second most important product. Today, however, oil and iron ore are as important. Oil is produced and refined near Luanda. Manganese and copper are also mined. The territory has several small hydro-electric plants, especially on the Catumbela, Dande and Kuanza rivers. The Benguela connects the port of Lobito with the mining area of Shaba (Katanga). Luanda is the other chief port.

History Angola's coastline was explored by the Portuguese in the 1480s and Angola became a major source of slaves. Large numbers were transported to Brazil and the population was greatly reduced. The early Portuguese settlements were on the coast at Luanda (founded 1575) and Benguela (founded 1617). After a brief period of Dutch control (1641–8), the Portuguese regained the region.

After World War II the government sponsored major settlement projects for Portuguese farm workers. Many black Africans opposed Portuguese rule and several nationalist groups organized armed resistance. Fighting between African guerillas and Portuguese troops began in 1961. Although fighting diminished in the mid-1960s, scattered fighting continued into the 1970's. Prior to independence in November 1975, fighting broke out between the three main nationalist groups, the MPLA and a joint command formed by the FNLA and UNITA. Many Europeans left the country. At independence, the MPLA controlled Cabinda and north-central Angola. The FNLA held the north and UNITA the south. The USSR, Cuba and some African countries supported the MPLA. Some western nations, including the US, together with China, South Africa and Zaire, supported the FNLA and UNITA. By early 1976, the MPLA forces had won control of most of the country and in February the Angolan People's Republic was recognized by the OAU.

ANNABA, leading port and one of the few good natural harbours of Algeria. Formerly called Bône, the port exports iron ore and phosphates and is a centre of automobile, chemical, oil and iron and steel industries. Pop. 158,000.

ARUSHA, regional capital in north-east Tanzania. It has been the headquarters of the East African Community since 1969. The surrounding region is important for coffee growing and mixed farming. Pop. 32,000.

ASMARA, capital of Eritrea province and second largest city of Ethiopia. It expanded rapidly in the 1930s as the leading city of the new Italian empire. Pop. 191,000 (1967).

ASMARA: A tree-lined highway.

ASWAN, the capital of Aswan province in southern Egypt, is situated on the NILE RIVER. The town is the terminus of the railway from Cairo. Aswan has a warm dry climate and is popular as a winter holiday resort. To the north is the first Aswan dam, completed in 1902, and 11 kilometres (7 miles) to the south is the first ASWAN HIGH DAM, inaugurated in 1968. Pop. 50,000.

ASWAN HIGH DAM, Egypt, lies 11 kilometres (7 miles) south of the town of Aswan and above the Aswan Dam (built 1902) on the NILE RIVER. The High Dam controls floodwater, making Egypt independent of the annual fluctuations of the Nile. It will also supply abundant electricity. The High Dam began to operate in 1968. Behind it stretches the new Lake NASSER.

ATBARA, a town and important route centre in Sudan. The town lies at the confluence of the Atbara and the Nile rivers. It is a junction of railways to Khartoum, Wadi Halfa and Port Sudan. Pop. 50,000.

ATLAS MOUNTAINS run parallel to the coast of north-west Africa through Morocco and Algeria. They include the chains of the Maritime, High and Sahara Atlas. Named after the mythical Greek god Atlas, they rise to an average height of 3,352 metres (11,000 feet), and form a barrier between the Mediterranean Sea and the sand dunes of the Sahara desert.

AWASH RIVER flows northwards along the Rift Valley in Ethiopia. The Koka Dam has harnessed the river to provide hydro-electric power and water for the irrigation of the cotton and sugar plantations of the Awash valley. The U.N. runs an agricultural research station in the valley.

BANTUSTANS, or 'Bantu Homelands' are the semi-independent states for Africans set up by the South African government as part of the policy of apartheid. Under the 1971 Bantu Homelands Constitution Act, each of the nine Bantustans has a Legislative Assembly and its own executive officials. The South African government has planned that the Bantustans will have 'total and complete independence' by 1979. However, eight of the nine Bantustans are divided into two or more separate blocks and are not economically viable as independent states. Many Africans migrate to the industrial areas of South Africa to work in the factories and mines. About half of the African population live officially in the Bantustans and all Africans are eligible to do so.

BARCE, a new city in Libya. It was built to replace the town of al Marj, which was destroyed by an earthquake in 1963. It is situated on the Jabal Akhdar (Green Mountain) in north-east Libya. It is surrounded by the agricultural region of the al Marj plain. Pop. 20,000.

BAROTSELAND (LOZI), province of Zambia and home of about 25 Barotse groups. It is now called Lozi after the main group that occupies the flood plain of the Zambezi. The farming and fishing economy is closely related to the annual floods of the ZAMBEZI RIVER.

BEAU BASSIN-ROSEHILL, town in Mauritius. It stands on the western slope of the central tableland and is mainly a residential area near PORT LOUIS. Pop. 66,000.

BANTUSTANS OF SOUTH AFRICA

Bantustan	Ethnic groups	Blocks	Population
Transkei	Xhosa	2	1,734,000
Ciskei	Xhosa	19	524,000
Kwazulu	Zulu	29	2,097,000
Lebowa	Pedi	3	2,019,000
Vhavenda	Venda	3	254,000
Gazankulu	Shangaan	4	267,000
Bophuthatswana	Tswana	19	884,000
Basotho Qua Qua	South Suthu	1	24,000
Swazi Territory	Swazi	2	118,000

▲ ATLAS MOUNTAINS: A rugged landscape.

BEIRA, a seaport of Mozambique. It is the chief port for Malawi, Zimbabwe and Zambia and also the SHABA region of Zaire, with which there are rail connections. Pop. 60,000.

BENGASI or **BENGHAZI,** joint capital with TRIPOLI of Libya. The country's chief seaport, it exports agricultural products, including sheep, wool and hides and skins. Encroaching sands have buried much of the original Greek settlement. Pop. 137,000 (1964).

BENGUELA, coastal town in West Angola. Founded in 1617, it is a commercial port which exports hides and cattle. Pop. 35,200.

BENIN, one of the most highly organized of early states in Nigeria, which became famous for its art. The name formerly applied to the whole Guinea coast from the VOLTA RIVER to lands east of the Niger delta.

BENIN, see DAHOMEY.

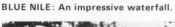
BLUE NILE: An impressive waterfall. ▼

AXUM, the ancient capital of Ethiopia. Ethiopians believe that it was the resting place of the Ark of the Covenant brought there by Menelik, son of King Solomon and the Queen of Sheba. It is famous for its ancient monuments and huge obelisks.

BAMBARI, town in the Central African Republic. It is the trading centre and capital of the Ouaka-Kotto rubber and cotton growing region. Pop. 31,000.

BANGUI, capital of Central African Republic. It lies on the west bank of the Ubangi River. A commercial and administrative centre, its port exports coffee, cotton, lumber and sisal.

BANGWEULU, LAKE, and its surrounding swamps lie in north-east Zambia in the country's heaviest rainfall area. The swamps are rich in bird and aquatic life. Samfya, at the south-west end of the lake, is a centre of the fishing industry.

BANJUL (formerly Bathurst), capital of Gambia. Founded by the British to suppress slave trading in 1816, it stands on the island of St. Mary, near the mouth of the GAMBIA RIVER. It is a river port and there is an international airport at Yundum. Pop. 43,000 (1967).

BOTSWANA: Roan antelope graze on the veld of the Chobe Game Reserve which is in northern Botswana.

BENIN CITY, capital of Midwest Nigeria. It lies on the Benin River in dense tropical forest north of the Niger delta. A walled city noted for brass-work and wood carvings, it is a centre of the lumber and rubber industries. Pop. 101,000 (1963).

BENONI, town in South Africa. Planned in 1903 as a gold mining town, it is now an important engineering centre of the Transvaal. Pop. 141,000.

BENUE RIVER, greatest tributary of the NIGER RIVER. Rising in Cameroon, it is navigable for much of its length.

BERBERA, port of the Somali Republic. A trading centre for nomadic herdsmen, it was formerly capital of the British Somaliland Protectorate. Pop. 12,000.

BERBERATI, town in Central African Republic. Pop. 21,000 (1966).

BETSIBOKA RIVER, Malagasy Republic. It rises on the plateau of the central highlands and flows northwest into the Mozambique Channel.

BIAFRA see NIGERIA.

BIGHT OF BENIN, bay to the north of the Gulf of Guinea. It extends along the coast from Ghana to the Niger delta.

BISSAU, capital and chief port of the Republic of Guinea-Bissau. Lying on the northern coastlands, it exports palm kernels, peanuts and rice.

BIZERTE, town in Tunisia, lies on a natural channel linking Lake Bizerte with the sea. It is a small commercial port which was an important French military base. Pop. 52,000.

BLANTYRE-LIMBE, commercial and industrial centre of Malawi. It is in the Shire Highlands, on the railroad from Salima to BEIRA. Blantyre was joined with Limbe in 1956. Pop. 110,000.

BLOEMFONTEIN, capital of Orange Free State and judicial capital of South Africa. It lies on a plateau at 1,450 metres (4,570 feet). A hub of communications, it is a leading distribution centre. Its fine public buildings include the National Museum, which contains the skull of Africanthropus Helmei Dreyer. Pop. 145,000.

BLUE NILE RIVER flows 1,600 kilometres (1,000 miles) from Lake TANA in Ethiopia, where it is called the Abbai, to join the WHITE NILE at KHARTOUM, in Sudan. The BLUE NILE provides over half the Nile's water volume. Its waters have carved spectacular gorges.

BOBO-DIOULASSO is a town in south-west Upper Volta. It is situated 320 kilometres (200 miles) south-west of OUAGADOUGOU, the capital. It is a centre for trade and agriculture. Processing factories produce soap and vegetable oils. A railway connects it with ABIDJAN. Pop. 38,000.

BODELE DEPRESSION is a low-lying area in northern Chad. It is situated between Lake CHAD, in the south, and the TIBESTI MOUNTAINS, in the north. Tobacco and cotton are grown in the area.

BOSOMTWE LAKE is an inland lake in Ghana with no visible outlet to the sea. It was formed either by a falling meteorite or by a volcanic eruption. It is a sacred lake of Ashanti people.

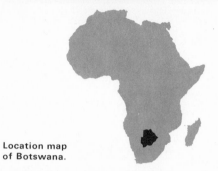

Location map of Botswana.

BOTSWANA is an independent republic in central southern Africa. It is bordered by South Africa to the south, Zimbabwe to the east and Namibia (South-West Africa) to the north and west. It covers 696,320 square kilometres (272,000 square miles) and has a population of 650,000.

People The population consists of two ethnic groups, of which the largest, Tswana (Bechuana) has over 280,000 members; the Bamangwato, Bakwena, Batwana and Bakgatla are the main clans or subgroups. The Bushmen in the Kalahari desert number a few hundred. About 3,900 Europeans and 3,500 Coloureds also live there. The most common language is Setswana (Chuana) and the official language is English. Apart from some Christians, the people practise their own religion. The main towns are the capital, GABERONE, FRANCISTOWN and SEROWE.

Land and Economy The eastern part of Botswana is well irrigated, but the south and west are part of the Kalahari desert. In the north is an extensive marshland, the Makarikari. The climate of the country is sub-tropical and dry.

Agriculture is the basis of the economy and raising beef cattle is by far the most important activity. Lobatse has one of the largest and most up-to-date abattoirs in the southern hemisphere. Fishing is carried out in the OKAVANGO and Chobe rivers.

There is almost no industry in Botswana, but in 1968, following diamond, copper and nickel finds, major mining developments began and production started in 1971. Aid for the mining industry has been obtained from the World Bank, the United States and Canada. Many men go annually to work in South African mines, and their earnings make an important contribution to the economy.

Communications are poor and the only railway line runs through the country from South Africa to Zimbabwe. A new road is being built to join Francistown with the Kazungula ferry on the Zambezi River, where Botswana has its only link with an independent black country—Zambia.

Unit of currency Rand

History Thomas Moffatt was the first missionary to visit Bechuanaland, as Botswana was then called. He became the father-in-law of Livingstone, who started his journeys from Moffatt's house in 1849. Botswana became important during the 'Scramble for Africa' as a link between South Africa and Rhodesia (now Zimbabwe). Following pressure from South-West Africa (now Namibia),

Britain declared a protectorate over Bechuanaland in 1885. During the 1890s, the Africans feared a takeover by Cecil RHODES' British South Africa Company. But after three senior chiefs had visited London and seen Queen Victoria in 1895, Britain confirmed the protectorate, although allowing the company to build the railway through to Zimbabwe. For most of the colonial period Bechuanaland was neglected, and South Africa constantly tried to have it incorporated into the Union. In 1965, an election took place, prior to independence, which was won overwhelmingly by the Botswana Democratic Party (BDP), led by Sir Seretse KHAMA.

Government Botswana is a presidential republic. A national assembly of 31 is elected by universal suffrage on a five-year basis, as is the president. The country is run by nine district councils. It is a member of the OAU, the Commonwealth and the UN.

BRAZZAVILLE, a river port on the north-west bank of the ZAIRE RIVER, is the capital of Congo. The city is 400 kilometres (250 miles) from the mouth of the Zaire and is connected by road and rail to the port of POINTE NOIRE. The city was founded in 1880 by the French explorer Pierre de BRAZZA. It is a trade and administrative centre. It has the largest airport in equatorial Africa.

BUGANDA, a region of south-central Uganda, lies north-west of Lake VICTORIA. With more than a million Baganda people, it was the most important of the four Bantu kingdoms of Uganda. The *kabakas* (rulers), once governed with the aid of a council called the *lukiko*. When Uganda became a British protectorate in the 1890s, Buganda received provincial status. However, in the early 1950s, the British temporarily exiled the kabaka Mutesa II. In 1966, after independence, Mutesa was deposed and exiled by Apolo Milton OBOTE, then prime minister. In the following year, the Bantu kingdoms were abolished, and Buganda was divided into four separate administrative districts.

BUJUMBURA, the capital of Burundi, stands on the shores of Lake TANGANYIKA. Since Burundi became independent, Bujumbura has grown rapidly as the administrative and communications centre of the country. It has factories for processing coffee and cotton. It also has an airport and a university. Pop. 90,000.

BUKAVU is the capital of Kivu province in Zaire. It lies on the southern shore of Lake KIVU, which borders Rwanda. Coffee and tea are grown on plantations and smallholdings in the surrounding area. Cattle are reared on the grasslands. Pop. 135,000.

BULAWAYO: Factory workers testing radios.

BULAWAYO, the second city of Zimbabwe, lies at the southern end of the high plateau in the south of the country. It was the original capital of the Matabele people and was named after Shaka's capital in Zululand. It is now a main railway centre. Industries include the manufacture of textiles, food and drink and steel. Pop. 280,000.

BURUNDI, a small independent republic in central Africa, borders Rwanda in the north, Tanzania in the south and east, and Zaire in the west. With an area of 27,512 square kilometres (10,747 square miles) and a population of about 3,546,000 it is very densely populated.

People Two distinct ethnic groups live in Burundi —the Hutu, who form most of the population, and the Tutsi, who, although they are in the minority, are the dominant people. The Tutsi consider the Hutu as their serfs. More than 100,000 Tutsi refugees, who fled from Rwanda in 1959 following a Hutu uprising, now live in Burundi. Kirundi, a Bantu language, is spoken throughout the country and French is also used. Many people are Roman Catholics, although the majority practise their ethnic region. The capital city is BUJUMBURA.

Land and Economy Eastern Burundi is a fertile plateau. Highland areas occupy the south and north-west of the country. In the west, the high ground slopes down to Lake TANGANYIKA and the Great Rift Valley.

Burundi's economy is almost exclusively agricultural and most farming is at subsistence level. The main food crops are bananas, beans, cassava and maize. Cattle, of which there are about 600,000 occupy 35 per cent of the available land, but are not selectively bred, nor sold. Coffee accounts for more than three-quarters of the country's exports and is bought mainly by the United States. Cotton and hides are exported in small quantities, together with some tin, which is mined in the north.

Unit of currency Franc

History Our knowledge of Burundi's history dates from the 1600s when Ntare, king of the Hima people invaded the country and gathered a number of Hutu and Tutsi clans into a small kingdom. In the reign of Mwami Rugamba (c. 1795–1852), the kingdom expanded, but it broke up when the king, or *mwami*, made his sons, the princes or *ganwa*, provincial rulers. When Europeans arrived in Burundi in the 1880s, it was a divided state. After the conference of Berlin (1885) Germany colonized the area until they were displaced by the Belgians in 1916. Burundi, together with the area that is now Rwanda, was mandated to Belgium as Ruanda-Urundi by the League of Nations in 1919. After World War II, the United Nations designated Ruanda-Urundi a Trust Territory. Burundi voted to become an independent monarchy by a referendum in 1961. A legislative assembly was elected and the country became independent the following year.

In 1966, Prince Charles Ndizeye took over as *mwami* from his father, Mwambutsa, after an attempted coup by Hutu army officers. Within 90 days Ndizeye was deposed by Tutsi army officers led by Captain Michel MICOMBERO. Burundi was proclaimed a republic in November 1966 and Micombero became its first president. To avoid a possible Hutu coup, the systematic murder of educated Hutu began in early 1972. Many thousands of teachers, soldiers, university students and even school children were killed. An attempted Hutu uprising was crushed in 1973 and Hutu refugees fled to Tanzania. Burundi troops launched attacks into Tanzania against the Hutu refugees. The Burundi Foreign Minister claimed that the refugees had attacked Burundi.

CABINDA is a small enclave of Angola situated on the Atlantic coast between Congo and Zaire. Since 1966, it has produced petroleum for export from an off-shore oil field. Pop. 60,000.

CABORA BASSA DAM is one of Africa's chief hydro-electric projects. It stands on the River Zambezi in Mozambique. The dam was completed in December 1974. It will eventually hold back a lake about 240 kilometres (150 miles) long and 38 kilometres (24 miles) wide. Its output of electricity, at the first stage, is 2,000 megawatts a year.

CAIRO (Al-Qahirah in Arabic) is the capital of the Arab Republic of Egypt and the largest city in Africa. It was founded near Fostat, or Old Cairo, on the River Nile in AD 969. It is an important industrial and educational centre, with three universities, including the al-Azhar religious university, founded in AD 970. Cairo has many ancient monuments and the world-famous Museum of Egyptian Antiquities. Pop. 5,000,000.

CAIRO: Like all Muslim cities, Cairo has many ancient mosques.

CALABAR, a river port and state capital in south-east Nigeria, lies on the left bank of the Calabar River in the Niger delta region. It is a centre of the Efik people, and trades in palm oil and kernels. Pop. 76,000.

CAMEROON is an independent republic in central west Africa. Its neighbours are Nigeria in the west, Chad and the Central African Republic in the east and Congo, Gabon and Equatorial Guinea in the south. Cameroon has an area of 469,455 square kilometres (183,381 square miles) and a population of 5,836,000.

People The many different ethnic groups in Cameroon, include Bamileke (1,500,000), Fulbe (350,000), Bassa (200,000), Bulu and Fang (170,000). French and English are the official languages. More than one-third of the people are Christians, one-fifth are Muslims and the remainder practise ethnic religions. The two main towns are YAOUNDÉ, the capital, and DOUALA.

Land and Economy Cameroon has a coastline facing the Atlantic on the Gulf of Guinea. Mount Cameroon, on the west coast, is the highest peak in West Africa at 4,070 metres (13,354 feet). A chain of mountains in the north-west rises to over 1,800 metres (6,000 feet) and then falls away to the lowlands that surround Lake CHAD in the extreme north. The high plateau in the centre of the country contrasts with the plain in the south. The climate is tropical in the north and equatorial in the south.

Agriculture is the mainstay of the Cameroon economy and employs about 85 per cent of the working population. Much of the farming is in the form of subsistence smallholdings and nomadic herding. Although the co-operative system is in use, only 5 per cent of the land is farmed by modern methods. Cocoa and coffee are the main export crops and bananas, maize and yams are grown for food. Cattle, sheep and goats are kept in large numbers and there are small freshwater and coastal fishing industries. Small quantities of gold, tin and calcium are mined and large deposits of bauxite and iron ore are beginning to be exploited. A substantial timber industry processes wood from Cameroon's 117,760 square kilometres (46,000 square miles) of forest. Other principal industries include aluminium refining and the manufacture of chemicals, furniture, metals and textiles.

Unit of currency Franc

History The first contacts between Cameroon and Europe came in the late 1400s, when the Portuguese arrived in the area. From the 1500s to the 1800s, slave traders visited the country and many of the people were carried away.

During the European 'Scramble for Africa' the Germans came to Cameroon and, in 1884, they declared a protectorate over the area and named it Kamerun. British and French troops occupied Kamerun during World War I and, at the end of the war, the territory was made a mandate of the League of Nations and divided between Britain and France. In 1961, following a referendum, the northern part of the British Cameroons joined Nigeria and the southern part joined with French Cameroon, which became independent in 1960, to form the modern Federal Republic of Cameroon. In 1970, Ahmadou AHIDJO was elected President for a third term of office.

Government Cameroon is a federal state consisting of two states. It has a national assembly elected by direct universal suffrage. Each of the two states also has its own government and an assembly. Cameroon is a member of the OAU, pursues a non-aligned policy between the West and the Communist countries and is an associate of the EEC.

CAMEROON: Women gather at a market in Marua, in northern Cameroon.

CANARY ISLANDS are a group of 13 Spanish islands in the Atlantic Ocean off the north-west coast of Africa. The seven main islands are Lanzarote and Fuerteventura, nearest the coast of Africa, Gran Canaria, TENERIFE, Gomera, LAS PALMAS and Hierro. They have a total land area of 7,418 square kilometres (2,898 square miles) and a total population of 944,000. The original inhabitants, the Guanches, were subdued by the end of the 1400s and became intermingled with the Spaniards, who now form the bulk of the population. The islands are volcanic and mountainous, rising to 3,706 metres (12,162 feet) in Tenerife. Rainfall is slight, and spring water is scarce. The chief exports are bananas and tomatoes, with smaller quantities of other fruit and vegetables. Tourism is very important to the economy of the islands. SANTA CRUZ DE TENERIFE, which has an oil refinery, and LAS PALMAS are important ports-of-call.

Known to the Romans as the Fortunate Isles, the Canary Islands were later neglected, until rediscovered, first by Malocello Lanzarote in 1312, and then by the Norman Jean de Bethencourt in 1402. Portugal and Spain disputed the islands until they were recognized as Spanish by the Treaty of Alcacova in 1479. The island group forms two administrative provinces of Spain, named Las Palmas de Gran Canaria and Santa Cruz de Tenerife.

CAPE AGULHAS, the southern-most tip of the African continent, is in South Africa, 190 kilometres (120 miles) south-east of CAPE TOWN. The name is Portuguese for 'needles' and the Cape has been the site of many shipwrecks.

CAPE COAST is a Ghanaian fishing port built on a natural breakwater. It is of historic interest, having been fought over by the Portuguese, Dutch and British, and is dominated by Cape Coast Castle, built by the British in 1682. Pop. 75,000.

CAPE GUARDAFUI, in Somalia, is the easternmost point of the African continent. It forms the tip of the 'Horn of Africa' and divides the Gulf of Aden from the Indian Ocean.

CAPE TOWN is situated on the Cape Peninsula between Table Bay and False Bay in the southwest of South Africa. Towering behind the city is TABLE MOUNTAIN. Cape Town was the site of the first Dutch settlement in 1652 and became the centre of the Dutch and British colonies. Today, it is a major port and manufacturing centre, and the seat of parliament. It has three universities and is a cultural centre of the country. Pop. 1,100,000.

CAPE VERDE, a peninsula on the coast of Senegal, is the westernmost point of Africa. Senegal's capital, DAKAR, is on its southern side.

CASABLANCA: A busy street scene in this Moroccan city.

CAPE VERDE ISLANDS are a group of 14 formerly Portuguese islands in the Atlantic Ocean, about 560 kilometres (350 miles) west of Cape Verde in Senegal. The population of 270,000 is made up of Africans, Creoles and Europeans. The islands are of volcanic origin and rise as high as 2,804 metres (9,201 feet). The climate is hot and there is little rainfall. Coffee, hides, nuts, salt and sugar are produced in small quantities. The islands are an important fuelling station for ships. The Portuguese discovered the islands in 1456, and populated them with slaves brought from Portuguese Guinea. Cape Verde Islands became independent in July 1975 and Aristides Pereira became the islands' first president.

CAPRIVI STRIP is a long narrow tongue of land forming part of Namibia (South-West Africa). It extends 400 kilometres (250 miles) eastwards from the north-eastern corner of Namibia and is only 40 kilometres (25 miles) wide in places. It lies between the ZAMBEZI and OKAVANGO rivers and has borders with Angola and Zambia in the north, and Zimbabwe and Botswana in the south. It was named after Count Caprivi, the German Chancellor who acquired it from Britain in 1890. It is now administered by South Africa as a restricted area because of military installations there. Much of the area is flooded during the year.

CARTHAGE was a city founded by the Phoenicians in 814 BC on what is now called the Bay of Tunis. It became the chief city for Phoenician activity in the western Mediterranean and a number of other colonies were administered from there, especially in Spain. Its most famous men were HAMILCAR and HANNIBAL. Carthage was destroyed by a Roman army in 146 BC.

CAPE TOWN: A view of the harbour with Table Mountain in the background.

CASABLANCA is a Moroccan port and provincial capital on the Atlantic Ocean. As the largest city and economic capital of the country, it handles three-quarters of Morocco's external trade, and possesses more than half of the industry, notably chemical products, glass, mechanical engineering, textiles and food processing. Pop. 1,250,000.

CASAMANCE RIVER is the main river of southern Senegal. About 160 kilometres (100 miles) long, it flows westwards into the Atlantic Ocean through a wide estuary. It gives its name to the Casamance region of Senegal.

Location map of the Central African Republic.

CENTRAL AFRICAN REPUBLIC lies in the centre of Africa to the north of the equator. It has borders with Chad in the north, Sudan in the east, Zaire and Congo in the south, and Cameroon in the west. With an area of 609,280 square kilometres (238,000 square miles), it has a population of 1,637,000.

People The people of the Central African Republic belong to a wide variety of ethnic groups. The most commonly spoken languages are Sango in the west, Zande and Banda in the east and Sara and Arabic in the north. French is the official language. Nearly two-thirds of the people practise ethnic religions. There are 276,000 Christians and about 50,000 Muslims. A quarter of the population lives in towns, the largest of which is BANGUI, the capital.

Land and Economy The Central African Republic occupies a large plateau of savanna country, lying between the western (Yade) and eastern (Bongo) massifs. The average temperature is 26°C (79°F). The northern area is very dry, and the south is tropical and wet.

The Central African Republic is one of the poorest countries in Africa and most of the people are engaged in subsistence farming. Cassava is the staple diet and other food crops include maize, millet, rice and sorghum. Coffee, cotton, rubber and tobacco are the main cash crops. Cattle are reared in areas that are free from tse-tse fly. Sheep, goats, pigs and poultry are also kept.

The country has 72,960 square kilometres (28,500 square miles) of forest and 12,800 of these are commercially viable. The main minerals are diamonds and uranium. Industry in the Central African Republic is mainly concerned with processing agricultural and mineral products. France, which buys most of the country's uranium, is the chief trading partner. Three game reserves cover one-third of the country.

Unit of currency Franc

History Little is known about the early history of the Central African Republic. The French established a settlement at Bangui in the late 1800s and in 1910 they incorporated the area into French Equatorial Africa. The Central African Republic became self-governing in 1958, received a new constitution in 1959 and gained independence in 1960. The first president, David DACKO, was overthrown in 1966 by army officers and replaced by Jean Bedel BOKASSA, the head of the army. The 1959 constitution was repealed and the national assembly was dissolved. An attempted coup against Bokassa in 1969 was defeated and its leaders were summarily tried and executed. Bokassa himself exercises control over the government and only one political party is permitted—the *Mouvement d'Evolution Sociale de l'Afrique Noire.*

CEUTA, a city on the Moroccan coast opposite Gibraltar, is under Spanish authority. An ancient town that experienced Phoenician, Greek, Roman and Arab occupation, it became Spanish in 1580. Since 1956, it has been a duty free port. It is governed by a mayor who is a member of parliament in Madrid. Pop. 76,000.

Location map
of Chad.

CHAD is an independent republic in central North Africa. Its neighbours are Libya in the north, Sudan in the east, the Central African Republic and Cameroon in the south, and Nigeria and Niger in the west. It is the fifth largest country in Africa in area—1,269,120 square kilometres —and has a population of 3,791,000.

People Chad is inhabited by Zaghawa and Masalit peoples in the east, Arabs and Tubu or Teda in the north, Kanuri, Hausa and Fulani in the west, Bagirmi and other, less numerous peoples in the south of the country. About 6,000 Europeans also live there. Apart from ethnic languages and dialects, the official language is French. Half of the people are Muslims and the rest, with the exception of 5 per cent who are Christians, practise ethnic religions. N'DJAMENA is the capital.

Land and Economy Chad is a large basin-shaped plain rising to 1,524 metres (5,000 feet) in the east and 3,350 metres (11,000 feet) in the north. To the north, Chad extends into the Sahara desert, where rainfall is less than 25 centimetres (10 inches) per year and temperatures vary between extremes of hot and cold by day and night. The central and southern regions have tropical climates which support savanna and grass plains. Lake CHAD, in the south, is surrounded by extensive marshes.

Little industrial development has occurred in Chad and farming is the mainstay of the economy. Cassava, maize, millet, rice and sorghum are the principal food crops. Cotton, grown in the south-west, is the major cash crop and an important export. Livestock, including 4,500,000 cattle and an equal number of sheep and goats, is raised. A considerable fishing industry, based on Lake Chad produces an annual catch of about 108,000 tonnes (110,000 tons). Natron (sodium bicarbonate), which is found on the shores of Lake Chad, is the only important mining product. Gum arabic is produced in the forested areas and is exported.

Unit of Currency Franc

History In the Middle Ages part of the area of what is now Chad was the empire of Kanem. Chad became a French protectorate in 1897, and in 1910 it was made part of French Equatorial Africa. In 1960, Chad became a fully independent republic within the French Community. In 1964, the country joined the UDEAC (Central African Customs and Economic Union). After independence, Chad was troubled by dissident groups in rebellion against the government of President Ngarta TOMBALBAYE. The Muslim Arab peoples of the northern region accused the government of favouring the black peoples of the south. The rebels were led by the Chad National Liberation Front (FROLINAT), whose leader was Dr. Abba Siddick. The Liberation Front was contained by the government with the help of French troops. In October that year, French troops withdrew at the request of President Malloum. President Tombalbaye was assassinated when the Army seized power in April 1975.

CHAD: Young tree seedlings being watered in a nursery in Chad.

Government After the assassination of Tombalbaye in 1975, Army chiefs announced the suspension of the constitution. Chad had a presidential government with a single party, the PPT (*Parti Progressiste Tchadien*). The party chose the president, who was then elected by the national assembly and endorsed by a national referendum. The national assembly was composed of 105 representatives elected every five years by universal suffrage.

CHAD, LAKE, lies in north-west central Africa at the meeting point of the boundaries of Chad, Niger, Nigeria and Cameroon. It is fed by the Chari River from the south and by many other streams, but has no outlet. Its size varies seasonally, from a maximum area of about 25,600 square kilometres (10,000 square miles) to only half that amount. In the south it is about 4.5 metres (15 feet) deep, and navigable; in the north-west it is only about 1 metre (3 feet) deep. Natron (sodium bicarbonate) is extracted from surrounding areas.

CHINGOLA town marks the northern end of the Zambian copperbelt. Most of its people are employed at the Nchanga mine, a huge open pit from which exceptionally rich ores are mined.

COMORO ISLANDS are a formerly French-ruled group of rugged islands in the Indian Ocean between the north of Madagascar and the African mainland. DZAOUDZI is the capital. The main inhabited islands are Ngazija (Grand Comoro), Anjouan, Mayotte and Moheli. These islands have a total area of 2,145 square kilometres (838 square miles) and a population of about 300,000. The people are chiefly Swahili-speaking Muslims of mixed African-Arab descent. The volcanic soil is very fertile and many tropical crops are grown, of which sugar and vanilla are the most important. The islands were annexed by France during the 1800s. In 1958, the islanders elected to remain subject to France, although they gained internal self-government. However, elections in December 1972 resulted in a victory for a coalition which favoured independence from France. An agreement signed in 1973 stated that full independence would be achieved within five years. In July 1975 the Comoro Islands made a unilateral declaration of independence (UDI). Mayotte, however, later decided to remain French.

CONAKRY, the capital and main seaport of Guinea, lies on the island of Tombo. A railway links it with the island centres of Fria and KANKAN. There is also an international airport. Conakry is the centre of the bauxite industry. Pop. 172,500.

Location map
of Congo.

CONGO is an independent republic situated astride the equator in West Central Africa. It is bordered by Cameroon and the Central African Republic in the north, Zaire in the east and south, and Gabon in the west. It has a small coastline on the Atlantic Ocean. Until 1971 the country was known as Congo Brazzaville. The country covers 355,840 square kilometres (139,000 square miles) and has a population of 1,300,000.

People Four main ethnic groups inhabit Congo— the Bakongo (45 per cent) the Teke (20 per cent) the Bobangi (16 per cent) and the Gabonais (15 per cent), all are Bantu-speaking. The official language is French. More than half of the people follow ethnic religions. The remainder are Christians, with the exception of a Muslim community of about 5,000 people. Four out of every ten people live in towns, of which BRAZZAVILLE, the capital, POINTE NOIRE, Dolisie and Jacob are the largest.

Land and Economy The ZAIRE RIVER Basin in the north, is an area of low-lying swampy land. In the south, the Bateke plateau and the Mayombe escarpment are separated by the Niari River valley. The higher parts are grassland and the river valleys, which cut through them, support savanna or forest. The coastal plain extends about 65 kilometres (40 miles) inland. The Zaire River and its tributary, the Ubangi, form the greater part of the country's eastern border. The temperature averages 24°C (75°F) and the annual rainfall is between 100 and 120 centimetres.

More than half of the working population is employed in agriculture, mostly in smallholdings. Bananas and cassava are the main food crops, and coffee, cocoa, groundnuts, sugar cane and tobacco are cultivated as cash crops. A new fishing industry is being developed on the coast at Pointe Noire. Forests cover large areas in Congo and the timber industry is of economic importance, lumber being a principal export. The mining of cassiterite, copper, gold and lead has been important in the past, but known deposits of these minerals are dwindling. In recent years some of the largest reserves of potash in the world have been found in Congo and mining operations began in 1969. It is hoped that potash will become a major earner of foreign currency in the future. Industrialization is growing fast and important products include chemicals, forestry products and textiles.

Unit of currency Franc

History Congo was made a French protectorate in 1880 and became part of French Equatorial Africa in 1910. The country remained faithful to the allied side in World War II. It gained its independence in 1960 and Fulbert YOULOU became the first president. In 1963, he was overthrown and replaced by Alphonse MASSEMBA-DEBAT, who held office as president until 1968. During this period, the government followed left-wing policies, nationalized industry and established relations with Russia and China.

In 1968 various factions staged coups and counter-coups but, by the end of the year, Major Marien NGOUABI had consolidated his position as the new president. An attempted coup in February 1972 was followed by a period of unrest. In February 1973 the government announced that it had uncovered another plot. In March 1973, it was announced that Lt. Ange Diawara, leader of the attempted coup in 1972, had been killed.

Government A constitutional referendum in 1973 resulted in the creation of a State Council, a Council of Ministers, and a 115-member National Assembly. The elected president would serve for five-year terms. Since 1968, the government has enacted various radical policies, including the abolition of the power of chiefs and the granting of land to peasants.

COTONOU is the largest city in Benin (Dahomey). Situated on the Bight of Benin to the west of PORTO NOVO, it is an important seaport. In the 1960s the port was developed to take ocean-going shipping. Cotonou is a commercial and industrial centre. Products include beer, textiles and vegetable oils. The city has an international airport and a university. Pop. 120,000.

CURE-PIPE, Mauritius, is a residential town on the island's central plateau. It is about 30 kilometres (20 miles) from PORT LOUIS, the capital, to which it is connected by a railway. Pop. 53,000.

Location map of Dahomey (Benin).

DAHOMEY (Benin), a narrow country in West Africa, has a small coastline on the Gulf of Guinea. The country is sandwiched between Togo in the west and Nigeria in the east. It is bordered by Upper Volta in the north-west and Niger in the north-east. With an area of 111,316 square kilometres (43,483 square miles), Dahomey has a population of 2,869,000.

People The inhabitants of Dahomey belong to more than 50 different ethnic groups including Adja, Bariba, Fon, Fula (Peul), Somba and Yoruba peoples. The main languages are Fon in the south, Ewe in the west, Yoruba in the east and Fulani (Peul) Borgu and Hausa in the north. French is the official language. About 65 per cent of the people practise indigenous religions and the remainder are either Christians or Muslims, in about equal proportions. PORTO NOVO, the capital, and COTONOU are the two most important towns.

Land and Economy Dahomey has a flat coastline with no natural harbours. The coastal plain reaches inland about 80 kilometres (50 miles) and much of it is covered by rain forest. The land rises to over 610 metres (2,000 feet) in the north-west and the higher ground is grassland. The coastal area has a wet tropical climate and the country becomes progressively drier to the north.

The economy of Dahomey is almost completely dependent upon agriculture and about nine out of every ten people are engaged in subsistence farming. Cassava, maize, millet, rice, sweet potatoes and yams are grown as food crops. Palm oil is the country's major export.

Industry has still to be developed. But there are some factories that process agricultural products, notably palm oil. Dahomey is known to have deposits of minerals, but these have not yet been fully exploited. Oil is drilled by offshore rigs.

Unit of currency Franc

History According to tradition, Dahomey was the location of three kingdoms that were founded by three brothers in the 1600s—Adjatche (Porto Novo), Abomey and Allada. It is known that the rulers of the area that is now Dahomey based their power on trade with European slavers. In 1863,

DAKAR: Sandanga market in Dakar, Senegal's capital city.

DAHOMEY (BENIN): Cotonou harbour. Fishing is important to the country's economy.

Sodji, the king of Porto Novo, put his kingdom under French protection. By the beginning of the 1900s, France had subdued the whole country and in 1904 it became a territory of French West Africa. After World War II, Dahomey was made an overseas territory of France. Internal self-government was achieved in 1958 and full independence in 1960.

Since Dahomey became independent, there have been periods of civilian government, interrupted by military regimes. This chronic instability has resulted from allegiances among Dahomeyans to three regional leaders: MAGA, Apithy and Ahomadegbe. A military coup in October 1972 marked the breakdown of an experiment in which all three leaders ruled as a presidential council. Major Matthieu KEREKOU became head of state. In Nov-

ember 1975, Kerekou announced that Dahomey would be known as the People's Republic of Benin.

DAKAR, main seaport and capital of Senegal, lies on the southern side of the CAPE VERDE peninsula. It has one of West Africa's best harbours. The city has a university and television and radio stations. Chemicals, light engineering goods, palm oil products and textiles are produced. Founded in 1857, Dakar was once capital of French West Africa. Pop. 436,000.

DAR ES SALAAM, the first capital of Tanzania. It is also the principal port, and road, rail and air centre of the country. It was founded in 1862 by Sayyid Majid, Sultan of Zanzibar. The city's original name was Mzizima. Cement, glass and textiles are produced. Pop. 344,000.

DESSIE is an important Ethiopian commercial town on the main road north from ADDIS ABABA to ASMARA. Trade in grain, hides, honey and beeswax centres on Dessie. Pop. 43,000.

DIEGO-SUAREZ, a town in the north of the Malagasy Republic, boasts one of the most beautiful bays in the world. The site of a French military base, its population is cosmopolitan, including Comorians, Chinese, Indians and Malagasy. Products include coffee and peanuts. Pop. 38,000.

DIREDAWA, in eastern Ethiopia, is the country's third largest town. Diredawa was built at the beginning of the 1900s alongside the ADDIS ABABA-DJIBOUTI railway. It has some light industry and coffee is now cultivated in the area near the town of HARAR. Pop. 51,000.

DJIBOUTI, capital of the French territory of Afars and Issas in north-east Africa, lies on the Gulf of Tadjoura, an inlet of the Gulf of Aden. Founded as a port in 1888, it became the territory's capital in 1892. Djibouti is the eastern terminal of the railway from Addis Ababa, Ethiopia. Much of Ethiopia's foreign trade passes through the port. Djibouti's importance was reduced by the closing of the SUEZ CANAL in 1968. Pop. 62,000.

DODOMA, a town in central Tanzania. In 1973, the Tanzanian government announced that Dodoma would become capital of Tanzania within 10 years. Pop. 708,000.

DOUALA, the leading port and major industrial centre of Cameroon, lies on the Bight of Biafra. It is connected by rail to YAOUNDE, the capital. Its products include beer, insecticide, shoes and vegetable oils. Pop. 250,000.

DRAKENSBERG MOUNTAINS, a range stretching 1,600 kilometres (1,000 miles) in south-eastern Africa rising to over 3,350 metres (11,000 feet) on the Lesotho borders. They are made up of basalt and volcanic rock and face the coastal plain in a steep escarpment. Several high road passes cross the range.

DURBAN is the second port and third city of South Africa. It is the centre of South Africa's sugar-growing area. It was named after a Cape Governor in the 1800s and was the centre of the British colony of Natal from 1824. The population includes many Asians, whose ancestors were brought there to work in the sugar industry in the 1860s. Pop. 843,000.

DZAOUDZI, the capital of the Comoro Islands in the Indian Ocean. The town is situated on Pamanzi islet and is encircled by the larger island of Mayotte. Many of the people work in government. Pop. 2,000.

EAST LONDON is a port in eastern Cape, South Africa. The city was built up after 1845, mainly by English settlers. It borders on the Ciskei and acts as a port for the products of the hinterland. It has textile and motor assembly plant industries. Pop. 137,000.

EDWARD, LAKE see IDI AMIN DADA, LAKE

Location map
of Egypt.

EGYPT, officially called the Arab Republic of Egypt (A.R.E.), has an area of 989,855 square kilometres (386,662 square miles). It is bordered by Libya to the west and Sudan in the south. In the north, the country has a coastline along the Mediterranean sea which stretches for 900 kilometres (565 miles). To the east Egypt has a coastline on the Red Sea stretching for 1,360 kilometres

(850 miles). Egypt is joined to the Asian mainland by the SINAI PENINSULA. The Israeli army occupied the peninsula in the Six Day War of 1967. After the war, Egypt's eastern land border with Israel was marked by the SUEZ CANAL. The population of Egypt is about 35,000,000.

People The Egyptian people are chiefly of Arab and Turkish ancestry. The Egyptian language has been Arabic since the Arab conquest of AD 640. Nomadic Berbers, who live in the semi-desert regions, and Italians and Greeks, who live in the cities form small minority groups. Most Egyptians are Sunni Muslims but about seven per cent of the people are Coptic Christians. Almost all Egyptians live in the fertile valley of the NILE RIVER and the Nile delta. CAIRO, the capital is the largest city in Africa. It is followed in size by ALEXANDRIA, GIZA and PORT SAID.

Land and Economy Most of the country consists of stony desert. The Western Desert is situated to the west of the Nile, extending into Libya. In the north of the Western Desert is the QATTARA DEPRESSION which sinks to 130 metres (440 feet) below sea level. In the south-west of Egypt the desert rises to a plateau of over 900 metres (3,000 feet). The most important feature of Egypt is the fertile valley of the Nile. Every year the river overflows its banks and floods the lowlands. This annual flooding deposits alluvial soils which make this one of the most fertile regions in the world. The Egyptian climate is generally hot and dry. In some southern regions there may be no rainfall for several years. Northern Egypt has the largest rainfall.

Only about 5 per cent of the land in Egypt is suitable for agriculture. The land which can be successfully cultivated is the Nile delta and valley. Soil fertility in this area is so high that there may be as many as three crops in one year. Cotton is Egypt's most important cash crop. Wheat, maize, rice, sugar and other crops are grown for home use and export. Enough oil has been found in the Western Desert to provide fuel for export as well as for home use. Lake NASSER, formed by the ASWAN HIGH DAM provides irrigation for crops. The dam itself is an important source of hydroelectricity. In Cairo, Alexandria, and other large cities of the Nile delta, there are oil-refining and steel manufacturing industries and textile factories. Egypt's chief ports are Alexandria, Suez and Port Said.

Unit of currency Egyptian pound

History Ancient Egypt was ruled from 2850-341 BC by thirty distinct dynasties. In 332 BC Egypt was conquered by Alexander the Great and, on his death, the country was ruled by Alexander's general, Ptolemy. Descendants of Ptolemy ruled Egypt until the death of Cleopatra in 30 BC. Egypt then became part of the Roman Empire and was known as the 'Granary of Rome'. When the Roman empire was divided in AD 395, Egypt remained a province of the East Roman Empire. Christianity became the official religion and Egypt became the centre of the Christian Coptic Church.

Egypt fell to Arab invaders in AD 640. Many Egyptians adopted the religion of Islam and the Arabic language. In AD 969, Egypt was conquered by the Shi'ite Arab Fatimid dynasty from Tunisia and a capital, Cairo was founded in AD 970. Egypt was ruled by the Fatimids until 1171 when Saladin took Egypt and united it with Syria. In 1250 Egypt was seized by the Mamluks, a people descended from former Turkish and Circassian war captives. The Mamluks ruled Egypt for 250 years. During this time Egypt became an important military, commercial and cultural centre. In 1517 Egypt was conquered by Ottoman Sultan Selim II (the 'Fierce'). For 300 years Egypt remained a province of the Ottoman Empire.

In 1798 Egypt was invaded by France. Napoleon Bonaparte defeated the Mamluks, who had remained in power under the Ottoman rule, at the Battle of the Pyramids. The French occupied Egypt until 1801. In 1805 Mohammed Ali Pasha, the Ottoman governor began a programme of

modernization in Egypt. Mohammed Ali invited French and Italian advisers to assist with his programme. Eventually, in 1841, Mohammed Ali was able to defeat the Ottoman sultan in battle and became hereditary ruler of Egypt. The successors of Mohammed Ali caused a decline in Egypt's prosperity even though they devised such schemes as the Suez Canal, which was opened in 1869. Discontent among the people led to a revolt by Arabi Pasha in 1882. This revolt led to military intervention and occupation by the British. In 1914 Britain made Egypt a 'protectorate' and completely severed the links between Egypt and the Ottoman Empire. In 1922 the 'protectorate' was ended and Egypt became a monarchy with Fuad I as King. In 1936 Faruk succeeded Fuad and the Anglo-Egyptian treaty was signed. British forces in Egypt were withdrawn to the Canal Zone.

During the World War II (1939–45), Egypt helped Britain to defeat the German and Italian forces in North Africa. After the war, nationalist feelings grew stronger. In 1952, the Egyptian Army led by Col. Nasser seized power, and exiled King Faruk. In 1953 Egypt was declared a republic and Col. NASSER became president in 1954. In the same year, Britain agreed to recall all troops from Egypt. President Nasser nationalized the Suez Canal in 1956. Britain and France did not wish to lose control of the Canal and invaded Egypt. Opposition from other foreign powers, however, caused a withdrawal of troops. Having successfully withstood this attack, President Nasser's popularity in the Arab world led Egypt to join with Syria to form the United Arab Republic. Syria, however, broke away from the union in 1961. Increased tension between Egypt and Israel and the closure of the straits of Tiran brought war with Israel in 1967. The Egyptian Army in Sinai was defeated by the Israelis after the Egyptian Air Force was destroyed. President Nasser died in 1970 and was succeeded by Anwar as-SADAT.

On October 6, 1973, Arab-Israeli hostilities broke out again. Egypt launched an offensive across the Suez Canal. After some very heavy tank battles, a cease-fire was proposed by the United Nations on October 22. Fighting continued, however, and the Israeli forces crossed to the west bank of the Suez Canal. On November 11, Egypt and Israel signed a cease-fire agreement. The Israeli troops later withdrew from the west bank of the Suez Canal. In September 1975, Egypt and Israel signed an agreement creating a United Nations buffer zone in Sinai. Egypt also agreed to allow Israel to use the reopened Suez Canal.

Government The Army controls political power in Egypt. There is a National Assembly which is elected by universal suffrage. The National Assembly appoints the President, who is the supreme commander of the armed forces.

ELDORET is a Kenyan town 190 kilometres (118 miles) north-east of NAIROBI in the foothills of MOUNT ELGON. An administrative and tourist centre, it provides services for visitors to western and northern Kenya. Pop. 11,600.

EL OBEID, in Sudan, is the capital of Kordofan province. It was seized by the Egyptians in 1821, and was captured by the MAHDI in 1883, when the old town was wholly destroyed. It was rebuilt in 1889. Pop. 76,000.

ENTEBBE, a Ugandan town on the northern shore of Lake VICTORIA, lies about 30 kilometres (19 miles) south-west of the capital, KAMPALA. It is just north of the equator. It has an international airport, and is also a major residential area for the civil service. Pop. 21,000.

ENUGU, the capital of Nigeria's East-Central State, lies on the railway from PORT HARCOURT to KANO and MAIDUGURI. It is the centre of the coal mining industry of the region. Pop. 165,000.

DRAKENSBERG MOUNTAINS: This rugged range is located in south-eastern Africa.

EGYPT: *Above left* An interior wall painting in the Temple of the Nobles at Thebes.
Above right Large-wheeled tractors are ideal for motoring over loose sand.
Left The gold mask of Tutankhamun, in Cairo Museum.
Right Cotton spinning. Cotton is the country's chief cash crop.

Location map
of Equatorial Guinea.

EQUATORIAL GUINEA is a small independent republic in West Africa. It consists of a mainland area, Rio Muni, which is bounded by Cameroon in the north and Gabon in the east and south, and the island of Macias Nguema Biyoga (formerly Fernando Póo) in the Bight of Biafra. The total area is 27,724 square kilometres. Pop. 290,000.

People On Macias Nguema Biyoga, the Bubi are the most numerous people and there are also 2,000 people of mixed descent. On the mainland, the Fang people make up the majority. Bubi and Fang are Bantu languages. About 4,000 Europeans and 40,000 Nigerian immigrants, mostly Ibos, also live on the mainland. Spanish is the official language. Most people practise traditional African religions. The capital, Bata is on the mainland.

Land and Economy The mainland rises from the coastal plain to the Cristal Mountains inland, which average about 1,220 metres (4,000 feet). Macias Nguema Biyoga is a volcanic island rising to 3,100 metres (10,190 feet).

The economy of the mainland depends heavily on the timber industry and many people work in lumber camps. The volcanic soil of Macias Nguema Biyoga is very fertile and cocoa and coffee are cultivated and exported.

Unit of Currency Peseta

History Spain acquired Macias Nguema Biyoga from Portugal in 1778 and established its claim to the mainland in 1885. Independence was granted in 1968, when Francisco Macias Nguema became the first president of the new republic.

Government Equatorial Guinea is a one-party democratic republic. It is governed by a president who is elected every five years by universal suffrage, and a national assembly with 35 members.

ERITREA see ETHIOPIA

Location map
of Ethiopia.

ETHIOPIA lies in north-eastern Africa. Its neighbours are the Sudan in the west, Kenya in the south, and Somalia, and the territory of the Afars and Issas in the east. In the north-east, Ethiopia has a coastline on the Red Sea of more than 800 kilometres (500 miles). The area of the country is 1,216,678 square kilometres (475,265 square miles) and the population is about 26,076,000.

People The two largest ethnic groups of Ethiopia are Cushites, who include Galla and Somali peoples, and Semites, who include the Amhara, the ruling group, and the Tigre. Nilotic groups live in the south-west of the country. Amharic is the country's official language but many others are spoken. About half the people practise Coptic Christianity, the official traditional religion. The rest are mainly Muslims. ADDIS ABABA is the capital.

Land and Economy A high mountainous plateau cut into two by the Rift Valley, extends over the centre of the country. Surrounding lowlands consist of rain forest in the south-west, savanna in the south-east and a coastal plain in the north. Ethiopia is divided into three zones: the lowlands, known as the *kolla*; the sub-tropical zone that extends from 1,500 to 2,200 metres (5,000 to 7,000 feet) above sea level which is called the *woina dega*; and the temperate highlands called the *dega*. The high ground is covered with natural juniper forests and with acacia savanna. The climate is divided into wet and dry seasons, with the rainy season occurring from July to September. Most rain falls in the south west of the country and on the higher ground. In the *woina dega*, temperatures rise to about 21°C (70°F) in the daytime but fall sharply at night. The coastal plain in the north is one of the hottest regions in the world.

Four-fifths of the people make their living by farming, most of them in the fertile *woina dega*. Coffee, grown in the lowlands, is the most important crop and provides two-thirds of Ethiopia's exports. Other crops grown include cotton, durra sorghum, maize and sugar in the lowlands, and cereals, oil seeds and pulses, together with some livestock, on the higher ground.

The mineral potential is largely unknown, although some exploration has taken place. Some light industry is centred on Addis Ababa, Diredawa and Asmara, although industrial products account for less than one per cent of Ethiopia's exports. Much of Ethiopia's international trade is handled by the port of DJIBOUTI in the territory of the Afars and Issas.

There are 24,000 kilometres (15,000 miles) of road in Ethiopia, and two railways link Addis Ababa to Djibouti and to Asmara and Massawa.

ETHIOPIA: A view of Addis Ababa, Ethiopia's capital city.

Unit of currency Dollar

History Early Negro inhabitants of Ethiopia were displaced by the expansion of the civilization of KUSH. In turn, this was infiltrated by Semitic migrants from Arabia in the 700s BC and in the first century AD a kingdom centred on the city of AXUM began to emerge. The Axumites traded with Greece and adopted Christianity in the AD 300s. The spread of Islam in the AD 700s destroyed the power of the Axumite kingdom and reduced it to the area of the Ethiopian central plateau, where it finally disintegrated into several semi-independent provinces.

The Emperor THEODORE II succeeded in re-unifying the country in 1855, but his successor, Yohannes allowed the Italians to colonize the northern province of Eritrea. In the late 1800s, Italy attempted to colonize Ethiopia, but was defeated by the Emperor MENELIK II at the battle of Adowa in 1896. Because of this victory, Ethiopia is the only African country never to have been colonized.

In 1935, the Italians again invaded Ethiopia and despite HAILE SELASSIE's protests to the League of Nations, their airplanes and superior weapons enabled them to occupy it. Independence was regained in 1941 when joint British and Ethiopian forces drove the Italians out.

Eritrea, a former Italian territory, was officially federated with Ethiopia in 1952 and, ten years later, this action was endorsed in a referendum. However, a rebel group, the Eritrean Liberation Front, worked to reverse this decision.

After his return to Ethiopia in 1941, Emperor Haile Selassie introduced various constitutional reforms to make the country more democratic, but he retained supreme power. In 1960, a group of army officers attempted a coup, but the Emperor put down the rebellion. In the 1960s and 1970s, Ethiopia faced many problems. Fighting with Somalia over border disputes in the early 1960s ended when a peace agreement was signed in 1964. In the early 1970s, drought led to starvation in many areas. Unemployment and rises in the cost of living caused unrest. In February 1974, the government resigned. A succession of governments failed to restore order. A group of soldiers formed a Provisional Military Administrative Committee, called the Dergue. The Dergue began to govern the country in August. The Dergue deposed Haile Selassie in September and, in November, 60 prominent Ethiopians, including two ex-prime ministers, were executed.

Resistance in Eritrea increased but the Dergue condemned the secessionist aims of the Eritrean Liberation Front. Fighting occurred on a large scale in Eritrea in 1975. In March 1975, the Dergue announced that all land would be nationalized and that Ethiopia would become a socialist republic.

ETOSHA PAN is a salt pan in the northern part of Namibia (South-West Africa), about 1,000 metres (3,400 feet) above sea level. With an area of 5,888 square kilometres (2,300 square miles), it is the largest salt pan in Africa. It lies at the centre of the Etosha game reserve. During the rainy season, it is flooded by rivers from the north, but most of the water is lost through evaporation.

FEZ or Fes, originally Faas, a Moroccan provincial capital in the plain of Sais, was the traditional capital of North Morocco. It is now a residential city with some light industry, particularly tobacco and food processing. It is a centre for traditional handicrafts. The fez, the famous Turkish hat, was first manufactured there. Pop. 243,000.

FIANARANTSOA is an administrative centre in the uplands of the Malagasy Republic. Pop. 39,000.

FORT-LAMY see N'DJAMENA.

FORT PORTAL, a town and provincial capital of western Uganda, lies near the border with Zaire. It is about 250 kilometres (160 miles) west of KAMPALA.

FORT VICTORIA, in south-eastern Zimbabwe was an early white settler town. It is now a farming centre and there is some mining in the district. Nearby are the famous ZIMBABWE RUINS. Pop. 13,000.

FOUTA DJALLON is a mountainous plateau of fine scenery in the centre of Guinea. It forms the region known as Middle Guinea and covers about 76,800 square kilometres (30,000 square miles). The highest peak is Tamgue at a height of 1,515 metres (4,970 feet). The Fouta Djallon is mainly inhabited by the cattle-raising Fulani (Fulbe) people. The NIGER and SENEGAL rivers have their source there.

ETHIOPIA: The ancient churches at Lalibela in northern Ethiopia were cut out of rock.

FEZ: A bustling street scene in this Moroccan provincial capital.

GABON: Omar Bongo became president of Gabon in 1967, succeeding Leon Mba. Bongo had previously served as vice-president.

GABERONE has been the capital of Botswana since 1965. Originally a small market town on the South Africa–Zimbabwe railway, it has grown as an administrative centre and as a communications centre. It has an airport and a radio station. It was previously the capital of the Batlokwa people. Pop. 27,000.

GABES is a coastal town in the south-east of Tunisia. The main industries are the manufacture of chemicals and fertilizers. Pop. 32,000.

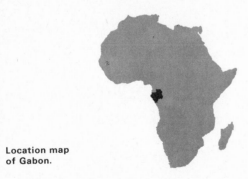

Location map of Gabon.

FRANCISTOWN is a commercial and industrial centre in northern Botswana and the largest town of the country. It is a centre for the processing of wildgame skins and an important ivory market. Pop. 41,000.

FREETOWN, a deep-water seaport and capital of Sierra Leone, lies on the northern shore of the rocky Sierra Leone Peninsula on the north-west coast. Among the city's features are a cathedral, college and museum. Industries include the refining of oil and the production of beer and shoes. Freetown was founded in 1788 as a settlement for freed African slaves. Pop. 200,000.

FUNCHAL is the capital and administrative centre of the Madeira Islands in the Atlantic Ocean. The town is built on the south coast of Madeira island on the lower slopes of the mountain. There is a cathedral dating from the late 1400s. The main occupations are fishing and agriculture. Pop. 95,000.

GABON, an independent republic on the west coast of central Africa, has borders with Congo in the east and south, and Equatorial Guinea and Cameroon in the north. The country, which is situated on the equator, has an area of 261,760 square kilometres (102,250 square miles) and a population of 500,000.

People The Fang people are the chief ethnic group in Gabon, numbering 180,000. Other groups include the Echira (92,000), the Adouma (60,000), the Okande (25,000) and the Kota (25,000). The official language is French. The population is equally divided between Christians and those who practise traditional African religions. One out of every four people live in towns, the largest of which are LIBREVILLE, the capital, PORT GENTIL and LAMBARÉNÉ.

Land and Economy Much of Gabon is highland, which, in places, rises to over 1,500 metres (5,000 feet). The high ground is cut into by the deep river valleys of the OGOUÉ RIVER and its tributaries. These valleys make communications difficult. The Atlantic coastline, which stretches for about 800 kilometres (500 miles), is swampy and indented with lagoons. Gabon has a tropical climate with a long and a short rainy season. Rainfall is abundant, and some parts of the country receive as much as 250 centimetres (100 inches) annually. The average temperature is 25°C (77°F).

By African standards, Gabon is a prosperous country, with an annual income per person of US $540. This prosperity is due to large mineral deposits and valuable hardwood forests. Although only five per cent of the country is under cultivation, four-fifths of the working population are engaged in agriculture. Cassava is the main food crop and cocoa, coffee, palm oil and rice are grown as cash crops. Forests cover 85 per cent of the country and timber production reaches nearly 1,000,000 tons a year. Timber has been the mainstay of the economy until recently, but has now been overtaken in importance by mining.

The major mineral resources of Gabon are uranium, which has estimated reserves of 1,000,000 tons; manganese with reserves of 200 million tons; and high grade iron ore, with reserves of 800 million tons. Small oilfields and reserves of natural gas have also been found. Poor communications have hampered the extraction of minerals. Gabon has a favourable balance of trade. Her main trading partners are France, the United States and West Germany.

Unit of currency Franc C.F.A.

History Gabon was first visited by the Portuguese in the late 1400s. The French established a naval and trading base near Libreville in the 1840s, and missionaries and colonists followed. Gabon became a colony within French Equatorial Africa in 1919. The country achieved internal self-government in 1957 and full independence as a republic three years later. The head of government from 1957, Leon Mba, became the first president. He was re-elected in 1967, but died shortly afterwards and was succeeded by Vice-President Omar BONGO. After independence, Gabon maintained close relations with France and an attempted coup in 1964 was put down with the aid of French troops. Gabon was one of the few African countries to recognize Biafra during the Nigerian civil war and this led to strained relations with Nigeria for a period.

Government In 1967 President Bongo revised the constitution and announced the formation of a new political party, the Gabonese Democratic Party. At the same time, he declared Gabon a one-party state. Gabon is a member of the Central African Customs Union (UDEAC) and an associate member of the EEC.

GAFSA, a town in central Tunisia, is the centre of the country's phosphate mining area. Phosphates are Tunisia's most important export. Dates are also grown and exported. Pop. 32,000.

Location map
of Gambia.

GAMBIA, a West African country extending inland from the Atlantic coast along the GAMBIA RIVER, is the smallest state in Africa. The narrow territory, which is 480 kilometres (300 miles) long, is like a finger pointing inland into Senegal, which surrounds it on three sides. Gambia covers 10,240 square kilometres (4,000 square miles) and has a population of about 493,000.

People The main ethnic groups of Gambia are the Mandingo (Mandinka or Bambara), Fula, Wolof, Jola and Serer. The capital BANJUL, formerly Bathurst, is located on St. Mary's Island at the mouth of the river. The official language is English, and Islam is the chief religion.

Land and Economy The Gambia river forms a valley in the surrounding Senegambian plateau. It has three main regions: the valley floor, often swampy, with fertile soil deposited by the river; the plateau edge, which is irregular, hilly and weathered; the plateau itself, which extends across the border from Senegal and is covered with poor, sandstone soils. The climate is tropical, with a dry season from November to April. Vegetation is mostly savanna, with a riverside forest strip.

Crops grown for local consumption include maize, millet and rice. The economy depends largely on groundnuts, the chief export crop. Gambia has no large-scale industry, but some cotton textiles are made. Communications are poor, with few metalled roads, and most passengers and goods are carried by river boats.

Unit of currency Dalasi

History Portuguese navigators first visited the Gambia River in 1455. English and French traders built forts near the river mouth in the 1600s and 1700s. In 1816, the British founded Bathurst, which, from 1821, was governed as part of Sierra Leone. In 1889, Britain obtained narrow strips of territory on either side of the Gambia River up to 480 kilometres (300 miles) inland. This territory became a British protectorate in 1894.

Gambia obtained internal self-government in 1962 and became an independent country within the Commonwealth in 1965. Sir Dawda JAWARA, leader of the People's Progressive Party, became prime minister. During the 1960s Gambia and Senegal signed agreements to follow joint development projects and to co-ordinate defence and foreign policy. In 1970, Gambia became a republic, with Sir Dawda Jawara as first president.

Government Gambia's republican constitution provides for a president and vice-president, elected for five-year terms. There is a 40-member house of representatives. Of these, 32 are elected and 8 are chosen by the government and chiefs.

GAMBIA RIVER, in West Africa, rises in the FOUTA DJALLON mountains of Guinea and flows north-west through Senegal and west through Gambia to the Atlantic Ocean at BANJUL (formerly Bathurst). About one-third of its 730 kilometres (460 miles) are navigable.

GAROUA, a market town in the north of Cameroon, lies in the Adamawa district on the BENUE RIVER.

GEZIRA (Jazira), in Sudan, is the triangular area between the BLUE NILE and the WHITE NILE south of Khartoum. A government-controlled project irrigates the area as a co-operative project with the cultivators to grow millet and cotton, Sudan's largest export crop.

GAMBIA: Stalls on Wellington Street, Banjul, Gambia's capital (formerly called Bathurst).

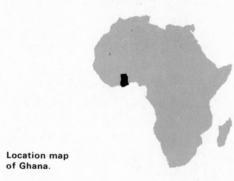

Location map
of Ghana.

GHANA, is an independent republic in West Africa, covering 235,116 square kilometres (91,842 square miles). It is bounded to the north by Upper Volta, to the east by Togo, to the west by Ivory Coast and to the south by the Atlantic Ocean. It has a population of 9,087,000.

People The people in Ghana originally came from the north and the east. In the southern forest region live the Akan (Asante, Twi and Fante) who form 45 per cent of the total population. Inhabiting the eastern region are the Ewe and Gan-Adangbe. The Guang and the Brong live in central Ghana. In the northern savanna region live the Dagomba (Dagbane), Grusi (Tamprusi), Mamprussi, Dagarti (Dagari or Dagati) and Kusasi. The majority of the population practise ethnic religions, about a third are Christians and there are some Muslims. ACCRA, the capital, is the largest city. Other important towns are KUMASI, Tamale and ports of CAPE COAST, SEKONDI-TAKORADI and TEMA.

Land and Economy Ghana is a low-lying country of savanna and forest, crossed by a network of streams and rivers. It has two major lakes: the man-made Lake VOLTA and the natural and sacred Lake BOSOMTWE. The dusty Harmattan wind blows from the Sahara from January to March and monsoon winds blow from the Atlantic from May to September. The average temperature is 27°C (80°F), the average rainfall is 100–180 centimetres (40–70 inches) a year and the humidity may range from 65 per cent in the day to 100 per cent at night.

Ghana's economy depends mainly on cocoa, of which it is the world's largest producer. Such an economy can be threatened too easily by fluctuations in world demand, and much effort is being made to increase the production of other crops. The cotton, oilpalm, rubber, sugar and tobacco industries are all being encouraged.

Ghana's second most important industry is timber. Ghana has over 150 species of trees, including wawa, mahogany and sapele. The country

exports timber and logs and has recently begun to produce veneers and plywoods. Ghana has long been famous for gold and is sixth among the world producers. It is the world's second largest producer of rough diamonds.

On the coast, the main source of income is fishing, and the industry based on Tema is being modernized. Off the coast, some oil and gas have been found, although their importance is not yet established. Other industries in Ghana include drinks manufacturing and engineering. One-third of Ghana's cheap electricity produced by the VOLTA DAM is used by an aluminium smelter.

Unit of currency Cedi

History The history of Ghana, or the Gold Coast as it was once known, is concerned with the gold and slave trades. From the 1400s to the 1800s the Portuguese, Dutch, Danish, French and English fought each other for control of the trade, and today their forts can still be seen. The coastal peoples traded with the Europeans while the people inland, who mined the gold, fought each for control of the trade routes.

On the coast the English were victorious, while inland the Ashanti grew rich and powerful, trading not only with the coast but with the Arab camel caravans that crossed the Sahara. Their first king was Osei Tutu, who built up a nation in the 1600s that was to withstand the British until 1901. He made his capital at Kumasi and built a magnificent palace. He presented the Golden Stool to the different peoples he had conquered in order to enshrine the nation's soul and symbolize its unity. He also laid down laws and procedures for all aspects of life and religion.

Much of this civilization survives to this day— the brass goldweights, the bright Kente cloths, the heavy gold jewellery and the architecture.

Modern Ghana is named after an ancient and very successful empire. In 1949, Kwame NKRUMAH founded the Convention People's Party and following Ghana's first general election in 1951, became prime minister. In 1957, Ghana became the first British African colony to receive independence. Nkrumah led the country until 1966 when he was deposed by a military coup. In 1969 the country returned to civilian rule under Dr. Kofi BUSIA but another military coup in January, 1972 brought Colonel Ignatius ACHEAMPONG to power.

Government Ghana is governed by the National Redemption Council whose chairman is Colonel Ignatius Acheampong. The council consists of officers of the armed forces. The various ministries are headed by 13 commissioners, one of whom is a civilian.

GHANA, an ancient kingdom 1,600 kilometres (1,000 miles) north of modern Ghana, was famous for its gold. It was possibly powerful as early as the AD 400s. It controlled gold prices, imposed taxes and dealt in slaves until its downfall in 1203, which was largely caused by the Almoravids, a Muslim sect. See MOROCCO, History.

GISENYI is a Rwandan port on the north-east shore of Lake KIVU, and is the country's main link with neighbouring Zaire. It caters for tourists visiting the volcanic regions of north-west Rwanda.

GIUBA RIVER or Juba River, rises in the Bali Highlands of south-east Ethiopia and flows for 1,600 kilometres (1,000 miles) through the plain of southern Somalia to enter the Indian Ocean near the port of Kisimayu. The lower course is navigable to shallow-draught vessels.

GIZA is a city on the west bank of the Nile south-west of Cairo, and the capital of the province of the same name. Near it are the ruins of Memphis and, to the south, the three great pyramids of Gizeh. Pop. over 250,000.

GONDAR, in northern Ethiopia, was the capital of the country from the 1500s until the mid 1800s, when THEODORE II moved the capital to Magdala. Several emperors built their castles at Gondar, which has now become a tourist attraction. A school for religious instruction is sited there. Pop. 25,000.

GHANA: The main post office in Accra.

GUINEA: Dancers on the road to Kindia.

Location map
of Guinea.

GUINEA, a republic in West Africa, is bordered by the Atlantic Ocean to the west, Guinea-Bissau, Senegal and Mali to the north, Ivory Coast to the east and Liberia and Sierra Leone to the south. Guinea covers 243,011 square kilometres and has a population of about 3,702,000.

People The main ethnic groups are the Peuls (Fulani), Malinke (Manding) and Soussous (Susu). Most of the peoples are Muslims. The official language is French. The capital, CONAKRY, KANKAN and KINDIA are the main towns.

Land and Economy The coast of Guinea is low and fringed with mangrove swamps and islands. Conakry, the capital, stands on Tombo Island. Lower Guinea is a coastal plain crossed by several winding rivers which form deltas. About 48 kilometres (30 miles) inland, the Kakoulima massif, formed from volcanic rock, rises to more than 900 metres (3,000 feet). Middle Guinea is formed by

the uplands of the FOUTA DJALLON massif. It covers about 76,800 square kilometres (30,000 square miles). Upper Guinea, in the north-east, consists of grassy plains. Southern Guinea is mountainous and forested. The highest peak, Mount Nimba, which rises to a height of 1,768 metres (5,800 feet), is in this region. The climate of Guinea is humid and tropical, with a rainy season from June to December.

Until independence in 1958, the economy was mainly based on farming. Export crops include coffee, pineapples and bananas. Rice and maize are grown as food crops. However, Guinea does not grow enough of these food crops and has to import some of its needs. Cattle are raised in the Fouta Djallon region.

Guinea has rich mineral deposits, including bauxite, iron ore, alumina and diamonds. Since independence the government has made great efforts to increase mineral production, especially of bauxite, and minerals are now the main exports.

The main industries of Guinea are cigarette production, furniture manufacture, textile printing and vehicle assembly. Guinea's rivers provide hydro-electricity. There are two railways, one from Conakry to Kankan and another from Conakry to Fria. About 16,000 kilometres (10,000 miles) of roads link the main cities and towns. Some centres are also linked by air services.

Unit of currency Guinea franc

History By about 1500, the Malinke people ruled Upper Guinea as the ancient kingdom of Mali, and the Peuls had established their rule over

Middle Guinea. The Soussous, related to the Malinke took control of the Conakry region at this time. The Portuguese first visited the Guinea coast in the 1400s and in the next 300 years, the area became a centre of operations for European slave traders.

In the 1860s, the French made treaties with coastal chiefs and began to penetrate the interior. By the 1880s, Southern Guinea was a French colony. However, Guinean chiefs resisted the French conquest, and the country did not come completely under French rule until 1911.

After World War II (1939–45), Sekou TOURÉ became the main nationalist leader. He and his party, the *Parti Démocratique de Guinée* (PDG) organized the people for independence. In 1958, when France offered its West African territories the choice of full independence or continued association with France, Guinea voted for independence. France reacted by cutting off all aid and withdrawing its administrators. Guinea survived with the help of aid from communist countries. On independence, Touré took office as head of state. He was re-elected in 1961, 1963 and 1968. In 1970, government forces defeated an invasion by Guinean exiles aided by foreign forces, generally believed to be Portuguese. Further border incidents occurred in 1973.

Government Guinea is a republic, with the head of state elected for a seven-year term. The national assembly has 75 elected members. The only political party is the PDG.

Location map
of Guinea-Bissau.

GUINEA-BISSAU, formerly Portuguese Guinea, is a territory in West Africa. It is bordered on the south-west by the Atlantic Ocean, on the north by Senegal and on the south-east by Guinea. It covers an area of 35,697 square kilometres (13,944 square miles) and has a population of 482,000.

People Various ethnic groups make up the population, most of whom are Muslims. The official language is Portuguese, but most of the people speak Cape Verde Creole. BISSAU, the capital, Bolama and Cacheu are the main towns.

Land and Economy The forested coastal area is low-lying and fringed with many small islands. Most of the interior is swampy, with some forest.

Guinea-Bissau's products include cassava, cattle, groundnuts, maize, palm oil and rice.

Unit of Currency Conto

History Portuguese traders reached the coast of Guinea by the 1400s but did not finally conquer the country until 1814. In 1962, the African Party for the Independence of Guinea and Cape Verde (PAIGC), led by Amilcar CABRAL (who was assassinated in 1973), launched an anti-Portuguese liberation war. By the early 1970s, the PAIGC controlled much of the country. In September 1974, Portugal conceded independence to Guinea-Bissau.

GUINEA, GULF OF, is a great bay of the Atlantic Ocean on the west-central coast of Africa, and includes the BIGHT OF BENIN. It washes the shores of Ghana, Togo, Dahomey and western Nigeria. It includes the Bight of Biafra.

GWELO is a mining and manufacturing town in the midlands of Zimbabwe. It was founded in 1894. The mining of gold and other minerals and the manufacture of shoes and glass are the main industries. Pop. 50,000.

HARAR a walled city, which was once an Islamic state, is still a Muslim centre in eastern Ethiopia. It is the only place where the Harari language, one of the Semitic languages, is still spoken. It stands on a mountain pass near the new town of DIREDAWA. Harar houses a teacher training institute and a military academy. Pop. 43,000.

HARGEISA, a town in north Somalia, was formerly the capital of British Somaliland. It is now a regional and district administrative centre.

HUAMBO see NOVA LISBOA.

IBADAN, a university and manufacturing city in Nigeria, lies about 140 kilometres (88 miles) north-east of LAGOS. It is the capital of the Western State, and has a radio station. It is a centre of Yoruba language and culture. Pop. 627,000.

IDI AMIN DADA, LAKE (formerly Lake Edward), lies in East Africa on the border between south-west Uganda and north-east Zaire. Its area is about 2,125 square kilometres (830 square miles). Its outlet is the Semlike River, which flows into Lake MOBUTU SESE SEKO (formerly Lake Albert).

IFE, a historic university town in Nigeria's Western State, lies close to the northern edge of the Nigerian forest. Ife is an ancient capital and royal residence of the Yoruba peoples, founded in about AD 1200. Pop. 155,000.

ILORIN, capital of Kwara State, western Nigeria. It is a market centre of the Yoruba people. It has an important trade in palm oil and rubber. Pop. 248,000.

INGA DAM is a project on the ZAIRE RIVER in Zaire. The site is 40 kilometres (25 miles) north of the port of MATADI and is part of the largest hydro-electric power scheme in Africa. The project has a maximum potential of 30,000 megawatts, distributed by high tension power lines to KINSHASA and eventually to the SHABA copper belt. The first stage began operation in November, 1972.

ISMAILIA is an Egyptian town on the western shore of Lake Timsah (part of the Suez Canal) about halfway between Port Said and Suez. It is the administrative headquarters of the Suez Canal Authority. The town was named after Ismail Pasha, the Khedive or Viceroy of Egypt when the canal was opened in 1869. Pop. about 150,000.

Location map
of Ivory Coast.

IVORY COAST is a square-shaped country in West Africa with a coastline on the Gulf of Guinea. It has borders with Liberia and Guinea in the west, Mali and Upper Volta in the north, and Ghana in the east. With an area of 318,728 square kilometres (124,503 square miles), it has a population of about 3,750,000.

People East Ivory Coast is inhabited by the Baule, Anyi and other peoples of the Akan ethnic group. The Djimini and Senoufo peoples live in the north-eastern part of the country. The Manding (Bambara and Dyula) live in the north. Most of the European minority live and work in Abidjan. Most people practise traditional religions, but there are sizeable minorities of Muslims and Christians. French is the official language. Nearly one-third of the people live in towns, of which ABIDJAN, the capital, Bouake and Gagnoa are the largest.

Land and Economy Ivory Coast is divided into three major geographical areas. The coastal region, which is indented with lagoons and swamps, is covered with tropical rain forest and extends inland for about 290 kilometres (180 miles). This gives way to dryer, wooded areas in the centre of the country, and eventually to grasslands in the north. The forested Guinea highlands rise to over 1,500 metres (5,000 feet) in the west. Three main rivers run from north to south—the Sassandra, the Bandama and the Comoe. The Cavalla River forms part of Ivory Coast's border with Liberia. The country has a tropical climate, and rainfall and temperatures are high.

The industrial economy of the Ivory Coast has prospered and expanded since independence in 1960 largely as a result of deliberate economic policies and political stability which has attracted foreign capital to the country. More than two-thirds of the people are peasant farmers. Cotton, groundnuts, maize and rice are grown and consumed locally. Coffee and cotton are the principal export crops. Pineapples, which are canned in local factories, and rubber are also produced. Timber, from the extensive forested areas, forms an important part of the economy and is exported in large quantities. Most of the country's industry processes agricultural products and timber. There are over 50 factories in Abidjan which produce electrical goods, assembled automobiles and plastics. Textiles, soap and metal goods are also manufactured. Most factories are foreign owned; they have greatly improved the prosperity of Ivory Coast. A hydro-electric power station on the Bia river provides power. In 1968 there was a balance of payments surplus of £21,200,000.

Unit of currency Franc

History Ivory Coast was declared a French colony in 1893, and by 1898 African resistance had been overcome. In 1904, Ivory Coast was made part of French West Africa. Agitation for independence began in 1946, when Felix HOUPHOUET-BOIGNY founded the *Parti Démocratique de la Côte d'Ivoire* (PDCI). In 1958, autonomy was granted and two years later Ivory Coast became an independent Republic. Houphouet-Boigny, who had led the independence movement throughout French West Africa, became the first President. He was re-elected in 1965. By employing foreign economic consultants and encouraging foreign businesses, he has made Ivory Coast an economically strong country. However, industrialization has created problems—the cities have become overcrowded by people moving in from the country areas in search of work and unrest is growing at the lack of Africanization in business. An attempted military plot to overthrow the government of Ivory Coast was discovered in June 1973.

Government Ivory Coast is a one-party state, that party being the PDCI. The national assembly has 85 members, who are elected every five years through direct vote. Ivory Coast is an associate member of the EEC and a member of the loose organization of West African states (Dahomey, Ivory Coast, Niger and Upper Volta) known as the *Conseil de l'Entente*.

IWO, a Yoruba city, lies in Nigeria's Western State. It is near the LAGOS–KANO railway to the north of IBADAN. Pop. 188,000.

JAMESTOWN is the capital of ST. HELENA, an island in the Atlantic Ocean. It lies in the north-west of the island on St. James Bay. It was once important as a coaling station and watering point for ships. The cathedral and the governor's palace are outside the town in the cooler highlands. Pop. 1,550.

JIMMA is an agricultural town in south-west Ethiopia. It is the centre of Ethiopia's main coffee-growing area, and is surrounded by natural rain forest where coffee, the largest export crop, grows wild. Pop. 40,000.

JINJA, the second largest town in Uganda, lies in the south-east of the country at the northern end of Lake VICTORIA. It is linked with the town of Njeru to form a large conurbation. It is a military centre and site of the Owen Falls Dam. The chief products are textiles and steel. Pop. 52,000.

JOHANNESBURG is the largest city and chief industrial, financial and communications centre of South Africa. It was founded in 1886 during the Gold Rush to the centre of the WITWATERSRAND and grew very rapidly with the gold industry. It now contains Witwatersrand University. The Jan Smuts international airport is nearby and the large African city of Soweto is on the outskirts. Pop. 1,433,000.

JOS, a tin-mining town, lies in the extreme north of Nigeria's Benue-Plateau State, of which it is the capital. It is on a branch of the railway from the Lake Chad region to PORT HARCOURT. Pop. 90,000.

KABELEGA FALLS, in Uganda, are on the VICTORIA NILE just north-east of Lake MOBUTU SESE SEKO. The falls are 36 metres (188 feet) high. They were once called the Murchison Falls.

KABWE is the capital of Central Province, Zambia. It was known as Broken Hill until 1964. Zinc and lead are mined nearby in the only major mine outside the Copperbelt. It is the garrison town of the Zambian Army.

KADUNA, the capital of Nigeria's North-Central State, lies on the LAGOS-KANO railway. The town has a radio station and a polytechnic college. Pop. 178,000.

KAEDI, in Mauritania, lies on the north shore of the SENEGAL RIVER. It is the most important commercial centre of eastern Mauritania.

KAFUE RIVER rises north of Zambia's copper-belt and joins the River ZAMBEZI at Chirundu in the south. After flowing southward it turns east across the Kafue flats and enters the Kafue gorge, where the level falls sharply by 600 metres (2,000 feet) in 30 kilometres (20 miles).

KAGERA RIVER is formed by the joining of the RUVUVU and Nyavarongo rivers. It flows north along the border between Rwanda and Tanzania and then east, forming the frontier between Tanzania and Uganda for a short distance then flowing into Tanzania alone until it reaches Lake VICTORIA.

KAINJI DAM see NEW BUSSA.

KAIROUAN see QUAYRAWAN.

JOHANNESBURG: A view of the city from the air.

KANKAN, a town in eastern Guinea, lies at the terminus of the railway from CONAKRY, and is at the junction of several roads. Pop. 76,000.

KANO is the capital city of Kano state in northern Nigeria. Founded in the AD 1000s, it was the capital of the Habe state until taken by the Fulani Muslims in 1807. It fell to the British in 1903. It is now an important centre for the vegetable oil processing industry. It has an international airport.

KANYE, in Botswana, is the market centre for an agricultural area which is irrigated by a nearby dam. It is situated south of GABERONES, the capital, and is the capital of the Bangwakese people. It is an asbestos mining centre. Pop. 34,000.

KAOLACK, in western Senegal, lies on the SALOUM RIVER, south-east of DAKAR. Pop. 96,000.

KARIBA LAKE is 280 kilometres (175 miles) long. It was formed after the building of the Kariba Dam on the Zambezi River. The dam is 128 metres (420 feet) high. The Zambia–Zimbabwe border runs through the man-made lake and the electricity supplies of both countries depend on the Kariba hydro-electric scheme.

KALAHARI: This desert and semi-desert region lies in Botswana and Namibia.

KALAHARI is a huge semi-desert region, which extends over 560,000 square kilometres (350,000 square miles) of western Botswana and eastern Namibia (South-West Africa). Parts of it are covered with sparse scrub vegetation and it contains a few scattered water holes. Small clans of nomadic Bushmen live there.

KAMPALA, capital of Uganda, lies about 30 kilometres (20 miles) north of Lake VICTORIA. It was also capital of the old BUGANDA kingdom, now the province of Buganda. Kampala is on the railway from Kasese in western Uganda to MOMBASA in Kenya. Its international airport is at nearby ENTEBBE. Makerere university is situated there and there is a television station. Products include metal goods and tobacco. Pop. 332,000.

KA MPFUMO see LOURENÇO MARQUES.

KANANGA is the capital of West Kasai province, Zaire. Its old name was Luluabourg. Rubber, sugar and timber are produced in the surrounding rain forests, and industrial diamonds are mined to the south-west. These products are sent by rail to Ilebo and road to KINSHASA. Pop. 60,000.

KANEM is a region covering about 35,000 square kilometres (22,000 square miles) in Chad, to the north-east of Lake CHAD. A powerful state was founded there in the AD 1000s. In the 1200s Kanem became subject to Bornu. Together, as Kanem-Bornu, they formed a strong empire which lasted until the 1800s. The chief town was Mao.

KARIBA LAKE: This lake *above* lies behind Kariba dam.
KANO: The great Kano mosque *below* is encircled by sprawling houses.

KARNAK is a town on the east bank of the Nile in southern Egypt. It stands on the site of the ancient capital of Thebes. It contains the remains of the temple of Amon and other ruins.

KAROO are areas of dry plateau land in the Cape province of South Africa. The Great Karoo and the Little Karoo are situated on 'steps' between the coastal ranges and the escarpment and are important for merino sheep and angora goats.

KASAI RIVER is a tributary of the ZAIRE RIVER in Zaire. From its source in eastern Angola it flows north along the border with SHABA province into West Kasai province. There, it widens and turns north-west to the Zaire River. It is an important part of the route from the copper belt of Shaba and Zambia.

KASSALA, the capital of Kassala province, Sudan, was founded by the Egyptians in about 1840. It is situated in some of the most fertile land in the country. It produces millet.

KAYES is a town on the Senegal River in south-west Mali. For two months of the year, it is the highest navigable point on the river.

KEETMANSHOOP is a town in Namibia (South-West Africa). It is situated in the south of the central plateau at an altitude of 1,152 metres (3,782 feet). Named after a German merchant who founded a mission station on the site in 1866, it is now the centre of the sheep-farming district and marakul wool industry. Pop. 10,000.

**Location map
of Kenya.**

KENYA, is an independent republic in East Africa. It has borders with Tanzania in the south, Uganda in the west, Sudan and Ethiopia in the north, and Somalia in the north-east. It has a coastline on the Indian Ocean. The country has a population of 12,482,000 and an area of 575,898 square kilometres (224,960 square miles).

People About 40 separate ethnic groups live in Kenya. The largest are the Kikuyu (2,201,000), the Kamba (1,198,000), the Luo (1,521,000) and the Luhya (1,453,000). The main minorities are the Asians (139,000), Europeans (40,000) and Arabs (28,000). Most people speak Swahili which, with English, is the official language. About a third of the people are Christians, Islam is the religion of a fifth, whilst the others practise ethnic religions. NAIROBI, the capital, is the largest city, followed by MOMBASA, NAKURU and KISUMU.

Land and Economy The north and north-east of Kenya is a dry semi-desert that covers more than a third of the country. The Kenya highlands in the south-west where most people live have a warm climate and receive a rainfall of about 75 cms a year. The GREAT RIFT VALLEY bisects the highlands from north to south. To the west, towards Lake VICTORIA, lie fertile grasslands that provide good agricultural land. The narrow coastal strip is both humid and hot, and is covered by swamps and rain forest. Temperatures and rainfall vary greatly throughout Kenya.

Kenya's economy is basically agricultural, most farming taking place in the central area of the country, although hardy cattle and camels are raised in the semi-desert areas in the north. Coffee, dairy products, hides, meat, pyrethrum, sisal and tea are the major agricultural products and they also form the bulk of Kenya's exports. The country has developed many secondary industries that process both local raw materials (to make, for example, blankets, margarine, paint and soap) and imported raw materials (to make such products as plastics and cement). The Mombasa-Uganda railway runs across the country and there are over 1,600 kilometres (1,000 miles) of metalled roads. Kenya is pursuing a policy of africanization.

Unit of currency Kenya Shilling.

History Muslims from South Arabia colonized the Kenya coast from the AD 700s. They made their living through trade and agriculture and established several prosperous city states along the coast. It was they who pioneered the first trading routes into the interior. The Portuguese landed in Mombasa in 1498, made it their headquarters in 1593, and were expelled by the Arabs in 1731. The sultan of Zanzibar conquered Mombasa in 1838.

The activities of the Imperial British East Africa Company led to British involvement in the area. The British established a protectorate and founded NAIROBI in 1895. Many Africans fought bitterly against the imposition of British rule, but the country was occupied by 1906. The building of the Mombasa–Uganda railway opened up the interior of Kenya to effective administration, as well as to Christian missionaries and European settlers.

Africans had no political rights in the new colony and some of their land was taken over, especially in the fertile highlands, traditionally occupied by the Kikuyu and Masai peoples. African nationalist movements began with the East African Association, whose leader, Harry THUKU, was deported in 1922. Later political activity came to be dominated by the Kikuyu and Luo people and was closely connected with grievances over land and labour. This activity culminated in the emergency period of 1952–60, when the 'Mau Mau' engaged in guerilla war against the colonial system. Jomo KENYATTA, later to become Kenya's first president, was accused of organizing the movement and was detained until 1961. The guerillas were decimated after a long and bitter struggle in which 100,000 of their suspected supporters were detained.

In 1961, universal suffrage was introduced and in the following election the Kenya African National Union (KANU) gained a majority over the Kenya African Democratic Union (KADU). However, KANU refused to form a government until their leader, Kenyatta, had been released from detention and so KADU took power. Full internal self-government was granted on June 1, 1963, and new elections were held, in which KANU were successful. On December 12, 1963, Kenya became independent with Kenyatta as its first prime minister. One year later, Kenya declared itself a republic within the Commonwealth. In 1965 the KADU party disbanded itself and joined with KANU. A new party, the Kenya Peoples Union (KPU) was formed in 1966, but was banned by Kenyatta three years later, leaving Kenya a one-party state. In 1967, Kenya became a member of the East African Community, together with Uganda and Tanzania. This organization co-operates in economic activities and certain services affecting the area as a whole.

Government Kenya has a strong central government with a 170-member parliament. All seats are held by the governing party, KANU. The country is divided into eight provinces, administered by centrally appointed commissioners.

KHARTOUM, the capital of the Republic of Sudan, is situated where the BLUE NILE and WHITE NILE join. It was founded by Egyptians in 1822, and occupied by the MAHDI in 1885. Lord Kitchener rebuilt it as a spacious new town in 1899. Pop. 280,000.

KHARTOUM NORTH (or Halfaya), a suburb 4 kilometres (2.5 miles) from KHARTOUM on the left bank of the NILE, is chiefly important as a residential quarter, with barracks and warehouses. Pop. 138,000.

KIGALI, the capital of Rwanda, is the country's administrative and communications centre. It was founded at the turn of the century by the German colonialists. It has an airport and is the business centre of the mining industry. Pop. 25,000.

KIGOMA, is the main Tanzanian port of Lake TANGANYIKA, on which it operates a steamship service. It is the principal port for trade with Zaire. It is also the terminal for a railway which reaches DAR ES SALAAM.

KILIMANJARO see MOUNT KILIMANJARO.

KIMA, Tanzania, is the name of three adjacent places. Kilwa Kisiwani, founded in AD 957, was capital of a sultanate and one of the most important Swahili trading towns from the 1100s to the 1500s. Kilwa Masoko is the modern headquarters of the Kilwa area, and Kilwa Kivinje, was a former slave-trading centre founded in about 1800.

KIMBERLEY, in northern Cape province, is the diamond mining centre of South Africa. It grew rapidly after the discovery of diamonds in 1870, and became linked with the coast by rail. It has had only limited industrial growth and is a regional centre for Griqualand. Pop. 96,000.

KINDIA, a town in Guinea, lies in the west of the country, on the railway 95 kilometres (60 miles) north-east of CONAKRY. It is a bauxite mining centre. Pop. 55,000.

KINSHASA, is the capital and main industrial centre of Zaire. Located on the east bank of the ZAIRE RIVER at its widest point, the city is a collection point for export products which are sent by rail to the port of MATADI. The rapids on the lower reaches of the Zaire River prevent any navigation. Most trading and manufacturing organizations in Zaire are established in the Kinshasa area. Kinshasa was formerly called Léopoldville. Just south of the city is the famous Université Lovanium. Pop. 1,323,000.

KISANGANI is the capital of Upper Zaire province, Zaire. The town lies close to the equator, situated on the ZAIRE RIVER just below the point where it is called the LUALABA RIVER. It is the centre of a rich agricultural region that produces coffee, cocoa, cotton, palm oil and timber. There is a university and an international airport. Kisangani was earlier called Stanleyville. Pop. 230,000.

KISUMU, a port on Lake VICTORIA, is the chief town of Nyanza province in the west of Kenya. Situated 340 kilometres (214 miles) from NAIROBI, it is the terminal of rail and road routes and the site of an international airport. Pop. 32,000.

KITEGA, in the geographical centre of Burundi, was the ancient capital of the *mwami* (Tutsi king). It is today little more than an overgrown village with an airfield, and a thriving market. Pop. 5,000.

KITWE is the second largest city in Zambia and lies at the centre of the copperbelt. Two major copper mines provide employment. Secondary industries include iron founding, precision engineering, printing and maize milling. Pop. 250,000.

KIVU, LAKE, 95 kilometres (60 miles) long and 48 kilometres (30 miles) wide, forms part of the border between Rwanda and Zaire. Deposits of methane gas lie beneath the deepest parts of the lake which reach down to 490 metres (1,600 feet). The main ports on the lake are BUKAVU, Goma, GISENYI and Changugu.

KORDOFAN PLATEAU, in Kordofan Province, Sudan is an area of about 332,800 square kilometres (130,000 square miles) of barren undulating plain averaging 460 metres (1,500 feet) above sea level. It is inhabited by nomads and farmers of mixed livestock.

KOUDOUGOU, in Upper Volta, lies 88 kilometres (55 miles) west of OUAGADOUGOU, to which it is connected by rail. It is an agricultural centre and processes goods including shea nut butter. Nearby are accessible deposits of chrome and manganese ore. Pop. 41,000.

KUFRA OASIS is a group of small settlements in south-east Libya. Kufra (Kufrah) was sacred to the former royal family of IDRIS I (the Sanussi). Since 1968, the underground water of the area has been used to irrigate alfalfa fodder for sheep.

KUMASI, a city in Ghana, was founded in about 1700 as the Ashanti capital. It now has a university, a large hospital and a modern cultural centre and is second only to ACCRA. It is a major commercial centre for cocoa and timber. Pop. 320,000.

KUNENE (CUNENE) RIVER rises in central Angola and runs on a southerly course for 700 kilometres (450 miles) until it bends west to form a border stretching for 290 kilometres (180 miles) between Angola and Namibia.

KUSH was an ancient kingdom south of Nubia and originally an Egyptian colony. Kush expanded after 1000 BC with the decline of the Egyptian civilization. At the height of its power, around 300 BC, Kush's influence extended from Ethiopia to Niger. MEROE, the capital, was sacked by the Axumites in AD 4 and the kingdom disintegrated.

KWANGO RIVER rises in northern Angola and runs north-west into Zaire, joining the KASAI RIVER at Bandundu. Kwango province, named after it, is inhabited by the warlike Ba-Yaka.

KWANZA (CUANZA) RIVER is the longest river in Angola. It flows north-west from the central plateau for 950 kilometres (600 miles) to the sea, draining a large interior area. It is navigable for 190 kilometres (120 miles) from the sea. The river supplies power to a hydro-electric station, Cambambe, in the north.

KYOGA LAKE lies in the centre of Uganda and covers about 2,560 square kilometres (1,000 square miles). Its shores have many gulfs. The VICTORIA NILE flows through it.

KENYA: *Above* Coffee on a smallholding. Coffee is one of the country's chief exports.

KENYA: *Right* A typical Kenyan landscape with an elephant browsing on the savanna near a road.

KENYA: *Above* A view of the city of Nairobi, Kenya's capital, with President Jomo Kenyatta (inset).

KENYA: *Right* Young lionesses in Tsavo National Park. Kenya's fascinating wildlife is a major tourist attraction.

LABE, a cattle marketing town, lies in the FOUTA DJALLON region of west-central Guinea. It is the main town of the Peul people. Pop. 283,000.

LAGOS, a seaport and the capital of Nigeria, is located on marshy Lagos Island off the south-western coast. It is connected by rail to the northern centre of KANO, and has extensive docks. One of the fastest-growing cities of West Africa, Lagos has many fine modern buildings and a university. Products include beer, cement, chemicals and textiles. The name, which is Portuguese for 'lake' or 'lagoon', was given to it by the Portuguese in the 1400s because of the many lagoons of the region. Pop. 875,000.

LAMBARENE, a town of western Gabon, lies on the lower OGOUÉ RIVER. It is the site of the hospital and medical settlement first established by Dr. Albert SCHWEITZER in 1913. Pop. 7,000.

LAMU is a town in Kenya on the off-shore island of the same name. It was founded in the AD 700s as an independent republic. It has a small port and now exports mangrove poles for shipbuilding, coconut oil, charcoal and fish. Lamu is also a centre of Swahili literature and art and of Islamic studies.

LAS PALMAS, the largest town in the Canary Islands, is the capital of one of the two provinces of Spain formed by the islands. It is situated in the north-east of the island of Gran Canaria. Its harbour is much used as a port-of-call, and many ships refuel there.

Location map
of Lesotho.

LESOTHO is a small land-locked mountainous country, situated in the south-east of southern Africa. It is surrounded on all sides by South Africa. With an area of 29,993 square kilometres (11,716 square miles) Lesotho has a population of more than one million.

People Nearly all the people of Lesotho, with the exception of a 3,000-strong minority of white South Africans, Asians and Coloureds, belong to the Basotho ethnic group. Sotho and English are the official languages. More than half the people are Christians. The remainder practise their traditional religions. Most people live in rural areas, and MASERU, the capital, is the only town of any size. Roma is a famous university.

Land and Economy Two-thirds of Lesotho are mountainous, rising to over 3,350 metres (11,000 feet) in the DRAKENSBERGS in the south and east, and to over 2,750 metres (9,000 feet) in the Maluti Mountains in the north. The valleys of the ORANGE and Caledon rivers and their tributaries cut into the high ground. The climate varies according to the altitude. Rainfall averages about 70 centimetres (28 inches), but is sporadic.

Much of Lesotho's soil is of poor quality. Subsistence farming, which employs most of the people, does not provide enough food to feed the whole country. Maize, sorghum, wheat and vegetables are the main food crops. Livestock is reared on the rough pastures of the uplands. Cattle, mohair goats and sheep are important to the economy and their products form a major proportion of Lesotho's exports. Some diamond mining is carried on in the north, but the yield is low. Industrial activity is limited to small-scale factories, mainly in Maseru, which produce candles, carpets, tyres and cut diamonds. Lesotho's main source of

LESOTHO: Primary school children at Makhalanyane, in Lesotho.

foreign income is from workers who take jobs as miners or labourers in South Africa. About 45 per cent of the male adult labour force work in South Africa and bring home their wages.

Unit of currency Rand

History The Basotho first became a nation in what is now Lesotho in the 1820s. King MOSHOE-SHOE I united them after they had suffered great depredations from the Zulus and Matabeles. Under Moshoeshoe's leadership, they resisted the attacks of the Nguni, and maintained their independence in the face of Boer and British colonial forces. In 1884, Lesotho became a British protectorate under the name of Basutoland. The protectorate was administered largely by the local chiefs under the supervision of a resident commissioner. Nationalist agitation for independence developed in the 1950s under Ntsu MOKHEHLE's Basutoland Congress Party (BCP). However, Chief Leabua JONATHAN's Basutoland National Party (BNP), which was more conservative and favoured close links with South Africa, narrowly won the pre-independence elections in 1965 and formed the first government. Basutoland became an independent kingdom in 1966, having successfully resisted incorporation into South Africa. Elections were held in 1970, and the BCP claimed a victory, but Chief Jonathan declared that the result was void. A state of emergency was declared and opposition leaders and supporters were detained. King MOSHOESHOE II, who had previously had disagreements with Chief Jonathan, went into exile for eight months. All political activity was suspended. In 1971 the political detainees were released, but the government continued to ban the opposition. In 1974, Chief Jonathan denounced a plot to overthrow the government.

Location map
of Liberia.

LIBERIA, the oldest independent republic in West Africa, is bordered by the Atlantic Ocean to the south-west, Sierra Leone to the north-west, and Guinea and Ivory Coast to the north-east and east. Liberia covers 110,080 square kilometres (43,000 square miles). Pop. 1,232,000.

LIBYA: Salting skins. Cured hides and skins are important agricultural exports.

People About one out of 100 Liberians is descended from free Afro-American slaves. These people, the Americo-Liberians, have controlled the political and economic life of the country. The indigenous peoples are divided into four main language groups: (1) the Kru, the largest group, who inhabit the southern coastal area; (2) the Mande-tan group, including the Vai people of the northern coastal area; (3) the Mande-fu group in the north; and (4) the West Atlantic group in the west. The official language is English. The capital is MONROVIA.

Land and Economy The coastal areas are low-lying with many lagoons and tidal creeks. Inland is a plateau region of grassland, averaging about 900 metres (3,000 feet) above sea level. In the north, bordering Guinea and Ivory Coast, are highlands. Large areas are forested. The climate is equatorial, with a dry season from November to March. Coastal areas have the greatest rainfall.

Until the early 1960s, Liberia's economy depended mainly on exports of rubber. However, by the 1970s Liberia's iron ore exports were worth nearly twice as much as rubber exports. Agricultural products include bananas, cocoa, coffee, palm oil and kernels, sugar and rice. Liberia encourages foreign ships to register under the Liberian flag by levying a low tax on ship owners. For this reason, the country appears to have one of the world's largest merchant fleets.

Unit of currency U.S. dollar

History In 1820, the American Colonization Society sent a party of 88 freed Afro-American slaves to Liberia. A settlement was founded on Sherbo Island, but most of the colonists died of malaria or moved to Sierra Leone. After another unsuccessful expedition, a third one, in 1822, founded Monrovia. In 1847, Liberia became independent. For many years the colonists sought to pacify the peoples of the interior, to defend themselves against neighbouring colonial powers and to achieve economic stability. In 1926, the Firestone Rubber Company of the United States bought a 99-year lease for up to 405,000 hectares (1 million acres) of Liberian territory for rubber production. In the 1930s, Firestone's labour policies in Liberia provoked international protests. The Liberian government resisted attempts by the League of Nations to impose reforms. However, it finally signed a new agreement with Firestone that reduced the company's economic hold on the country. In 1944 when William TUBMAN became president, Liberia began an 'open door' policy for foreign investment and many United States and European Companies established industries. However, the government holds a 50 per cent stake in many of the foreign companies. Tubman also

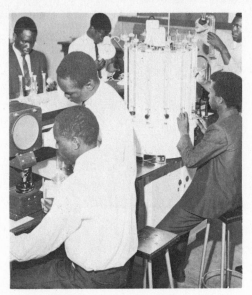

LUSAKA: Students at work in a laboratory in the University of Zambia, Lusaka.

introduced universal suffrage, and lessened the power of the Americo-Liberian minority. In 1971, Vice-President William TOLBERT succeeded Tubman as president.

Government Liberia's constitution, modelled on that of the United States, provides for a legislature consisting of a 17-member senate and a 53-member house of representatives. The government is headed by the president, who is elected for eight years initially, and then for any number of four-year terms.

LIBREVILLE, a seaport and the capital of Gabon, lies on the northern side of the mouth of the Gabon River. It was founded as a settlement for free slaves in 1849. The town has a university and contains the headquarters of uranium and manganese mining companies. Pop. 75,000.

Location map of Libya.

LIBYA is a republic on the Mediterranean coast of North Africa. It is bordered by Egypt and Sudan in the east, Chad and Niger in the south, and Algeria and Tunisia in the west. Since 1969, Libya has become rich through the exploitation of its vast oil reserves. Covering an area of 2,073,600 square kilometres (810,000 square miles), Libya has an estimated population of 2,240,000.

People The original inhabitants of Libya were Berbers. This group now forms only five per cent of the population, and most of them live in remote areas in the north-west. Because of successive invasions by Mediterranean peoples and trading links with Africa south of the Sahara, Libya has a mixed ethnic heritage. Most people are descended from the Arabs who settled in Libya between the 600s and 1000s. As a result, Libyans speak Arabic and are Muslims. The chief centres are the twin capitals, BENGASI and TRIPOLI.

Land and Economy Nearly 90 per cent of Libya is desert or semi-desert. Huge dry basins of rock and sand cover most of the country. The highest land, 2,290 metres (7,500 feet) above sea-level, is in the south-east. Rainfall is sparse. Tripoli in the north-west, receives 35 centimetres a year.

Today, Libya's economy almost entirely depends upon petroleum production. About half of the population work in agriculture, although less than one per cent of the land is cultivated. Cereals, citrus fruits, groundnuts and olives are grown mainly for Libyan use. About one-tenth of Libya is poor grazing land used to raise livestock—cattle, camels, sheep and goats. The contribution of agriculture to the national income has declined from more than 90 per cent in the 1950s to less than 5 per cent in 1972.

The export of petroleum began in 1961 and grew at the rate of between 15 and 20 per cent annually between 1965 and 1969. By 1969, output had risen to 125 million tons per year, and Libyan oil earnings were higher than any other African or Middle Eastern country. Because the Libyan government decided to conserve its oil resources, oil production decreased after 1969. Earnings, however, increased because the price of petroleum rose. Chemical industries based on oil are the most successful industrial enterprise. The expansion of other industries has been hampered by the shortage of skilled labour. Because of its oil production, Libya has the highest income per head in Africa, in 1968 it was £565.

Unit of currency Libyan dinar

History Ancient Roman authors gave the name Libya to the area of North Africa west of Egypt. Greeks, Phoenicians and Romans colonized Cyrenaica and other coastal areas, but were resisted by the people of Germa (the Garamantes) who lived in the remote south. Byzantine influence replaced that of Rome in the AD 300s in the coastal cities of Tripolitania—Sabrata, Oea (Tripoli) and Leptis Magna—and in the Pentapolis (including Cyrene and Apollonia) in Cyrenaica. The area was invaded by Arabs in the 600s. Later, the area was subject to a number of foreign regimes, including Spanish, Maltese, Turkish (until 1911), Italian (until 1943) and British, before ultimate independence in 1951.

Libya was a constitutional monarchy until September 1, 1969, when IDRIS I was overthrown by a revolutionary movement led by a group of young army officers, under Muammar al GADDAFI. After the revolution, Libya took an increasingly militant line in both internal and international policies. Colonel Gaddafi adopted a policy of unrelenting opposition to Israel, and gave support to Palestinian guerilla organizations. 'Arabization' was achieved in Libya with the assistance of trained personnel from Egypt. In 1971, a treaty was signed with Syria and Egypt to form the Federation of Arab Republics. Libya and Egypt set a target of September 1973 for the merger of their countries. But in August 1973, Presidents Gaddafi and SADAT agreed on a more gradual approach to unity.

Government The army-dominated Revolutionary Command Council governs the country through a cabinet of about 20 ministers. For administrative purposes, the country is divided into ten *muhafadat* (provinces).

LIKASI, is a town in SHABA province, Zaire. It is the most important centre of the copper, cobalt and zinc mining industries and is on the railway from LUBUMBASHI to Ilebo and to LOBITO in Angola. Pop. 74,000.

LILONGWE is the capital of Malawi. It is situated in the central region at the junction of roads leading southward to BLANTYRE–LIMBE, northward to Tunduma on the border of Zambia and Tanzania, and westward to LUSAKA. Pop. 20,000.

LIMPOPO RIVER is one of the major rivers of southern Africa. It rises in the Magaliesberg Mountains, near PRETORIA in South Africa, and flows 1,440 kilometres (900 miles) to reach the coast of Mozambique just north of LOURENÇO MARQUES. It forms the South African border with Botswana and Zimbabwe.

LIVINGSTONE see MARAMBA.

LOBATSE, a town in Botswana situated on the southern border with South Africa. The town has one of the most modern abattoirs in Africa and is

the centre for the beef cattle industry. Hides, carcasses and canned meat are produced there and exported, mainly to South Africa. Pop. 24,000.

LOBITO is a port on the coast of Angola. Together with the old city of BENGUELA to the south, it forms a combined urban complex, with administrative, trading, and fishing activities. Lobito is the terminus of the Benguela Railway which runs west from the SHABA province of Zaire. Pop. 100,000.

LOME, the capital and main sea port of Togo, is the chief commercial centre of the country. Cotton ginning is an important industry and exports include phosphates, cacao, palm kernels and coffee. It has an airport and is linked with the interior by rail. Pop. 148,500.

LOURENÇO MARQUES, renamed Maputo in 1976, is the capital and commercial centre of Mozambique. Situated on the southern coast, it has acted as the main outlet for trade to and from South Africa since the construction of a railway to Pretoria in 1895. The settlement was established in 1544, by a Portuguese trader called Lourenço Marques. The port handles 9,700,000 tonnes (9,500,000 tons) of cargo per year. Pop. 250,000.

LOVANIUM is part of the National University of Zaire. It was founded in 1954 just outside KINSHASA by the Roman Catholic University of Louvain in Belgium and financed by Roman Catholic sources. In 1971, Lovanium, together with the Protestant university at KISANGANI and the state university at LUBUMBASHI, were reconstituted as campuses of the National University of Zaire.

LUALABA RIVER, forms the eastern arm of the main stream of the ZAIRE RIVER. From its source in southern SHABA province, it flows north through Kivu and Upper Zaire provinces. Just south of KISANGANI, the river passes through cataracts and rapids and the river is known as the Zaire River.

LUANDA is the capital and main economic centre of Angola. Its deep-water port handles most of Angola's overseas trade. Most of the country's industry is situated in and around Luanda. Coffee, cotton and sugar are exported from there. Products include paper, shoes and textiles. Pop. 500,000.

LUANGWA RIVER, which crosses eastern Zambia from north-east to south-west, follows a rift valley. With its main tributary, the Lumsemfwa River, it drains most of eastern Zambia.

LUANSHYA, the most southerly of the towns on Zambia's copperbelt, is the site of Roan-Antelope, the oldest operating copper mine in Zambia. Secondary industries include mining machinery, furniture and clothing. Pop. 110,000.

LUAPULA RIVER rises in SHABA province, Zaire but flows for most of its length through Zambia. From its source near the Zambian border, it follows a northern course to the Lake BENGUELA in north-eastern Zambia.

LUBANGO see SA DA BANDEIRA.

LUBUMBASHI is the capital of SHABA province, Zaire. It is a distribution centre for copper and other mining products of Shaba, which are sent mainly by rail to Ilebo and LOBITO. The city was the capital of the secessionist state of Katanga (now Shaba) from July, 1960 to January, 1963. It was the former headquarters of the *Union Minière du Haut Katanga* which controlled the copper industry until 1966. Pop. 318,000.

LUDERITZ is a port in Namibia (South-West Africa) to the south of WALVIS BAY. Lüderitz and Walvis Bay are the only two safe anchorages along the entire Namibian coast. It has lobster fishing and canning industries. Pop. 7,000.

LUSAKA, capital of Zambia, is the commercial centre of the country and the seat of government. Many modern government offices have grown up round the old colonial buildings. The University of Zambia, and the copper-domed national assembly building are within the city boundary. It has an international airport. Pop. 347,000.

LUXOR is an Egyptian city, standing on the east bank of the Nile in southern Egypt. It has magnificent temple ruins, including the great temple of Amon. Pop. 30,000.

MADAGASCAR, the world's fourth largest island, lies off the south-east coast of Africa. See MALAGASY REPUBLIC.

MADEIRA ISLANDS are a small Portuguese group of islands which lie in the Atlantic Ocean, off the north-west coast of Africa. Madeira is the main island. The others are Porto Santo, the Desertas, and the Selvagens to the south. The population of 283,000 is of Portuguese descent mixed with elements of the Italian, Jewish, Moorish and Negro peoples. The island of Madeira is of volcanic origin and rises to a summit of 1,860 metres (6,105 feet). The climate is mild and the annual rainfall averages 66 centimetres (26 inches). FUNCHAL is the capital of Madeira.

Fishing and farming are the main occupations on the island. Bananas, coffee, dates and sugar cane are grown in the coastal regions and, on the higher ground, vines and oranges are cultivated. Temperate fruits and vegetables flourish above 600 metres (2,000 feet). A mainstay of the economy of Madeira is the famous fortified wine of the same name. Canned fish, fruit, local handicrafts and sugar are also exported. The islands were first settled by the Portuguese in 1419, and, despite periods of occupation by the Spanish and the British, the islands remain a possession of Portugal.

MAFEKING is a town in the northern Cape province of South Africa. It was the scene of a famous battle in the Anglo-Boer War in 1899–1900. Until 1961, it was the administrative capital of the Bechuanaland Protectorate (now Botswana). It is now a railway centre and the seat of the Bophutatswana Bantustan administration.

MAGADI, LAKE, in Kenya, lies on the floor of the Rift Valley, 145 kilometres (90 miles) south-west of NAIROBI. The lake is 20 kilometres (12.5 miles) long. Trona deposits, from which soda ash is refined, are mined there.

MAIDUGURI, a town in Nigeria, lies in the Lake CHAD region. It is the capital of the country's North-Eastern state, and the terminus of the railway from PORT HARCOURT. Pop. 166,000.

MAJUNGA is a town on the north-west coast of the Malagasy Republic at the mouth of the BETSIBOKA RIVER. Pop. 43,000.

Location map of Malagasy Republic.

MALAGASY REPUBLIC is the official name of the country consisting of Madagascar, the world's fourth largest island, and some other small islands in the Indian Ocean. Separated from the African continent by the MOZAMBIQUE CHANNEL, Madagascar has a unique animal life. It is the home of the true lemurs. Madagascar covers 588,800 square kilometres (230,000 square miles) and has a population of 7,700,000.

People The Malagasy people are divided into about 20 main groups, the largest of which is the Merina group. Frenchmen, Comorians, Indians and Taiwan Chinese also live in the country. Malagasy, a language of Indonesian origin, is the chief language, but French is also an official language. The capital is TANANARIVE. Other towns include DIÉGO-SUAREZ, FIANARANTSOA, MAJUNGA, TAMATAVE and TULEAR.

Land and Economy Down the centre of the island runs the High Plateau from which mountains rise. The High Plateau divides Madagascar both climatically and economically. Along the east

coast is a narrow, well-populated belt of hot tropical forest with high rainfall. The western lowlands are used for cattle rearing. The climate becomes increasingly dry to the south.

The economy is based on farming. Subsistence foods include cassava, maize, meat, rice and sweet potatoes. Chief export crops include cloves, coffee, rice, sugar and vanilla. Most manufacturing plants process farm produce. Madagascar's main imports are chemicals, food and drink, manufactured goods, textiles and fuel, and transport equipment. France is by far Madagascar's most important trading partner. An underpopulated country, Madagascar suffers from insufficient communications.

Unit of currency Malagasy franc

History The original people came to Madagascar from Indonesia before AD 1000. Later immigrants were Bantu peoples from Africa, and Arabs. Several kingdoms existed in the 1600s, before the great King Andrianampoinimerina (1787–1810) unified the Merina people. Under his successor Radama I (1810–1828), the Merina conquered two-thirds of the island. In the 1800s, the French and English became interested in Madagascar. The Merina aristocracy under prime minister Rainilaiarivony, tried to preserve their independence and also to modernize the country. But the French declared Madagascar a protectorate in 1885 and captured Tananarive in 1895.

The country was pacified by the French General Gallieni, who abolished the monarchy. But nationalist opposition continued and many thousands were killed in a rebellion in 1947. Madagascar finally became independent in 1960, with Philibert TSIRANANA as president. Tsiranana's Social Democrat party stayed in power until 1972, when it was replaced by a military and civilian government led by General Gabriel RAMANANTSOA, following disturbances. Tsiranana was accused of being too pro-French, and his party of failing to develop the economy. Ramanantsoa sought to revise French-Malagasy aid agreements and changed Tsiranana's foreign policy. He opened relations with communist countries, but he did not cut his country's tie with the West. Ramanantsoa stood down from the presidency in February 1975. His successor, Colonel Richard Ratsimandrava was killed by gunmen after only six days in office. Ratsimandrava was succeeded by General Gilles Andriamahazo.

MALAWI: Fishermen haul in nets in the Shire River, near the town of Mangoche.

Location map of Malawi.

MALAWI is a landlocked country in eastern central Africa. Long and narrow, it measures 930 kilometres (580 miles) from north to south, and between 80 and 160 kilometres (50 and 100 miles) from east to west. It has borders with Tanzania in the north, Mozambique in the east and south, and Zambia in the west. Lake Nyasa stretches along 580 kilometres (360 miles) of the eastern border. With an area of 116,436 square kilometres (45,483 square miles), Malawi has a population of 4,800,000.

People The major ethnic groups of Malawi are the Nyanja/Chewa of the central and southern regions, the Tumbuka of the north, and the Yao and Lomwe of the south-east. The Tonga, who live beside Lake Nyasa, and three separate groups of Ngoni are the most important smaller groups. About 11,000 Asians and 7,000 Europeans also live in Malawi. English, Nyanja/Chewa and Tumbuka are the official languages, and Nyanja/Chewa is the *lingua franca*. Although Malawi is densely populated, with about 40 people per square kilometre (100 people per square mile), only one out of every 20 Malawians lives in a town. BLANTYRE–LIMBE is the largest town. LILONGWE replaced ZOMBA as the capital in January 1975.

Land and Economy The Rift Valley, at the floor of which lies Lake Nyasa, runs from north to south down the eastern part of the country. A high plateau, rising to over 1,220 metres (4,000 feet), occupies the land to the west of the Rift Valley. Mountains, rising to over 2,750 metres (9,000 feet), lie to the north and south of the lake. Temperatures and rainfall vary greatly according to the altitude.

Agriculture is the most important factor in the Malawi economy. Tea and tobacco, grown on plantations, are the chief export crops, and coffee, cotton and sugar are grown as cash crops. Maize and rice provide the staple diet. Malawi has little industry, but there are deposits of coal and bauxite.

MALI: A large baobab tree provides shade for villagers.

Unit of currency Kwacha

History The name Malawi is a form of Maravi, the name of the empire which the Portuguese encountered in the 1500s. Dr. David LIVINGSTONE discovered Lake Nyasa in 1859. At that time, the area was in turmoil, owing to the invasion of Ngoni peoples from across the Zambezi River. European missionaries and settlers followed Livingstone, and, in 1892, the area, then known as Nyasaland, became the British Central African Protectorate. In 1953, Nyasaland was joined to the federation of North and South Rhodesia. The Africans opposed the federation and began to agitate against it. The independence movement was led by Dr. Hastings Kamuzu BANDA, leader of the Nyasaland African Congress Party. Britain granted the country a new constitution and in the elections that followed, the Malawi Congress Party won a majority in the legislative assembly.

In 1963, Nyasaland left the Rhodesian federation, and the following year, the country became independent as Malawi. In 1966, Malawi became a republic within the Commonwealth with Dr. Banda as the first president.

Government Malawi is a one-party state ruled by the Malawi Congress Party. Dr. Banda was made president for life in 1970. He governs the country with the aid of ten cabinet ministers. There is no vice-president or prime minister. The national assembly has 63 members who are elected by universal suffrage. For administrative purposes, the country is divided into three regions: north, central and south.

Location map of Mali.

MALI is a landlocked republic in West Africa. It is bordered on the north by Algeria, on the west by Mauritania, Senegal and Guinea, on the south by Ivory Coast and Upper Volta, and on the east by Niger. It covers 1,225,643 square kilometres (478,767 square miles) and has a population of 5,345,000.

People The main groups include the Malinké, Dioula, Bambara, Sarakole and Bozo. Most Malians are Muslims, although some follow traditional religions and a few are Christians. The official language is French. The capital is Bamako, and other centres include KAYES, TIMBUKTU, MOPTI, SEGOU, SICASSOU and Gao.

Land and Economy Mali consists of two main regions, the Sahara desert in the north and savanna in the south. The great bend of the NIGER RIVER passes through central and western Mali. The climate is hot and dry.

Mali's economy depends mainly on livestock (cattle, sheep and goats). Leather, hides and some animals are exported. Crops include cotton, groundnuts and rice, which are exported, and maize, millet and sorghum. River fishing is important. Mali has deposits of manganese and bauxite, but they have not been mined because of their remote location.

A railway links Mali with Senegal and the Atlantic coast. The Niger River is navigable for long stretches. Air services link Bamako with Senegal and Ivory Coast.

Unit of currency Malian franc

History In the AD 700s caravan routes between the Niger and North Africa carried a rich trade through Mali. Empires founded around the southern starting points of these routes included ancient GHANA, and SONGHAI. Sundiata Keita, King of Mali, conquered Ghana in about 1240. After the decline of Mali in the late 1500s, Tuareg, Fulani and Bambara peoples migrated to the Niger valley. The French conquered the country in 1893. Until 1958, Mali was known as the French Sudan. Then it became a self-governing state of the French Community, as the Sudanese Republic. In the following year, it formed the Mali Federation with Senegal, but this broke up in 1960. In the same year, the country became a separate independent republic, as Mali. Modibo KEITA was president, but in 1968 he was deposed by a group of army officers and Moussa TRAORE became president.

Government The constitution of 1960 provided for a national assembly with legislative power with members elected for five-year terms by universal suffrage. The president, who is head of state, leads the government and chooses its members, including the prime minister.

MALI, an ancient African empire, was centred on the upper Niger valley in the western Sudan region. Following the decline of ancient GHANA in the AD 1100s, Sundiata, the leader of a Mane clan further to the south, laid the foundations of the Mali empire. He reigned as *mansa* (emperor) from about 1230 to 1255. Mali reached its greatest extent in the 1300s. From their capital, Niani, the Mali emperors controlled territory to the Atlantic in the west, as far as the desert to the north, and to Hausaland in the south-east. However, after 1400, internal rivalry weakened Mali, and much of its territory was conquered by SONGHAI.

MALINDI is an expanding town on the Kenyan coast 120 kilometres (75 miles) north of MOMBASA. It is a tourist centre and the small port supports a fishing industry. Pop. 11,000.

MANZEL BOURGUIBA is a modern manufacturing town in northern Tunisia. A steel plant started production there in 1965. Pop. 33,000.

MANZINI, the second town of Swaziland, is situated in the central Middleveld. It was the main centre for settlers and was known as Bremersdorp. It was renamed Manzini in 1962.

MAPUTO see LOURENÇO MARQUES.

MARAMBA (formerly Livingstone), capital of South province, Zambia's richest agricultural area, lies close to the Victoria Falls. It was originally named after Dr. David LIVINGSTONE, the first European to see the falls. A popular tourist centre, it has a fine cultural and anthropological museum, and an international airport. Pop. 50,000.

MARRAKECH is a provincial capital and urban prefecture in the plain of the Hawz in southern Morocco. Founded in 1070, it was the point of departure for the Almoravid conquest. Today, it is the main market of southern Morocco. Pop. 262,000.

MARRAKECH: The Medina in Marrakech.

MARRA MOUNTAINS (Jebel Marra) are the highest range in Sudan, the highest peak reaching 3,088 metres (10,130 feet). An ancient trade route over the adjoining Mardi plateau, connects the Lake CHAD and NILE areas.

MASERU, the capital of Lesotho and the principal town, is situated on a bluff over the Caledon River on the South African border. It has some small scale industry. Two hotels and a casino attract gamblers from South Africa, where gambling is illegal. Pop. 20,000.

MASSAWA is an Ethiopian commercial and military port on the Red Sea.

MATADI is the principal port of Zaire and the capital of Lower Zaire province. It is 380 kilometres (237 miles) upstream on the south side of the ZAIRE RIVER estuary. Pop. 59,000.

Location map
of Mauritania.

MAURITANIA

MAURITANIA, an Islamic republic in West Africa, is bordered on the south by Senegal, on the east by Mali and the Algerian Sahara, on the north by the Spanish Sahara and on the west by the Atlantic Ocean. The area of Mauritania is 1,070,080 square kilometres (418,000 square miles) and the population is 1,200,000.

People Approximately four out of every five Mauritanians are Moors of Berber/Arab descent. The remainder are Black African peoples, mainly Peul, Wolof and Sarakole, living in the south. The official language is French and the *lingua franca* is Arabic. More than 90 per cent of the people are rural, and NOUAKCHOTT, the capital, is the only large town.

Land and Economy Most of Mauritania forms part of the western SAHARA desert and is composed of bare rock and sand, broken up by rocky hills and depressions. The SENEGAL RIVER forms the southern border. The southern region has a moister climate with rainfall generally reaching 50 centimetres (20 inches) a year. Most of the permanent population live in this area because the rich soils enable them to raise crops and livestock.

Agriculture is the chief occupation in Mauritania. The Arab population follow a nomadic, pastoral way of life, raising sheep and camels. Dates, groundnuts, millet, rice and yams are grown as food crops in the southern part of the country. Fishing, based on Port Etienne, is an important industry and dried fish are exported to other parts of Africa. The exploitation of mineral resources, especially that of iron ore near Idjil north of the Adrar Mountains, has become of great economic importance. Reserves of at least 153 million tonnes (150 million tons) of high-grade iron have been discovered, and are being exploited by an international consortium, MiFerMa. A railway has been constructed to transport the iron to the sea at Port Etienne. The other important metal is copper, which is mined at Akjoujit in western Mauritania.

Unit of currency Ougiya

History The original inhabitants of Mauritania were a Black people, who followed an agricultural way of life. In the 1200s, the Almoravids, a Berber dynasty inspired by the Islamic religion, invaded the country. They were followed, in the 1300s, by Arab peoples, who migrated from the north-east and enslaved the Berber population. Trading contact with Europeans began in the 1500s with the arrival of the Portuguese. The French made Mauritania a protectorate in 1903 and gradually subdued the country. In 1920, it was made a colony within French West Africa. Internal self-government, within the French Community, was granted in 1958, and in 1960, despite claims by Morocco that Mauritania should be made part of it, the country became fully independent. The following year, Mokhtar Ould DADDAH was elected president. In the 1970s, Mauritania claimed SPANISH SAHARA. In late 1975, it established a presence in southern Spanish Sahara.

Government A one-party state was declared in 1965 and the various existing parties joined together to form the *Parti du Peuple Mauritanien* (PPM). The country is governed by the president, a government council of ministers and a national assembly of 50 elected members.

MAURITANIA: Camels are often used for transport in Mauritania because they are able to travel for long periods without drinking.

MAURITIUS, a volcanic island in the Indian Ocean, lies 800 kilometres (500 miles) east of the island of Madagascar. It covers an area of 1,843 kilometres (720 square miles) and has a population of 851,000. It is about 36 kilometres (23 miles) wide. and 58 kilometres (36 miles) long.

People Two-thirds of the people of Mauritius are Indians. Most of the others are of mixed African-European or Indian-European descent. Most people speak Mauritian Creole. French and English are the official languages. The chief religions are Hinduism and Roman Catholicism. The largest towns are PORT LOUIS, the capital, and CURE-PIPE.

Land and Economy The island was formed by volcanoes. A high plateau rises to over 600 metres (2,000 feet) in the centre of the island. The climate is sub-tropical, and marked variations occur between summer and winter temperatures.

The economy of Mauritius is chiefly agricultural. Sugar, the most important crop and major export, is planted on 86,600 out of the 93,100 hectares (214,000 out of the 230,000 acres) of the land suitable for cultivation. Sugar-cane processing is the most important industry. Other crops grown include aloes, maize, tea, cassava and tobacco.

Unit of currency Rupee

History Mauritius was discovered by Portuguese sailors in 1502. It was then uninhabited. In 1638 and again in 1664–1710, the Dutch made unsuccessful attempts to settle the island and gave it its name. The French colonized Mauritius in 1714. They planted sugar plantations and imported slaves from India and also from Africa and China. The British annexed the island in 1810, but the people retained the French language and traditions. Mauritius became independent from Britain in 1968, following violent rioting caused by racial tensions and unemployment. Following independence, the island was ruled by an elected government led by the prime minister, Sir Seewoosagur RAMGOOLAM.

MBABANE, capital and main town of Swaziland, was established in 1909. It is the seat of government, has some small industry and is a tourist centre. Pop. 18,000.

MBANDAKA is the capital of Equatorial province, Zaire, and was formerly called Coquilhatville. Coffee, cocoa and cotton are grown widely in the area, which is mainly tropical rain forest. The town is sited on the navigable part of the ZAIRE RIVER, just north of the junction with the Oubangui tributary. Pop. 38,000.

MBUJI MAYI is the capital of East Kasai province, Zaire. It is the centre of industrial diamond production in Zaire, and supplies 90 per cent of world output. Pop. 256,000.

MEKNES is a Moroccan provincial capital southwest of FEZ. It is an ancient city with many splendid monuments. It is now a commercial and industrial centre, particularly for textiles, cement and food processing. Pop. 205,000.

MELANGE is the capital of the Malange district in northern Angola. It is an agricultural market town for the main products of the region: cassava, cotton, maize and sisal. Pop. 32,000.

MELILLA is a free port on the Mediterranean coast of Morocco. Spanish since 1496, it is governed by a mayor and the population is mainly Spanish. It exports lead and iron ore extracted from mines in the hinterland in the Eastern Rif. Pop. 81,000.

MEMPHIS was the capital of the ancient kingdom of Egypt from 2600 to 2190 BC. It was near the modern city of Gizeh. Ruined buildings and the remains of temples mark the site of Memphis.

MERCA is a seaport in southern Somalia, on the Indian Ocean coast. It serves the agricultural region of the SHEBELLE RIVER. Pop. 56,000.

MEROE (or Merowe), in Sudan, was the capital of the ancient state of KUSH from the 500s BC to the AD 300s. Remains of temples, pyramids, tombs and other buildings have recently been excavated. The inscriptions on them are written in an unknown language.

MITUMBA MOUNTAINS stretch from southern SHABA, in Zaire, along the eastern border of Zaire as far as Uganda. They rise to over 4,900 metres (16,000 feet) above sea level. Although just south of the equator, the high peaks are permanently snow-capped. The range continues further north as the RUWENZORI MOUNTAINS.

MOBUTU SESE SEKO, LAKE (formerly Lake Albert), lies in East Africa. Its western half is in Zaire and its eastern half in Uganda. It covers 5,284 square kilometres (2,064 square miles) and is about 32 kilometres (20 miles) wide from east to west and 160 kilometres (100 miles) long. At its south-west end, the lake receives the Semlike River, the outlet of Lake IDI AMIN DADA (formerly Lake Edward). At its north-east corner, it receives the VICTORIA NILE. Its outlet, at the northern end, is the NILE RIVER. In 1972, Zaire and Uganda named the lake after Zaire's president.

MOGADISCIO is the capital of Somalia and one of its chief ports. It was founded in the AD 1000s or earlier, by Arab merchants. It became an independent trading state, but was later conquered by the Somali. It serves the agricultural region of the SHEBELLE RIVER. Pop. 200,000.

MOLEPOLOLE is an agricultural market town in Botswana, situated on the fringes of the KALAHARI desert. Pop. 30,000.

MOMBASA, the main port of Kenya, serves as a trade centre for the whole coastal region and is the site of many light industries. It is also one of the major centres of Swahili cultural activity. Founded before AD 1000 as an independent Islamic city state, Mombasa became the capital of Portuguese East Africa from 1593 to 1731. In 1895, the British built the Uganda railway, which made Mombasa the main port of Kenya. Pop. 247,000.

MONROVIA, a seaport and the capital of Liberia, lies on Cape Mesurado. Mining and rubber companies have their headquarters there and cement is manufactured. Monrovia is the site of the University of Liberia. An international airport connects the city with the rest of Africa. Monrovia was founded in 1822 by the American Colonization Society and named after President James Monroe of the United States. Pop. 180,000.

MOROCCO: Donkeys are used to carry dates to market.

MOPTI, a town in Mali, lies on the NIGER RIVER. It is a market town for the surrounding agricultural area. The area is very dry and depends on the annual flooding of the Niger for irrigation. Pop. 30,000.

Location map of Morocco.

MOROCCO is a kingdom in north-west Africa, bordered by Spanish Sahara in the south, and by Algeria in the south-east and east. It has a coastline on the Mediterranean and the Atlantic, and is separated from Europe by the Strait of Gibraltar. Morocco has an area of about 441,344 square kilometres (172,400 square miles) and a population of 15,800,000. See SPANISH SAHARA.

People Most Moroccans are Arabs and Arabic is the official language. About 35 per cent of the people are Berbers, who have their own language. Most Berbers live in the mountainous regions of the country. The Islamic religion is practised by almost all the people. The most important towns are RABAT, the capital, CASABLANCA, FEZ, MARRAKECH and TANGIER. The towns of CEUTA and MELILLA in the north are administered by Spain.

Land and Economy Morocco is dominated by mountain chains. In the north-east, the Rif Mountains run parallel to the Mediterranean coast. To the south, the Middle, Grand and Anti ATLAS ranges run in a south-westerly direction, almost to the Atlantic coast. West of the mountains is a large plateau with depressions in the interior. To the east of the Atlas ranges, a high plain stretches southwards to the Sahara.

West Morocco has a warm climate, with a rainfall of about 38 centimetres (15 inches) a year. The south and east of the country is arid and summer temperatures rise above 50°C (122°F) in the daytime.

Agriculture forms an important part of Morocco's economy. Arab farmers in the western region grow cereals, rice, vegetables and vines. The Berbers in the highland regions raise camels, sheep and goats and grow crops for their own needs.

In recent years, mining has become increasingly important in Morocco. Large deposits of phosphates are exploited to make Morocco the world's second biggest producer. Cobalt, iron ore, lead and manganese are also mined. Food processing is the most important industry, but the production of chemicals and textiles is gaining in importance.

Unit of currency Dirham

History Parts of Morocco were occupied successively by Phoenicians, Romans and Vandals from the 500s BC until the country was conquered by the Arabs at the beginning of the AD 700s. In the early 1100s, the Almoravids, a Muslim movement from the Sahara, united the country under one rule for the first time. The Almoravids and their successors, the Almohads, conquered most of North Africa and large areas of Spain. Arab power declined in the 1200s and Spain and Portugal gained control of many of the ports of northern Morocco. In the early 1500s, the country was re-united under the Sa'di dynasty and most European possessions were re-taken. In the 1800s, European pressure on Morocco increased and in 1912 the country became a French protectorate, with the exception of the north which was put under Spanish control. The movement for independence gained much popular support in the 1930s. Muhammad V, the young sultan, became its figurehead. During World War II, Muhammad V began to assert his authority and his right to rule. In 1953, he was deposed by the French. Following the Algerian revolt and violent action by Moroccan nationalists in 1954, the French allowed Muhammad to return to the throne. In 1956, Morocco became independent as a constitutional monarchy. Muhammad died in 1961 and was succeeded by his son, who was crowned as HASSAN II. Two unsuccessful military coups against Hassan took place in 1971 and 1972.

Government Morocco is ruled by the king, with the assistance of a two-chamber national assembly elected by universal suffrage.

MOROGORO is a regional capital in east-central Tanzania chiefly important for sisal growing and agriculture. It was founded in the 1800s as the capital of a small Arab sultanate.

MOSHI, a town on the south slopes of MOUNT KILIMANJARO in north-eastern Tanzania. Pop. 28,000.

MOULOUYA RIVER, in eastern Morocco, flows into the Mediterranean Sea and is 400 kilometres (250 miles) long. It has irrigation dams.

MOUNT CAMEROON is a mountainous massif near the coast of north-western Cameroon. Rising to 4,070 metres (13,353 feet), it is the highest point in west-central Africa.

MOUNT ELGON, a volcanic peak in East Africa, lies on the border between Uganda and Kenya, north-east of LAKE VICTORIA. It is 4,320 metres (14,176 feet) high.

MOUNT KENYA is the second highest mountain in Africa and the highest in Kenya. It reaches 5,200 metres (17,058 feet), with a subsidiary peak of 3,894 metres (12,776 feet). Situated about 160 kilometres (100 miles) north-east of NAIROBI, it is the site of a national park and is a tourist attraction. The country has taken its name from the mountain.

MOUNT KILIMANJARO, in Tanzania, is the highest mountain in Africa, 5,895 metres (19,340 feet). The peak is covered with snow all year round. The lower slopes, inhabited by the Chagga people, are a rich coffee and banana-growing region.

MEKNES: A view of the town.

Location map
of Mozambique.

MOZAMBIQUE, formerly the second-largest Portuguese territory in Africa, is situated between Tanzania to the north, Malawi, Zambia, and Zimbabwe to the west, and South Africa and Swaziland to the south. To the east it has a coast line 2,800 kilometres (1,750 miles) long on the Indian Ocean. With an area of 762,791 square kilometres (297,731 square miles), it has a population of 8,519,000. The country is becoming increasingly known in Africa as Msumbiji.

People The people, who all speak Bantu languages, are divided into several ethnic groups. In the north are the Yao and Makonde; in the west, the Tete, Nyanja, Nsengo, Nkunda, Ndau and Tswa. Along the coast are the Makua and Shanga; and in the south are the Ronga. Portuguese is the official language. Swahili is the common language in the north, and Ronga (Tsonga) in the south. LOURENÇO MARQUES, now Maputo, and the port of BEIRA are the largest towns.

Land and Economy The country consists of low-lying coastal plains, rising gradually into a zone of uplands 245–600 metres (800–2,000 feet) above sea level. In the Tete and Niassa districts, the land rises in the north-east to 1,520 metres (5,000 feet) above sea level. Rivers include the LIMPOPO, Rovumba and ZAMBEZI.

The economy is based on cash crop production, transport services, and the export of migrant labour, mainly to South Africa. The six main crops —cashew nuts, copra, cotton, sisal, sugar and tea— are produced on European-owned plantations by African farmers. The highly developed railway and port facilities serve the transit trade of Mozambique's neighbours. Secondary industry is limited to processing agricultural produce in the Lourenço Marques area. The Cabora Bassa hydro-electric scheme is intended to provide power.

Unit of currency Conto

History In early times, the country was dominated by African kingdoms, such as the Monomotapa kingdom of the 1500s and by Arab traders on the coast. The Portuguese explorer Vasco da Gama anchored off Mozambique Island in 1498, and Portuguese colonization began in 1505. For 300 years they achieved only limited control, and conquest of the interior only began in the 1800s. The frontier with British Central and South Africa was fixed in 1891, but African resistance continued up to 1905. During the early 1900s Portugal organized a colonial system in Mozambique. However, a rise in African nationalism in the 1960s brought an increased demand for independence. From 1964 to 1974, the Mozambique Liberation Front (FRELIMO) waged a guerilla war against the Portuguese forces. In 1974, a coup took place in Portugal and a more liberal government took power. In September 1974, Portugal finally agreed to grant independence on June 25, 1975. Samora MACHEL became the first president.

Government On June 25 1975, the government announced a constitution, renaming the country the People's Republic of Mozambique. Power was vested in FRELIMO and the president of FRELIMO would be president of the nation. The president governs with a council of ministers. The legislative body, a 210-member People's Assembly, includes FRELIMO's leaders and representatives of the armed forces and of mass organizations.

MOZAMBIQUE is a city and port on an island off the northern coast of Mozambique, 785 kilometres (490 miles) north of BEIRA. Originally an Arab trade centre, it became the chief Portuguese defensive point for 300 years after 1948. In that year, it was reached by the explorer Vasco da Gama. Its Swahili name is Msumbiji.

MOZAMBIQUE CHANNEL is a stretch of the Indian Ocean about 400 kilometres (250 miles) wide between the island of Madagascar and Mozambique.

MUCHINGA MOUNTAINS form a ridge across eastern Zambia rising to 2,150 metres (7,000 feet) at its western end and reaching 1,220 to 1,370 metres (4,000 to 4,500 feet) throughout its length.

MUFULIRA is near Zambia's largest copper mine, which has extensive underground operations. Production fell after a disaster in 1970, but is now returning to full capacity.

MWANZA, in Tanzania, is a regional headquarters and port on Lake VICTORIA. It is the chief town of a prosperous cotton-growing and cattle-rearing region. Pop. 35,000.

MWERU LAKE, on Zambia's northern border, forms part of the headwaters of the ZAIRE RIVER. Bream is caught there and sold to traders from the copperbelt area.

NAIROBI, the capital of Kenya, is situated 1,668 metres (5,475 feet) above sea level and is 480 kilometres (300 miles) west of the port of MOMBASA. It was founded in 1899 as a railhead camp on the line being built between Mombasa and Uganda. The city is the seat of government and a centre of administration, communications and commerce. It supports a variety of light manufacturing industries. Pop. 509,000.

NAIVASHA, LAKE, is a small Kenyan lake situated 80 Kms. north-west of NAIROBI. It is a tourist centre and has a bird sanctuary on Crescent Island. Hippopotami and tilapia fish are found in the lake and abundant bird life.

NAKURU is a Kenyan town, situated in the southern Rift Valley, in the heart of the country's richest agricultural area. It is a communications centre. Nearby is the Nakuru national park, one of the finest bird sanctuaries in the world with a huge flamingo population. Pop. 47,000.

NAMIB DESERT extends along Namibia's coastline for almost 1,000 miles (1,600 kilometres). It varies in width from 30 to 90 miles (48 to 144 kilometres), and covers 15 per cent of the total land of Namibia. Rainfall throughout the desert is less than 2.54 centimetres (one inch) per year. Chains of sand dunes 1,000 feet (304 metres) high are found in the centre. The southern part has large deposits of gem diamonds.

Location map
of Namibia.

NAMIBIA is a South African controlled territory in southern Africa. The legal authority over Namibia is claimed by the United Nations. It has borders with Angola in the north, with Botswana in the east, with South Africa in the south. It has a coast on the Atlantic in the west. With an area of 816,220 square kilometres (318,836 square miles), Namibia has a population of 749,000.

People About 631,000 Africans, 90,000 Europeans and 28,000 Coloureds live in Namibia. The largest ethnic group is the Ovambo who inhabit the northern part of the country. Kwanyama and Herero are the principal languages. Afrikaans and English are the official languages. German is also spoken. WINDHOEK is the capital.

Land and Economy Most of Namibia is occupied by the central highlands, which rise to 2,438 metres (8,000 feet) above sea level. Along the Atlantic coast, the Namib desert stretches for almost 1,600 kilometres (1,000 miles). In the east, the highlands merge into the Kalahari semi-desert.

Agriculture in Namibia is mainly concerned with the commercial production of beef and dairy products, and karakul (persian lamb) pelts. The climate is dry and food and cash crops are not produced on a large scale. Subsistence farming is carried on in the north, but foodstuffs have to be imported from South Africa. The fishing industry produces tinned pilchards, fish oil and meal, and lobsters. Mining is the most important factor in the Namibian economy. Important minerals include gem diamonds, copper, lead, and zinc.

Unit of currency Rand

History In the late 1800s, Germany took advantage of conflict between Herero and Damara peoples to declare a protectorate over Namibia in 1884. South African forces occupied Namibia in 1915 during World War I and, in 1919, the League of Nations placed the country under South African administration as a mandated territory. In 1946, South Africa refused to accept United Nations trusteeship over the territory and continued to rule it, despite African demands for independence. These demands led to the formation of nationalist groups, including the South West African Peoples Organization (SWAPO) in 1959. In 1966, SWAPO began guerilla activity against South African forces in the Caprivi strip. In 1971, the World Court of Justice ruled that South Africa's administration was illegal. In 1972, the U.N. Secretary-General Kurt Waldheim began negotiations with South Africa, aimed at self-determination and independence for Namibia. These negotiations were unsuccessful and were halted by the U.N. Security Council in December 1973. Meanwhile, South Africa continued its policy of establishing BANTUSTANS in Namibia.

Government A legislative assembly, elected by the European population, and an administrator, appointed by the South African government, rule the country. Since the German colonial period, Namibia has been divided into two administrative areas—the 'police zone' in the south where most Europeans live, and the 'northern native reserves'. in 1968, ten Bantustans were set up.

NASSER, LAKE, is the artificial lake formed by the Aswan High Dam, which holds back the waters of the Nile, in Egypt. The lake, part of which is in Sudan, is 480 kilometres (300 miles) long and up to 48 kilometres (30 miles) wide.

NATRON, LAKE, in Tanzania, covers about 563 square kilometres (220 square miles). Its soda content is alloyed with salt and is not exploitable.

N'DJAMENA capital of Chad, lies on the Chari River in the south-western part of the country. It was founded by the French as a military station. Its industries include flour milling and sugar refining. Pop. 179,000.

NDOLA, capital of Western province, Zambia, is the gateway to the copperbelt. It is a major commercial centre and has an international airport.

NEW BUSSA, a town in the Kwana State of Nigeria. New Bussa is growing in importance due to the Kainji Dam which has been built there, across the River Niger. It is thought that hydro-electricity from Kainji would be sufficient to supply most of Nigeria's needs.

NGORONGORO CRATER, in the Serengeti national park, Tanzania, is a volcanic crater rich in wildlife. It is visited by many tourists.

NIAMEY, capital of the Republic of Niger is on the NIGER RIVER about half way between the frontiers of Mali and Nigeria. Roads link it with Gao in Mali, COTONOU in Dahomey and ABIDJAN in Ivory Coast. Pop. 42,000.

**Location map
of Niger.**

NIGER, an independent republic of West Africa, is bordered on the north by Algeria and Libya, on the south by Upper Volta, Benin and Nigeria on the west by Mali and on the east by Chad. With an area of 1,175,500 square kilometres (459,180 square miles), it has a population of 4,476,000.

People Hausa make up almost half of the population. Other important groups are the Djerma-Songhai, Peul (Fulani) and Tuareg peoples. Most people live in the southern half of the country. French is the official language and Islam is the main religion. Less than two per cent of the people live in towns. The capital is NIAMEY. ZINDER, Maradi, Tahoua and Agadès are the other important towns.

Land and Economy The country can be roughly divided into three zones: the south-west, where the Niger River valley is sufficiently fertile to maintain a settled agriculture; the south and south-east, which is savanna country, leading down to Lake CHAD; the northern part, which extends into the Sahara. The AIR MOUNTAINS are a range in the northern part of the central region, rising to 2,133 metres (7,000 feet).

Most people are engaged in agriculture, the most important crops being groundnuts and rice. Cassava, cotton, millet, sugar and tobacco are also grown wherever water supplies are sufficient—mainly in the valleys of the Niger and Maradi rivers. Sheep, goats and, above all, cattle are raised largely for the Nigerian market.

At present there is little exploitation of mineral resources, although deposits of copper, iron, tin, tungsten and uranium have been found. Uranium, which is being mined in the Agadès area with French assistance, is the most important mineral. Cassiterite, a tin-bearing ore, is mined in the southern central region.

Unit of currency C.F.A. Franc

History The southern part of Niger was the northern fringe of Hausaland, where the typical walled cities gave rise to a number of Muslim states in the 1500s. In 1906, the region was effectively occupied by France, and became part of French West Africa. Political parties appeared shortly before independence in 1960. The Sawabi party was declared illegal in 1959, and remained so under the government of its rival, the Parti Progressiste Nigérien (PPN) led by president Hamani DIORI. A military group, led by Colonel Seyni KOUNTCHE, seized power from Diori in April 1974.

Government After independence Niger became a republic, with a president elected every five years by direct universal suffrage and a national assembly of 50 members. After the coup of 1974, the leader, Colonel Kountche, suspended the constitution and dissolved the national assembly. A supreme military council, with a cabinet of 11 army officers, was formed to rule the country.

NIGER RIVER rises in Guinea's FOUTA DJALLON region near the Sierra Leone border. It flows for about 4,160 kilometres (2,600 miles), making a great curve north-east then south-east through Mali, to form part of the border with Dahomey. It then passes through Nigeria to the sea. Its middle course is navigable for about 1,600 kilometres (1,000 miles). However, boats cannot pass all the way along because of rapids and sandbars. Its main tributary is the BENUE. The Niger ends in a delta of about 35,840 square kilometres.

▲ **LAKE NAKURU:** This Kenyan lake, *above*, lies within a national park, which is one of the world's finest bird sanctuaries. Flamingos and pelicans are among the birds to be seen on Lake Nakuru.

◄ **NAMIBIA:** This strange rock feature, *left*, was worn away by wind erosion. It is called the 'Finger of God'.

**NIGER, a market ►
scene in the town
of Agades.**

NAMIBIA: Walvis Bay
is Namibia's main
port.   ▼

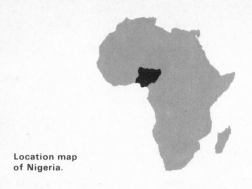

Location map
of Nigeria.

NIGERIA is an independent federal republic in West Africa. Its area is 911,360 square kilometres (356,000 square miles). Provisional 1974 census figures gave the population as 79.75 millions—a sixth of the total population of Africa. Nigeria is the potential giant of Africa. Since the end of the civil war (1967–70) the country has had a rapidly increasing influence on African politics and has faced the rest of the world with growing political confidence. The country borders Benin (Dahomey) in the west, Niger in the north, and Chad and Cameroon in the east. It has a coastline of about 760 kilometres (475 miles) on the Gulf of Guinea.

People There are about 250 ethnic groups in Nigeria, each with its own language. The most important are the Hausa, Kanouri and Fulani in the northern region, the Igbo in the south-east and the Yoruba in the west. The official languages are Hausa, Igbo and Yoruba. About 47 per cent of the population are Muslims, and 35 per cent are Christians. The remaining 18 per cent practise traditional ethnic religions. Nigeria with 170 people per square mile is densely populated by African standards. Although only 16 per cent of the population live in towns, the country has many well-developed cities, including LAGOS, the capital, IBADAN, KANO and Ogbomosho.

Land and Economy The coastal region of Nigeria is indented with lagoons and much of it is covered with mangrove swamps. The delta of the NIGER RIVER covers a wide area. Rainfall is high on the coast, with an annual average of about 381 centimetres (150 inches). Inland, tropical forests to the north of the coastal strip give way to savanna country in the centre of the country. Plateaux rise

NIGERIA: This bronze cockerel was made at Benin and decorated the altars of the queen mothers.

to over 457 metres (1,500 feet) to the west and east of the Niger River valley. The BENUE RIVER joins the Niger in the centre of Nigeria. North of this junction, the Niger flows from the north-west and the Benue from the north-east. Between the valleys of the Niger and the Benue, the land rises to over 914 metres (3,000 feet) and then drops down to below 457 metres (1,500 feet) in the far north. Most of the central and northern regions are covered in savanna. The land becomes swamp in the north-east in the area of Lake CHAD. The annual rainfall in the north averages about 50 centimetres (20 inches) and temperatures range between 38°C (100°F) and 42°C (108°F).

Nigeria has an enormous economic potential, and since the end of the civil war the economy has expanded rapidly. Nearly four out of every five people work in agriculture and agricultural products form half Nigeria's exports. Nigeria exports more groundnuts and palm-oil products than any other African country and also produces cocoa, cotton and rubber in large quantities. Bananas, cassava, maize, millet, rice, sorghum and yams are grown as food crops. Livestock is extensively reared and it is estimated that Nigeria has over 21 million goats, 11 million cattle and over 7 million sheep. Fishing produces about 50,800 tonnes (50,000 tons) of fish every year. Forests cover a third of the country and wood production in 1969 was 3,489,960 cubic metres (11,450,000 cubic feet).

The discovery of oil has revolutionized the Nigerian economy and the country now ranks third in economic power in Africa, after South Africa and Egypt. Oil now accounts for half of the country's exports. In 1972, 1,818,000 barrels of oil were produced per day. This amounted to nearly one-third of the production of Saudi Arabia. The chief importers of Nigerian oil in 1973 were the United States, Britain, the West Indies, Holland and France. Known reserves will permit this rate of production to continue for 20 years. Nigeria has extensive coal deposits and rich sources of natural gas.

Industry is mainly concerned with processing the country's agricultural products. In 1970, a four-year plan was begun to expand and diversify Nigeria's industry. Although the annual gross national product is about £2,000 million, the average income per person is less than £30 per year. This is due to the great size of the population. The government aims to double this amount by 1985.

Nigeria has a well-developed transport system. There are over 3,520 kilometres (2,200 miles) of railway line, serving most parts of the country. Of the 80,000 kilometres (50,000 miles) of roads, nearly 16,000 kilometres (10,000 miles) have all-weather tarred surfaces. Civil aviation is important and the main centres are connected with regular air services. Nigerian airliners also fly to other parts of Africa, Europe and the United States.

Unit of currency Naira

History The first known Nigerian culture was that of NOK, which was in existence over 2,000 years ago. In 1486, the first contacts with Europe were made when the Portuguese penetrated inland from the coast to the ancient kingdom of BENIN. During the 1700s, the peoples in the south of Nigeria suffered greatly from the ravages of the slave traders. Islam had been widely practised in the north of the country since the 1300s, and in the 1800s, the Fulani created a Muslim empire and set up a system of emirs to rule it. This was known as the caliphate of Sokoto.

The British occupied Lagos in 1861. During the latter half of the 1800s, they spread their influence over the country, mainly through the activities of the Royal Niger Company. In 1893, Britain proclaimed the Niger Coast Protectorate and in 1900 the colony of Southern Nigeria was set up. A protectorate was proclaimed over Northern Nigeria in 1906 and in 1914 the two protectorates merged to form the basis of modern Nigeria. The

first Governor General of the colony, Lord Lugard set up an indirect federal system of colonial government.

After World War II, Nigeria began to prepare for independence. A central council was set up which was advised by three regional councils from the north, east and west. In 1954, the country became a federal state and the regional councils increased in importance. Sir Abubakar Tafawa BALEWA became the first prime minister of the federation and continued to hold this post after the election of 1959. Nigeria gained independence in 1960. Following a referendum in 1961, the western region of the United Nations Trust Territory of the Cameroons became part of Nigeria. Nigeria became a republic in 1963.

Disputes between the main ethnic groups in Nigeria, which included arguments about the distribution of seats in the federal parliament led to the breakdown of the political system at the beginning of 1966. In January of that year, a military coup overthrew Balewa's government and killed him. General AGUIYI-IRONSI, an Igbo, emerged as head of state. He set up a strong central government and repealed the original constitution. Fearing domination by the Ibos, army officers from the northern parts of the country staged a coup in July, 1966, and killed Aguiyi-Ironsi. Fighting between the Igbos and the Hausas broke out and about one million Igbos living in the north became refugees. General Yakubu Gowon became the new president of Nigeria and restored order through a federal military government which he led until he was deposed in July 1975.

In May, 1967, Nigeria was split into 12 regions. The old Eastern Region, under Lieutenant-Colonel OJUKWU, its military commander, then declared its secession from the federation and renamed itself Biafra. In July, the federal government began a military campaign to end this secession and a civil war began which lasted for 30 months. The fighting was bitter and large areas of the country were devastated. The federal government effectively blockaded Biafra and the breakaway province suffered from widespread starvation. In January 1970, Biafra surrendered and accepted the rule of the federal government. During the war, most of the major powers, including Britain, the United States, Russia and France, became involved on one of the two sides. The total casualties of the war are estimated as high as one million people.

After the war, the federal government re-established its control over the whole country, following a humane and highly successful policy of reconciliation. The Igbos were rehabilitated and brought back into the mainstream of Nigerian life. Great efforts were made to repair the damage, both physical and mental, that had been caused by the war. The humanitarian treatment of the Ibos greatly enhanced Nigeria's reputation with the rest of the world.

Since the civil war, the Nigerian federal government has concentrated on unifying the country and preventing the re-appearance of ethnic jealousies. It has also taken important steps to strengthen and expand the Nigerian economy. In 1971, it announced that 26 types of business—mainly those needing low investment—were to be owned only by Nigerians. It was expected that a three year transition period would be needed to complete the Africanization of businesses in this category. Foreign owned companies have been encouraged to raise capital from Nigerian investors. Also in 1971, the government established the National Oil Corporation and took a 35 per cent shareholding in the French oil company SAFRAP. It has made agreements with other oil companies and the eventual aim is to extend government control over 51 per cent of the oil industry.

Nigeria has played an increasingly important part in African and world politics since 1970. Relations with Ivory Coast, Gabon, Tanzania, and Zambia were strained for a while after the war, as a result of the former's support of Biafra. For the same reason Nigeria's attitude towards France has been cool. Britain is Nigeria's most important trading partner, both for imports and exports. Although the relationship was difficult for a while after the war, owing to Britain's refusal actively to support the government, it improved in the early 1970s.

General Murtala Muhammed overthrew General Gowon in July 1975, but was assassinated in February 1976 and replaced by Lt.-General Obasanjo.

Government Nigeria is ruled by the supreme military council. The council appoints commissioners to run the departments (ministries) of the federal military government. The country is divided into 12 regions administered by state military governors, who are also members of the supreme military council. No internal political activity has been allowed in Nigeria since the civil war and new laws are in the form of decrees. In 1976, plans were announced for the formation of nineteen states, rather than twelve, when the country returns to civilian rule in 1979.

NILE RIVER (*Al Bahr el Nil* in Arabic) is the largest river in the world. Its length has been variously calculated, because of its many sources. But it is generally accepted as 6,699 kilometres (4,187 miles). This distance is measured from the point where the river enters the Mediterranean Sea along the Rossetta branch of its delta to its furthest source a few miles east of Lake Kivu. Here it is known as the Lukarara River. The source of the Nile was a fascinating mystery for several English explorers of the 19th century. John Speke first recognized Lake VICTORIA as a main source in 1858. Sir Samuel and Lady Baker discovered the Lake MOBUTU SESE SEKO source in 1864.

The Nile has three main streams: the White Nile, the Blue Nile and the Nile proper, formed when the White and Blue Niles meet at KHARTOUM. The basin of the three streams covers about one-tenth of Africa's land surface. The Nile is navigable for 1,520 kilometres (950 miles) from the sea as far as the ASWAN HIGH DAM. Rapids and cataracts above the dam and its lake, Lake NASSER, make navigation difficult but some stretches can be used by river transport. Dense masses of vegetation in the Sudan, known as the *sudd*, blocked the river in the 19th century. These have now been cleared to improve navigation.

The dams along the Nile, notably the Sennar Dam and the Aswan High Dam control flood waters and distribute it for irrigation evenly throughout the year and provide hydro-electric power. The population of the basin supported by the Nile now exceeds 50 millions.

NOK is a village in northern Nigeria, south-west of lake CHAD. It was inhabited by an African farming civilization by about 1000 BC. For this reason, the civilization that developed between that time and about AD 200 is known as Nok culture. Nok craftsmen produced stone tools and jewellery and developed a tradition of fine terracotta sculpture.

NOUAKCHOTT, the capital city of Mauritania, is situated near the Atlantic coast. Until 1957, the country was administered from SAINT LOUIS in Senegal, and in 1958, Nouakchott was only a small village. The transfer of administrative services was completed in 1961. Pop. 20,000.

NOVA LISBOA, renamed Huambo in 1975, is the capital of Huambo district in central Angola. It acts as the collection centre for the farm products of the central plateau. Pop. 45,000.

NUBIA was the name that classical and Arab writers gave to the land adjoining the NILE between ASWAN and modern KHARTOUM. The Romans called the inhabitants, a people of Negro stock, Nobatae. In the AD 500s, they formed a Christian kingdom which lasted until 1317.

NUMIDIA was the Roman name for an ancient kingdom which existed in the coastal area of present-day Algeria and western Morocco, from the 200s BC to 106 BC.

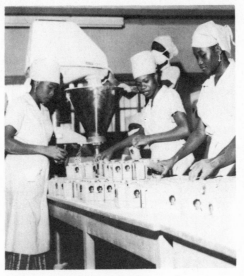

NIGERIA: A cosmetics factory in Lagos, the capital.

NIGERIA: A swamp drilling barge in Eastern Nigeria. The discovery of oil has revolutionized Nigeria's economy. ▶

NIGERIA: Pyramids made of sacks of groundnuts, or peanuts, at Kano ready to be exported.

NYASA, LAKE, has a length of 568 kilometres (355 miles) and a maximum width of 80 kilometres (50 miles). Its height above sea level is about 487 metres (1,600 feet). The lake abounds in fish and is drained by the Shire River into the ZAMBEZI.

OGBOMOSHO, a city in Nigeria, lies in the country's Western state, about 80 kilometres (50 miles) north-north-west of IBADAN. Pop. 380,000.

OGOUE RIVER is the chief river of Gabon. About 1,120 kilometres (700 miles) long, it flows westwards into the Atlantic Ocean south of Cape Lopez. It is navigable for about 400 kilometres.

OKAVANGO RIVER rises in Angola in the Bie plateau, where it is known as the Cubango. It flows east, forming the border between Angola and Namibia, and then turns south-east to flow across the CAPRIVI STRIP into Botswana. It then disappears into the OKAVANGO SWAMP.

OKAVANGO SWAMP occupies a large basin in northern Botswana. The swamp is fed by the OKAVANGO RIVER and is choked with papyrus reed. In time of floods, the excess water is drained away by the Thamalakane River into the Makarikari salt pans.

OMDURMAN is the second largest city in Sudan. It is situated north of KHARTOUM on the NILE RIVER. It is an ancient city and an Islamic centre. The College of Arabic and Islamic Studies is situated there. The Sudanese radio and television services operate from Omdurman. The MAHDI is buried there and his tomb is visited by pilgrims. Pop. 273,000.

ONITSHA, a town on the NIGER RIVER, lies in Nigeria's East-Central state and is a commercial and market centre. Pop. 194,000.

ORANGE RIVER is the major river of South Africa. Rising on Mount-aux-Sources in the DRAKENSBERG MOUNTAINS it flows for 2,176 kilometres (1,360 miles) through Lesotho across South Africa and into the south Atlantic Ocean at the border with Namibia (South-West Africa). In the Orange Free State, a giant hydro-electric power and irrigation project is being constructed on the Orange river.

OSHOGBO, a city in western Nigeria, lies on the railway route about 80 kilometres (50 miles) north-east of IBADAN. Pop. 248,000.

OUAGADOUGOU, the capital of Upper Volta, is the commercial centre of an agricultural region. Its industries process agricultural products into shea butter, vegetable oils, soap and textiles. It is a route centre with rail connections to Ivory Coast and an airport. Pop. 79,000.

OUJDA, a provincial capital in eastern Morocco, is a commercial and administrative centre producing wine, fruit and cereals. Pop. 139,000.

OYO, an historic town in Nigeria, lies about 50 kilometres (32 miles) north of IBADAN. The former Yoruba state of Oyo made its capital there when the original capital, Old Oyo, became difficult to defend from Muslim nomads. Oyo's power collapsed in the 1800s, when it was squeezed between conquest from the north by Muslim Fulanis and by the rise of European power on the coast. It is now a gold mining centre. Pop. 134,000.

PALIME, in Togo, is linked with the port of LOME, 104 kilometres (65 miles) to the south-east by rail. It sends cacao, palm oil and cotton there from its important agricultural region.

PALMA is an island in the Canary Islands. Its main feature is the volcanic crater La Gran Caldera de Tabouriente. Its capital is Santa Cruz de la Palma. The total area is 720 square kilometres (281 square miles). Pop. 4,000.

PEMBA ISLAND lies just north of Zanzibar in the Indian Ocean, south-east of Mombasa. It joined the Republic of Tanzania in 1964. The island contributes more than half of the clove crop, which is the main export of the islands.

PRETORIA: The Union buildings at Pretoria, South Africa's administrative capital.

PIETERMARITZBURG, in Natal, South Africa, was founded in 1838 by Boertrekkers. It was both a Boer and British administrative centre in the 1800s and became the capital of Natal province. Pop. 113,000.

POINTE NOIRE, the main port of Congo, lies on the Atlantic coast 400 kilometres (250 miles) west of BRAZZAVILLE. Potassium is mined in the district and deposits of off-shore oil are exploited. Shoe manufacturing and timber processing are the main industries. Pop. 100,000.

PORT ELIZABETH is a major port and industrial centre in the Eastern Cape of South Africa. It was established by English settlers in 1820 and is now a centre for the clothing and car industries. Pop. 469,000.

PORT-GENTIL, the leading seaport of Gabon, lies 160 kilometres (100 miles) south-west of LIBREVILLE, the capital. It serves as a major outlet for Gabon's mineral and timber exports. Pop. 30,000.

PORT HARCOURT, the second port of Nigeria, lies near the mouth of the Bonny River. Founded as a coal port in 1914, it now has important petroleum refineries. Pop. 213,000.

PORT LOUIS, the capital of Mauritius, was founded by the French in 1723. Lying on the north-west coast of the island, it is the country's major port. Pop. 135,000.

PORTO NOVO is the capital of Benin (Dahomey) on the Ouémé River near the coast. It is connected by rail to COTONOU. Pop. 71,000.

PORT SAID is a seaport at the Mediterranean end of the Suez Canal. It was named after Said Pasha, Viceroy of Egypt.

PORT SUDAN, on the Red Sea, is Sudan's main port. It is connected by rail to KHARTOUM, which lies 792 kilometres to the south-west. Founded in 1905, the town exports goods both from Sudan and from Ethiopia. Pop. 116,000.

PORTUGUESE GUINEA see GUINEA-BISSAU.

PORT VICTORIA, the capital of the Seychelles Islands, is on the island of Mahé. Founded in 1768 by the French, it is the chief port of the Seychelles. Pop. 10,500.

PRAIA, the capital of the Cape Verde Islands, is on the south-east coast of Sao Tiago. The main occupation is fishing. Pop. 32,000.

PRETORIA, is the administrative capital of South Africa. It was named after the Reverend Pretorius and was the capital of the 19th-century Transvaal Republic. The city is situated on the High Veld, 60 kilometres (38 miles) north of JOHANNESBURG. It contains some heavy industry (coal and steel) and a university. Pop. 562,000.

PRINCIPE see SÃO TOMÉ and PRINCIPE.

QATTARA DEPRESSION, is an irregularly shaped depression in the desert of north-western Egypt. The depression is up to 320 kilometres (200 miles) long and is 160 kilometres (100 miles) wide at its widest point. The lowest point lies 134 metres (440 feet) below sea level. The Egyptian government plans to build a canal from the Mediterranean to the Qattara Depression to turn it into a lake.

QAYRAWAN is a Tunisian centre of pilgrimage for Muslims. It is sited on the dry plains south of the Dorsale plateau. The great mosque was built in the late 600s. The city also has an Islamic university. Carpet making is the main industry. The city attracts many tourists. Pop. 46,000.

QUE QUE is a small town in the Zimbabwean midlands. It is notable for gold mining and a major iron and steel plant. Pop. 38,000.

RABAT, the capital of Morocco, is situated on the Atlantic coast on the left bank of the estuary of the Bou-Regreg. The town, founded in 1160, has medieval monuments and a modern city. It has some light industry and a university. Pop. 261,000.

REUNION, a French island in the Indian Ocean, lies 640 kilometres (400 miles) east of Malagasy and measures about 64 by 80 kilometres (40 by 50 miles). The population of 474,000 is mainly French-Creole. The capital is SAINT DENIS. The island is of volcanic origin and rises to two peaks, the Piton de Neiges, which is 3,069 metres (10,069 feet), and the still active volcano Fournaise. Temperatures on the coastal lowlands average 27°C (80°F) and the annual rainfall from the south-east trade winds is 254 centimetres (100 inches) per year on the windward side of the island and 76 centimetres (30 inches) per year on the leeward. Sugar is the most important crop and rum is exported. Other products include cassava, vanilla, and tapioca. Manufactured goods include chocolate, vegetable oil and cigarettes.

Réunion was discovered by the Portuguese in the 1500s and settled by the French in 1642. During its history, the island has been named Bourbon, Buonaparte and finally Réunion in 1848.

REY MALABO (formerly Santa Isabel), is the chief town on the island of Macias Nguema Biyoga (formerly FERNANDO PÓO) and the capital of EQUATORIAL GUINEA. The town has an airport and a radio station, and is the marketing centre for the cocoa grown on the island. Pop. 37,000.

RHODESIA see ZIMBABWE

ROBERTSPORT, a seaport of Liberia, lies on the coast north-west of MONROVIA. Iron ore and rubber are exported from there.

ROKEL RIVER, the main river of Sierra Leone, rises in the country's north-eastern uplands and flows for about 480 kilometres (300 miles) south-west and west into the Atlantic Ocean.

ROSEIRES DAM (properly Al-Rusayris), in Sudan, was built in 1960–65 at the southern limit of navigation on the NILE. It irrigates more than 121,404 hectares (3 million acres) and also provides hydro-electric power.

RABAT: A ceremonial guard of the royal palace in Rabat.

RUDOLF, LAKE see TURKANA, LAKE

RUFIJI RIVER drains 175,360 square kilometres (68,500 square miles) of Tanzania and is the site of an important rice-growing scheme.

RUFISQUE, a town of western Senegal, lies about 16 kilometres (10 miles) east of CAPE VERDE, near DAKAR. Pop. 48,000.

RUKWA LAKE, in south-west Tanzania, varies in area according to the rainfall. It has an important tilapia fishing industry.

RUVUBU RIVER rises in southern Burundi and flows north-east to form a section of the Tanzania–Burundi border. It joins the KAGERA RIVER 48 kilometres (30 miles) south-east of the Rwandan town of Kiibungu.

RUWENZORI MOUNTAINS extend for about 120 kilometres (75 miles) along the border between Zaire and Uganda and reach a height of over 4,876 metres (16,000 feet). Although the range crosses the equator, the highest peaks are permanently snow-capped. Mount Margherita which is 5,119 metres (16,795 feet) is the third highest peak in Africa after MOUNT KILIMANJARO and MOUNT KENYA. The mountains are one of the few remaining areas where the rare mountain gorilla can be found.

RUZIZI RIVER flows from Lake KIVU into Lake TANGANYIKA, forming the border between Burundi and Zaire. Rapids occur in its upper reaches. It provides water for a fertile cotton-growing area. The river forms part of the great Lualaba-Congo system.

Location map of Rwanda.

RWANDA is a small landlocked independent republic in Central Africa just to the south of the equator. It has borders with Zaire in the west,

Uganda in the north, Tanzania in the east and Burundi in the south. With an area of 26,330 kilometres (10,166 square miles) and a population of 3,896,000, it has the highest population density in Africa which is 148 people per square kilometre (about 380 people per square mile).

People Most Rwandans are descended from Hutu peoples who settled in the area over one thousand years ago. The tall proud Tutsi and the Twa (pygmies) make up the rest of the population. The official languages are French and Kinyarwanda. About half of the people are Christians, mainly Roman Catholics, and the other half practise ethnic religions. KIGALI the capital, is the only centre with more than 20,000 inhabitants.

Land and Economy Western Rwanda is mountainous rising to over 4,267 metres (14,000 feet) in the north-west. To the east, the land falls away to

RWANDA: An agricultural landscape outside Kigali, the capital.

high plateaux, cut into by many river valleys. Part of the western border of Rwanda lies through Lake KIVU which is part of the Great Rift Valley of East Africa.

Rainfall and temperatures vary throughout the country. The Rift Valley area is the hottest part, with temperatures averaging over 21°C (70°F). The wettest area is the western mountainous region, which has an annual rainfall of over 152 centimetres (60 inches). All the eastern plateaux, at one time, were forested, but today almost all the trees have been cleared for farming. Over-grazing by livestock and heavy rains have caused erosion of the topsoil in the west of the country. This has caused hardship for many farmers.

Rwanda's economy is based on farming, and 90 per cent of the population are engaged in agriculture, mostly at subsistence level. Coffee is the most important export crop, and cotton, pyrethrum and tea are secondary cash crops. The chief food crop is bananas, followed by beans, peas, sorghum and sweet potatoes. Mining is the only important industry. Four Belgian companies extract and export cassiterite, wolframite and other ores. Over-population, lack of natural resources and poor soil combine to hinder the development of the Rwandan economy.

Unit of currency Franc

History In the 1500s, bands of migrant Tutsi herdsmen began to arrive in Rwanda. In the 1700s, the Tutsi conquered the Hutu and established a feudal system. The Hutu worked as serfs in return for protection and use of the Tutsi cattle.

The Germans colonized Rwanda and Burundi at the end of the 1800s and named the area Ruanda-Urundi. In 1916, Germany lost the colony to Belgium. The colony became a League of Nations Mandate administered by Belgium in 1924 and a United Nations Trust Territory after World War II. The Belgians failed to reform the feudal system and in 1959, the Hutu rebelled against their Tutsi overlords. The Tutsi *mwami* (king) and thousands of his followers fled to Burundi. In 1961, Rwandans voted in favour of becoming a republic, independent of Burundi. Independence was achieved in 1962 and the Parmehutu party which had campaigned for Hutu rights, was elected to power. Its leader, Gregoire KAYIBANDA, became the first president of Rwanda. On July 5, 1973, Kayibanda was deposed by his defence minister, General Juvenal Habyalimana, who became president and head of the government of Rwanda.

SA DA BANDEIRA, renamed Lubango in 1976, is the capital of Huila district in south-western Angola. Mainly an agricultural centre, it is surrounded by an extensive cattle-ranching and sheep rearing region. Pop. 32,000.

SAHARA is the Arabic word for 'the deserts'. The Sahara is the largest desert in the world, occupying an area of about 8,320,000 square kilometres (3,250,000 square miles) in North Africa. It stretches more than 4,800 kilometres (3,000 miles) from the NILE valley to the Atlantic Ocean and about 1,600 kilometres (1,000 miles) from the ATLAS MOUNTAINS to the Sudanese savanna. It was formed about 4,000 years ago by the drying-up of savanna country which supported hunting and farming communities. Today, it is made up of huge wastes of sand (*ergs*) and bare rock (*hammada*), and by the AHAGGAR and TIBESTI mountains.

The few people who live in the Sahara make their living by farming around the oases or by herding camels, goats and sheep. The caravan routes that cross the desert are very ancient. They were once important trade routes, carrying cloth, gold, salt and slaves to and from the African kingdoms to the south. Today, the main economic resources are oil and natural gas in Libya and Algeria, and iron ore in Mauritania and Spanish Sahara.

SAINT DENIS, the capital and administrative centre of Réunion, lies on the northern side of the island. Agricultural products are processed there. Pop. 85,000.

SAINT HELENA is a British island in the South Atlantic situated 1,920 kilometres (1,200 miles) west of Angola. The population of about 5,000 is a mixture of Europeans, Africans and Asians. The island has an area of 120 square kilometres (47 square miles). St. Helena is of volcanic origin, rising to 824 metres (2,704 feet) at Diane's Peak (Mount Actaeon) and cut by rapid streams into deep gorges. An average of 101 centimetres (40 inches) of rain falls each year in the mountains whilst the coast receives eight inches. On the coast temperatures average 21°C (70°F). JAMESTOWN, the capital, was once a famous port of call for refuelling ships and is now a cable station. Fibre, rope and twine made from flax are exported. St. Helena was discovered in 1502 by the Portuguese, annexed by the Dutch in 1633 and taken under the control of the British East India Company in 1673. The island became a British Crown Colony in 1834.

SAINT LOUIS, a city and seaport of Senegal, lies on Saint Louis Island at the mouth of the Senegal River. It is connected by rail to DAKAR. Saint Louis was founded by the French in 1658. It was a former capital of Senegal and, for a short time, of French West Africa. Pop. 81,000.

SAINT PAUL, the original settlement and port of Réunion, lies on the north-west coast. Agricultural products include rum. Pop. 43,000.

SAINT PIERRE, the chief town of the south of Réunion is a fishing port. Its agricultural processing industries include extracting essence from locally grown geranium seeds. Pop. 40,000.

SALISBURY, the capital and main city of Zimbabwe, was founded by settlers in 1890 and named after Lord Salisbury then the British prime minister. At an altitude of 1,478 metres (4,850 feet), it is at the northern end of the central high veld. It is the seat of government and the commercial heart of the country. The centres of the tobacco industry and many secondary industries are in Salisbury. Pop. 463,000.

SALOUM RIVER, in Senegal, is about 160 kilometres (100 miles) long. It flows westwards into the Atlantic just north of Gambia. It has a wide mouth with many islands and is navigable for about 96 kilometres (60 miles).

SAN ANTONIO see SÃO TOMÉ and PRINCIPE.

SANTA CRUZ DE TENERIFE is the capital of one of the two provinces that make up the CANARY ISLANDS. The city has a harbour and is an important port. It has an oil refinery. Pop. 133,000.

SÃO TOMÉ, the capital of SÃO TOMÉ and PRINCIPE, lies on the north-east coast of the island of Sao Tomé. It is a port with a good harbour in Ana de Chaves Bay. It is connected by rail with the cocoa farms and coffee plantations. Pop. 7,800.

SÃO TOMÉ and **PRINCIPE,** are two islands in the Gulf of Guinea. The two islands have a total area of 952 square kilometres (372 square miles) and a population of 75,000. São Tomé has a steep rocky coast and is of volcanic origin. The island rises to Pico de São Tomé which is 2,023 metres high (6,640 feet). Its position, almost on the equator, gives the island a hot and humid climate with a long rainy season. Cocoa, coffee, copra, kola nuts and oilpalms are the main products. Industrial processing includes soap and palm oil.

Principe, or Princes Island, is also of volcanic origin rising to 947 metres (3,110 feet). Smaller than São Tomé, the chief town is San António in the east. Cacao, coffee and coconuts are grown. Smaller islands in the group are Pedras Tinhosas and Rolas.

The islands were discovered by the Portuguese in 1470, and were an overseas province of Portugal until their independence in July 1975.

SAQQARA, an Egyptian village in the province of Gizeh, stands near the ruins of the ancient Egyptian capital of Memphis. It was the necropolis (city of the dead) for Memphis and it contains several pyramids. The best known is the step pyramid of Zoser (2600 to 2550 BC) which was built by Imhotep.

SARH, the second largest town in Chad, lies on the Chari River in tne south of the country. It was established as a military base by the French and was called Fort-Archambault until 1972. There is an airport, and cotton textiles are manufactured. Pop. 44,000.

SEGOU, a town on the Niger River, is in southern Mali. It is a market for agricultural produce and textiles are also manufactured. Pop. 30,000.

SEKONDI-TAKORADI is Ghana's second largest port. Opened in 1926, with 89 hectares (220 acres) of enclosed water it handles the bulk of Ghana's export trade. It is a centre for the timber trade, mining and engineering. Pop. 75,450.

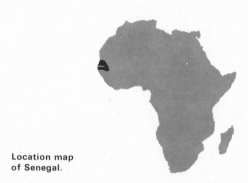

Location map of Senegal.

SENEGAL, the most westerly country of Africa, borders the Atlantic Ocean to the west, Mauritania to the north, Mali to the east and Guinea and Guinea-Bissau to the south. Gambia cuts into the south of Senegal along the Gambia River. Senegal covers 197,120 kilometres (77,000 square miles), and has a population of 3,780,000.

People The main peoples of Senegal are the Wolof (35 per cent of the population), Peul (17 per cent), Serer (16.5 per cent), Toucouleur, or Fula (6.5 per cent) and Lebon. The official language is French although most people are Muslims. The capital is DAKAR. Other cities include SAINT LOUIS (the former capital), KAOLACK, THIÉS and ZINGUINCHOR.

Land and Economy Senegal's coast is mostly low-lying, and the interior is mostly lowland, except for the south-east. The lower SENEGAL RIVER and its main tributary, the Faleme, form Senegal's northern and eastern borders.

The climate over most of the country is like the Sudan's (midway between dry desert and moist tropics). In the north it is Sahelian, typical of the southern edge of the Sahara. The rainy season is from June to November in the Sudanese zone. It begins later in the north.

Senegal has to import some of its foodstuffs, such as rice, maize and other staple crops. Groundnuts are the major cash crop and account for 80 per cent of the country's total exports. Mineral resources include phosphate, which is mined for export. Fishing, especially for tuna, market gardening and tourism are growing in importance. More than half of Senegal's exports go to France.

Senegal is one of the most industrialized countries in western Africa. Its industries range from groundnut oil mills to textiles, beer, cigarettes and oil refining. Communications are good. Long stretches of the rivers are navigable and all the main towns and cities are linked by road. A railway links DAKAR with KAOLACK, Touba and Bamako the Mali capital. Another railway links Dakar with the port of SAINT LOUIS, which has an international airport.

Unit of currency CFA franc

History Senegal owes its name to the Zenega, a Berber people who were possibly already living there in Roman times. After AD 1000 they were converted to Islam. In about 1400, Fulani invaders established themselves in the middle Senegal River. On the coast, the Wolof founded a kingdom, which was later divided into four states, Dyolof, Walo, Cayor and Baol. In 1445 the Portuguese explorer Dinas Dias, reached the mouth of the River Senegal and trading stations were later established. Other Europeans followed the Portuguese. The Dutch founded Goree trading station in 1621 and the French built a fort at Saint Louis in 1638. Senegal was an English colony from 1758 to 1817 when it was retaken by the French. DAKAR was founded in 1857, and grew rapidly as the capital of French West Africa. In 1946, Senegal became an overseas territory of France. In 1957–58, several French-speaking West African countries, including Senegal, failed to form a federation. An attempt to form a federation between Senegal and Mali (1959–60) also failed. Dakar, which had been built as a capital for the whole of French West Africa, became 'top-heavy', because the Senegal hinterland was too small to support it. Senegal's industries, built up to supply a federal French West African market, were left with only the small home market when the Mali Federation collapsed. In 1960, Léopold Sédar SENGHOR became president of the independent republic of Senegal. In 1962, his Prime Minister, Mamadou DIA, tried to seize power but failed. Students' riots and workers' strikes, similar to those in Paris, occurred in Dakar in 1968. In the 1970s, Senghor's government under prime minister Abdou Diouf achieved greater political stability.

Government Senegal is a one-party state. All the 80 members of the legislative assembly elected for a four year term, belong to the Senegalese Progressive Union (PUS). The president has full control of the government although in 1970 the post of prime minister was re-created. The country is divided into 13 administrative units for local government.

SENEGAL RIVER, in West Africa, rises in the FOUTA DJALLON highlands of Guinea near the Sierra Leone border. It flows north-west through Mali. It then forms the northern boundary of Senegal, and empties into the Atlantic at SAINT LOUIS. It is about 1,680 kilometres (1,050 miles) long. The main tributary of the Senegal river is the Falémé in East Senegal.

SENNAR DAM, in Sudan, was built between 1922 and 1925 on the BLUE NILE RIVER. Formerly known as the Makwar Dam, it provides water for the Gezira cotton scheme which provides Sudan's most valuable export.

SEROWE, in Botswana, is situated 288 kilometres (180 miles) north of GABERONES, the capital. It is an agricultural market town and the capital of the Bamangwato people. Pop. 34,000.

▲ Salisbury: A view by night.

◄ SENEGAL: The Fulani (or Peul) people have a semi-nomadic way of life. *Left,* they are shown how to use oxen for farming.

SAQQARA: The step pyramid of Zoser was built between 4,570 and 4,220 years ago. ▼

SEYCHELLES ISLANDS are a group of 90 small islands in the Indian Ocean about 1,760 kilometres (1,100 miles) east of the Kenya coast. The population of 55,000 in 1971 is made up of French, Indians, Chinese, Africans and Creoles. English is the official language although Creole is widely spoken. Most people are Roman Catholics. The main occupations are the cultivation of vanilla and coconut palms, and the manufacture of coconut products. Salted fish and tortoise-shell are also important exports. The tourist industry is growing. The islands were first discovered by the Portuguese in 1502. They were annexed by the French in 1756 and by the British in 1810. The Seychelles became a British crown colony in 1903. Since 1970, they have had internal self government through an elected legislative assembly. Plans are now being made to grant the Seychelles independence in 1976.

SFAX, Tunisia, is a major port and manufacturing centre. The modern docks and factories are sited close to the old walled city. Exports include phosphates and olive oil and other agricultural products. Fishing is also a very important industry. Pop. 70,000.

SHABA, formerly called Katanga, is a province in south-eastern Zaire. It is populated by the Baluba, the most numerous of the Bantu peoples. Shaba is one of the major mining areas of Africa. Large deposits of copper, cobalt, coal, manganese, uranium and zinc are worked in this province. It was partly colonized by Swahili merchants after the decline of the Lunda empire. The Belgians occupied it in 1895.

SHEBELLE RIVER rises in the highlands of south-east Ethiopia and flows south, for 2,000 kilometres (1,250 miles), to water the plain of southern Somalia. It does not enter the sea, but drains swamps near the mouth of the GIUBA RIVER.

SICASSOU, Mali's third largest town, is a market centre in the south near the border with Ivory Coast.

SIDI IFNI was the capital of the former Spanish province of Ifni on the west coast of Morocco between the SAHARA desert and the Atlantic Ocean. It was ceded to Spain in 1860 and reverted to Morocco in 1969. Pop. 8,300.

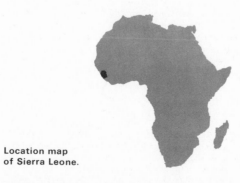

Location map of Sierra Leone.

SIERRA LEONE, a republic in West Africa, is bordered by the Atlantic Ocean to the west, by Guinea to the north and east and by Liberia to the south-east. Founded in 1787 as a settlement for freed slaves, Sierra Leone covers an area of 70,910 square kilometres (27,699 square miles) and has a population of 2,861,000.

People The descendants of the ex-slave settlers, known as Creoles, and the African peoples make up the population of Sierra Leone. The largest groups are the Temne of the north-west, and the Mende of the south. One third of the people are Muslims, five per cent are Christians and the rest follow their ethnic religions. English is the official language of Sierra Leone. Its capital is FREETOWN. Other towns include Bo, Kenema and Makeni.

Land and Economy Sierra Leone is situated on the Atlantic slopes of the high plateau that separates the tributaries of the upper Niger River from the shorter rivers that flow straight to the Atlantic. The country has a low coastal plain about 32 kilometres (20 miles) wide rising to broad lowlands with some hills. Inland, a plateau rises to more than 609 metres (2,000 feet). The rocky peninsula on the north-west coast, the Sierra Leone, on which the capital, FREETOWN, stands, gives the country its name. The climate is tropical, but because the country is geographically varied, there are wide differences in rainfall and temperature. Inland, it is cooler and drier.

Nearly 80 per cent of Sierra Leoneans work on the land as subsistence farmers. Rice is grown, but also has to be imported. The main export crops include cassava, cocoa, coffee, ginger, kola nuts and palm kernels. More than 80 per cent of Sierra Leone's exports are made up of diamonds, iron ore, bauxite, rutile and other minerals. Diamond smuggling has been a great problem. Industries include oil refining and diamond cutting and polishing.

Unit of currency Leone

History Sierra Leone was founded on land bought from the Temne King, Naimbanna, in 1787. In 1808, it became a British crown colony. At Fourah Bay College, founded in 1827, Creole Sierra Leoneans trained as clerks, teachers, lawyers and doctors, for English-speaking West Africa. The resulting Creole domination of the country was resented by the African peoples of the country. In the 1950s, the Sierra Leone People's Party (SLPP) under Sir Milton MARGAI overcame Creole influence and won the elections of 1957 with the support of 'native' Sierra Leoneans. After Sierra Leone became independent in 1961, the SLPP was re-elected. Following Margai's death in 1964, he was succeeded as prime minister by his brother, Sir Albert MARGAI. The opposition All People's Congress led by Siaka STEVENS, won the election of 1967, but was prevented from taking office by the army. Military government followed, but in 1968, Stevens finally became prime minister. Sierra Leone became a republic in 1971 and Stevens took office as the first president.

Government Sierra Leone's legislature, the House of Representatives, has 66 elected members, 12 paramount chiefs and a speaker. Elections are held every five years. The cabinet has 20 ministers, including the prime minister, who is chosen by the president.

SINAI PENINSULA is a desert peninsula which separates Egypt in Africa from the mainland of Asia. The peninsula is roughly triangular, bounded by the Mediterranean in the north, the Gulf of Suez in the south-west, and the Gulf of Aqaba in the south-east. The peninsula is mostly desert and mountain. There are oil wells near the coast of the Gulf of Suez. An ancient Orthodox monastery is sited on Mount Catherine. Sinai was occupied by Israel during the Six Day War of 1967.

SOBAT RIVER, is one of the NILE RIVER's tributaries. It rises in south-west Ethiopia and, after 736 kilometres (460 miles), joins the WHITE NILE south of Malakal in Sudan.

SOKODE, in Togo, lies 304 kilometres (190 miles) north of LOME to which it is linked by road, and rail. It is a commercial and agricultural centre for cotton, groundnuts, shea nuts and kapok. Pop. 4,000.

Location map
of Somalia.

SOMALIA, now known as the Somali Democratic Republic, is an independent state situated on the 'Horn' of north-east Africa. It is bounded by Kenya, Ethiopia and the French territory of Afars and Issas, and has coastlines on the Indian Ocean and the Gulf of Aden. Somalia has an area of 630,156 square kilometres (246,155 square miles) and a population of over three million.

People Most people are Somalis, a Cushitic people. In the south, many of the inhabitants are descended from the original Bantu-speaking population. Arabs are the main minority group. Somali is the official language while English is used in contact with the outside world and is taught in secondary schools. In contrast, Arabic is used in the instruction of Islam, the state religion, and in ritual. Less than one out of every ten people live in towns. The largest town is MOGADISCIO, the capital.

Land and Economy Northern Somalia is a large dry plateau, which is semi-mountainous. Much of the southern region is semi-desert, but there is a large fertile area which is watered by the Juba and Shebelle rivers.

The herding of livestock is the most important factor in the Somali economy. About three-quarters of the working population are employed in raising cattle, camels, goats and sheep, and many of the herders still follow a nomadic life. Livestock and livestock products form the major part of Somalia's exports. In the fertile southern region, bananas, sugar cane and fruits are grown on plantations as cash crops. Maize, sorghum and various beans are grown in this area as food crops. Somalia has meat and fish processing industries and leather, cloth, plastic and sugar factories. Mining activity is slight, although uranium and oil have been discovered.

Unit of currency Somalo

History The Somali people first lived in the north of the country. In about the AD 900s, they were converted to Islam, and at the same time began to spread south.

In 1884, the north of the Somali territory became a British protectorate. The south was taken by Italy and became the colony of Somalia in 1905. Other areas came under the control of France and Ethiopia. Between 1900 and 1920 a religious leader, Sayyid Muhammad Abdille Hasan, led a holy war against British, Italian and Ethiopian forces, but was finally defeated.

In 1940, the Italians conquered British Somaliland, but in the following year British forces reconquered it and the whole of Somalia. However, the former boundaries were restored after the war, and in 1950, Italy began to administer the southern part of the country under the trusteeship of the United Nations, while preparing it for independence. In 1960, both the Italian and the British territories became independent, and were united as the Somali Republic, a parliamentary democracy modelled on both the British and Italian systems. This continued until 1969, when the president, Abderashid Ali SHERMARKE, was assassinated. The army with the help of the police, took power in a bloodless coup. The National Assembly was dissolved and the country renamed the Somali Democratic Republic.

Government Somalia is governed by the Supreme Revolutionary Council, composed of military members and by the council of Secretaries,

SOUTH AFRICA: A decorated Ndebele village near Pretoria.

which includes both military and civilian members. The president of the Supreme Revolutionary Council and head of state is Major-general Mohamed SIAD BARRE, a self-proclaimed Marxist.

SONGHAI, in west-central Sudan, was an African empire in the region of the NIGER RIVER. Its kings were originally vassals of MALI, but by the early 1400s the Songhai rulers broke away and began to conquer Mali territories. Under SONNI ALI (1464–92) and his successors, Songhai became even greater than Mali. Its chief centres were Gao, the capital, and TIMBUKTU, a centre of Islamic learning. Internal rivalry and raids by the Moroccans caused the collapse of Songhai by the early 1600s.

SOUSSE is a port and manufacturing centre on the eastern Tunisian coast, with industries including vehicle assembly. Sousse exports phosphates, olive oil and esparto. There is also a fishing industry. Pop. 58,000.

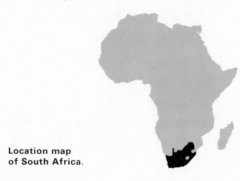

Location map
of South Africa.

SOUTH AFRICA, by far the most highly industrialized country in Africa, lies at the southern tip of the continent, with coastlines on both the Atlantic and Indian Oceans. It borders Namibia (South-West Africa), Botswana, Zimbabwe and Mozambique, which all lie to the north. The independent country of Lesotho is completely surrounded by South African territory. The port of Walvis Bay on the coast of Namibia is a South African possession. South Africa has an area of 1,206,900 square kilometres (471,445 square miles). In 1974 the estimated population numbered 24,887,000.

People South Africa's population contains four distinct groups. Making up more than 70 per cent of the total are the 17,712,000 Africans. Europeans number 4,160,000 (about 17 per cent), and Asians and people of mixed descent number 3,015,000 (about 12 per cent). The Africans belong to various ethnic groups, of which the Xhosa, Zulu and Sotho are the largest, each with more than two million members. Most Europeans are either descendants

of the early Dutch settlers, known as Afrikaners, or are descended from British settlers. A number of the Europeans have French or German ancestry. The Coloured people are the result of intermarriage between the early European settlers and the indigenous people. The Asian population are descended from labourers who came to South Africa in the second half of the 19th century to work on sugar plantations. A few Bushmen survive in the dry regions in the west of the country.

English and Afrikaans, a language descended from Dutch, are the official languages and many Europeans speak both. The Africans speak Bantu languages, and the Asians speak Gujerati, Tamil, Urdu and Hindi. Many people are Christians. The Dutch Reformed Church is the largest denomination, with over two million members. Many people practise Islam and traditional African religions. The Jewish community numbers more than 100,000.

South Africa is the most urbanized country on the continent, and nearly half the population live in towns. CAPE TOWN is the legislative capital and PRETORIA the administrative capital. JOHANNESBURG is the largest city and is the commercial and industrial centre of South Africa.

SOUTH AFRICA: The beautiful protea is South Africa's national flower.

Land and Economy Most of South Africa is a vast plateau, part of which is called the High Veld. This is open grassland and is between 1,219 and 1,828 metres (4,000 and 6,000 feet) above sea level. The plateau is bounded by an escarpment facing towards the ocean. This includes the DRAKENSBERG, which rise to nearly 3,352 metres (11,000 feet) in the south-east. South Africa, which becomes increasingly dry towards the north-central area, touches on the southern fringe of the KALAHARI Desert. The Great KAROO Desert lies in the south-west of the country.

The main rivers of South Africa are the ORANGE RIVER, which flows across the country from east to west into the Atlantic Ocean and the VAAL.

The South African climate is mainly temperate because of the altitude, with a sub-tropical area in the north, and a Mediterranean climate in the area of the Western Cape. Temperatures vary from 21°C to 27°C (70°F to 80°F) in the summer and 7°C to 13°C (45°F to 55°F) in the winter. Rainfall, which mostly occurs in the summer months, comes mainly from the east. The eastern and southern coastal belts are the wettest areas with up to 127 centimetres (50 inches) a year. Towards the west, the rainfall diminishes to less than 50 centimetres (20 inches) a year.

Agriculture is very important in South Africa, and agricultural products account for half the exports, if gold is excluded. Maize is the most important crop, and over five million tonnes are produced annually. Other food crops include oats, wheat, barley and sorghum. Regional variations in climate mean that South Africa can produce a wide range of cash crops, which include apples, bananas, citrus fruits, grapes, groundnuts, pineapples and sugar cane. Grapes for wine are

SOUTH AFRICA: A misty lake scene in Kruger National Park.

SOUTH AFRICA: A view of Cape Town and Table Bay.

cultivated in the area around the Cape.

Livestock is a major factor in the South African economy. Nearly 40 million sheep are reared and wool is the second export after gold. Cattle, goats and pigs are also reared in large numbers.

Gold was first discovered in the area now known as the Witwatersrand in the north-east of the country in 1886. This area now produces more than 60 per cent of the world's gold. Diamonds are mined near Kimberley in the centre of the country, South Africa being one of the world's leading producers. Other minerals mined and exported include antimony, asbestos, chrome, coal, copper, iron ore, manganese and platinum. Excluding gold, minerals make up about one third of the country's exports.

Since World War II, South Africa has greatly increased her industrial capacity, mainly in Johannesburg and the surrounding area. South African industry is mainly concerned with the processing of natural resources. The textile industry produces wool. Iron and steel, and chemical works are important. A number of factories assemble automobiles from parts imported from Europe and America. Electricity is mainly supplied from coal-fired power stations. However, a country-wide scheme of hydro-electric dams is under construction. This scheme will also provide water for irrigation. An experimental nuclear power station is being developed. Communications are good and a network of roads and narrow gauge railways covers the country. An internal air service connects most of the large centres.

Unit of currency Rand

History Historians believe that the original inhabitants of South Africa were nomadic hunters, Hottentots and Bushmen. Two distinct linguistic groups of Bantu speaking peoples migrated to South Africa between AD 1100 and 1800. The Nguni settled on the coastal belt as far south as the Great Fish River. The Sotho occupied the High Veld.

The first European settlement was established at the Cape by Jan van Riebeck in 1652 for the Dutch East India Company. Settlers from other European countries followed the Dutch and in the early 1700s, began to expand inland from the coast. In the 1800s, a succession of disputes with the Africans over land occurred.

In the first half of the 1800s, two major historical events changed the relationship between the Africans and the Europeans—the Mfecane and the Great Trek. The Mfecane, a dispersal of the African peoples from the area was caused by the formation of the powerful Zulu nation under SHAKA in 1817. The Zulus, who are a Nguni people, expanded, conquering and incorporating other Nguni groups.

Some of these groups, forced out by Zulu pressure, migrated to the north and west, causing the disruption of the Sotho peoples. The southern Sotho formed themselves into the Basotho nation and settled in the area that is now Lesotho. The Ndebele of Zimbabwe, the Ngoni of Tanzania and Malawi, and the Shagaan of Mozambique are all descended from Nguni groups forced out of South Africa by the Mfecane.

The Great Trek began in 1835. The British had gained control of the Cape in 1795. From then on, they began to exert increasing pressure on the descendants of the Dutch settlers, who were known as Boers (farmers). In 1806, the Cape became a British colony. To escape the restrictions of British rule, the Boers began to migrate northwards and eastwards. This migration was known as the Great Trek. By the 1850s, despite conflict with the Zulus, two independent Boer republics had been established: the Orange Free State and the South African Republic (now the Transvaal). A similar republic in Natal had been destroyed by the British. The British made Natal a colony, and the land occupied by the southern Sotho became a British protectorate. Meanwhile the British recognized the independent Boer republic.

By 1870, the Zulu kingdom had been weakened and was finally defeated by the British in 1879.

The discovery of diamonds at Kimberley in 1870, and gold on the Witwatersrand in 1886 caused the next changes in South Africa. The Witwatersrand developed into the centre of the gold rush. Most of the mining was controlled by British businessmen, of whom Cecil RHODES was the most successful. The expansion of British industrial interests in the Transvaal led to conflict between the British and the Boers. This came to a head with the Anglo-Boer wars (1880–81) and (1899–1902). In spite of setbacks early in the second war, the British defeated the Boers, who acknowledged British sovereignty over the Transvaal and the Orange Free State.

A compromise between the Boers and the British was achieved by the formation of the Union of South Africa in 1910. The two British colonies and the two Boer republics were joined together, although they retained some independence.

The South African economy expanded rapidly during the 1920s and 30s, and the industrial cities grew correspondingly. The dividing line between the Africans and the Europeans became more marked, and, in 1936, laws were passed that defined the status of the Africans. Their right to vote was restricted, and they were only allowed to have 13 per cent of the land area of South Africa to themselves.

In 1948, the National Party, led by Daniel

MALAN, won the general election and replaced the United party of Jan SMUTS. The National Party favoured the policy of apartheid or separate development. Apartheid called for the formation of separate societies for the Europeans, the Africans, the Asians and the Coloureds. The Malan government passed various laws to implement apartheid. African workers were forbidden to strike. Residential areas were strictly segregated into 'black' and 'white' areas. Travel restrictions were imposed on the Africans and the police acquired wide powers. Malan's successors, Johannes Strijdom (1954–58), Hendrik VERWOERD (1958–66) and Balthazar Johannes VORSTER (1966–   ), have followed the apartheid policy. In 1959, the Bantu self-government act was passed. This provided for the formation of internally self-governing BANTU-STANS or African homelands, within South Africa.

The introduction of apartheid provoked bitter political opposition from the Africans. In 1960, South African security forces fired on a crowd of Africans who were demonstrating outside a police station at Sharpeville, killing 56 of them. The government declared a state of emergency and banned the leading African political parties—the African National Congress (ANC) and the Pan African Congress (PAC).

Apartheid has provoked international criticism of South Africa, especially from the newly independent African nations. In 1961, South Africa left the Commonwealth and became a republic.

In the late 1960s, South Africa began a policy of trying to establish contacts with other nations in Africa, with the declared aim of providing general economic assistance. In 1974, prime minister Vorster declared his aim as peaceful co-existence in Africa. In view of the problems of southern Africa, he participated with the presidents of Botswana, Tanzania and Zambia in trying to achieve a political settlement for Zimbabwe.

Government South Africa is a republic. The major executive power lies with the prime minister, who heads a 166-seat House of Assembly, elected by Europeans over 18 years of age. The House of Assembly and the provincial councils elect 42 of the 54 members of the Senate. The president who is a non-executive head of state appoints 12 more senators. The four South African provinces each have an elected council.

As part of the apartheid policy, new political institutions under the ultimate control of the central government have been established for the Africans, the Asians and the Coloureds. Eight Bantustans, which correspond to ethnic groups have their own governments. The Coloured Persons' Representative Council and the Indian Council represent the Coloureds and the Asians.

SOUTH-WEST AFRICA see NAMIBIA. The name Namibia was given to South-West Africa by the United Nations General Assembly on June 12, 1968. African leaders from the country, which is ruled by South Africa, suggested the name.

SPANISH SAHARA, a former Spanish territory in north-west Africa, has an area of 362,912 square kilometres (102,700 square miles), with a population of about 50,000, mostly Arabs and Berbers. It is now called Western Sahara.

The country is mostly semi-desert and many people are nomadic hardsmen. Fishing is important, but the massive deposits of phosphates in the north are the territory's chief resource.

The Spanish colonized the area in the late 1800s and agreed frontiers with France in 1912. In the 1970s, both Morocco and Mauritania claimed the territory, but the World Court could not affirm historical legal ties between them and the territory. In Spanish Sahara, an Algerian-backed nationalist group opposed their neighbours' claims and demanded independence. Spain agreed to withdraw in early 1976, leaving Morocco in control of the north, with Mauritania in the south. Algeria opposed this agreement and Saharan nationalists fought with Moroccans and Mauritians.

STEPHANIE, LAKE, is the southernmost of a line of Ethiopian lakes lying in the Rift Valley. Lake Stephanie lies parallel to Lake TURKANA.

Location map of Sudan.

SUDAN, an independent republic in north-east Africa, is the largest country on the continent. It has borders with Ethiopia in the east; Kenya, Uganda and Zaire in the south; the Central African Republic, Chad and Libya in the west; and Egypt in the north. It has 640 kilometres (400 miles) of coastline on the Red Sea. The Sudan's area is 2,476,800 square kilometres (967,500 square miles) and the population numbers about 17,000,000.

People The northern Sudan is inhabited by Arabs and Nubians, whilst Black peoples live in the southern part of the country. The Arabs of the north are Muslims; the peoples of the south mostly practise their own religions. The official language is Arabic but peoples of the south speak over a hundred different languages. Most people live in the fertile valleys of the WHITE NILE and its tributaries. OMDURMAN and KHARTOUM, the capital, are the largest cities.

Land and Economy Most of the northern Sudan is taken up with the Libyan and Nubian deserts, which are separated by the narrow valley of the Nile. To the south, the desert gives way to grasslands and then to savanna country. Southern Sudan has an equatorial climate which supports forest. The mountainous regions are along the Red Sea coast and in the extreme south-east. Rainfall is irregular over most of the country.

Farming is the most important occupation. Cotton, grown in the region of the GEZIRA irrigation scheme, where the Blue and White Niles meet, is the most important cash crop. The Sudan produces four-fifths of the world's supply of gum arabic. Food crops include cassava, groundnuts, maize, millet, rice and sweet potatoes. There is some industry, which processes agricultural products. The country has large deposits of asbestos and smaller quantities of chromite, iron ore, gold, gypsum and manganese.

Unit of currency Sudan pound

SPANISH SAHARA: A street in Aiún, the newly-built capital of the country.

History The first Sudanese culture was that of Meroe, which flourished from about BC 670. The Romans penetrated Nubia in AD 203. The Christian Nubian kingdom resisted Islam for many centuries, from AD 641 until it was conquered by the Arabs in 1366. The Funj kings ruled the Gezira until the Turks invaded the Sudan in 1520, but it was not finally subdued until 1821, when an Egyptian army conquered it. An independent movement was created by the MAHDI, a messianic Muslim leader, in 1881. In 1899, an Anglo-Egyptian army defeated the Mahdi's successor and Sudan came under joint British and Egyptian control as the Anglo-Egyptian Sudan.

The Sudan became an independent republic in 1956. Two years later a military coup was staged and General Abboud became president of the country. He ruled until 1964, when he resigned and was succeeded by a civilian government led by Muhammad Ahmad MAHJOUB. The population of the south rebelled against the government and civil war broke out. In 1969, Colonel Jaarfar al-NIMEIRY came to power through another military coup and in 1971, he survived a further coup. He rules through the Revolutionary Council.

One of the chief problems faced by the country from 1964 was a civil war between peoples of the North (Muslim Arabs and Nubians) and South (Nilo-Hamitic and Negro peoples). This war ended in March 1972 with an agreement which granted the South considerable autonomy.

SUEZ is an important seaport and Egypt's main outlet to the east. It lies at the southern end of the Suez Canal and at the head of the Gulf of Suez. It has a large oil refinery and chemical industries.

SUEZ CANAL connects the Red Sea with the Mediterranean. It is 160 kilometres (100 miles) long and runs from the town of Suez to Port Said at the northern end. Ferdinand de Lesseps built the canal with Egyptian and international finance between 1859 and 1869. The canal considerably cut the sea journeys from Europe to Asia. In 1878, the British bought a controlling interest in the Suez Canal Company from Egypt. In 1956, the Egyptian president, Gamel Abdel NASSER, nationalized the canal and a joint British and French force made an unsuccessful attempt to occupy the canal. The canal was closed after the Israeli occupation of the Sinai peninsula in 1967 but was reopened in 1975.

SUDAN: This statue at Juba symbolizes the unity of the peoples of the north and south.

SUEZ, GULF OF, is the north-western branch of the Red Sea that separates continental Egypt from the Sinai peninsula. It is about 320 kilometres (200 miles) long and about 48 kilometres (30 miles) wide at its widest part.

SWAKOPMUND is a town in Namibia. It is situated at the mouth of the Swakop River, just north of WALVIS BAY. The town is a popular resort and the administration has its head-quarters there during December and January. Guano and salt are produced. Pop. 6,000.

Location map of Swaziland.

SWAZILAND is a small, independent, landlocked kingdom in southern Africa. It has an eastern border with Mozambique, but is almost surrounded by South Africa. The country has an area of 1,716,480 square kilometres (6,705 square miles) and a population of 460,000.

People The main ethnic group are the Swazis, a Bantu people of the Nguni sub-family. Another 12,000 non-Swazis, mostly Europeans, live in the country. Most people practise their traditional religions, although some are Christians. English is the official language, but Swati is the language most commonly spoken. The main towns are the capital, MBABANE, and MANZINI.

Land and Economy Swaziland is divided into three geographical areas: the Highveld in the west, which rises to 914 metres (3,000 feet) and is mountainous; the Middleveld, which is between 304 and 609 metres (1,000 and 2,000 feet) and hilly; and the Lowveld, in the east, which is a low plain below 304 metres (1,000 feet). Rainfall varies in the three regions, from 140 centimetres (55 inches) a year in the west, to 63 centimetres (25 inches) in the east. Temperatures are sub-tropical.

SUDAN: *Above* Firewood is transported by dhows to Khartoum.

SWAZILAND: *Far right* King Sobhuza II.

Most people are subsistence farmers, and agriculture is the mainstay of the economy. Maize, millet, rice and sorghum are the chief food crops. Citrus fruits, cotton and sugar are cultivated as cash crops. The rearing of livestock, and forestry also, plays an important part in the economy. Minerals are of increasing importance Deposits of asbestos, coal and iron are exploited, and tin and gold are also mined. Most industry is concerned with the processing of agricultural products. The major trading partner is South Africa, with which Swaziland has a customs union.

Unit of currency Rand

History The Swazi first moved into the area in the 1820s, as a result of Zulu pressure from the south. After 1850, European settlers began to arrive in the area, and in 1903 following the Boer War, the British took effective control of the country. Swaziland gained internal self-government in 1967, and full independence the following year.

Government Under the 1967 constitution, Swaziland is ruled by the Ngwenyama (king) with the assistance of an Assembly and a Senate, which are partly elected and partly appointed by the king. King SOBHUZA II (who had been king, with limited powers, since 1921) became the ruler on independence and in the election the royalist Imbokodvo party won a majority, which it retained in the 1972 election. In 1973, King Sobhuza repealed the constitution, abolished parliament and political parties and initiated rule by proclamation, with all power vested in himself and his council.

TABLE MOUNTAIN rises to 1,082 metres (3,550 feet) immediately behind CAPE TOWN. It is flat topped and often covered by a 'table cloth' of thin cloud.

TABORA, capital of the Western Region of Tanzania, was founded by traders from Zanzibar in 1844, at the point where their caravan routes from Lake TANGANYIKA and to Lake VICTORIA met. The city is the centre of an important agricultural area.

TAMATAVE is the chief port of the Malagasy Republic, lying on the east coast. Roads and a single-track railway carry the country's trade between Tamatave and the capital TANANARIVE.

TANANARIVE: A market scene in the capital of the Malagasy Republic.

TANA, LAKE, is a crater lake in Ethiopia covering an area of 3,200 square kilometres (1,250 square miles) and lying 1,800 metres (6,000 feet) above sea level. It is Ethiopia's largest lake and is the source of the BLUE NILE, which flows from the lake over the Tissisat Falls.

TANA RIVER is the longest river in Kenya. It has many sources in MOUNT KENYA and the Aberdare highlands. It runs down for 640 kilometres (400 miles) to the coast in Lamu district where it has formed a small delta. At Kindaruma it serves a hydro-electric scheme.

TANANARIVE, the capital of the Malagasy Republic, lies on the high plateau just east of the geographical centre of the country. It became the island's capital in the time of King Andrianampoinimerina (1787–1810), when marshes were drained around the seven hills on which the city stands. Wood and brick houses now crowd the hillsides, which are criss-crossed with stone steps. The Zoma (Friday market), one of the biggest in Africa, is held at the city's centre. Pop. 342,000.

TANGA, in Tanzania, is a regional capital, deep-water seaport and communications centre. The railway runs to MOSHI and ARUSHA, where it joins the railway from MOMBASA. Tanga is connected by road with DAR ES SALAAM and NAIROBI. The chief exports from the area are coffee and sisal. Tanga is also a traditional centre of Swahili literature. Pop. 61,000.

TANGANYIKA, LAKE, lies along the borders of Burundi and Tanzania on its eastern shore, and Zaire and Zambia on its western shore. It has an area of 32,512 square kilometres (12,700 square miles).

TANGIER, in Morocco, is situated on the Straits of Gibraltar. It was a free port under international control until integrated with Morocco in 1956. Its economic privileges were abolished in 1960. The industries of Tangier include textiles, tyres and shipyards. Pop. 142,000.

Location map of Tanzania.

TANZANIA, officially called the United Republic of Tanzania, is the largest country in East Africa. It lies just to the south of the equator and has 800 kilometres (500 miles) of coastline bordering the Indian Ocean to the east. Its neighbours are: to the north, Kenya and Uganda; to the west, Rwanda, Burundi and Zaire; to the south, Zambia, Malawi and Mozambique. Tanzania covers an area of 927,845 square kilometres (362,440 square miles) and has a population of 14,758,000.

People Most Tanzanians speak Bantu languages. The main ethnic groups are the Sukuma, Nyamwezi, Ha, Makonde, Gogo, Haya, Chagga and Hehe. Asians (85,000), Arabs (26,000) and Europeans (15,000) are the chief minority groups. English and Swahili are the two official languages, whilst Islam and Christianity are the main religions. DAR ES SALAAM is the main port and first capital. DODOMA will be the new capital. TANGA, TABORA, MWANZA, ARUSHA, and MOSHI are main towns.

Land and Economy A high plateau in the centre of Tanzania rises from 1,200 metres (3,900 feet) to 1,600 metres (5,200 feet). The country also has the highest mountain in Africa, Kilimanjaro which is 5,895 metres (19,340 feet) high, and parts of two of Africa's greatest lakes, TANGANYIKA and VICTORIA. The climate on the coast is humid and tropical but the interior is hot and dry.

Tanzania has an agricultural economy and most people are subsistence farmers. The country's main crops include sisal (of which Tanzania is the world's largest producer), cashew nuts, coffee, cotton, sugar, tea, tobacco and wheat. Zanzibar and Pemba are the world's largest producers of cloves, which are a major export product. Cattle and sheep farming and the timber industry are also important. Fishing is based on both the lakes and the Indian Ocean. The textile, leather and hide industries are well developed and diamonds are mined, but apart from these, there is little industry. The country has poor communications with less than 1,600 kilometres (1,000 miles) of tarred roads.

After the 1967 Arusha Declaration, in which President Nyerere committed the country to socialism and economic independence, Tanzania nationalized all foreign banks, insurance companies and European owned farms. The Ujamaa village policy was also implemented in 1967. It aimed to concentrate a predominantly scattered rural population into cooperative villages of up to 3,000 people. Five million people now live in such centres. In 1970, the government, with Chinese help, began building the Tanzam railway which will run for 1,600 kilometres (1,000 miles), linking Dar es Salaam with the Zambian Copperbelt.

Unit of currency Tanzania Shilling

History Kilwa and Zanzibar are the oldest towns in Tanzania. They were founded by the Shirazi people in the 11th century. Kilwa was occupied by the Portuguese in the early 16th century and by the French in the 18th century. The Arabs took Zanzibar in the 17th century. In the early 19th century the towns along the coast had to accept the rule of the sultans of Zanzibar. They founded Dar es Salaam and controlled the slave trade from Lake TANGANYIKA (Ujiji) to Bagamoyo. In 1884, the German, Carl Peters, first came to East Africa. The treaties he forced various chiefs to sign were the basis of German claims to colonize the territory.

In 1888, when the German East Africa Company tried to move its operations inland, it was fiercely opposed and met with continuing opposition until 1891. The Germans finally subdued the area in 1907 after the famous Maji Maji uprising.

After World War I, German East Africa was given as a Mandate of the League of Nations to Britain and renamed Tanganyika. In 1945, it became a British Trusteeship Territory of the United Nations. In 1954, Julius NYERERE formed the Tanganyika African National Union (TANU) and by 1960, it was clear that he enjoyed the confidence of the people. Tanganyika became independent on December 9, 1961, and Nyerere became president. The country adopted a one-party constitution in 1963 and the first elections under it were held two years later. In 1964, after an army mutiny, Nyerere disbanded the army and formed instead the People's Defence Force, (PDF). Following the revolution in Zanzibar, Tanganyika united with Zanzibar in April 1964 to become the United Republic of Tanzania. In 1967, the Arusha Declaration (Tanzania's Declaration of Socialism) was published. In April 1972 the first vice-president, Sheikh Abeid KARUME of Zanzibar was assassinated. He was succeeded by Sheikh Aboud JUMBE. Tanzania is a member of the OAU, the Commonwealth and the UN. The country has gained much influence in African politics as a result of its policies of socialism and non-alignment.

Government Tanzania has a one-party presidential regime. The National Assembly has legislative powers and the country has a permanent commission of inquiry to protect the rights of citizens under the constitution. The only political parties allowed are TANU on the mainland and the Afro-Shirazi Party (ASP) on Zanzibar and Pemba. For administrative purposes the country is divided into 20 regions (three of them in Zanzibar). Each region comes under a regional commissioner. The Arusha Declaration is the key to Tanzanian politics and by the early 1970s the 'Arusha spirit' was beginning to take effect as more and more people came to live in Ujamaa (self-help) villages. Other aspects of Arusha socialism have been successfully extended into many fields of life. President Nyerere hopes to decentralise his government and move his capital from Dar es Salaam to Dodoma by 1985.

TEMA, opened in 1962, is Ghana's chief port and industrial centre, with over 100 factories and industries. It has a modern fish storage plant and market, and one of the largest artificial harbours in the world—about 200 hectares of sheltered water.

TENERIFE is the largest and most important of the Canary Islands, covering 2,035 square kilometres (795 square miles). The capital is SANTA CRUZ. Two other large towns, La Ortova and La Laguna, are both holiday resorts. Its main products are fruit and vegetables.

TETOUAN, a Moroccan provincial capital near the Mediterranean, was the former capital of Spanish Morocco. It is now a residential town with some light industry, mainly food processing and tobacco. Pop. 101,000.

THEBES was the capital of Ancient Egypt from 2190 to 2040 BC. It was the centre for the worship of the god Amon. The city stood on the banks of the Nile on the site of present-day Luxor. The ruined temples of Luxor and Karnak are among the relics of Thebes.

THIES, a city in Senegal, lies about 65 kilometres (40 miles) inland from CAPE VERDE, on the railway from DAKAR to Mali. It is a centre for the mining of calcium and aluminium phosphates.

THIKA, in Kenya, is an important industrial satellite town of NAIROBI. It lies 48 kilometres (30 miles) north-east of the capital and is the site of coffee-pulping, sisal-processing, textile and fruit-canning factories. Pop. 18,000.

TIBESTI MOUNTAINS lie in the SAHARA region in the north-west of Chad. The highest peak is Emi Koussi at 3,414 metres (11,201 feet). The mountains are inhabited by the Teda people.

TIMBUKTU, a historic town in Mali, lies near the NIGER RIVER east of Lake Faguibine. Timbuktu was settled in the AD 1000s by Saharan Tuareg people who intermingled with Negro Mande people. Timbuktu developed rapidly because it was at the cross-roads of the Saharan caravan routes. From about 1400 it was one of the great cities of the SONGHAI empire. Its schools and mosques attracted students from many parts of the Islamic world. Following its capture by the Moroccans in 1591, Timbuktu declined and was plundered several times. It became French in 1893, and in 1958, part of Mali. Its great mosque and many ruins can still be seen. Pop. 8,000.

TOBRUK is a port and centre of regional administration in the extreme east of Libya. In 1967, Tobruk became a major oil port with the opening of the loading facilities at Marsa Harega. These handle crude oil from the Serif field. Pop. 20,000.

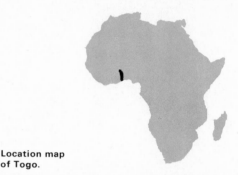

Location map of Togo.

TOGO, a small country in West Africa, is bordered by Ghana to the west, Upper Volta to the north and Benin to the east. It has an area of 55,352 square kilometres (21,622 square miles) and a population of 2,166,000. It has a coastline extending for 65 kilometres on the Gulf of Guinea.

People The Ewe people live in the southern half of Togo, and various ethnic groups, of whom the Kabre are the largest, inhabit the north of the country. French is the official language, but Ewe is more widely spoken than any of the other languages. Most people practise ethnic religions, although there are some Muslims in the north of country. LOME is the capital and major port, whilst other important towns are PALIME and SOKODE.

Land and Economy The Togo Mountains run from south-west to north-east across the country. Grasslands lie on both sides of the mountains and there is a well-watered coastal plain. Togo's climate is both hot and humid with a high rainfall, especially in the south. The economy is mostly agricultural. Cocoa, coffee, and palm nuts, grown on plantations in the south, are the most important crops and the chief export products. Much of the farming is at subsistence level, and many of the farmers are sharecroppers who give a proportion of their produce to their landlords as rent. There is light engineering and phosphates are mined.

Unit of currency Franc

History The Portuguese reached Lomé in the 1400s, but the country of Togo was created by German colonization at the end of the 1800s. It then included part of Ghana. After the defeat of Germany in World War I, the country was divided into two parts, each of which was under a League of Nations Mandate. Western Togo was administered by Britain and was eventually incorporated into Ghana in 1957 after a referendum. Eastern Togo was administered by the French until 1960, when it became independent. Agitation for independence in the 1950s was led by the *Comité de l'Unité Togolaise* party of Sylvanus Olympio, who became the country's first president. His government was overthrown by a military coup in 1963 and he was killed. A period of unstable civilian government followed under the nominal authority of Nicholas GRUNITZKY. In 1967, the military again intervened and assumed direct control of the government. Lieutenant-colonel (now General) Etienne EYADEMA became president.

◄ TANZANIA: A street scene in Zanzibar. In 1964, Zanzibar and Tanganyika formed the United Republic of Tanzania.

TANZANIA: A peaceful beach near Bagamoya, a coastal town in Tanzania. ►

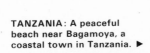

TANZANIA: A vegetable market. ►

◄ TETOUAN: This Moroccan city nestles at the foot of a mountain in the Er Rif.

TOGO: A fisherman casts his net into a coastal lagoon. ▼

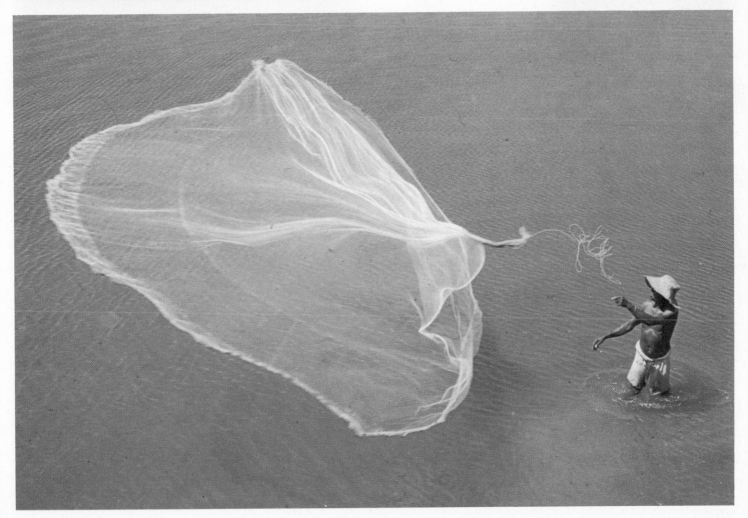

TRIPOLI is the joint capital (with Benghazi) and the largest port of Libya. An administrative and commercial centre, it is the headquarters of most ministries and of foreign oil companies. Tripoli's industries include tobacco manufacture and food processing. There is also a university. Tripoli was founded by the Greeks and formed part of the Roman empire until it was conquered by the Arabs in AD 689. Pop. 237,000.

TSUMEB is a base metal mining centre in northern Namibia. The Tsumeb mine produces large quantities of copper, lead, silver and zinc. It is the biggest employer of migrant labour in the country.

TUGELA RIVER rises at Mont aux Sources in the DRAKENSBERG MOUNTAINS in South Africa and flows for 320 kilometres (200 miles) to the Indian Ocean north of Durban. Along its course it passes over the Tugela Falls, an almost vertical drop of 550 metres (1,800 feet). The Tugela Basin is the site planned for massive hydro-electric power and industrial development.

TULEAR is a town on the east coast of the Malagasy Republic. It lies in the driest region of the country. Pop. 34,000.

TUNIS is the capital and main port of Tunisia. A traditional Muslim town, it was considerably extended during the French colonial period (1881–1956) with broad boulevards and spacious suburbs. It is now the centre of national government, commerce and university education. Major manufacturing plants include vehicle assembly and food processing. Pop. 660,000.

Location map
of Tunisia.

TUNISIA is an independent republic on the Mediterranean coast of North Africa. It has borders with Algeria to the west, and with Libya to the south and east. The country has an area of 123,700 square kilometres (48,319 square miles) and a population of 5,641,000.

People Arabs form the majority of the population and the Arabic language and the Islamic religion are the dominant cultural forces. The original inhabitants were Berbers, who now live in the less fertile interior. Minority groups include Jews, French and Italians. Besides Arabic, the French language is widely used and is taught in schools. About 45 per cent of Tunisia's people live in towns, the most important of which are TUNIS, the capital, and SFAX.

Land and Economy Tunisia lies at the eastern end of the ATLAS MOUNTAINS. They extend through the centre of the country as the Dorsale, which divides the Mjerda Valley, with its Mediterranean climate, in the north, from the desert regions in the south. In the southern region, rainfall can be less than 10 centimetres (4 inches) a year, and summer temperatures reach 49°C (120°F). To the north of the Dorsale, rainfall, which occurs in winter, varies between 40 and 50 centimetres (16 and 20 inches) annually. Temperatures average 26°C (79°F) at Tunis and 33°C (91°F) inland at GAFSA.

Half the Tunisian people are engaged in agriculture and about two-thirds of the country is used for this purpose. Barley, maize, oats, sorghum and wheat are grown as food crops. Dates, figs, grapes, olives and oranges are cultivated as cash crops and exported. Although agriculture is a major occupation, it only contributes one-fifth of the national income. The variable rainfall often makes crop yields uncertain.

Mining is important to the Tunisian economy and phosphates account for 35 per cent of the country's exports. Iron ore, lead, potash and zinc are also mined. A limited petroleum industry and a refinery at BIZERTE supplies enough petroleum for local consumption with a small surplus for export abroad.

Food processing, including wine making, is the most important industry. Chemical processing and the manufacture of cement, clothing and steel are becoming increasingly important. Tourism is the most rapidly expanding industry.

Unit of currency Dinar

History The original inhabitants of Tunisia were Berbers. The Phoenicians colonized the country and built the city of CARTHAGE in 814 BC. This became the centre of a powerful empire until its destruction by the Romans in 146 BC. St Augustine lived there from AD 354 to 430. The leader of the Vandal invaders, Genseric, conquered the city in 439 AD. A century later, in 533, Carthage was conquered by the Byzantines.

In 650 Carthage was taken by the Arabs, who established the Islamic religion. QAYRAWAN became the capital of West Africa and its famous mosque was built between 772 and 836. From 800 to 909 the Aghlabids ruled Tunis as an independent dynasty. The famous historian Ibn Khaldun was born in Tunis in 1332. The Hafsids ruled Tunis from 1228 to 1510 when the Spaniards took it. In 1574, Tunisia was conquered by the Turkish Ottoman empire. The Turks governed Tunisia until the country gained its independence in 1956.

The first government after independence was a constitutional monarchy, but in 1957 the *Bey* (king) was ousted and a republic was proclaimed. Since then, Habib BOURGUIBA, the first president has remained in power, largely through his control of the only political party, the Destourian Socialist Party. In 1974, Tunisia and Libya announced their intention to merge as one nation at some point in the future.

TURKANA, LAKE, situated on the northern border of Kenya, extends slightly into Ethiopia. It is 374 metres (1,230 feet) above sea level, with a length of 246 kilometres (154 miles), and a width of between 16 and 32 kilometres (10 and 20 miles). The area of the lake is 7,022 square kilometres (2,743 square miles).

TUNISIA: A view of Sousse, a coastal town in north-eastern Tunisia.

Location map
of Uganda.

U GANDA, a republic in East Africa, is bounded on the north by Sudan, on the east by Kenya, on the south by Tanzania and Rwanda and on the west by Zaire. It covers 233,303 square kilometres (91,134 square miles), including 41,892 square kilometres (16,364 square miles) of lakes and swamps. The population is 11,172,000.

People About two-thirds of the people live in the southern part of the country and belong to the Bantu language group. This group includes the Baganda, the largest group, the Banyoro, Batoro, Banyankore, Basoga, Bagisu, Bakiga and Bakonjo peoples. Non-Bantu peoples of the north include the Lango, Acholi, Alur, Iteso and Lugbara. In all, about 40 ethnic groups live in Uganda. Half the people are Christians and the others follow traditional religions. The official language is English, although Swahili is widely spoken. KAMPALA, the capital, JINJA, Mbale and Kabale are the largest towns.

Land and Economy Most of Uganda is between 900 and 1,500 metres (3,000 and 5,000 feet) above sea level. The BUGANDA region, north-west of Lake VICTORIA, consists of flat-topped hills separated by broad valleys. Central and northern Uganda is a vast plain, covered with wooded savanna and broken by a few hills. On the eastern border are the forested uplands of the MOUNT ELGON region. The forested RUWENZORI MOUNTAINS, reaching a height of more than 4,800 metres (16,000 feet) are on Uganda's south-west border. Lake Idi Amin Dada (formerly Lake Edward) lies to the south, Lake MOBUTU SESE SEKO (formerly Lake Albert) is to the north, and Lake GEORGE is to the east. In the south-east, the overflow of Lake VICTORIA passes through the Owen Falls Dam at Jinja to form the VICTORIA NILE.

Uganda has some of the most fertile land in East Africa and farming is the basis of the economy.

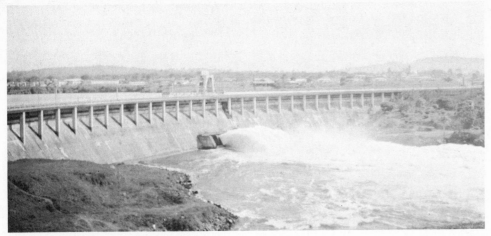

UGANDA: The Owen Falls hydro-electric power station at Jinja is an important source of electricity for industry.

The country produces nearly all its own food, and farm products provide more than four fifths of its exports. The main food crops are bananas, millet, sorghum, maize and cassava. Groundnuts and sesame are also grown. The main export crops are coffee, cotton, sugar, tea and tobacco. Livestock raising (cattle, sheep and goats) is important, and Uganda's forests produce valuable timber, including mahogany. Uganda's lakes provide much fish. Mineral resources include copper, tin, tungsten and clay. The main industries are food processing, cotton textiles, copper smelting, brewing, cigarette production and cement manufacture. Power is provided by the Owen Falls hydro-electric station.

Uganda's main trading partners are the United States, Britain, Japan, Canada, India and neighbouring Kenya and Tanzania.

Uganda has good communications with roads and internal air services linking Kampala with many centres. Railway and water transport services handle most of Uganda's trade. A railway from the Kenyan port of Mombasa to Kasese in western Uganda connects with Tororo, Jinja and Kampala. Ferry services on Lake VICTORIA link several towns. Kampala's international airport at nearby ENTEBBE is connected with many local airfields through internal air services.

Unit of currency Uganda Shilling

History Before 1850, Nilotic peoples (the Alur, Acholi, Lango and Luo) migrated into the Uganda area from the north, where they mingled with the Bantu already in the region. From the late 13th century, a powerful kingdom, Buganda, grew up. European missionaries were active in the area, but the Buganda *kabakas* (kings) limited their influence. However, in 1893 Buganda became a British protectorate. By an agreement of 1900, the British recognized the kabaka as the ruler of his people as long as he recognised the authority of the protectorate. This arrangement was the basis of British–Bugandan relationships for the next 50 years. Meanwhile, by 1914, the rest of Uganda had come under British administration. After 1900, the economy developed rapidly. Many Asians, who had been brought by the British to build the railway, settled and played an important part in Uganda's business and industry.

In 1962, Uganda became independent and Buganda was given a federal relationship with the rest of the country. The prime minister was Apolo Milton OBOTE and the first president (elected in 1963) was the Bugandan kabaka, Mutesa II. In 1966, Obote deposed the Kabaka and took over the presidency. In 1971, Obote himself was deposed and the army commander, Idi AMIN, became president. In 1972, Amin expelled more than 50,000 Ugandan Asians, on the grounds that they controlled too much of the country's economy. At the same time, his army defeated an invasion attempt from Tanzania by exiled supporters of Obote.

Government The constitution of 1967 provided for a legislature of 82 directly-elected members. The monarchy was abolished and the president became head of state and head of the government. He has many powers, including the power to pass certain laws.

UJIJI, near Lake TANGANYIKA in Tanzania, is famous as the place where Henry Morton STANLEY met David LIVINGSTONE in 1871. It was an entrepôt town on the former trade route between Zaire and the coast.

UMTALI is a Zimbabwean town in the Eastern Highlands near the Mozambique border. Founded in the 1890s, it supports some secondary industry, including car assembly, and is a major rail communications link with the coast. Umtali is also a major tourist centre. Pop. 50,000.

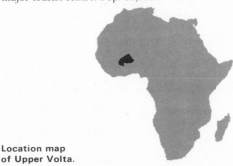

Location map of Upper Volta.

UPPER VOLTA is a landlocked country in West Africa. It is bordered by Mali on the west and north, Niger on the east, and Benin, Togo, Ghana and Ivory Coast in the south. It has an area of 272,794 square kilometres (106,560 square miles) and a population of 5,384,000.

People The Mossi are the most numerous group in Upper Volta, making up almost half the population. The principal minority peoples are the Fulani, Lobi, Mandinka, Bobo, and Senoufo. Most of the people follow traditional African religions. 20 per cent are Muslims and about 5 per cent are Christians. French is the official language. OUAGADOUGOU is the capital of Upper Volta, and BOBO-DIOULASSO and KOUDOUGOU are the only other large towns.

Land and Economy Upper Volta is made up of a large plateau which rises to over 450 metres (1,500 feet) in the north of the country. This plateau is split up by the valleys of the main rivers: the Black, White and Red Voltas, and their tributaries. The country receives an average of about 90 centimetres (35 inches) of rain annually. The north of the country borders the Sahara and is very dry. In 1973, this area had not had any rainfall for seven years. Temperatures rise to over 32°C (90°F) in the hot season.

The economy of Upper Volta depends on agriculture. Much of the soil is of poor quality and the raising of livestock, chiefly cattle, is important. Maize, millet, rice and sorghum are grown as food crops. Recently, the cultivation of cotton and groundnuts has increased and these cash crops are

now being exported. One of the most important sources of foreign currency is the wages sent home by Upper Volta agricultural labourers who go to work on the plantations in neighbouring Ivory Coast and Ghana. However, these states have recently restricted this practice. Until 1966, gold was an export, but the mines have now been worked out. Large reserves of manganese have been discovered in the north-east of the country, although they have not yet been exploited. The economy of Upper Volta is hindered by the lack of access to the sea. A railway line from Ouagadougou carries most of the country's international trade.

Unit of currency Franc

History King Baba founded the Mossi kingdom shortly after AD 1300. The French subdued the territory which is now Upper Volta in 1896, and later divided the area between Ivory Coast, Mali and Niger. In 1947, it was reconstituted as a separate colony and in 1960, it became independent. The first government was formed by the *Union Démocratique Voltaique,* whose leader, Maurice Yaméogo, became the first president of the country. In 1966, this government was overthrown by a military coup led by Sangoulé LAMIZANA, after a year of civil disorder. The military government made a number of decrees ordering austerity in an attempt to improve the low standard of living. In 1971, Upper Volta returned to partial civilian rule, but President Lamizana restored military rule in 1974 and the National Assembly was dissolved.

VAAL RIVER runs through South Africa for 1,120 kilometres (700 miles) from the south-eastern Transvaal to join the ORANGE RIVER near KIMBERLEY. It supplies water to the WITWATERSRAND, the Orange Free State goldfields, and to the Vaal-Hertz irrigation scheme near Kimberley.

VALLEY OF THE KINGS lies in the mountains to the west of the Ancient Egyptian capital of Thebes. The valley contains the tombs of many kings and officials of the 18th and 20th dynasties (1555 to 1085 BC). Archaeologists have excavated many of the tombs. The most valuable and spectacular finds were made at the tomb of Tut-Ankh-Amun which was opened in 1922.

VEREENIGING is a town on the VAAL RIVER in the southern Transvaal, South Africa. It is a centre of a coal-mining area and of the Vaal Triangle heavy industrial region. Pop. 90,000.

VICTORIA FALLS lie on the Zambezi River between Zambia and Zimbabwe. The falls are 108 metres (355 feet) high.

VICTORIA FALLS: The local name for the falls is Mose-la-Tunya.

VICTORIA, LAKE, or Victoria Nyanza, Africa's largest lake, covers 68,680 square kilometres (26,828 square miles). Its northern half is in Uganda and its southern half in Tanzania. In the north-east, it borders on Kenya. About 1,134 metres (3,720 feet) above sea level, it is 400 kilometres (250 miles) from north to south and 320 kilometres (200 miles) from east to west. Its greatest depth is 80 metres (270 feet), and its shores are indented with deep gulfs. Many rivers flow into the lake, draining from the nearby uplands. The largest is the KAGERA RIVER. However, the lake is filled mainly by rainfall. Its only outlet is the VICTORIA NILE. Steamer services link the main ports on its shores: ENTEBBE (Uganda), KISUMU (Kenya), and MWANZA and Bukoba (Tanzania).

VICTORIA NILE is the section of the NILE RIVER running for 480 kilometres (300 miles) that connects Lakes VICTORIA, KYOGA and MOBUTU SESE SEKO in East Africa. It is fed by the overflow of Lake Victoria, which leaves the northern end of the lake at Ripon Falls. It flows north to and through Lake Kyoga, then north-west over Kabelega (formerly Murchison) Falls into the north-eastern corner of Lake MOBUTU SESE SEKO.

VICTORIA NYANZA see VICTORIA, LAKE.

VOLTA, LAKE, Ghana's largest lake, covering 8,640 square kilometres (3,375 square miles), was created in 1965 when the VOLTA RIVER was dammed to provide hydro-electricity. It is hoped that the lake will provide fish and irrigate the surrounding land for rice.

VOLTA RIVER, Ghana's most important river, has its source in Upper Volta. A dam was constructed across it at Akasombo in 1965. The water from the resulting Lake VOLTA now provides hydro-electricity and water for irrigation.

WADI HALFA, the capital of Northern Province in the Sudan, was founded by the British in 1884. It is the northern terminus of the Sudan railway. The town stands on the banks of the NILE. Much of the surrounding region has been flooded by Lake NASSER.

WADI MEDANI, the capital of Blue Nile Province, in the Sudan, is the main administrative centre of the GEZIRA Cotton Scheme. It is a manufacturing and commercial centre, and a market for goods exchanged between the Sudan and Ethiopia. Pop. 79,000.

WALVIS BAY is the main port of Namibia (South-West Africa) and the centre of the seasonal inshore fishing industry that operates from March to August. The town and an enclave of 1,111 square kilometres (434 square miles) were annexed to the British Cape Colony in 1878 and remain technically part of the present-day Cape Province of South Africa. Pop. 19,500.

WANKIE is a mining town in south-west Zimbabwe near the ZAMBEZI RIVER. It is the site of Africa's largest coal mine, which supplies much of central Africa. Coal reserves are estimated at 714 million tonnes (700 million tons) and production runs at 4.1 million tonnes (4 million tons) a year. A major disaster in 1972 killed 467 miners. The main game park in Zimbabwe is also at Wankie. Pop. 22,000.

WAU, capital of Bahrel Ghazal province in Sudan.

WESTERN SAHARA see SPANISH SAHARA.

WHITE NILE RIVER, the longest branch of the Nile, joins the BLUE NILE at KHARTOUM. It contributes less than a third of the Nile's volume of water. Above the point where the WHITE NILE crosses the Sudan–Uganda border it becomes known as the Albert Nile. Its higher reaches consist of numerous rivers and head-streams, that rise over a wide area of the East African plateau and flow into Lake MOBUTU SESE SEKO.

WINDHOEK is the administrative and commercial capital of Namibia (South-West Africa). It is situated in the central plateau 1,670 metres (5,500 feet) above sea level. It was founded in

1890 by the German military governor Kurt von François on the site of an existing Afrikaner settlement. Pop. 65,000.

WITWATERSRAND is the industrial region of southern Transvaal, South Africa. The region includes the cities of JOHANNESBURG and PRETORIA. More than half of South Africa's industry is located in the Witwatersrand. The region is an important coal-mining area and the centre of South Africa's gold-mining industry.

YAOUNDÉ, the capital of Cameroon, lies about 200 kilometres (125 miles) east of the coast. Cameroon's sugar and rubber industries have their headquarters here and cigarettes are manufactured. It is the site of a university and a radio station. Yaoundé is connected to the port of DOUALA by rail. Pop. 178,000.

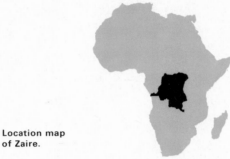

Location map of Zaire.

ZAIRE, an independent republic in central Africa, is the second largest country in the continent, with an area of 2,292,091 square kilometres (895,348 square miles). In colonial times, Zaire was called the Belgian Congo. From independence, in 1960, until 1971, the country was known as the Democratic Republic of the Congo or Congo (Kinshasa).

The country surrounds the basin of the ZAIRE RIVER, stretching from the Atlantic coast to the Rift Valley in the east. It has borders with nine other countries: Angola, Congo, Central African Republic, Sudan, Uganda, Rwanda, Burundi, Tanzania and Zambia. In 1970, a census put the population at 24,222,000.

People Most people belong to the Bantu-speaking peoples of central Africa. The largest ethnic groups are the Bakongo, Baluba, Balunda and Bamongo. Pygmies live in the dense equatorial rain forest that covers much of Zaire. The European minority numbers about 30,000. About 150 different dialects are spoken in Zaire. French is the official language and Kiswahili and Lingala are also used as common tongues. About half of the people are Christians, mainly Roman Catholic, while the remainder follow traditional African religions. KINSHASA, the capital is the largest town, with a population of more than 1,500,000, followed by LUBUMBASHI and KISANGANI.

Land and Economy Much of Zaire is occupied by a huge shallow depression formed by the Zaire River and its tributaries. Much of the interior consists of plateau land which rises to mountains in the east. The mountains, which are between 1,500 and 5,000 metres (5,000 and 16,000 feet) above sea level, extend along Zaire's eastern border, where they include the RUWENZORI range, to Shaba province in the south. Tropical rain forest covers the central part of the country, with savanna in the north and south, and grasslands on the higher ground in the east. The climate is tropical, with high temperatures and an annual rainfall of between 150 and 200 centimetres.

Agriculture plays an important role in the economy of Zaire and about three-quarters of the people work in farming. The main cash crops are cocoa, coffee, cotton, palm oil, rubber, sugar and tea. Cassava, maize and millet are widely grown as food crops. Zaire's extensive forests support a timber industry. Ebony is among the rare hardwoods which are exported from Zaire.

Zaire is very rich in mineral resources. Copper, mined in Shaba province, is the most important mining product. In 1970, it accounted for half of Zaire's total exports. The Union Minière du Haut Katanga, a Belgian company, controlled the copper mining industry, and thus the whole economy until 1966. In that year, it was taken over by the Gecamines company, which is 60 per cent government-owned.

Zaire is the world's main producer of industrial diamonds, which are mined in Kasai province in the southern-central region. Other important minerals include cassiterite, cobalt, gold, manganese, uranium and zinc. Although small deposits of oil have been discovered on Zaire's 80 kilometre (50 mile) coastline, they are not commercially viable.

The Zaire River and its tributaries provide a great potential for hydro-electric power. In 1972, the first stage of the Inga dam project was put into operation near Matadi, on the Zaire estuary. When this project is completed, it will be the largest hydro-electric complex in the world. The major part of Zaire's electricity supply comes from 30 small hydro-electric projects throughout the country. Nearly three-quarters of the power is used in the Shaba copper belt for the refining of copper ore.

Industry, apart from the processing of mineral products, is centred on Kinshasa. Beer, cement, cigarettes, fuel oils and textiles are among the goods produced for home consumption. Zaire has more than 4,800 kilometres (3,000 miles) of railway line and about 1,600 kilometres (1,000 miles) of all-weather roads.

Unit of currency Zaire

History Well organized states, such as the kingdoms of Kongo and Baluba, existed in Zaire from the 1300s and 1400s respectively. The Portuguese landed at the mouth of the Zaire River in 1482. The king of the Kongo sent ambassadors to their king. These returned in 1491 with Portuguese artisans, who built the first Christian church south of the equator. The conquests of the Kongo kings in Central Zaire brought many slaves who were shipped away by the Portuguese. The kingdom of Kasanje in Kwango lasted from about 1600 to 1911. During this time, the Kazembe kings ruled south-eastern Katanga from 1700.

In 1874–7, Henry Morton STANLEY explored the Zaire River and paved the way for the European colonization of Zaire. In 1884, Zaire became the 'Congo Free State' which was the personal property of King Léopold II of Belgium. Leopold granted concessions to companies to extract the wild rubber growing in the forests. The brutal treatment of the local people led the Belgian government to take control of the colony in 1908.

Independence movements in other parts of Africa stimulated a similar movement in Zaire in the 1950s, and in 1959, the colonial administration allowed the formation of political parties and promised independence. In January 1960, African leaders attended talks in Brussels, and independence was set for the 30th June that year. A government was formed with Joseph KASAVUBU as head of state and Patrice LUMUMBA as prime minister.

Five days after independence mutinies in the army, the *Force Publique*, over pay and continued control by Belgian officers, led to the departure of Europeans and the intervention of Belgian troops. At the same time, Moise TSHOMBE declared the secession of Katanga province (now SHABA). The government appealed to the United Nations, which sent a multi-national force and economic aid. Although Belgian troops withdrew, Katanga's secession continued, with Tshombe recruiting mercenaries and withholding mining revenues from the central government. In September 1960, Kasavubu dismissed Lumumba, and Colonel MOBUTU SESE SEKO, head of the renamed Congolese National Army, appointed a caretaker administration. Lumumba was captured when he tried to escape to Kisangani, where his supporters were in control. In January 1961, he was flown to Katanga where he died under mysterious circumstances.

A new central government was formed in August, 1961. Katanga was occupied by UN troops in January 1963, but Lumumbist revolts broke out in Bandundu, Kivu and Upper Zaire. The UN force withdrew in June 1964, and in July Tshombe returned from exile to head a new central government. A joint campaign by the army and mercenary forces defeated the rebellions in early 1965. Elections held later in the year led to renewed political in-fighting, and Tshombe was dismissed by Kasavubu in October. The Army High Command decided to take power and Mobutu, now General, announced his assumption of the presidency and the appointment of a civilian government on November 25th, 1965. Mercenary-led revolts in 1966 and 1967 were defeated, and Mobutu was elected president in the elections held in 1970.

Since 1970, the government has followed a policy of 'authenticité'. This involves the stamping out of colonial and ethnic influences through the reorganization of the economy and the education system, the Africanization of names.

ZAIRE: A building site in Kinshasa, the capital of Zaire.

ZAIRE: The Inga Dam, north of Matadi is part of the largest hydro-electric project in Africa. The project was begun in 1972 and will supply Kinshasa and Shaba.

Government Under the constitution introduced in 1967, the president is elected for a seven-year term, and the 420 members of the national assembly for five-year terms.

The *Mouvement Populaire de la Révolution* (MPR), founded by President Mobutu Sese Seko, is the sole political party. Government decisions are taken by the MPR political bureau. The country is administered in eight provinces, Lower Zaire, Badundu, Equateur, Upper Zaire, Eastern Kasai, Western Kasai, Shaba, Kivu and the city of Kinshasa. In external affairs Zaire is a member of the OAU and has associate status with the EEC through the Yaoundé Convention.

ZAIRE RIVER is the second longest river in Africa. It was formerly called the Congo River. From its source in the plateau of southern SHABA, the river flows for 4,640 kilometres (2,900 miles) to the sea, in a great arc first north-west and then south-west. It is fed by many tributaries from both sides of the equator and in places it widens into lakes and rushes through rapids. The river is navigable from the Atlantic to MATADI, from KINSHASA to KISANGANI, and from Ponthierville to Kindu. Together with linking roads and railways, the Zaire forms a major transport system and is a source of hydro-electric power.

ZAMBEZI RIVER is the fourth longest river in Africa. It flows 3,500 kilometres (2,200 miles) from its source in north-west Zambia, through Angola,

between Zambia and Zimbabwe and across Mozambique to its mouth in the Indian Ocean north of BEIRA. Its course contains the VICTORIA FALLS, KARIBA LAKE and Kariba Dam and the CABORA BASSA DAM in Mozambique.

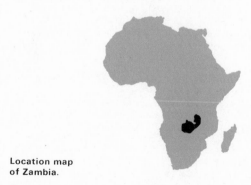

Location map of Zambia.

ZAMBIA is an independent republic, situated inland south of the equator. It was formerly the British protectorate of Northern Rhodesia. It has borders with Zaire in the north, Tanzania, Malawi and Mozambique in the east, Zimbabwe, Botswana and Namibia (South-West Africa) in the south, and Angola in the west. Zambia covers an area of 743,903 square kilometres (290,587 square miles) and has a population of 4,751,000.

People Zambia is inhabited by more than 70 African ethnic groups, speaking six major languages. Minorities of 43,000 Europeans and 8,000 Asians also live there. Bemba and Nyanja are the most widely spoken African languages, and the official language is English. Most people follow traditional African religions, but one out of every five Zambians are Christians. LUSAKA is the capital and other important towns include NDOLA, KITWE, MUFULIRA and MARAMBA.

Land and Economy Zambia is situated on a high plateau, about 1,200 metres (4,000 feet) above sea level. In the north-east, this rises to over 2,100 metres (7,000 feet) in the MUCHINGA MOUNTAINS. Much of the country is savanna. The soil is rich in minerals but not very fertile. The plateau is cut into by the valleys of the ZAMBEZI, LUANGWA and KAFUE rivers and their tributaries. The principal lakes are Lake BANGWEULU and Lake MWERU in the north, and the artificially created Lake KARIBA on the southern border. Temperatures reach 38°C (100°F) in the hot season but are cooler for most of the year. Rainfall is highest in the northern part of the country, which receives about 130 centimetres (50 inches) annually.

Most Zambians are farmers, many of them at subsistence level. Groundnuts, maize, fruit and vegetables are grown as food crops. Sugar is produced in the south and government development schemes encourage smallholders to grow tobacco and cotton as cash crops.

The mainstay of the Zambian economy is the mining of copper, which accounts for more than 90 per cent of the country's exports. Although the economy is affected by fluctuations in the world price of copper (the price fell from £589 per ton in 1970 to £441 per ton in 1971), its export gives Zambia a considerable balance of payments surplus. Other minerals mined include coal, cobalt, lead, silver and zinc. Zambian industry processes minerals and agricultural products. Power is supplied by the hydro-electric scheme at the Kariba dam, and by a second hydro-electric dam on the KAFUE RIVER.

Transportation of exports is a problem for Zambia. Until 1975, the only rail link with the coast ran through Zimbabwe, and the Zambian government wished to be free of this dependence. A railway (known as the Uhuru or Tanzam railway) running for 1,870 kilometres (1,160 miles), built with Chinese help, now runs from Zambia to the port of Dar es Salaam in Tanzania. An oil pipeline from Dar es Salaam was completed in 1968.

ZAMBIA: President Kaunda has played an important part in O.A.U. affairs.

Unit of currency Kwacha

History The Lunda Empire was founded in what is now Zambia in about 1550 and lasted more than three centuries. The Bemba settled in what is now north-eastern Zambia after 1600. Barotseland was a kingdom in 1848.

Dr. David LIVINGSTONE explored this part of Africa in 1854. The area became known as Northern Rhodesia and, shortly afterwards, the British South Africa Company began to administer it under Royal Charter. In 1924 control of Northern Rhodesia passed from the Company to the British Colonial Office and the country became a British protectorate.

The discovery of large reserves of copper in the 1930s and 1940s encouraged many Europeans to emigrate to Northern Rhodesia and they began to demand greater independence from Britain. To meet these demands, the British government formed, in 1953, the Federation of Rhodesia (including Northern and Southern Rhodesia) and Nyasaland. However, the Federation was ruled by a white-dominated government and was not acceptable to the African majority. The Federation was dissolved in 1963, and in the following year Northern Rhodesia became fully independent and was renamed Zambia. Southern Rhodesia became known simply as 'Rhodesia'.

Kenneth KAUNDA, leader of the United National Independence Party (UNIP), came to power as Zambia's first president and was re-elected in 1968.

The Zambian government had condemned the white-dominated regimes of 'Rhodesia' and South Africa and has called for strong measures against them. In 1973, 'Rhodesia' closed her border with Zambia in retaliation against Zambia's support of guerrilla operations against her. In 1974–5, President Kaunda was involved in initiatives to arrive at a settlement in Zimbabwe.

Government A new constitution came into force in 1972, which established Zambia as a one-party democracy—that party being UNIP. The first elections under the new constitution were held in December 1973 and President Kaunda was re-elected for a third term of office. Zambia is a member of the Commonwealth, OAU and UN.

ZANZIBAR ISLAND is situated in the Indian Ocean opposite Bagamoyo in Tanzania. It was known to Arab sailors in early times and is called Unguja by the Swahili. The earliest building is the much-restored mosque at Kizimkazi, which was built in AD 1107. The Portuguese occupied the island from 1506 until 1698, when it was captured and annexed by the Omani Arabs who held it (under British Protectorate 1885–1963) until 1964. Following the revolution in January 1964, it united with Tanganyika to form Tanzania.

ZANZIBAR TOWN, on ZANZIBAR ISLAND, was in existence in the Middle Ages. However, it was built mainly after 1806 when Sayid Said Sultan of Oman and Muscat made it his capital. The town became the centre of an extensive trade in ivory and slaves, which reached as far as Zaire and Zambia. For its wealth the town now relies on its port and light industry and local crafts. Pop. 57,000.

ZARIA is a university city in Nigeria's North-Central State. It was the capital of the Habe state of Zazzau from the 1500s and was taken over by the Fulani in the 1800s. The British occupied it in 1901. It is the site of Ahmadu Bello university, the largest in Nigeria. The industries include printing. Pop. 166,000.

Location map of Zimbabwe.

ZIMBABWE, called 'Rhodesia' by its illegal white government, is a country in Southern Africa. It is legally a British colony situated between the ZAMBEZI RIVER in the north and the LIMPOPO RIVER in the south. It has common boundaries with Zambia, Mozambique, South Africa and Botswana. The country has an area of 384,852 square kilometres and a population of 6,100,000.

People There are 5,400,000 Africans in Zimbabwe and the chief ethnic groups are the Shona and Ndebele. Minorities of 262,000 Europeans, mostly of British descent, and 28,000 Asians and Coloureds also live in Zimbabwe. The official language is English. About one out of every five people live in towns, of which the largest are the capital SALISBURY, BULAWAYO, GWELO and UMTALI.

Land and Economy Most of the country forms a high plateau, which drops away to the valleys of the Zambezi in the north and the Limpopo in the south. The high land in the centre of the country is about 1,524 metres (5,000 feet) above sea level. The natural vegetation is savanna. Temperatures range from 27°C (80°F) in summer to about 10°C (50°F) in the winter. Rainfall varies throughout the country, from 101 centimetres (40 inches) per year in the east to 50 centimetres (20 inches) in the west and less than 38 centimetres (15 inches) in the southern lowlands.

Zimbabwe's mineral wealth is the most important factor in the economy. But most people work in subsistence farming. Maize and wheat are grown as food crops. Zimbabwe is one of the world's leading producers of tobacco, and, until recently, it was the major export product. Citrus fruits, cotton, and sugar are also grown as cash crops and cattle are extensively reared.

Zimbabwe has large reserves of asbestos, chrome copper and nickel. The coal mine at WANKIE is the largest in the world. Zimbabwe's industries make a wide range of products, including chemicals, clothing, metal goods and textiles. Food and tobacco processing is also important. Power is provided by the Kariba hydro-electric scheme on the Zambezi River, which Zimbabwe operates jointly with Zambia.

Unit of currency Dollar

History Archaeological remains indicate Iron Age settlement existed from about AD 300. The ZIM-BABWE RUINS reveal that a fairly sophisticated civilization was in existence in the 10th century. From 1100 to 1800, the area was ruled by the Rozwe clan of the Shona people. The first contact with Europe came in the 1500s when Portuguese traders penetrated inland from the east coast. But this contact was broken in the 1700s. In the 1830s, Mzilikazi's Ndebele people, driven northwards by the Boers and Zulus, overran and dominated most of the area.

In the 1880s, the British South Africa Company, under the direction of Cecil RHODES, obtained mining rights from Lobengula, the Ndebele king. During the 1890s, British settlers moved into the area, which became known as Rhodesia, and defeated the Shona and Ndebele with the aid of British troops. From 1898 to 1923, Rhodesia was governed partly by a British High Commissioner at the Cape, and partly by an administration composed of settlers and company officials. In 1922, the settlers voted in favour of Rhodesia remaining independent from South Africa, and in 1923 Southern Rhodesia became a self-governing British colony.

In 1953, European politicians formed a federation of Southern Rhodesia (now Zimbabwe), Northern Rhodesia (now Zambia) and Nyasaland (now Malawi) with its capital at Salisbury. Under the premiership of Garfield TODD, attempts were made to give increased power to the African majority. The Africans considered these moves did not go far enough and rejected them. The African National Congress was formed to campaign for political freedom.

The federation broke up in 1964, Zambia and Malawi became independent, but Southern Rhodesia refused to grant the concessions demanded by Britain. These concessions would have given the country independence with African majority rule. In 1965 Ian SMITH, the prime minister, made a unilateral declaration of independence (UDI).

After UDI, 'Rhodesia' became isolated from most of the rest of the world. Economic sanctions, advocated by Britain and supported by the UN, seriously affected its economy but failed to gain any political results. Various unsuccessful attempts were made by Britain to achieve a settlement of the dispute, and guerilla activities began in the 1970s. In 1974, the prime minister of South Africa and the presidents of Botswana, Tanzania and Zambia intervened to try to achieve a settlement between Ian Smith's government and the chief nationalist politicians, Bishop MUZOREWA, Joshua NKOMO and Ndabaningi SITHOLE. Negotiations continued in 1975 and 1976. 'Rhodesia' became increasingly known in Africa as Zimbabwe.

Government 'Rhodesia' was declared a republic in 1970. Under this constitution, it is governed by a president, a Senate and a house of assembly. The Senate consists of 23 members (10 whites elected by white MPs; 10 chiefs; and 3 appointed by the president). The House of Assembly consists of 66 members (50 elected by white voters and 16 blacks, half elected by a black voters' roll and half elected by the chiefs).

ZIMBABWE RUINS, in Zimbabwe, are the remains of buildings, including a temple and a citadel, built by an early African civilization. They probably date as far back as the AD 200s. The architecture of high walls with ornamental friezes and round towers of perfectly fitting stones is unique in Sub-Saharan Africa.

ZINDER is the traditional capital of Damagaram Province in Niger. The province was the transition zone between the territories of the nomads of the north and the Hausa of the south. Zinder lies at the crossroads linking NIAMEY with Chad and Agades with KANO in Nigeria. Pop. 24,000.

ZINGUINCHOR, capital of the CASAMANCE region of southern Senegal, lies between Gambia and Guinea-Bissau. Pop. 46,000.

ZOMBA is the former capital of Malawi. It is situated approximately 880 metres (2,900 feet) above sea level on the lower slopes of Zomba Mountain. Pop. 20,000.

ZULA, a seaport town in Ethiopia. It is situated on the Gulf of Zula. It became an Italian protectorate in 1888 and part of Eritrea in 1890.

Map of Vegetation

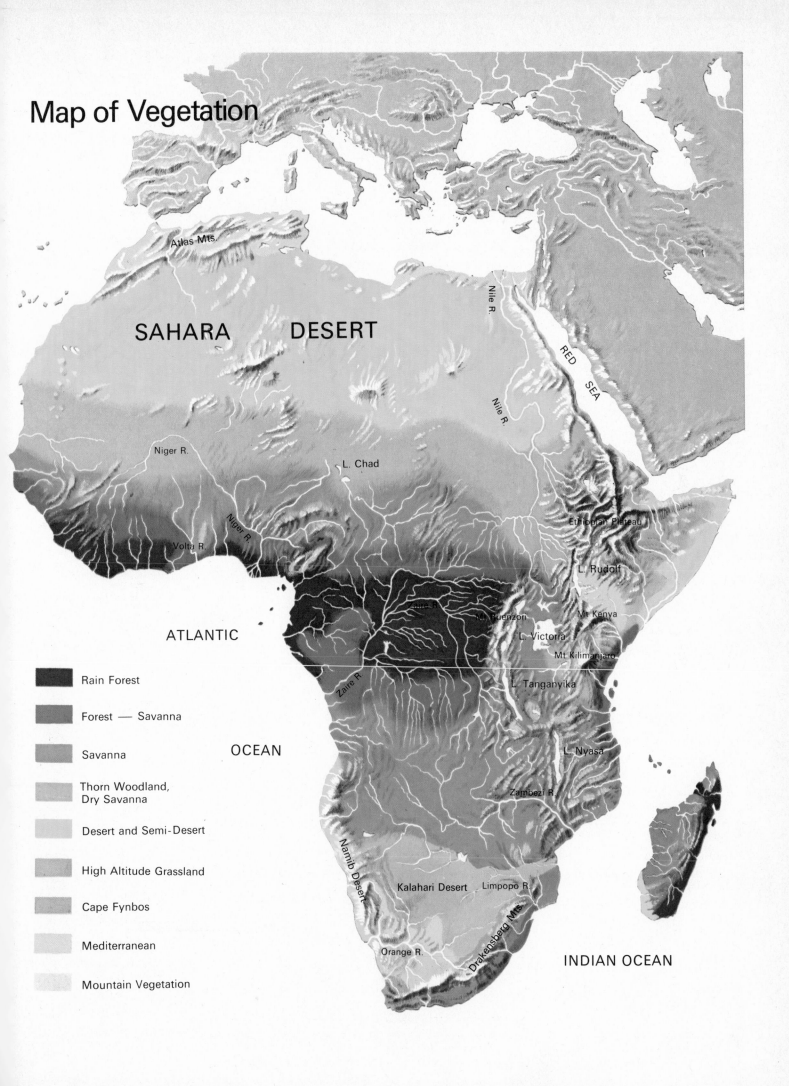

Atlas Mts.

SAHARA DESERT

Nile R.

RED SEA

Niger R.

L. Chad

Niger R.

Volta R.

Ethiopian Plateau

L. Rudolf

Zaire R.

ATLANTIC

Mt Ruenzori

Mt Kenya

L. Victoria

Mt Kilimanjaro

Zaire R.

OCEAN

L. Tanganyika

L. Nyasa

Zambezi R.

Namib Desert

High Altitude Grassland

Cape Fynbos

Kalahari Desert

Limpopo R.

Mediterranean

Mountain Vegetation

Orange R.

Drakensberg Mts.

INDIAN OCEAN

Rain Forest

Forest — Savanna

Savanna

Thorn Woodland,
Dry Savanna

Desert and Semi-Desert

VEGETATION

NOTE: See page 129 for a map of African Vegetation Regions.

Africa is a continent with a fascinating and varied plant life. Rolling grasslands flecked with flat-topped acacia trees merge into wide regions of thorny scrub dotted with swollen-trunked baobabs. The arid dunes of the deserts are sharply contrasted against the lush equatorial rain forests and mangrove swamps. These different types of vegetation have evolved in Africa over millions of years, gently adapting to the changing patterns of climate, surface features and soils. Agricultural plants are described in the section on *Food and Farming* on pages 44–47.

Climate and Surface Features In Africa, rainfall is the most important factor affecting the growth of plants. A belt of rich, luxuriant rain forest lies along the equator where the rainfall is high. To the north and south of this forest are belts of drier vegetation. These regions merge into the Sahara desert in the north and the Namib desert in the south-west. This pattern is broken by high plateaux and mountains down the eastern side of Africa, which receive enough rain for forests to grow. At the top and bottom of the continent there are sub-tropical zones with a Mediterranean type of climate and scrub vegetation with leathery leaves. There are no sharp boundaries between the main types of vegetation. The divisions on a map can give only a rough indication of the major vegetation changes. Local variations occur within the main types. For example, in the dry semi-desert and savanna regions, belts of rich, green vegetation often grow beside the rivers.

Effects of Fire and Grazing Natural fires, started by lightning or sparks from falling rocks have affected the growth of plant life over millions of years. Man often starts fires deliberately on the grasslands to get fresh green grass for domestic herds. Frequent burning may change the vegetation patterns quite drastically.

Grazing and browsing by wild animals also affect the growth of vegetation in savanna regions. The different feeding habits of wild herbivores keep a balanced ecosystem. For example, buffalo feed on tussocky grass and prevent it from spreading. This provides space for short, creeping grasses which are eaten by animals such as hippos and warthogs. Domestic cattle, on the other hand, eat a variety of grasses and overgraze them. They also need plenty of water and pollute water holes by trampling the ground around them. Overgrazing by cattle can remove the protective cover of vegetation, so that the top-soil is blown away.

Plant Adaptation and Migration It is easy to see how some plants have adapted to local conditions. For example, *succulent* (fleshy) plants such as aloes are characteristic of dry places. These plants have evolved special ways of reducing water loss such as having spines instead of leaves.

Changes of climate and land surface over long

▲ The planting of trees and shrubs in over-grazed areas can help to prevent top-soil from being blown away.

Soils
The type and depth of the soil affects the water available to plants. Water soon evaporates from shallow soil. But on deep, porous soil, water seeps down to a level, called the *water table*, where only long roots can reach it. Water runs off rocky slopes and collects in valleys where rich vegetation grows. Clay soils retain more water than sandy soils and provide different growth conditions. In some soils, high concentrations of mineral salts limit plant growth.

A bush fire in acacia savanna. Fires are often started deliberately to clear ground for cultivation. ▼

periods of time allow some plants to develop new forms and also enable them to migrate. Forms which are not adapted to the new conditions gradually die out. Many such changes must have occurred in Africa. Lake Chad was once much larger than it is now, and fossils of savanna animals have been found in the western Sahara. This suggests that, long ago, parts of the Saharan region had far more rainfall and a different vegetation from that of today. In East Africa, volcanoes and rifts have completely changed the landscape, and provided new growing conditions for plants.

The cacti of America, and the euphorbias of tropical Africa look similar but are not in fact closely related. These two families have developed separately in each region. The prickly pear *Opuntia* is an American cactus which was introduced into Africa by man. This plant was able to spread rapidly across Africa. The rest of the cactus family, however, was prevented from spreading naturally by the Atlantic Ocean which acted as a barrier. This shows that plants will spread until they are halted by some climatic or physical barrier.

VEGETATION REGIONS

African vegetation can be looked at under the following headings: lowland rain forests; mountains; deciduous woodland and wooded grassland; dry thorn woodland, grassland and semi-desert; deserts; swamps; and Mediterranean regions.

Lowland Rain Forest

Many people outside Africa imagine that the lowland rain forest is a dark, thick mass of tangled vegetation with massive trees. This was the impression given by early explorers. They often travelled along rivers and paths where the bright sunlight encourages plant growth, forming a tangled jungle. In the depths of the forest itself the continuous canopy of leaves reduces the amount of sunlight that reaches the lower layers. Therefore few plants grow on the forest floor.

For many hundreds of years, farmers have been

clearing patches of the original *primary forest*. After clearing the land, they cultivate it for a few years, and then as the soil becomes less fertile, they abandon it. This type of farming is called *shifting cultivation*. In abandoned clearings, quick-growing but short-lived trees, such as the umbrella tree, flourish at first. But umbrella tree seedlings cannot grow in the shade produced by their parents. As a result, seedlings of larger trees, which can grow in shade, gradually replace the umbrella trees. *Secondary forests* take about 100 years to become re-established in the clearings. It may take 250 years for the last signs of disturbance to disappear. The most dense area of lowland rain forest is in a belt extending from south-eastern Nigeria, through Cameroon and Gabon, to eastern Zaire. This belt receives more than 180 centimetres (70 inches) of rain every year and there is no dry season. Similar forests extend westward to Guinea and, in patches, to the East African coast.

In the lowland forest, most trees are 20–30 metres (70–100 feet) tall. The leaves form a continuous cover, or *canopy*. Some taller trees rise above the canopy to heights of up to 45 metres (150 feet). Smaller trees grow in a layer beneath the canopy. Below this is a layer of shrubs. Few herbs and grasses grow on the forest floor because light cannot filter through the dense canopy. Many woody climbers, however, can reach up to the light using the trees as support. The branches of the trees are sometimes covered with ferns, mosses and many orchids. Such clinging plants, called *epiphytes*, can grow far above the ground. This is because some can absorb water direct from the moist air while others use water

▲ Many beautiful orchids grow on the forest trees of Africa. Most of them are fairly small, but this Malagasy orchid, *Angraecum sesquipedale*, has flowers 15 centimetres across.

A wide expanse of forest in eastern Zaire. Here the mountain forests of eastern Africa spread down to the great lowland rain forest of the Zaire basin. ▼

which collects on the tree branches.

Lowland forest trees are usually tall and slender, with pale, smooth trunks. Their root systems are often shallow, but they may have trunks which are fluted or buttressed at the base to give the trees support. The trees usually have oval dark green leaves which end in a narrow point or drip tip. The fruits of these trees are often attractive to bats, birds and monkeys, which disperse the seeds. Trees that reach above the canopy may have flat fruits or seeds, which can be carried by the wind.

Many species of tree grow in the forests. Individual species tend to be scattered and do not grow in pure *stands*, or large groups. Extraction of valuable timber trees, such as African mahoganies and other hardwoods, is therefore very difficult, because they are widely spaced. African lowland forests have fewer species than Asian or American rain forests. This may be the result of past climatic changes, which reduced the size of the African forests.

Away from the equator, the annual rainfall is smaller. More important, the rainfall is less evenly distributed. Such differences in climate determine the boundary of the forest. The forest ends in a narrow zone of small trees, shrubs and green grass. This vegetation tends to halt the fires that sweep through the neighbouring wooded grasslands in the dry season. Towards the edge of the rain forest is a zone which has a dry season. Some of the trees are *deciduous,* losing their leaves in the dry season to avoid water loss. Much of the forest in West Africa is partly deciduous. Large areas of forest have been cleared, to produce wooded grassland.

Mountains

Upland evergreen or mountain forests grow like islands down the eastern side of Africa. These forests are very similar to one another, although they are far apart. They were probably joined together when the climate was cooler and moister. Similar forests grow south of the tropics and down at sea level in the eastern Cape Province of South Africa. Mountain forests are not so tall and dense as the lowland forests and contain fewer species. The trees are more varied in shape and tend to grow in groups. Conifers do not grow in the lowland forests, but juniper and widdringtonia ('cedar') grow on the drier sides of the mountains.

On the slopes of the larger tropical mountains, there are vegetation zones which vary according to their altitude. These zones include forest, bamboo thickets and sub-alpine scrub forest. The forests are fringed by bushland. In regions that have been cultivated, grassland and bushland have extended and only patches of forest remain. Higher still there is a scrub of giant heaths (*Erica* and *Philippia*). Gradually, this scrub becomes a moorland which stretches up to the snowline on the highest mountains. Plants on this moorland are adapted to rapid temperature changes. The days may be hot, but the nights can be freezing cold. Grasses form clumps or tussocks with masses of dead leaves that protect the growing centre. Shrubby plants often have small leathery leaves covered in hairs. The giant groundsels (*Senecio*) and lobelias have massive leaf rosettes, and they keep their old, dead leaves as a thick insulating cover. Giant senecios may also develop a thick, corky bark to protect them from the cold. Sometimes the leaves of the moorland plants are adapted to curl up over the tender shoots at night. Some giant lobelias produce a special substance from their leaf-bases. This prevents the water caught in the leaf rosettes from freezing.

Similar species of plants grow on widely separated mountain tops. Seeds may perhaps have been carried by cyclones.

VEGETATION ZONES ON MOUNT KILIMANJARO

The Peak Above 4,800 metres, the region of permanent snow and ice.
Alpine Tundra Above 3,900 metres, the rainfall is less than 15 centimetres. Few plants can survive.
Upland Moor Up to 3,900 metres, plant species are found similar to those of temperate regions.
Upland Grassland At 3,000 metres, the rainfall suddenly decreases and the forest disappears.
Mountain Rain Forest From 1,650 metres to 3,000 metres, rainfall increases to about 152 centimetres.
Savanna On the lower slopes, rainfall is less than 76 centimetres per year.

Snow and Ice
4,800 metres

Alpine Tundra
3,900 metres

Upland Moor
3,300 metres

Upland Grassland
3,000 metres

Mountain
Rain Forest
1,650 metres

Savanna

A valley in the Balé mountains of Ethiopia. The large spiky-leaved plants in the picture are giant lobelias. These plants are found only above 3,300 metres on African mountains. ▼

Deciduous Woodland and Wooded Grassland

A large area around the lowland forest is covered by deciduous woodland and wooded grassland (called *savanna*). Here the rainfall is more than 90 centimetres (35 inches) a year, but there is a marked dry season. Bush fires often break out during the dry season. The grasses tend to grow in clumps. The plants of the savanna may be annuals which can complete their life-cycle before the next dry season. The perennial herbs often have woody underground root stocks and their stems die back every year. The trees often have thick, protective corky bark and well-developed root systems. Some trees have specially adapted seedlings, which behave like herbs. They die back each season, until the seedling is strong enough to grow into a mature tree.

Trees and shrubs often lose their leaves in the dry season. New leaves are often put out just before the rain breaks. Within a few weeks of the rain, the appearance of the savanna changes completely. Bright green grass springs up and fresh leaves and colourful flowers appear almost like magic.

The northern savanna belt is only 450–800 kilometres (300–500 miles) wide, but it stretches 5,600 kilometres (3,500 miles) from east to west. Two zones occur: the southern Guinea zone and the northern Sudan zone. In the Guinea zone, the southern part is a broad-leaved mixed woodland. Further north it becomes open wooded grassland with fewer tree species. The Sudan savanna receives less rain and there is a long dry season. The grasses tend to be shorter and the seeds can lie dormant for several years if the rains fail. The grasses provide good grazing for about two months every year, but even in the dry season they provide good standing hay. This area is very suitable for grazing.

An enormous area of deciduous woodland called *miombo* grows in south-central Africa, from Tanzania southward to the Limpopo River and westward to Angola. In many places the trees are tall and almost continuous so that fires are less severe. Miombo contains at least three times as many plant species as the northern savannas.

Dry Thorn Woodland, Grassland and Semi-Desert

Around the wooded grasslands lies a large region which receives less than 80 centimetres (30 inches) of rain every year. Because of this dry climate tall perennial grasses are less successful, and so serious bush fires are less common. Depending on rainfall, the vegetation varies from dry, thorny woodland and deciduous bushland with little grass, to wooded grassland or open grassy plains. In the driest parts there is semi-desert, which consists of bare areas of soil with scattered low, shrubby plants, juicy succulents, and a few small trees. Acacias with their tiny leaves and thorny stems are the most characteristic trees and shrubs in this region.

Plants of these dry areas are adapted to survive drought rather than fire. A corky bark serves both purposes, but hairs or a waxy covering on leaves may also help to reduce water loss. Plants often store water in soft inner tissues. For example, the baobab tree stores water in spongy tissues in its trunk. This stored water keeps the tree alive during the dry season. During severe drought, elephants may rip through the bark with their tusks and dig out the water-filled tissues. Aloes and sansevierias have thick, succulent leaves which store water. Euphorbias and stapeliads are virtually leafless, but they have juicy green stems.

The branches of trees of the dry regions are often spiny. This helps to discourage browsing animals. Acacia trees are usually flat-topped with spreading branches which protect the central growing point from browsers and provide shade.

The roots of plants growing in dry places reach down to water supplies far below the surface of the soil. Some plants, such as lilies, die back in dry conditions and survive from reserves stored in underground roots and bulbs. Other plants survive the droughts by remaining as seeds for most of the year. After rain has soaked the parched ground, the seeds begin to grow. They are able to bloom and produce seeds very quickly, sometimes within a few weeks.

A narrow belt of semi-desert spreads across the continent between the Sudan savanna and the Sahara. This is called the Sahel savanna. The region consists mainly of small acacias and other narrow-leaved trees with a sparse cover of grasses. The valleys and areas where water seeps underground have better grass with taller acacia trees, doum palms (*Hyphaene*) and the desert date.

Another belt of dry vegetation extends behind the coast of the north-eastern Horn of Africa down to Tanzania and southwards into the hotter, drier parts of the miombo region. Rainfall is low and erratic, but tends to fall in two seasons which start in about April and November. There is a dense growth of small thorny trees, often succulent or semi-succulent. Shrubs called commiphoras are very common, but there are also many acacias, euphorbias and baobabs. In hot, dry places in the eastern Rift Valley and around the northern coasts, bushland changes to semi-desert and desert. Open grassy plains on shallow, mostly clay soils cover large areas east of Lake Victoria. In southern Africa there is an enormous area of dry thorn woodland called the Kalahari region. Further south, this thins out into the semi-desert of the Karroo and Namib areas.

Most of the Karroo region lies south of the Orange River in South Africa. It consists of a rather flat dry area behind the Cape Mountains. There is a very low rainfall in this region, only 12–35 centimetres (5–15 inches) per year. The plants here are similar to the plants which grow in the Cape. They include a great variety of succulents, particularly the colourful mesembryanthemums, but also spiny euphorbias, crassulas, stapeliads and aloes. A characteristic plant of the Karroo region is *lithops* or livingstone daisy. This plant is related to the fleshy-leafed mesembryanthemum but it has evolved pebble-like leaves. This adaptation enables the plant to escape the attention of animals. To the east and north-east, where the land gradually rises to the magnificent Drakensberg mountain range, there is an almost treeless expanse of tussock grassland, called the High Veld.

Far left Aloes, such as *Aloe marlothii* from Botswana and the Transvaal, are common in the drier parts of Africa. *Above* The baobab, *Adansonia digitata*, has a soft, pulpy trunk which stores water.

Above Dragon's blood trees growing in northern Somalia. *Below* The brilliant fireball lily grows in forest clearings.

◄ Some plants, such as date palms, can grow in sand. Their deep roots reach down to underground water supplies.

Mangrove swamps occur in tropical river estuaries. The fine salty mud has little oxygen. Some mangrove trees, such as this *Rhizophora* on the Kenya coast, put up breathing roots. These roots also trap silt brought down by the river. ▼

Deserts

There are very few plants in the desert regions. Large areas of desert are completely bare. The plants which do grow in the arid regions are all adapted to survive during droughts. In many cases, leaves are reduced to spines and frequently stems are adapted for water storage. There is no sharp line dividing the semi-desert and desert. The vegetation thins out gradually.

The Sahara is the world's largest desert. It is about 1,600 kilometres (1,000 miles) wide and 4,800 kilometres (3,000 miles) long. There is evidence that, within the last 5,000 years, parts of the western half of the desert had a fair cover of vegetation. But today, the rainfall is less than 25 centimetres (10 inches) a year and it may only rain in one year out of ten. Any rain that falls on the bare, rocky plateaux, or *hamadas*, flows swiftly downhill, carrying a mass of silt and stones down to the plains. Strong winds blow across the plains, and in places fine silt and sand is piled up into dunes or *ergs*. In other areas there are rocky deserts or *regs*. These have little plant life, because the stones get very hot.

Some plants will grow in sandy places, especially in valleys and basins where deep-rooted plants can reach down to underground water supplies. The green oases around springs and wells have been planted with date palms.

Smaller areas of desert occur in the East African Rift Valley and the coastal regions of north-eastern

Africa. The Danakil depression in northern Ethiopia is also a desert region, together with the area east of Lake Turkana in Kenya.

The Namib desert stretches in a strip about 48 kilometres (30 miles) wide along the coast of Angola and Namibia. Fog brought inland at night by sea breezes condenses on rocks, providing a little moisture. This enables lichens and small succulents to grow. Most of the coastal strip, however, is bare and gravelly, or has large sand dunes. The most famous plant of this region is *Welwitschia*, or miracle plant, the only survivor of a group of plants distantly related to the conifers. It has a short trunk and two large, strap-like trailing leaves, which grow slowly throughout its long life.

Swamps

There are large mangrove swamps in river estuaries from Gambia to Liberia, in the Niger delta, and at the mouth of the Zaire river. Mangrove swamps also occur on the east coast from Somalia to Mozambique with the largest areas in the deltas of the Rufiji and Zambezi rivers.

Mangrove swamps are usually found in inlets sheltered from strong waves. They form dense forests of small evergreen trees with bright green leathery leaves. The trees are often partly supported by *prop roots*. Prop roots curve out from the stem several feet above the base of the tree and enter the mud some distance away from the taproot. Sometimes mangrove trees have *breathing roots,* which stick up vertically above the mud. The roots trap silt brought down by the river. The silt builds up in layers and eventually forms dry land. Other species of tree then colonize the new coastline.

Freshwater swamp forests can be found inland in places that are sometimes flooded. The largest area occurs in the Zaire basin, but such swamps are fairly common throughout the lowland forest region. Trees with prop roots or breathing roots, together with a number of palms, are typical of these areas.

Lush, swamp vegetation grows in shallow lakes or slow-moving rivers in the tropics. The largest area of swamps is in the upper drainage basin of the White Nile. The river broadens out into a vast region of shallow lakes in southern Sudan, known as the *sudd*. Floating plants such as water lilies, the Nile cabbage (*Pistia*) and the floating grass (*Vossia*), form a loose, tangled mat on the surface. As the mat becomes thicker, papyrus, a giant sedge growing up 4.5 metres (15 feet) tall, becomes established. It produces a soggy mass of floating vegetation, which sometimes drifts off in rafts. In slightly drier areas, swamps of bulrushes (*Typha*), reeds (*Phragmites*) and various sedges replace the papyrus. Beyond the swamps, where flooding is seasonal, grassland with palms and acacia develops.

Large swamps and flood plains can be found along such great rivers as the Niger and Zambezi, in places where the rivers cross flattish ground. Swamps also occur in inland drainage basins which have no outlet to the sea, such as Lake Chad, the Okavango

▲ **Papyrus plants form huge floating mats in tropical swamps. Water lilies and floating grass soon invade channels cut through the papyrus.**

Above **Proteas are very common in the *fynbos* scrub of the Cape region of South Africa. *Below* Spring flowers, mostly annuals, give a mass of colour on cleared ground in Cape Province, South Africa. These plants grow, flower and set seed very quickly.**

delta and parts of the Rift Valley. In hotter, drier areas, large quantities of mineral salts accumulate. Most plants cannot grow in soil which has a high salt content and so the vegetation is limited.

Mediterranean Regions

The far north and south of Africa have a Mediterranean type of climate, with mild wet winters and hot dry summers. The plants of these regions consist mainly of wiry shrubs with mostly small leathery leaves. This type of vegetation is called *macchia* (Italian) or *maquis* (French). The Cape macchia or *fynbos* (Afrikaans) has also a number of larger shrubs. Macchia plants flower and grow mainly in the spring. They are adapted to survive periodic fires during the dry summer. Many plants store food underground in bulbs, rhizomes or swollen rootstocks. There are few grasses but in the Cape, reed-like plants belonging to the family Restionaceae are common.

The fynbos extends from the coast to the high mountain tops in the south-western and southern Cape Province. This region has many different local climatic conditions, and a great variety of plants. The heather and protea families are particularly characteristic. Remnants of conifer forest can be found in the south-western mountains. Forests similar to those of tropical mountains are found near sea level, in the eastern, wetter area.

The North African macchia is well-developed along the coasts and mountain foothills from Morocco to Tunisia. The characteristic plants including heathers, broom (*Cytisus*), gorse (*Ulex*), lavender, rosemary and sun rose (*Cistus*), are mostly related to those of Mediterranean Europe and western Asia. The coastal plain probably once had grasslands and light woodlands of olive and cork oak, but cultivation has long replaced most of the natural vegetation. On the mountains, oak forest gradually changes higher up to conifer forests of cedars, firs and pines.

WILDLIFE

Zoologists divide Africa into two separate regions. The area inland from the North African Mediterranean coast belongs to the *Palaearctic* region. This region also includes Europe and parts of Asia. Africa to the south of the Atlas mountains is called the *Ethiopian* region. The 'Ethiopian region' should not be confused with the modern country of Ethiopia. The ecological term probably arose because all of Africa was known as Ethiopia in classical times. The island of Madagascar is usually accepted as part of the Ethiopian region, but its animal life is quite different from that of the rest of Africa.

Palaearctic Region

In many ways the animal life of the Palaearctic region is more European than African. This fact is most obvious in the mammal population. Deer and wild boar live in North Africa, but are not found in any other part of the continent. However, the region does have animals that are typical of other parts of Africa, including the jackal and the leopard. Some smaller mammals, such as the mongoose and genet, live in both the Palaearctic and the Ethiopian regions. The only North African monkey is the barbary ape, which has more in common with the monkeys of Asia than with those of Africa. The bird life of the Palaearctic region has many European types, such as wood pigeons, blackbirds and chaffinches.

Historical evidence shows that the animal life of North Africa has not always been the same as it is now. The lions, to which the Christians were thrown in the Roman circuses 2,000 years ago, came from North Africa. North Africa must then have looked very similar to present-day East Africa. At that time, lions, leopards, elephants, giraffes and many antelopes inhabited the area. Zoologists believe that many of the Ethiopian type animals of North Africa died out during the Roman period. Those left died out over the following centuries. One species, the bubal hartebeest, survived until the 1800s. The animal life that has survived in North Africa is mainly Palaearctic and it is these animals which now live in the area.

The Ethiopian Region

The Ethiopian region, most of Africa, is particularly rich in mammals. It contains 38 separate families of mammals, excluding bats. Many of them live only in Africa. Aardvarks, giraffes and hippopotamuses are among the animals which are not found anywhere else in the world. Many species of primates, the animals most closely related to man, inhabit Africa. They include two of the world's four species of great apes—the gorilla and the chimpanzee.

The animal life of the Ethiopian region is spread unevenly over the African continent. Indeed, concentrations of animals are found in certain areas of Africa, namely areas most suitable for their growth and survival. For example, a species that lives in an equatorial rain forest is specially suited to living under the conditions found there. If such an animal was transported to a desert area, it would be unable to adapt its life-style to desert conditions and would soon die. Different environments are the key to the distribution of the many animal species throughout the continent. Rainfall, temperature, soil conditions and the presence of other animals all combine to make certain areas suitable for one species and unsuitable for another.

A young male lion wedges himself comfortably in the fork of a tree to avoid the hot afternoon sun. Lions, being large, heavy cats, do not normally climb trees. In the Ruwenzori National Park, Uganda, however, some of the lions have adopted this unusual habit. ▶

◀ Zebras grazing on grasslands in East Africa. African grasslands have the greatest variety and largest populations of grazing mammals in the world.

THE MAIN WILDLIFE REGIONS
Deserts

The desert areas of Africa include the Sahara, which is the largest desert in the world with an area of about 8,960,000 square kilometres (3,500,000 square miles). Extensive deserts also exist in the south-west of the continent—the Karoo, Kalahari and Namib deserts. The largest of these deserts, the Kalahari, is in fact semi-desert and resembles savanna. Although almost no surface water occurs, underground supplies exist beneath the sand and can be reached by deeper rooted plants, such as trees.

The animal life of the Sahara is very sparse and few large animals live there. One large animal, the addax, has several adaptations for desert life. It can go without water for long periods and has large splayed hooves to prevent the addax from sinking into the sand. Because it is light in colour, its body absorbs less heat than animals with darker coats.

Large desert mammals have made other adaptations to the conditions. Surface water is often non-existent, but the animals can obtain liquid from the moisture in the plants that they eat and from the dew that forms on the vegetation at night.

Few large mammals could survive the extremely high temperature of the desert. Their bodies would absorb more heat than they could lose and they would die of heat stroke. Desert animals, such as the camel, the donkey and the addax, survive because they are adapted to tolerate a rise in the

Wild camels, descendants of domestic herds, graze in the Libyan desert. ▲

Right This desert adder, *Bitis Peringuey*, uses a twisting motion called 'side-winding' to move up the side of a sand dune. *Below* The fennec fox lives in the arid areas of North Africa.

body temperature during the day. This absorbed heat is lost to the atmosphere during the cold nights. Lack of water can cause a rise in the concentration of the blood which would be fatal to most animals. However, the desert animals can survive this condition to a much higher degree than animals that have not adapted to desert conditions.

Most desert animals are small, and survive the harsh conditions by avoiding them. Small animals can burrow under the sand, where the temperature is lower, or they can crawl under stones, where the atmosphere is moister. Desert species of animals are normally smaller than related species that live in cooler, wetter climates. For example, the fennec fox is much smaller than foxes from other habitats.

Surprisingly, some amphibians live in the desert. Frogs do occur, but toads, which spend more time on land and which have drier skins, are more common. Toads avoid the desert's heat by burrowing into the sand or under stones. Like desert mammals, they have physiological adaptations which enable them to survive when water is in short supply. Desert toads, however, need water for reproduction. Toads lay eggs in pools created by rainstorms and the tadpoles develop rapidly into adult toads before the pools dry out.

Reptiles are well adapted to living in deserts. Most are predators and obtain water from the animals on which they feed. Their dry skin reduces water loss. They also produce solid waste rather than urine and this feature helps them to conserve moisture.

Few birds live in the deserts. Most are predators, because too little vegetation exists to support plant-eating birds. Some birds can live in very dry areas because they can fly great distances quickly to find food and water. For example, the sand grouse, which needs to drink regularly, can be found in the driest part of the desert. It survives because it stays within a day's flight from the nearest water. The sand grouse has also learnt to carry water to its young by soaking its breast feathers in water as it drinks. Birds have a higher body temperature than most mammals, and can therefore absorb more heat without suffering any ill effects.

◀ Hyraxes appear at dusk to feed on twigs and leaves, uttering an amazingly loud, raucous call. These little animals, no bigger than a rabbit, are thought to be distant relatives of the elephant.

Mountains

Many mountains in Africa are volcanic in origin. The highest, Mount Kilimanjaro, is an extinct volcano. The volcanoes of East and Central Africa, most of which are extinct, are of great interest to the zoologist.

The mountain sides are covered by forests which were once part of a continuous rain forest all over central Africa. For this reason species of birds and small mammals which are typical of the West African rain forests are also found on the slopes of Mount Kenya and the Aberdare highlands in East Africa. They are known as relict species because they were left behind when the forests retreated. There are few large mammals in this category but the bongo, a shy antelope, is an example of such an animal species.

A rich variety of large mammals lives on the slopes of the extinct volcanoes of East Africa. Leopard, buffalo, elephant and giant forest hog inhabit the wooded mountain sides. Sun-birds are, perhaps, the most typical group of birds found in these mountains. Sun-birds have a similar ecological role to the humming-birds of the Americas. They feed on the nectar of flowers and help the pollination of the flowers by carrying the pollen from one flower to another. Unlike humming-birds, however, sun-birds rarely hover in front of a flower when feeding.

The Ruwenzori Mountains of Uganda, also known as the 'Mountains of the Moon', were formed at the same time as the Rift Valley system. The vegetation of the Ruwenzoris is of great interest and contains giant lobelias, tree heathers and giant groundsels. Among the animals found there is the tiny hyrax, a distant cousin of the elephant but the size of a rabbit. The raucous voice of the hyrax is out of all proportion to its size.

A string of volcanoes further south runs from Rwanda and Uganda into Zaire. These mountains are important as the habitat of the small remaining population of mountain gorillas. Gorillas live only in Africa and most belong to the lowland sub-species which is found in West Africa. The mountain gorilla is larger and shaggier than its lowland cousins. A third race of gorillas has recently been identified in the lowland forests of eastern Zaire and western Uganda. This race was previously thought to be the mountain gorilla. In the light of this discovery, the surviving numbers of the mountain type are even fewer than was thought.

Ethiopia is a very mountainous country, with mountain ranges rising from a plateau of high land. The Ethiopian highlands support a very interesting animal life, which includes some species found nowhere else in Africa. Among them are the gelada baboon and the Abyssinian ibex, which is a goat and more typical of the Palaearctic region than the Ethiopian. The mountain nyala, a large kudu-like antelope, also lives only in the Ethiopian highlands.

A zone of bamboo is often found on the mountainside at about 2,500 to 3,000 metres (8,000 to 10,000 feet) but there are few signs of wild life in the tall, gloomy bamboo thickets, apart from a duiker or two. However, elephants visit the region to feed on the seedlings and clear a passage through the otherwise impenetrable stalks.

The black sunbird, *Chalcomita amethystina*, uses its long, curved beak for sipping nectar from large flowers. ▼

Forests

The forests of Africa are the main habitat of the primates, the group of animals closest to man on the evolutionary scale. The primates include lemurs, bush-babies, monkeys and great apes. The chimpanzee, the ape that most resembles man psychologically, is a species of the West African forests, although its range extends into Central and East Africa.

Recently, much research has been carried out into the behaviour of chimpanzees, both in the wild and in captivity. The results show, among other things, that the chimpanzee can adapt to its environment far better than other animals. Chimpanzees can form and use primitive tools. For example, they use thin straight twigs to extract termites from their nests. Some chimpanzees feed on meat as well as the insects and fruit which were formerly thought to make up their diet. Most authorities agree that there is only one species of chimpanzee, with perhaps four sub-species. The pigmy chimpanzee is markedly different from other races and may well be considered a separate species. Most monkeys live in forests, and the rain forest of West Africa is particularly rich in species. Among the West African species is the large colourful mandrill, which has a limited distribution there. The mangabeys, which belong to the genus *Cercocebus*, are found in the equatorial rain forests of central Africa as far east as Uganda. The colobus monkeys inhabit a large area of equatorial Africa from Senegal across to Ethiopia.

At least six species of colobus occur with many sub-species. They differ from other monkeys in having only four fingers, the thumb being absent or very small. They are well suited to forest life and live on a diet of leaves. Their digestive systems are adapted to this diet in the manner of grass-eating animals. The Abyssinian black and white colobus is the most handsome species. Its general colour is black, but it has a 'cape' of long white hair falling from its shoulders down its back, and a white bushy tip to its tail. The dullest and smallest species is the olive colobus of West Africa. This monkey is unique in that the female carries her young in her mouth, in the manner of a dog or cat.

The pigmy hippopotamus is another animal of the equatorial rain forest and has a very limited range in West Africa. The pigmy hippopotamus lives in swampy forests and spends far more of its time on dry land than the more familiar common hippopotamus. It does not have the protruding eyes and nostrils that enable the common hippopotamus to spend much of its time almost completely submerged.

The central forests of Zaire are inhabited by the okapi. This animal, which was discovered only some 60 years ago, is the only living relative of the giraffe. It is similar to the giraffe in appearance, with a sloping back, although it has a shorter neck. The inaccessible regions in which the okapi lives and its extreme shyness have prevented any extensive study of the animal.

Many of the smaller antelopes live in the forests. They include bushbuck, duikers and the royal antelope. The royal antelope is the smallest of the African antelopes and is not much bigger than a European hare.

▲ A jewel of the forest, this nesting flycatcher awaits the return of its mate.

A beautiful crowned hawk eagle. This impressive bird, the largest African eagle, often feeds on monkeys snatched from the forest tree-tops. ▼

▲ The grey parrot is a natural mimic and imitates the call of other forest birds.

140

Many forest antelopes, including the okapi, have stripes on their skins, which serve as good camouflage in the thick undergrowth.

The buffalo is also found in the West African forests. But it is a very different animal from the large black buffalo of the eastern plains. The forest buffalo is small and red in colour, with straight vertical horns, while the Cape buffalo of East and South Africa is far more massive and has horns spreading sideways from its forehead. The forest buffalo of West Africa is sometimes known as a bush cow. Although the two types of buffalo are very different in appearance, they both belong to the same buffalo species.

Certain races of buffalo found in areas between the Cape and forest varieties show characteristics of both types. An intermediate type of buffalo inhabits the Guinea savanna and the Nile Basin. This type resembles the Cape buffalo, but is slightly smaller and many individuals are red.

The change in colouring between East and West Africa is not confined to the buffalo. In West Africa the bushbuck is red, while in East Africa, the adult male bushbuck develops an almost black colouration. The same difference can be seen with the bush pig.

The leopard, which feeds on monkeys, bush pigs and the smaller antelopes is the only large predator of the forests. The leopards of the equatorial rain forests are of the usual spotted variety. A few of those that live in the mountain forests to the east may be black in colour.

The elephants of the rain forest belong to the same species as the elephants living in the savanna. However, they do belong to a different sub-species. They are shorter at the shoulder and have rounder ears. Their tusks are longer and straighter than those of the savanna elephant. Forest elephants were once tamed by Indian *mahouts* (elephant drivers) in Zaire.

Among the forest birds is the largest of African eagles, the crowned hawk eagle. This bird flies low over the tree tops, and snatches monkeys from the upper branches. Hornbills, turacos and parrots are the birds most likely to be seen in the dense vegetation of the rain forest. They attract attention by their bright colouring and raucous calls. The Congo peacock, first discovered in 1937, is one of the most unusual birds in the rain forest. The pheasants and peafowls, the family to which the Congo peacock belongs, are Asian birds. The Congo peacock is the only representative of the family found in Africa, many thousands of miles away from its nearest relative.

The insect life of rain forests is very rich. Any traveller in the forest is bound to notice the huge, brightly coloured butterflies and the many biting insects. Huge centipedes, snake-like millipedes, long-legged spiders and columns of ferocious safari ants are among the creatures that crawl over the forest floor. Termites are common. Travellers in the forest are bound to be struck by the widely varying sizes and shapes of termite nests.

▲ The cool, damp shadows of the forests provide a habitat for many amphibians, such as this tree frog. The tree frog has suction pads on its toes which enable it to cling to leaf surfaces.

The bush-baby is a small ▶ *nocturnal*, or night-active animal which lives in the forest tree-tops. It is named for its babylike cries.

The African forests are full of insects and invertebrates. This huge, long-legged spider waits in its web for an unwary insect. ▼

◄ A young female vervet monkey cuddles her baby protectively. Vervets feed on the grasslands during the day, but never move far away from the trees where they sleep.

The spotted, or laughing hyaena is one of the scavengers of the savanna. Hyaenas also hunt at night, often in packs numbering up to thirty. ▼

Aardvark

Pangolin

Left Termites build huge earth mounds, sticking the soil particles together with saliva. *Above* The termites' fortress is no defence against the aardvark and pangolin.

The Savanna

The savanna is one of the major wildlife habitats of Africa, but the term has no precise scientific definition. The word *savanna* originally came from South America, where it is used to describe the great prairies of tall pampas grass that stretch over the continent. In Africa, savanna can refer to anything from treeless scrub and grassy plains to near woodland. However, the ground vegetation of the savannas is always grass.

Much savanna country is either treeless or only sparsely wooded. Some savannas, such as the short-grass plains of northern Tanzania, are treeless because of the shallow depth of soil. In other areas, such as the southern part of Kabalega National Park in Uganda, elephants have destroyed the trees. In some cases, the farming activities of man have created savanna country where the original vegetation was thick woodland or forest. Where man has cut down the original trees and cleared the undergrowth by slash and burn methods, the result is a *derived* or *fire-induced* savanna. Recently, the term *woodland savanna* has been coined for this type of grassland.

The savannas support a profusion of animal species. Some species, such as buffalo, elephant, giraffe and warthog, are found in all types of savanna. Nowhere else in the world can one find the *ungulates* (hoofed mammals) in such large numbers. Most of them belong to the family *Bovidae* which has evolved into a wide variety of species. Birds are present in huge numbers in the savannas. Vultures and large birds of prey live beside a bewildering variety of bustards, herons, plovers, storks and a host of smaller birds, often magnificently coloured. Reptiles are well represented, with lizards, tortoises and snakes.

Many species of snakes occur in the savanna but they are not often seen because of their retiring habits. Most are harmless to man but some, such as the cobras and vipers, are very poisonous. The forest-dwelling green mamba and the black mamba which lives in more open country, are perhaps the most dangerous. Next is the spitting cobra, which can project venom over a distance of about three metres (ten feet) and which aims unerringly for the eyes. Although very painful, such an attack rarely causes permanent harm provided the poison is washed out at once.

Of the many insect species that inhabit the savanna, the termite is the most conspicuous because of the tall nests that dot the plains. Termites support many insectivorous animals. Birds feed on the winged adults, whilst aardvarks, aardwolves (a kind of hyaena) and pangolins dig into the nests and eat the workers and the grubs.

The elephant is found in all types of savanna and is highly important ecologically to the other animals and to the habitat itself. Elephants are destructive feeders. Purely vegetarian, they feed both on grass and on leaves and shoots. They help to maintain the savanna by uprooting and pruning back bushes and by destroying trees. However, the presence of too many elephants can harm the savanna to such an extent that it becomes derelict and of no use to any other animal.

When elephants had the whole of Africa to wander over, their destruction of habitat was not a serious problem. Elephants would range over a wide area and any vegetation that had become damaged by elephant feeding would have time to regenerate itself before they returned. The spread of the human population has now forced the elephants into smaller areas. For example, in the 1930s, elephants ranged over three-quarters of the area of Uganda, but in the early 1970s, they were confined to less than one-fifth of the country.

The presence of elephants in the same area for the whole year round has, in some cases, led to the desolation of the savanna environment. The destruction of trees is harmful to the elephants themselves. They require trees for food as well as for shade, because grass alone does not provide a sufficient diet. The destruction of trees has also had an adverse effect on other browsing mammals and on birds. Most national parks with large elephant populations have suffered from the effects of what has come to be known as the 'Elephant Problem'. Such parks include Kabalega Park in Uganda and Tsavo Park in Kenya.

The solution of the Elephant Problem is a matter of argument among scientists. Some feel that nature will solve the problem if it is allowed to take its course. This happened in Tsavo Park in 1971, when a severe drought caused the deaths of more than 3,000 elephants. Death was due not to thirst, but to

▲ Elephants can do great damage to the savanna if they are too numerous. They can easily break down a tree to reach the tender shoots and branches on the tree-tops.

◄ Elephants in the Luangwa Valley National Park, Zambia. Elephants often cross the Luangwa River to invade the surrounding country outside the park.

starvation. The drought reduced the amount of nourishment in the vegetation to the point where it would no longer support the elephants.

Others argue that natural disasters such as this are wasteful and inhumane. It is also felt that irreversible damage may be done to some habitats before 'natural' control comes into play. Kabalega Park, for example, is unlikely to suffer from drought. The elephants there have not declined in numbers, but they have suffered in health. The elephants have made adaptations to limit the growth of the population. The intervals between calving have grown longer, and young elephants take longer to reach maturity. Meanwhile, the population remains at its original size and continues to damage the habitat. If the natural control of numbers is allowed to run its course, it may be many years before the elephant population drops to a reasonable level. By that time, the park may have been irreparably damaged. It has been suggested that man should intervene and reduce the number of elephants and this would seem to be the logical solution to the Elephant Problem. However, what is not clear is the level to which the elephant population should be reduced before they cease to have a damaging effect on the environment.

◄ The long neck of the giraffe enables it to feed on the young leaves at the tops of acacia trees.

143

The Sudanese Semi-desert

South of the Sahara, the desert gradually gives way to vegetated country as the rainfall increases, until the well-wooded grasslands of the Guinea savanna are reached. The transition zone between the desert and the Guinea savanna has no distinct borders. However, it forms a belt of savanna called the Sudanese semi-desert stretching from West Africa to the Nile. Much of it is made up of areas of grassland dotted with a few stunted trees. Most of the people who live there keep herds of animals. Their large flocks of scrawny goats are causing the spread of desert conditions and soil erosion by overgrazing the sparse vegetation.

Gazelles are the most typical wild mammals of the Sudanese semi-desert. The red-fronted and dorcas gazelles are small and are similar in size and appearance to the Thomson's gazelle of East Africa. The dama gazelle is bigger and is the largest member of the gazelle family. It is very handsome, with its irregular red and white markings. The gazelles and the scimitar-horned oryx, another mammal typical of the region, are true desert animals. Many species from this region are nomadic, wandering over vast areas in search of the short-lived flush of grass that follows each irregular rainstorm. The ostrich, the largest of all birds, is another nomadic grazer, although it is also found in other parts of Africa. Ostriches are flightless birds but they have immensely strong legs which speed them away from danger. Adult ostriches can run very fast, achieving speeds of up to 65 km.p.h. (40 m.p.h.).

Predatory mammals are few, but they include the cheetah. This elegant cat is the fastest sprinter in the world. It can reach about 95 km.p.h. (60 m.p.h.) over short distances. The cheetah preys on the swift gazelles, dashing after a selected victim and swiftly bringing it down. The nocturnal caracal, an African lynx, takes animals up to the size of small antelopes and it can bring down birds in flight by leaping up at them. The bat-eared fox, with its large ears typical of desert animals, lives in this region, preying on small mammals and insects. Various insect predators, including spiders and scorpions, also live in the semi-desert region.

Because the rainfall is irregular, many species of grass have to survive long periods of drought in seed form. This provides the food for many seed-eating birds, such as weaver birds. Many of the seed-eaters are migratory and may do considerable damage to crops in other parts of Africa.

Migration and the nomadic life are typical of the Sudanese semi-desert, as in any difficult environment. Even some of the insect life is migratory and many locust swarms come from this area. The erratic and unpredictable rainfall forces the animals of the Sudanese semi-desert to adopt the nomadic way of life.

The Guinea Savannas

Towards the southern part of the Sudanese semi-desert, more large animal species appear and the land gradually merges into the Guinea savannas.

▲ Weaver birds weave intricate grass nests using their beaks and claws. They often build over water to avoid such predators as snakes.

◄ The ostrich is the world's largest bird. It can run at speeds of up to 64 km.p.h. The young chicks, coloured to match the savanna grass, can run from danger as soon as they are hatched.

◄ The defassa waterbuck is a large, thickset antelope usually found near water on the African savannas.

◄ The graceful impala is famous for its ability to leap great distances. Leaps of well over 9 metres have been recorded.

144

They stretch across much of Africa from Senegal and Guinea to the Nile Basin.

The Guinea savannas contain a variety of large mammal species, but they do not support many individuals in comparison with other African savannas. The reason for the lack of numbers is unclear, because the vegetation and the rainfall are as favourable in the Guinea savannas as in other parts of Africa. Perhaps the answer lies in the human history of the area. Advanced civilizations, with good internal communications and contacts with the outside world, have existed in West Africa for hundreds of years. It is possible that the large mammals of the Guinea savannas suffered from over-contact with man in the same way as the animals of the Palaearctic region of North Africa. Efforts are being made to increase the animal populations in the national parks and game reserves of the Guinea savannas.

Typical antelope of the region include roan, waterbuck, bushbuck, kob and hartebeest. Buffalo, which are between the Cape and forest varieties in size, are not uncommon. The Guinea savannas are the home of the western variety of giraffe, but over-shooting has made it rare. The giant, or Lord Derby's, eland is also sadly reduced in numbers in the western part of its range, but the central African race is still holding its own. A few elephants inhabit the region but no rhinoceroses nor zebras live there. Predators are rare and, although lions occur, they are seldom seen.

The bird life of the Guinea savannas is rich, particularly around the flood plains of the many rivers that flow through the area. Woodland birds are found in the forests near the rivers themselves. Many of the birds are migratory visitors, coming from the Palaearctic region as well as from other parts of Africa.

The Nile Basin
The savanna of the Nile Basin lies interspersed between lakes and swamps. The grasslands are covered with bushes and candelabra trees. Much of Uganda, including the two major national parks, Kabalega and Ruwenzori, is of this nature. By East African standards, relatively few animal species inhabit the area. However, the number of individuals is higher than elsewhere in Africa. The Nile Basin's *biomass* (the total weight of living matter) is greater than that of any other part of Africa. One of the reasons for this is the large number of the bigger animals, such as elephant, hippopotamus and buffalo. Antelope are abundant in the Nile Basin. Many belong to the West African species, such as bushbuck, hartebeest, kob, topi and waterbuck. The antelopes provide the food for lions, leopards, hyaenas and a variety of smaller carnivores. Cheetahs do not inhabit this region because the terrain is not suited to their hunting techniques.

The Nile Basin is one of the major habitats of the Nile crocodile. Kabalega National Park, south of the Kabalega Falls in Uganda, contains the largest crocodile population of any African national park.

However, the crocodile population has declined alarmingly in recent years and is now numbered in hundreds rather than thousands. The poaching of adult crocodiles for their hides and a decline in breeding has been the cause of the reduction in numbers. Visiting tourists have been the main cause of the failure in the breeding. Crocodiles nest on sandy shores and bury their eggs about 30 centimetres (1 foot) below the surface. The female guards the eggs and when the baby crocodiles hatch, she has to dig them out of the sand. She remains with them for several months after hatching to protect them from predators. The motor launches carrying the tourists frighten the female crocodiles away from the nesting sites. Once this has happened, baboons, marabou storks and monitor lizards dig up the eggs and eat them. If the female is disturbed too often, she may desert the nest site completely. Even if the eggs do hatch out, the baby crocodiles will be unable to dig their way to the surface and will die. Fortunately this problem has been recognized and tourist launches are forbidden to approach the nesting sites during the breeding season.

In other parts of the Nile Basin, the pest-control policies of game departments have greatly reduced the crocodile populations. Crocodiles are dangerous to man, and they do eat fish. But the argument that they harm the commercial fishing industries may not be valid. Crocodiles probably eat mainly the commercially unimportant predators and so they may be beneficial to the fishing industry by keeping the predatory fish in check.

Large numbers of crocodiles still survive in Lake Turkana in northern Kenya. The area is isolated and this fact has helped to protect them. Also, their skins are warty as a result of the alkaline waters of the lake. Because of this, their skins are not commercially valuable and poachers do not hunt them for the leather trade.

▲ **Hippopotamuses are very common in the waters of the Nile basin. They leave the water at night to graze on the river banks.**

The crocodile is the nearest living relative of the dinosaur. It lives along river banks and feeds on fish but occasionally catches land mammals. ▼

The Nyika

The Nyika is a thick dense scrubland that stretches for about 950 kilometres (600 miles) across the border between Kenya and Tanzania and extends to within 320 kilometres (200 miles) of the coast. Because the nyika is mostly scrubland, covered with bushes and trees, it supports a variety of browsing animals. Large mammals and big herds of antelopes are not often seen there. Among the

The black rhino is well ▶ adapted to browsing on shrubs and trees of the Nyika. It has a pointed upper lip which it can use for picking leaves and shoots. The black rhino is the most common rhino species, mainly because it can survive in areas where grass is scarce.

The slender gerenuk has the habit of standing on its hind legs to feed. It plucks the leaves of acacias, using its lips and long tongue. ▼

animals present are the lesser kudu, a shy elegant animal, and the gerenuk, a long necked gazelle which is able to browse to a height of 2.5 metres (8 feet) when it stands on its hind legs.

A wide variety of ungulates live in the nyika, including beisa oryx, bushbuck, Coke's hartebeest, eland, giraffe, warthog and zebra, together with several species of duikers and other small antelopes. Another inhabitant of the nyika is the klipspringer. This small antelope, which lives on rocky outcrops, has cylindrical hooves, like blocks of rubber. These hooves give a sure grip and enable it to stand on small pinnacles of slippery rock. The klipspringer is also unusual for its hair, which is brittle and spine-like.

The black rhinoceros is more common in the nyika than anywhere else. The conservation of the bushland is vital to the survival of this declining species. The black rhinoceros is a browser, eating leaves and shoots, unlike its larger and far rarer relative, the white rhinoceros, which is a grazer. The Tsavo National Park of Kenya, which lies within the nyika contains as many as 9,000 black rhinoceroses and is of tremendous importance to the survival of the species.

Most African carnivores are represented in the nyika. Many of the male lions there do not have manes, and this may be an adaptation to life in the thick bush vegetation. Prey is scarcer in the nyika than in the grassland savannas, but it is easier to catch because the thick cover makes stalking easier. Rainfall is low and springs provide water for the wildlife. The antelopes have to crowd around the few available water holes where they may be easily taken. Hippopotamuses and crocodiles are also found at the water holes.

The elephant is undoubtedly the most ecologically important of the mammals of the nyika. Its activities contribute greatly to the well-being of the rest of the wildlife. As it passes through the scrubland, the elephant leaves behind it a trail of uprooted bushes and felled trees. Grasses grow in the spaces and provide fuel for bushfires that clear the dead timber. Open glades are created, providing grazing and making the area more attractive to other animals.

The elephant plays another important role by providing water for other species during the dry season. When the surface water has dried up, the elephant digs down to water several feet below the dry river beds. After it has drunk its fill, other animals can drink at these 'wells', which may be the only source of water for many miles around.

The nyika supports a colourful and abundant birdlife. Hornbills, which are smaller and drabber than the forest species are often seen around the safari lodges of Tsavo National Park. Starlings, weavers and rollers are all common, but perhaps the most conspicuous bird of all is the golden pipit. The pipit is not particularly noticeable when perched, but the bright canary yellow of the underside of the wings attracts attention as it flies across the scrub.

▲ Flamingos on Lake Nakuru in Kenya. This soda lake has a very plentiful supply of microscopic plants and animals which provide food for the flamingos.

Top The wide East African grasslands are able to support huge herds of wildebeeste. During the dry season, the herds, each one often numbering as many as 10,000, migrate in search of fresh pastures.

hunting dog, as well as two species of hyaena, are in abundance. Many smaller carnivores, such as serval, ratel, mongoose, civet and genet, also occur.

The large herds of herbivores, such as zebra and wildebeeste, are the most distinctive feature of the East African grasslands. The migration of these herds across the Serengeti plains of northern Tanzania is one of the greatest wildlife spectacles in the world. At one time, such migrations were common in Africa, but they have now largely ceased, either because of the destruction of the animal populations or because human settlements have created barriers across the migration routes. For example, it is known that the springbok of South Africa once made migrations in huge numbers, similar to those made by the animals of northern Tanzania.

The migrations of large mammals are governed by cycles of rainfall and drought. In the rainy season, species migrate to areas that would be uninhabitable during the dry season. In the Serengeti area, the herds of wildebeeste and zebra move onto the grass plains during November, when the short rains occur, and spend the next five months there. When the dry weather begins in May or early June, the animals disperse to the north and west of the Serengeti park, where permanent water exists. These migrations, particularly the one in May, are spectacular to watch. Thousands upon thousands of animals walk in the same direction in columns that stretch for kilometres. Although the migrations are on such a large scale, they may only take a few days to complete.

The migrations of the herbivores control the movements of the carnivores. The lions of the Serengeti include some nomadic individuals, which follow the herds. The hyaenas of the area are active predators rather than scavengers. They hunt in packs, like the wolves of northern America and Europe, and will attack animals as large as zebra.

The floor of the Rift Valley in the region of the East African grasslands is covered by many large lakes which are important sanctuaries for water birds. Lake Nakuru is one of the most spectacular and is now a national park. It contains millions of lesser flamingos, with a substantial number of greater flamingos. The flamingos do not breed there, however, because they require complete freedom from disturbance and their breeding grounds have only recently been discovered in the more remote lakes of the Rift Valley. Flamingos nest at the water's edge on small raised cones of mud which are very vulnerable to changes in the lake level.

Although found together, the two species of flamingo do not compete for food. The lesser flamingo feeds on the surface of the water, mainly on blue-green algae, while the greater takes water shrimps and other small creatures from the mud bottom. Both species feed with the head held upside down while water is sucked into the mouth and forced out again by the fleshy tongue. A mesh at each side of the bill retains the solid food material, which is then swallowed.

The East African Grasslands

The East African grasslands lie between the nyika to the east and the Nile basin to the west. The savanna is park-like, with fairly short grass dotted with fig and acacia trees, but with few of the bushes which are such a feature of the Nile basin grasslands. The Nairobi National Park and the big national parks and reserves of southern Kenya and northern Tanzania are examples of this type of savanna. Vast numbers of herbivores, referred to as 'plains game', roam the grasslands. They include not only the antelopes found in the Nile basin, but also gazelles, wildebeestes and zebras.

Nearly all types of African mammal, except those typical of the forests and mountains are present on the grasslands. Elephant, rhinoceros, giraffe and, where there is suitable water, hippopotamus occur in limited numbers. Many species of antelopes, from the largest in the world, the eland to the tiny dikdik and klipspringer, inhabit the region. Carnivores, including lion, leopard, cheetah and

The Miombo

The miombo lies to the south of the East African grasslands and stretches right across the continent to the south of the Nile basin and the equatorial rain forest. The miombo, which covers an area of about 3,840,000 square kilometres (1,500,000 square miles), is woodland rather than grassland, although the grass growing between the trees is sufficient to support grazing mammals. The miombo includes the savannas of Zambia, Zimbabwe and southern Tanzania, where the Ruaha National Park is a good example. Large mammals inhabit the area, but not in such great numbers as in the grasslands to the north. They include the puku, a type of kob, Lichtenstein's hartebeest, lechwe, buffalo, reedbuck, greater kudu and sable antelope.

Conditions in the miombo are harsher than in the East African savannas. The soil is of poorer quality and water is scarce. Rainfall is less and only occurs during six months of the year.

The Bushveld

South of the miombo woodland is an area of savanna with a temperate climate which is known as the bushveld. Although the area is covered with bush, it is very dry.

The variety of large mammals living in the bushveld is as great as in most other parts of Africa, but the number of individuals is low. The Kruger National Park in South Africa is an example of this type of savanna. Elephant, rhinoceros, hippopotamus, buffalo, giraffe, eland, greater kudu, wildebeest, zebra, roan and sable antelope, and a form of topi known as a tsessebe are among the many species that live in the bushveld. The animal population of the bushveld has much in common with those of the East African grasslands and the nyika, further north.

The Highveld

The highveld in southern South Africa consists of rolling grasslands at a height of between 1,500 and 3,000 metres (5,500 and 11,000 feet) above sea level. This area has been inhabited by man for many years and much of it is farmed. As a result, little of the original wildlife survives today. Bad farming methods have led to serious soil erosion over much of the highveld. Some of the original wild animals still inhabit the region, but most of the wildlife has been re-introduced into the area by man. Conservation and re-stocking for hunting purposes are among the reasons why this has been done.

Reedbuck and Vaal rhebuck (no relation) are among the animals that live in the highveld. The springbok once lived in huge migratory herds in the highveld before the coming of man. The quagga, an extinct race of zebra, was another inhabitant of the region. Other animals, although greatly reduced in numbers, have managed to escape total extinction. They include the rare white-tailed wildebeest, which has survived on a few farms and small reserves as a result of protection. The blesbok, a form of topi, almost exterminated in the 1800s, has also increased in numbers dramatically due to protection. The lion of the highveld is now extinct. It is said to have been a particularly magnificent creature, with a thick black mane.

▲ A grey heron on its nest in the Luangwa Valley National Park, Zambia. Herons have long legs and beaks which enable them to catch fish in shallow waters.

Top right The spiny tenrec found on the island of Madagascar. The tenrec can have litters of up to 24 young, more than any other mammal.

Sable antelope drinking at a water hole in the Kruger National Park, South Africa. ▼

Madagascar

The island of Madagascar, now known as the Malagasy Republic, has been separated from the African mainland for at least 60 million years. During this period, an animal life has evolved there which is quite distinct from that of the rest of Africa. Among the mammals present are the lemurs, the most primitive of the primates. Lemurs were once common in other parts of the world, but most species are now extinct. Although a few related forms of lemur, the lorises, are found in mainland Africa and south-west Asia, Madagascar is the only location where lemurs have survived successfully.

Lemurs are forest animals, living in the rain forests which fringe the island. In size, they vary from the tiny mouse lemurs, which are only 12 centimetres (5 inches) in length, to the indri which is 90 centimetres (3 feet) long and is able to walk upright. One of the rarest lemurs is the aye-aye, of which perhaps only 20 individuals remain. The aye-aye has a long, stick-like middle finger, which it uses to extract insects from crevices and to comb its fur. In recent years, much of the forest in which the lemurs live, has been cut down and the whole lemur family is in danger of extinction.

The second group of animals that are unique to Madagascar are the tenrecs. The 20 species of tenrecs vary in size from 12 to 40 centimetres (5 to 15 inches) and they have evolved in a number of different forms. Some tenrecs have spines all over their backs rather like hedgehogs. Others resemble moles or shrews. The web-footed tenrec is only about 12 centimetres in length.

The lemurs and the tenrecs resemble the marsupials of Australia in that various species have evolved with body forms resembling those of other mammals, for example, the mouse lemur and the hedgehog tenrec. The geographical isolation of Madagascar left various ecological niches empty, which the two groups have filled.

The bird life of Madagascar contains several peculiar species, but, because of the great mobility of birds, most of them are similar to the species on the mainland. The reptiles, amphibians and insects all show the same trend, with many native Madagascar species having similarity to African species.

THE MAJOR AFRICAN GAME RESERVES AND NATIONAL PARKS

Benin (Dahomey)	Parc National de la Bouclé de la Pendjari (2,786 square kilometres)	Situated on the alluvial plain of Pendjari river. Consists mainly of Savanna and bush. Sp. elephant, hippo, crocodile, many antelope sp., lion, leopard, cheetah, warthog crested crane, marabou.
Ethiopia	Awash National Park (1,212 square kilometres)	Situated in the valley of Awash river. Grassy plains and thorny bush. Sp. oryx, zebra, gazelle, reedbuck, waterbuck, hippo, ostrich, bee-eater, kori bustard.
Kenya	Lake Nakuru National Park (30,173 hectares)	Lake Nakuru (13 kilometres long and 6 kilometres wide). Chiefly a bird sanctuary. Famous for the huge population of flamingoes.
	Masai Amboseli National Park (Over 2,590 square kilometres)	Dry plains covered in volcanic ash. Sp. rhino, elephant, buffalo, leopard, cheetah, giraffe, zebra, wildebeeste, many antelope and gazelle sp. lion, rich bird life.
	Tsavo National Park (20,808 square kilometres)	Open grassland, volcanic hills, river regions (Tsavo and Athi rivers). Sp. elephant, giraffe, buffalo, black rhino, lion, leopard, hippo, zebra, many antelope sp., monkeys.
Malawi	Kasungu National Park (2,048 square kilometres)	Wooded hills, grassy valleys. Sp. zebra, buffalo, hartebeest, kudu, roan, reedbuck, eland, oribi, elephant, waterbuck, rhino, lion, cheetah, and leopard.
Mali	Parc National de la Bouclé du Baoule (3,540 square kilometres)	Sandstone plateau. Sp. gazelle, eland, giraffe, hippo, lion, elephant, buffalo.
Mozambique	Gorongoza National Park (5,957 square kilometres)	Thorn scrub, palm jungle, open grassland, marshes. Sp. lion, elephant, buffalo, zebra, hartebeeste, bushbuck, many antelope sp. leopard, monkey, hippo, crocodile. Rich in water birds.
Nigeria	Yankari Game Reserve (3,315 square kilometres)	Wooded savanna and marshy forest. Sp. elephant, hippo, lion, leopard, cheetah, crocodile, hunting dog, many antelope and monkey sp.
South Africa	Kalahari Gemsbok National Park (9,583 square kilometres)	Dry sand dunes and plains. Sp. gemsbok, springbok, eland, lion, ant bear, warthog, ostrich, kudu, leopard, cheetah. jackal, secretary birds and many other sp.
	Kruger National Park (20,720 square kilometres)	Grassy plains crossed by rivers, thorny bush, forested hills. Sp. buffalo, many antelope sp., giraffe, leopard, lion, hippo, ostrich, monkeys, warthog, white rhino.
Sudan	Dinder National Park (7,122 square kilometres)	Thick savanna bush. Sp. lion, buffalo, elephant, black rhino, hyaena, jackal, many antelope and gazelle sp.
Tanzania	Ngorongoro National Park (264 square kilometres)	Ngorongoro crater—huge cap of an extinct volcano. Habitats range from tropical forest to dry plains. Sp. black rhino, buffalo, lion, leopard, elephant, cheetah, hunting dog. hyaena, wildebeeste, zebra, many antelope and gazelle sp., monkeys, birds of prey and other bird sp.
	Serengeti National Park (14,763 square kilometres)	Vast grassy plains. Famous for annual migrations of thousands of gnu and other grazing animals. Sp. wildebeeste, zebras, gazelles, lion, leopard, hyaena, hunting dog, cheetah, black rhino, giraffe, buffalo, many antelope sp., rich bird life.
Uganda	Ruwenzori National Park (2,227 square kilometres)	Lakes, hills, open plains, forest. Sp. topi, kob, buffalo, elephant, lion (tree-climbing), hippo, giant forest hog, warthog, leopard, rich bird life.
Zaire	Virunga National Park (8,091 square kilometres)	Volcanic mountainous regions, forest, wooded savanna, lakes and rivers. Sp. rare mountain gorilla, chimpanzee, tree hyrax, buffalo, many antelope, leopard, lion, okapi.
Zambia	Kafue National Park (22,403 square kilometres)	Huge plateau with rich vegetation ranging from forest to wooded grassland. Kafue river. Sp. hippo, buffalo, elephant, zebra, black rhino, lion, many antelope sp. Rich bird life.
	Luangwa Valley National Park (15,540 square kilometres)	Valley of Luangwa river, river pools, mopani woodland. Sp. elephant, hippo, buffalo, zebra, giraffe, many antelope sp. lion, leopard, crocodile, black rhino, wildebeeste, birds of prey, bee-eaters.
Zimbabwe	Wankie National Park (12,950 square kilometres)	Dry plains, scrub, forest. Sp. elephant, buffalo, white and black rhino, leopard, cheetah, jackal, crocodile, lion, ostrich, baboon, hippos, giraffe, sable and other antelope sp.

N.B. Sp. is an abbreviation for species.

EARLY ART

ART IN NORTH AFRICA

Ancient Egyptian Art One of the earliest centres of civilization was the Nile valley. Guarded by deserts and seas, this region was fairly secure from attack. As a result, many arts emerged there. The schools of architecture, sculpture and painting created in ancient Egypt spread across the lands of the eastern Mediterranean and influenced much subsequent development. Architecture was the chief art form in the Nile valley. Both painting and sculpture were considered more as decorations of buildings rather than as separate art forms.

From the Nile delta upstream into the Sudan, the Nile valley contains the remains of magnificent temples and tombs. The great temple of Karnak is the most impressive of the temples. The pyramids of Giza, one of the seven wonders of the world, are the most impressive of the tombs. The thought of death seems to have overshadowed the minds of Egyptians. As soon as he came to the throne, a pharaoh would start work on his tomb.

Egyptian Tombs People were once buried in the sand, and the sand preserved their bodies. This led to the belief that, in order to obtain life after death, it was necessary to *mummify* or preserve the body. Elaborate precautions were taken to safeguard the mummies.

The earliest tombs were of the *mastaba* type. These tombs were so called, because the oblong room above ground in a tomb resembled a stone bench, or *mastaba* in Arabic. From this upper chamber, an underground shaft led to the actual tomb, which was carefully concealed.

The earliest pyramid, that of Saqqara, was built by the architect Imhotep, who lived around 2680 B.C. It is a stepped pyramid, consisting basically of six *mastabas* which diminish in size one above the other. From this beginning developed the majesty of the Giza pyramids. The Giza pyramids were originally faced with polished stone so that they gleamed in the sunlight.

Northern Egypt contains more than 60 pyramids. But later dynasties built tombs that were hollowed out of rock, such as those in the Valley of the Kings near Luxor. In this valley, the marvels of Tutankhamun's tomb were uncovered in 1922. The walls of these tombs were painted with scenes from everyday life and also with sections from the Book of the Dead, an instruction book for the soul after death. These scenes often reached considerable artistic heights, with superbly detailed and carefully studied figures. Because the tombs contained examples of everything that the soul might need after death, including furniture and clothing, we have learned a great deal about the everyday life of the ancient Egyptians.

Egyptian Temples The great Egyptian temples of Abydos, Denderah, Karnak, uxor, Edfu, Kom Ombos, Philae and Abu Simbel cover a period of more than 2,000 years. The stark simplicity of one

▲ The great temple of Karnak, the most impressive of the ancient Egyptian temples.

Below right The imposing ruins of the Roman city of Leptis Magna situated near Tripoli.

The interior of a *mastaba* at Saqqara. *Mastabas* were the earliest type of tomb and consisted of an oblong room above ground with a shaft leading to an underground chamber where the body was concealed.▼

of the earliest monuments, that of the Sphinx at Giza, contrasts with the greater richness of the temples of the Ptolemaic pharaohs (323–30 B.C.). These elaborate temples were influenced by Greek and Roman architecture.

All the Egyptian temples, however, have one factor in common. They were all designed on the *trabeate*, or post and lintel, principle. The dome was unknown in ancient Egypt, and a forest of columns was required to roof the great halls. Perhaps the finest example is the great Hypostyle Hall of the temple of Karnak. This immense hall has 134 pillars arranged in 16 rows. The pillars of the central two rows are nearly 24 metres (80 feet) high and more than 1.8 metres (6 feet) in diameter. The central two rows are higher than the rest, so as to form a *clerestory*, an upper story with windows, through which light filtered into the hall. The walls and columns are covered with carvings and inscriptions, all of which were originally coloured.

Egyptian Painting was apparently always used for decoration, either of buildings or of articles of furniture. During Egyptian history, however, it developed greatly. In general, a certain rigid style is associated with Egyptian painting, such as the formalized style adopted for painting human profiles. But at times, a superb naturalism emerged. This was especially noticeable in the 18th dynasty (1575–?1308 B.C.). Artists had always been given freedom to depict flowers, birds, animals and even slaves naturally. In the 18th dynasty, they used this freedom in formal portraits, even those of the royal family, with delightful results.

Egyptian Sculpture, especially royal portrait sculpture, was one of the earliest expressions of the Egyptian genius for art. Again, sculpture was closely associated with architecture. Statues were always designed for a special setting, usually in a temple. These magnificent, usually idealized representations of men and gods have a smooth serenity, resulting both from the pose and from the highly polished stone. The sculptor, like the painter, was restricted by conventional formulae. But within these formal poses, there were many possibilities for originality and many of these statues were fine portraits. Some smaller pieces are incredibly lively, and in the 18th dynasty were apparently purely ornamental.

Roman Art Painting and sculpture continued to flourish in Egypt, even when the Roman empire was spreading over the whole Mediterranean world. Some of the finest existing Roman monuments were built in North Africa. These monuments demonstrate the wealth and importance of North Africa at that time. Some of the Roman mosaics in Africa are as fine if not better than those from other parts of the Roman world.

The highly stylised beauty of Egyptian art can be seen in this wall painting on a tomb at Thebes. Wall paintings were a form of decoration often used by the Egyptians. Many examples of this art have been preserved, due to the hot, dry climate of North Africa.

Islamic Art

While the Roman arts flourished, the Egyptian style continued in the form of Coptic art. This was originally folk art, but it became that of the Coptic Church. It combined with the art of Byzantium to produce Christian art. In turn, this helped to create the art of Islam.

The art of Islam is unique and unmistakable. However, it drew its inspiration from three main sources: the classical Hellenistic tradition which survived in the Byzantine empire; the art of the great Sasanian Persian empire; and the Coptic art of Egypt all became part of the Islamic world from the outset, and so generated ideas from within.

Islamic North Africa has always developed around three main points: Egypt; Ifriqiya (now Tunisia); and Morocco. Eastern Libya has tended to follow Egypt. Western Libya and eastern Algeria have grouped with Tunisia. Western Algeria has usually been artistically linked with Morocco. These divisions have not always been followed politically. But artistically, these were the three great centres,

The beautiful skyline of the Sultan Hasan Mosque in Cairo. This mosque was built in 1362. ▼

152

whose influence spread in all directions. Of the three, the greatest and most important has always been Egypt. At times, however, the other two centres have seriously challenged Egypt's position.

Islamic Egypt Ideas of architecture in Islamic Egypt were absorbed from all parts of the Muslim world. These ideas were then transformed into purely Egyptian forms. Whatever the original material, all the Egyptian structures were built in stone.

The dome made its first appearance in Egypt under Byzantine influence. In the hands of Muslim architects, the dome was used in the most impressive way, and its surface was covered with delicate carvings. Today Cairo is a city of domes and minarets. These structures give Cairo one of the most exciting skylines of any city. Inside the mosques coloured stones, marbles and, sometimes, ceramic tiles are richly inlaid. *Stucco* (plaster) and carved wood are also used. The wooden ceilings of mosques were often painted, although only with geometrical and plant designs. Superbly painted and gilded glass lamps hang in groups from the ceilings. The floors glow with richly coloured rugs and carpets. Intricately carved brass or bronze tables and braziers add to the comfort. These are also used in private houses.

As in ancient Egypt, all the arts were once again grouped into a place of worship. Only the painter is not truly represented, because the Koran is the one book which is never illustrated with miniatures. However, a great school of painting existed in North Africa, especially from the 900s to the 1100s under the brilliant Fatimid dynasty, although very few works survive.

Ifriqiya and Central North Africa was the home of a series of dynasties. Each ruled with great magnificence until the whole area was destroyed by the invasion of the Banu Hilal in the mid-1000s. These

▲ For hundreds of years rugs and carpets have been woven using the traditional Islamic designs and rich, glowing colours.

Below left The interior of the Sidi bu Medien Mosque at Tlemcen in Algeria.

Below right The mosque at Qayrawan in Tunisia. Qayrawan is a centre of pilgrimage for Muslims. The mosque, which was begun in the late 600s is one of the finest mosques in Africa.

Bedouin Arabs destroyed the towns, without which arts cannot exist. The civilization only revived after the arrival of the Turks in the 1500s.

Before the invasion of the mid-1000s, the richness of the art of this region was well known. Palaces and mosques abounded and were richly decorated, as can be seen from remains. The oldest and most splendid of the mosques is that of Qayrawan, Tunisia, to which successive rulers have added, making it a living museum of all styles. The art of Central North Africa was so important that, even after the Muslims had lost Sicily in the 1000s, the Norman kings of Sicily still built and decorated in the Islamic style. The beginnings of the later Italian Renaissance, the rebirth of art and learning, can be traced back to an Islamic origin through the flourishing of Sicilian Norman culture.

Morocco and Western North Africa have always developed separately, although common factors and designs run through the Islamic world. Architecturally, Morocco has been linked much more closely with Spain than with the rest of Africa. This also applied to other arts. It was especially true of ceramics which, in Islamic society, can certainly be regarded as one of the fine arts. In this field, the threefold division of North Africa was very strong. Egypt was a pottery centre for itself. Tunisia supplied the whole of Central North Africa. Morocco had a quite separate school.

The Artistic Influence of North Africa From earliest times, North Africa has been an artistic centre of great importance. In ancient times, Egyptian styles influenced development throughout the eastern Mediterranean. Indirectly, through Rome and Byzantium, it influenced the entire Mediterranean region. Later, this North African style permeated Islam and so penetrated to Europe. Such an important force naturally also made itself felt to the south of the Sahara.

ART SOUTH OF THE SAHARA

Origins Historians are now beginning to get a clearer picture of the complex artistic influences and developments that span Africa south of the Sahara. The details of such developments are still obscure. But it seems that the origins can be sought in the once grassy Sahara, some 5,000 years ago.

In this remote period, rock paintings and relief carvings were made. Examples have been found in the Tassil-n-Ajjer mountains in south-eastern Algeria in the central Sahara. These paintings show scenes of daily life, hunting, and religious ceremonies. They are very complex and are painted with great beauty. Paintings and reliefs on rock cliffs are found throughout most of Africa. They are the works of various peoples using different styles. Scholars once believed that the Sahara had been a barrier against cultural contacts. But we now know that this was not so. It was through the migrations of the original Saharan peoples that some of the belief and social structures reflected in the arts of Black Africa were spread throughout the continent.

East African Art

Kush and Axum In the east, the ancient civilizations of Kush in the Sudan and Axum in Ethiopia provide links with ancient Egypt.

The rulers of Kush became independent of ancient Egypt around 750 B.C. They established a powerful empire along the upper Nile in Nubia. With capitals at Napata and Meroe, Kush evolved a distinct art of its own. It borrowed heavily from Egypt, but also from civilizations as far apart as Syria and China. However, it still remained profoundly African in spirit.

The art that flourished in the Ethiopian interior from the 400s B.C. until the start of the Christian era had its origins in ancient Arabia. The civilization of the early Ethiopian period, which had its cultural and political centre at Axum, produced massive architectural structures built in limestone blocks and monumental *steles* (slabs) carved out of basalt.

Christian Art in Ethiopia At the beginning of the Christian era, Ethiopian art started to evolve in a unique fashion. Its development was virtually independent from the rest of Africa. The reasons for this isolation were religious, political and geographical.

The Christian art of Ethiopia included religious architecture that was strikingly original. This architecture included monolithic churches carved from solid rock, such as those at Lalibela, in northern Eritrea. There are also rectangular stone churches, such as that of the monastery of Dabra Dammo in Agamo. Many others are decorated with sculptural reliefs and paintings.

Islamic Influences From the A.D. 700s Islam spread throughout northern Africa to cover all the area from the Atlantic Ocean to the Red Sea and beyond. By the early 1100s, it had spread southward along the coast of present-day Tanzania. Here it created the distinctive African culture of the

Above The outer facade of a ruined mosque excavated at Gedi in Kenya.
Below A Christian church at Lalibela, in northern Ethiopia. Like the Axum obelisk, this church is carved from solid rock.

Swahili-speaking coastal peoples who lived in a string of coastal and island trading city-states. From the 800s, these cities acted as depots for the exchange of goods between the African interior, the Indian Ocean and the Middle East.

Swahili architecture used coral stone masonry to sober and original effect. Large towns, such as the excavated town of Gedi in Kenya and Kilwa in Tanzania, had palaces and mosques as well as elaborate tombs decorated with Chinese pottery. In later times, a sophisticated urban culture flourished in the more northerly islands of the Kenyan coast. There, a distinctive architecture was developed with tall, elegant houses that were richly decorated inside with stucco.

▲ The 20 metre-high obelisk or *stelae* at Axum in Ethiopia. The obelisk is made from a solid piece of rock and doors and windows are carved in its sides.

West African Art

In West Africa, great trading empires grew and expanded from the 800s to the 1600s. The oldest of these west African empires was ancient Ghana, whose capital Kumbi Saleh was recently excavated. The capitals of Mali, Songhai and Kanem-Bornu, are now being excavated. These were great cities, lying at the cross-roads of trading routes. They were centres of learning and culture, where scholars gathered from far and wide. They were the equals of the greatest medieval European and Islamic cities of the time. They included such places as Timbuktu, Jenne and Gao. These cities linked the West African civilizations with the Islamic world at a time when Islamic civilization was reaching its height. In art, however, deeply rooted and original forms were maintained. This art was characterized by an emphasis on three-dimensional modelling, despite the Islamic preference for abstract and non-figurative art. Two of the best-known groups of African sculptors belong to this region, although they are outside Islamic influence. They are the Bambara and the Dogon.

Bambara Sculpture The Bambara excel in wooden sculpture. The masks, ancestor figures and musical instruments that they carve vary according to their function and also according to the secret society that uses them. In their most typical form, the masks represent a human face surmounted by straight horns, decorated with cowrie shells. Other masks are representations of animals in human forms or humans in animal forms. These masks are decorated with copper and are used in dramatic representations of myths.

Dogon Sculpture The Dogon peoples carve masks in the likeness of a dead being, man or animal. These masks are intended to capture the life force that escaped at the moment of death. Others are carved in separate but inter-related planes, with an emphasis on sharp angles. Such masks are most effective when seen in movement during ritual dances. Beautiful headpieces, designed to be seen in profile, are carved in the shape of stylized antelopes.

Nok, Ife and Benin Along the Atlantic coast, from Senegal to the delta of the Niger River, the Guinean peoples also developed great empires. The art of these peoples is of great sophistication and beauty, both naturalistic and abstract.

Powerful and haunting clay sculptures have been found at Nok, a village in northern Nigeria. These clay sculptures date back to about 900 B.C. They probably influenced the sculptures of clay heads at Ife (A.D. 700s–1400s).

The masterpieces of African metal-work—the famous commemorative heads of dead rulers and their wives—were made in the imperial capitals of Ife and Benin, in Nigeria. Skilful methods were used for these portraits, as well as for bronze plaques with reliefs, depicting scenes of courtly life and divine symbols. Such objects decorated the palaces of the west African rulers, whose power they represented.

West African Forest Cultures In the forests of West Africa, wood sculpture flourished, especially in the form of ritual masks with strong, jutting forms. The Dan peoples have produced some beautiful masks. The Baule, among the best sculptors of west Africa, carve exquisite objects for daily use. They also carve beautiful ceremonial objects such as spoons, dishes, stools, carved doors and the *daule* (small carved drumsticks) as well as masks and statues of ancestor-figures. The Ashanti gold weights with their geometric and figurative designs are considered to be masterpieces. West African forest peoples also developed weaving, pottery, metalwork and sculpture of the highest quality.

An ivory pendant mask worn by the Oba (King) of Benin as a costume ornament. This mask, which was probably made during the early sixteenth century, is one of the most beautiful examples of early Nigerian art. The delicately carved mask is only nineteen centimetres high. On the top is carved a tiara of miniature Portuguese heads.

Top A dramatic terracotta head found at Nok, a village in northern Nigeria. It probably dates back to about 900 BC.

Centre An Igbo pottery ornament which relates to the Yam festival.

Bottom A terracotta head, probably dating from the 11th century, found at Ife, in Nigeria.

155

Bantu Art From Nigeria southwards, the geographical and ethnic diversity of Africa has produced a great number of cultures and artistic styles. These are loosely grouped together as 'Bantu'. The chief art form is sculpture.

It is very difficult to establish a chronological sequence for sculptures, when the material used is wood. This material is very fragile in hot climates, and Europeans destroyed most of the pieces that they found. Most of the known Bantu sculpture was made in the last 200 years. However, there is evidence of the continuity, variety and richness of the artists' imagination and skill.

Bantu sculpture, whether Mpongwe painted masks in their serene beauty, Baluba ceremonial stools, or contemporary Shona sculptures in stone, is generally stylized. It does not aim to represent reality, but a mythical or supernatural-fantastic world. Non-essential details are discarded, although the details may be very realistic. Body distortions are common. These are not the result of a lack of skill, but of a deliberate choice according to certain accepted conventions.

ARCHITECTURE

Although little known, African architecture perhaps summarizes best the social and philosophical beliefs, and the strongly three-dimensional sculptural quality of most African art. African architecture must rank with other great architecture of the world.

The varieties of plan and building material cover a vast range. The houses, circular or rectangular, often have painted walls or sculptured reliefs. For example, the mosques of West Africa vary from the basic Islamic plan. Some have mud walls built in a pyramidal structure resting on a permanent wooden scaffolding. However, the mosques of Mopti reflect the mask forms of the Dogon peoples because of their strong vertical emphasis.

The same sculptural effect on a grand scale is achieved in the stone buildings of Zimbabwe in central Africa. Zimbabwe is the best known of a series of religious and political centres built all over the region. The impressive stone buildings date from about A.D. 1100.

Perhaps the greatness of African architecture lies in its functional quality. It is in the village, or *kraal*, that the integration of art with life is best expressed. The architecture and the decoration of the buildings reveal complex symbolism.

The Influence of Black African Art Since the end of the 1800s, Black African art has been collected by foreigners. It has also inspired great European artists, such as Pablo Picasso and Amedeo Modigliani. African art, especially sculpture, combines symbolic content with the most sophisticated forms. However, western artists have been mainly interested in the form, whereas western anthropologists have concentrated on the content or meaning of the art. Because the true quality of this art lies in a combination of both content and form, it seems even today to be inadequately appreciated.

▲ A wooden Baluba sceptre from Zaire. It is carved in the shape of a young girl and decorated with beads.

The conical tower ▶ which forms part of the famous Zimbabwe Ruins. This tower is thought to have been built in the 15th century.

◀ The mosque at Mopti in Mali. The Muslims of West Africa adapted the traditional Islamic mosque design, using wooden scaffolding with mud walls.

ART TODAY

Ethnic sculpture in the classical African tradition is almost everywhere in decline. This is because the religious groups and other institutions which inspired it are themselves disappearing in modern society. Classic African art and art forms inspired and influenced a whole generation of modern European artists, and one of the more interesting features of the present African art scene is a noticeable reverse influence, in technique rather than style or content, from Europe to Africa.

A disconcerting distraction for the serious art student has been the dramatic growth of what is known as airport art—the sale of mass-produced carvings of animals and modern copies, or even forgeries, of traditional masterpieces in response to the apparently insatiable demand from outside Africa for African art and curios. Yet even this carving industry has not been a total artistic disaster. Among the Makonde carvers of Mozambique and southern Tanzania there are some fine individual artists who daringly combine the constraints of their classical inspiration with the liveliness of modern innovation in works of tremendous talent.

One of the more refreshing discoveries in recent years has been the urban folk art among the Igbo and Yoruba of Nigeria. This has been described by Ulli Beier in two books. He writes: 'The spirit of optimism and the sense of High-life that preceded independence throughout West Africa created many exuberant art forms: cement lions on Yoruba houses, popular shop signs in Igbo cities, paintings on lorries

▲ A lino-cut by the Kenyan artist Hezbon Owiti, 1966.

A painting on cloth by Twins Seven Seven called *The Angry Hen*.   ▼

and in bars, cement sculpture on tombs, new styles in dress, batiks, embroidery, etc.' Even more strange and original are the mud sculptures of the *mbari* houses (Igbo temples to the gods), where dozens of brightly painted groups of figures represent not only the gods, but ordinary men and women at work, as well as domestic and wild animals.

In contrast to the temples, non-religious forms of 'total' art—including music, dancing, theatre and art exhibitions—have been fostered by some of the new art centres. The most famous, Mbari Mbayo, was founded by Ulli Beier and Duro Lapido at Oshogbo in Western Nigeria. During the 1960s they organized several summer schools which were attended by visitors from other parts of Nigeria. It was at Oshogbo that Ulli Beier discovered the versatile talents of Twins Seven Seven. This young artist, who is also a gifted musician, actor and dancer, has in recent years exhibited his pictures in London and New York. His speciality is ink drawing coloured in with gouache and then varnished.

The bronze sculpture of Vincent Kofi of Ghana (*Awakening Africa*) and Ben Enwonwu of Nigeria (*The Awakening*) showed that some contemporary artists are looking for a symbolism related to the aspirations of their people. One of the best painters, Malangatana Valente of Mozambique, harks back to ethnic motifs in his use of grimacing mask-like faces, often viewed frontally. This use of the ethnic style is also seen in the wood sculpture produced under the encouragement of certain missionaries. This

▲ A bead mosaic by the Oshogbo artist Jimoh Buraimoh.

Christian statuary retains some of the traditional features of ethnic sculpture, as can be seen, for example, in the *Madonna and Child* reproduced on this page. The rigid, forward-facing pose and the symmetry of the two figures, as well as the large size of the heads, follow the classical pattern.

Some artists have wanted to make a clean break with the past, at least in their use of new media. These media include aluminium panels (Adebisi Akanji), beaten copper reliefs (Asiru Olatunde), beadwork mosaics (Jimoh Buraimoh), as well as a large range of graphics. One of the most original sculptors working in Africa today is Francis Nnagenda from Uganda, who makes welded metal sculpture. His figures tend towards monumental size, reaching heights of nearly 4 metres (12 feet).

The flourishing departments of fine arts at the universities have also produced a new generation of painters and sculptors who are themselves influencing the artists of tomorrow. There are Elimo Njau, Louis Mbughuni, Eliabu Moshi, Kiasi Nikwitikie and Sam Ntiro from Tanzania; Gregory Muloba, Ali Darwash, Elisha Gatu, Faiz Hyder, Samuel Wanjau, Hezron Watindi, Lee Kanyare, Hezbon Owiti and Louis Mwaniki from Kenya; Mukiibe-Mugalala, Brother Anthony, M. O. Buluma, Francis Musango, Lwanyaga Musoke, Theresa Musoke, Nasa Tumwesige, Moses Ssonko, Muhammed Kamulegeya and Eli Kyeyune from Uganda; Demas Nwoko and Bruce Onabrakpeya from Nigeria; Wosene Boghossian and Abdel Rahman Sherif from Ethiopia; and Clark Andriambelo from Malagasy. Modern African art is among the most innovative, provocative and refreshing anywhere in the world today.

▲ A bronze sculpture called *Head of a Fulani Girl* by the Nigerian artist Ben Enwonwu.

Crazy Ones Don't Touch Me, a painting by Malangatana Valente of Mozambique. ▼

◄ A sculpture of the Madonna and Child carved in odante wood by the Ghanaian artist Vincent Kofi, 1957–8.

MUSIC AND DANCE

◄ Moroccan musicians

◄ Drummers at Maramba, Zambia. The complex and exciting fighting rhythms of drumming are a special feature of African music.

A Zulu dance. Dance is the full expression of African music. Rhythm, movement and music combine to form a single art form. ▼

Music and Dance South of the Sahara
Africa has a fine musical tradition. In some places, such as North Africa and along the East coast, some of the music has been strongly influenced by the Arabs. However, this article concentrates on the indigenous music of Africa.

Melody Most African tunes start high and gradually fall until they reach the end. Most African languages are *tonal*—that is, a word consists not only of syllables, but also of the high, middle or low voice on which one pronounces them. To change the pitch of voice will alter the meaning of the words. It is clear, therefore, that the tune of a song must, as far as possible, follow the up and down pitches of the words so as to preserve their correct meaning.

Songs are usually in 'call-and-response' form. A leader sings parts of a verse and the audience joins in at the right places. There are also songs sung by one person, although these are much less usual. In solo songs, professional singers praise leaders or relate the history of their people.

Some peoples sing all songs in unison and they have no harmony. Most groups, however, use a simple harmony called *organum*. This is achieved in two ways. The first way involves adding a tune a fourth (four notes) below the main tune. This is the same tune starting four notes lower. For example:

Main tune	f m r d	F E D C
		or
Harmony	d t_1 l_1 s_1	C B A G

The second way involves adding a tune only a third (three notes) below the main tune. For example:

Main tune	f m r d	F E D C
		or
	r d t_1 l_1	D C B A

Usually, each group of peoples has its own style, singing all songs in either one or other of the above styles. They do not mix them. A few groups sing in more complex harmony.

Rhythm The chief feature of African music is its rhythm. There are two kinds of rhythm: *regular* rhythm; and *irregular* rhythm. The usual way of beating time is by hand-clapping. The examples in Box 1 show the two kinds of rhythm, the handclaps falling on **1**. In the second example, the third and fifth note have three units of time, and the others have only two. The rhythm therefore divides time into unequal pieces. It is irregular.

In western singing and clapping, the strong beats of the tune keep in step with the claps. In Africa, the strong beats in the tune do not always fall on the claps. There is therefore a fight between the song and the clap rhythms. The same happens if bells or rattles are used with the song. This *fighting* of rhythm is the special feature of African music.

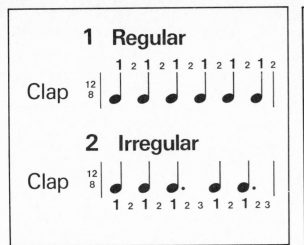

1 Regular

Clap

2 Irregular

Clap

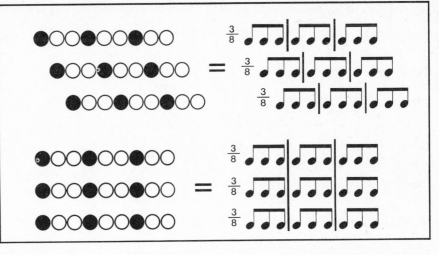

Above The box shows two kinds of rhythm, the handclaps falling on 1. The first example shows *regular* rhythm. In the second example of *irregular* rhythm the third and fifth note have three units of time while the others have only two.
Right The first example in this box shows an African drumming pattern with shifted rhythm. The second example shows a European drumming pattern with the beats all coinciding.

Drumming The fighting of rhythms is the basic feature of African drumming. Let us take three drums, each beating triple time—three beats in a bar, with the first beat as the strong one. Europeans would tend to put these together so that the number 1 beats all coincide. The second example in Box 2 shows this pattern of rhythm. Africans, however, will shift the rhythm of the second drum, so that its number 1 beat falls either on the second or the third beat of the first drum. See the first example in Box 2.

Normally, there are at least three drums in African drumming. The small drum keeps playing a simple rhythm. Then the big master-drum comes in. In every dance, the master has several long patterns of irregular rhythms. He starts playing one pattern. The middle drum then plays the proper reply. Each master-drum pattern has its own proper reply on the middle drum. When people start dancing, the master-drummer starts playing variations on his pattern. His object is to suit the style of the dancers, and make them enthusiastic.

▲ A Zambian dancer.

Felix Cobbson, a Ewe drummer from Ghana, teaches an enthusiastic group of English children the rhythms of African drumming. ▼

Dancing An African dance is the full expression of African music. Together, the dancers and musicians make a single art form. There may be a bell, rattles, song, hand-clapping, and then at least three drums all crossing their rhythms. Yet all these elements are kept strictly in time. The dancers choose one instrument to guide their feet, so all the other rhythms are fighting them. This is the thrill of an African dance.

Dances are used not only for general recreation or beer parties. They are also performed to celebrate the main events in life—birth, marriage, sickness, and death. In parts of Africa, especially West Africa, there are religious sects, each of which has its own special dances. There are also professional solo dancers who earn their living by dancing.

Other Instruments Besides drums, Africa is rich in other instruments. A few of the many instruments common in Africa are xylophones and hand-pianos, stringed instruments, flutes, trumpets, horns, bells and rattles. There is evidence that xylophones were brought to Africa from Indonesia around 400 BC. Some trumpets and kettle-drums are clearly the result of Arab influence.

Recent Musical Developments Recently, a new style of music has developed in Africa. It is often called *neo-folk music*, because it is both new and it is made by the people themselves. It has various names. There is 'high-life' in Ghana, 'Congo' music, and 'cheta' in Malawi. This music is the result of European and American influence in Africa. European and American musicians have introduced their rhythm, harmony and instruments, especially accordions, guitars and brass instruments. Africans have taken some of these features and welded them into their own musical system.

The same process happened in America, where the American Blacks, the descendants of African slaves, have created *jazz*. This music consists of a basic European rhythm on top of which other instruments fight against it in the African style and produce syncopation. Indeed, in jazz, the improvised saxophone or cornet solos are much like the variations that an African master-drummer would create on his drum. Songs like the 'blues' express the same feelings and ideas that Africans often use in their own songs.

SPORT

Athletics The Kenyans have led the conquest of world athletic honours, followed by other East Africans, Ethiopians and North Africans. Most have been runners of the longer distances, for most of them come from mountainous regions. A runner who lives and trains at 1,800 metres (6,000 feet) above sea level, as did the Ethiopian Abebe Bikila or the Tanzanian Filbert Bayi, has a great advantage in longer races over a runner born at sea level. His lungs are used to coping with the shortage of oxygen in the rarefied atmosphere. This was shown dramatically in the 1968 Olympics in Mexico City, 2,239 metres (7,347 feet) up. Africans from mountainous regions or who had trained at altitude took most of the medals in the longer events. When such runners compete at sea level, the advantage is greater—like taking weights off the feet.

But altitude does not explain all the successes of African runners. They also have a fresh approach to tactics. They are not afraid of leading from start to finish, as Bayi did in the 1974 Commonwealth Games 1,500-metre race. In 1975, he broke the world record in 3 min. 51 sec. Men like Bayi and the Kenyan Ben Jipcho run naturally, because in the past they ran long distances to school daily.

The first African athlete of international stature was Alain Mimoun O'Kacha, an Algerian who ran under his French nationality. Although overshadowed by the great Emil Zatopek for most of his career, he at last won an Olympic gold medal in the marathon in 1956 at the age of 35. In the same Olympics Black African runners showed their growing strength in world athletics. Nyandika Maiyoro of Kenya finished 7th in the 5,000-metre race. But in the 1960 Olympics he improved his time and position and became the idol of men such as Keino and Jipcho.

But it was an Ethiopian, Abebe Bikila, winner of the marathon, who caught the world's admiration in 1960. His retention of the marathon title in 1964 added to the stature of African athletics. Kipchoge Keino of Kenya emerged as the new star of Africa in 1965. African successes in the 1968 Mexico Olympics, two Commonwealth Games, the 1972 Munich Olympics and the 2nd African Games held in Lagos in January 1973 have confirmed how much potential is still to be tapped in Africa.

Nearly all the stars so far have been runners of the longer distances, but already Africans are showing what they can do in other events. Ghana has good sprinters in George Daniels and Ohene Karikari and a long and triple jumper, Joshuah Owusu, who is nearing world class. The Nigerians are also getting stronger in the sprints and field events. Chad and Ivory Coast have already produced good high jumpers and discus throwers.

Women are also competing more now. Modupe Oshikoya of Nigeria won the long jump at the 1974 Commonwealth Games, as well as coming close to beating the British 1972 Olympic champion, Mary Peters, at the pentathlon. A 17-year old Kenyan girl, Sabina Chebichi, cut 7 seconds off her best time to take the bronze medal in the 800-metre race.

George Daniels, Ghanaian sprinter, running the 100 metres.

Elizabeth Chelimo, Kenyan sprinter, at the 1974 Commonwealth Games at Christchurch, New Zealand.

The 3,000 metre final at the 1974 Commonwealth Games. Mogaka (414) of Kenya is leading, followed by the Kenyans Jipcho (404) and Biwott (402).

Athletics

				hr	min	sec
400 m	3rd.	J. Sang	(Kenya)			44.92
800 m	3rd.	M. Boit	(Kenya)		1	46.0
1,500 m	2nd.	K. Keino	(Kenya)		3	36.8
5,000 m	2nd.	M. Gammoudi	(Tunisia)		13	27.4
10,000 m	3rd.	M. Yifter	(Ethiopia)		27	41.0
Marathon	3rd.	M. Wolde	(Ethiopia)	2	15	8.4
400 m hurdles	1st.	J. Akii-Bua	(Uganda)			47.82
3,000 m steeplechase	1st.	K. Keino	(Kenya)		8	23.6
	2nd.	B. Jipcho	(Kenya)		8	24.6
4 x 400 m relay	1st.	Kenya			2	59.8

Boxing

Flyweight	Silver	L. Rwabogo	(Uganda)
Featherweight	Silver	P. Waruinge	(Kenya)
Lightweight	Bronze	S. Mbugua	(Kenya)
Light-Welterweight	Bronze	I. Daborg	(Nigeria)
Welterweight	Bronze	D. Murunga	(Kenya)
Middleweight	Bronze	P. Amartey	(Ghana)
Light-Heavyweight	Bronze	I. Ikhouria	(Nigeria)

◄ **The Zaire football team during the 1974 World Cup series. Second from the right in the top row is Bwanga, who was named Best African Footballer in 1973.**

Left **Modupe Oshikoya of Nigeria winning the long jump at the 1974 Commonwealth Games.**
Right **Eusebio, of Mozambique, one of the world's most outstanding football players.**

Association Football Football is the most popular game in Africa as a whole. It is encouraged by governments, who assist wherever possible with training facilities and financial grants. The countries most successful at football seem to be those without great track and field athletes—Egypt, Zaire, Guinea, Zambia, Morocco and Ivory Coast. Egypt has long competed internationally. It beat European teams in the 1924 and 1928 Olympics, and played superbly against Hungary in the 1934 World Cup. Morocco also has a fine record in international football. In the 1970 World Cup finals in Mexico, Morocco led West Germany 1–0 before losing 2–1, and drew with Bulgaria 1–1. Zaire entered the finals of the 1974 World Cup played in Munich. Africa has justified its inclusion as a separate qualifying zone in the World Cup.

The two big competitions in Africa are the African Nations Cup, held about every two years, and the African Champion Clubs Cup. Egypt has won the Nations Cup several times. Vita of Zaire beat Asante Kotoko of Ghana for the Champion Clubs Cup in December 1973. The other leading clubs are Ismailia of Egypt, Canon of Yaounde (Cameroon) and Mazembe of Lubumbashi (Zaire). In East Africa, Young Africans and Simba are Tanzania's best teams; Gor Mahia in Kenya and Mufulira Wanderers in Zambia. Vita's key defender, Bwanga, was named Best African Footballer of 1973, but, in general, teams are more important than outstanding individuals. Some of the best players including Eusebio and Salif Keita of Mali have left their homelands for the star treatment and high pay of European teams.

Boxing Africans were often seen in professional fights in England and France in the 1950s and 1960s, but few had the chance to go for big titles. Two Nigerians, however, who moved to England in the 1950s did succeed against the odds and they became world champions—Hogan 'Kid' Bassey and Dick Tiger. Two other boxers, Rafiu King Joe of Nigeria and Floyd Robertson of Ghana, later fought for the world featherweight title and failed. One of the best African boxers Sugar Ray Adigun, lives in France.

The formation of the African Boxing Union and the staging of the first professional fight in Africa in 1973 are signs that African boxers' fortunes will not be in foreigners' hands for much longer. More boxers of the calibre of Makhloufli of Algeria and Allotey and Tetteh, both of Ghana, should emerge.

In amateur boxing the East Africans usually dominate both the African Championships and the Commonwealth Games.

Other sports Basketball is popular in the French-speaking states, but African teams have made little impact at world level. Tennis is played at a high standard in South Africa, Egypt and Nigeria. Rugby football is popular in South Africa and has a growing following in the rest of the continent. Cricket is also popular in southern, east and central Africa. Hockey championships are held in East Africa, and swimming as a competitive sport is growing in popularity in West Africa.

AFRICA PAST AND PRESENT

◄ Charles Darwin pioneered the study of evolution. He was the first scientist to adopt the theory that man had a common ancestor with the higher apes of Africa.

In 1961 Dr Louis Leakey found a skull (*right*) of a man-like creature at the Olduvai Gorge in Tanzania. This skull is estimated to be about 1,750,000 years old. On the left is a chimpanzee skull.   ▼

The Dawn of Mankind

Scientists still argue among themselves about the origin and evolution of mankind. Fresh discoveries are still being made, but their meaning is uncertain. Argument is likely to continue. The work of archaeologists is slow, and new discoveries depend largely on chance. Most scientists agree that the origins of man are still a mystery.

The Work of Darwin In the 1800s the British scientist Charles Darwin crystallized all knowledge up to that time in his great work *On the Origin of Species by Means of Natural Selection or Preservation of Favoured Races in the Struggle for Life*. This book appeared in 1859 and was followed in 1871 by the *Descent of Man, and Selection in Relation to Sex*. He also wrote many other works. In his books Darwin stated that man probably had a common ancestor with the higher apes. Because the higher apes are found in Africa, he supposed that man originated there.

This theory was generally accepted until an ancient skull was discovered later in Java. This discovery suggested that man may have originated in Asia. But in recent times there have been many more discoveries of fossil remains of earlier apes, described as *pongoids*, and of 'near men', called

australopithecines, in eastern and southern Africa. Because of these finds, modern scientists again favour an African origin for man.

Research in Africa The site in Africa where the most important discoveries have been made is the Olduvai Gorge in north-western Tanzania. This gorge is not far from the game reserves of Ngorongoro Crater and the Serengeti. Another site, east of Lake Turkana in Kenya, promises to be of equal importance, as also does the Afar Valley site in north-eastern Ethiopia.

The Olduvai Gorge cuts through the floor of the great African Rift Valley. It is 92 metres (300 feet) deep and, along its sides, is a series of rock layers formed from the sediment that piled up in what was then a lake. These rock layers include deposits made by lakeside dwellers over many millions of years. From the 1930s onwards the Olduvai Gorge was excavated by the late Dr. Louis and Mary Leakey.

In 1959 Mary Leakey found a fossil skull about 1,750,000 years old. This creature, eventually named *Australopithecus boisei*, was *hominid*, or man-like, rather than *pongoid*, or ape-like. However, soon afterwards in 1960, Dr. Leakey discovered equally old remains of a much more man-like creature, given the name *Homo habilis*. It appeared, therefore,

that these very different man-like creatures lived at about the same time. *Homo habilis* obviously used stone tools, since these were found with his remains. Dr. Leakey pointed out that although chimpanzees were known to make tools of a regular pattern, only man-like creatures were known to make stone cutting tools of this kind. Similar tools have been found in early deposits in Morocco.

Homo habilis was physically distinct from other primates of his day. He had a large brain and an upright posture, walking on two legs. His arms were therefore freed for grasping. An even more important difference was his opposable thumbs. Unlike the thumbs of apes, opposable thumbs can be moved to touch the finger-tips. This special feature of *Homo habilis* enabled him to handle tools with greater precision. Further fossil remains of this type have been found in the Transvaal, and near Lake Chad.

Recently Richard Leakey, son of Dr. Leakey, has made other discoveries east of Lake Turkana in Kenya. These discoveries include fossils of australopithecines and of *Homo erectus*, which represents a further stage in man's development. The dating of the *Homo erectus* fossil is between 1,000,000 and 2,600,000 years old. But this dating is uncertain and may be revised.

Another problem arose at this site. A skull was found, dated provisionally at 1,500,000 years old, which appears to be of the *Homo sapiens* type. The term *Homo sapiens* is now used for modern man, regardless of race. If this skull is in fact *Homo sapiens*, then its owner must also have lived alongside the less man-like australopithecines. There are, therefore, many problems yet to be solved in establishing how *Homo habilis* evolved into *Homo erectus* and then into *Homo sapiens*.

The Acheulian Age in Africa The relationship between the earliest representatives of what was to become mankind is highly obscure. Also, no precise relationship has been established with the men (*Homo erectus*) who made the earliest tools in the Acheulian Age, or early Stone Age culture. The Acheulian Age lasted from 60,000 to 10,000 years ago. Acheulian remains have been found in western Asia, eastern India, southern Europe and England. But in Africa Acheulian sites are far more numerous than elsewhere. Africa appears to have been the centre of this early Stone Age culture, from which the art of tool-making evolved and spread. At this time African inventiveness far outstripped technological development in any other known region on earth.

If we ignore the dating of the *Homo sapiens* skull found by Richard Leakey, it was during the Acheulian Age and not later than 35,000 years ago that *Homo erectus*, who was mainly a grassland hunter and gatherer, gradually gave way to *Homo sapiens*. *Homo sapiens* then came to occupy the equatorial forest and desert regions of Africa. But other forms of man had also appeared by this time. They included Neanderthal Man, named after a valley in Germany where his fossils were first found. Only *Homo sapiens*, however, survived until modern times.

A reconstruction of Australopithecus, a man-like creature. This early man lived about 1,750,000 years ago in East Africa. ▶

Cultural Developments Between 35,000 and 10,000 years ago, there was considerable variation in the types of tools that were used. There was also, according to the prehistorian J. D. Clark, 'a new self-awareness or concern for matters that had no relation to fulfilling such biological needs as, for example, hunting or mating'. This is shown by the burial of the dead together with food and weapons. This demonstrates a belief in survival after death. It also implies that there was some concept of religion that affected not only the dead, but also imposed some duty on the living. This ritual indicates more complicated social behaviour. It is likely that, at this time, languages developed. Words were needed not simply for the names of everyday objects, but also for abstract concepts. During the new Stone Age that followed, agriculture began and animals were domesticated.

Ancient Egypt

Some prehistorians believe that the invention of agriculture was made in western Asia about 6000 BC. The domestication of sheep and cattle, and the invention of pottery happened about the same time. Not long afterwards, people began to use metals. Bronze tools replaced tools of stone.

These new arts soon reached Egypt. By 3000 BC the Sahara, which had once been a grassland where men could live and find plenty of game for hunting, was drying up. Its people had to leave. They settled along the North African coast or in the grasslands to the south. But in the Nile valley there was always plenty of water. Every year the river brought down a fresh supply of soil from Ethiopia and Uganda.

Gradually the swamps of the Nile delta were cleared and settled by farmers. Some came from higher up the valley, and others from the neighbouring lands of Asia. At first the people settled in small villages. Later they formed larger settlements. They built houses of sun-dried bricks. They found out how to make glass. They used copper and bronze, and began to irrigate the fields.

Life was possible in Egypt only within reach of the Nile. Ancient Egypt therefore consisted of a narrow ribbon of cultivated land along the Nile from Wadi Halfa northward.

Though small, Egypt fell naturally into two parts. The narrow strip to the south was called Upper Egypt. There the desert pressed close to the river. The other part was the broader delta of Lower

Egypt to the north. All Egypt, Upper and Lower, was under pressure from the Negro peoples further south. Lower Egypt was under pressure from the nomadic shepherds of Asia and Libya.

About 3000 BC or a little earlier, a man named Menes from Lower Egypt conquered Upper Egypt. He made himself king of the whole country. He fixed the capital of Egypt at Memphis, almost opposite modern Cairo. Cairo itself was built by the Arabs only 1,300 years ago. After the time of Menes there was a strong feeling that Egypt was one country and that Upper and Lower Egypt ought to hold together. They did not always do so. From time to time civil wars split them apart. Sometimes they were reunited under the rule of Upper Egypt. Thebes, capital of Upper Egypt, became for a time the capital of the whole country.

During the 200 years after Menes's reign, Egypt made great progress. The people began to use stone instead of mud for building. The kings sent to Syria for timber, because Egypt had no large trees. Priests invented the art of writing. Historians believe them to be the first people in the world to do so. Egyptian writing was pictorial. One picture or a group of pictures represented a word. The papyrus reed grew in the Nile delta. From it the Egyptians made paper and pens. They wrote in black ink.

The Sphinx and Great Pyramid of Cheops at Giza. The building of the Egyptian pyramids was an incredible feat of architecture. It took 30 years to build this tomb. ▼

Four or five hundred years later Egyptian civilization was even more impressive. At this time great stone temples and pyramids were built. The priests were strongly organized and the worship of the god Ra and of the king, who was supposed to be the son of Ra, was carried on with great magnificence.

The Spread of Egyptian Civilization Just as Egypt had learned the beginnings of art, agriculture and craftsmanship from its Asian neighbours, so now all its neighbours in Asia and elsewhere were eager to learn what they could of civilization as Egypt had developed it. The ancient Greeks learned these arts and techniques from Egypt, and Greece taught the rest of Europe.

Almost certainly the peoples of Africa to the south also learned pottery making, weaving, agriculture and other arts from Egypt. They may have taken from Egypt the idea of the divine king. In some respects Africans learned less from Egypt than did the Greeks and other Europeans. This was because their circumstances and communications were more difficult. For example, the use of the ox-drawn plough and of the wheel spread to Europe, but not to the rest of Africa.

In Lower Egypt, the fields were broad and there were plenty of oxen with ample fodder. Higher up the Nile, the cultivated land might be only half a mile wide, so that little could be spared for cattle feed. Without oxen, and in small fields divided by irrigation ditches, the plough was not practicable. The hoe was a better implement. Without draught animals the wheel was also of little use.

Similarly, Egyptian arts and crafts, writing and splendid buildings all depended on wealth. They were only possible if there were nobles and priests

The head of a colossal red granite statue of Tuthmosis, king of Egypt, found at Karnak. ▼

who had leisure to think of such things and the money to spend on them. The basis of Egyptian wealth was broad, fertile fields and hard-working peasants.

The more spectacular aspects of Egyptian civilization could not be copied in the rest of Africa. But pottery, weaving, agriculture and cattle rearing spread up the Nile and were diffused along the routes of trade and migration all over Africa.

Ancient Egypt was a bronze-using civilization. The use of iron began quite late in Egyptian history. But bronze tools were not used elsewhere in Africa in ancient times. The Africans to the south passed straight from the Stone Age to the Iron Age. At Meroe in Nubia, between the fifth and sixth cataracts of the Nile, large deposits of iron ore were found. From Meroe, the use of iron spread all over Africa.

A kingdom grew up in Nubia called Kush. The Kushitic kings copied Egyptian civilization. They built temples and pyramids after the Egyptian style though not to Egyptian standards. Kush was conquered by Egypt and remained under Egyptian rule for about 400 years. Then, about 1000 BC, it became independent. It was possibly from Kush that a knowledge of Egyptian ways spread into the rest of Africa.

Egypt's decline In the last thousand years BC, Egyptian power declined. Egypt was conquered by foreign foes, first by Kush, then by Assyria, and then by Persia. In 332 BC, Egypt became part of the Empire of Alexander the Great, who founded the city of Alexandria. After Alexander's death, his general PTOLEMY took possession of Egypt. Ptolemy's descendants ruled it until 30 BC.

◄ A detail from the Book of the Dead of Lady Gheritwebeshet drawn on papyrus. The scene depicts ploughing, sowing and harvesting.

A bronze Egyptian cat, ► dated about 30 BC. The cat was considered to be sacred by the ancient Egyptians.

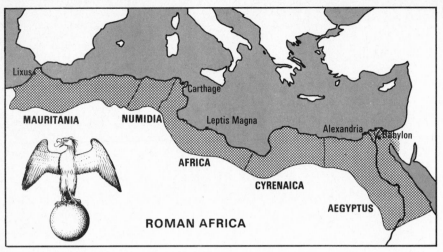

ROMAN AFRICA

Carthage and Rome

The peoples living to the west of Egypt, between the desert and the sea, belonged to the Mediterranean group. About 814 BC, seamen from Tyre and Sidon, Semitic trading cities on the Lebanon coast, founded a colony at Carthage about six kilometres from the centre of the modern city of Tunis. Carthage quickly became the centre of a commercial empire. Carthaginian colonies were founded all along the Mediterranean coast from Tangier to Tripoli, as well as in Spain, Sicily and Sardinia.

In 262 BC war broke out between Carthage and the rising power of Rome. Three long wars were fought between the two powers. They ended in 146 BC with the destruction of Carthage. Though the Berber people gave the Roman armies much trouble before they were finally brought under control, the whole of North Africa became a Roman province. In 30 BC Egypt also became Roman. For 500 years North Africa was part of the Roman empire. It became thoroughly Romanized. Its wheatfields were one of Rome's main sources of food.

In AD 429 Roman Africa was invaded by the Vandals, barbarians who had fought and conquered their way across Germany, France and Spain. They crossed the Strait of Gibraltar to establish a new kingdom in Africa. In AD 439 they took Carthage, and quickly conquered all the coastal lands of Algeria and Tunisia. Egypt and the Libyan coast remained in Roman hands.

Though Roman Africa was well developed, there is no evidence that Roman civilization spread beyond the frontier. The Romans introduced the camel from Arabia. They formed a camel corps in their army to deal with desert raiding bands. This introduction of the camel was the most permanent result of the Roman conquest. It made travel possible across the Sahara.

◄ This terracotta head was made by people whose culture is known as Nok, after the village where the first of this kind of statuette was discovered. The Nok civilization dates back to 900 BC.

A head, probably ► representing an early Oni of Ife excavated at Ife, Nigeria. This head is made from an alloy of copper and zinc and is thought to date from 1300 AD.

The ruins of Carthage recall the greatness that the ancient city once achieved as centre of a great commercial empire. ▼

Early Developments in West Africa

Little is yet known of the earliest history of the peoples of West Africa south of the Sahara. About 900 BC a group of people living in northern Nigeria produced very distinctive statuettes in baked clay. The culture of these people is called the Nok culture. Nok is a village where the first statuette was discovered in 1931. Historians know little about the Nok culture. Only the statuettes survived, because damp and termites have destroyed many relics of the culture, although excavations are still to take place. But it seems possible that the Nok culture may have lasted until about AD 900.

The art of lost-wax casting in bronze is known all over West Africa. But some of its early examples, the famous Ife bronzes, are probably not older than AD 1000. It would seem, then, that although the art was known in ancient Egypt, it probably reached West Africa across the Saharan trade routes in Muslim times. By about 300 BC, iron-working had spread all along the savanna belt of West Africa. New groups of craftsmen and traders emerged from the societies previously based on subsistence farming.

The Bantu About 100 BC a major group of peoples arose consisting of the Bantu-speaking people. They may have arisen somewhere in the Congo (now Zaire) basin or, more likely, in the mountains of Cameroon. As they multiplied, they moved southward and eastward through the Congo valley and on to the East Africa plateau. The Bantu used iron. They grew millet and kept goats, later also cows. They moved slowly. By about AD 900 they had reached as far south as Sofala in Mozambique. The southernmost of the Bantu peoples, the Xhosa, arrived at the Fish River in South Africa in 1776.

During their migration some of the Bantu peoples developed the art of irrigation by water-channels dug along the contours of hills— that is, the channels followed a level course. Although most Bantu lost the art of contour-irrigation, some still preserve it. In the greater part of the lands that they occupied there was no suitable building stone and, for this reason, they built huts of wattle. At various places in East and Central Africa, where a supply of suitable stone was available, some people erected stone buildings. The most famous were at Zimbabwe, in central Africa. The date of Zimbabwe is uncertain. The site was first occupied by an iron-using people about AD 300 but most of the principal existing buildings were erected around 1400. These buildings continued to be enlarged until about 1830.

Historians consider that by about AD 1000 the whole of East and Central Africa was occupied by the Bantu. Older inhabitants, such as the Hottentots and Bushmen, could not hold back the Bantu with their iron spears and their greater numbers. Enough of the Bushmen and others were absorbed into the Bantu to impart to some of the southern Bantu languages their characteristic clicks. But most were destroyed or pushed into less desirable places, such as the Kalahari. A few remained as isolated groups of hunters and food-gatherers. They were surrounded by the Bantu.

Nubia and the Arabs Meanwhile, the state of Kush in the Nile valley was becoming weaker. It was conquered by Rome, and parts of its northern lands were annexed. To the south-east, a new state grew up with its capital at Axum in the Ethiopian mountains. It was successful, because it controlled the coast of Eritrea and the sea trade route to southern Arabia. Its rulers spoke a Semitic language. Thanks to elaborate irrigation, southern Arabia was greener and more fruitful than it is today. About AD 350 Axum conquered Kush, and the state of Kush broke into two—the kingdom of Dongola and the kingdom of Alwa. Alwa had its capital at Soba on the Blue Nile. By the mid-500s, all three Nubian kingdoms—Dongola, Alwa and Axum—had become Christian.

The trade which Axum maintained with Arabia was important, because Yemen was the chief source of incense, which was in great demand in ancient times. Not only was southern Arabia productive, but its people were great traders and seamen. They explored the Indian Ocean, and discovered the regular monsoon winds. These winds make it easy

▲ This Chinese flask, made in about AD 1300 was found in Tanzania. Trade between East Africa and China occurred from about the mid-1100s.

Bushmen paintings of ▶ hunters and eland in Ndema Gorge, Natal. Some Bushmen paintings are of ancient origin.

Most of the Zimbabwe ruins were probably built around 1400, but the site was occupied from about AD 300. ▼

for a sailing ship to go from East Africa to India between May and October and to return between November and April. They pushed on down the East African coast. After AD 700 they founded such trading settlements as Kismayu, Mogadiscio, Gedi, Malindi, Mombasa, Kilwa and many more. They inter-married with the Bantu people of the coast, and a mixed language and culture, Swahili, grew up in the coastal region. From East Africa, the Arabs exported ivory, slaves, gold and copper. They brought in manufactured goods from Asia, including such luxuries as Chinese silk and porcelain after about AD 1150. They introduced valuable new crops, including the banana and the Asiatic yam.

The influence of Islam

When Islam was founded by Muhammad (*c.* AD 570–632), the links between East Africa and Arabia were strengthened. Groups of merchants from southern Arabia and Persia emigrated to the East African coastal towns. Around 1100, Islam spread along the East African coast. Its influence extended as far south as Sofala, in what is now Mozambique, the coast of the island of Madagascar and the Comoro Islands. But in medieval times Islam did not penetrate to the African peoples who lived inland. Elsewhere in Africa, however, Islam did penetrate rapidly and deeply. The Arabs conquered Egypt in 641. By the end of the century they had carried Islam to the Atlantic Ocean.

In 711, the Berber leader Tarik crossed the Strait of Gibraltar and began the Muslim conquest of Spain. The word Gibraltar comes from the term Jabal-al-Tarik, which means 'the hill of Tarik'. In southern Spain and northern Africa, a flourishing Muslim civilization grew up. It developed art, literature and architecture. It preserved ancient Greek literature and thought as well as Egyptian science and mathematics.

The Christian kingdoms of Alwa, Dongola and Axum then had to face increasing pressure from Islam. The Muslim rulers of Egypt, like their predecessors, the Pharaohs, often attacked Nubia. From about 750 onwards a new Muslim threat developed

▲ Arab dhows were used from ancient times for trade and were important in the spread of Islam into Africa.

A detail from an early map of North Africa drawn by the Majorcan cartographer Abraham Cresques in 1375. ▼

from the east. Arab immigrants came across the Red Sea and settled on the Blue Nile upstream from Soba, the capital of Alwa. This new Muslim settlement developed into a strong state called Funj, and it cut off the southernmost kingdom of Axum from the other two.

Muslims from Egypt fanned out westward along the savanna and founded other Muslim states, such as Kordofan and Darfur. Dongola thus became hemmed in. In 1351 it had to surrender to Egypt its territory north of the third cataract. Axum, harried by the Muslims of Funj and by new Muslim immigrants coming in from the Gulf of Aden, retreated into the mountains. There, the people developed into the isolated Christian kingdom of Ethiopia. Its memory was preserved in the stories of the Christian king Prester John. Christian Ethiopia was a powerful stimulus to the crusading and exploring spirit of western Europe.

Dongola and Alwa stood out against the rising Muslim tide. From 1517 onwards Egypt and nearly the whole of the North African coast came under Turkish rule. The Turks, having already occupied much of south-eastern Europe, launched a powerful attack on Alwa and Dongola. They colonized the country with Muslims from Europe. There were still Christian churches in Nubia in the early part of the 1500s. But Christianity was probably extinguished there by Turkish colonization.

The Saharan Trade Routes The Sahara had never become so dry as to be totally uninhabitable. However, without the introduction of the camel, it could have been inhabited only by farmers and herdsmen moving from one oasis to another. The distance that they could move had to be within range of the endurance of their sheep and goats. With the camel longer journeys became possible.

Regular trade routes developed from one oasis to another across the desert. The desert itself produced salt. The savanna country south of the desert produced gold, ivory, slaves, hides and skins, the basis of the famous Moroccan leather trade. The forest country produced kola nuts. These nuts were important because, although they were a mild stimulant, even strict Muslims were permitted to eat them. Muslim theologians held that the ban on alcohol in the Koran did not apply to kola nuts. North of the desert there was all the rich produce of the Muslim world and of the East. This produce included Damascus steel, silk and cotton fabrics from India and China, tools, manufactured goods of all kinds, and books.

Contacts with the Western Sudan The most important routes to the western Sudan, the name commonly used for West Africa south of the Sahara, started from Morocco and Tunis. The southern oases of Bilma and Agades brought one route from Tunis into the savanna country of northern Nigeria. Other routes reached the Niger River near Timbuktu. An important route from Sijilmasa in Morocco kept well to the west. It reached the savanna in what is now the country of Mali between the Niger and the Senegal rivers. In those days, this region was one of the main gold-producing areas. At the head of this westernmost trade route, the earliest of the medieval kingdoms of the western Sudan developed. This was the kingdom of Ghana.

The Western Sudan Knowledge of ancient Ghana, and of its successor ancient Mali, is limited. Most information came from geographers, not historians. Arab geographers of North Africa wrote descriptions of these kingdoms. The most notable of these writers was AL BAKRI. He did not himself visit Ghana. He described it as it was in 1068 from information given him by merchants and others who knew the country. IBN BATTUTA, who travelled over the whole Muslim world from his home in Tangier as far as India and China, spent some months in Mali during 1353. He left a full description of his experiences.

There are occasional references in the works of other geographers. In the 1600s the Sudanese writer Ibn-al-Mukhtar wrote a history called *Tarikh al-Fettach*. Another Sudanese historian, Es-Sadi, wrote *Tarikh al-Sudan*. But these works, though reasonably full on events that occurred in the later kingdom of Songhai, tells us hardly anything about Ghana and not very much about Ghana's successor, Mali. Archaeologists have so far discovered few datable objects and no historical inscriptions. All three kingdoms were basically Negro and non-Muslim.

With the camel as a means of transport, the Sahara was easily crossed by the Arabs. They travelled in caravans to trade with the peoples south of the Sahara and their scholars recorded much information about the kingdoms and empires that flourished in West Africa in the Middle Ages.

The Great Mosque at Djenné (or Jenné) in Mali. Djenné was probably founded in the AD 700s by the Songhai people, but it became an especially important commercial centre between 1100 and 1500. ▼

Ancient Ghana According to the *Tarikh al-Sudan* the early kings of Ghana were 'white'. It is possible that the kingdom began when Arab or Berber merchant-adventurers, with camels or horses and with superior weapons, established authority over the Soninke people. But this 'white' ruling dynasty, if it ever existed, was overthrown by a Negro dynasty. Al-Bakri wrote that in his day the king of Ghana was not a Muslim, although there was a strong Muslim influence in the country. The king whom he mentioned, named Tenkamenin, came to the throne in succession to his mother's brother, who had been buried in the traditional fashion with human sacrifices and with a store of food, drink and clothing for his use in the spirit-world.

Throughout medieval history, the trade pattern remained the same. The Sudanese kingdoms were subject to the same conditions and the same temptations. The Arab or Berber desert peoples controlled the caravan routes across the desert and the supply of the desert products, including the salt of Taghaza and Taodeni and the copper of Takedda.

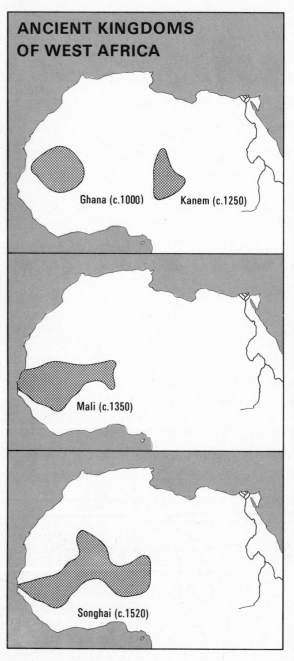

ANCIENT KINGDOMS OF WEST AFRICA

Ghana (c.1000)   Kanem (c.1250)

Mali (c.1350)

Songhai (c.1520)

Above and below Ancient brass weights used for weighing gold dust in Ashanti, Ghana.

◀ Maps showing the major ancient kingdoms and empires of West Africa.

The Western Sudanese kingdoms never controlled the forest country which supplied kola nuts. They did not usually control the gold mines. They were always tempted to try and gain control of the supplies of the caravan routes, and so cut out several sets of middlemen's profits.

In 992, Ghana captured its chief trading rival, the Berber town of Audoghast on the northern road. But this attack on a Muslim town produced a reaction. The Almoravid movement, which began 50 years later, was one of the many religious reform movements which arose from time to time in the Muslim world. It reunited all the Berber tribes and conquered all Morocco and Muslim Spain. It recaptured Audoghast, and in 1076 the Almoravid leader Abu Bakr conquered Ghana itself.

Ancient Mali After the Almoravid conquest, the kingdom of Ghana fell to pieces. Later there was a revival. Under the leadership of a man named Sundiata (or Mari Diata, 1230–55), a new kingdom began to grow up on the headwaters of the Niger River. It developed into the state of Mali. Mali was powerful for about 150 years.

Its most famous king was Mansa MUSA (1307–1332), a grandson of Sundiata. When Mansa Musa went on pilgrimage to Mecca in 1324, he travelled with a large escort. He was the talk of the town of Cairo for his piety and generosity, and his people's good behaviour. Under Mansa Musa the kingdom of Mali became famous in the Muslim world. It was also known to European map-makers. Musa entered into diplomatic relations with several Muslim states. He took trouble to attract to his kingdom scholars and theologians from as far afield as Syria.

The authority of the king of Mali stretched from his capital at Niani (near the modern town of Bamako) over the headwaters of the Niger and Senegal rivers. It included the gold-bearing area. It reached the Niger as far as Gao, but the important city of Jenne was independent. Mali controlled the salt of Taghaza and the copper of Takedda. The kingdom in its heyday was about 1,600 kilometres across in each direction. On the east, its power was checked by three states—the Songhai people of the middle Niger, the Berbers of Agades, and the Moshi kingdoms of Ouagadougou and Yatenga.

The Arab traveller Ibn Battuta, speaking 30 years after Musa's day in the time of Mansa Sulaiman (1341–60), was impressed by the number of lawyers and educated men he found in Mali. He noted that there were many books and that great care was taken over children's schooling. He praised the music and dancing and other entertainments and was impressed by the beautiful clothes made of fine materials imported from Egypt. He also mentioned the absolute security and peacefulness everywhere, and the upright administration of justice.

There was no coined money. Gold dust was used for large payments, and cowrie shells for small change. But in small villages there was still much barter. For this purpose Ibn Battuta found it convenient to carry salt, beads and spices on his travels. Having travelled to India and China, Ibn Battuta thought little of the mud brick architecture of Mali. He disliked the customs of reckoning succession through the mother, and of showing reverence to the king by pouring dust on one's head. As a strict Muslim, he was shocked by the way women moved freely in society.

All these western Sudanese kingdoms were strong and stable as long as the king was known to be active. It took three months to cross Mali from side to side. There were no natural frontiers. There were many varieties of language and custom. Literacy was restricted to a small class of learned men and officials. Administration had to be decentralized. Rebellion and corruption within, and attack from foes outside, were held in check only as long as the king kept moving with a strong cavalry force. In this way, he showed and enforced his authority.

Songhai The Songhai people had their capital at Gao on the Niger River. For many years, they were dominated by Mali. But at the end of the 1300s, they freed themselves. Under their king SONNI ALI (1464–92), they expanded their power greatly. They captured the university town of Timbuktu, which the desert Berbers had taken from Mali 30 years earlier. They captured Jenne, which had always defied Mali and defeated the Mossi.

On Sonni Ali's death in 1492, the throne was usurped by his great minister Askia Muhammad Abu-Bakr, who ruled for 30 years with great military glory. The minister had the reputation of being a

▲ An Ashanti terracotta funerary head found in Ghana.

great supporter of learning and an upholder of the Faith. But after him the dynasty became weaker.

The Songhai capture of the Taghaza saltmines irritated the king of Morocco. Morocco was a dangerous enemy. It had been strengthened by the immigration of the Muslims of Granada, who had been expelled when Spain conquered it in 1492. Morocco had been enriched in 1578 when it inflicted a crushing defeat on a Portuguese invading army and held half the Portuguese nobility to ransom. In 1590, the Sharif of Morocco, having spent his money lavishly on buying the latest firearms from Elizabeth I of England, invaded Songhai and conquered it. All the learned men of Songhai were deported to Morocco. Their books were confiscated or destroyed. The cultural and economic development of western Sudan received a shock.

The Moorish army of occupation refused to recross the desert. It remained and set itself up as a rather feeble independent state. Islam ceased to be a state religion and lingered on merely as a personal religion. New kingdoms then arose with pagan rulers. But the tradition of Ghana, Mali and Songhai remained alive.

Hausaland and Kanem-Bornu During the 1000s and 1100s a group of states was growing up just east of the Songhai. These were the Hausa states. Islam came to them in the 1300s. They grew strong enough to win their freedom again after having been conquered by Askia Muhammad. Further east still the Kanuri, whose rulers became Muslim in the 1000s, built up the strong state of Kanem-Bornu. Kanem-Bornu had two periods of glory. The first was in the 1100s and 1200s when its power reached as far west as Kano and as far east as Wadai. The second was contemporary with Askia Muhammad.

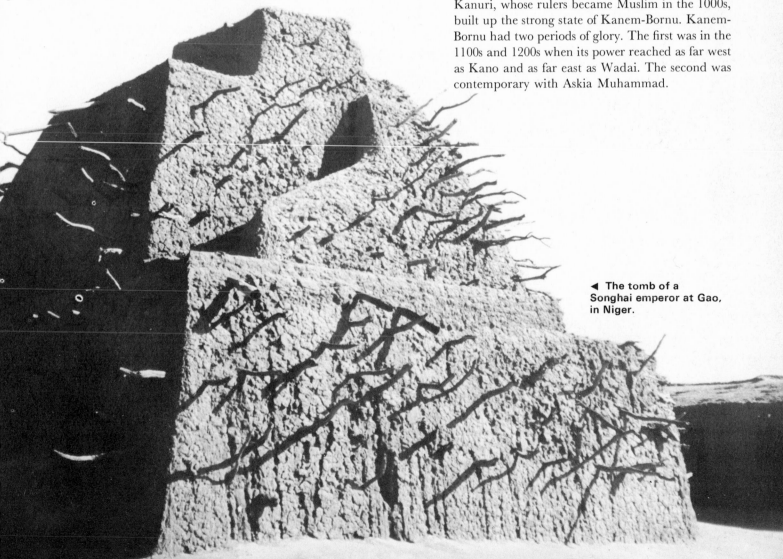

◀ The tomb of a Songhai emperor at Gao, in Niger.

East and Central Africa

In the region of the great lakes, new states were rising through the fusion of pastoral with agricultural peoples. The Bahima or Bachwezi culture flourished in modern Uganda between 1350 and 1500. About 1500, the Bachwezi were overthrown by Luo immigrants from the north-east. The Bachwezi state of Kitara broke up. From its fragments, there developed the states of Bunyoro, Ankole, Toro, Buganda and others, which lasted until modern times.

In the 1400s a string of kingdoms arose which stretched from the northern part of modern Angola through the modern Republic of Zaire as far as Zimbabwe. Some of these were highly centralized. Others were loose federations each under a hereditary ruler. The best known was the Kingdom of Kongo. About 1450, far away to the south-east a group of Shona clans crossed the Zambezi into what is now Zimbabwe. Their war-chief was so great a fighter that the earlier Bantu peoples, whom he met and conquered, nicknamed him 'the great plunderer', Mwana Mtapa. He took the nickname as a title of honour. The centralized kingdom, which he founded, became rich and famous for its gold, which was exported to the Arabs at Sofala. The name 'Monomotapa' (whether as the name of a man or of his country) was heard of in Europe and marked on European maps. The Portuguese had heard of him. They had also heard of Sonni Ali of Songhai. Everyone in Europe had heard of Prester John. The Portuguese formed the idea of establishing relations with these great kings.

Early European Contact The Portuguese led the way in early European contacts with Africa. There were good reasons for this. Nearly the whole of Spain and Portugal had at one time been occupied by Muslims from North Africa. Ever since 711, the Christians had been engaged in an up-and-down struggle to reconquer the peninsula, and Portugal was eager to carry the war into Africa. Castile and Aragon were active in European politics. Portugal was poor and remote, and Africa was its one outlet. The Portuguese had hopes of tapping the valuable Sahara trade from the south.

In 1299, Europe was startled by the publication of Marco Polo's account of his long stay in China. For the first time people in Europe learned that there was a great civilized country at the ends of the earth, beyond the Turks and the nomads of Asia. The Turks had reduced trade with the Far East to a mere trickle. That trickle was monopolized by Venice. Genoa, the great rival of Venice, tried but failed to outflank the Turks and reach China by sea. Portuguese seamen, learning from the Genoese, picked up the idea. Prince Henry the Navigator of Portugal (1394–1461) read Marco Polo's book and determined to explore the African coast.

In 1418 the Portuguese reached Madeira, and in 1439 the Azores. But the survey of the unpromising desert coast of north-west Africa was slow at first. In 1442, they picked up the first gold at Rio de Oro. In 1446 they passed beyond the desert

and saw green trees at the mouth of the Senegal River. After that, progress was quicker. In 1460 they reached Sierra Leone and in 1471 the Gold Coast. In 1484 they sailed up the Congo River, which they called Zaire from the Kongo word *zaidi* meaning 'water'. In 1488 they came to Table Bay and sailed a little way further into the Indian Ocean.

The European Circumnavigation of Africa

The breakthrough came in 1498, when Vasco da Gama sailed up the east coast of Africa. He found the gold of Sofala and heard that Monomotapa was not far away. He visited the wealthy Arab trading cities. He obtained an Arab pilot Ibn Majid, at Malindi. The pilot guided him to India on the winds of the monsoon. In less than 20 years, after the conquest of Malacca in 1511, the Portuguese established their power in the East Indies. They had done it all without Spain. The king of Spain decided to back Christopher Columbus. Spanish efforts then went into opening up the New World which Columbus discovered.

Early Settlements and Trade The Portuguese did not push all their effort into this circumnavigation. With permission from Sonni Ali of Songhai, they occupied a trading post for a few years at Wadan on the western Sahara route. They sent missions to Mali and to Timbuktu. But such isolated ventures in the interior were less effective than the string of fortified posts which the Portuguese were building along the Guinea coast.

The Moorish conquest of Songhai in 1591 weakened the trading links between the Sudan and North Africa. The Moors on the Niger made themselves independent, and the king of Morocco was occupied in fighting the Turks, who had already seized Tunis and Algiers.

The appearance of the Portuguese on the Guinea coast in time transformed the whole pattern of West African trade. The savanna country, formerly the centre of civilization, gradually became a remote backwater. But the coastal peoples were now on the main highway of world trade.

The Portuguese had thus succeeded in one of their three main objectives. They had tapped the Guinea gold trade. By 1505 they succeeded in a second. Their posts at Quelimane and Sofala tapped the gold supply of Monomotapa. Later in the 1500s the Portuguese tried to conquer and hold the gold-producing country for themselves. But the attempt failed and the gold supply came to an end.

Their third objective was to get in touch with Prester John. In 1487 Pedro da Covilhao left Portugal on this diplomatic mission. Four years later, he found his way into Ethiopia by way of the Red Sea, and resided at the Ethiopian court from 1491–1525. But although the Christian kingdom really existed, it was a disappointment to the Portuguese. Hemmed in by Muslims, the Christian Ethiopians could not hope to lead a victorious crusade. What was worse from the point of view of the Roman Catholic Portuguese, the Ethiopian Church did not acknowledge the authority of Rome. It did not welcome Catholic missionaries.

A superb Benin bronze ▶ figure of a Portuguese musketeer armed with a flintlock. This figure was probably made in the 1600s. The Portuguese had established relations with the kingdom of Benin in the previous century.

In 1498 the Portuguese explorer Vasco da Gama became the first man to circumnavigate the continent of Africa. ▼

The Beginnings of the Slave Trade Gold was what the Portuguese most wanted, and at various places they found it. They also began the slave trade in a small way. In the early 1500s there was a fashion in Europe for Negro domestic servants. In spite of papal disapproval, the Portuguese bought slaves in Africa to supply this comparatively small market. The slave trade began on a large scale in 1517, when Spain began importing slaves for labour in American mines and plantations. English, French and Dutch soon joined the trade.

Throughout the 1500s, the Portuguese held strings of fortified trading posts both on the eastern and western coasts. They entered into relations with various West African states, especially Benin (a small kingdom in Nigeria that was notable for its art) and Kongo. Both of these states surprised the Portuguese by their wealth and culture. In the Indian Ocean, the Portuguese had an ambitious commercial empire. Its headquarters and naval base was at Goa in India. Malindi and Mombasa were trading stations on the route to India.

The stations on the west coast of Africa came under increasing attack from the Dutch. Between 1637 and 1642 the Dutch captured all the Portuguese forts in the Gold Coast and Angola. In the Indian Ocean the Dutch attacked the Portuguese settlements in the Spice Islands. Between 1698 and 1739 the Arabs captured all the East African stations north of Cape Delgado.

The slave trade quickly came to be more important than the trade in gold, ivory and other produce. The administration of the whole of the coastal region of West Africa, from the Senegal River down to Angola, was reorganized to supply slaves. In exchange, Africa received liquor, firearms, European manufactured goods, textiles and hardware.

New African states developed, such as Ashanti and Dahomey, whose economic life depended to a significant extent on their activity as wholesale suppliers of slaves to the African coastal middlemen who sold them to the Europeans. This continuous export of people had a depressing effect on African cultural and economic development.

A slave ship. The Atlantic slave trade was at its height between the 1500s and 1800s. ▼

▲ **Jan van Riebeck was a Dutch surgeon who established the first European settlement in southern Africa—Cape Town. The chief purpose of this settlement was to supply ships en route between Europe and Asia with water and fresh food.**

A map showing the routes of some of the most important European explorers. ▼

Interest in the Interior Meanwhile, Europe knew nothing of the interior of Africa. The Africans kept the Europeans pinned to their coastal settlements. The source of the Nile was a mystery. The existence of the Niger was known, but most geographers thought that it flowed east to join the Nile. No one suspected that the creeks from Benin to Calabar in Nigeria formed the delta of the Niger.

In 1652 the Dutch planted a settlement at Cape Town. They grew fruit and vegetables and raised sheep and cattle, to supply their ships with fresh provisions for the long voyage to the East Indies. But the huge empty continent lured the settlers away from their cabbage patches and cow sheds. In spite of prohibitions they insisted on moving inland. In 1776 the advancing Dutch settlers met the southern-most parties of the advancing Bantu-speaking peoples. The Dutch and Bantu became direct competitors for the grazing lands. In this way, the South African racial problem first arose.

The European penetration of the interior of Africa began partly through the missionary and humanitarian movement in Britain in the 1700s. It was also partly due to the geographical interest in Captain Cook's explorations in the Pacific.

One of the earliest anti-slavery measures was the purchase in 1787 of a small piece of land at Sierra Leone to be a home for freed slaves, Freetown. Protestant Christian missionary work began almost at once. It began on the Gold Coast in 1827 and in Kenya in 1844.

THE EXPLORERS

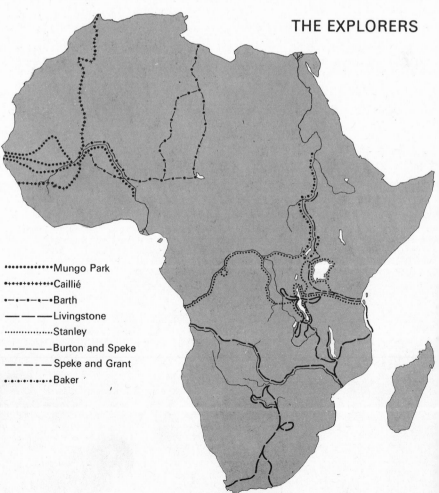

•••••••••••Mungo Park
•+•+•+•+•+•Caillié
•–•–•–•Barth
————Livingstone
••••••••••••Stanley
———————Burton and Speke
— — — — Speke and Grant
•–•–•–•Baker

Interior Exploration Early European explorers aimed at solving the mystery of the Niger River. The Scotsman Mungo PARK found the source of the Niger and sailed down it to the Bussa rapids, where he was drowned. His work was continued by others. In 1830, the Niger was found to flow into the delta which the British called the Oil Rivers. Consequently it was shown that the Niger and the Nile were not connected.

The Frenchman René CAILLE crossed the Sahara and saw Timbuktu. In the 1850s, the German traveller Heinrich BARTH explored the Saharan trade routes. He exposed the Arab slave trade, which was being run from West Africa.

In 1841 the greatest explorer of all, David LIVINGSTONE, set out on the first of his three great journeys. Between 1841 and his death in the heart of Africa 31 years later, Livingstone crossed the continent from Quelimane (Mozambique) to Luanda (Angola). He discovered the Victoria Falls and explored the course of the Zambezi. He visited Lake Nyasa and trod and retrod the country around Lake Tanganyika.

Livingstone, more than anyone else, showed that it was possible for Europeans to live and work happily in central Africa. He broke the terror of the unknown that had held back Europeans for so long. Another result of Livingstone's travels was that Europe was awakened to the brutality of the Arab slave trade in East Africa. The desire to police the interior of Africa and stop slavery at its source was one of the motives for European colonization. Another reason was that Europeans realized from the accounts of explorers that Africa was a huge continent on their doorstep which was awaiting exploitation. The possibilities of trade were not lost on an industrializing Europe.

Two German missionaries, Johann Ludwig Krapf and Johannes Rebmann, set out from their base near Mombasa in the 1840s. They saw the snows of Mount Kenya and Kilimanjaro. From 1856 onward great efforts were made to discover the source of the Nile. The Englishman John Hanning SPEKE saw Lake Victoria in 1858. Two years later, with his colleague James GRANT, he entered Uganda and saw the Nile leaving Lake Victoria at Jinja.

Henry Morton STANLEY's great journey of 1874–6 explored the shores of lakes Victoria and Tanganyika, and proved that they were not connected. Stanley then carried out one of Livingstone's unfulfilled projects. He went down the Lualaba River to the Congo River and then, negotiating many rapids, journeyed down to the Atlantic Ocean. By 1890 the geography of the Niger, Congo and Nile basins was well known.

John Hanning Speke ▶ was the first European to locate the source of the Nile.

◀ David Livingstone was the most remarkable of all European explorers in Africa. His reports helped to accelerate the ending of slavery.

David Livingstone and Henry Morton Stanley explored Lake Tanganyika together. Later, Stanley explored the Zaire basin. ▼

Early Colonization After the missionaries and the explorers came commercial men and imperialists. Who could tell what undiscovered wealth lay in Africa?

In the 1830s the French had annexed Algeria although many bitter campaigns still had to be fought to keep it. In the 1850s they pushed inland from their bases on the Senegal coast and occupied the area at the upper reaches of the Niger. The British annexed Lagos in 1861. In 1874 they proclaimed a colony over the coastal region of the Gold Coast. Following Stanley's exploration of the Congo basin, King Léopold II of Belgium formed the International African Association to open up the region, apparently in the interests of civilization and science, but also for commercial reasons. Trade rivalry began to develop. It included rivalry for the ivory of Uganda and the Congo basin, and also for the palm-oil of the Niger delta.

North Africa Napoleon's invasion of Egypt in 1798 had focused European attention upon the Nile valley—both for its ancient wonders and its strategic importance.

During the 1860s, Egypt was ruled by Khedive Ismail, an energetic man, who did much to modernize his country. He spent money on education and irrigation. He also had ambitious plans for opening up the Sudan. He employed the explorer Samuel BAKER and the British General Gordon for this purpose. In 1869, the Suez Canal was opened. The canal brought not only India, but also East Africa, much nearer to Europe. The canal was especially important to the British, who regarded it as the 'lifeline' of their empire. In 1874, the British prime minister, Benjamin Disraeli, purchased some 40 per cent of the Suez Canal shares, giving Britain effective control of the Suez Canal Company.

Egypt faced financial difficulties. The reformer Ismail did not know how to manage money. Eventually his financial problems led to the appointment of a Franco-British dual control over Egyptian finances. This provoked a nationalist rising under ARABI PASHA. In 1882 Britain sent troops to occupy Egypt for a few months while British financial administrators set the country on its feet again.

This action earned Britain the hostility of France. As a result France became Britain's rival everywhere in Africa. This rivalry continued until the early part of the 1900s when the British and French governments, in the face of a threat from Germany, came to a comprehensive agreement and formed a dual *entente* (agreement or understanding). Britain found it easier to send troops into Egypt than to withdraw them, and the troops stayed on for more than 70 years.

In 1885, General Gordon was killed when the town of Khartoum fell to the MAHDI, a religious leader in the Sudan. In 1898, the British General Kitchener led a joint Anglo-Egyptian expedition up the Nile to defeat the Sudanese at the battle of Omdurman. An Anglo-Egyptian Condominium (an arrangement for joint rule) was then established over the Sudan. The British considered the Sudan to be of great strategic importance, because it controlled the Upper Nile. This in turn controlled Egypt, which contained the Suez Canal.

Steadily from 1880 onward, France expanded its interests in North and West Africa. After Britain's occupation of Egypt, France speeded up its activities. The French established a protectorate over Tunisia in 1883. Much later, following the *entente* between Britain and France in 1904, Britain recognized France's special rights in Morocco. In 1911, the Italians invaded and colonized Tripoli (now Libya).

A detail from a painting of the Battle of Isandhlwana (1879) fought between the Zulus, under their king, Cetewayo, and the British. The Zulus won this battle. ▼

178

The Scramble for Africa In the second half of the 1800s, Africa was transformed in European eyes from a dark and dangerous continent to one of immense possibilities and opportunities. After the British occupation of Egypt and the Belgian interest in the Congo, the so-called 'scramble for Africa' began.

Two things sparked off the scramble. First King Léopold of the Belgians had established the International African Association 'for the purpose of promoting the civilization and commerce of Africa and for other human and benevolent purposes'. Léopold's pressure for international recognition of what was shortly to become the Congo Free State led to the holding of the Berlin Conference of 1884–5, under the chairmanship of the German statesman Otto von Bismarck.

The second cause of the scramble was the tension between France and Germany in Europe. This tension persuaded Bismarck, whose own policy was opposed to colonial expansion, to do his utmost to embroil France and Britain in Africa. This would leave Germany freer to pursue its ambitions in Europe.

The Berlin Conference laid down rules for avoiding dangerous quarrels over African soil. However,

Above left Arabi Pasha opposed the increasing foreign influence in Egypt in the late 1800s. He led an uprising in 1881–2, but was defeated by the British at the battle of Tel el Kebir in 1882.

Above centre The British General Gordon was killed at Khartoum in 1885 by the troops of the Mahdi.

Above right The Mahdi led a revolt against Turkish oppression in the Sudan. By 1885 he controlled the entire country.

The painting *Inside the 2nd Brigade Square* shows the battle of Tamai (1884) in the First Sudan War. ▼

these same rules made it inevitable that Africa should be rapidly parcelled up into colonies. No Africans were present at the conference. Afterwards the scramble proceeded at great speed.

The French annexed the great bulk of West and Equatorial Africa, apart from the four British West African enclaves of Gambia, Sierra Leone, the Gold Coast and Nigeria. Nigeria's northern borders were not finally settled between France and Britain until just before World War I. The Congo Free State became the property of the King of Belgium.

Following an Anglo-German treaty in 1890, Britain consolidated its East African possessions. Britain proclaimed a protectorate over Zanzibar and the coastal strip of Kenya that year. In 1894, it proclaimed another protectorate over Uganda and a third over East Africa (later Kenya Colony) in 1895. Germany also established its East African colony, which was later called Tanganyika.

Southern Africa Meanwhile in southern Africa, the discovery of diamonds in 1869 and then gold in 1886 had spurred the British to renewed economic interest in colonial expansion. The Portuguese, encouraged by Germany, were moving inland in both Angola and Mozambique.

The British, seeing the possibility of being cut off from their possessions to the north, annexed Bechuanaland (now Botswana). This prevented a joint German–Portuguese advance. The Portuguese had been hoping to link their colonies in south-eastern and south-western Africa. At the same time, Germany had been trying to move across the continent along the Caprivi Strip. In 1890 Cecil RHODES sent a joint Anglo-Afrikaner ·column of settlers to establish 'Rhodesia'. Britain annexed Northern Rhodesia (now Zambia) and Nyasaland (now Malawi).

Quite suddenly the scramble was over. In a very short time, practically all of Africa had been annexed into the empires of Britain, France, Germany, Portugal and, a little later, Belgium and Italy. For a time only Liberia and Ethiopia managed to maintain a precarious independence.

Imperial Consolidation Once the scramble was over, the European powers forgot about their new territories in Africa to an astonishing extent. Increasingly they turned their attention toward each other in a tense Europe, which was heading toward World War I.

In the African colonies, the main objective of the administrations was consolidation. In many areas Africans resisted colonial rule, because they saw no point in giving their allegiance to foreign powers. For example, between 1895 and 1908 the British sent no less than five expeditions of 'pacification' against the Nandi of East Africa alone. In 1905 in German East Africa, the heroic Maji-Maji Rebellion was put down only with great loss of life. In German South-West Africa (now Namibia), a Herero revolt in 1903 led to a brutal war of extermination by the Germans.

In South Africa war between the British and the Afrikaners broke out in 1899. It was called the Boer War. Britain won this war only after mobilizing an army of 250,000. Peace came in 1902. The Union of South Africa was established in 1910 and the country was given dominion status—that is, it became self-governing. Effectively, therefore, Britain passed over control of the African population of the Union to the white settler minority.

In 1908, a scandal in the Congo burst upon the world. Until then, the Congo Free State had been run as the personal possession of King Leopold. But news of forced labour and atrocities of an appalling nature became public knowledge. The Belgian parliament then took over the Free State from the king. The country became the Belgian Congo.

World War I (1914–1918) ended German colonial power in Africa. Joint Anglo-French expeditions took over German Kamerun and Togoland. An expedition from South Africa took over German South-West Africa. In German East Africa, an Anglo-Boer, Indian and African force fought a four-year campaign against the Germans. At the end of the war the newly founded League of Nations declared the German colonies to be *mandates*—that is, countries whose government was granted to other powers, acting for the League of Nations.

German East Africa became the British Mandate of Tanganyika. German South-West Africa was mandated to South Africa. The German Kamerun and Togoland were both split between Britain and France. Many Africans had served as soldiers or porters in the imperial armies. One result of this was the return home in 1918 of a generation of young Africans, who began to question the whole basis of European power in Africa.

A column of troops advancing during the Boer War. The war was fought in South Africa from 1899 to 1902 between the British and the Boer settlers. ▼

◄ During World War I, the King's African Rifles engaged in a four-year campaign against German troops in East Africa. The photograph shows a K.A.R. machine-gun crew.

Colonial Stagnation The period between World Wars I and II saw little political progress in most of colonial Africa. Serious disturbances took place in Egypt in 1922 against British occupation. In 1936, and Anglo-Egyptian treaty was signed to last 20 years.

In 1923, bitter rivalry between British and Indian settlers in Kenya resulted in the Devonshire Declaration. This stated that the interests of the Africans must be paramount and protected against any settlers. Although this was not acted upon for another 40 years, the statement provided a vital tool in the hands of African nationalists.

In 1923 Britain granted an unusual constitution to the Colony of Southern Rhodesia. It enabled the minority group of white settlers to control the internal government of the colony. This gave the settlers effective political power up to 1965, when they illegally declared the colony independent.

The great world slump of 1929 hit the colonial economies of Africa, especially such commodities as copper in the Congo and Northern Rhodesia. In 1935, Italy made clear its intention of annexing Ethiopia. After a period of attempted appeasement by the great powers, Italy invaded and conquered Ethiopia in 1936. For a few years only Liberia, which was dominated by American finance, was free of actual colonial occupation.

World War II (1939–1945) saw major fighting in Egypt and Libya. Finally, the Italians and their allies, the Germans, were driven out of North Africa in 1943. Another major event in Africa was the British campaign against the Italians in East Africa. This led to the liberation of Ethiopia and Somalia in 1941. The Free French used their West and Equatorial African colonies as bases while France was occupied by the Germans.

Nigeria and Ghana both made major economic contributions to the British war effort, as well as supplying base facilities. Southern Rhodesia was used as a centre to train the British Air Force. A major road, the Great North Road, was built from Salisbury through Northern Rhodesia (Zambia) to Nairobi in Kenya. This road became a supply route for war supplies from South Africa to the British forces in the Middle East.

Africa was no longer a political backwater. It proved to be strategically and economically vital to the imperial powers. This lesson was not lost on a new generation of African nationalists. Above all the war meant that 250,000 Africans served with British armies all over the world fighting for 'democratic freedoms'. When they returned home, they again found themselves colonial subject people. As a result the African ex-servicemen became the shock troops of the coming nationalist revolt against imperialism.

The Rise of African Nationalism In 1945, the imperial powers hoped to return to the pre-war situation. But too many forces were working against them. First, the collapse of the European powers in Asia against the Japanese onslaught had showed that a European power could be defeated by a non-

European power. This defeat destroyed the myth that they were invincible. Second, the granting of independence to British India in 1947 spurred African nationalists to demand independence for themselves. Third, the collapse of the French in Indo-China in 1954 encouraged the nationalist revolt in Algeria.

Fourth, the emergence of the United States and the Soviet Union as world super-powers helped to end European colonialism. Both super-powers, for different reasons, encouraged the break-up of the old empires. Fifth, in colony after colony, such nationalist leaders as Sekou TOURE of Guinea, Jomo KENYATTA of Kenya, Kwame NKRUMAH of the Gold Coast and Colonel Gamal Abdel NASSER of Egypt, demanded independence.

Italian war planes being refuelled and overhauled in Italian Somaliland (part of present-day Somalia) in 1935. These planes were used to attack Ethiopia which had successfully resisted colonization and remained independent. The Italians were finally defeated by Ethiopian and British troops in 1942. ▼

World War II British infantrymen using an abandoned tank as cover. They are advancing towards enemy positions during the Battle of El Alamein.

Bren gunners on the East African front during World War II. ▼

The Advance to Independence Two events in 1952 signalled the coming triumph of nationalism. The first was the July revolution in Egypt which ended the rule of King Farouk and brought Colonel Nasser to power and made Cairo the centre of anti-colonial agitation for the next decade. The second event in 1952 was the outbreak of a nationalist revolt in Kenya that was called the Mau Mau. This revolt was followed by a state of emergency in Kenya.

The Mau Mau rebellion resulted in a total of 13,500 dead and many thousands wounded. At its height 10,000 British troops were stationed in the colony. The emergency continued until 1959. It cost Britain £55 million. Mau Mau was a vital factor in persuading the British to decolonize. The British government decided that the cost of similar rebellions in its other African colonies would outweigh the value of trying to hold on against the people's wishes. The Gold Coast colony was then promised independence as a new republic in 1954 under one-time philosophy teacher Dr. Kwame Nkrumah if he obtained a 'reasonable majority' in the country's elections.

The next advances toward independence came in 1956. First Britain and Egypt terminated the Anglo-Egyptian Condominium over the Sudan, which became independent that January. Second, the French, having lost their colonial war in Indo-China, decided to make Morocco and Tunisia independent.

The French then concentrated their energies and military strength upon holding Algeria. Algeria had about a million *colons*, or French settlers. Seven years bitter fighting in Algeria effectively ended French colonial power in North Africa. At the peak of the war, about half a million French soldiers were in Algeria. Before Algeria finally became independent in 1962, many of the French settlers had returned to France.

In 1956, there was the failure of the Anglo-French invasion of Suez, following Nasser's nationalization of the Suez Canal. The failure of the British and the French demonstrated to exultant African nationalists that the two greatest colonial powers could be stopped by an African state. This was another lesson to imperial powers that military force alone was not enough to keep their empires in order.

In March, 1957, Britain gave independence to the Gold Coast, which was renamed Ghana. This enabled one of Africa's most able and articulate leaders, Kwame Nkrumah, to become for the next three years the chief spokesman for African nationalist aspirations on the world stage. He fulfilled this role to great effect.

A few years later the whole of colonial Africa, with the exception of Portuguese Angola and Mozambique; Rhodesia (Zimbabwe); South Africa and South-West Africa (Namibia) in the south, and enclaves like the French Territory of the Afars and Issas, became independent.

President Nasser of Egypt being acclaimed after the announcement of the nationalization of the Suez Canal in 1956. The canal is one of the world's most important waterways for international shipping.

Many ships were sunk in the Suez Canal during the Anglo-French invasion of Suez in 1956. ▼

The French Approach France had evolved a more centralized approach to the government of its African colonies than had Britain. Leading African politicians served as deputies in the French Assembly in Paris many years before independence. But between 1945 and 1958, France went through a period of great political instability. Finally, General Charles de Gaulle came to power in 1958 as prime minister. Later he became the first president of the Fifth Republic.

At that time, African politicians in the French empire were not agreed about independence. Many regarded themselves as part of a greater France, certainly in cultural terms. Consequently, a debate occurred about political advance. This debate took the form of an argument about the merits of either a federal republic or of a confederal commonwealth. De Gaulle himself discouraged regional groupings and unification among the various parts of French-speaking Africa.

Federation or Independence In 1958, de Gaulle proposed a federation whose members would 'enjoy autonomy and dispose of their own affairs'. But they would not be specifically recognized as states. They would have representation in the French senate. The African territories, said de Gaulle, must choose once and for all between this federation and secession. Once the constitution had been accepted, they could not then talk of independence. There was to be a vote for 'yes' or 'no' in each of France's African territories.

'Yes' meant that a voter favoured membership of a form of federal state—a Franco-African Community. 'No' meant independence. African pressure produced an amendment. After five years, a state might change its mind and request independence, thereby ceasing to be a community member.

De Gaulle toured the territories in August, 1958, encouraging a 'yes' vote. Voting took place in September and every territory voted 'yes' except for Guinea which voted 'no'. Guinea immediately became independent on October 2. The French at once ended all aid to Guinea.

Movement to Full Independence The Community did not last long. In the first place, Cameroon and Togo were both United Nations trust territories. Both had as neighbours sister trust territories having similar peoples under British rule. In agreement with the U.N. and Britain, both countries emerged as fully independent and re-united in 1960. Apart from this, however, it soon became clear that the French Community was not a true federation. Many Africans regarded it as a mask for continuing French control.

In 1958–60, several members of the community opted for full independence. Once such moves began, they undermined the whole concept of the community which, by 1960, was on the verge of disintegration. France faced the inevitable. In September, 1960, it sponsored the admission to the U.N. of 12 new independent black African states. France held on, however, to the Territory of the Afars and Issas after a referendum of the people.

▲ Dr. Kwame Nkrumah (left) greets the Duchess of Kent and introduces her to his ministers when the Duchess arrived to represent Britain at the Ghana independence celebrations.

An Algerian nationalist ▶ demonstration in the streets of Algiers in 1960. Algeria won its independence in 1962.

General de Gaulle, President of France, arriving in the Ivory Coast in 1958. During his 1958 tour, de Gaulle proposed that the French African territories should join France in a federation. All territories, except Guinea, voted 'yes', but in 1960 the Ivory Coast declared itself an independent republic. ▼

▲ In British territories, all stamps from the colonial era bore the head of the British monarch.

Dr. Julius Nyerere of Tanzania was carried shoulder-high after leaving Government House in Dar es Salaam in 1961. He had just announced that his country would become independent that year. ▶

The British Approach As nationalist pressures mounted, the British dealt with each colonial question. However, this usually meant that the degree and speed with which progress toward independence was achieved was governed by the presence or absence of a white settler minority.

British West Africa set the pace. The territories had a long tradition of political activity among Africans. There were also no white settlers to slow down the advance to independence. Following Ghana's independence in 1957, Britain's colonial giant, Nigeria, became independent in 1960, and Sierra Leone and Gambia came next. The year 1960 was very significant in Britain's changing relationship with its African colonies. The British prime minister Harold Macmillan toured Commonwealth Africa and gave his famous 'Wind of Change' speech in South Africa. This speech heralded the British decision to decolonize the remainder of British Africa.

British East Africa Kenya was dominated by white settler politicians. Land hunger among the Kikuyu, Kenya's largest ethnic group, and opposition to settler rule had produced Mau Mau. The Kenyan settlers accepted the inevitable onset of independence at the beginning of the 1960s. Tanganyika became independent in 1961, Uganda in 1962, and Kenya and Zanzibar at the end of 1963.

British Central Africa was even more dominated by the powerful white minority of Southern Rhodesia. A Central African Federation of Northern and Southern Rhodesia, together with Nyasaland, was formed in 1953. This federation was set up against the opposition of almost all politically active Africans in the three territories. By the late 1950s, it had become clear that the white minority in Southern Rhodesia intended to maintain its political control. African opposition to federation and demands for independence were spearheaded by Joshua NKOMO in Southern Rhodesia, Harry Nkumbula, and Kenneth KAUNDA in Northern Rhodesia, and Hastings Kamuzu BANDA in Nyasaland. Banda had returned home at the end of the 1950s after 30 years outside Africa. So effective was African opposition from 1959 onwards that Britain disbanded the Federation at the end of 1963.

In 1964, first Nyasaland, renamed Malawi, and then Northern Rhodesia, renamed Zambia, became independent. For a year after Zambia's independence in October, 1964, the white government of Southern Rhodesia tried to persuade the British government to hand over full power to it. When Britain refused, the Southern Rhodesian government made an illegal and unilateral (one-sided) declaration of independence (UDI) on November 11, 1965.

Enclaves in Southern Africa Apart from British Somaliland, which was united with Italian Somaliland to form the Somali Republic in 1960, and Mauritius, which became independent in 1968, Britain's remaining African territories consisted of three enclaves in southern Africa. These were Basutoland, Bechuanaland and Swaziland. Britain's policies in these three countries had been largely determined by Britain's relations with South Africa. This came about because South Africa dominated the economies of these countries. Following UDI in 'Rhodesia', however, Britain wished to tidy up the remnants of its African empire. It granted independence to Bechuanaland, as Botswana, and Basutoland, as Lesotho, in 1966. Swaziland became independent in 1968.

Pan-Africanism Dreams of pan-Africanism had dominated the thinking of African intellectuals and their supporters in the West Indies and the United States long before independence became a reality. After Ghana became independent in 1957, Kwame Nkrumah became the leading advocate of pan-African moves toward continental unity.

To further this aim, the first conference of eight independent African states was held at Accra in Ghana in 1958. It was attended by Egypt, Ethiopia, Ghana, Liberia, Libya, Morocco, Sudan and Tunisia. The conference united in declaring war on colonialism. It opposed South Africa's racial policies and promised support for the nationalists fighting in Algeria. It also marked the start of African policies of non-alignment (to avoid becoming a committed supporter of the super-powers).

Over the next three years conferences were held at Addis Ababa in 1960 and at Brazzaville, Casablanca and Monrovia in 1961. But by 1961, rifts began to develop between the emerging groups.

The Addis Ababa conference was attended by 12 states, plus the Algerian provisional government. The states represented were Cameroon, Ethiopia, Ghana, Guinea, Liberia, Libya, Morocco, Nigeria, Somalia, Sudan, Tunisia and Egypt. A split developed when Nigeria attacked Nkrumah's concept of pan-Africanism as premature.

For a short time in 1960, the African states presented a single front to the United Nations and to the world. By the end of the year, however, this unity had disappeared. A quarrel developed between Morocco and Mauritania, and Tunisia supported Mauritania. Then there was disagreement over a common approach to the crisis in the former Belgian Congo.

Former British Central Africa faced many problems as colonialism was coming to an end in Africa. In 1953, a Central African Federation was established, consisting of Nyasaland, Northern Rhodesia and Southern Rhodesia (now Malawi, Zambia and Zimbabwe). African opposition to the federation was spearheaded by such leaders as Joshua Nkomo, Dr. Banda and Kenneth Kaunda (*bottom left*). The federation was dissolved in 1963. Malawi and Zambia became independent in 1964. The photograph (*bottom right*) shows Kenneth Kaunda lighting torches at the Zambian independence celebrations. The torches were carried to Zambian villages to herald independence. Southern Rhodesia (Zimbabwe), however, did not achieve majority rule and independence. In 1965, the European minority government illegally proclaimed the country independent from Britain. The photograph (*below left*) shows prime minister Ian Smith making this announcement. This move was strongly opposed by African nationalist leaders and, at Britain's request, the United Nations imposed economic sanctions on the illegal régime.

The OAU In 1961, two groups had emerged. The *Monrovia states*, named after a meeting in Monrovia, Liberia, contained a majority of the independent states, including Nigeria. It was described as 'moderate', and it hoped to mediate with France over Algeria.

The *Casablanca powers*, named after a meeting in Casablanca, Morocco, also in 1961, formed a smaller, more radical group, consisting of Ghana, Guinea, Mali, Morocco, the UAR and the Algerian provisional government. Efforts to heal the breach between the groups culminated in the 1963 meeting in Addis-Ababa. At this meeting, the Organization of African Unity (OAU) was founded.

Regional Groupings Although continental unity was proving impractical, some smaller regional groupings began to emerge. The Conakry declaration of May 1, 1959, announced a union between Ghana and Guinea. Later, for a short time, these two countries were joined by Mali. In the north the possibility of a Maghreb Federation between Algeria, Morocco and Tunisia came to nothing. This also was the fate of another possible union between Egypt, Sudan and Uganda.

Independence for Somalia, consisting of British and Italian Somaliland in 1960, created pressures on Ethiopia and Kenya where Somalis lived. Two border wars continued until well into the 1960s.

But in East Africa, PAFMECA (Pan-African Movement for East and Central Africa), later known as PAFMECSA with the addition of southern Africa, emerged as perhaps the most hopeful of the regional groupings. Its early aspirations were tempered by the realities of power politics.

Attempts to form an East African Federation between Kenya, Tanzania and Uganda petered out by the mid-1960s. However, the more practical East African Common Market (EACM) did emerge. Although the EACM faced many difficulties, it both survived and provided economic advantages for each of its three members. It was formalized by a treaty which established the East African Community.

Crisis in the Congo When the Belgian Congo achieved independence on June 30, 1960, it was estimated that there were only 17 graduates from a total population of about 17 million. This lack of preparation meant that the Congo, rich in mineral resources but with poor communications, was liable to face crisis if the government ever broke down.

This crisis occurred as a result of internal political rivalries and powerful external pressures. The army mutinied within a week of independence. By July 11, Katanga (now Shaba) under its provincial prime minister Moise TSHOMBE announced secession. Katanga contained most of the country's minerals that were then being exploited. Deep distrust also existed between Joseph KASAVUBU, the country's first president, and Patrice LUMUMBA, the first national prime minister. They worked together for a short time, but they soon quarrelled.

UN Intervention Following Katangan secession, Lumumba appealed to the United Nations for assistance in maintaining law and order. UN forces soon arrived. Later Lumumba appealed to the Russians for support. However, the Americans backed Kasavubu, who meanwhile had dismissed Lumumba's government. Finally backed by the United States and other western countries, Kasavubu's representatives were seated at the UN. Kasavubu appointed Albert Kalonji prime minister. Lumumba, for his own protection, was put under a UN guard. But Lumumba escaped and was captured when trying to escape to Kisangani, which was controlled by his supporters. In January 1961 he died under mysterious circumstances in Katanga.

After his death Lumumba became a martyr in the eyes of African nationalists in other parts of the continent. The UN Secretary General Dag Hammarskjold was then killed in a mysterious plane crash in Northern Rhodesia, while on his way to a secret meeting with Tshombe. After these events, the situation in the Congo became extremely complicated. There were attacks upon and massacres of the whites, many of whom fled the country. There was ethnic warfare and cold war and big business intrigues. The emergence of groups of hired soldiers, called *mercenaries*, helped prolong the fighting for several years until the word 'Congo' became synonymous with disaster.

Effects of the Crisis The events in the Congo frightened African leaders throughout the continent. A breakdown of law and order in a new state was something every African leader wished to avoid. What was worse, and for them far more frightening, was the cynical way in which the big powers had moved into the Congo affair for their own reasons.

African leaders were alarmed by the apparent partiality of the UN toward the western viewpoint, the pursuit of cold war interests by the Americans and Russians, and the backstage intrigues of some big business corporations. These manoeuvres, as well as the conduct of the white mercenaries, convinced Africans that their independence was precarious. They considered that, in any crisis, they would probably be at the mercy of outside influences.

▲ Congolese government troops sought to restore order in Zaire after the crisis of 1960.

In 1960, Moise Tshombe (*above*), the secessionist leader of Katanga (now Shaba), a province rich in minerals, opposed Patrice Lumumba (*right*), Zaire's first prime minister, UN personnel (*below*) played an important part in ending the fighting.

Economic Sanctions in 'Rhodesia' When 'Rhodesia' made its unilateral declaration of independence on November 11, 1965, many African leaders called on Britain to use force to put down this rebellion. They had long demanded that Britain should curtail the powers of the white settlers and ensure African majority rule in the country. The reaction of the British Government was to impose sanctions against the white settlers.

As a result, the OAU went into emergency session. It passed a resolution calling on its members to break off diplomatic relations with Britain by December 10, 1965, unless it had taken far tougher action by that date. However, when December 10 arrived, only 9 out of the 36 members of the OAU broke off relations with Britain.

The Nigerian prime minister, Abubakar Tafawa BALEWA, called for a Commonwealth conference on 'Rhodesia'. This conference met at Lagos in January, 1966. It reluctantly agreed to give Britain until June to make sanctions work. Then a full-scale Commonwealth conference should be held. In April, 1966, the British navy blockaded Beira in Mozambique to stop oil supplies reaching 'Rhodesia'.

Attempts to find Agreements In September a Commonwealth conference in London called for sterner measures. In December, the British prime minister Harold Wilson met Ian SMITH, 'Rhodesia's' prime minister. The two leaders negotiated an agreement which was later rejected in 'Rhodesia'. Britain then asked the United Nations to call upon all of its members to impose economic sanctions.

Full-scale sanctions were called for by the UN in May, 1968. By the end of 1968 Britain again attempted to come to an agreement with 'Rhodesia', but this was also unsuccessful. In 1971, the British foreign secretary Sir Alec Douglas Home, negotiated with Ian Smith in Salisbury. They agreed a settlement but also agreed that it should be approved by the people of 'Rhodesia' as a whole. To test opinion, the British sent a commission under Lord Pearce to Zimbabwe in January, 1972. The commission reported that the Africans were overwhelmingly opposed to the agreement.

South Africa and Its Neighbours South Africa's policy of separate development for its peoples or *apartheid*, is condemned by black Africa. It has been opposed by every meeting of African heads of state. South Africa is by far the most powerful state in Africa. It is capable of organizing an army of about 250,000 in an emergency. South Africa's strength only adds fear and frustration to African opposition.

At the first meeting of the OAU in 1963, a resolution called on all members to boycott South Africa. Following UDI 'Rhodesia' and the intensification of the guerilla wars in the Portuguese territories of Angola, Guinea-Bissau, and Mozambique, the white minority governments were drawn closer together.

The two exile groups from South Africa, the African National Congress (ANC) and the Pan-Africanist Congress (PAC), began to work more closely with the exiled Zimbabwean groups, the

▼ Britain introduced a policy of economic sanctions against the white minority government of 'Rhodesia' (Zimbabwe). The photograph shows a British frigate stopping a Greek tanker from landing oil for the rebel country.

Zimbabwe African People's Union (ZAPU), the Zimbabwe African National Union (ZANU) and the Front for the Liberation of Zimbabwe (FROLIZI).

The claims of these organizations for support caused quarrels among African nations. Some African countries supported the OAU condemnation of South Africa in theory, but did little about it in practice. Others, notably Tanzania and Zambia, provided money, bases and training facilities. They also took in refugees from the south. In 1975 the OAU tried to form one nationalist group in Zimbabwe, linking them in the African National Council led by Bishop Muzorewa. But differences soon emerged between the leaders.

▲ South Africa's racial policies remain a problem for Africa. Typical notices show the distinction made between 'whites' and 'non-whites' in South Africa.

► The leading advocates of majority rule in Zimbabwe, Joshua Nkomo (*left*) and the Rev. Ndabaningi Sithole (*right*).

Namibia (South-West Africa) German South-West Africa was mandated to South Africa in 1919. Because South Africa had imposed apartheid there and not prepared the territory for independence, the UN revoked the mandate in 1966. It put the territory under direct UN administration, setting up a Council for Namibia. South Africa ignored this decision and proceeded to establish a white area, two coloured areas and nine African homelands. In 1972, however, the UN Secretary-General Kurt Waldheim had talks with the South African government. These talks ended in 1973. Although South Africa continued its policy of establishing Bantustans in Namibia, the South African prime minister was reported in 1975 to have agreed to Namibian independence, providing a peaceful handover of power could be negotiated.

Botswana, Lesotho and Swaziland These three independent states are surrounded in part or entirely by South African territory. Because all their imports and exports must pass through South Africa, they have a customs union with it.

South Africa and Black Africa South Africa maintained considerable military commitments in southern Africa. There were South African troops and a major air base in the Caprivi Strip on the opposite shore of the Zambezi River from Zambia. South African troops were also stationed along the Zambezi.

▲ In the late 1960s and 1970s, South African troops patrolled key areas in southern Africa including the Caprivi Strip.

Dr. Banda, president of Malawi visited South Africa to meet prime minister, Johannes Vorster in 1971 as part of the policy of dialogue.
▼

Dialogues Differences between black Africa and South Africa have led to a 'dialogue' between them. Toward the end of the 1960s the South African prime minister said that, provided African countries respected and did not interfere with South Africa's internal policies, South Africa would be willing to enter into diplomatic relations, to trade and to give aid.

There have been two main African reactions to this 'outward looking' policy. The first, represented by Malawi Malagasy and Ivory Coast, was a willingness to enter into a dialogue with South Africa. Thus South Africa had both trade and aid agreements with Malagasy and Malawi, although Malagasy abandoned the dialogue policy after the fall of President TSIRANANA in 1972. Hastings Kamuzu Banda of Malawi exchanged trade missions with South Africa in 1967. He and the South African prime minister, Mr. VORSTER, then exchanged visits in 1971. This was the first time ever that a South African prime minister had gone on a state visit to a black African country, or that a black head of state had visited South Africa.

The second school of thought was represented by the 1969 Lusaka Manifesto, which was signed by 14 countries in East and Central Africa. This manifesto spurned any form of dialogue with South Africa as long as apartheid was maintained.

South Africa's race policies were regarded as a threat by most black African leaders. While South Africa continued to separate the races and support minority regimes in 'Rhodesia' and the Portuguese territories, many observers believed that race conflicts in southern Africa would increase.

However, in 1974 the situation in southern Africa changed greatly. The government of Portugal, which had conducted wars against the nationalist groups in its African territories, was overthrown in a coup in April, 1974. In the months that followed, independence agreements were negotiated for Guinea-Bissau (September, 1974), Mozambique (June, 1975) and Angola (November, 1975). One of the reasons for the rapid moves toward independence was the view of Portugal's new leaders that no military solution was possible in these African territories. In the 1970s more than two-fifths of Portugal's budget was spent on the three African wars. Portugal had maintained armies of about 55,000 in Angola, 40,000 in Mozambique and 35,000 in Guinea-Bissau.

Independence for Mozambique and Angola increased the pressure on 'Rhodesia' to find a settlement. In late 1974, the South African prime minister was involved with the presidents of Botswana, Tanzania and Zambia in attempts to arrive at a solution to the problem of 'Rhodesia'. These attempts received a setback in December 1974, when Ian Smith's regime in 'Rhodesia' refused to accept African majority rule within a short period, but negotiations continued into 1976. The success of the Communist-backed MPLA in Angola put further pressure on South Africa to reach an agreement with black Africa.

Former Portuguese Territories Portugal described its three former African territories as 'overseas Portugal'. The largest territory, Angola, is the richest in resources. In 1956, the main nationalist movement, the People's Movement for the Liberation of Angola (MPLA), was formed. In 1961 it launched an armed struggle against the Portuguese. Other Angolan nationalist groups are the Union of Angolan Peoples (FNLA) and the National Union for the Total Independence of Angola (UNITA). When Angola became independent in November 1975, the FNLA and UNITA opposed the MPLA. But the MPLA, supported by the USSR and Cuban forces, won control of the country and set up the Angolan People's Republic.

In the second largest territory, Mozambique, the chief nationalist group is the Mozambique Liberation Front (FRELIMO). The front launched an armed struggle in 1964 and by the early 1970s it claimed control over much of the north. In 1974, following the independence agreement, FRELIMO set up a provisional government and the FRELIMO leader Samora MACHEL became the president of Mozambique.

The third territory was the small Guinea-Bissau. There, the nationalist movement was called the African Independence Party of Guinea and Cape Verde Islands (PAIGC). Formed in 1956, this movement launched its armed struggle in 1963. By 1972, it claimed control over two-thirds of the countryside. The 1974 independence agreement applied only to Guinea-Bissau, but Portugal also declared the Cape Verde Islands independent in July 1975 with Mr. A. Pereira as the country's first president.

Economic Progress during recent years has been uneven. However, development has been faster and often more spectacular than it was during the colonial era. Most African states are still mainly farming societies. Major advances in industrialization have occurred mainly in areas with rich mineral resources, such as oil and natural gas in Algeria, oil in Nigeria, and copper in Zambia.

▲ During the war in Angola, villagers were often transferred from areas where freedom fighters were active.

Posters on a wall in ▶ Luanda, Angola, recall the Portuguese attempts to create a multi-racial system in the country.

Below left FRELIMO guerillas examine the wreck of a plane in the Cabo Delgado province of Mozambique.

Below right Samora Machel, the FRELIMO leader, addresses a group of villagers in Cabo Delgado province. Machel became president of the Peoples Republic of Mozambique on 25 June 1975.

Aid After the formation of the EEC (European Economic Community, or Common Market), the ex-colonies of France, Belgium and Italy were invited to apply for associate status. In this way, African countries could obtain free access to the market and obtain aid. They were still able to protect their own infant industries.

Apart from connexions with the European Common Market, most African countries obtained much of their aid from the old colonial powers. However, increasingly since independence, they have also got assistance from the Scandinavian countries, the United States and Canada, and from China, Russia and the socialist world.

About half of British bilateral aid goes to Commonwealth countries in Africa. This included in 1972 the presence of more than 10,000 aid personnel. An even higher proportion of French bilateral aid goes to its former colonies in Africa. Much aid has taken the form of trained personnel, especially secondary school teachers. Some has been in the form of grants-in-aid to the budgets of the poorest countries. The balance of aid has been in the form of loans for a wide variety of projects. The largest and most spectacular of these projects have been such developments as the Aswan Dam in Egypt (financed by the Russians), the Volta River Project in Ghana, and the Uhuru (or Tanzam) railway linking Zambia's copper belt with Dar es Salaam in Tanzania (financed by the Chinese).

Changing Policies Most investment in Africa still comes from the west. Increasingly, however, African countries have adopted socialist policies. Western businessmen have become more wary of investing

capital in African commercial ventures.

Toward the end of the 1960s, Botswana wanted to exploit new finds of diamonds and copper. This could only be done through the huge mining corporations, South African, British, American and Canadian. Following discussions, the Botswana government's share was only 15 per cent.

Because of such problems, Africans have become increasingly alarmed at the extent to which so many of their economies are dominated by foreign financial interests. One result of this concern was the Arusha Declaration of February, 1967. In this declaration, President NYERERE of Tanzania put forward a socialist theory of development. He conconcluded that a developing country should control its own resources. Tanzania then nationalized banks and insurance companies. This action sparked off a series of whole or partial take-overs of foreign assets in other countries at the end of the 1960s.

Zambia took over 51 per cent of foreign assets, including the copper industry. Uganda produced the Poor Man's Charter in May, 1970—another statement of socialist principles. Sudan and Somalia nationalized foreign companies. Algeria nationalized the oil industry. Nigeria ensured that the government had the majority control of its oil. Libya both nationalized its oil and led the oil-producing countries in making demands for higher payments for the major importers.

In the 1970s there was a new spirit of African scepticism about the intentions of those who offered aid or investments. The Tanzanian slogan of 'self-reliance' became increasingly popular elsewhere in Africa.

Below left President Nyerere, one of the leading philosopher-statesmen of Africa, delivers his famous 'Arusha Declaration' of 1967. In it he defined the role of socialism in a country such as Tanzania.

Below right Laying the first section of track of the Uhuru railway between Tanzania and Zambia. The Chinese helped in the construction of this line, which will open up many productive areas.

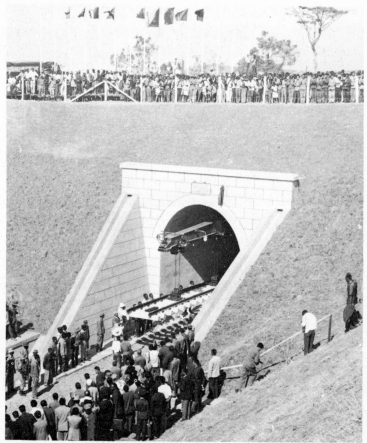

Political Upheavals The 1960s was a period of political upheaval. The new regimes grappled with problems of government and came to terms with difficulties arising from their colonial past. Some states favoured pro-western forms of development, as in Kenya. Some maintained close relations with the old colonial power, such as the Ivory Coast with France. Some adopted socialist policies, as in Tanzania.

In some territories independence was followed by periods of great conflict. Zaire was the first to suffer. Conflict continued until 1965 when General Joseph MOBUTU became president. He first restored law and order and then brought back an increasing measure of prosperity. In the neighbouring states of Rwanda and Burundi, clashes between the Tutsi and the Hutu led to massacres in the early 1960s. This was repeated on an even greater scale in Burundi in 1972.

In January, 1964, an anti-Arab revolution occurred in Zanzibar. A most significant result of the Zanzibar revolution was union with Tanganyika in April, 1964. The union was finally renamed Tanzania.

In 1966, tensions between the regions in Nigeria, resulting from the federal system of government left by Britain, led to a breakdown of law and order. This was followed by a civil war when the Igbos of the Eastern Region tried to secede from Nigeria and set up a new state called Biafra. Finally the federal government, under General GOWON, won the war and Biafra did not secede. During the conflict many hundreds of thousands of Nigerians died either in battle or from starvation.

Below left **Federal troops fought during the Civil War from 1967 to 1970 to maintain the unity of Nigeria.**

Below right **During the civil war in Nigeria, civilians suffered when transport became difficult and food supplies were cut off. International assistance was provided and the photograph shows milk being distributed to children.**

There have been other disturbances in Africa since independence. This is hardly surprising when more than 40 new states have emerged within a few years. Africans have to work out the kind of political and economic systems that they wish to pursue. They have to reconcile ethnic and language differences among their peoples. They also have to come to terms with powerful external influences.

Some African states are among the poorest in the world. However, against great economic odds, most of them have made major advances since independence. Educational opportunities, business chances and political participation have to some extent been brought within the reach of the majority. Africa in the 1960s and 1970s also produced some notable leaders, as well as some new experiments in politics.

The post-independence period was also marked by the emergence of one-party states or the rise of military dictatorships, following many coups and civil disturbances. However, most observers agree that the astonishing achievement is that so few major upheavals took place in Africa during the 1960s.

The Future Africa still faces many problems of economic development and political stability. There are external pressures from the super-powers, as well as from the old colonial powers. Internally Africa is still dangerously divided between independent countries north of the Zambezi and the white minority regimes to the south.

Despite all these problems, however, African countries have emerged as a vital and important group whose collective voice can no longer be ignored in world councils.

GOVERNMENT AND DIPLOMACY

Traditional Government

Before Europeans colonized the continent, Africa had a wide variety of political institutions. In West Africa especially, there was a tradition of complex institutions which served great kingdoms and empires, such as ancient Ghana, Mali and Songhai.

Social organization ranged from roving bands with simple institutions to highly developed states. The small roving band was the most simple grouping. Its only 'official' was the headman. Such bands, however, could grow in size and become powerful forces. As they moved, raided and took captives, so they became unwieldy. Some of them would then break away from the band and set up separate kingdoms, while the main band moved on. For example, the Ndebele were one such band in southern Africa that finally settled in Rhodesia (Zimbabwe).

At the other extreme from the roving band was the settled kingdom. The most sophisticated of these kingdoms were mainly in West Africa at the southern end of the old trading routes across the Sahara.

In some cases, the colonial powers hastened a process of cohesion within a single ethnic group. For example, the Igbos of eastern Nigeria once lived in many small, detached groups. However, the British recognized and emphasized the similarities between them. They treated them as a single people. As a result, the Igbos came to think of themselves as one ethnic group covering a wide area.

In other cases, the colonialists came into contact with a settled regime that had existed for a very long time. For example, the Kingdom of Barotseland (now part of modern Zambia) had an aristocratic ruling class, the Lozi, who had evolved a highly sophisticated system of rule. This kingdom had absorbed many groups. Captives became subjects after a generation or so. Such kingdoms were to make treaties with European chartered companies or with representatives of the colonial powers.

Many of the larger African kingdoms or states were varied in composition. The ruling class often consisted of one ethnic group, such as the Tutsi of Burundi and Rwanda or the Lozi of Barotseland. Their subjects were often of a different group or groups. The subject groups kept their own languages and customs. They saw no reason to adopt those of their rulers.

Problems of Traditional Government

The problems faced by African rulers were common to most of Africa. How much power could be given to officials who lived far away without encouraging rebellion, especially in view of the poor communications? How strong could a ruler be permitted to become before he turned into a tyrant? What checks upon him were possible? How could revenue be raised and collected? How could the continuity of the government be ensured by a form of regulated succession?

Military control by the king was difficult. Before large quantities of firearms became available, all men had similar weapons and few kings could afford standing armies. As a result, breakaways were

◄ Early explorers, such as John Hanning Speke and his companion James Grant, received much help from local rulers during their travels. The drawing shows a reconstruction of the scene when Speke and Grant sought the assistance of a king in Uganda when they were searching for the source of the Blue Nile in the early 1860s.

frequent. The threat of a breakaway was one of the main checks on an unpopular ruler. The king was responsible for the well-being of the kingdom. His position was enhanced by rituals, which were controlled by some form of priest class. Catastrophes were often blamed on the king. After a major catastrophe, the king was likely to be deposed.

One of the greatest states in the second half of the 1800s was that ruled over by Sokoto. This state was an alliance of Fulani states in Niger, Nigeria and Northern Cameroon. The Fulani maintained control through their cavalry. In the rain forests to the south, where the cavalry could not operate, the Yoruba were free of their control. Many Fulani customs were a mixture of those of the conquered Hausa with Islamic customs from the north.

The Yoruba of western Nigeria had evolved a highly complex system of government by the time that the British arrived. The king was responsible for the welfare of the state, but had little to do with the day-to-day administration. Officials were not dependent on the king. Usually, fees were attached to their various offices. The officials recruited the armies. The cities in Yorubaland were dominated by secret societies. Those Yoruba who broke laws were more likely to be committing offences against a group or a particular secret society, rather than against the kingdom.

Below left Sir Edward Mutesa inspecting his troops on his birthday celebrations in 1951. Sir Edward was the last *kabaka* (king) of Buganda, a rich province within Uganda. Deposed in 1966, he died in Britain three years later.

Below right the Oba (or king) of Benin, an ancient state in Nigeria known for its superb court art. Unlike the kabaka of Uganda, the Oba of Benin still has an administrative role in contemporary Nigeria.

In neighbouring Dahomey, on the other hand, real power rested in the hands of the king in council. The king controlled appointments and the army. Among the Yoruba, a man was first a member of a society or group and second a citizen of the state. However, in Dahomey (now Benin), it was the other way round—a man was first a citizen of the state and only secondly a member of a group.

Quite different developments had occurred elsewhere in Africa. In the south, Shaka Zulu, a military genius, had created a powerful military despotism. Even though it was on the decline in 1870, the Zulu kingdom still comprised about a million people.

In East Africa, the Baganda, under a line of able kings, had secularized the office of kingship. They had destroyed the hereditary basis of other offices in the state. The king controlled all appointments, although there were some checks on him.

Social and political responsibilities, checks and balances, took different forms in various parts of the continent. Among some East African peoples, the system of dividing people into sets according to age was highly evolved. Men were divided into initiates, warriors and elders. Each group, both individually and collectively, was responsible for certain duties. Most African societies had systems of corporate lineages or kin groups.

Colonial Rule

Changes in Traditional Government When the Europeans arrived, they misunderstood many of the existing customs. For example, in East Africa, newcomers were permitted to settle and were allotted land that was not in use. At the same time, the local people expected the newcomers to acknowledge the overlordship of the ruler by making gifts. Europeans assumed too often that their gifts provided them in return with title to the land. They thought that they had purchased a freehold, as would have been the case in Europe. This was not so.

During the period of colonization, these various institutions of government were seriously undermined, although the African people often fiercely resisted the superior European technology. Generally, the colonizers deliberately adopted a policy of downgrading the people they had conquered. An ethnic or organized group became known as a 'tribe'. The king or head of state became a 'chief'. Such terms implied that the units of people were smaller, and the rulers less civilized than they really were. This made it easier to justify colonial expansion.

From 1870 to 1900, colonial rule was established over most of Africa. With their superior science and wealth, Europeans could do more or less what they liked and go where they pleased.

The colonizers publicly declared that the African people were backward and their societies primitive. They then justified imperialism by claiming that Europe was bringing order and civilization to Africa. Much of the early colonization, however, was carried out by chartered companies, as in German and British East Africa and in southern Africa. These companies were often short of money. As a result, despite their technological superiority, many early colonists were weaker than the people they wished to rule. To avoid clashes that they doubted they could win, they made treaties with the more highly organized states or groups that they met.

A regular colonial system of government was known as *indirect rule*. According to this system, chiefs, ranging from local headmen to powerful rulers, were confirmed in their localized powers provided that they assisted the colonial authorities. The chiefs were expected to act as recruiting agents for men to work on European plantations or in the mines, and to assist European officials in the collection of taxes. When chiefs were not prepared to act as agents of colonialism, they were deposed and replaced by others.

Nationalism and Government The emergence of nationalist leaders, who were to lead the colonies to independence, speeded up the pace of change.

In essence, the nationalist leader had to satisfy the requirements of leadership that were previously filled by traditional rulers. A nationalist leader had to provide a standard for his followers. He had to be acceptable to all the various groups in the territory and be a focus for political integration. He then became a symbol of a new community.

In most colonies, there was at first very limited political participation of any kind for the Africans. Agitation for a greater say in government, the rise of trade unions, or demands for social equality at first often produced a colonial reaction of repression. Continued agitation, sometimes violence, persuaded the colonial government to come to terms with the rising tide of nationalism. The colonial government then became more accommodating. It relaxed its rules and provided new constitutions.

At this stage, the nationalist movement began to organize itself into a political party. Again and again, these parties were mass movements, embracing all African groups within the colony, including would-be oppositions. In this last phase, the colonial officials provided the focus of attention as the enemy. This general pattern of constitutional development may be traced from three examples: Ivory Coast, Kenya, and Nigeria.

▲ Sir Harry Johnston became one of Britain's chief colonial diplomats in Africa. He established Malawi (then Nyasaland) as a British territory.

British colonial rule was maintained by district commissioners and other officials who maintained the law in local courts. Colonial administrators relied on local officials for advice on customs. ▼

Lord Lugard, Britain's ▶ leading colonial administrator, established 'indirect rule' in Nigeria. This system maintained the power of local rulers, provided that they assisted the colonial administrators.

Ivory Coast The Ivory Coast Democratic Party went through three phases. At first (1946–51), it took the form of a protest movement. The colonial regime at that time provided limited opportunities for African participation. Then it became a political party (1952–8). Greater opportunities were open to Africans and the party's chief aim was independence. The third phase came after independence, when it became the government party, the all-embracing source of power and patronage.

There was no question of competition between two or more parties to determine who would govern. Rather, the party consisted of an elite that ruled through a mass movement. This movement was representative of most sections of the population. As the ruling party after independence, it became increasingly paternalist.

Nigeria A constitution, introduced in 1946, set up Houses of Assembly in the Northern, Eastern and Western provinces. There was a Legislative Council at the centre with an unofficial African majority. Members of the Houses of Assembly were chosen by the African authorities. But the assemblies had no legislative powers, only advisory ones. The British governor remained president of the Legislative Council. The key to power remained the Executive Council (or cabinet) which was controlled by the governor.

By 1951 nationalist pressures had increased so much that this constitution was outdated. A new one was then introduced. It came into force in 1952, establishing semi-responsible government and maintaining the unity of the country but it also provided regional autonomy. The regions were given executive councils, and the Regional Assemblies had legislative and financial powers. Indirect elections through electoral colleges followed. The elections were fought on party lines. The parties were based on the regions. The result of this system was that the regions were strong and the central government was weak.

Throughout the 1950s, the constitution was constantly modified. The adaptations were aimed at balancing the powers of the regions and the central government. The end product was a federal constitution which gave great power to the regions. A federal election in 1959 provided Nigeria with the government that led it to gain its independence in 1960.

Kenya was a British colony with a substantial number of European settlers. The settlers assumed that eventually they would rule the colony. Much of the colony's history was concerned with their attempts to gain absolute political control. In the Legislative Council, whites represented the interests of the Africans. Between World Wars I and II, the settlers demanded their own government. Although the British Colonial Office gave way to many of the demands, it did not surrender final authority to the settlers.

The central and most powerful ethnic group in Kenya was the Kikuyu. Early on in the colonial period, the Kikuyu pressed their land and nationa-list claims against the settlers. Finally the increasingly bitter struggle between the Kikuyu and the settlers culminated in the Mau Mau rebellion of 1952–9. It was Mau Mau that led to the final independence struggle and ensured the emergence of a successful militant nationalism. At the height of the struggle, there was a split in the ranks of the settlers. Some remained opposed to majority rule, but some allied themselves with the colonial authorities in helping to introduce representative government.

Jomo Kenyatta, now President of Kenya, attended the 5th Pan-African Conference held in Manchester, Britain in 1945. This conference was important for developing the idea of Pan-Africanism and African unity against colonialism.

An early pre-independence rally organized by the Tanganyika African National Union (TANU) and addressed by *Mwalimu* (teacher) Julius Nyerere. Following independence in 1961, TANU became the governing party of the country.

Government Since Independence

In the 10 years following independence, country after country in Africa rejected the political system that they had inherited from the colonial era. Why did this happen? First the colonial powers could only establish a system that they fully understood. In effect, this meant that the system was a copy of their own. Had they offered anything else the nationalists would probably have rejected it as second best.

Second, in almost all cases, the establishment of a full-scale political system was only achieved a very short time before independence. Little opportunity existed for it to take root. Even so, this does not mean that it was necessarily the right form of government. It was simply the only form that the colonial power could reasonably hand on.

At independence the nationalist governments all faced the same broad problems. They were concerned with nation-building, the achievement of unity, and the reconciliation of the claims of different groups and regions. They wanted to provide universal education and they needed to search for competent people to fill all the posts of a modern society. Against this background, the new states had to decide what kind of government was most suitable for dealing with their problems.

Most people claim that the system of government in their own country is the best of all possible systems. This is hardly ever true, except in the narrow sense that a system may best suit a certain country at a particular time in its history.

In some countries, such as Botswana and Swaziland, the two-party system of democracy was retained. Some countries, such as Tanzania and Zambia, adopted one-party constitutions, although democracy is preserved through the party by participation of the people. Some countries, such as Uganda and Zaire, experienced military take-overs leading to one-party systems or military rule.

The argument for the one-party state in Africa has probably been best explained by President Julius Nyerere of Tanzania. He said that the people became unified in the nationalist struggle for independence. Why, he argued, should artificial disunity be created by insisting on a two-party system? Nyerere also stated that the social and economic rifts in society that produced such a system in Britain do not exist in Tanzania.

Military governments have come to power in Africa so often after coups that the question of the standing of African armies has become important. The army has emerged as a vital political force in many states. It represents the chief alternative to a party system as a means of government.

African Armies Between 1960 and 1972 some 30 African states experienced one or more coups or military disturbances. At the start of 1976, 21 out of 46 countries were run by military governments which came to power by coups.

Some 23 African countries, including South Africa, spent 10 per cent or more of their budgets on defence in 1969, and four of these spent more than 20 per cent. Between 1968 and 1972, the average rise in the armed forces of African states was at the rate of 10 per cent more a year. By the end of the 1960s, there was a steady arms build-up taking place in Africa. By the beginning of the 1970s, all the African armies combined totalled more than 7,000,000 men. Several factors explain this build-up.

President Amin of ▶
Uganda congratulates
President Mobutu Sese
Seko of Zaire in 1972
after awarding him the
Order of the Source of
the Blue Nile. Both
presidents have
vigorously pursued a
policy of Africanization
in their countries.

A FRELIMO commander ▶
addressing a meeting in
Beira on September 25,
1974, the anniversary of
the armed struggle in
Mozambique.

The impressive Parliament
Building at Gaberone in
Botswana. ▼

Increase in Defence Expenditure Before the civil war (1967–70), the Nigerian army numbered 12,000. The war led to a rapid increase of forces and importation of arms, mainly from Britain and the Soviet Union. By 1972, the army numbered about 250,000. Egypt has long maintained one of the largest armies in Africa. It is a major importer of arms, chiefly from the Soviet Union. However, in Egypt's case, the chief reason for this is the continuing confrontation with Israel. Both Ethiopia and Somalia have large and expanding armies. This largely results from their border quarrel.

In January, 1971, a coup brought General Idi Amin to power in Uganda. Since then the army has been expanded and by 1974, it numbered at least 12,000 men. In Uganda's case there was some justification for a fair-sized army before the coup. In the years following independence there were troubles with Rwanda, disturbances in the Congo, and a civil war in the neighbouring Sudan. All these problems made it necessary for Uganda to patrol its borders. Since coming to power, Amin has also clashed with another neighbour, Tanzania. In 1971 and 1972, there was border fighting.

After 1964, when there were army mutinies in Kenya, Tanzania and Uganda, President Nyerere of Tanzania first disbanded his army and built up a People's Militia to a figure of about 10,000. The militia has had two main tasks since 1970. Bad relations with Uganda produced border incidents. There were also threats from the Portuguese in Mozambique, as the FRELIMO guerillas who had been trained in Tanzania increasingly put the Portuguese on the defensive.

The greatest military build-up in Africa was in the south. Apart from the bitter struggle between the Portuguese and Amilcar Cabral's PAIGC in Guinea-Bissau, the Portuguese also fought a war in Mozambique between 1964 and 1974. Mozambique became independent in June, 1975. Another war in Angola was waged between 1961 and 1974. After Angolan independence in November 1975, the MPLA fought against the FNLA and UNITA and by early 1976 had won control of the country.

In Zimbabwe (Rhodesia), up to 3,000 white troops are stationed in rotation along the Zambezi. The South Africans also have forward bases in the Caprivi Strip and in early 1976 fought in Angola against the MPLA forces.

In 1971 South Africa's defence budget was £185 million. The only items that South Africa cannot manufacture itself are warships and long-range fighter planes. With its regular forces, para-military police and white reservists, South Africa could summon 250,000 white troops within 10 days following an emergency. These forces are trained first to put down an internal revolt. Second, they are trained to counter a major attack from black African states to the north. A Security Council resolution of the UN in 1963 called on all member states to ban the sale of arms to South Africa. But during 1969 and 1970, South Africa imported more arms than all the rest of Africa combined.

Military Governments The army in Africa has emerged in many states as the only alternative means of government. It has done so by mounting coups against unpopular or corrupt regimes. Because of its success, governments have found it hard to deny the economic demands of growing armies on their national budgets. Once the army has achieved a position of strength, it becomes difficult if not impossible to dislodge it from its position of political power.

Coups are most likely to take place when a political regime is the only one permitted in a country, and is not checked by active public opinion. However, more African states today are making provision for the expression of public opinion. In such circumstances, coups are less likely. Many people think that military regimes form 'law and order' governments of a conservative kind.

However, an examination of a few of the military governments in Africa disproves this idea. For example, the military president of Congo (Brazzaville) is a Marxist. Colonel Gaddafi of Libya is a progressive and revolutionary man. Two of the most successful rulers in Africa, the late Colonel Nasser in Egypt and General Mobutu in Zaire, founded political parties as the surest way to preserve their power and keep the revolutions going in the direction they desired. In fact, most military regimes have turned to civilians to help them rule.

Problems of Military Governments Military governments face many great disadvantages. They can easily become machines, which keep government going but which do not provide the essential political thought and innovations that any society needs. By their nature, military governments can harbour corruption if they deny or suppress free speech and effective opposition. Too frequently they ensure the continuation of those practices that they came to power to suppress. Military governments can create a false sense of unity and security. The temptation of would-be reformers is then to mount another coup. The second coup is often led by younger and more radical soldiers than their predecessors.

Because of its wars and tensions, Africa has become a major field in which all the big powers sell arms. One of the sources of arms, France, has agreements with 14 states that its army will intervene on request. Clearly, African armies will continue to wield great power and influence in the 1970s.

International Affairs African countries try repeatedly to act together. There are several organizations through which they can do this. Problems of unity, however, often make such action difficult. Differing political attitudes, poor inter-African communications and varying states of economic development all contribute to disunity. However, all African states face the same problems. This often enables them to speak with one voice.

The Commonwealth Thirteen African countries, the ex-British colonies, belong to the Commonwealth. They are Gambia, Ghana, Nigeria and

President Gaddafi of Libya came to power in 1961. He has pursued a policy of 'Arabization', much like the policy of Africanization in states to the south. He has also been a stern opponent of Israel.

▲ President Kerekou of Dahomey and President Gowon of Nigeria signing a friendship treaty between their two countries in 1973. Co-operation between independent nations has been a feature of the new Africa.

Sierra Leone from West Africa; Kenya, Malawi, Tanzania, Uganda and Zambia from East Africa; Botswana, Lesotho and Swaziland from southern Africa; and Mauritius. It has been reported that Namibia (South-West Africa) will be offered Commonwealth membership when it becomes independent.

The Commonwealth is an important political forum for those states, and a means of influencing some non-African countries. Commonwealth conferences since 1965 have spent much time discussing Rhodesia (Zimbabwe). Many observers believe that, without Commonwealth pressure, Britain might have recognized the illegal regime. Similarly, at the 1971 conference, African and Asian members restrained British policy concerning arms sales to South Africa.

The Organization of African Unity The achievements of the OAU, since it was set up in 1963, have depended on the collective will of its members. As an organization, it is easy to criticize. But it has some concrete successes to its credit.

First, by uniting the rival Monrovia and Casablanca groups, it prevented black Africa splitting into blocs. In January, 1961, delegates from Morocco, Ghana, Guinea, Mali, the United Arab Republic, Libya and the Algerian Provisional Government had met in Casablanca and adopted a number of resolutions on African problems. They were militant in their attitudes. Later that year, in May, delegates from some 20 states met at Monrovia, in Liberia. Their views were more moderate than those of the Casablanca group. A split between the groups threatened African unity.

Second, by its resolution that all members should accept the inherited colonial boundaries, it prevented border incidents and wars of adjustment that could have brought chaos to Africa. It has also tried, with varying degrees of success, to produce united action over 'Rhodesia' and South Africa.

By the beginning of 1972 many observers felt that OAU was no longer effective. The 1972 meeting at Rabat, however, appeared to give the organization a new lease of life. A new secretary-general, Nzo Ekangaki of Cameroon, was appointed. The conference ended the dispute between Guinea and Senegal. It saw the formal signing of a protocol between Algeria and Morocco, ending their border dispute. It admitted representatives of guerrilla movements as full members of the conference and promised them more aid. With all its difficulties, the OAU acts as a mediator. It also helps to create a sense of continental purpose. In early 1976 the OAU was bitterly divided over support for the various nationalist factions in the war that followed Angolan independence. Eventually a majority emerged that supported the Russian-backed MPLA led by Agostinho Neto.

The United Nations Four political problems have so far dominated African activities at the UN. They are South Africa, decolonization, 'Rhodesia', and, until 1974, the Portuguese territories.

In 1952, South Africa's policy of apartheid was first debated at the World Assembly. As a result the UN called for the breaking of diplomatic relations and for trade boycotts of South Africa. In the 1970s UN pressure on South Africa mounted over the issue of Namibia. The General Assembly (but not the Security Council) voted for South Africa's expulsion from the UN in 1974. Increasingly, during the 1950s, the UN was used as a base for the campaign for decolonization. African pressures at the UN forced Britain to mount an oil blockade of Beira in 1966. In 1970 a UN Commission stopped further Portuguese intervention in Guinea.

The UN also played a major part in the Congo crisis between 1960 and 1965. When it came to an end, the UN had spent $392.8 million, while 20,000 troops from 23 countries had served in the UN force.

Between 1947 and 1969, World Bank loans to Africa totalled $1,700 million. The Economic Commission for Africa (ECA) at Addis Ababa, Ethiopia, had a budget of $5,479,000 in 1971. It has been responsible for much regional co-operation, the establishment of the African Development Bank, the starting of the trans-Saharan highway and the Mombasa–Lagos trans-continental road.

▲ Judith Todd, daughter of Garfield Todd, demonstrating against the policies of the white 'Rhodesian' government.

Below left Black and white women demonstrate against police action in South Africa in 1974. The police had arrested 37 people at a pro-FRELIMO rally in Durban.

Below right Rwandan and Nigerian delegates negotiating with the European Economic Community over future trade relations.

WHO'S WHO

An alphabetical guide to famous African personalities

Abboud, Ibrahim (1900–), became president, prime minister and army commander-in-chief of Sudan in 1958 when he overthrew the government of Abdullah Khalil in a bloodless coup. In 1964, he was replaced by a civilian government. Abboud fought with the Sudanese contingent of the British army during World War II in North Africa.

Abd al-Kadir (1807–83) was an Algerian hero who tried to prevent the French conquest of Algeria in the early 1800s. After the French conquered Algiers in 1830, he was chosen by the Arab tribes of Oran as emir. From 1832 to 1847 he skilfully fought the French invaders. In 1835 he crushed the French at the battle of Makta. Finally driven into Morocco, he surrendered to the French in 1847. He was sent to France, but died in Damascus, Syria.

Abd al-Krim (1880–1963) was a Moroccan chief who led revolts against Spanish and French colonial rule in Morocco in the 1920s. Defeated by combined Spanish and French forces in 1926, he was exiled to the French island of Réunion. In 1947, when being taken to France, he jumped ship and escaped to Egypt, where he continued his anti-colonial work.

Abd al-Mumin (1101?–63), an Arab chief, founded the political power of the Almohad (unitarian) Muslim dynasty of northern Africa in the 1100s. He was a disciple of Muhammad ibn-Tumart, the spiritual founder of the Almohads. In a series of campaigns beginning in 1139, al-Mumin and his followers extended their power into Morocco and Algeria. In 1146–7 they overthrew the Almoravid dynasty in Spain and took control.

Abrahams, Peter (1919–), a leading South African writer, was born in Transvaal and educated in Johannesburg. He left Africa at the age of 20, but many of his works have African themes. His books include his autobiography *Tell Freedom, Song of the City* (1945), *Wild Conquest* (1951), *Return to Goli* (1953) and *A Wreath for Udomo* (1956).

Ibrahim Abboud

Acheampong, Ignatius Kutu (1931–), a Ghanaian colonel, led the military coup which overthrew the government of Kofi Busia in January 1972. Born in Kumasi, Ghana, he received military training in Britain and served with the United Nations force in Congo (now Zaire) in 1962–3. From 1966 he was chairman of Ghana's western region administration, and was appointed acting commander of the first brigade of the Ghana army in 1971. After the overthrow of Busia's government he became chairman of the National Redemption Council government. In addition to being chairman, he also took responsibility for defence and finance.

Achebe, Chinua (1930–), a leading Nigerian novelist and poet, was educated at Government college, Umuahia, and at the university college, Ibadan. He worked for the Nigerian Broadcasting Corporation from 1954 to 1966 and became a senior research fellow at the Institute of African Studies of the University of Nigeria in 1967. Achebe won several literary awards for his books, which include *Things Fall Apart* (1958), *No Longer at Ease* (1960), *Arrow of God* (1964), *Chike and the River* (1966), *Man of the People* (1966), and *Girls at War* (1972).

Adoula, Cyrille (1921–), a leading politician of Zaire, was born in Kinshasa. He received a secondary education and, in the 1950s, was an active trade unionist. From 1960 to 1961, he was minister of the interior and was prime minister from 1961 to 1964. During the late 1960s, he served as Zaire's ambassador to Belgium, Luxembourg and the European Economic Community, and to the U.S.

Afewerk, Tekle (1932–) an Ethiopian artist, was born at Ankober, Shoa. He studied art in London. Afewerk received a commission to design stained glass windows for Africa Hall, Addis Ababa. His other works include murals, mosaics, frescoes, sculpture, drawings and designs for Ethiopian stamps.

Aguiyi-Ironsi, Johnson (1925–66), a Nigerian army commander, headed the short-lived military government that took power after the army overthrew the federal government of Sir Abubakar Tafawa Balewa in January 1966. This coup threatened northern control of the federal government, and in July 1966 northern army officers rebelled. Aguiyi-Ironsi was killed and his government overthrown. General Yakubu Gowon succeeded him as head of state. Aguiyi-Ironsi was a British-trained officer. In 1965, with the rank of major-general, he became the first Nigerian to command the Nigerian army.

Ahidjo, Ahmadou (1924–), became president of the Cameroon Federal Republic in 1961. Before that, he had headed a semi-independent government in French Cameroon (1958–60). From 1960 to 1961, he was president of the Cameroon Republic. He retained this office when the East and West Cameroons joined in 1961 to form a federation. Born at Garoua, Cameroon, Ahidjo worked as a radio operator before his election to the First Assembly of East Cameroon in 1947.

Ahmed, Jamel Mohammed (1917–), a leading Sudanese writer and former diplomat, was educated at Gordon College, Khartoum, and in Britain. He served as Sudanese ambassador to several Arab countries, Ethiopia and Britain. He was Sudan's delegate to the United Nations and served as permanent under-secretary at the Sudanese ministry of foreign affairs before retiring in 1970. His books include *Africa Rediscovered* (1963).

Jamel Mohammed Ahmed

Akii-Bua, John, a Ugandan hurdler, began hurdling in 1967 but progressed so rapidly that in 1970 he was fourth in the Commonwealth Games 400-metre hurdles. In 1971 he won the event for Africa in a match against the United States with a time of 49 seconds. At the Munich Olympics of 1972, he created a new world record of 47.8 seconds with a technically faultless style.

Aklilou Abte-Wold, Teshafi Teezaz (1912–74), was prime minister of Ethiopia from 1961 until he was overthrown in February 1974. Educated at the French Lycée in Alexandria, Egypt, and in France, he began his political career as Ethiopian chargé d'affaires in Paris (1936–40). From 1943 to 1949, he was vice-minister for foreign affairs, becoming minister in 1949. He held a variety of important posts in the 1950s before becoming deputy prime minister in 1958. He was executed in November, 1974.

Al-Bakri (?–1094) was a great Arab geographer. Born either in Moorish Spain or Africa, he studied at Córdoba, Spain. His works are among the oldest surviving records of Arab–Spanish geographers. His chief work, *Book of the Roads and Provinces*, contains historical material and information about the peoples of his time as well as geographical description. Much of our knowledge of ancient Ghana comes from the writings of Al-Bakri, although he never travelled south of the Sahara.

Al Mu'izz (?–976) was the fourth caliph or *imam* of the Fatimid Arab dynasty. During his reign Egypt was conquered and remained under Fatimid rule for 200 years. When al-Mu'izz succeeded his father al-Mansur in 953, his authority extended over present-day Morocco, Algeria and Tunisia. After the death of the Arab ruler of Egypt, al-Mu'izz's armies conquered Egypt in 969, establishing the Fatimid capital at Cairo.

Amin, Idi (1925–), a Ugandan army officer and a Muslim, became president of Uganda in January 1971 after a military coup had deposed the former president, Milton Obote. Amin joined the King's African Rifles in 1946 and from 1964 to 1971 was Uganda's army commander with the rank of major-general. In 1972, Amin ordered the expulsion of tens of thousands of Asians from Uganda in the interests of the 'economic war'. He also broke off relations with Israel and has taken a marked pro-Arab stance in foreign affairs.

Amr-Ibn al-As (580?–664) was an Arab leader who conquered Egypt in the 600s. Born in Mecca, Arabia, he became a Muslim in 629, having earlier been an enemy of Muhammad. In 636 the caliph Abu Bakr gave him command of one of the three forces invading Palestine, from where Amr-Ibn al-As invaded Egypt in 639. There, after the fall of Alexandria and Tripoli (642–3), he founded Cairo (then Fustat). He was removed from the Egyptian command by the caliph Othman, but later became governor of Egypt until his death.

Ankrah, Joseph Arthur (1915–), lieutenant-general of the Ghanaian army, was chairman of the National Liberation Council (NLC) of Ghana from 1966 to 1969. The NLC was set up following the overthrow of the former president Kwame NKRUMAH. Born in southern Ghana, Ankrah was educated in Accra and saw service in World War II and as a brigadier in the United Nations Congo operation in 1960–1. Ankrah remained chairman of the NLC, as well as chief of defence staff, until a few months before the general election of August 1969, after which a civilian government took office.

Antubam, Kofi (1922–64), was a Ghanaian artist who studied in London. He held one-man shows in Europe and represented the modern African school of art which, while drawing on tradition, has new content. His work included the Ghanaian state regalia and murals in the United Nations buildings in Geneva. He founded the Ghana Society of Artists and helped found the Ghana National Museum.

Apithy, Sourou Migan (1913–), was president of the republic of Dahomey from 1964 to 1965, and became a member of the presidential council of Dahomey from 1970 to 1972. His political career began in the 1940s, when he was a Dahomeyan deputy in the French parliament. From 1958–9 he was prime minister of the provisional government of Dahomey and from 1960 to 1963 ambassador to France, Britain and Switzerland.

Dr. Nnamdi Azikiwe   **Sir Abubakar Tafawa Balewa**

Arabi Pasha (1840?–1911) was an Egyptian army officer who led a revolt against foreign influence and Turkish overlordship in Egypt in 1881–2. He succeeded in forcing the Khedive, Tewfik Pasha, to set up a nationalist ministry with himself as war minister. When the British took the Khedive under their protection, he declared Arabi Pasha a rebel. A British force then defeated Arabi Pasha at the battle of Tel el Kebir in 1882. The Khedive was restored, Arabi Pasha was exiled to Ceylon, and Egypt came under British control.

Armah, Ayi Kwei (1939–) is a Ghanaian writer who has lived for many years outside his own country. He began his writing career contributing articles to various magazines and writing short stories. His major works are his novels: *The Beautyful Ones Are Not Yet Born* (1968), a biting criticism of modern Africa; *Fragments* (1970), a semi-autobiographical novel about a child who does not match his parents expectations of him; *Two Thousand Seasons*, an attack on Western values in African society; and *Why Are We So Blest?* Armah was born at Takoradi, Ghana, and later studied at Harvard University in the United States.

Awolowo, Obafemi (1909–), a Nigerian statesman and writer, was born at Ijebu, Nigeria, and educated in Nigeria and Britain. He worked in several professions before becoming a solicitor and advocate of the Nigerian supreme court (1947–51). From 1954 to 1959 he was premier of Nigeria's western region, and from 1960 to 1962 he led the Opposition in the federal parliament. In 1967 he became chancellor of the university of Ife. His books include *Path to Nigerian Freedom; Thoughts on the Nigerian Constitution*, and an autobiography, *Awo*.

Awoonor, Kofi (1935–), a Ghanaian poet and editor, was born in Keta, Ghana. His publications include *Poems from Ghana* (edited 1969) and *Rediscovery*. He was educated at Achimota secondary school and the university of Ghana. He later worked for the Ghana Film Industry Corporation.

Aye, Hippolyte (1932–), an Ivory Coast politician and doctor, became minister of health and population in 1970. Born in Anoumako, Abidjan, he studied medicine in France. From 1966 to 1969 he was assistant head of the clinical department at the medical school of Abidjan university. In 1970 he served as president of the general assembly of the World Health Organization.

Azikiwe, Nnamdi (1904–), a Nigerian statesman, was the first president of Nigeria (1963–6). Born at Zungeru, northern Nigeria, he had his university education in the United States. In the late 1930s he took a leading part in the emerging Nigerian nationalist movement and founded a chain of newspapers. In the 1940s he became president of the National Council of Nigeria and Cameroon. From 1954 to 1959, he was the premier of the eastern region and from 1960 to 1963 he was governor general of Nigeria. While in Britain in 1966, Azikiwe was deposed by a military uprising. He returned home as a private citizen.

Baker, **Sir Samuel White** (1821–93), a British explorer, was one of the first Europeans known to have seen the sources of the River Nile. Accompanied by his wife, he went to Africa in 1861. After exploring the Nile tributaries on the Sudan-Ethiopian border, Baker sailed up the White Nile to Gondokoro, Sudan, where he met John Hanning SPEKE. In 1864, guided by Speke's information, he reached and named Lake Albert (now Mobutu Sese Seko), which proved to be part of the Nile system.

Balewa, Sir Abubakar Tafawa (1912–66), became Nigeria's first federal prime minister in 1957, and received a knighthood when Nigeria became independent in 1960. He was killed in a military uprising in 1966. Balewa was born at Bauchi in northern Nigeria. He became a member of the Northern People's Congress and was elected to the Nigerian Federal Assembly in 1947.

Banda, Hastings Kamuzu (1906–), became president of Malawi when it became a republic in 1966. Born in Kasungu district, Nyasaland (now Malawi), he studied medicine in the US. Banda practised as a doctor in Britain and Ghana before returning to Nyasaland to become president-general of the African National Congress in 1958. In 1960 he became leader of the Malawi Congress Party and from 1964 to 1966 was prime minister.

Barnard, Christiaan Neethling (1922–), a South African heart surgeon, in 1967 performed the world's first successful heart transplant operation. Born in Cape Province and educated at the university of Cape Town, Barnard graduated in 1947 and worked for some years as a doctor before studying heart surgery in the US. On his return, he worked at Groote Schuur hospital in Cape Town, and became head of the cardiac research and surgery department in the university medical faculty. There he developed the Barnard valve, for use in open-heart surgery.

Dr Hasting Kamuzu Banda

Christiaan Neethling Barnard (*centre*) at a press conference.

Bassey, Hogan 'Kid' (real name **Okon**), a Nigerian world-class boxer was born in Calabar in 1932. He won his country's flyweight title when only 17. He made his home in Liverpool, England, in 1951. Having taken the Empire featherweight title in 1955, he went on to win the world championship in 1957.

Bayero, Alhaji Abdullahi (?–1953), was emir of Kano in northern Nigeria from 1926 until his death. He was greatly revered in Kano for his learning and for his Islamic piety. A college in Kano of the Ahmadu Bello university is named after him.

Bayero Alhaji Ado (1930–), became emir of Kano in northern Nigeria in 1963. Educated at Ahmadu Bello university, he became chief of police. He served as Nigerian ambassador to Senegal before becoming emir and also was a member of the Northern house of assembly.

Bayi, Filbert, a Tanzanian 1,500-metre runner, was born in 1953 near Arusha in the foothills of Mt. Kilimanjaro. He became known in 1973 when he ran a series of 1,500-metre and mile races in times close to world records. He likes to lead and usually runs the first 800 metres at a blistering pace of around 1 minute 50 seconds. In Stockholm, in July 1973, he used this tactic to force Ben Jipcho to run the second fastest mile time ever (3 minutes 52.0 seconds) and himself the third fastest (3 minutes 52.6 seconds). In the 1974 Commonwealth Games he led from the start of the 1,500-metre race. He defeated the best field of 1,500-metre runners ever assembled, with a record-beating 3 minutes 32.2 seconds. In May 1975 at Kingston, Jamaica, Bayi made a new world record for the mile of 3 minutes 51 seconds.

Bello, Sir Ahmadu (1910–66), was Sardauna (ruler) of Sokoto in northern Nigeria and great-great-grandson of the reformer Uthman dan FODIO. He became minister of Northern Nigeria in 1952 and later premier of the Northern Region. He was also the leader of the Northern Nigerian political party NPC. He wrote an autobiography entitled *My Life*. He was assassinated during the military coup of January, 1966.

Ben Bella, Ahmed (1916–), was the first prime minister, and later, president of Algeria after independence in 1962. He served in the French army in World War II. In 1945, he joined the Algerian People's Party. As one of the nine 'historic leaders' of the FLN in 1954, he helped to launch the Algerian rebellion which eventually led to independence. He was captured by the French in 1956, but was released in 1962 to become prime minister of the new independent Algeria. He was overthrown by an army coup led by Houari BOUMEDIENNE in 1965.

Beti, Mongo (1932–), a Cameroonian writer, has written several novels, including *Le Pauvre Christ de Bomba* (1956), a satire on colonial rule. He was educated in Yaoundé and the Sorbonne, Paris.

Bikila, Abebe, was probably the greatest marathon runner of all time. Born in Mout province in Ethiopia in 1932, he was unknown outside his own country until the Rome Olympics of 1960. There he took the gold medal in the marathon, running in bare feet and recording the fastest time ever—2 hours 15 minutes and 16.2 seconds—for the 26 miles 385 yards. In the 1964 Olympics in Tokyo, he became the first man to retain a marathon title with a new record time of 2 hours 12 minutes 11.2 seconds. Illness forced him to miss the 1968 Olympics. He was paralysed by a car crash the following year and died in 1973.

Blyden, Edward Wilmot (1832–1912), a West Indian-born Liberian scholar, diplomat and writer, became president of Liberia College in 1880. In 1892 he became Liberia's ambassador to Britain. In his writings Blyden developed the idea of African personality, which became an important theme of subsequent Pan-Africanist thinking.

Bokassa, Jean Bédel (1921–), Central African Republic army officer and politician, became president in 1966, succeeding David DACKO. Bokassa took over the posts of prime minister and minister of defence in the same year, and later several other ministries. He was educated at M'Baiki, Bangui and Brazzaville. He became a captain in the French army and, in the early 1960s, organized the army of the Central African Republic. He became commander-in-chief in 1963.

Jean Bédel Bokassa

Houari Boumedienne

Habib Ben Ali Bourguiba

Amilcar Cabral

Bongo, Omar (formerly **Bernard-Albert**) (1935–), became president of the republic of Gabon in 1967. Born at Lewai, Franceville, he became a civil servant. He held the vice-presidency from March to December 1967. He then became president as well as prime minister, and also headed the ministries of defence, information and planning. In 1968, he founded and became general secretary of the Democratic Party of Gabon.

Botha, General Louis (1862–1919), a South African politician and soldier, was born in Greytown, Natal, the son of a Voortrekker. In 1884 he played a leading role in setting up the Vryheid New Republic in the Orange Free State. During the Anglo-Boer War, he was commandant-general of the Transvaal forces. Having been prominent in the peace treaty, he became leader of the Het Volk party with its policy of reconciliation. In 1907, he was prime minister of the Transvaal and became South Africa's first prime minister at Union in 1910.

Boumedienne, Houari (1925–), became president of Algeria, following a military coup in 1965. He studied and taught Arabic in Tunis and Cairo until he returned to Algeria to join the FLN. In 1957, he became head of the rebel command in the region of Oran. As the chief Algerian military leader, he helped Ahmed BEN BELLA to power in 1962. Three years later Boumedienne led the military coup which deposed Ben Bella.

Bourguiba, Habib Ben Ali (1903–), the first president of Tunisia, was educated in Tunis and Paris. He returned to Tunis in 1930 to run a nationalist newspaper, and in 1934, was a founder of the Neo-Destour Party. The party was banned by the French and he was imprisoned. He left Tunisia after World War II, and returned in 1951, but was again imprisoned from 1952 to 1954 for his political activities. In March 1956, when full independence was declared, he became prime minister of Tunisia. The next year, after the abolition of the monarchy of the Bey, Bourguiba was unanimously elected president by the constituent assembly.

Boye, Ibrahima (1924–), a Senegalese judge, was born in Saint Louis, and educated in France at Montpelier University. In 1961, after holding several important legal positions in Guinea, Dahomey and Ivory Coast, he became attorney-general of Senegal. In 1968 he became chairman of the United Nations permanent commission on human rights as well as Senegal's ambassador to the UN and a member of the UN security council.

Brazza, Pierre Paul François Camille Savorgnan de (1852–1905), a French naval officer, played a major part in founding the French Congo colony (now the Republic of the Congo). While serving off the West African coast he obtained permission to explore the Ogooué River. He founded a settlement that later became Brazzaville, and made many treaties with African chiefs.

Brooks, Angie Elizabeth (1928–), a Liberian lawyer and United Nations official, was born in Montserrado county. She was educated at the university of Liberia and at universities in the United States and Britain. In 1954, she became Liberian delegate to the UN. In 1969–70, she was the president of the 24th session of the UN general assembly.

Bruce, James (1730–94), a Scot, was one of the first Europeans to explore Ethiopia and the sources of the River Nile. From 1763 to 1765, he served as British consul in Algiers. He spent the next three years travelling in the Mediterranean countries of Africa and Asia. Then he set off from Alexandria to reach the source of the Nile. He arrived at Gondar, then the capital of Ethiopia, in 1770. The Ethiopian royal family helped him to reach the source of the Blue Nile.

Burton, Sir Richard Francis (1821–90), a British soldier and diplomat, explored extensively in Africa. In 1857, he and John Hanning SPEKE set out to find the sources of the River Nile. They reached Lake Tanganyika in 1858, after a hard journey. Burton fell ill and did not accompany Speke on a further part of the trip in which he found Lake Victoria. Burton joined the British diplomatic service in 1861, and became consul at Fernando Póo. While there he explored Dahomey, the Gold Coast (Ghana), and Benin, in Nigeria. His books include *First Footsteps in East Africa* (1856), *Wanderings in West Africa* (1863) and *To the Gold Coast for Gold* (1883).

Busia, Dr. Kofi Abrefa (1913–), a Ghanaian academic and politician, was educated in Ghana and England and held visiting professorships in the United States, Holland and Mexico. A long-standing opponent of Dr. Kwame NKRUMAH, Busia was made adviser to the National Liberation Council in 1966 after Nkrumah was deposed and prime minister in 1969. His government promoted Ghanaian business by africanizing firms belonging to foreigners. When he was deposed in 1972, he went into voluntary exile.

Buthelezi, Chief Gatsha (1924–), a South African politician, was appointed leader of Kwa Zulu in 1971. Kwa Zulu is a large Bantustan, or 'homeland'. Born into the Zulu royal family, he studied at Fort Hare University College. During the 1960s, he worked as a clerk for the government. In 1970, he was elected leader of the Zulu Territorial Authority, set up under the apartheid policy of 'Bantu homelands'. Since then, he has emerged as an important African spokesman working within the South African system, while arguing for radical changes.

Cabral, Amilcar (1924–73), led the struggle against Portuguese rule in Guinea-Bissau until his assassination in 1973. Born in Bafata, Guinea, he was educated in São Vicente and in Lisbon, Portugal, where he trained as an agronomist. In the early 1950s, he worked for the Portuguese administration in Guinea. In 1956, he founded the Guinea and Cape Verde Independence Party (PAIGC) and was a founder member of the Popular Movement for the Liberation of Angola (MPLA). In 1963, he led the PAIGC against the Portuguese.

Cabral, Luiz (1929–) one of the founders of the liberation movement PAIGC in Guinea-Bissau in 1956. Born and educated at Bafata, he became involved in trade unionism when working as a clerk. After a violent strike in 1959, he had to flee the country. During the following years he played an active part in gaining foreign support for PAIGC.

Caillé, René Auguste (1799–1838), was the first European to visit Timbuktu, Mali, and return to tell of his experiences. Caillé, who spoke Arabic, posed as an Egyptian trader. He set out from Kakondy, in Guinea in April 1827. He reached Timbuktu in April 1828, and spent several days exploring it. Then he joined a caravan travelling north and reached Tangier, Morocco, five months later.

Cetewayo (?–1884) became king of the Zulu nation in 1873. During his reign, the powerful Zulu nation was almost destroyed by white settlers and British imperial policy. Having resisted Boer incursions from the north, the Zulus were attacked by a British army, which, after initial heavy losses, overcame the Zulus in 1879. Cetewayo was imprisoned in Cape Town but allowed to return in 1883. He died a year later and the Zulu power was broken.

Chilembwe, John (1871–1915), was founder of the independent Provident Industrial Mission at Mbombwe in Malawi. He led a 12-day rebellion against British rule in 1915, in which three Europeans were killed. Chilembwe himself was shot near the Mozambique border. The revolt was caused by the bad social and economic conditions of the African workers and by the forceful recruitment of African soldiers for the British army. Chilembwe, with his motto 'strike a blow and die', stands as an early national hero in the fight for freedom.

Chona, Mathias Mainza (1930–), became Vice-President of Zambia in 1970 and Prime Minister in 1973. His legal career began when he became an interpreter in the High Court. He then studied law in England, qualifying as a barrister in 1958. On returning home, he entered politics and, in 1959, founded the United National Independence Party (UNIP). He then handed over the leadership to Kenneth Kaunda, on Kaunda's release from prison in 1960. Chona resigned as Prime Minister in May 1975.

Clapperton, Hugh (1788–1827), a Scottish sailor, was sent by the British government in 1822 to find the source of the River Niger. With two companions, he travelled across the Sahara to Bornu, Nigeria, and Lake Chad, and reached as far west as Sokoto, Nigeria. In December, 1825, he headed another expedition, starting from Lagos. He and his servant again reached Sokoto, where Clapperton died.

Cleopatra VII (69–30 BC) was born in Alexandria and ruled as queen of Egypt from 51 to 30 BC. Julius Caesar supported her against a rival claimant to the throne. Cleopatra became Caesar's lover and bore him a son. After Caesar's murder, she captivated Marcus Antonius and supported him in the Roman civil war against Octavian. After the defeat of Antonius in the naval battle of Actium in 31 BC, Egypt was conquered by Octavius and Cleopatra committed suicide by snake-bite.

Covilhão, Pedro da (1400s–1500s), was one of the earliest Portuguese explorers of Ethiopia. In 1487, he and a companion, Alfonso de Paiva, were sent by King John of Portugal to find the legendary kingdom of Prester John. Covilhão's travels took him to India, Egypt and Arabia. About 1490, he reached Zeila (now in Somalia), and travelled inland to Ethiopia. He settled there and married an Ethiopian woman. When a Portuguese mission reached Ethiopia 30 years later, he helped to arrange trade and other contacts.

Dacko, David (1930–), a Central African Republic politician, was educated at the Ecole Normale, Brazzaville. From 1957 to 1958 he was minister of agriculture in the Central African government council; from 1958 to 1959 he was minister of the interior in the provisional Central African government. He became prime minister of the Central African Republic in 1959, and in 1960, president and minister of defence. In 1966, he was replaced by Jean Bédel Bokassa, following a coup.

Daddah, Moktar Ould (1924–), became premier of Mauritania in 1958 and president in 1961. He first worked as an interpreter and then studied law. In 1957, he became a territorial councillor. As president, he holds the office of secretary general of the *Parti du Peuple Mauritanien*. He was chairman of the OAU in 1971–2.

Cetewayo

Danquah, Dr. Joseph Boakye (1895–1965), a Ghanaian lawyer and politician, studied law in London. In 1947, he formed the United Gold Coast Convention and invited Dr. Kwame Nkrumah to be its secretary. Danquah believed in 'self-government as soon as possible', while Nkrumah wanted 'self-government now'. In 1949, Nkrumah formed his own party. Danquah ran against Nkrumah for the first presidency in 1960. He died while imprisoned by Nkrumah.

Delamere, Lord (?–1931) settled in Kenya in 1903. He introduced various crops and livestock into the country. He became a voice of the European settlers in their campaign against the British colonial policies. His reactionary views provided some links with the other races in Kenya.

Denham, Dixon (1786–1828), an English soldier, accompanied Hugh Clapperton and Walter Oudney in an expedition to find the source of the River Niger in 1822. They crossed the Sahara from Tripoli to Lake Chad. Denham explored the region around the lake while the others travelled further west.

Dia, Mamadou (1910–), a Senegalese politician, became a councillor for Senegal in 1946. In 1952, he became a grand councillor for French West Africa and a deputy at the French national assembly. He became vice-president of the Senegalese council of ministers in 1957, and president in the following year. From 1959 to 1960, he was vice-president of the short-lived Mali federation, before becoming president of the council of ministers of Senegal at independence in 1960. In December 1962, Dia's government was overthrown and he was sentenced to life detention in 1963. He was unconditionally released in 1974. Dia published several works on economics and politics.

Dias de Novais, Paulo (1500s), was a Portuguese military leader who played a large part in the conquest of the Ndongo kingdom in Angola. He began his campaign from Luanda in 1576.

Dingane (?–1843) was a Zulu king in the 19th century. The half-brother of Shaka, he was involved in his assassination and succeeded him as king in 1828. He built up relations with the small white colony at Port Natal and with missionaries, as well as furthering Shaka's policy of making Zulu power supreme. In 1838, he encountered the Voortrekkers under Pieter Retief, and Dingane's army inflicted a crushing defeat on them. The Voortrekkers took their revenge at the battle of Blood River and Dingane fled into Swaziland, where he was assassinated in 1843.

Dingiswayo (?–1818) was a Nguni chief of the Mthethwa people in south-eastern South Africa in the late 1700s. He pioneered new tribal structures, such as the age grade system, and military organizations and expanded his domain through the merger of different groups. He provided his successor, Shaka, with the base for the militant expansion.

Diop, Alioune (1910–), a Senegalese writer and publisher, was born in Saint Louis. In 1947, he founded the journal *Présence Africaine*. He organized the International World Congress of Black Writers and Artists in 1956, and in 1957 became secretary-general of the African Cultural Society. He has served as president of the International Congress of Africanists, and also as the president of the World Festival of Negro Art.

Diori, Hamani (1906–), became president of Niger on independence in 1960. He was a deputy in the French parliament for Niger in the years 1946–51 and 1956–9. As president, he survived an assassination attempt in 1965, and was last re-elected in 1970. He was deposed in 1974 by a military coup led by Lieutenant-Colonel Seyni Kountche.

Dlamini, Prince Makhosini (1914–), became Prime Minister of Swaziland in 1967, and led his country to independence in 1968. He worked as a teacher until 1947, when he entered politics, sitting on elected councils and working as a rural development officer. In 1964, he became leader of the royalist Imbokodvo party, which has been in power since independence.

Dos Santos, Maralino (1929–), the first vice-president of Mozambique, was a leading figure in the struggle for independence from Portuguese rule. Born in Lourenço Marques and educated in Lisbon and Paris, he became vice-president of FRELIMO in 1970.

Emin Pasha (1840–92) was a German-born administrator who became *pasha* (governor) of Equatoria province of Sudan. He was born Eduard Schnitzer of Jewish parents. In 1865, he became a Muslim and adopted the name Emin ('the faithful one'). In 1875, he entered the Egyptian service as a medical officer. The British general Charles Gordon made him pasha of Equatoria in 1878. The Mahdi rebellion of 1885 isolated Emin for three years until he was rescued by Henry Morton Stanley. He was murdered by slave traders at Stanley Falls, on the River Zaire, while working for the German East Africa Company.

Enahoro, Chief Anthony (1923–), a Nigerian journalist, was born in the Uromi Ishan division of the Mid-Western state, and was educated there and at King's College, Lagos. In the 1950s he became minister of home affairs for the Western region. In 1963, he was extradited from Britain to Nigeria and imprisoned for treason until 1966. In 1967, he became the Federal Commissioner for information and labour. Enahoro has published his autobiography, *Fugitive Offender*.

Eusebio da Silva Ferreira is probably the greatest of all African-born footballers and one of the best strikers in the world. Born in 1942 in Lourenço Marques, Mozambique, he was qualified to play for Portugal. After joining Benfica club of Lisbon, he helped his team to beat Real Madrid for the European Cup in 1962. He was the leading goal-scorer in Portugal in every season from 1964 to 1968 and was voted European Footballer of the Year in 1965. He was top scorer, with nine goals, in the 1966 World Cup. He has been called the 'European Pele' and perhaps more accurately, the 'Black Panther', because of his electrifying sprints when attacking the opposing team's goal.

Eyadema, Etienne Gnassingbe (1935–), a Togolese army officer, became president and minister of defence of Togo in April 1967, after seizing power three months earlier. Born at Pya in the Lama Kora District, he served in the French army from 1953 to 1961. He became an officer in 1963, and was appointed chief of staff of the Togo army in 1965. In 1969, he became president of the Togolese People's Assembly.

Fodio, Uthman dan (1754–1817), was an Islamic scholar and reformer. After a career of itinerant preaching in the Habe kingdoms of Gobir and Zamfara, he led a successful *jihad* (Islamic holy war) which resulted in the setting up of the Fulani Caliphate of Sokoto. He was the author of books and tracts in classical Arabic on theological subjects, and of verse in Fulfulde and Hausa.

Forster, Isaac (1903–), a Senegalese judge, was appointed to the international court of justice at The Hague, Netherlands, in 1964. From 1958 to 1960 he had been secretary-general of the Senegalese government and from 1960 to 1964 he had served as first president of the Senegalese supreme court.

Fugard, Athol (1932–), a leading South African playwright and actor, is one of the leaders of the 'Sestiger' group (meaning Sixties) of Afrikaans writers who grew to prominence during the 1960s, and who represent a marked break from traditional Afrikaaner culture and literature. His main plays include *The Blood Knot; Hello and Goodbye; People are Living Here; Boesman and Lena; Sizwe Bansi is Dead; The Island.*

Gaddafi, Colonel Muammar al (1938–), became president of Libya in 1969 after an army coup had deposed King IDRIS I. At that time, he was a captain in the Libyan army. As president, he pursued policies of economic and political union with other Arab states. He used some of Libya's

Etienne Gnassingbe Eyadema

oil wealth to extend military and economic aid to other Arab and African countries, such as Uganda. He nationalized the British Petroleum interests in Libya and forced the oil companies to pay more for crude oil exported from Libya. His oil policies, his expulsion of former Italian settlers and his statements opposing other Arab monarchs, especially those of Jordan and Morocco, have made him a controversial figure around the world. A staunch Muslim, Gaddafi is totally committed to the ideals of Arab unity and self-determination. He was born to a semi-nomadic family in the Surt area of Libya.

Gammoudi, Mohammed, born in 1938, is a Tunisian long-distance runner, consistently of world class over a number of years. He has won medals in three Olympic Games. In the 1964 Tokyo Olympics he gained a silver medal, beating the world record-holder Ron Clarke. In 1968, his best year, he won the International Cross-Country Championship in his own country, the military championship in Greece (he is a lieutenant in the Tunisian Army) and the 5,000-metre race in the Mexico Olympics, beating Kipchoge Keino. He also took the bronze medal in the 10,000-metres. In the Munich Olympics of 1972, he just failed to win the 5,000-metres and gained a silver medal.

Gardiner, Robert (1914–), is a Ghanaian international administrator. Born in Kumasi, he was educated in Ghana, Sierra Leone and England. He was head of university departments in Sierra Leone and Nigeria and at one stage responsible for the entire civil service in Ghana. In 1959, he was appointed officer in charge of the UN operation in the Congo and Executive Secretary of the UN Economic Commission for Africa.

Gizenga, Antoine (1925–), a Zairian politician, became deputy premier of the first independence government of Zaire in 1960. He was educated at mission schools and was a mission worker before entering politics. In 1959, he helped found the *Parti Solidaire Africain* (PSA), which won 13 seats in the 1960 election. He joined with Patrice LUMUMBA to form a coalition government. After Lumumba's dismissal, he continued in office as vice-premier in the coalition government until 1962, when he was dismissed and detained. He was finally released in 1965.

Gordimer, Nadine (1923–), is the leading white English-speaking novelist in South Africa. Since the beginning of the 1950s, she has written many novels and short stories and won many literary awards. Her novels sensitively reflect the dilemmas of whites in Africa, and include *The Lying Days; A World of Strangers; The Late Bourgeois World; A Guest of Honour.* In 1974, she won the Booker prize for fiction with her novel *A Conservationist.*

Gowon, Yakubu (1934–), a Nigerian army officer, became head of state and commander-in-chief of the Nigerian army in 1966. Born in Lur Pankshin division of Benue-Plateau state, he was educated in Zaria and at military colleges in Britain. In 1960, he became an officer in the Nigerian army and until 1961 he served in the United Nations force in Congo (now Zaire). In 1966, he was appointed chief of staff, and the following year he became a major-general. His steady leadership of the federal side during the Nigerian civil war (1967–70) helped ensure Nigeria's survival as a state. He was deposed by a coup in July 1975.

Graaff, Sir de Villiers (1913–), a South African politician, was educated at universities in Cape Town, Oxford, and Leyden (Holland). He was elected as a Member of Parliament for the United Party in 1948 and became leader of the party in 1956. As the leader of the opposition in parliament, he has opposed the Nationalist Party, which has retained the support of the white electorate. In formal opposition to the 'apartheid' policy, Graaff has developed the policy of 'federation' of the race groups, which differs only in detail from the policy of the Nationalist Party.

Yakubu Gowon

Grant, James Augustus (1827–92), a Scottish soldier and botanist, helped John Hanning SPEKE to trace the source of the River Nile back to Lake Victoria in 1860–3. In 1868, as a lieutenant-colonel, Grant took part in the expedition to Ethiopia to free British officials imprisoned by the Emperor Theodore.

Grunitzky, Nicholas (1913–), a Togolese politician, trained as an engineer and mathematician in France. From 1951 to 1956 he was a Togolese representative to the French national assembly. He was a founder of the Togolese Progress Party. In 1956–8 he was prime minister. In 1959, he formed the Togolese People's Democratic Union. In 1962 he was president of the provisional government. From 1963 to 1967 he was president.

Guggisberg, Sir Gordon (1869–1930), a Canadian, was governor of the Gold Coast (now Ghana) from 1919 to 1927. He was a practical idealist, convinced of African potential, and he worked hard to improve relations between the British and the Africans. Among other activities, he started the building of new railways and roads, the installation of telephone and telegraph systems, the construction of Takoradi Harbour, and many hospitals and dispensaries.

Haile Selassie I

Haile Selassie I (1892–1975), emperor of Ethiopia from 1930 until 1974, was born Ras Tafari and was the cousin of Emperor MENELIK II. In 1910, he became the governor of Hara province and regent to the Empress Zaudita, Menelik's daughter, in 1916. As regent he carried out a programme of modernization, which included the eradication of slavery. In 1923, Ethiopia joined the League of Nations and Ras Tafari toured Europe. He became emperor in 1930, taking the title Haile Selassie (meaning power of the trinity) and the following year he introduced Ethiopia's first written constitution. During the Italian invasion in 1935, he went into exile in Britain. He returned in 1941. A firm believer and active supporter of Pan-African unity, he served as president of the OAU. He acted as a peace-maker in African affairs and mediated in the Nigerian and Sudanese civil wars. In 1974 he was stripped of all his powers by the Dergue, a Committee of the Armed Forces.

Hamilcar, Barca (270–229 BC), was a Carthaginian general who became commander of the Carthaginian army in Sicily in 247 BC. He conducted many successful engagements in Sicily. He conquered many new areas of Spain and Sardinia for Carthage between 237 and 228 BC. His most famous son was HANNIBAL.

Hannibal (247–183 BC) commanded the armies of the ancient Phoenician city of Carthage in their wars with the Romans. In 218 BC he led his army from Spain, through France and over the Alps, into Italy, where he defeated the Romans at the battle of Cannae. He returned to Carthage, but was defeated by the Romans at the battle of Zawa in 203 BC. In 183 BC he poisoned himself to avoid being captured by a superior Roman force.

Hassan II (1929–), king of Morocco, was born in Rabat. The elder son of MOHAMMED V, he was officially designated heir to the throne in 1957. He married in 1961, and succeeded to the throne in that year. Two unsuccessful military coups to overthrow him occurred in 1971 and 1972. In 1975 he led Moroccan attempts to annex Spanish Sahara.

Herzog, General James Barry Munnik (1866–1942), was a South African politician and soldier. He studied law and became a judge in the Transvaal in the 1890s. As general of the Orange Free State forces, he took part in the Anglo-Boer war and afterwards became the political leader of the Orange Free State. He joined the cabinet at Union in 1910. His opposition to General BOTHA led him to resign in 1913, and form the National Party. In 1924, the National Party, in alliance with the Labour Party came to power, and Herzog became prime minister. He remained in this post until 1939, in alliance with Jan SMUTS in the United South African National Party after 1932.

Houphouet-Boigny, Felix (1905–), was elected President of Ivory Coast at independence in 1960, and re-elected in 1965. He took up politics in 1944, becoming President of the Syndicat Agricole Africain. A year later he founded the PDCI (Parti Démocratique de la Côte d'Ivoire). He was a member of the post-war constituent assembly of French West Africa in 1946, and was elected to the French National Assembly in the same year. In 1959, he founded the group of French-speaking West African countries known as the Conseil de l'Entente, comprising Niger, Upper Volta, Dahomey and Ivory Coast.

Huggins, Godfrey (later Lord Malvern) (1883–1971), was a Rhodesian politician born in England. He trained as a doctor before going to Rhodesia in 1911, where he set up a medical practice. He was elected to the Legislative Council in 1923 and in 1933 became prime minister and minister of native affairs. He remained in this position until he took over the premiership of the Central African Federation in 1953. As prime minister of the Federation he attempted to implement 'racial partnership'.

Hassan II

Hussein, Abdirazak Haji (1924–), was prime minister of the Somali Republic in 1964–7. In 1944, he joined the Somali Youth League, the chief independence party. He became president of the League in 1955 and first entered parliament in 1959. In 1960, he became minister of the interior in the first independent Somali government, and later minister of public works. Hussein has been held in detention since 1969, when his government was taken over by the military.

Ibn Battuta (1304–68) was a Moroccan explorer. He began his travels with a journey to Mecca, which continued as a 24 year tour of Asia. During this journey he visited Zeila, Mombasa, and Kilwa on the East African coast. In 1352, he crossed the Sahara from Tangier to the empire of Songhai, whose capital was Timbuktu. From there he ventured into the old Mali empire, and explored part of the River Niger.

Ibn Hawqal (AD 900s) was an Arab traveller and geographer. He set out from Baghdad in 943 on an extensive series of journeys through Asia and Africa, which he recorded in the important geographical work *Kitab al-masalik wa l-mamalik* (Book of Routes and Kingdoms).

Ibn Khaldun (1332–1406) was an Arab historian, philosopher and politician. He was born in Tunis and entered its ruler's service. A series of political intrigues took him to the courts at Fez, Granada, Bougie, and Biskra. North-western Africa became too unsafe for him, and he went to Egypt, where he was appointed a judge. He wrote a history of the Arab peoples, *Kitab al 'Ibar* (Book of Examples).

Ibn Tumart (1078?–1130), a Berber religious Muslim leader, founded the Muslim Almohad (unitarian) movement, which, after his death, formed a powerful state with its capital at Marrakech, Morocco. Ibn Tumart spent many years studying Islamic thought in the Middle East, and returned to his native Morocco to lead a religious reform movement. The Almoravid rulers of Marrakech objected to his preaching, and he was forced to flee to the Atlas mountains, where he began a rebellion and started the Almohad state.

Ibrahim Pasha (1789–1848) was the son of MOHAMMED ALI PASHA and his chief general. He led the Egyptian armies in their conquest of Arabia and Syria. The period of his governorship of Syria was one of stability and prosperity.

Idris I (1890–) was king of Libya from 1951, when the country became independent until he was deposed by a revolution in 1969. During World War I, he became leader of the Sanussi religious order. As such, he led the Libyan struggle for independence from the Italians and was eventually forced to go into exile in Egypt. He returned to Libya in 1947. He remained a remote figure during his reign and was abroad when the revolution against him took place.

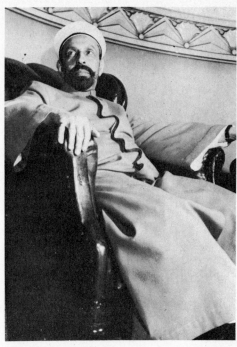
Idris I

Idris Alooma (1575?–1617) was the most important *mai*, or king, of Bornu (now part of northern Nigeria). He united Bornu after a series of wars during which he conquered the Marghai, Gamergum, and Mandara peoples to the south. He also subdued Kanem, north of Lake Chad. A devout Muslim, he built mosques and did his best to spread Islam throughout his lands.

Idris Ibn Adb Allah (?–795), Idris I, was a refugee from Arabia who founded the dynasty of the Idrisids in northern Morocco in AD 788. He claimed descent from the caliph Ali, son-in-law of the prophet Muhammad. Idris was poisoned in AD 795 by Harun al Rashid at Oulili (Volubilis).

Ileo, Joseph (1921–), a Zairian politician, was prime minister of Zaire from January to August in 1961. Educated at mission school, he worked as an accountant before entering politics. In 1958, he was co-founder, with Patrice LUMUMBA, of the *Mouvement National Congolais* (MNC), but led a breakaway faction from it in 1959. He was prime minister of the provisional federal government in 1961. Since then he has held various government posts. In 1969, he became a member of the political bureau of the *Mouvement Populaire de la Révolution* founded by President MOBUTU.

Imhotep lived about 2600 BC and was an Egyptian physician and architect. He built the famous step pyramid at Saqqara.

Issa, Abdullahi (1922–), a Somali political leader, was a founder member, in 1943, of the Somali Youth League, which became the principal independence party. In 1947 he was made its secretary general. In 1959, he became the first prime minister of the Somali parliament. In 1960, in the newly independent Somali Republic, he was appointed minister for foreign affairs. He subsequently held the posts of minister for health and labour (1964) and minister of industry and commerce (1966). After the military takeover in 1969, he was placed in detention.

Jawara, Sir Dawda Kairaba (1924–), became president of Gambia in 1970. Born in Barajally, MacCarthy Island, he was educated at Bathurst, at Achimota College in Ghana and at Glasgow university in Britain. During the 1950s he worked as a veterinary officer. In 1960, he became leader of the People's Progressive Party and minister of education. He was prime minister from 1963 to 1970.

Jipcho, Ben, is a Kenyan runner. Born in 1943, he is younger than Kipchoge KEINO, who at first overshadowed him. In the 1968 Olympics 1,500-metre race won by Keino, Jipcho was tenth. But he was second to Keino in the 1972 Olympics steeplechase. In 1973, he equalled the world steeplechase record and then lowered it to 8 minutes 14 seconds.

Jonathan, Chief Leabua (1914–), became prime minister of Lesotho in 1966. In the 1930s, he worked in the South African gold mines. Since 1937, he has been involved in politics and administration—firstly as a local official, then as a member of the district and national councils in 1954. In 1959, he founded the Basutoland National Party (BNP) which lost the 1960 election. In 1965, he led the BNP to victory in the election and his country to independence in 1966. As prime minister he also acted as minister of external and internal affairs and defence. After the 1970 election, he declared a state of emergency and annulled the results. Having put down the opposition, he declared a 'political holiday' and in 1973 made attempts to reconstitute the national assembly. In early 1974 he suppressed an attempted insurrection.

Jumbe, Sheikh Aboud (1920–), succeeded Sheik KARUME as first vice-president of Tanzania and chairman of the revolutionary council of Zanzibar when Karume was assassinated in 1972. He joined Karume's Afro-Shirazi party in 1953, having previously had his own party, the Zanzibar National Union. He held office under Karume as minister of state with responsibility for religious affairs.

Chief Leabua Jonathan ▶

Ben Jipcho ▼

Kadalie, Clements (1896–), was an African trade union leader in South Africa in the 1920s. In 1919 he formed the Industrial and Commercial Union (ICU) for dock workers. The union was centrally involved in successful strikes at that period. It grew to become a general union for Africans throughout South Africa and beyond, with an estimated membership in 1928 of 250,000. Kadalie was its national secretary until 1929. By 1930, internal divisions had caused the union to collapse.

Kano, Alhaji Aminu (1920–), is a Nigerian politician and author. He worked as a schoolteacher and, in 1947, he founded the Northern Teachers' Association. He became president of a political party called the Northern Elements Political Union (NEPU) in 1954. Elected to the house of representatives in 1959, he became deputy chief whip in the coalition government. He has written plays and songs in Hausa and is the author of articles and pamphlets criticizing the colonial Northern Nigerian Native Authority.

Kapwepwe, Simon Mwanza (1922–), a Zambian politician, first qualified as a teacher. He joined the African National Congress (ANC) and in 1956 became its treasurer. In 1958, he broke away from ANC to form the Zambia National Congress (ZNC) with Kenneth KAUNDA, and later joined the United National Independence Party (UNIP) after ZNC had been banned. Kapwepwe was vice-president of Zambia in 1967–70, but resigned from the government in 1971 to form the opposition United Progressive Party (UPP).

Karume, Sheikh Abeid (1905–72), became ruler of Zanzibar through a revolution only 32 days after the country had become independent in 1964. He had previously led the Afro-Shirazi party that had campaigned for the African government of Zanzibar. As president, Karume established ties with Russia and China and accepted aid and military missions from them. He governed Zanzibar through the revolutionary council and held the post of first vice-president of Tanzania until his assassination.

Kasavubu, Joseph Ileo (1910–69), the first president of Zaire, held office from 1960 to 1965. After attending Roman Catholic seminaries, he qualified as a teacher in 1940. In 1958, he was elected mayor of a commune and demanded self-government and elections. As the leader of the Alliance des Bakongo (ABAKO), he favoured a federal state and was opposed to Patrice LUMUMBA's policies of creating a strong central government in Zaire. The post-independence elections gave neither side a complete majority. A compromise resulted in Lumumba becoming prime minister and Kasavubu becoming president. After Lumumba's murder, Kasavubu presided over the governments of Joseph ILEO and Moise TSHOMBE.

Kashim, Shettima (later Sir Kashim Ibrahim) (1910–), worked first as a teacher and later as a local government official in northern Nigeria. He was appointed *waziri* (vizier) of Bornu in 1955 and became minister of social services in the federal Nigerian government. From 1962 until the military coup of 1966, he was the first governor of Northern Nigeria. In 1967, he became chancellor of Ibadan university.

Kaunda, Kenneth David (1924–), became the first president of Zambia in 1964. He joined the African National Congress (ANC) in 1952 and became a district organizer and later secretary general. After criticisms of Harry NKUMBULA's leadership, Kaunda left the ANC to form the Zambia National Congress (ZNC) in 1958. ZNC was banned by the colonial government and Kaunda served nine months in prison. He became leader of the United National Independence Party after his release in 1960. He is the creator of the political philosophy of Humanism and has played a leading role in the pressures for independence in Zimbabwe and Mozambique.

Kawawa, Rashidi Mfaume (1929–), became prime minister and second vice-president of Tanzania in 1972. As vice-president of the Tanganyikan African National Union party, he held office as prime minister in the period between independence and the election of Julius NYERERE as President in 1962. He had previously held the posts of minister of local government and housing, and minister without portfolio. He has been very active in promoting the policy of Ujamaa villages and socialism in Tanzania.

Kenneth David Kaunda

Kayibanda, Grégoire (1924–), became president of Rwanda when it became independent in 1962. He was overthrown by the Defence Minister, General Habyalimana, in 1973. Before entering politics, he worked as a teacher. From 1955 to 1958 he was the editor of a Roman Catholic newspaper in Rwanda.

Keino, Kipchoge, a Kenyan runner, born in 1940, was inspired by Kenya's first great athlete Nyandika Maiyoro. He made a big impression in the 1964 Tokyo Olympics without actually getting a medal. But in 1965 he beat the world record-holder Ron Clarke and set new world records for the 3,000-metres (7 minutes 39.6 seconds) and 5,000-metres (13 minutes 24.2 seconds). In the 1966 Commonwealth Games, he won the three-mile and mile races. His time for the mile was the second fastest ever (3 minutes 53.4 seconds). Then came gold medals in the 1968 Olympics 1,500-metres, the 1970 Commonwealth 1,500-metres and the 1972 Olympics steeplechase, as well as medals in other events.

Grégoire Kayibanda

Kipchoge Keino

Mzee Jomo Kenyatta

Keita, Fodeba (1921–), a Guinean writer and politician was born in Siguiri and studied law at the Sorbonne, Paris. In 1958, he founded the Guinean National Ballet, and in the same year became minister of the interior and of security. He later occupied other ministerial post. Among his books are *African Poems; The African Theatre; The School Master* and *The Men of the Dance.*

Keita, Modibo (1915–), was president of Mali from 1960 to 1968. Educated at Dakar, Senegal, he was *conseiller général* for French Sudan in the mid-1950s and deputy to the French national assembly. From 1958 to 1960 he was president of the constituent assembly at Dakar. For most of his term as president of Mali, Keita was also minister of defence. He received the Lenin peace prize in 1962.

Keita, Salif, a Malian footballer known as 'Domingo' is considered by some to be the best player in Africa. Born in 1946, he played for Real Bamako and Mali's national team before joining St. Etienne in France in 1967. Almost at once, he helped his new team to the league and cup championships. A fast-running striker, he has scored an average of 25 goals a season. He was voted African Footballer of the Year in 1970.

Kenyatta, Mzee Jomo (1893–), president of Kenya, was born at Ichaweri, near Nairobi. His early education was at the Church of Scotland mission in Kikuyu. He became a court interpreter and later supervisor in the Nairobi municipal council water department. In 1928, he became general-secretary of the Kikuyu Central Association and later studied at the London School of Economics and visited Moscow and western Europe. He also took a prominent part in the Fifth Pan African Congress which was held at Manchester, England, in 1945. In 1947, he was president of the Kenya African Union and in 1952 he was arrested on suspicion of leading the 'Mau Mau' rebellion. Sentenced to seven years' imprisonment and detention thereafter, he was eventually released in 1961. As leader of the Kenya African National Union, he took office as Kenya's first prime minister in June 1963. He became president when Kenya became a republic in December 1964. In 1938 he published *Facing Mount Kenya*, a sociological study of his own people and has written other political books such as *Kenya, the Land of Conflict* (1945).

Kerekou, Major Matthieu (1933–), became head of state and head of the government of Dahomey in 1972. His accession to power followed a coup which overthrew the Presidential Council which had ruled the country from 1970.

Khalifa, Ser al-Khatim (1919–), a Sudanese politician and educationist, was educated at Gordon college, Khartoum. He served as a teacher at Gordon college and at Bakht er-Roda teacher training institute. He was principal of Khartoum technical institute in 1960–4 and 1965–6, and a deputy under-secretary at the ministry of education. He was prime minister briefly in 1964 and again in 1964–5. He was ambassador to Italy in 1966–8 and ambassador to Britain in 1968–9.

Khama, Sir Seretse, KBE (1921–), president of Botswana, was educated at Tiger Kloof, Adams college and Lovedale. He graduated at Fort Hare and went on to take a degree at Balliol college, Oxford. He practised law at the Inner Temple, London, and later in Botswana. In 1950, he was exiled until 1956. He served on the African Advisory Council and the Joint Advisory Council and was elected to the legislative council. He founded the BDP (Botswana Democratic Party) in 1962 and became its first president. In 1965, he was elected to the legislative assembly (now national assembly) and the following year he became the first president of Botswana.

Kimathi, Dedan (1931–57) became leader, in 1953, of the Mau Mau freedom fighters in Kenya during the struggle against colonial rule. He was born at Gakanga in Nyeri District and, after his school education, followed various jobs before becoming interested in politics. In 1952, he moved to the forests of the Aberdares where he organised Mau Mau resistance to the British. Four years later he was captured and hanged at Nairobi prison.

Kingsley, Mary Henrietta (1862–1900), an English author and explorer, understood the people of Africa as few Europeans of her time did. She made her first visit to West Africa in 1893, and a year later travelled up the Ogooué River by canoe from the coast of Gabon. She insisted that African customs ought to be respected, and that the people should be administered through their own rulers.

Kiwanuka, Kabimu Mugumba Benedicto (1922–72?), was a Ugandan judge and politician. He was educated in Basutoland and in Britain. He became president-general of the Uganda Democratic Party, and in 1961 a government minister. He was chief minister from 1961 to 1962, when he became prime minister. In 1963, and again in 1964, he was arrested, but charges against him were dropped. He was imprisoned from 1969 to 1971, when the government of Apolo Milton Obote fell. Kiwanuka then became chief justice, but in 1972 he disappeared.

Koroma, Sorie Ibrahim (1930–), became prime minister and vice-president of Sierra Leone in 1971. Born in Port Loko, he was educated in Freetown, Sierra Leone, and in Ibadan, Nigeria. A member of parliament from 1962 to 1965, he was re-elected in 1967. He became minister of agriculture and natural resources in 1969.

Kountche, Seyni (1931–), became president of Niger in 1974 when he led a successful military coup against President Hamani Diori. Kountche was previously the army chief of staff. After the coup, Kountche established, together with 10 other army officers, a Supreme Military Council to govern Niger. Kountche was declared head of state, head of the Council and Minister of Economic Affairs.

Kruger, Stephanus Johannes Paulus (1825–1904), was a South African politician, and the father-figure of Afrikaaner Republicanism. He was born in the East Cape and trekked to the Transvaal as a small boy. A leading figure in the Trekker republics, he led resistance to British annexation in 1870. He became president of the South African Republic in 1883 at the time when the gold rush to the Witwatersrand was under way. He resisted British imperial interests, both commercial and military. When war broke out in 1889, he went into exile in Europe.

Sir Seretse Khama

Stephanus Johannes Paulus Kruger

Kutako, Hosea (1870–1970), was paramount chief of the Herero people of Namibia (South-West Africa), and a lifelong opponent of colonial rule. In 1904, he opposed the German colonial administration. In 1925 and again in 1946, he resisted moves by the South African government to move the Hereros to infertile land to make way for white settlers. Kutako also opposed the incorporation of his country into South Africa. He sent a number of protest petitions to the United Nations, which drew attention to the position of the Africans in his country.

La Guma, Alex (1925–), a South African writer, was born into the Cape Town Coloured community. He became politically active in the 1950s and was a defendant in the Treason Trial after 1956. He wrote for various left-wing newspapers before being placed under house arrest and imprisoned. He left South Africa in 1967, and now lives in exile in Britain. He has written many short stories and his novels include *A Walk in the Night* (1962) and *And a Threefold Cord* (1967).

Lamizana, Sangoulé (1916–), an Upper Volta army officer and politician, was born at Dianra Tougan. After serving with the French army in World War II and in Indochina, he became chief of staff of the Upper Volta army in 1961. He became president in 1966. Lamizana introduced a mixed army/civilian type of government in 1971 but in 1974 he dismissed the prime minister, Gérard OUEDRAOGO, and abolished civilian participation in government.

Lander, John (1807–39), a British explorer, accompanied his brother Richard in 1830, on his journey to explore the lower part of the River Niger. During their expedition, they proved that a number of rivers flowing into the Gulf of Guinea were in fact the mouths of the Niger delta.

Lander, Richard Lemon (1804–34), a British traveller, was one of the main explorers of the River Niger. He began his exploration as servant to Hugh CLAPPERTON in 1825. In 1830, the British government sent Lander and his brother John to explore the lower part of the Niger. The brothers discovered the River Benue, the Niger's chief tributary.

Laye, Camara (1924–), a Guinean writer, was born in Kouroussa. He was educated in Conakry, Guinea, and in Paris, and became a civil servant. Among his books are *L'Enfant Noir* (1953), *Le Regard du Roi* (1955) and *Dramouss* (1967). He has also written several short stories.

Leakey, Louis Seymour Bazett (1903–72), was a famous archaeologist. With his wife, Mary, he was the discoverer of the proconsul skull on Rusinga Island, Lake Victoria during excavations from 1942 to 1948 and of the important remains of a man-like animal now known as *Australopithecus bosei* in Olduvai Gorge, Tanzania (1959). In 1960 he found the remains of *Homo habilis*, a tool-using creature who lived about 1,800,000 years ago! Leakey was born in Kabete, near Nairobi, Kenya and was educated in East Africa, at Oxford and in California. He was the curator of the Coryndon Museum, Nairobi, from 1940 to 1961 and the author of many archaeological works, for example *Stone Age Africa* (1936) and *Adam's Ancestors* (1953).

Lesseps, Ferdinand Marie de (1805–94), a French diplomat and engineer, planned and supervised the cutting of the Suez Canal. He became interested in the idea of the canal while serving as a consul at Alexandria and Cairo. When he retired from the diplomatic service in 1849, he revived the idea and secured a concession from Said Pasha, the viceroy of Egypt. Work on the canal began in 1859 and was completed in 1869.

Livingstone, David (1813–73), a Scottish missionary doctor, brought much of south-central Africa to the knowledge of the outside world. He began his missionary work at Lepelole, Botswana, where he studied African languages and customs. In 1849, he crossed the Kalahari Desert to Lake Ngami, where he came into contact with the slave trade. From Lake Ngami he explored westwards to the coast at Luanda, Angola, and eastwards down the Zambezi to Mozambique. After an illness, he explored the Zambezi area. In 1866, he led another expedition to find the sources of the Congo and Nile rivers. No news was heard of him for three years, until an expedition led by Henry Morton STANLEY found him at Ujiji, by Lake Tanganyika. He died two years later, still exploring.

David Livingstone

Lobengula (1836–93) was a Matabele king in Zimbabwe. He succeeded his father MZILIKAZI in 1868, by which time he ruled a large part of what was to become 'Rhodesia'. He was involved with the missionaries and then commercial interests spreading out from the south. Having signed away mineral rights, he was overwhelmed by the force of the settlers and the colonial army.

Lugard, Frederick John Dealtry (1858–1945), a British colonial administrator, was governor-general of Nigeria from 1914–19. He began his career as a soldier and, in 1888, led an expedition against Arab slave traders on Lake Nyasa. In the 1890s, the British East Africa Company sent Lugard to Uganda, where he established British control. He served in Nigeria from 1894 to 1906, returning to Nigeria in 1912 as governor. In his book *The Dual Mandate* (1922), he laid down the principles of Indirect Rule.

Lumumba, Patrice (1925–61), was the first prime minister of Zaire. He worked as a postal clerk before he became a leading trade unionist. In 1958, he was co-founder of the Mouvement National Congolais. This organization followed a policy of national unity and was opposed to most other independence groups which favoured tribal separatism. The MNC failed to win a clear majority in the post-independence election and Lumumba formed a coalition government with Joseph KASAVUBU. Lumumba was prime minister and minister of defence from June to September 1960, when Kasavubu dismissed him. Although guarded by United Nations troops, he was captured and it was reported that he was finally shot by the troops of Moise TSHOMBE.

Luthuli, Chief Albert John (1898–1967), was a South African chief and politician. He was born in Zimbabwe but grew up in his family's home in Natal. He studied and later taught at Adams college near Durban until 1936. In the 1950s, he became president of the African National Congress and was removed from his chieftainship by the government. He was arrested in 1956 on treason charges but released. In 1960, he was awarded the Nobel Peace Prize in recognition of his work for peaceful change and moderation in South Africa. His autobiography *Let My People Go* was published in 1962.

Machel, Samora (1933–) became the first president of Mozambique after the country was granted independence in July 1975. From 1970 he was head of the liberation movement FRELIMO. Born in Gaza, he had a brief education before becoming a medical assistant, but soon turned to nationalist politics. He joined FRELIMO in 1963.

Macias Nguema, Francisco (1922–), became president of Equatorial Guinea in 1968. Born in Nsegayong on the Rio Muni mainland, he was educated at Catholic schools in Rio Muni. In 1944, he became a coffee planter and joined the colonial administration. Entering politics in 1963, he was vice-president of the administrative council from 1964 to 1968, when he became president and minister of defence.

Maga, Hubert (1916–), a former Dahomey president, was elected as one of Dahomey's two representatives to the French national assembly in 1951 and served as secretary of state for labour in the Gaillard French government in 1957–8. In Dahomey he created the Groupe Ethnique du Nord party and in 1956 the Mouvement Démocratique Dahoméen. He became head of government in 1959 and president of Dahomey on independence in 1960. A military coup removed him from power in 1961. Maga returned formally to Dahomey politics in 1970 as a member of a three-man presidential council and served his turn as its first leader from 1970–2.

Mahdi (1843–85). Muhammad Ahmad ibn-Seyyid Abdullah, called the Mahdi, was a Dongola boat-builder's son. Born in Sudan, he joined the al-Sammaniyah Islamic religious fraternity in 1861. In 1871, he built a monastery on Aba Island in the White Nile. In March 1881, having gained many followers, he proclaimed himself al-Mahdi, and called on his people to revolt against Turkish oppression. By 1885, he had gained control of the entire country, but died suddenly in June that year.

Mahjoub, Muhammad Ahmad (1908–), is a Sudanese lawyer, politician and poet. He was educated at Gordon college and Khartoum law school and practised as a solicitor from 1958 to 1964. In 1947, he was a delegate to the UN. He was elected to parliament as a non-party candidate in the 1954 election. He was leader of the opposition in 1954–6, minister of foreign affairs in 1956–8 and 1964–5, and prime minister in 1965–6 and 1967–9. He has published several distinguished volumes of Arabic poetry.

Makhloufli, Ould, is an Algerian lightweight boxer rapidly approaching world class. In 1973 he won the first professional bout organized in Africa beating the Ghanaian Tetteh on points. On an off-day in January 1974, he lost to Amaya of Panama in Paris but intends eventually to try for the world title.

Mancham, James Richard (1939–), became the chief minister of the Seychelles Islands when the legislative assembly was formed in 1970. He read law in Britain and was called to the bar in 1961. After further legal studies at the university of Paris, he returned to practise in the Seychelles in 1962. In 1963, he founded the Seychelles Democratic Party which won a majority in the new assembly.

Ferdinand Marie de Lesseps

Mandela, Nelson Rolihlahla (1918–), a South African lawyer and politician, was the acknowledged leader of the African National Congress (ANC) after its banning in 1961. He was born the son of a chief in the Transkei and attended Fort Hare university college and Witwatersrand university. He practised law from 1952 and became an organizer for the African National Congress. A key defendant in the Treason Trial, 1956–61, he was acquitted. He operated 'underground' after 1961 and was arrested and found guilty of sabotage and terrorism. He was sentenced to life imprisonment on Robben Island. His writings and speeches are collected in *No Easy Walk to Freedom*.

Marchand, Jean Baptiste (1863–1934), a French soldier, led a number of expeditions to explore French West Africa. In 1897, he set out from Brazzaville under orders to cross to the River Nile to establish French rights there. Marchand reached Fashoda (now Kodok, in Sudan) in July 1898. There he encountered British forces under Herbert Kitchener. A crisis between Britain and France followed, which ended when France agreed that Fashoda came under British influence.

Margai, Sir Albert Michael (1910–), a Sierra Leone lawyer, was prime minister from 1964 to 1967. He was educated at Catholic schools in Bonthe and Freetown, and in London. Margai was a member of the legislative council in 1951, and from then until 1957 was minister of education, welfare and local government. He was minister of finance from 1962 to 1964, when he became prime minister succeeding his brother who died. Margai was a member of the Sierra Leone People's Party from 1951 to 1958, when he became a founder member of the People's National Party.

Margai, Sir Milton (1895–1964), became prime minister of Sierra Leone in 1958. Born at Gbangbatoke, he was educated in Sierra Leone and in Britain, where he studied medicine. He entered the Sierra Leone legislative council in 1951. He was prime minister when Sierra Leone became independent in 1961, and continued in office until his death in 1964.

Masire, Quet K. J. (1925–), is a Botswana politician and journalist. He is a member of the Bangwaketse Tribal Council, the African Council and the National Assembly. He was a founder member of the Botswana Democratic Party and has been secretary-general since its founding. He is the editor of the party paper—*Therisanyo*. In 1965, he was elected to the legislative assembly and became deputy prime minister. Since September 1966, he has been vice-president and minister of development planning for Botswana.

Massamba-Debat, Alphonse (1921–), a Congolese politician, was trained as a teacher and became headmaster of primary schools in Mossendjo and Brazzaville. In 1959, he became a member of the legislative assembly. During 1963, he headed the provisional government and was minister of defence. He became president in that year, remaining in office until 1968. He was arrested in 1969 when he was deposed by Marien Ngouabi.

Matanzima, Chief Kaiser (1915–), is a South African lawyer and politician and chief minister of the Transkei Bantustan. He was educated at Lovedale Mission and Fort Hare university college. He took up politics, eventually becoming head of the Transkei in 1961 and its chief minister in 1963, through his support for government policies. Since 1968, he has begun to make demands for land and links with other Bantustans.

Mboumoua, Eteki, a Cameroonian, succeeded his fellow Cameroonian, Nzo Ekangaki, as Secretary General of the OAU in 1974. Ekangaki had been elected in 1972 to serve a four-year term, but he resigned after only two years in office as OAU Secretary General.

Mboya, Thomas Joseph (Tom) (1930–69), was a Kenyan politician. He was born on Rusinga Island, Lake Victoria, and educated at Holy Ghost College, Mangu and at Ruskin College, Oxford university. He was a founder of the Nairobi People's Convention Party, general-secretary of the Kenya Federation of Labour, and rapidly became an important figure on the international labour scene. In 1959 he became Nairobi's representative in the legislative council, and in 1960, he was one of the founders of the Kenya African National Union, of which he later became general-secretary. He was appointed Minister of Labour (1962), Justice and Constitutional Affairs (1963) and Minister for Economic Development (1964). He was assassinated in Nairobi.

Medhen, Tsegaye Gabre (1935–), is an Ethiopian poet and playwright working in both Amharic and English. After receiving training in theatrical arts in Britain and America, he was director of the National Theatre in Addis Ababa from 1965 to 1972, when he resigned from the post. He now lives in West Africa.

Menelik II (?–1913) was king of southern Ethiopia from 1865 and became emperor in 1889. He defeated Italian efforts to colonize Ethiopia at the battle of Adowa in 1896 and so preserved Ethiopian independence when the European colonial powers were engaged in the 'Scramble for Africa'. Modernization introduced by Menelik included the Addis Ababa to Djibouti railway, a national currency, extended diplomatic relations, the national bank and modern roads. He moved the capital to Addis Ababa in 1887.

Menelik II

Micombero, Michel (1940–), became president of Burundi in November 1966. In 1960–2 he attended the Ecole Royale Militaire in Brussels. He then returned to Burundi to become assistant commander-in-chief of the Burundi national army. By 1965 he was secretary of state for the army. On the accession of Prince Charles as *mwami* (king), Micombero was asked to form a government on July 12, 1966.

Mobutu Sese Seko (1930–) became president of Zaire in 1965. He joined the Mouvement National Congolais and attended the pre-independence talks in 1960. On independence he became Colonel Chief-of-Staff of the Congolese army. In September 1960, following the dismissal of prime minister Patrice Lumumba by President Kasavubu, Mobutu intervened and set up a caretaker government of 'commissioners'. The following year, Mobutu restored Kasavubu to power. Mobutu became commander-in-chief of the army and led the attacks on the secessionist state of Katanga. In 1965, Mobutu deposed Kasavubu as president. In 1966, he became prime minister and minister of defence. He established the Mouvement Populaire de la Révolution (MPR) and declared it the sole authority.

Mohammad V (1909–61), king of Morocco, was the third son of Mulay Yusuf and became sultan in 1927. He governed with the full agreement of France until 1952, when he declared that he favoured independence for Morocco. Deposed in 1953, he was exiled in 1954 to Corsica, and then to Madagascar. He was replaced as sultan by Mohammad ben Arafa, but restored in 1955. After independence, on March 2, 1956, he took the title of king in 1957. In 1960 he took over the government.

Michel Micombero   Mobutu Sese Seko

Mohammed Ali Pasha (1769–1849) became the viceroy of Egypt in 1804. At that time, Egypt was part of the Turkish empire. During his reign, Mohammed Ali conquered parts of Syria and Sudan. He also waged two wars against his overlord, the Sultan of Turkey, in 1832 and 1839. As a result of these wars, Mohammed Ali and his successors became independent rulers of Egypt, paying only lip service to the Sultan. Mohammed Ali's greatest achievements were his administrative and social reforms.

Moi, Daniel Toroitich arap (1924–), became Kenya's minister for home affairs in 1964 and vice president in 1967. Born in Baringo District, northwest Kenya, Moi became a teacher and was assistant principal of Tambach Teachers' Training College from 1949 to 1954 before his election to Kenya's legislative council in 1954. In 1962 he became minister for education and in the following year was elected to Kenya's House of Representatives.

Mokhehle, Ntsu (1918–), was leader of the opposition Basutoland Congress Party (BCP) in Lesotho. He was active in the African National Council (ANC) Youth League and in the politics of Basutoland (now Lesotho). He became a teacher and formed the BCP in 1952. As the first major nationalist party, BCP won the election of 1960, but narrowly lost in 1965 to the Basutoland National Party (BNP). After apparent victory in the 1970 election he was imprisoned with many others of his party and not released until 1972.

Mondlane, Eduardo (1920–69), a Mozambique nationalist leader, was president of the Mozambique Liberation Front (FRELIMO) from 1962. He was educated at mission school and at universities in South Africa, Portugal and the United States. In 1962, he helped to organize FRELIMO from existing independence movements in Tanzania. Guerrilla activities began in northern Mozambique in 1964 and spread to other parts of the country. Mondlane often visited areas controlled by FRELIMO and publicized the movement abroad.

Moshoeshoe I (1786–1870), the founder of the Basotho nation, was born in the north of Lesotho, the son of a minor chief. When the wars of the 'Mfecane' (dispersal) spread into the Caledon valley after 1818, he gathered scattered groups together for protection, firstly on a mountain in the north and, in 1822, at the impregnable fortress of Thaba Bosiu. The Basotho grew and prospered, resisted the Boer trekkers and eventually became allied to the British colony at the Cape. He established the dynasty of Basotho paramount chiefs.

Gamal Abdel Nasser became president of Egypt in 1954. ▶

Moshoeshoe II (Constantine Bereng Seeiso, 1938–) is the king of Lesotho and great-grandson of that nation's founder. He was educated at Roma College in Lesotho and at Ampleforth College and Oxford university in England. In 1960, he succeeded to the throne. At independence, he became the constitutional monarch but has since been in conflict with the government of Chief JONATHAN. In 1970, he went into exile for nine months and lost most of his constitutional powers.

Mphahlele, Ezekiel (1919–), is a South African writer and critic. His autobiographical novel *Down Second Avenue* is perhaps the best account of the life and conditions of urban Africans in the 1940s and 1950s. Born in Pretoria, he became a teacher in Orlando, Johannesburg. His teaching was restricted by his political activities and he became fiction editor of *Drum* magazine. From 1957, he lived in exile, writing and teaching in Nigeria, France and the United States. His other works include *The Wanderers* and a book of criticism *The African Image*.

Musa (reigned mid-1300s) was the best-known *mansa* (emperor) of the old West African empire of Mali. He ruled while Mali was at the height of its power and wealth. Some time before 1350, Musa, a Muslim, made a pilgrimage to Mecca in Arabia. When he passed through Cairo, he brought so much gold with him that the value of the metal in Egypt declined as a result. Musa's fame reached Europe and in 1375 his likeness and Mali appeared on the first-known map of West Africa drawn in Europe.

Muzorewa, Abel Tendekayi (1925–), is a Zimbabwean bishop and political leader. He attended theological colleges in the United States from 1958 to 1963 and then worked for various Christian bodies in Zimbabwe before becoming bishop of the United Methodist Church in 1968. His movements within the country were restricted by the 'Rhodesian' government. In 1971 he organized a letter to the British government and, having been appointed founding president of the African National Council in December 1971, he led the successful opposition to the proposals for the settlement of Zimbabwe's independence dispute with Britain. He later attended the unsuccessful talks concerning Zimbabwe's future which were held in late 1974.

Mzilikazi (about 1790–1868) was a Nguni leader in southern Africa in the 1800s. He became a general in SHAKA's Zulu army after 1818. In 1822 he broke away from Shaka with a small *impi* (regiment of about 200) and for 16 years moved across the High Veld conquering and absorbing weaker groups. Contact with the Tswana chiefdoms, the Griqua and finally military defeat by the Voortrekkers drove him across the Limpopo River where he founded the Ndebele kingdom around his capital Bulawayo. There he established control over much of the Shona territory.

Nasser, Gamal Abdel (1918–70), was president of Egypt from 1954 until his death. In 1952, as a lieutenant-colonel, he masterminded the Egyptian revolution and, in 1953, the abolition of the monarchy. As president, he brought Egypt into inter-Arab and international politics. He defeated the combined French and British attempt to seize the nationalized Suez Canal in 1956. He did much to modernize Egypt by introducing land reforms and encouraging industrialization. He was responsible for the building of the Aswan High Dam. On the defeat of the Egyptian army by Israel in June, 1967, Nasser resigned, but was recalled by popular acclaim. He died of a heart attack.

Bishop Abel Tendekayi Muzorewa

Neto, Antonio Agostinho (1922–), an Angolan doctor and poet, became president of the *Movimento Popular de Libertação de Angola* (MPLA) in 1962. In 1947, he went to Portugal to study medicine. In Portugal he was arrested in 1952 and 1957 for his anti-colonialist political activities. He returned to Angola to practise medicine and joined the MPLA. In 1962, he was exiled to the Cape Verde Islands, but later escaped to Congo. Neto planned guerrilla campaigns against the Portuguese throughout the 1960s. In 1968, he transferred the MPLA headquarters from Zaire to the interior of Angola. In 1975–6 Neto led the MPLA to victory in the Angolan civil war.

Ngouabi, Marien (1938–), a Congolese army officer, became his country's head of state in 1969. A former paratroop commander, he became chief of the general staff and head of the national revolutionary council in 1968. In 1970 as head of state, he became president of the central committee and political bureau of the Congolese Workers' Party (PCT).

Ngugi wa Thiongo (James Ngugi) (1938–) is one of Kenya's best-known novelists. He was born in Limuru and educated at Alliance High School and at Makerere and Leeds universities. His best-known works are *Weep Not Child* (1964), *The River Between* (1965) and *A Grain of Wheat* (1967).

Nimeiry, Ja'afar al- (1930–), became president of the revolutionary council of Sudan in 1969. He was educated at the military academy in Khartoum and in Germany and the United States. In 1966–9 he was in charge of Shendi district. On May 25, 1969, he led the military coup which overthrew Ismail al-Azhari's government. He was elected president in 1971. He combined the presidency with the posts of minister of defence, and commander-in-chief.

Nkomo, Joshua (1917–), is a Zimbabwean politician. He was educated at Adams College, Natal, and at the University of South Africa, Johannesburg. He became president of the African National Congress (ANC) in 1957 and went into exile when the ANC was banned in 1959. He returned to Zimbabwe in 1961 and became president of the Zimbabwe African Peoples Union (ZAPU). He was imprisoned on a charge of terrorism in 1963. He was placed in detention in 1964 and in 1968 an order was made detaining him for a further five years until 1974. In 1972, he gave evidence to the Pearce Commission investigating support for Zimbabwean independence. In late 1974, Nkomo attended talks in Zambia, concerning a settlement in Zimbabwe. Afterwards, he returned to Zimbabwe and later reopened negotiations with Ian Smith.

Nkrumah, Dr. Kwame (1909–72), was prime minister of Ghana at independence in 1957. Three years later, when Ghana became a republic, he became its first president. He studied in America and in 1949 formed the Convention People's Party with its slogan 'self-government now'. He worked for a united Africa and revived the principle of African Personality. As president he was overthrown in 1966 and he took refuge in Guinea until his death. He wrote several books including *Ghana: The Autobiography of Kwame Nkrumah* and *I Speak of Freedom*.

Nkumbula, Harry (1916–), a Zambian politician, studied at Makerere College (now university), Uganda and at the London School of Economics. As leader of the African National Congress (ANC) he led the 1951–3 campaign against the federation of the Rhodesias and Nyasaland.

Noumazalay, Ambroise (1933–), a Congolese politician, was born in Brazzaville and studied at Toulouse university in France. From 1964 to 1966 he was first secretary of the National Revolutionary Movement and director of economic affairs. From 1966 to 1968 he was prime minister and minister of planning.

Ja'afar al-Nimeiry

Joshua Nkomo

Dr. Kwame Nkrumah

Mwalimu Julius Kambarage Nyerere

Nyerere, Mwalimu Julius Kambarage (1922–), became president of Tanzania when that country was formed by the union of Tanganyika and Zanzibar in 1964. He was educated at Makerere College (now university) and at Edinburgh university before becoming a teacher. In 1954, he became a founder member of the Tanganyika African National Union, of which he was elected president. He was returned to parliament in 1958 and took office as prime minister three years later. Following Tanganyikan independence in 1962, he became the country's first President. Nyerere has built up an international reputation as a political philosopher and continuously teaches the theory and practice of socialism. He has written several books, including *Freedom and Unity—Uhuru na Ujamaa; Uhuru na Umoja,* and *Freedom and Socialism.* He has also translated two of Shakespeare's plays into Swahili.

Obote, Apolo Milton (1924–), was president of Uganda from 1966 to 1971. He once worked as a labourer, clerk and salesman in Kenya and was a founder member of the Kenya African Union. From 1952 to 1960 he was a member of the Uganda National Congress. In 1960 he became a founder member of the Uganda People's Congress. He was leader of the opposition in 1961 and 1962, when he replaced Benedicto KIWANUKA as prime minister. In January 1971, while attending the Commonwealth conference in Singapore, Obote was deposed as president by Idi AMIN. He went into exile in Tanzania.

Odinga, Ajuma Oginga (1911–), was vice-president of Kenya from 1964 to 1966. He was educated at Alliance High School and Makerere College (now university). In 1957, he became a member of Kenya's Legislative Council, and in 1960, vice-president of the Kenya African National Union. On independence he became minister for home affairs and then vice-president. In 1966, he resigned and formed his own party, the Kenya People's Union. A 'little general election' was called, and he was returned to parliament and the KPU was recognized as an official opposition. He was detained in 1969 after disturbances following the assassination of Tom MBOYA, but was released in 1971. He wrote a biography called *Not Yet Uhuru.*

Ojukwu, Chukwuemeka Odumegwu (1933–), a Nigerian army officer and politician, led the Eastern Region of Nigeria in its unsuccessful attempt to form the breakaway state of Biafra in the civil war of 1967–70. Educated in Lagos and at Oxford university and military colleges in Britain, Ojukwu joined the Nigerian army in 1957. He served in the United Nations Congo (Zaire) operation in 1962, and, by 1963, reached the rank of lieutenant-colonel. In 1966, he became military governor of Eastern Nigeria and next year proclaimed its independence as Biafra. In January, 1970, shortly before the final defeat of his forces, he fled to Ivory Coast.

Oppenheimer, Harry Frederick (1908–), is a South African businessman and politician. He is the head of a vast business empire, centred on the Anglo-American Corporation, and is also chairman of De Beers Consolidated Mines.

Opuku Ware II (1919–) is a Ghanaian lawyer and traditional ruler. Educated in England, he followed a successful legal career in Ghana until 1970, when he was named ambassador to Rome. In July that year, he succeeded his uncle, Sir Osei Agyeman Prempeh II, as *asantehene* (king of the Ashantis).

Ouedraogo, Gérard Kango (1925–), an Upper Volta politician, became prime minister in 1971. A former ambassador to Britain, he was president of the Democratic Union of Volta. In 1974, he was relieved of his office by General LAMIZANA.

Okigbo, Christopher (1932–67?) is a Nigerian poet born in Ojoto, Nigeria. He is noted for his collections of poems, *Heavengate* (1962), *Limits, Silences, Distances* and *Path of Thunder.*

Ousmane, Sembene (1923–), is a Senegalese writer and film director who formerly worked as a plumber, bricklayer, mechanic and docker. In 1967, he was awarded first prize at the World Festival of Negro Arts in Dakar, and in 1968, he directed the film *Mandabi.* His books include *Le Docker Noir* (1956), *O pays, mon beau peuple* (1957), *Les Bouts de Bois de Dieu* (1960) and *Vehi Ciosane* (1965).

Oyono, Ferdinand Léopold (1924–), a Cameroonian diplomat, is also one of his country's leading authors. His books include *Une Vie de Boy; Le Vieux Nègre et la Médaille,* and *Le Pandémonium.* He served as Cameroonian ambassador to Liberia, and in the 1960s was ambassador to several European countries.

Park, Mungo (1771–1806), a Scottish surgeon, led two expeditions to try to find the source of the Niger River. In his first expedition, in 1795–6, he travelled up the Gambia River, and then journeyed eastwards with slave traders until he reached the Senegal River. After being imprisoned by a Moorish chief, he reached the Niger and explored part of it. On his second expedition, in 1805, he again reached the Niger and travelled down it by canoe. But he was drowned in the rapids at Bussa, Nigeria.

Paton, Alan Stewart (1903–), a writer and politician, became known as a spokesman of white liberalism in South Africa. Born in Natal, he attended Natal university before teaching from 1924 to 1936, and being principal of Diepkloof Reformatory for African boys on the Rand. He was founding president of the Liberal Party and a leader until its disbanding in 1968. In 1969 he became founding editor of the magazine *Reality.* His writings include novels *Cry, the Beloved Country* (1948), *Too Late the Phalarope* (1953), short stories *Debbie Go Home* (1961), a biography *Hofmeyr* (1965) and several non-fiction works.

p'Bitek, Okot (1931–) is a Ugandan writer, best known for his *Song of Lawino* (1966), *Song of Ocol* and *Two Songs,* satirical poems on Africa today. He was educated in Uganda and Britain.

211

Rabemananjara, Jacques (1913–), a Malagasy poet, dramatist and politician, was born in Tamatave. He entered the French colonial administration and studied in Paris. There, he wrote a play and several books of poetry. After the rebellion in 1947, Rabemananjara was imprisoned. Released in 1960, he joined Philibert TSIRANANA's government. By 1972, when the government fell, he was foreign secretary and a vice-president.

Ramanantsoa, Gabriel (1906–), was head of the Malagasy government from 1972 to 1975. He was educated in Tananarive, Marseilles, and the St. Cyr military academy, France. He served with the French army in Tunisia (1936–40), France (1940) and Vietnam (1953–5). In 1960, he became commander-in-chief of the Malagasy armed forces. He remained in this post until 1972, when he took power from Philibert TSIRANANA. Ramanantsoa stood down as head of the government in February 1975. His successor, Lieutenant-Colonel Richard Ratsimandrava, was assassinated after only six days in office.

Rameses was the name of several Pharaohs of Egypt during the 19th and 20th dynasties (1330 to 1085 BC). The most important of the pharaohs bearing the name was Rameses II, who ruled from 1290 to 1224 BC. He extended the Egyptian empire into Asia in wars with the Hittites. Rameses was one of the greatest builders of ancient Egypt. The temples of Luxor and Abu Simbel are among the monuments built by him which survive today.

Ramgoolam, Sir Seewoosagur (1900–), became the first premier of Mauritius in 1964. He studied medicine at Royal College, Curepipe, Mauritius and at University College Hospital, London. He then practised as a physician in Mauritius. In 1948, he became a Member of the Mauritian legislative and executive councils. In 1958–60, he was ministerial secretary to the treasury, and, in 1961, he became chief minister and minister of finance. Following constitutional changes in 1964, he became premier of Mauritius.

Ranaivo, Flavien (1914–), a Malagasy poet, became known for his use of the vernacular song and ballad forms. These forms had been used by Jean-Joseph Ravearivelo (1901–37), the father of modern Malagasy poetry. Some of Ranaivo's poems were included in Léopold SENGHOR's *Anthologie de la Nouvelle Poésie Nègre et Malgache*.

Anwar as-Sadat

Cecil John Rhodes (*left*) and Alfred Beit.

Albert Schweitzer

Retief, Pieter (1780–1838), was a leader of the Voortrekkers in South Africa. In 1814 he became a leader of the Boer settlers in the eastern Cape. He was the author of the famous manifesto, listing Boer grievances under British rule, which resulted in the Great Trek of 1836–7. He led one of the groups on to the High Veld and through to Natal, where he met DINGANE's Zulus. Following a cattle-stealing incident, Retief's expedition was wiped out by a Zulu *impi*.

Rhodes, Cecil John (1853–1902), was a businessman and politician in southern Africa and a pioneer British imperialist. Born in England, he went to Natal in 1870. He joined the 'diamond rush' at Kimberley and founded the De Beers Diamond Company, which acquired a near monopoly. He later expanded his business interests into gold and founded the Goldfields Company. His political career began as a Cape member of parliament in 1880. He was then a cabinet member before becoming prime minister in 1890. He annexed Bechuanaland, and colonized 'Rhodesia' by means of the Pioneer Column and the British South Africa Company.

Richards, Barry (1945–), a South African cricketer is a brilliant batsman and fielder. He has played for Natal, for two English counties and for South Australia, but he represented South Africa for only a short time before it was excluded from international cricket.

Roberto, Holden (1923–), is an Angolan nationalist and a leader of the *Frente Nacional de Libertação de Angola* (FNLA). Born in northern Angola, he was educated at mission schools in Zaire, where he spent much of his life. In 1954, he formed the União das Populações de Angola (UPA). In 1963, the UPA merged with other independence groups to form the FNLA. In 1974 Holden Roberto negotiated a cease-fire between the FNLA and the new Portuguese government. He led the FNLA delegation at the Angolan independence talks in Portugal in January 1975. After independence, the FNLA, led by Roberto, was defeated by the Communist-backed MPLA in the civil war waged for control of Angola.

Robert, Shaaban, OBE (1909–1962), one of the most important writers in modern Swahili literature, is the author of 13 volumes of collected works published as *Diwani ya Shaaban*. They include an autobiography, *Maisha Yanqu*, (my life), traditional tales and many poems. He was born at Vitambani, Tanzania and educated at Masimbazi and Dar es Salaam.

Sadat, Anwar as- (1918–), succeeded Gamal Abdel NASSER as president of Egypt in 1970. In 1971, he changed the official name of Egypt from the United Arab Republic to the Arab Republic of Egypt. He established close links with other Arab countries and emerged as the unofficial leader of the Arab world. In October 1973, he led Egypt in a combined attack with Syria on Israel to recover the territories occupied by Israel during the Six Day War of 1967.

Schweitzer, Albert (1875–1965), a German theologian, musician, philosopher and physician, spent most of his life running a hospital and leper colony at Lambaréné, in Gabon. After a short but brilliant career as an organist and scholar, Schweitzer gave up his posts and opportunities to work as a medical missionary in Africa. He made frequent visits to Europe, where he gave organ recitals and lectures to raise money for his work in Africa. He was awarded the Nobel peace prize for 1952.

Senghor, Léopold Sédar (1906–), a Senegalese politician and poet, became president of the Republic of Senegal in 1960. Educated in Dakar, Senegal, and in Paris, Senghor was a teacher in France during the 1930s and 1940s. From 1946 to 1958 he was a Senegalese deputy to the French national assembly, and from 1948 to 1958 he was a university professor. In 1959, he became president of the federal assembly of the short-lived Mali federation. He is the leader of the Progressive Union of Senegal. Renowned as one of Africa's leading men of letters, Senghor has published many collections of poetry. In his writings, Senghor has often reflected the concept of *Negritude*, a French word for 'blackness'. This concept involves the rejection of any imitation of European styles and the assertion of traditional African values.

Shaka (1787–1828) was a Zulu king. He became a general in DINGISWAYO's army and succeeded him as king in 1818. He devised new military strategies, new weapons and a standing army divided into *impis* (regiments). His military might and his conquests and absorption of surrounding peoples sparked off the *Mfecane* (dispersal), which had widespread repercussions throughout southern Africa.

Shepstone, Theophilus (1817–93), was a British colonial administrator in South Africa. As a Cape civil servant, he was in charge of 'native affairs' in Natal from 1845. He devised new policies of indirect rule, using tribal structures allying with chiefs and setting up separate 'native areas' in Zululand.

Shermarke, Abderashid Ali (1917–69) was president of the Somali Republic. As a young man, he joined the Somali Youth League, which became the main independence party, and was its secretary in 1948–51. In 1958, he took his doctorate in political science at Rome university. He was the first prime minister of the newly independent Somali Republic in 1960–4. In 1967, he became president, but was assassinated in October 1969.

Siad Barre, Mohamed, became president of the Somali Democratic Republic in 1968. He served in the police under both the British and Italian trust administrations, reaching the rank of major. On independence in 1960, he joined the army as colonel and rose to become brigadier-general. When the Army took over power in October 1969, he became president of the Supreme Revolutionary Council and head of state.

Léopold Sédar Senghor

Sithole, Rev. Ndabaningi (1920–), a Zimbabwean politician and writer, was educated at Waddilove Institute in Zimbabwe. He was a teacher from 1941 to 1955 and then trained at an American theological college for the ministry of the Congregational Church. Returning to Zimbabwe in 1958, he became president of the African Teachers Association, treasurer of the National Democratic Party (NDP) and later chairman of Zimbabwe African People's Union (ZAPU). In August 1963, a split in ZAPU led to the formation of Zimbabwe African National Union, with Sithole as leader. He was involved in unsuccessful talks with Ian Smith in 1974.

Smith, Ian Douglas (1919–), prime minister of Rhodesia, was born in Rhodesia and educated in Gwelo and at university in South Africa. During World War II, he was an air force pilot and afterwards a farmer. He was a member of the Southern Rhodesian legislative assembly from 1948 and of the federal parliament from 1953, where he was chief whip for the United Federal Party. A founding member of the Rhodesian Front in 1962, he took over leadership from Winston Field in 1964. Two years later, he won an overwhelming majority from the white electorate on the issue of independence. He declared independence from Britain in 1965.

Ian Douglas Smith   Jan Christiaan Smuts

Smuts, Jan Christiaan (1870–1950), a South African military leader and politician, was born in the Cape and educated at Stellenbosch and Cambridge universities. He practised law in Johannesburg from 1896. He became a Boer leader in the Anglo-Boer War and at the peace conference in 1902. Reconciled to the terms of the peace settlement, he joined General BOTHA's government at Union in 1910. He joined the British war cabinet during World War I and was involved in the establishment of the League of Nations. He succeeded Botha as South African prime minister in 1919, but, following the suppression of the Rand revolt, he was defeated in 1924. In 1933, he joined with General HERZOG in the United Party and was his deputy until 1939. Smuts then became prime minister again until his defeat by the Nationalists in 1948.

Sobhuza II (1899–), *ngwenyama* (king) of Swaziland since 1921, became the country's head of state on independence in 1968. The son of King Ngwana V, he was educated at Lovedale college in the Cape. In the 1920s and 1930s, he campaigned against the alienation of Swaziland by European settlers. In the 1960s and 1970s, he followed a policy of co-operation with whites and has retained wide powers.

Sobukwe, Robert Mangaliso (1924–), a South African politician, was educated at Fort Hare university college and became a lecturer at Witwatersrand university. He was active in the African National Congress (ANC), but in 1959 broke away to become the founding leader of the Pan African Congress. He led the campaign against the pass laws which ended with the Sharpeville massacre. He was detained in 1960 and was kept in prison until 1969.

Sonni Ali (reigned about 1464–92) was a great soldier-emperor of the old West African empire of Songhai. In the 1300s the kings of Songhai ruled the area around Gao on the middle Niger River, but paid tribute to the emperors of Mali. However, in the 1400s, Mali's power declined, and Sonni Ali conquered Mali territories and built up the Songhai empire. Under his successor Muhammad, the Songhai empire became even larger than Mali had been.

Soyinka, Wole (1934–), a leading Nigerian writer, was born at Abeokuta. He was educated at Ibadan university and at Leeds university, Britain. During the 1960s, he lectured at the universities of Ife and Lagos. He was a political prisoner from 1967

to 1969, during the Nigerian civil war. Since 1969, he has directed the drama school of Ibadan university. His published plays include *The Lion and the Jewel* (1959), *A Dance of the Forests* (1960), *The Strong Breed* (1962), *Kongi's Harvest* . (1965) and *Madmen and Specialists* (1971). He has also written several novels, including *The Interpreters*, and some poetry. He also wrote *The Man Who Died*, a harrowing account of his experiences in prison during the Nigerian Civil War.

Speke, John Hanning (1827–64), an English soldier, was the first European to see Lake Victoria. He proved that it was one of the sources of the Nile. Speke's first expedition to Africa, with Richard BURTON, was to Somalia and Ethiopia in 1854. On his second, also with Burton, Speke reached lakes Tanganyika and Victoria.

Rev. Ndabaningi Sithole

CAPTAIN SPEKE.

John Hanning Speke

Reginald Stephen Garfield Todd
with his daughter Judith.

William Richard Tolbert

William Vacanarat Shadrach Tubman

Stanley, Sir Henry Morton (1841–1904), a British-American journalist, was sent to Africa in 1871 by a New York newspaper to find the British missionary David LIVINGSTONE. The two men met on the shores of Lake Tanganyika. After Livingstone died, Stanley decided to carry on his exploration of Africa. He explored lakes Victoria and Tanganyika and then struck westwards. He proved that a central African river called the Lualaba was in fact the Congo (now called the Zaire River).

Stevens, Siaka Probyn (1905–), became president of Sierra Leone in 1971. Born in Moyamba, he was educated in Freetown and worked as a railwayman and a miner. He became an active trade unionist and in 1947–8 attended Ruskin college, Oxford. During the 1950s he was a member of the Sierra Leone legislative council and was a government minister in 1951. He was deputy leader of the People's National Party in 1958–60. Since then, he has led the All People's Congress. Although elected prime minister in 1967, he was exiled and did not resume his post until 1968. He remained prime minister on becoming president.

Sutherland, Efua Theodora (1924–), is a Ghanaian playwright, poet and authoress and an important figure in Ghanaian theatre. In 1958, she founded a programme of experimental theatre and built the Ghana Drama Studio, a striking open-air theatre in Accra. In 1963, she began a programme of research into African literature and drama at the University of Ghana.

Suzman, Helen (1917–), is a South African politician. She was educated at convent school and Witwatersrand university. During World War II, she worked as a statistician and afterwards lectured on economic history. She was elected as a United Party member of parliament in 1953. She left the party in 1958 to help form the Progressive Party and was its only member of parliament for 16 years. During that time she was a vigorous opponent of the racial legislation of the Nationalist Party government of South Africa.

Siaka Probyn Stevens (*seated centre*)
with Fidel Castro (*seated left*) the Cuban leader.

Theodore II (Tewodros) (1818–68), the son of an Ethiopian chieftain, became emperor of Ethiopia in 1855, when he defeated Ras Ali, the ruler of the capital, Gondar, and overcame opposition by the semi-independent provincial nobles and the Church. He unified the empire and moved the capital to Magdala. Magdala fortress was captured by a British expedition sent to rescue foreigners imprisoned there. Theodore committed suicide to avoid capture by the British.

Thuku, Harry (1895–1970), was the first well-known African nationalist leader in Kenya. He was born near Kambui Hill, Kiambu, and was educated at the Gospel Missionary Society School, Kambui. In 1921, he formed the East African Association (a multi-tribal political organization) and campaigned against the pass laws. When he was arrested in 1922, the crowd trying to free him was fired on by the police and 21 people were killed. Thuku was detained from 1922 to 1930. On his release, he became leader of the Kikuyu Central Association, which later split. Thuku then formed the more passive Kikuyu Provincial Association, which opposed the 'Mau Mau' militants.

Tiger, Dick, was a Nigerian boxer who spent 17 years in the ring and won two world titles. He moved to Liverpool, England, in 1955. He took the Empire middleweight title from Pat McAteer in 1958 but lost it for a short time in 1960. He became the N.B.A. world champion in 1962 but then lost to Joey Giardello. Champion again in 1965, he lost to Emile Griffith in the following year. But he came back again to take the world light heavyweight title in 1966 and kept it until he was knocked out by Bob Foster in 1968.

Todd, Reginald Stephen Garfield (1908–), a Rhodesian politician, was born and educated in New Zealand and later studied in South Africa. He went to Rhodesia as a missionary in 1938 and was a mission superintendent at Dadaya until 1953. As member of parliament from 1946, he became prime minister of Southern Rhodesia on the formation of the Central African Federation. By 1958, his liberal policies caused his party, the United Federal Party (UFP), to reject him in favour of Sir Edgar Whitehead. He was involved in forming other parties as his sympathies moved closer to the African nationalists. From 1962 he retired to his ranch, where he was placed under government restriction in 1965 to 1966 and 1972 to 1976. Garfield Todd's daughter Judith, who is a journalist, has also campaigned on behalf of the African Nationalists.

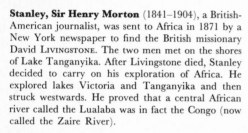

Toiva ja Toiva, Herman (1924–), a Namibian nationalist, became a founder of the South-West African Peoples Organization (SWAPO). Educated at mission school, he joined the South African army during World War II and afterwards became a miner on the Witwatersrand. He moved to Cape Town and became active in nationalist politics, but was expelled from South Africa in 1957. Returning to Namibia, he became northern regional secretary of SWAPO. He was arrested following SWAPO guerrilla attacks on South African posts in 1966. In 1968, he was sentenced to life imprisonment.

Tolbert, William Richard, Jr. (1913–), became president of Liberia in 1971. Educated at Liberia college (now the University of Liberia), he joined the Liberian treasury in 1935. From 1943 to 1951, he was a member of the house of representatives, and from 1951 to 1971 he was vice-president. In 1965 and 1966, he was president of the World Baptist Alliance.

Tombalbaye, Ngarta (1918–75), a former businessman and school official, became president of Chad in 1962. He was vice-president from 1957 to 1958 and prime minister from 1959 to 1960. Before becoming president in 1962 he also held several other top government jobs. He was secretary general of the Chad Progressive Party (PPT). He was assassinated during an army coup in April 1975.

Sékou Touré

Touré, Sékou (1922–), a Guinean politician and trade unionist, became head of state of Guinea in October 1958, after his country chose independence from France. Educated in Conakry, Touré became an active trade unionist and politician in the 1940s. In 1952, he became secretary-general of the Guinea Democratic Party and in 1956, mayor of Conakry and a Guinean deputy to the French national assembly. After becoming head of state in 1958, Touré was re-elected in 1961, 1963 and 1968. He was awarded the Lenin peace prize in 1960.

Traore, Moussa (1936–), a Mali politician and army officer, became president of Mali in 1968. Born at Kayes, he was educated at the Cadets' college, Kati. He became a non-commissioned officer in the French army and had military training in France. From 1964 to 1968, when he became president, he was an officer on the staff of the armed forces college at Kati. Traore is Commander in Chief of the Armed Forces in Mali.

Tshekedi Khama (1905–59) became chief regent of the Bamangwato of Bechuanaland (now Botswana) in 1926. In 1934, he successfully opposed the incorporation of Bechuanaland into South Africa. He became a member of the African Advisory Council in 1939. Following disagreements with Seretse KHAMA in 1949, he went into voluntary exile and was then banished. He returned home as a private citizen three years later, and in 1955 renounced all claims to chieftainship.

Philibert Tsiranana

Tshombe, Moise Kapenda (1919–69), a Zairian politician, was the leader of the secessionist state of Katanga from 1960 to 1963. He was educated at mission school and became a businessman. In 1959, he helped found the Confédération des Associations du Katanga (CONAKAT), which had the support of Belgian business interests. CONAKAT gained control of the Katanga provincial assembly in the 1960 election, and shortly afterwards, Tshombe declared Katanga's secession. Katanga was occupied by United Nations troops in 1963 and Tshombe went into exile. In 1964 he was recalled to lead the central government of Zaire, but the following year he resigned and again went into exile. The Kinshasa high court sentenced him to death in 1967. Shortly afterwards, his plane was hijacked to Algiers, where he was placed under house arrest until his death.

Tsiranana, Philibert (1912–), was president of the Malagasy Republic (1959–72). Born of a peasant family in northern Madagascar, he began his education at the age of 12. From 1946 to 1950 he trained at Montpelier, France. His political rise was swift. In 1956, he became a member of the representative assembly, in 1957 a French deputy, and in 1958 deputy head of the Malagasy government. He was elected president in 1959, and re-elected in 1966 and 1972. His policies were mildly socialist, pro-French and strongly anti-communist. He was overthrown in 1972 by General Gabriel RAMANANTSOA who subsequently stood down.

Tubman, William Vacanarat Shadrach (1895–1971), a Liberian lawyer and statesman, was president of Liberia from 1944 to 1971. After having worked as a teacher and then as a lawyer, he was an associate justice of the Liberian supreme court from 1937 to 1944. During Tubman's presidency, Liberia adopted an 'open-door' policy for foreign investment that speeded the country's economic and social development. This policy reduced Liberia's dependence on the United States, which, in 1944, had been overwhelming.

Tutuola, Amos (1920–), a leading Nigerian writer, was born at Abeokuta and educated at mission schools. After working on his father's farm he trained as a coppersmith, then served with the British air force in World War II. From 1945, he worked for the Nigerian Broadcasting Corporation at Ibadan. His books include *The Palm-Wine Drinkard* (1952), *My Life in the Bush of Ghosts* (1954), *The Brave African Huntress* (1958) and *Ajaiyi and His Inherited Poverty* (1967).

Van Riebeck, Johan (Jan) (1618–67), one of the first white settlers in South Africa, was born in Holland. He was appointed by the Dutch East India Company as commander of a trading post to be established in Table Bay, following promising reports on the site. He arrived in 1652 with 90 men. Before he left, ten years later, he set up the port of De Kaap (Cape), a fortress and a small community.

Verwoerd, Dr. Hendrik Frensch (1901–66), a former prime minister of South Africa, was born in Holland. He went to South Africa as a child and attended universities in Stellenbosch, in Europe and in the United States. From 1927, he was a professor in social sciences at Stellenbosch and was involved in political and welfare work among poor Afrikaaners. He was editor of the Nationalist newspaper *Die Transvaler* from 1937 to 1948, when he joined the new government as a senator. As minister of 'native affairs' he was largely responsible for developing the policy of apartheid, which he furthered as prime minister.

Vorster, Balthazar Johannes (1915–), became prime minister of South Africa in 1966. Born in the Cape, he trained as a lawyer at Stellenbosch university. During World War II, he was interned for his pro-Nazi involvement. He practised as a lawyer and entered parliament in 1953. He was a member of the cabinet from 1958, first as deputy minister of education and then as minister of justice. He succeeded Hendrik VERWOERD as prime minister in 1966 and his period in office has been characterized by attempts to open diplomatic contacts with Black Africa with offers to help accelerate the independence of Rhodesia and Namibia.

Balthazar Johannes Vorster   Sir Roy Welensky

Welensky, Sir Roland (Roy) (1907–), a politician, was born and educated in Rhodesia. He worked on Rhodesia Railways from 1924 to 1953, mainly in Northern Rhodesia (now Zambia). He was a member of the legislative council of Northern Rhodesia from 1938 to 1953 and held various offices. He became deputy prime minister of the Central African Federation in 1953 and minister of transport and prime minister from 1956 to 1963, but was unable to avoid the disintegration of the Federation.

Youlou, Fulbert (1917–), a Congolese politician and priest, was educated at Brazzaville seminary and ordained in 1946. A former mayor of Brazzaville he also held several government posts. From 1960 to 1963 he was president of the republic.

Zobel, Joseph (1915–), a novelist now living in Senegal was born in Martinique, in the West Indies. From 1946 to 1950 he studied at the Sorbonne university in Paris. He later became the director of national broadcasting and cultural services in Dakar. His novels include *Diab'là* and *Les Jours Immobiles*. He has also published short stories.

215

Bibliography

Peoples of Africa

Bohannan, Paul, *African Outline: a General Introduction*, Penguin, London, 1966

Caldwell, John C., and Okonjo, Chukuka, eds., *The Population of Tropical Africa*, Columbia University Press, New York, 1968

Castle, E. B., *Growing Up in East Africa*, Oxford University Press, London, 1966

Haag. Michael von, *Egypt. The Land and its People*, Macdonald Educational, London, 1975

Hiernaux, Jean, *Peoples of Africa*, Weidenfeld and Nicolson, London, 1974

Legum, Colin, ed., *Africa: a Handbook to a Continent*, Penguin, London, 1969

Mair, Lucy P., *African Societies*, Cambridge University Press, London, 1974

Murdock, George P., *Africa: its Peoples and their Culture History*, McGraw-Hill, New York, 1959

Paulme, Denise, *Women of Tropical Africa*, Routledge and Kegan Paul, London, 1971

Seligman, Charles G., *Races of Africa*, Oxford University Press, London, 1966

Skinner, Elliot P., *Peoples and Cultures of Africa*, Doubleday, 1973

Synge, Richard, *Nigeria. The Land and its People*, Macdonald Educational, London, 1975

Languages of Africa

Alexandre, Pierre, *Languages and Language in Black Africa*, Northwestern University Press, Evanston, 1972

Dalby, David, *Black through White: Patterns of Communication in Africa and the New World*, Indiana University African Studies Program, Bloomington, 1972

Greenberg, Joseph H., *The Languages of Africa*, 1963

Religions

Beetham, Thomas A., *Christianity and the New Africa*, Pall Mall Press, London, 1967

Mbiti, John S., *African Religion and Philosophy*, Heinemann, London, 1969

Mugambi and Kofi, eds., *African and Black Theology*, AACC-Transafrica

Parrinder, Edward G. S., *African Traditional Religion*, Sheldon Press, London, 1974

Trimingham, J. S., *Islam in West Africa*, Oxford University Press, London, 1962

Trimingham, J. S., *Islam in East Africa*, Oxford University Press, London, 1964

Wilson, Monica, *Religion and the Transformation of Society: a Study in Social Change in Africa*, Cambridge University Press, London, 1971

Traditional Literature

Arnott, Kathleen, *African Myths and Legends*, Oxford University Press, London, 1962

Arnott, Kathleen, *African Fairy Tales*, Frederick Muller, London, 1970

Dorson, Richard M., *African Folklore*, Indiana University Press, Bloomington, 1972

Drachler, Jacob, *African Heritage: Intimate Views of the Black African from Life, Love and Literature*, Crowell-Collier, New York, 1963

Hughes, Langston, *Poems from Black Africa*, Indiana University Press, Bloomington, 1963

Nunn, Jessie A., *African Folk Tales*, Funk and Wagnalls, New York, 1969

Radin, Paul, *African Folk Tales and Sculpture*, Secker and Warburg, London, 1965

Rutherfoord, Peggy, *African Voices: an Anthology of African Writing*, Vanguard Press, New York, 1960

Modern Literature

Allen, J. W. T., *Tende: Six Examples of Swahili Classical Verse Form*, Heinemann, London, 1971

Cartey, Wilfred, *Whispers from a Continent: the Literature of Contemporary Black Africa*, Heinemann, London, 1971

Edmann, *Who's Who in African Literature*, 1972

Kemoli, *Criticism in Afro-Caribbean Literature*, EALB, 1975

Economy

Annual Reports of Government Departments

Clare, Roger, *The Third World*, Macdonald Educational, London, 1974

Hutton, ed., *Urban Challenge in East Africa*, East African Publishing House, Nairobi

Oxford Regional Economic Atlas: Africa, Oxford University Press, London, 1965

Russell, E. W., *East Africa: its Peoples and Resources*, Oxford University Press in association with David Hawkins, 1971

Stamp, L. D., and Morgan, W. T. M., *Africa: a Study in Tropical Development*, Wiley, New York, 1972

Tropical Agricultural Series: *Rice, Coconut, Bananas*, etc., Longman, London

Food and Farming

Kyesimira, *Agricultural Export Development*, East African Publishing House, Nairobi

Industry

Ewing, A. F., *Industry in Africa*, Oxford University Press, London, 1968

Energy Resources

Manners, G., *The Geography of Energy*, Hutchinson, London, 1971

Moxon, J., *Volta, Man's Greatest Lake*, Deutsch, London, 1969

Rubin, N., and Warren, W. M., eds., *Dams in Africa*, London, 1968

Mining and Minerals

de Kun, N., *The Mineral Resources of Africa*, Elsevier, Amsterdam, 1965

Transport

Day, J. R., *Railways of Southern and Northern Africa*, London, 1963

Hoyle, *Seaports of East Africa*, East African Publishing House, Nairobi

O'Connor, A. M., *Railways and Development in Uganda*, Nairobi, 1965

Ridley, A., *An Illustrated History of Transport*, London, 1969

Communications

Annual Reports of Government Departments, e.g. Post and Telecommunications, Broadcasting Services

Ainslie, R., *The Press in Africa: Communications Past and Present*, London, 1969

Condon, J. C., 'Nation Building and Image Building in the Tanzanian Press', *Journal of Modern African Studies*, Volume V, 1967

Doob, L. V., *Communication in Africa: a Search for Boundaries*, New Haven, 1961

Omu, F. I. A., 'The Dilemma of Press Freedom in Colonial Africa', *Journal of African History*, Volume IX, 1968

Education

Jolly, *Education in Africa; Research and Action*, East African Publishing House, Nairobi

Jolly, *Planning Education for African Development*, East African Publishing House, Nairobi

King, M., *Pan Africanism and Education*, Oxford University Press, London

McNown, *Technical Education in Africa*, East African Publishing House, Nairobi

Ward, W. E. F., and White, L. W., *East Africa, a Century of Change*, Allen and Unwin, London, 1971

Health and Medicine

Brant, J., *Health and the Developing World*, Cornell University Press, Ithaca and London, 1969

Davey, T. H., and Wilson, T., *The Control of Disease in the Tropics*, Lewis, London, 1965

Dubos, M., *Man, Medicine and Environment*, Penguin, London, 1970

Ebrahim, *Child Care in the Tropics*, EALB

Gould, ed., *Health and Diseases in Africa*, EALB, 1971

King, M., ed., *Medical Care in Developing Countries*, Oxford University Press, Lusaka and London, 1966

The Land

Grove, A. T., *Africa South of the Sahara*, Oxford University Press, London, 1970

Hance, W. A., *The Geography of Modern Africa*, Columbia University Press, New York, 1964

Schulthess, Emil, *Africa*, Collins, London, 1959

Geology and Soils

Bridges, E. M., *World Soils*, Cambridge University Press, Cambridge, 1970

Cahen, L., and Snelling, N. J., *The Geochronology of Equatorial Africa*, North Holland Publishing Company, Amsterdam, 1966

Calder, Nigel, *Restless Earth*, British Broadcasting Company, London, 1972

Eyre, S. R., *Vegetation and Soils*, Arnold, London, 1968

Furon, R., *Geology of Africa*, Oliver and Boyd, Edinburgh, 1963

The Story of the Earth, Her Majesty's Stationery Office, London, 1972

Holmes, A., *Principles of Physical Geology*, Nelson, London and Edinburgh, 1965

King, L. C., *The Morphology of the Earth*, Oliver and Boyd, Edinburgh, 1967

Ecology

Brown, L., *Africa. A Natural History*, Hamish Hamilton, 1965

Myers, N., *The Long African Day*, Cassell Collier Macmillan, 1973

Vegetation

Hedberg, I., and Hedberg, O., *Conservation of Vegetation South of the Sahara*, Acta Phytogeographica Suecica 54, Uppsala, 1968

Hopkins, B., *Forest and Savanna*, Heinemann, London, 1965

Dale and Greenaway, *Kenya's Trees and Shrubs*, Hatchards, London

Fitzgerald, Vesey, *Grasslands of East Africa*, East African Publishing House, Nairobi 1974

Lawson, G. W., *Plant Life in West Africa*, Oxford University Press, London, 1966

Morrison, L., *East African Vegetation*, Longman, London, 1974

Nielson, M. S., *Introduction to the Flowering Plants of West Africa*, University of London Press, London, 1965

Polunin, N., *Introduction to Plant Geography*, Longmans Green, London, 1960

Walter, H., *Ecology of Tropical and Subtropical Vegetation*, Oliver and Boyd, Edinburgh, 1971

Wildlife

Brown, L., *African Birds of Prey*, Collins, London, 1970

Cloudsley Thompson, J. L., *The Zoology of Tropical Africa*, Weidenfeld and Nicolson, London, 1969

Dorset, J., and Dandelot, P., *A Field Guide to the larger Mammals of Africa*, Collins, London, 1970

Mackworth-Praed, G. W., and Grant, C. H. E., *African Handbook of Birds*, series I volume I, 1952, volume 2, 1955, series II volume I, 1962

Moreau, R. E., *The Bird Faunas of Africa and its Islands*, Academic Press, London, 1965

Morrison, L., *East African Vegetation*, Longman, London, 1974

Williams, John G., *A Field Guide to the Birds of East and Central Africa*, Collins, London, 1963

Art

Beier, Ulli, *Art in Nigeria*, Cambridge University Press, London, 1960

Beier, Ulli, *Contemporary Art in Africa*, Pall Mall Press, London, 1968

Dick-Read, R., *Sanamu, Adventures in Search of African Art*, Rupert Hart Davis, London, 1964

Elisofon, E., and Fagg, W., *The Sculpture of Africa*, Thames and Hudson, London, 1958

Jones, A. M., *Africa and Indonesia*, E. J. Brill, Leyden, 1971

Korn, Jörn, *Modern Makonde Art*, Hamlyn, London, 1960

Lamb, Venice, *West African Weaving*, Duckworth, London, 1975

Music and Dance

Blacking, John, *Venda Children's Songs*, Witwatersrand University Press, Johannesburg, 1967

Jones, A. M., *Studies in African Music*, Oxford University Press, London, 1959

Acknowledgements

Jones, A. M., and Kombe, L., *The Icila Dance, Old Style*, Longmans Green for the African Music Society, Roodepoort, South Africa, London, 1952

Kirby, P. R., *The Musical Instruments of the Native Races of South Africa*, Oxford University Press, London, 1953

Nketia, J. H., *Drumming in Akan Communities of Ghana*, Nelson, Edinburgh, 1963.

Tracey, Hugh, *Chopi Musicians*, Oxford University Press for the International African Institute, 1970

Sport

Amin, Mohamed, and Moll, Peter, *Kenya's World Beating Athletes*, East African Publishing House, Nairobi

Amin, Mohamed, and Moll, Peter, *The East African Safari Rally Comes of Age*, Heinemann Education (East Africa)

Cullen, *Crash Strike (Big Game Fishing)*, East African Publishing House, Nairobi

History

Ade Ajayi, J. F., and Espie, I., eds., *A Thousand Years of West African History*, Ibadan University Press and Nelson

Davidson, Basil, *The African Past*, Longman, London, 1964

Hargreaves, John D., *West Africa, the Former French States*, Prentice Hall, Englewood Cliffs, New Jersey, 1967

Ions, Veronica, *Egyptian Mythology*, Hamlyn, London

Leakey, L. S. B., *By the Evidence*, Harcourt Brace Javanovich, London, 1975

Ogot, B. A., and Kieran, J. A., eds., *Zamani*, Longman, London, 1968

Oliver, R., and Fage, J. D., *A Short History of Africa*, Rex Collings, London, 1974

Perham, Margery, *Lugard*, Collins, London, 1956

Posnansky, M., *The Pre-History of East Africa*, Oxford University Press, London

The Oxford History of East Africa, Oxford University Press, London, Volume I 1963, Volume II 1965

Walker, E. A., *History of Southern Africa*, Longman, London, 1959

Ward, W. E. F., *A History of Africa*, Allen and Unwin, London, Volume I 1960, Volume II 1963, Volume III 1968

Ward, W. E. F., and White, L. W., *East Africa, A Century of Change*, Allen and Unwin, London, 1971

Government and Diplomacy

African Contempory Records, Volumes I-VI, Rex Collings, London

Beshir, M. O., *Revolution and Nationalism in the Sudan*, Rex Collings, London, 1974

Cliff and Saul, *Socialism in Tanzania*, East African Publishing House, Nairobi, 1972

Gibson, Richard, *Liberation Movements in Africa*, Oxford University Press, London, 1972

Legum, Colin, *Africa: a Handbook to a Continent*, Penguin, London, 1969

Leys, Colin, *Underdevelopment in Kenya*, Heinemann, London, 1972

Ranger, T. O., *The African Voice in Southern Rhodesia*, East African Publishing House, Nairobi

Seidmann, *Comparative Development Strategies in East Africa*, East African Publishing House, Nairobi

Famous People

Dickie, John, and Rake, Alan, *Who's Who in Africa*, African Buyer and Trader (Publications), London, 1973

Kwame Nkrumah, Panaf Books Great Lives Series, London, 1974

Murray-Brown, Jeremy, *Kenyatta*, Fontana, London, 1974

Patrice Lumumba, Panaf Books Great Lives Series, London, 1973

Short, Philip, *Banda*, Routledge and Kegan Paul, London, 1974

Smith, William Edgett, *Nyerere of Tanzania*, Gollancz, London, 1973

Photographers

The Publishers wish to thank the following people, organizations and agencies for their assistance and for making available the material in their collections.

Algerian Embassy P. 202(TL); Anglo-American Corporation (CA) Ltd. P. 55(B); Owen Barnes P. 163 (Zaire football team and Eusebio), 204; Botswana Information Service pages 89(T), 196, 207(CR); Donald Bowen, Commonwealth Institute pages 158(BL), 159(TL), 159(TR), 159(BL); British Museum pages 18(T), 112, 155(L), 155(TR), 155(CR), 155(BR), 167(T), 167(BR), 168(CR); Embassy of Burundi page 209(TL); Camera Press pages 83(L), 202(B); J. Allan Cash pages 16(BR), 16(TL), 29(B), 31(T), 37(L), 39, 81(C), 90(B), 98, 108, 111(CR), 117(BR), 118(T), 123(B), 136, 157, 166, 170(T); Cassell & Co. Ltd, London pages 179(TL), 179(C); Central Press Photos page 213(TR); Charter Consolidated Ltd page 53(B); CIBA-GEIGY (UK) Ltd page 86(T); Roger Clare pages 31(B), 125(T); Dr Nicholas Cohen pages 15, 40, 70(T), 74(B), 75, 76(T); Rex Collings Ltd page 22 (The Man Died); Compix pages 61, 106, 123(CR); East African Publishing House page 23 (Song of Lawino); Egyptian Tourist Office pages 95, 151; Ethiopian Airlines page 97(TL); Ethiopian Tourist Office pages 9(3), 87(B), 88(B), 96, 154(B); FAO pages 10, 44(T), 44(B), 45(T), 45(B), 46(CR), 47(BL), 47(BR), 48(B), 56(C), 65(L), 65(R), 77, 83(R), 85, 92, 103(TL), 104(TR), 117(BL); Fontana Paperbacks pages 22-23 (The Gab Boys); Let My People Go; A Dream of Africa; More Voices of Africa); Werner Forman Archive pages 16(TR), 150(BL), 152, 154(L), 156(R), 167(BL), 168(B), 168(CL), 169(T), 171(B), 172, 173(T), 173(B), 175; Fox Photos pages 181(T), 182(B); Peter Fraenkel pages 18(B), 24, 25, 26(R), 29(T), 29(C), 34, 35, 42, 58(BR), 78, 103(C), 107(T), 111(B), 119(R), 120(L), 123(TR), 124, 128, 134(T), 156(BL); Gabon Embassy page 97(TR); Geographical Magazine page 9(2); David Goldblatt page 23 (Nadine Gordimer); Guinea Information Service page 215(CL); Brian Hawkes pages 79(T), 103(B), 133(TR), 133(BR), 139(T), 140(TL), 141(BL), 142(T), 142(B), 144(TR), 144(C), 144(B), 145(B), 146(T), 147(T), 147(B); Heinemann Educational pages 22-3 (A grain of Wheat; Zambia shall be Free); F. N. Hepper page 130(B); Allan Hutchison pages 39, 49, 56-7, 103(inset), 112, 113(B), 115(B), 120(R), 127(T), 127(B), 188(T), 189(T), 189(C), 189(BR), 189(BL), 195(B), 197(B), 198(B), 199(BL), 199(BR); Anthony Hutt pages 150(T), 150(BR), 153(BL), 153(BR); Imperial War Museum pages 180(B), 181(BL), 181(BR); Industrial Diamond Information Bureau page 55(C); International Red Cross page 74; Mrs Jeffes page 135(B); Dalu Jones pages 81(B), 90(T), 99(B), 103(TR), 135(T), 170(B); Kenya Information Service pages 7(R), 50(T), 59(B), 66(C), 84(T), 196, 207(TR); Keystone Press pages 164, 182(T), 183(C), 183(B), 184, 186(TL), 186(TR), 186(B), 187(T), 187(B), 191(BL), 197(T), 199(T), 200(BL), 211(CL); Cathy Kilpatrick pages 199(L), 133(TL); Jan Knappert page 9(BL); E. D. Lacey pages 162-3, 206(BL), 207(TL); Lesotho Information Service pages 74(TR), 206(CL), 210(TL); Liberian Embassy pages 214(TC), 214(TR); Libyan Embassy page 198(T); Macdonald Educational pages 22-3, 58(BL), 64(T), 64(B); Mansell Collection pages 164(L), 174, 176(T), 176(B), 177(TL), 177(TR), 179(TR), 194(T), 194(BR), 208(T), 208(B), 209(C), 212(TL), 213(BR); Mary Evans Picture Library pages 171(T), 177(B), 192, 203; Mauritania Information Service page 203; R. M. Melville page 133(CR); Middle East Archives pages 69(TR), 69(BR); Moroccan Tourist Office pages 9(4), 88(T), 91(T), 97(BL), 107(B), 109(B), 115(T), 122(CL), 160(T), 205(TL); Pat Morris pages 130(T), 132, 143(T); Mozambique Tourist Office page 90; Museum Angewandte Kunst page 153(T); D. Napper page 134(B); NASA page 82; National Army Museum pages 178, 179(B), 180(C); NHPA/A. M. Anderson page 137; NHPA/M. Tomkinson page 138(T); NHPA/A. Bannister page 138(C); NHPA/P. Johnson page 138(B); NHPA/P. Johnson page 139(B); NHPA/K. B. Newman page 140; NHPA/A. Bannister page 141(T); NHPA/P. Johnson page 141(BR); NHPA/P. Johnson page 142(C); NHPA/L. A. Wilkinson page 146(B); NHPA/P. Johnson page 149; Nigerian Information Service pages 7(T), 50(C), 50(B), 101(B), 113(TL), 193(BR), 201(BR), 203, 204(T); Nobel Foundation page 212(TR); Panaf Books page 22 (I Speak of Freedom); James Pickerell (International Development Association) pages 46(BR), 67(T), 67(C), 67(B); Dr R. M. Polhill page 131(B); Popperfoto pages 164(B), 183(T), 185(BL), 187(C), 188(B), 190(BL), 191(BR); Publicare pages 143(B), 144(TL); Radio Times Hulton Picture Library pages 193(BL), 194(C), 195(T); Rhodesia Information Service pages 32(R), 46, 51(B), 51(T), 84(B), 89(B), 101(C), 117(T), 125(B), 169(B), 185(TL), 213(TL), 215(CR); Rwanda Information Service page 206(BR); SATOUR pages 11, 32(L), 37(R), 21, 43, 46(BL), 54, 55(T), 91(B), 95(B), 100, 101(T), 111(CL), 114, 148(B), 160(B), 169(C), 201, 207(BR), 213; Jurgen Schadeberg page 62(T); Senegalese Embassy page 213(CL); Shell Photographic Service pages 52(T), 52(R), 72, 113(TR); South African Embassy pages 201, 207(BR), 213(CT), 215; J. Stewart page 131(T); Sudanese Embassy pages 200, 211(TL); Syndication International pages 201(T), 204(BR), 205, 209(TR), 210(C), 211(BL), 214(TL); Tanzania Information Service page 211(TR); Togolese Embassy page 204(BL); Topix pages 22 (Chinua Achebe), 161(B); Tunisian Embassy pages 26(L), 202(TC); United Nations pages 93(T), 121(TL); UNESCO pages 65 (T/P. Larsen), 68 (B/J. Mohr), 68 T/D. Roger), 69 (L/P. Vagliani); T. G. Usborne pages 79(L), 86(B), 109(T), 111(T), 123(TL), 135(C); U.S.P.G. pages 9(1), 19(TL), 19(BR), 56(T), 59(C), 60, 63(T), 66(B), 76(C), 104(TL); Keith Wicks pages 16(BL), 66(T), 118(B); World Health Organisation (WHO) page 70(B); Zambia Information Services pages 7(BL), 10, 53(T), 56(B), 62(B), 63(B), 80, 81(T), 105, 128, 140(TR), 143(C), 161, 145(T), 145(C), 148(T), 160(C), 161(T), 185(BR), 190(BR), 206(T).

N.B. The bracketed letters which follow the page numbers indicate the position of the illustration on each page, e.g. TR = Top Right, BL = Below Left.

Artists

The diagrams and drawings in this book are the work of the following art agencies and artists: Andrzej Bielecki, Eric Jewell Associates, George Thompson, Tudor Art Agency, Maurice Wilson.

Index

How to use this Index

The Encyclopedia of Africa is divided into general chapters and three A-Z sections. This index does not include all the entries from the *Guide to Peoples and Languages* (pages 24-43). If you wish to find information concerning one of Africa's peoples or languages, you must turn to that section. This index, however, does include entries from the A-Z *Gazetteer of Places* and *Who's Who*, because supplementary information about people and places can be found elsewhere in the book. For example, if you require information about Kenya, you will see that the Gazetteer entry on this country appears under Kenya in the Index. Specific information on particular topics concerning Kenya is then listed in alphabetical order with page references.

Note: entries appearing in the *Gazetteer of Places* have (G) following the appropriate page numbers. Page numbers in bold typeface indicate pages on which illustrations occur.

A

Aba 86 (G)
Abaya, Lake 86 (G)
Abbai *see* Blue Nile River
Abboud, Ibrahim 200, **200**
Abd al-Kadir 200
Abd al-Krim 200
Abd al-Mumin 200
Abeokuta 86 (G)
Abrahams, Peter 23, 200
Abu Simbel 86 (G), **86**
Accra 86 (G), **99**
Acheampong, Ignatius Kutu 200
Achebe, Chinua 23, 200
Acheulian Age 165
Achimota College 63
Addis Ababa 86 (G), **96**
Adoula, Cyrille 200
Afar 86 (G)
Afewerk, Tekle 200
Africa, *Area* 78; space photograph **82**
Africa, *European circumnavigation of* 174; *Scramble for* 179
African National Congress 187
African unity 185, 198, 199
Afrikaans 11, **12**
Agades **111**
Aggrey, Dr 63
Agriculture 44, 50; *Development of* 46; *see also* Farming
Aguiyi-Ironsi, Johnson 200
Ahaggar Mountains 79, 86 (G)
Ahidjo, Ahmadou 200
Ahmed, Jamel Mohammed 200, **200**
Ahmed, Sultan, tomb of **9**
Air Mountains 86 (G)
Air movements 82
Air transport 57
Aiun 86 (G), **120**
Akan language 14
Akii-bua, John 200
Aklilou Abte-Wold, Teshafi Teezaz 200
Al-Azhar 69, **69**
Al Bakri 171, 200
Albert, Lake *see* Mobutu Sese Seko, Lake
Alexander the Great 167
Alexandria 86 (G)
Alexandrines 68
Al Fayum 86 (G)
Algeria 86 (G); *French domination* 69, 182; *Government* 87 (G); *History* 87 (G); *Independence* 183; *Land and economy* 86 (G); *Natural Gas* 52; *People* 86 (G)
Algiers 87 (G)
Almoravid movement 172

Al Mu'izz 200
Aloes **133**
Altitude, *Effects on climate* 83; *Map* **78**
Aluminium 54, 55
Alur 15
Alwa 170
Amharic 20
Amin, Idi **196**, 197, 200
Amphibians 138, **141**
Amr-Ibn al-A's 201
Anaemia, *Sickle-cell* 72
Anglo-Egyptian Condominium 182
Anglo-Egyptian treaty 181
Angola 87 (G), 189, **189**; *Government* 87 (G); *History* 87 (G); *Independence* 188; *Land and economy* 87 (G); *People* 87 (G)
Animal life, *see* Wildlife
Animism 8, 16
Ankrah, Joseph Arthur 201
Annaba 87 (G)
Antelopes **89**, 140, 145, **148**
Antubam, Kofi 201
Apartheid 187, 199
Apithy, Sourou Migan 201
Arabi Pasha 178, **179**, 201
Arabia 169, 170
Arabic, *language* 9, 15; *Literature* 20
Arabs 7, 8, 68, 74, 153
Archaeology 164
Architecture 154, 156-7
Area of Africa 78
Armah, Ayi Kwei 201
Armies 196-8
Arms 196, 197
Art, *Airport* 158; *Ancient Egyptian* 150, 151; *Bantu* 156; *Black African* 156; *Christian in Ethiopia* 154; *Coptic* 152; *Early* 150-7; *East Africa* 154; *Ethiopian* 154; *Islamic* 152, 154; *Modern* 158-9; *New media* 159; *North Africa* 150; *Pictorial* 158; *Roman* 151; *South of Sahara* 154; *Total* 158; *Urban folk* 158; *West Africa* 155
Arts and Crafts Training Centre **65**
Arusha 87 (G)
Arusha Declaration 190, **190**
Ashanti 25, **25**
Askia Muhammad Abu-Bakr 173
Asmara 87 (G)
Aswan 88 (G)
Aswan High Dam 53, 88 (G)
Atbara 88 (G)
Athletes and Athletics 162
Atlas Mountains 79, 88 (G), **88**
Australopithecus 164, **165**
Automobile industry 50

Awash National Park 149
Awash River 88 (G)
Awolowo, Obafemi 201
Awoonor, Kofi 201
Axum 88 (G), 154, 169
Aye, Hippolyte 201
Azikiwe, Nnamdi 201, **201**

B

Bachwezi 174
Baganda 193
Baker, Sir Samuel White 178, 201
Bale mountains **132**
Balewa, Sir Abubakar Tafawa 187, 201, **201**
Baluba sceptre **156**
Bambara Sculpture 155
Bambari 88 (G)
Bamum 10
Banda, Hastings Kamuzu 184, 188, **188**, 201, **201**
Banganda 74
Bangui 88 (G)
Bangweulu, Lake 88 (G)
Banjul 88 (G)
Bantu 7, 169; *Art* 156; *Languages* 9, 11, 13, **13**
Bantustans 88 (G)
Baobab tree **107**, **133**
Barge 88 (G)
Barnard, Christian Neethling 201, **201**
Barotseland Lozi 88(G)
Barth, Heinrich 177
Basotho 74
Bassey, Hogan 'Kid' 201
Basutoland 184
Bathurst *see* Banjul
Bauxite 54
Bayero, Alhaji Abdullahi 201
Bayero, Alhaji Ado 201
Bayi, Filbert 201
Beau Bassin-Rosehill 88 (G)
Bechuanaland 184
Bedouins 7, **26**
Beier, Ulli 158
Beira 88 (G)
Beit, Alfred **212**
Belgian Congo 180, 186
Belgian influence 179
Bello, Sir Ahmadu 201
Ben Bella, Ahmed 202
Bengasi (Benghazi) 88 (G)
Benguela 88 (G)
Benin *see* Dahomey
Benin (Nigeria) 88, 89
Benin, *Language* 14; *Metal-work* 155; *Oba of* **193**

Benoni 89 (G)
Benue River 89 (G)
Berbera 89 (G)
Berberati 89 (G)
Berbers 20, **26**, **42**
Berlin Conference 179
Beti, Mongo 202
Betsiboka River 89 (G)
Biafra *see* Nigeria
Bight of Benin 89 (G)
Bikila, Abebe 162, 202
Bilharzia 71, 72, **72**, 73, 75, **75**
Bini 14
Birdlife 138, 141, 142, 145, 146, 149
Birth control 75
Bissau 89 (G)
Biwott **162**
Bizerte 89 (G)
Black Africa, *and South Africa* 188; *Art* 156
Black sunbird **139**
Blantyre-Limbe 89 (G)
Blesbok 148
Bloemfontein 89 (G)
Blue Nile 78, 80, 89 (G), **89**, **192**
Blyden, Edward Wilmot 202
Bobo-Dioulasso 89 (G)
Bodele Depression 89 (G)
Boer War 180, **180**
Bokassa, Jean Bédel 202, **202**
Bongo (Antelope) 140
Bongo, Omar **97**, 202
Bornu 20
Bosomtwe, Lake 89 (G)
Botha, General Louis 202
Botswana 12, 89 (G), 188; *Government* 89 (G); *History* 89 (G); *Land and economy* 89 (G); *People* 89 (G)
Boumedienne, Houari 202, **202**
Bourguiba, Habib Ben Ali 202, **202**
Boxing 163
Boye, Ibrahima 202
Brain pressure, *Relief of* 70
Brass weights **172**
Brazza, Pierre Paul Francois Camille Savorgnan de 202
Brazzaville 89 (G)
British Central Africa 184
British East Africa 184
British West Africa 184
Broadcasting service 59, **59**
Bronze 167, 168
Brooks, Angie Elizabeth 202
Bruce, James 202
Brutus, Denius 23
Buffalo 141
Buganda 9, 89 (G)
Bujumbura 89 (G)

Bukavu 89 (G)
Bulawayo 89 (G)
Buraimoh, Jimoh 159
Burial 165
Burton, Sir Richard Francis 202
Burundi 10, 90 (G); *History* 90 (G);
    Land and economy 90 (G);
    People 90 (G)
Bushbaby 141
Bushbuck 141
Bush fire 130
Bushmen 7, 8, 32, 169
Bushveld, *Wildlife* 148
Busia, Dr Kofi Abrefa 202
Buthelezi, Chief Gatsha 202
Bwanga 163

C

Cabinda 90 (G)
Cabora Bassa Dam 51, 53, 90 (G)
Cabral, Amilcar 202, 202
Cabral, Louis 203
Caillé, René Auguste 177, 203
Cairo 90 (G), 90, 153, 166
Calabar 90 (G)
Camels 56, 108, 137, 138, 168,
    171, 171
Cameroon 90 (G); *Government* 90
    (G); *History* 90 (G); *Land and
    economy* 90 (G); *Languages* 10;
    People 90 (G)
Cameroon, Mount 79, 109 (G)
Canary Islands 91 (G)
Cancer 71-2
Cape Agulhas 91 (G)
Cape Coast 91 (G)
Cape Guardafui 91 (G)
Cape Town 91 (G), 91, 119, 176
Cape Verde 91 (G)
Cape Verde Islands 91 (G)
Caprivi Strip 91 (G), 188
Carthage 91 (G), 168, 168
Casablanca 91 (G), 91
Casablanca powers 185
Casamance River 91 (G)
Cassava 45
Castro, Fidel 214
Cat, *Egyptian* 167
Central Africa 174; *Language* 10
Central African Federation 185
Central African Republic 91 (G);
    History 91 (G); *Land and
    Economy* 91 (G); *People* 91 (G)
Cereals 45
Cetewayo 203, 203
Ceuta 92 (G)
Chad 92 (G), 92; *Basin* 79;
    Government 92 (G); *History* 92
    (G); *Land and Economy* 92 (G);
    People 92 (G)
Chad, Lake 79, 92 (G), 130
Cheetah 144
Chelimo, Elizabeth 162
Chi-Chewa 11
Chiefs 194
Children, *Nutritional deficiency
    disorders* 74
Chilembwe, John 203
Chimpanzees 140
Chingola 92 (G)
Chinua Achebe 22
Chobe Game Reserve 89
Cholera 73, 77
Chona, Mathias Mainza 203
Christian Art in Ethiopia 154
Christianity 16, 16, 17, 19, 170
Chromium ore 54, 55
Clapperton, Hugh 203
Clark, J. D. 165
Cleopatra VII 203
Climate 82-3, 130
Climatic regions 83

Clinics 75
Cloete, Stuart 23
Coal and coal mining 52, 53, 84
Coastal Lands 81
Cobalt 54
Cobbson, Felix 161
Coffee 46, 103
Colobus 140
Colonization 177-81, 184, 185, 194,
    194
Columbus, Christopher 174
Commonwealth conferences 198
Commonwealth countries 198
Commonwealth games 162
Communications 58
Community development 66-7
Community health 76
Comoro Islands 92 (G)
Conakry 92 (G)
Conakry declaration 185
Congo 92 (G); *Crisis in* 199;
    Government 93 (G); *History* 92
    (G); *Land and economy* 92 (G);
    People 92 (G)
Congo peacock 141
Congo Swahili 9
Constitutional development,
    Pattern of 194
Continental drift 84, 85
Co-operatives 47
Copper 54, 55
Coptic art 152
Coptic language 20, 68
Cosmetics 113
Cotonou 93 (G)
Cotonou harbour 93
Cotton 95
Coups *see* Government, *Military*
Covilhao, Pedro da 203
Crocodiles 145, 145
Crops, *Cash crops* 45, 46;
    Improvement 47; *Protection* 47;
    Regional subsistence 45
Cultural developments 165
Cure-Pipe 93 (G)
Cushitic Languages 28

D

Dacko, David 203
Daddah, Moktar Ould 203
Dahomey, 93 (G) 193; *History* 93 (G);
    Land and economy 93 (G);
    People 93 (G)
Dakar 93 (G), 93
Dams 51, 53, 53; *see also* under
    specific names
Danakil depression 134
Dance 99, 160, 160, 161, 161
Daniels, George 162
Danquah, Dr Joseph Boakye 203
Dar Es Salaam 93 (G)
Darwin, Charles 164, 164
Defassa waterbuck 144
Defence 196, 197
Deficiency disease 72, 74, 74
de Gaulle, General Charles 183, 183
Delamere, Lord 203
Denham, Dixon 203
Desert adder 137
Deserts 45, 79, 101, 137; *Vegetation*
    134; *Wildlife* 138; *see also* Semi-
    desert
Dessie 93 (G)
Development policies 190
Devonshire Declaration 181; *White
    Paper* 65
Dhows 170
Dia, Mamadou 203
Dialects 7
Diamonds 50, 54, 55, 55, 179
Dias de Novais, Paulo 203
Diego-Suarez 94 (G)

Dinder National Park 149
Dingane 203
Dingiswayo 203
Dinka 15
Diop, Alioune 203
Diop, Birago 23
Diop, David 23
Diophantus 203
Diori, Hamani 203
Diphtheria 73, 77
Diplomacy 192-9
Diredawa 94 (G)
Diseases 70-7, 71; *Bacterial* 73;
    Communicable 73; *Control of* 73;
    Deficiency 72; *Degenerative* 72;
    Endemic 70; *Epidemic* 70;
    Geography of 72, 74, 74;
    Hereditary 72; *Infectious* 72, 73;
    Major 71; *Nutritional* 72;
    Pandemic 70; *Stress* 72; *Tropical*
    72; *Virus* 73; *see also* Health
Disraeli, Benjamin 178
Djenne 171
Djibouti 94 (G)
Dlamini, Prince Makhosini 203
Docks 57
Doctors 77
Dodoma 94 (G)
Dogon Sculpture 155
Dongola 170
Donkeys 109
Dos Santos, Maralino 203
Douala 94 (G)
Dragon's blood trees 133
Drainage patterns, *Map* 78
Drakensberg Mountains 94 (G), 94
Drought 74, 83
Drumming 160, 161, 161
Durban 94 (G)
Dutch settlers 176
Dwarfism 72
Dysentery 71, 73
Dzaoudzi 94 (G)

E

Eagles 140, 141
East Africa 174; *Art* 154;
    Grasslands, (Wildlife) 147;
    Language 9; *Volcanoes* 78
East African Common Market
    (EACM) 185
East African Community 185
East London 94 (G)
Economic Commission for Africa 199
Economic progress 189
Edo 14
Education 60-9, 60; *Adult* 65, 67;
    Attitude in Europe after 1850 60;
    Belgian colonial 63; *British
    colonial* 63; *Colonial* 60, 63;
    Colonial policy differences 64;
    Curricula and methods 67;
    Development since independence
    69; *Early European* 60; *French
    colonial* 63; *German colonial* 63;
    Higher 63; *Independence* 65;
    Language problems 62; *Mass* 66;
    North Africa 68-9; *Portuguese
    colonial* 60, 63, 66; *Priorities and
    needs* 67; *Problems* 60, 62;
    Progress 65; *Society and* 66;
    Text-books 62; *University* 66
Edward, Lake *see* Idi Amin Dada, Lake
Egypt 8, 53, 94 (G), 178, 181;
    Ancient 68, 166-7; *Army* 197;
    Art 150, 151; *Civilization* 167;
    Decline 167; *Government* 94 (G);
    History 94 (G); *Industry* 51;
    Islamic 153; *Land and economy*
    94 (G); *Painting* 151; *People*
    94 (G); *Pyramids* 117, 150, 166,
    167; *Sculpture* 151; *Temples* 150;

Egypt (cont.) *Tombs* 150; *Universities*
    69; *Writing* 166
Ekangaki, Nzo 199
Eldoret 94 (G)
Electricity 52-3
Elephants 141-3, 143, 146
Elgon, Mount 78, 109 (G)
El Obeid 94 (G)
Emin Pasha 203
Enahoro, Chief Anthony 203
Energy resources 52-3, 52
Entebbe 94 (G)
Enugu 94 (G)
Environments 8
Enwonwu, Ben 159
Epiphytes 131
Epworth Mission 84
Equatorial Guinea 96 (G);
    Government 96 (G); *History*
    96 (G); *Land and economy* 96 (G);
    People 96 (G)
Eritrea *see* Ethiopia
Ethiopia 44, 46, 96 (G); *Art* 154;
    Christian Art 154; *History* 96 (G);
    Italian invasion 181; *Land and
    economy* 96 (G); *Language* 15;
    Mountains 78; *People* 96 (G);
    War with Italy 181; *Wildlife* 136,
    139
Ethnic groups 7-8, 192
Etosha Pan 96 (G)
European Economic Community
    190, 199
European influence 7, 8, 60, 176, 177,
    194
Eusebio da Silva Ferreira 163, 204
Evolution 164
Ewe 14
Excavations 164
Exploration 174, 176, 176, 177
Exports 50-51; *Fish* 48; *Groundnuts*
    113; *Minerals* 54; *Mining* 50;
    Oil 52
Eyadema, Etienna Gnassingbe 204,
    204

F

Falasha 15
Family spacing 75
Famine 74
Fanagalo 11, 12
Fang 28
Fante 29
Farming 8, 44-7, 67; *Cash crop* 45;
    Importance of 44; *Livestock* 45;
    Physical problems 46; *Shifting
    cultivation* 131; *Solutions to
    problems* 47; *Subsistence* 44;
    Traditional method 44
Farouk, King 182
Fellahin 8
Fennec fox 137
Fertilizers 47, 47
Fetishes 17, 18
Fez (Fes) 96 (G), 97
Fianarantsoa 96 (G)
Filariasis 71
Fireball lily 133
Fish, *Protein from* 48
Fishing 8, 48, 48, 49, 106, 123
Fishing Festival 49
Flamingos 147, 147
Flooding 83
Flycatcher 140
FNLA (Union of Angolan Peoples)
    189
Fodio, Uthman dan 204
Food 45, 50; *Nutritional content* 74;
    Shortage of 74
Food and Farming 44-7
Football 163, 163
Fold belts 84

Forests 45, 46, 130, **131**, 132;
    Wildlife 140-41, **141**
Forster, Isaac 204
Fort Portal 96 (G)
Fort Victoria 96 (G)
Forty-Lamy *see* N'Djamena
Fossil remains 164, 165
Fourah Bay College 66
Fouta Djallon 96 (G)
Fragmentation belt 9
France, *influence of*
    178, 182, 183
Francistown 97 (G)
Freetown 97 (G)
FRELIMO (Mozambique
    Liberation Front) 189, **196**;
    Guerillas **189**
French West Africa, *Education* 63
FROLIZI (Front for the Liberation of
    Zimbabwe) 187
Fruit-growing **51**
Fugard, Athol 204
Fula **10**, 14, 20, **29**, 117
Fulani *see* Fula
Fulbe *see* Fula
Funchal 97 (G)
Fungal infections 73
Fynbos 135

G

Gaberone 97 (G)
Gabes 97 (G)
Gabon 97 (G), **97**; *History* 97 (G);
    Government 97 (G); *Land and
    economy* 97 (G); *People* 97 (G)
Gaddafi, Colonel Muammar al **198**,
    204
Gafsa 97 (G)
Galla 15
Gambia 98 (G), **98**; *Government*
    98 (G); *History* 98 (G); *Land and
    economy* 98 (G); *People* 98 (G)
Gambia River 98 (G)
Game Reserves 149
Gammoudi, Mohammed 204
Gardiner, Robert 204
Garoua 98 (G)
Gazelles 144, 146
Gedi **154**
Ge'ez 15, 20
Geology 84-5
Gerenuk 146, **146**
German East Africa 180
German influence 179, 180
German South-West Africa 188
Gezira (Jazira) 98 (G)
Ghana 98 (G), 182; *Ancient* 171,
    172, **172**; *Government* 98 (G);
    History 98 (G); *Independence*
    183; *Industry* 51; *Land and
    economy* 98 (G); *People* 98 (G);
    Power 53
Giraffe **143**
Gisenyi 98 (G)
Giuba River 98 (G)
Gizeh 98 (G)
Gizenga, Antoine 204
Glossopteris 84
GNP (Gross national product) 44, 46,
    50
Gnu 148
Gods *see* Religion
Gold 54, **54**, 174, 176, 179
Gold Coast 182, **182**; *Education* 65;
    Schools 63
Golden pipet 146
Gondar 98 (G)
Gondwanaland 84
Gonorrhoea 71
Gordimer, Nadine **23**, 204
Gordon, General 178, **179**
Gorillas 139

Government 192-9; *Colonial Rule*
    194; *Since Independence* 196;
    Ivory Coast 195; *Kenya* 195;
    Military 196, 198; *Nigeria* 195;
    Traditional 192, 194
Gowon, Yakubu 191, **198**, 204, **204**
Graaff, Sir de Villiers 204
Grant, James 177, 192
Grant, James Augustus 204
Grasslands, *Vegetation* 132-3;
    Wooded 132; *Wildlife* 147
Great Erg **79**
Great Lakes 45
Gross National Product 44, 46, 50
Groundnuts **113**
Groundsels 132
Grunitzky, Nicholas 204
Guggisberg, Sir Gordon 204
Guinea 45, 99 (G), 183; *Bauxite* 55;
    Government 99 (G); *History*
    99 (G); *Land and economy* 99 (G);
    People 99 (G)
Guinea, Gulf of 99 (G)
Guinea Savannas, *Wildlife* 144-5
Guinea-Bissau 99 (G), 188, 189;
    Land and economy 99 (G);
    People 99 (G)
Gur languages 14
Gwelo 99 (G)

H

Haile Selassie I **204**, 205
Hamilcar, Barca 205
Hannibal 205
Harar 100 (G)
Hargeisa 100 (G)
Hassan II 205, **205**
Hausa, *Literature* 15, 20
Hausaland 173
Health 70-77; *Centres* 77;
    Community 76; *Man-made
    hazards* 75; *Priorities in care* 76;
    Services 77; *Statistics* 72; *see also*
    Diseases
Heron **148**
Herzog, General James Barry Munnik
    205
Hides **104**
High Veld 133; *Wildlife* 148
Hippopotamus 140, **145**
Homo erectus 165
Homo habilis 164
Homo sapiens 165
Hornbills 146
Hospitals 77
Hottentots, 8, **32**
Houphouet-Boigny, Felix 205
Hova 12
Huambo *see* Nova Lisboa
Huggins, Godfrey 205
Humus 85
Hussein, Abdirazak Haji 205
Hyaenas **142**, 149
Hydroelectric power 51, 53, **53**, 80,
    125, **127**
Hypostyle Hall 151
Hyrax 139, **139**

I

Ibadan 100 (G)
Ibn-al-Mukhtar 171
Ibn Battuta 171, 172, 205
Ibn Hawqal 205
Ibn Khaldun 205
Ibn Tumart 205
Ibrahim Pasha 205
Idi Amin Dada, Lake 100 (G)
Idris I 205, **205**
Idris Alooma 205
Idris Ibn Adb Allah 205

Ife 100 (G), **168**; *Metalwork* 155
Igbo 15
Ileo, Joseph 205
Illness *see* Diseases
Ilorin 100 (G)
Imhotep 205
Immunisation 73, 76, 77
Impala **144**
Independence 182-4; *Education for*
    65; *Government since* 196;
    Literature 22
Indirect rule 194
Industrialization, problems of 51
Industry 50-51, **50**; *Capital intensive*
    51; *Egypt* 51; *Ghana* 51; *Labour
    intensive* 51; *Nigeria* 51; *South
    Africa* 50; *Zimbabwe* 51
Influenza 73
Inga Dam 100 (G), **127**
Initiation ceremonies 18
Inland Waterways 56
Insect life **73**, 141, 142
International affairs 198
Investment 47, 51, 190
Iron and iron ore 54, 55, 167
Irrigation **45**, 47
Isandhlawana, *Battle of* **178**
Islam 16, 17, 173; *Art* 152, 154;
    Influence of 170
Islamic Egypt 153
Ismailia 100 (G)
Issa 86 (G)
Issa, Abdullahi 205
Italy, *War with Ethiopia* **181**
Ivory Coast 100 (G), **183**;
    Constitutional development 195;
    Government 100 (G); *History*
    100 (G); *Land and economy*
    100 (G); *People* 100 (G)
Iwo 100 (G)

J

Jamestown 100 (G)
Jawara, Sir Dawda Jairaba 205
Jazz 161
Jebel Mara 79
Jimma 100 (G)
Jinja 53, 100 (G), **125**
Jipcho Ben, **162**, 206, **206**
Johannesburg 100 (G), **100**
Johnston, Sir Harry **194**
Jonathan, Chief Leabua 206, **206**
Jos 100 (G)
Juba River *see* Giuba River
Jumbe, Sheikh Aboud 206

K

Kabalega park 143
Kabalega Falls 100 (G)
Kabwe 100 (G)
Kadalie, Clements 206
Kaduna 100 (G)
Kaedi 100 (G)
Kafue National Park 149
Kafue River 100 (G)
Kagera River 100 (G)
Kainji Dam 53, 110 (G)
Kairouan *see* Quayrawan
Kalahari 101 (G), **101**
Kalahari basin 79
Kalahari Gemsbok National Park 149
Kalanga 11
Kamba 19
Kampala 101 (G)
Kananga 101 (G)
Kanem 101 (G)
Kanem-Bornu 173
Kankan 101 (G)
Kano 101 (G), **101**
Kano, Alhaji Aminu 206

Kanuri 20, **31**
Kanye 101 (G)
Kaolack 101 (G)
Kapwepwe, Simon Mwanza 206
Karamojong **31**
Karanga 11
Kariba dam 53, 101 (G)
Kariba Lake 81, 101 (G), **101**
Karnak 101 (G); *Temple* 101 (G),
    150, 151
Karoo 101 (G), 133
Karroo rock system 84
Karume, Sheikh Abeid 206
Kasai River 101 (G)
Kasavubu, Joseph Ileo 206
Kashim, Shettima 206
Kassala 101 (G)
Katanga 186
Kaunda, Kenneth David **128**, 184,
    185, 206, **206**
Kawawa, Rashidi Mfaume 206
Kayes 101 (G)
Kayibanda, Grégoire 206, **206**
Keetmanshoop 101 (G)
Keino, Kipchoge 162, 206, **207**
Keita, Fodeba 207
Keita, Modibo 207
Keita, Salif 207
Kenya **7**, 102 (G), 181, 182, 184;
    Constitutional development 195;
    Government 102 (G); *History*
    102 (G); *Independence* **196**;
    Land and economy 102 (G);
    Literature 21; *People* 102 (G);
    Schools 63
Kenya Coast Literary Swahili 9
Kenya, Mount 78, **84**, 109 (G)
Kenyatta, Jomo 22, **195**, 207, **207**
Kerekou, Major Matthieu, **198**, 207
Khalifa, Ser al-Khatim 207
Khama, Sir Seretse **66**, 207, **207**
Khartoum 102 (G), 178
Khartoum North (Halfaya) 102 (G)
Khedive Ismail 178
Khoi-San 9, **32**
Kigali 102 (G)
Kigoma 102 (G)
Ki-Kongo 11
Kikuyu **7**, 22
Kilimanjaro, Mount **78**, 109 (G), 132
Kima 102 (G)
Kimathi, Dedan 207
Kimberley 55, 102 (G)
Kimbundu 10
Ki-Ngazija 10
Kings, *Ancient Egyptian* 166, 167;
    Ancient Ghana 172; *Traditional
    African* 192-3
King's African Rifles **180**
Kingsley, Mary Henrietta 207
Kinshasa 102 (G), **127**
Kisangani 102 (G)
Kisumu 102 (G)
Kitchener, General 178
Kitega 102 (G)
Kitwe 102 (G)
Kiungwana 9
Kivu, Lake 102 (G)
Kiwanuka, Kabimu Mugumba
    Benedicto 207
Klipspringer 146
Kofi, Vincent **159**
Kongo 174
Kordofan Plateau 102 (G)
Korekore 11
Koroma, Sorie Ibrahim 207
Koudougou 102 (G)
Kountche, Seyni 207
Krapf, Johann Ludwig 177
Kruger National Park **119**, 148
Kruger, Stephanus Johannes Paulus
    207, **207**
Kumasi 102 (G)

Kunene (Cunene) River 102 (G)
Kush 102 (G), 154, 167, 169
Kutako, Hosea 207
Kwa languages 14
Kwango River 102 (G)
Kwanza (Cuanza) River 102 (G)
Kwashiorkor 74, 75
Kyoga Lake 102 (G)

L

Labe 104 (G)
La Guma, Alex 208
Lagos 104 (G)
Lagos University 65
Lake Nakuru National Park 149
Lakes 48, 56, 80
Lalibela 97, 154
Lambarene 104 (G)
Lamizana, Sangoulé 208
Lamu 104 (G)
Land reform 47
Lander, John 208
Lander, Richard Lemon 208
Languages 7, 9, 10, 11, 12-15, 20;
    Bantu 9, 11, 13, 13; Central Africa
    10; East Africa 9; Four main
    groups 9; Guide 24-43; Malagasy
    Republic 12; North-East Africa 15;
    Northern Africa 12, 15; Scripts 11;
    South Africa 11; South of
    Equator 9; Swahili 9, 20; West
    Africa 12, 14
Lapido, Duro 158
Las Palmas 104 (G)
Lava 79
Laye, Camara 208
Leakey, Louis and Mary 164, 164, 208
Leakey, Richard 165
Leishmaniasis 73
Lemur 149
Leopard 141
Leprosy 71
Leptis Magna 150
Lesotho 12, 104 (G) 188; History
    104 (G); People 104 (G)
Lesseps, Ferdinand Marie de 208, 208
Lesser kudu 146
Lianja, Legend of 10, 21
Liberia 45, 104 (G); Government
    105 (G); History 104 (G); Land
    and economy 104 (G); Iron ore 55;
    People 104 (G)
Libreville 105 (G)
Libya 105 (G); History 105 (G);
    Land and economy 105 (G); Oil
    52; People 105 (G)
Likasi 105 (G)
Lilongwe 105 (G)
Lilongwe Land Development
    Programme 67
Limpopo River 105 (G)
Lingala 10
Lions 136, 136 146
Literature 20-23; Animal fables 21;
    Arabic script 20; Early written 20;
    French African 23; Modern 22-3;
    South Africa 23; Swahili 20;
    Traditional 20-21; Traditional
    songs 21; Traditional themes and
    forms 21
Lithops 133
Livestock 45
Livingstone see Maramba
Livingstone daisy 133
Livingstone, David 177, 177 208,
    208
Loa Loa 73
Lobelias 132, 132
Lobengula 208
Lobito 105 (G)
Lome 105 (G)
Lourenço Marques 105 (G)

Lovanium, 105 (G)
Lowland areas 79
Lozi 34
Lualaba River 105 (G)
Luanda 105 (G)
Luangwa Valley National Park 143,
    149
Luangwa River 105 (G)
Luansha 105 (G)
Luapula River 105 (G)
Lubango see Sa da Bandeira
Lubumbashi 105 (G)
Luderitz 105 (G)
Lugard (Lord), Frederick John
    Dealtry 194, 208
Lumumba, Patrice 186, 208
Lusaka 105 (G)
Lusaka Manifesto 188
Luthuli, Chief Albert John 208
Luxor 105 (G)

M

Machel, Samora 189, 208
Macias Nguema, Francisco 208
Madagascar see Malagasy Republic
Madeira Islands 106 (G)
Madrassahs 69
Maga, Hubert 208
Macchia 135
Mafeking 106 (G)
Magadi, Lake 106 (G)
Mahdi 179, 208
Mahjoub, Muhammad Ahmad 208
Maiduguri 106 (G)
Maiyoro, Nyandika 162
Maize 45, 74
Majunga 106 (G)
Makhalanyane 104
Makhloufli, Ould 208
Malagasy Republic (Madagascar)
    9, 12, 14, 81, 106 (G); History
    106 (G); Land and economy 106
    (G); Language 12; Literature 20;
    People 106 (G); Wildlife 149
Malaria 70-3, 73
Malawi 106 (G), 184; Government
    107 (G); History 107 (G);
    Independence 185; Land and
    economy 106 (G); Language 11;
    People 106 (G)
Mali 20, 107 (G), 171; Ancient 172;
    Government 107 (G); History
    107 (G); Land and economy
    107 (G); People 107 (G)
Malindi 107 (G)
Malnutrition 73, 74
Mancham, James Richard 208
Mande languages 14, 20
Mandela, Nelson Rolihlahla 209
Mangabey 140
Manganese 55
Mangrove swamps 134, 135
Manufacturing 50
Manzel Bourguiba 107 (G)
Manzini 107 (G)
Maps, Altitude 78; Ancient kingdoms
    and empires of West Africa 172;
    Bantu languages 13; Diseases 71;
    Drainage patterns 78; Energy
    resources 52; Exploration 176;
    North African languages 12;
    Political 6; Population distribution
    8; Railway network 57; Rainfall
    82; Rift valleys 85; Temperature
    82; Vegetation 129, 129
Maputo see Lourenço Marques
Marabout of Senegal 70
Maramba 107 (G)
Marasmus 74
Marchand, Jean Baptiste 209
Margai, Sir Albert Michael 209
Margai, Sir Milton 209

Marra Mountains 107 (G)
Marrakech 107 (G)
Masai 7, 35, 70
Masai Amboseli National Park 149
Masai Steppe 79
Maseru 107 (G)
Masire, Quet K. J. 209
Massamba-Debat, Alphonse 209
Massawa 107 (G)
Mastabas 150
Matanzima, Chief Kaiser 209
Matriarchies 8
Mau Mau 182, 184
Mauritania 108 (G); Government
    108 (G); History 108 (G); Land
    and economy 108 (G); People
    108 (G)
Mauritius 108 (G); History 108 (G);
    Land and economy 108 (G);
    People 108 (G)
Mbabane 108 (G)
Mbandaka 108 (G)
Mboumoua, Eteki 209
Mboya, Thomas Joseph (Tom) 22,
    209
Mbuji Mayi 108 (G)
Mbundu, Language 10
Measles 77
Medhen, Tsegaye Gabre 209
Medical auxiliaries 77
Medical schools 77
Medicine 70-7
    Glossary of terms 77
Medina 107
Mediterranean Regions, Vegetation
    135
Meknes 108 (G), 109
Melange 108 (G)
Melilla 108 (G)
Memphis 108 (G)
Menelik II 209, 209
Menes 166
Merca 108 (G)
Merina 12
Meroe 108 (G)
Meru, Mount 78, 79
Metals 54
Metal-work 155
Mganga 70
Micombero, Michel 209, 209
Migrations, Wildlife 147
Military government see Government
Millet 45
Mineral resources 51, 54 5
Mining 50, 54, 54, 55; see also
    under specific minerals
Miombo 132, 133; Wildlife 148
Miracle plant 134
Missionaries 60, 63, 177
Mitumba Mountains 108 (G)
Mkomaindo Hospital 76
Mobutu, Sese Seko 191, 196, 209,
    209
Mobutu Sese Seko, Lake 108 (G)
Modern Art 158-9
Modern Literature 22-3
Mogaka, E. 162
Mohammed Ali Pasha 209
Mohammad V 209
Moi, Daniel Toroitich Arap 209
Mokkehle, Ntsu 209
Molepolole 108 (G)
Mombasa 108 (G)
Mondlane, Eduardo 209
Mongo-Nkundo 10
Monkey 136, 140, 142
Monrovia states 185
Moors 174
Mopane 132
Mopti 109 (G), 156
Morocco 44, 69, 109 (G) 173, 182;
    Art 153; Government 109 (G);
    History 109 (G); Land and
    economy 109 (G); People 109 (G)

Morogoro 109 (G)
Moroni 109 (G)
Mose-la-Tunya 125
    see also Victoria Falls
Moshoeshoe I 209
Moshoeshoe II 210, 210
Mosi 14
Mosques 16, 24, 69, 90, 101, 152,
    153, 153, 154, 156, 156, 171
Mosquito 72, 73
Mo-tswana 12
Moulouya River 109 (G)
Mountains 78-9; Atlas 79, 85;
    Ethiopian Highlands 78;
    Vegetation 132; Wildlife 139;
    see also under specific names
Mozambique 53, 110 (G), 188, 197;
    Government 110 (G); History
    110 (G); Land and economy
    110 (G); People 110 (G)
Mozambique Channel 110 (G)
Mozambique Liberation Front
    (FRELIMO) 189
Mphahlele, Ezekiel 210
MPLA (Peoples' Movement for the
    Liberation of Angola) 189
Mpondo 37
Msumbiji see Mozambique
Muchinga Mountains 110 (G)
Mufulira 110 (G)
Musa 172, 210
Music 20, 25, 160-1; Songs 21
Musical instruments 20, 161
Muslims 16, 170, 171
Mutesa, Sir Edward 193
Muzorewa, Bishop Abel Tendekayi
    210, 210
Mwanza 110 (G)
Mweru Lake 110 (G)
Mzilikazi 210

N

Nairobi 103, 110 (G)
Nairobi University 66
Naivasha, Lake 110 (G)
Nakuru 110 (G)
Nakuru, Lake 111, 147
Namib desert 110 (G), 134
Namibia 110 (G), 111, 188, 199;
    Government 110 (G); History
    110 (G); Land and economy
    110 (G); People 110 (G)
Nasser, Gamal Abdel 182, 182,
    210, 210
Nasser, Lake 110 (G)
National parks 143, 146, 148, 149
National Union for the Total
    Independence of Angola
    (UNITA) 189
Nationalism 181, 182, 194
Nationalist leaders 181, 194
Natron, Lake 110 (G)
Natural gas 52
Ndau 11
Ndebele 11, 37
N'Djamena 110 (G)
Ndola 110 (G)
Nefertiti 210
Neto, Antonio Agostinho 210
New Bussa 110 (G)
Newspapers 58, 59
Ngorongoro Crater 110 (G)
Ngorongoro National Park 149
Ngouabi, Marien 210
Ngugi wa Thiongo 210
Nguni 11
Niger 111 (G); Government 111 (G);
    History 111 (G); Land and
    economy 111 (G); People 111 (G)
Niger River 111 (G)
Nigeria 7, 112 (G), 191; Army 197;
    Art 155; Civil War 191;
    Constitutional development 195;

Nigeria (cont.) *Government* 113 (G);
  History 112 (G); *Indirect rule* **194**;
  Industry 51; *Land and economy*
  112 (G); *Language* 14; *Minerals*
  55; *Oil* 52; *People* 112 (G);
  Power 53
Nile Basin 145; *Wildlife* 145
Nile Delta 166
Nile River 80, **80**, 113 (G)
Nilotic languages 15
Nimeiry, Ja'afar al- 210, **211**
Nkomo, Joshua 184, 210, **211**
Nkrumah, Kwame 22, 182, **183**, 185,
  210, **211**
Nkumbula, Harry 184, 210
Nkundo 8, 10
Nnagenda, Francis 159
Nok 113 (G); *Civilization* **168**;
  Culture 168; *Sculptures* 155
North Africa, *Art* 150; *Artistic
  influence* 153; *Education* 68-9;
  Language 15; *History* 178;
  Universities 69
North-East Africa, *Language* 15
Northern Rhodesia 184 *see also*
  Zimbabwe
Nouakchott 113 (G)
Noumazalay, Ambroise 210
Nova Lisboa 113 (G)
Nubia 113 (G)
Nuer 15
Numidia 113 (G)
Nupe 14
Nurses 77
Nutrition 74
Nyanja 11, 21
Nyasa, Lake 113 (G)
Nyasaland *see* Malawi
Nyerere, Mwalimu Julius Kambarage
  23, **66**, **184**, 190, **190**, 197, 211
  211
Nyika, *Wildlife* 146

O

OAU *see* Organization of African
  Unity
Obelisk **154**
Obote, Apolo Milton 211
Ocean currents 83
Ochocerciasis 72
Odinga, Ajuma Oginga 22, 211
Ogbomosho 113 (G)
Ogoue River 113 (G)
Oil, *Drilling* 52, **113**; *Libya* 52;
  Nigeria 52
Ojukwu, Chukuemeka Odumegwu
  211
O'Kacha, Alain Mimoun 162
Okavango River 113 (G)
Okavango Swamp 113 (G)
Okigbo, Christopher 211
Olduvai Gorge 164, **164**
Olof 14
Olympic Games 162, 163
Omdurman 113 (G)
Onitsha 113 (G)
Oppenheimer, Harry Frederick 211
Opuku Ware II 211
Orange River 53, 81, 113 (G)
Orchids **130**
Organization of African Unity (OAU)
  185, 187, 199
Oromo language 15
Oshikoya, Modupe 162, **163**
Oshogbo 114 (G)
Ostrich 144, **144**
Ouagadougou 114 (G)
Ouedraogo, Gérard Kango 211
Oujda 114 (G)
Owen Falls 53, **125**
Owiti, Hezbon **158**
Oyo 114 (G)

Oyono, Ferdinand Leopold 211

P

Pack animals **56**
PAFMECA (Pan-African Movement
  for East and Central Africa) 185
PAIGC (African Independence Party
  of Guinea and Cape Verde Islands)
  189
Paintings 151, 154, **158**, **159**, **169**
  179
Palaeartic region, *Wildlife* 136
Palime 114 (G)
Palma 114 (G)
Pan-African Conference, Manchester
  195
Pan-Africanism 185
Pan-Africanist Congress 187
Pangea 84, 85
Papyrus plants 135, **135**
Parasites 73, **75**
Parc National de la Bouclé de la
  Pendjari 149
Parc National de la Bouclé du Baoule
  149
Park, Mungo 177, 211
Parrots **140**
Paton, Alan Stewart 23, 211
Patriarchies 8
p'Bitek, Okot 211
Peanuts **113**
Pellagra **74**
Pemba Island 114 (G)
Peneplain 85
Peoples 7-8; *Guide to* 24-43
Peoples' Movement for the Liberation
  of Angola (MPLA) 189
Pesticides **73**
Pietermaritzburg 114 (G)
Pigmy hippopotamus 140
Pipit 146
Plantains 45, 74
Plantations 46
Plants 130, **130**, 133; *Adaptation and
  migration* 130; *Clinging* 131;
  Desert 134; *Floating* 135;
  Moorland 132; *Succulent* 130;
  see also Vegetation Plateau of
  Southern Africa 79
Pneumoconiosis 75
Poetry *see* Literature
Pointe Noire 114 (G)
Politics *see* Government
Pollution 75
Polo, Marco 174
Poor Man's Charter 190
Population, *Distribution map* 8
Port Elizabeth 114 (G)
Port-Gentil 114 (G)
Port Harcourt 114 (G)
Port Louis 114 (G)
Port Said 114 (G)
Port Sudan 114 (G)
Port Victoria 114 (G)
Porto Novo 114 (G)
Portugal, influence of 174, **174**, 176,
  179, 188
Portuguese Guinea *see* Guinea-
  Bissau
Portuguese Territories 189
Postal services 58, **58**; *Postage
  stamps* **184**
Pottery **155**
Power resources *see* Energy resources
Power stations 52
Praia 114 (G)
Precambrian period 84
Pressure zones 82
Prester John 174
Pretoria 114 (G), **114**
Prickly pear 130
Priesthood **16**, 17

Principe *see* São Tomé and Principe
Protea **118**, **135**
Protectorates 179
Protein 48, 74
Proverbs 20, 21
Ptolemy 167
Pygmies 7, 8, **39**
Pyramids **117**, 150, **166**, 167

Q

Qattara Depression 79, 114 (G)
Qayrawan 114 (G), 153, **153**
Que Que 114 (G)
Qur'an (Koran) Sultan Shaban **69**

R

Ra 167
Rabat 114 (G), **115**
Rabemananjara, Jacques 212
Radio 59, **59**, **68**
Rail transport 56-7, **57**
Rain forests *see* Forests
Rainfall 82, 130-2; *Climatic types* 83;
  Maps **82**; *Seasonal pattern* 82;
  Seasonal variations 83
Ramanantsoa, Gabriel 212
Rameses 212
Ramgoolam, Sir Seewoosagur 212
Ranaivo, Flavien 212
Ras Dashen 78
Rebmann, Johannes 177
Religions 8, 16, **16**, 17-19; *Belief in a
  Supreme Being* 17; *Ethnic* 16;
  Gods 18; *Priesthood* **16**, 17;
  Spirits 18, 70; *Taboos* 19;
  Traditional 16
Reptiles 138
Retief, Pieter 212
Reunion 114 (G)
Rey Malabo 114 (G)
Rhinoceros 146, **146**
Rhodes, Cecil John 179, 212, **212**
Rhodesia *see* Zimbabwe
Rhodesia, Northern 184
Rhodesia, Southern 181, 184, 187,
  197
Richards, Barry 212
Rift Valley 78, 79, 85, **85**
River blindness 72
Rivers 56, 80, *see also* under names of
  rivers
Road transport **56**, 57, 181
Robert, Shaaban 21, 212
Roberto, Holden 212
Robertsport 114 (G)
Rocks 84
Rokel River 114 (G)
Roma University **66**
Roman Africa **168**, 169; *Art* 151;
  Ruins **86**
Roseires Dam 114 (G)
Rudolf, Lake *see* Turkana, Lake
Rufiji River 115 (G)
Rufisque 115 (G)
Rukwa Lake 115 (G)
Rundi 10
Ruvubu River 115 (G)
Ruwenzori Mountains 115 (G), 139
Ruwenzori National Park **136**, 149
Ruzizi River 115 (G)
Rwanda 10, 115 (G), **115**; *History*
  115 (G); *Land and economy*
  115 (G); *People* 115 (G)

S

Sa da Bandeira 87, 116 (G)
Sadat, Anwar as- 212, **212**
Sahal savanna 133

Sahara desert 45, 79, **79**, 116 (G),
  130, 134, 166; *Trade routes* 171;
  Wildlife 138
Saidon, Conte 23
Saint Denis 116 (G)
Saint Helena 116 (G)
Saint Louis 116 (G)
Saint Paul 116 (G)
Saint Pierre 116 (G)
Sakia **45**
Salisbury 116 (G), **117**
Saloum River 116 (G)
Salt marshes 79
Samburu **40**
San Antonio *see* São Tomé
Santa Cruz de Tenerife 116 (G)
São Tomé and Principe 116 (G)
Saqqara 116 (G)
Sarh 116 (G)
Savanna 45, 79, 130, 132; *Sahal* 133
  Wildlife 142-5
Schools and colleges **59**, 60, 61, 62,
  62, 63, **63**, 64-9
Scripts **11**
Sculpture, *Bambara* 155; *Bantu* 156;
  Dogon 155; *Egyptian* 151, *see also*
  chapters on Early Art and Art Today
Schweitzer, Albert 212, **212**
Sea transport *see* Ships and
  shipping
Segou 116 (G)
Sekondi-Takoradi 116 (G)
Semi-desert, *Vegetation* 133;
  Wildlife 138, 144
Semitic languages 20
Senecios 132
Senegal 14, 116 (G); *Government*
  116 (G); *History* 116 (G); *Land
  and economy* 116 (G); *Marabout
  of* 70; *People* 116 (G)
Senegal River 116 (G)
Senghor, Léopold Sédar 23, 212, **213**
Sennardam 116 (G)
Senufo 14
Serengeti National Park 149
Serowe 116 (G)
Se-tswana 12
Seychelles Islands 117 (G)
Sfax 117 (G)
Shaba 117 (G)
Shaka (Zulu) 193, 213
Shebelle River 117 (G)
Shepstone, Theophilus 213
Shermarke Abderashid Ali 213
Ships and shipping 56, **80**, 81, 169
Shona 11
Siad Barre, Mohamed 213
Sicassou 117 (G)
Sickle-cell anaemia 72
Sidi bu Medien mosque **153**
Sidi Ifni 117 (G)
Sierra Leone 45, 66, 117 (G);
  Government 117 (G); *History*
  117 (G); *Land and economy*
  117 (G); *People* 117 (G);
  Schools 63
Sinai Peninsula 117 (G)
Sisal **50**
Sithole, Rev. Ndabaningi 213, **213**
Skins **104**
Skulls (fossil) 164, 165
Slave trade 176, **176**, 177
Sleeping sickness *see*
  Trypanosomiasis
Smallholdings 46
Smallpox 73, 77
Smith, Ian Douglas **185**, 187, 213,
  213
Smuts, Jan Christiaan 213, **213**
Snails 73, 75
Snakes 142
Sobat River 117 (G)
Sobhuza II 121, 213
Sobukwe, Robert Mangaliso 213

Soils 46, 85; *Erosion* 45, 85, **85**
Sokode 117 (G)
Somali 7
Somalia 118 (G); *Government* 118 (G); *History* 118 (G); *Land and economy* 118 (G); *Language* 15; *Literature* 20; *People* 118 (G)
Songhai 118 (G), 173
Sonni Ali 173, 213
Sorghum 45
Sousse 118 (G), **124**
South Africa 118 (G), 180, 188, **199**; *Apartheid* 187, 199; *Coal mining* 52; *Defence* 197; *Energy* 53; *Gold fields* 54; *Government* 119 (G); *History* 119 (G); *Industry* 50; *Land and economy* 118 (G); *Languages* 11; *Literature* 23; *People* 118 (G); *Racial policies* **187**
South-West Africa 188, *see also* Namibia
Southern Rhodesia 181, *see also* Zimbabwe
Southern Sotho 12
Soyinka, Wole 23, 213
Spanish explorers 174
Spanish Sahara 120 (G)
Speke, John Hanning 177, **177**, **192**, 213, **213**
Sphinx 151, **166**
Spirits *see* Religion
Sport 162-3
Springbok 147
Stanley, Henry Morton 177, **177**, 214
Steel industry 51, **51**
Stephanie, Lake 120 (G)
Stevens, Siaka Probyn 214, **214**
Sudan 45, 120 (G), **120**, 171, 182; *Government* 120 (G); *History* 120 (G); *Land and economy* 120 (G); *People* 120 (G)
Sudd 80
Suez 120 (G); *Gulf of* 120 (G)
Suez Canal 120 (G), 178; *Crisis of 1956*, 182, **182**
Sultan Hasan Mosque **152**
Sun-birds 139
Sutherland, Efua Theodora 214
Suthu **41**
Suzman, Helen 214
Swahili, *Architecture* 154; *Dialects* 9; *Literature* 20
Swakopmund 120 (G)
Swamps, *Vegetation* 135
Swaziland 120 (G), 184, 188; *Government* 121 (G); *History* 121 (G); *Land and economy* 120 (G); *People* 120 (G)
Syphilis 71

T

Table Bay **119**
Table Mountain 121 (G)
Taboos 19
Tabora 121 (G)
Tamai, *Battle of* **179**
Tamatave 121 (G)
Tana, Lake 80, 121 (G)
Tana River 121 (G)
Tananarive 121 (G), **121**
Tanga 121 (G)
Tanganyika 180, 184
Tanganyika, Lake 80, **80**, 121 (G)
Tanganyika African National Union (TANU) 195
Tangier 121 (G)
Tanzania 21, 122 (G), **123**; *Co-operatives* 47; *Education for self-reliance* 67; *Government* 122 (G); *History* 122 (G); *Independence* **184**;

Tanzania (cont.) *Land and economy* 122 (G); *People* 122 (G); *Rail link to Zambia* **190**
Tanzania Standard Swahili 9
Tassil-n-Ajjer Mountains 154
Tea plantations **46**
Telecommunications 58
Telegraph services 58
Telephone services 58
Television 59, **59**, **68**
Tema 122 (G)
Temperature 82, **82**
Temples **95**, 150, **150**, 167
Tenerife 122 (G)
Tenkamenin 172
Tenrecs 149, **149**
Termites 141; *Nest* **142**
Terracotta heads **155**, **168**, **173**
Tetanus 77
Tetouan 122 (G), **123**,
Thebes **95**, 122 (G), 166
Theodore II 214
Thies 122 (G)
Thika 122 (G)
Thuku, Harry 214
Tibesti Mountains 79, 122 (G)
Tiger, Dick 214
Timbuktu 122 (G)
Timgad **86**
Tin 54, 55
Tississat waterfalls 80
Tobacco plants **67**
Tobruk 122 (G)
Todd, Judith **199**, **214**
Todd, Reginald Stephen Garfield 214, **214**
Togo 14, 122 (G); *History* 122 (G); *Land and economy* 122 (G); *People* 122 (G)
Toiva ja Toiva, Herman 215
Tolbert, William Richard 188, **214**, 215
Tombalbaye, Ngarta 215
Tombs, *Egyptian* 150; *Mastaba type* **150**
Totemism 19
Toubkal, Mount 79
Touré, Sékou 215, **215**
Trachoma **70**, 71, 72
Tractors **47**, **95**
Trade 172, 177; *Routes* 171
Transport 56, **56**, 57; *Air* 57; *Development* 56; *Rail* 56-7; *Road* **56**, 57, 181; *Sea* 56; *Inland water* 56
Traore, Moussa 215
Tree frog **141**
Trees 131, 132, 135
Tripoli 124 (G)
Trypanosomiasis 71, 72
Tsavo National Park **103**, 146, 149
Tsetse fly 72, **73**
Tshekedi Khama 215
Tshombe, Moise Kapenda **186**, 215
Tsiranana, Philibert 215, **215**
Tsumeb 124 (G)
Tuareg 7, **42**
Tuberculosis 71, 73, 75, 77
Tubman, William Vacanarat Shadrach **214**, 215
Tugela River 124 (G)
Tulear 124 (G)
Tunis 124 (G)
Tunisia 69, 124 (G), 153, 182; *Government* 124 (G); *History* 124 (G); *Land and economy* 124 (G); *People* 124 (G)
Turkana, Lake 124 (G), 145
Tutankhamun **95**, 150
Tuthmosis **167**
Tutuola, Amos 215
Twi language 14
Twins Seven Seven 158, **158**
Typhoid 73, **76**, 77

U

Uganda 124 (G); *Army* **197**; *Government* 125 (G); *History* 125 (G); *Land and economy* 124 (G); *Language* 9; *People* 124 (G)
Ujiji 125 (G)
Umbrella tree 131
Umbundu 10
Umtali 125 (G)
Ungulates 142, 146
Union of Angolan Peoples (FNLA) 189
UNITA (National Union for the Total Independence of Angola) 189
United Nations 199; *Intervention in Belgian Congo* 186; *Namibia* 188
Universities **59**, **65**, 66, **66**, 69
Upper Volta 125 (G); *History* 125 (G); *Land and economy* 125 (G); *People* 125 (G)

V

Vaal River 81, 125 (G)
Vaccination 73, 74, 76, 77, **77**
Valente, Malangatana 159
Valley of the Kings 125 (G)
Van Riebeck, Johan (Jan) **176**, 215
Vanadium 55
Vasco da Gama 174, **174**
Vegetation 130-5; *Effects of climate and surface features* 130; *Effects of fire and grazing* 130; *Types* 130; *Deciduous woodland* 132; *Deserts* 134; *Dry thorn woodland* 133; *Grassland* 133; *Lowland rain forests* 130; *Map of regions* **129**; *Mediterranean Regions* 135; *Mountains* 132; *Regions* 130; *Semi-desert* 133; *Swamps* 135; *Wooded grassland* 132
Venereal diseases 71
Vereeniging 125 (G)
Verwoerd, Dr. Hendrik Frensch 215
Victoria Falls 80, 81, **125**, 177
Victoria, Lake 80, 126 (G)
Victoria Nile 126 (G)
Victoria Nyanza *see* Victoria, Lake
Virunga National Park 149
Volcanoes 78, 79, **79**, 85, 139
Volta dam 53
Volta, Lake 126 (G)
Volta River 126 (G)
Vorster, Balthazar Johannes 188, **188**, 215, **215**

W

Wadi Halfa 126 (G)
Wadi Medani 126 (G)
Walvis Bay **111**, 126 (G)
Wankie 126 (G); *National Park* 149
Water birds 147
Water supplies 47, 83
Water transport 56
Waterways, *Inland* 56, *see also* Ships and shipping
Water wheels **45**
Weather 82-3
Weaver bird **144**
Welensky, Sir Roland (Roy) 215, **215**
Welwitschia 134
West Africa 171; *Ancient kingdoms and empires* **172**; *Art* 155; *Early developments* 168; *Forest Cultures* 155; *Language* 14
White Nile 80, 126 (G), 135
WHO (World Health Organization) 76
Whooping cough 73, 77
Wildebeeste 147, **147**

Wildlife 136-49; *Bushveld* 148; *Deserts* 138; *East African grasslands* 147; *Ethiopean region* 136; *Forests* 140-1; *Guinea savannas* 144-5; *Highveld* 148; *Malagasy Republic (Madagascar)* 149; *Migration* 147; *Miombo* 148; *Mountains* 139; *Nile Basin* 145; *Nyika* 146; *Palaeartic region* 136; *Regions* 138; *Savanna* 142-3; *Semi-desert* 138, 144
William Ponty college 63
Windhoek 126 (G)
Witwatersrand 126 (G)
Wolof 14
Woodland, *Deciduous* 132; *Dry Thorn* 133
World Bank 199
World Health Organisation (WHO) 76
World War I 180, **180**
World War II 181, **181**

X

Xhosa 11
X-rays **70**

Y

Yankari Game Reserve 149
Yaounde 126 (G)
Yaws 73
Yellow Fever 72, 73, 77
Yemen 169
Yoruba 14, 193
Youlou, Fulbert 215
'Youth and Society' organization **68**

Z

Zaire 10, 126 (G), **186**, 191; *Copper* 54; *Government* 127 (G); *History* 126 (G); *Land and economy* 126 (G); *People* 126 (G); *Wildlife* 140
Zaire River 53, 81, 127 (G)
Zambezi River 53, **80**, 81, 127 (G)
Zambia **7**, **10**, 127 (G), 184; *Copper* 54, **55**; *Government* 128 (G); *History* 128 (G); *Independence* 185; *Land and economy* 127 (G); *Languages* 17; *People* 127 (G); *University* **105**
ZANU (Zimbabwe African National Union) 187
Zanzibar **123**, 184, 191
Zanzibar Island 128 (G)
Zanzibar Town 128 (G)
ZAPU (Zimbabwe African People's Union) 187
Zaria 128 (G)
Zebra **136**, 147
Zimbabwe 128 (G), 169, 179, 181, 184, **185**, 197; *Economic sanctions* 187, **187**; *Government* 128 (G); *History* 128 (G); *Industry* 51; *Land and economy* 128 (G); *Language* 11; *Minerals* 55; *People* 128 (G); *Unilateral declaration of independence* 187
Zimbabwe African National Union (ZANU) 187
Zimbabwe African People's Union (ZAPU) 187
Zimbabwe Ruins 128 (G), **156**, **169**
Zinder 128 (G)
Zinguinchor 128 (G)
Zobel, Joseph 215
Zomba 128 (G)
Zula 128 (G)
Zulu **43**, 193; *Language* 11